**Fourth Edition**

# NEWS REPORTING
# AND WRITING

**Fourth Edition**

# NEWS REPORTING AND WRITING

THE MISSOURI GROUP:

Brian S. Brooks

George Kennedy

Daryl R. Moen

Don Ranly

School of Journalism
University of Missouri at Columbia

**St. Martin's Press**
New York

**Senior editor:** Cathy Pusateri
**Managing editor:** Patricia Mansfield-Phelan
**Project editor:** Elise Bauman
**Production supervisor:** Alan Fischer
**Text design:** Nancy B. Field
**Graphics:** G&H Soho
**Photo researcher:** Inge King
**Cover design:** Jeheber & Peace, Inc.

Library of Congress Catalog Card Number: 90–71645

For information, write:
St. Martin's Press, Inc.
175 Fifth Avenue
New York, NY 10010

ISBN: 0–312–04768–1

**Acknowledgments**

*Figure A, color insert.* Reprinted by permission of the *Atlanta Constitution.*
*Figure 1.1, page 7.* Reprinted by permission of the *Columbia Missourian.*
*Figure B, color insert.* Reprinted by permission of the American Society of Newspaper Editors.
*Figure C, color insert.* Reprinted by permission of the American Society of Newspaper Editors.
*Figure D, color insert.* Reprinted by permission of the American Society of Newspaper Editors.
*Figure 2.2, page 20.* Reprinted by permission of McCann-Erickson Worldwide.
*Figure 2.3, pages 23–24.* Reprinted by permission of the *Seattle Times.*
*Figure 3.1, page 50.* Front page from Sept. 23, 1991 of *USA Today.* Copyright © 1991, *USA Today.* Reprinted with permission.
*Page 157.* "Broad Spectrum of Events Honors Black History." From the February 2, 1990 edition of *The Miami Herald.* Reprinted by permission of The Miami Herald.
*Page 158.* "S. Florida Guarded by Hopes for More Change." From the February 12, 1990 edition of *The Miami Herald.* Reprinted by permission of The Miami Herald.
*Page 159.* "Blacks Reject Suarez's Olive Branch on Mandela." From the June 27, 1990 edition of *The Miami Herald.* Reprinted by permission of The Miami Herald.
*Page 159.* "Unofficially Mandela Day." From the June 29, 1990 edition of *The Miami Herald.* Reprinted by permission of The Miami Herald.

Acknowledgments and copyrights are continued at the back of the book on page 580, which constitutes an extension of the copyright page.

# Preface

Newspapers are trying to redefine news. This fourth edition of *News Reporting and Writing* recognizes that trend and advances it with new criteria for news judgment. This basic redefinition of news is only one of many important changes you will find in this edition.

Changes also are occurring rapidly in the methods journalists use to gather information. That's why you will find a greatly expanded chapter (Chapter Seven) on sources and searches. It contains the latest information about using computer data bases to assist journalists in their news-gathering efforts.

Changes are also occurring in the organization of the news room, where the visual techniques of storytelling have gained increasing respect and importance. Chapter Two shows how graphics editors are assuming new positions in the organizational structure and why.

Visual communication is particularly stressed in this new edition. Students will find it easier to use because of the many lists and boxes that have been highlighted to help them focus on important points in the text. We are trying not only to preach service journalism but also to practice it.

Of course, many of the writing examples are new, and many recent court cases dealing with issues pertinent to reporters are discussed in the press law chapter (Chapter Twenty-One). We have retained the popular exercise questions at the end of each chapter, while also expanding and updating the workbook. For the first time, software is available to accompany the text. Adopters can receive The St. Martin's Wire Service Hotline by calling 1–800–446–8923. Reacting to comments from our reviewers, we have not made any changes in the order of chapters for this edition. The book still is organized with chapter topics progressing from simple to complex, to permit teachers to use it through two semesters of reporting and writing instruction or to skip around as they see fit.

We want to thank our colleagues, Dr. Sandra Scott, a Missouri journalism professor and lawyer, who revised the chapter on press law and advised us on crime and the courts, and Prof. James K. Gentry, former director of Missouri's business journalism program, who revised the chapter on business and consumer reporting (Chapter Fifteen). We are grateful, too, to our colleagues across the country who provided us with helpful comments and suggestions for this fourth edition: Libby Allison, University of South Florida; Dorothy Bibbee, West Virginia University at Parksburg; Richard Cunningham, New York University; Donald Glynn, Niagara University; Barbara Hines, Howard University; Thomas B. Littlewood, University of Illinois Urbana-Champaign; Dave Nelson, Southwest Texas State University; Ed Rooney, Loyola University—Chicago; Howard Seemann, Humboldt State University; Jim Ylisela, Columbia College (Chicago); Carl Zablotny, John Carroll University; and Julie Zuehlke, Winona State University. We also thank our students—past and present—whose work we've drawn from to illustrate the principles of the book and from whom we've learned. Our wives, Anne, Robin, Nancy and Eva Joan, have been full partners in this project.

Brian S. Brooks    Daryl R. Moen

George Kennedy    Don Ranly

# Contents

## PART TWO

## Basic Skills    47

## PART SIX

## PART SEVEN

# PART ONE

# Introduction to the News

# 1

## The Nature of News

The most basic, most important and most difficult question in journalism can be asked in three words: *What is news?* It's a basic question for anyone beginning the study of journalism or for anyone who learns about the world— as most of us do—from journalists. It's an important question because the answer (or answers) will guide your work as a journalist and will determine what you receive as a consumer of journalism. It's a difficult question because there isn't and can't be a single, universal answer. Besides, the answers keep changing.

Even the dictionary, that basic tool of the journalist, isn't very helpful. Webster's defines *news* as ''a report of a recent event; new information; fresh tidings . . . any matter regarded as interesting to newspaper readers or news broadcast audiences.'' But just watch the evening news and then read your local paper, The New York Times and USA Today for the same day. Obviously, not every recent event or every fresh tiding gets reported. Just as obviously, journalists for different news organizations have different ideas about what will be interesting to their different audiences.

If you're a little confused at this point, you should be. Experienced journalists and scholars disagree about what news is and what it ought to be. Don't despair, though. There are broad areas of agreement—guidelines that the best journalists use, and that you can use, to determine which of every day's flood of events are most likely to be regarded as interesting by your particular audience. There are also two principles—accuracy and fairness— that don't change.

**In this chapter you will learn:**

1. The criteria that journalists are using today in deciding what news is.

2. How those criteria are changing and how the changes are shaping the journalism of tomorrow.

3. The challenges you will face in developing and applying news judgment.

4. How the unchanging principles of accuracy and fairness will help you meet the challenges of good journalism.

# What News Was, Is and (Probably) Will Be

For generations American journalists have used similar criteria in deciding the news value of each day's tidings; that is, to decide which among the almost infinite number of events, ideas and continuing controversies should be reported in the paper or on the broadcast news on any given day. Various editors, teachers and textbooks use varying labels for those criteria, but almost every journalist's list is similar to this one:

1. *Impact*—how many people an event or idea affects and how seriously it affects them determine its importance as news.

2. *Proximity*—the closer an issue or an event is to your audience, the greater the impact and news value it will have.

3. *Timeliness*—today's news is stale tomorrow.

4. *Prominence*—names make news; the bigger the name, the bigger the news.

5. *Novelty*—the unusual, the bizarre, the first or last or once-in-a-lifetime event is news.

6. *Conflict*—war, politics and crime are the most common news of all.

Just as important as these criteria, however, is the array of events and ideas to which the criteria are applied. Generations of American journalists have thought of news as coming mainly from capitols, courthouses, city halls and cops. With a few exceptions, such as murders, sports and natural disasters, news has focused on governmental issues. This was true, for the most part, in the 1950s. It was still true, with the range of subjects starting to broaden just a little, in the 1970s. By the 1990s, however, the broadening had become an explosion while the most important criteria could be boiled down to three: *relevance, usefulness* and *interest*.

The explosion of subject matter resulted from the belated recognition by journalists that government and politics were no longer—if they ever had been—the most interesting forces in American society. Nor were they the only important forces. People needed and wanted to know about everything from the biology of AIDS to the crisis in education, from Japanese business practices to the sex lives of the elderly. The traditional role of the press as schoolmaster of the people had to be expanded to cover the full curriculum of contemporary life.

A 1990 report by the American Society of Newspaper Editors (ASNE) summarized the findings of a research project intended to create a newspaper for the year 2000:

1. Readers want news in their newspapers.

2. Readers want news to be relevant and to focus on them and where they live.

3. Readers do not want their newspapers to ignore what is going on elsewhere in the nation and the world.

4. Readers are not fooled by gimmicks or fancy designs. They will accept gimmicks and fancy designs only if they seem relevant to stories, make the newspaper easier to use or make the information easier to grasp. If the gimmicks are self-conscious or the designs radical, readers will reject them for interfering with ease of readership.

5. Readers want practical and useful information that helps them live their lives. They want tips and advice. As the lifestyles of readers change, editors must produce newspapers that focus on how they live. . . .

You'll notice a certain repetition: Readers want, readers want. . . . This is the force that has driven, and will continue to drive, changes in journalists' definitions of news. Those generations of journalists who applied much the same criteria to much the same subjects knew they had readers, of course, and they cared—some—about giving those readers what they wanted. Today's and tomorrow's journalists will care a lot. Why? Competition.

When Americans of the 1990s want new information, fresh tidings or just entertainment, they have dozens of choices—daily newspapers, weekly newspapers, magazines of all descriptions, books, dozens of cable channels, radio, and increasingly interactive computers. Every publication, every voice, every screen is competing for the time, attention and money of people who don't have enough of any of these commodities to go around.

That's why the journalism of the 1990s and beyond must strive for relevance, usefulness and interest.

# How and Why News Is Being Redefined

Let's look at the new criteria for making news judgments to see how journalists apply them in deciding what news is. We'll look first at two front pages from 1991 newspapers. Then we'll look ahead.

Figure A in the color insert shows a front page of The Atlanta Constitution, which describes itself as "the South's Standard Newspaper." If you were to compare this page with one published 10 years ago, you would see that the standard is changing. Remember the tradition that news was mainly about government? Only two of the five stories on this front page deal with government, and neither is a traditional account of politics or bureaucracy. Instead, like many newspapers of the 1990s, the Constitution showcases stories its audience is more likely to need and want to read.

Relevant stories are those that have a direct impact on the lives of readers. That impact may be emotional, as with The Atlanta Constitution's photograph of baseball's opening day and the sensitive description of the Etowah River. The impact may come from war, as with the story about the aftermath of the Persian Gulf War. Or the impact may come from the story's touching on the health or welfare of readers or their children, as with the smoking-and-sports story and the story about the teaching of foreign languages to kindergartners.

When you are assessing the news value of a story or a potential story, your first question should be, "How will this affect the lives of my readers?" Events or ideas that are likely to touch the health, safety, environment or education of significant segments of the public provide the raw material for front-page stories in Atlanta or anywhere else. The more of your readers who may be affected and the more direct the effect, the more relevant—and therefore the more important—the story will be.

# COLUMBIA MISSOURIAN

WEATHER

There is a good chance of showers today and tonight. The high today will be 60, and the low tonight will be 50. Page 7A

No. 177 GOOD MORNING! It's Thursday, April 11, 1991 2 Sections — 18 Pages

## School bill's price goes up

### Reforms added to win approval

By MARY MICKLE
State Capitol Bureau

JEFFERSON CITY — House Speaker Bob Griffin said Wednesday that he will add more reforms for public schools to win the governor's approval of a Senate education and tax increase bill.

The result would be a package costing Missouri taxpayers $955 million.

Hours before Griffin's announcement, Gov. John Ashcroft repeated criticism that the Senate version — a $456 million tax package — costs too much and does too little.

"He's referring to the lack of reforms in elementary and secondary education," Griffin said. "I offer some reforms specified by the governor and hope to win his support."

The Senate passed the bill three weeks ago, 24-10. If the House passes the bill — sponsored by Sen. James Mathewson, D-Sedalia — it would return to the Senate for final approval.

Ashcroft's remarks were made at a meeting sponsored by Associated Industries of Missouri, before a group of about 1,700 manufacturers. Mathewson, who is Senate President Pro Tem, spoke to the group after the governor's remarks. He said Ashcroft should air his concerns about the bill before the House Budget Committee.

Griffin presented his reforms to that committee Wednesday night. They include: alternative certification for teachers, district report cards, drop-out definitions and reports and reduced class size.

Griffin said his reforms include everything the governor recommended his January address to the General Assembly, except Ashcroft's request for a 200-day school year.

In addition to these reforms, Griffin modified the public schools foundation formula and tacked on funding for

See BILL, Page 8A

## A taxing problem

### IRS says there's still filing time

By EDGAR FONSECA
Missourian staff writer

Five, four, three, two, one. ... April 15 is almost here with its tax-return deadline.

Haven't you filled out the form yet? Have you even picked it up?

You still have time. But if you don't do it, the IRS takes a dim view of the matter and can levy heavy penalties on non-filers.

An average of 150 people are requesting assistance daily at the local office of the Internal Revenue Service, said Gordon Nulty, an IRS employee. The office is in Room 116 in the Federal Building, 608 E. Cherry St.

As the deadline approaches, more and more people show up in Nulty's office, not only to pick up their forms, but also to untangle the fine points.

"What form do I need?" is the most common question people ask, Nulty said.

Nulty, along with Mary Long, try to answer the questions, but sometimes when they are at loss, they turn to bureaucrats in St. Louis for technical help.

Nulty said each year, more and more people come to the office with more and more complex questions. He said people ask about issues for which he hasn't been trained.

More than 2 million people are supposed to fill out tax returns in April in Missouri, an IRS spokeswoman in St. Louis said. As of March 30, 1,127,550 returns had been filed.

On Wednesday, Annette Weaver, owner of a book business in Columbia, requested help in understanding how to fill a form of depreciation and amortization. "It's very complicated," she said.

The rest of the forms were not difficult, she said. "It is a matter of keeping the records."

Tim Vierling, a doctor from Illinois who is visiting Columbia, also arrived at the IRS office. His main concern was to figure out what deductions he is eligible for. He picked up extra forms and said that he has been filling the forms

See TAX, Page 8A

JACKIE HOSEY/Missourian

Avalene Kruger said the closer it gets to April 15, the less she can see of her desk.

### Husband-wife combination a bit unusual

By VANESSA LU
Missourian staff writer

Leaky pipes and income-tax returns make for an unusual combination. But Avalene and Lou Kruger's newspaper ad offers the two in one — relief from draining income taxes and overtaxed plumbing.

The business is called Kruger Plumbing, Heating and Tax Service, run by the husband and wife team.

Avalene Kruger operates the tax service out of her home on Highway WW, seven miles east of Columbia, while her son, Greg, helps out his father with the plumbing and heating side of the business.

"It's two businesses combined into one, in essence," Avalene said. She got into the tax business by keeping the books for friends, including her husband, who started the plumbing and heating company in 1962.

Besides keeping the books for her husband, answering the phone during the day and raising three children, she worked evenings at a H&R Block office during the busy tax season in the late 1960s and early 1970s.

"Then I just started doing taxes on my own here," Avalene said. Some of her customers also use the Krugers for plumbing and heating problems. "We just laugh about the name."

The 66-year-old tax consultant sticks mainly to business and personal taxes. She even keeps the books for other plumbers in town.

Avalene said the last few days before the April 15 deadline are just "insane." The average cost for a basic personal tax return is $50.

She said she's been dreaming about whether particular forms have been filled out, what needs to be done and what forms have to be mailed. But it will all be over soon.

And Avalene says, "I'm going to sleep all day Tuesday."

# 4/11/91

**WHY WE DO WHAT WE DO.** Here at Boone County's Greatest Morning Newspaper, we intend to bring you news that's relevant, useful and interesting. That's why, for instance, you see on Page 1 today and most days stories about health and education. Those are Columbia's major industries and among nearly everyone's major concerns.

Of course, THE major concern this week — and one that creates another major industry — is taxes. I hope you find our Page 1 reporting today useful. I think you'll find it interesting. In any case, I welcome your reactions. My number is 882-5734.

— **George Kennedy, managing editor**

COLUMBIA

**TESTING YOUR SMARTS.** M.U. faculty have bristled at the idea of standardized student testing, and the university's new provost, Gerald Brouder, says questions remain about how useful it is. 8A

*Other local news*

- Using Earth to save energy. 7A

NATION

**YOU SCRATCH MY BACK . . .** Attorney General Dick Thornburgh raises the prospect that President Bush would pass the 'Brady bill' if Congress passes his anti-crime bill. 2A

**HISPANICS MAKE FEW GAINS.** The nation's fast-growing Hispanic population is still at the bottom of the economic ladder, a Census Bureau report indicates. 2A

*Other national news*

- Fans turn on New Kids. 2A
- Suicide attempt results in AIDS. 2A

SPORTS

**TIGERS TAKE TWO.** The Tiger baseball team swept a double-header against Missouri Western. Joe Winkler was 7-for-7 and scored seven runs. 1B

CORRECTION

**OOPS.** If you were confused by Wednesday's note here about President Bush coming to town for a soldier's funeral, you weren't alone. Bush is coming to town, but not ours.

CALENDAR

- The Jordan International Circus will appear at 7 p.m. at the Hearnes Center, 600 Stadium Blvd.
- Revivalist rock quartet Redd Kross and Chicago's gritty Eleventh Dream will kick off KCOU's Springfest at 9 p.m. at the Blue Note, 17 N. Ninth St.

## Fraternities launch spud warfare

By MELANIE SACKSON
Missourian staff writer

Spring is in the air. And so are golf balls, potatoes and even a chicken.

This week, Sigma Alpha Epsilon and Kappa Sigma members revived the annual tradition of launching golf balls and other objects at each other's houses via sling shots and golf clubs.

But at least one neighbor who lives between the two fraternities doesn't find their annual spring rivalry funny. The family has found golf balls on its lawn and roof and even in its living room.

Recognizing that golf balls could present a danger, members of Sigma Alpha Epsilon decided to use potatoes and hard-boiled eggs this spring. "A few days ago we shot a half a chicken," said Steve Marsh, a fraternity member.

They made the switch to food after some of the members' cars were dented. Some windows at the house also were broken last spring.

Neighbor Mary Jane Grundler has had enough.

"This happens every spring," said Grundler, who has had two windows broken by golf balls over the past several years. She said repeated calls to police have produced no results.

"The last time we called they said more stringent action would be taken the next time we called," she said. But the fraternities were just given warnings after calls Monday and Wednesday, she said.

Police Capt. Chris Egbert said he didn't know of any charges filed against either of the two fraternities. "If someone got hit, there could be an assault," he said.

So far, no injuries have been reported.

"I hope there's no more of it," Grundler said. "We don't like to complain, but it's a matter of danger."

## Army nurse speaks to son's class

### Woman recently returned from Gulf

By TRACY L. KING
Missourian staff writer

NICK WERTELECKI/Missourian

1st Lt. Diane Meek, an operating nurse who served in Saudi Arabia, spoke Wednesday at Mill Creek Elementary School.

Army 1st Lt. Diane Meek of Columbia spent nearly three months in Saudi Arabia. During that time, she dreamed that her two children visited her in the Middle East. In the dream her children were without gas masks — fearing for their safety — as she tried frantically to put them on a plane home.

Speaking to a fourth-grade class at Mill Creek Elementary School on Wednesday, Meek was quick to give her son, Darron, a hug whenever he was within arm's reach.

Just one week after returning home from Saudi Arabia, where she was stationed with the 904th medical detatchment, Meek had two messages for the students: Be proud you're an American and free, and don't take your friends for granted.

Darron, a fourth-grader at Mill Creek who said he had faith that his mother would return safely, never strayed far from her side during the presentation.

Before it, Meek was concerned that a discussion about Operation Desert Storm might upset the children.

The students, who had sent Valentine's Day cards to troops as a school project, appeared to be rather well-versed about the Gulf war. They asked about specific types of aircraft and weapons, whether she had lost any patients and whether she got to meet President Bush.

"No," Meek replied, "some people got to meet Stormin' Norman too, but I didn't."

Meek told the students about cultural differences between Americans and the people of the Middle East. She described how Kuwaiti people she met thought they could buy security and friendship with money.

"No matter how much money you have, you still need friends," she said.

Darron modeled a cap worn by Saudi Arabian schoolchildren. Meek told the students that women in Saudi Arabia don't have the same freedoms as American women.

"Being female, they never go out in society, like to go shopping," she said.

At that, the children gasped.

Saudi "men had a hard time accepting American women, unless we had on army uniforms. When I had my uniform on, I was like a man to them," she said.

Now that she's home, Meek, a nurse, doesn't want to return to work full time. "We take life for granted and I want to spend time with my kids."

These are brand names and prices of some of the bottled water available at Gerbes, 1729 W. Broadway:

| | |
|---|---|
| Diamond | $1.29/gall. |
| Finnegan's | $1.09/gall. |
| La Croix | 99 cents/32 oz. |
| Mtn. Valley | 99 cents/1.5-liter |
| Evian | $2.09/1.5-liter |
| Ozarka | $1.29/1.5-liter |
| Excelsior Spgs. | $1.39/1.5-liter |
| Talking Rain | $1.29/32 oz. |
| Canadian Spring | $1.19/25 oz. |
| Perrier | 99 cents/25 oz. |
| Chapelle | $1.49/23 oz. |
| Mendota Spring | $3.49/96 oz. |
| Klarbrunn | $2.79/72 oz. |

## People who shun tap water might not be gaining a thing

By LAURA WATILO
Missourian staff writer

Sharon Sessions rolled her cart through Gerbes grocery store Wednesday evening, scanning five rows of bottled waters. She bent down and picked a bottle from the lowest shelf.

"Columbia water tastes terrible," said Sessions, one of many bottled-water drinkers contributing to the industry's growth.

Consumption in the United States has increased nearly fourfold in 10 years.

What Sessions and others might not know is that plain tap water could be safer than some pricey bottled waters.

The General Accounting Office, a congressional watchdog agency, concluded that the Food and Drug Administration needs to do more to ensure that bottled water is safe.

Inadequate regulations mean "bottled water, including mineral water, might contain levels of potentially harmful contaminants that are not allowed in public drinking water," the report said.

**The Associated Press contributed some information for this report.**

**Figure 1.1 Front Page of the Columbia Missourian for April 11, 1991.**

Relevance, of course, depends on your audience. Issues that are relevant to readers in Atlanta may be meaningless to people in Columbia, Missouri. Look at Figure 1.1. The stories on this front page from the Columbia Missourian were written, edited and displayed using the same criteria as in Atlanta. There's an education story, a health story, a war-related story. But none is the same as the stories in The Atlanta Constitution. The audience is different. Readers in Columbia and Atlanta share many broad interests and concerns, as do people from Key West, Fla., to Anchorage, Alaska, but the specifics that yield stories are local. For instance, education is important in both Atlanta and Columbia, but the language instruction of Georgia kindergartners would be of little more interest to Columbians than the fate of a school tax proposal in Missouri would be to Atlantans. Journalists who want their work to be relevant can't be content with knowing the subject matter of their stories. They also must know the audiences for those stories.

The ASNE study quoted earlier and many other recent studies show that people want news they can use. *Usefulness* has become an increasingly important criterion for assessing the news value of stories and potential stories as journalists have become increasingly aware of the competition for readers' time. Usefulness takes several forms. In a broad sense, any story that tells readers what is going on in the world is useful to people in a free society—The Atlanta Constitution's story of the problems of Soviet leader Mikhail Gorbachev is a good example. A story whose content can help readers participate in their society is even more useful. You can imagine, for example, the argument and emotion on both sides of the debate over whether cigarette companies should sponsor sporting events. And in a university town such as Columbia, many readers will take a personal interest in any effort to raise money for education. However, the most direct form of usefulness enables readers to do something directly that they want or need to do—to take some action. This is why the Missourian, four days before the income tax deadline, printed on page one a couple of stories describing the progress of America's least-loved ritual and offering help to those who had yet to file their tax returns.

The concept of usefulness has given rise to new newspaper sections and consumer magazines devoted to *service journalism*, the aim of which is to show people how to solve problems, make better decisions and generally improve their lives. Readers' preference for useful stories is even changing the way journalists write their most serious work, the investigation or analysis. In many cases today—and probably many more tomorrow—investigative and analytical stories include a section or a separate story telling how the problem explained or the abuse exposed can be corrected.

The final criterion for judging news value, *interest*, is built on relevance and usefulness, but it goes beyond them. Stories that touch readers' lives, especially stories that tell them how to improve life, are likely to be interesting. That isn't guaranteed. As you will see in later chapters, storytelling is a craft that requires of its practitioners skill not only in choosing topics but in gathering information and in writing clear and compelling prose.

The most interesting stories are most likely to come from reporters who remember that, as the scholar James Carey put it, ''Journalism is a culture's conversation with itself.'' That conversation will be painfully dull if it doesn't include some drama, some humor and lots of humanity. In other words, relevance should be defined broadly and not restricted to the grimmer aspects of existence.

Notice, for example, that The Atlanta Constitution used for its main photograph on page one a shot of the crowd at the opening-day baseball game. That's hardly a momentous event, but it is one that captures the interest of more Americans every year than just about any other happening. Look, too, at the Missourian story headlined, ''Fraternities Launch Spud Warfare.'' The story begins, ''Spring is in the air. And so are golf balls, potatoes and even a chicken.''

Just as baseball marks the coming of spring in a major-league city, so do fraternity pranks signal the season in a college town. Both events are relevant to the lives of the papers' readers; neither is especially useful, but both are interesting. Both belong in the conversation.

The best stories meet all three criteria—relevance, usefulness and interest. Not every worthwhile story does. Some stories worth telling are relevant but useful only in the broadest sense. Some useful stories are interesting only to those who share the particular problem or need being addressed. And some stories are interesting just because of their novelty, the prominence of their subjects, or even because of the skill with which they are told. As the ASNE and other studies have found, today's readers want their newspapers to be complete.

Now let's take a quick look ahead. Figures B, C, and D in the color insert show prototype pages produced by newspaper editors trying to apply news judgment criteria to create papers for the 21st century. Figure B shows the front page of the hypothetical Suburban Star for Jan. 14, 2001. Study it for a moment and you'll see that the trends of 1990 may become the standards of the next decade. Relevance and usefulness are the keys. Notice the emphasis on making the newspaper easy to use—the roundup of national and international news with the reference to the full report, the editor's chatty column with phone numbers and index to the paper below it, the charts and maps that provide information quickly as well as ''Today's Tip,'' an example of news-you-can-use. (By the way, the prototype appears in full color to make locating particular stories even easier.) Note also the feature story about the presumed triumph of Pete Rose Jr., a story valued purely for entertainment and combining prominence with novelty, two traditional criteria that add up to interest.

Figure C shows The Star's version of the lifestyle section in the year 2001, called ''The Suburban Family.'' The dominant story, ''Timesavers,'' is a good example of service journalism. But everything on the page is selected to be directly relevant to the lives of the hypothetical readers of the future. It doesn't take much imagination to see why those readers would find the page interesting and useful.

A possible "tailored newspaper" of the not-very-distant future, Womenews, is shown in Figure D. It demonstrates a logical extension of another trend of the 1990s, an effort to meet the information needs of particular groups of readers. In this case, the group constitutes a majority of the population. Recent studies have shown, to the consternation of editors and publishers, that newspaper readership among women is declining. Some experts speculate that the decline may be due, at least in part, to the fact that traditional definitions of news and traditional sources of news have been predominantly male-dominated. Womenews illustrates one possible solution to this problem.

This solution emerged from a brainstorming session sponsored by New Directions for News, a think tank supported by the newspaper industry and headquartered at the University of Missouri. When the idea was proposed to women in a focus group interview, the initial reaction was hostile. The women, like members of minority groups, preferred to see their interests addressed as part of regular news coverage. Once they saw the section, however, focus group members found it (in words that may have a familiar look by now) relevant, useful and therefore interesting.

---

# "New News" Poses New Challenges to Journalists

---

When journalism has been done well, it always has been a demanding craft. Gathering information, organizing it coherently, placing it in context and writing it clearly—that is work that has tested the intelligence, skill and stamina of practitioners since Jonathan Swift kept his "Journal of a Plague Year." Now, in some ways, the demands are becoming even greater. Let's consider why.

First, the tools journalists use are becoming more powerful and more sophisticated. In later chapters you will be introduced to the most important of these tools—the computer. You will see how you can—and must—move beyond the keyboard to use the computer for such tasks as checking background information in the reference library, conducting data-base searches that extend reporting beyond the interview, even performing analyses of budget data and surveys. With better tools, you'll be expected to produce better stories.

Second, the requirement to report and write stories that are relevant, useful and interesting means that the days of the reporter-as-recorder are numbered. Not so long ago, most reporters and editors were content with, for example, a story about a city council meeting that accurately recorded who said what to whom. Today, and tomorrow even more, a reporter who covers such a meeting is expected to tell her or his readers not only what was said but what the discussion means to the readers. Busy people don't have the time or inclination to read stories of no apparent relevance to them, so reporters must have the ability to spot significance and explain it. This kind of journalism—you might call it reporting in contrast to recording—requires an in-depth understanding of topics and a high level of writing skill.

Third, the steadily lengthening list of legitimate subjects of news stories requires of reporters both broader knowledge than ever before and an ability to seek out and use new kinds of sources.

The Orange County Register, competing for readers in media-rich southern California, has taken the lead in meeting this challenge. In 1990 the Register attracted widespread attention in the industry by declaring itself, in the words of editor N. Christian Anderson, a "newspaper without walls." The "walls" Anderson referred to are the traditional beats newspapers long have used to organize their coverage—city hall, courthouse, police, schools, business, and so on. The Register replaced these institution-based assignments with a broad set of assignments-by-topic. The topics included Southern California culture, relationships, making money, learning, houses and "getting around" (transportation and related issues). Within particular topics, for instance, a shopping mall reporter was part of the culture team and "friends and lovers" became part of relationships coverage.

Although the Register went further faster than other U.S. papers, its general direction was not unique. Rather, the direction was established tentatively more than 20 years earlier, when journalists began having to learn how to cover the social and political movements that were changing American life. Probably the first of these was the civil rights movement of the 1960s. Then came the emergence as powerful forces of women, the young, consumers, environmentalists, gays and others. The agendas and tactics of these movements differed, but collectively they forced journalists away from their traditional reliance on elected officials, government bureaucrats and business leaders as the sources of news. Martin Luther King Jr., Gloria Steinem, Ralph Nader, Cesar Chavez, Barry Commoner—none of them held political office or occupied a position of economic power—but they and dozens like them captured the attention and the headlines of America. Journalists had to learn how to find, deal with and evaluate newsmakers who lacked the traditional kinds of "official" credentials and who, in many cases, were highly suspicious of mainstream journalists.

You will have to do the same thing. You can't cover relationships by interviewing the mayor (unless, of course, you're writing about her or his relationships; but that's another story). You won't make sense of shopping malls by talking to a press officer at the U.S. Department of Commerce. To track down these new kinds of news, reporters must as never before draw on broad interests and broad educations.

The journalists of the 1990s and beyond need to know more than earlier generations about a growing number of issues, including biology (AIDS isn't going away), sociology (minorities are becoming the majority), statistics (it's a quantitative world out there) and the other disciplines that help explain an increasingly complicated and interrelated world. You are only beginning a learning process that, if you make your career in journalism, must be a continuing commitment.

# Accuracy, Fairness and the Problem of Objectivity

Amidst all the changes that are sweeping American journalism as the 20th century draws to a close, two traditions remain central. The first is the *professional ethic* that demands of every journalist accuracy and fairness. The second, more difficult to explain and easier to attack, is the tradition of objectivity. The two come together when we try to sum up what it is that reporters and editors are trying to do with their work.

The goal for which most journalists strive has seldom been expressed any better than in a phrase used by Bob Woodward, a great reporter and later an editor of The Washington Post. Woodward was defending in court an investigative story published by the Post. The story, he said, was ''the best obtainable version of the truth.''

A grander-sounding goal would be ''the truth,'' unmodified. But Woodward's phrase, while paying homage to the ideal, recognizes the realities of life and the limitations of journalism. After centuries of argument, philosophers and theologians have been unable to agree on just what truth is. Even if there were agreement on that basic question, how likely is it that the Catholic Church and the Planned Parenthood organization would agree on the ''truth'' about abortion, or that a president and his challenger would agree on the ''truth'' about the state of the American economy?

In American daily journalism, that kind of dispute is left to be fought out among the partisans on all sides, on the editorial pages and in commentaries.

The reporter's usual role is simply to find and write the facts. The trouble is, that turns out often to be not so simple.

Sometimes it's hard to get the facts. The committee searching for a new university president announces that the field of candidates has been narrowed to five, but the names of the five are not released. Committee members are sworn to secrecy. What can you do to get the names? Should you try?

Sometimes it's hard to tell what the facts mean. The state supreme court refuses to hear a case in which legislators are questioning the constitutionality of a state spending limit. The court says only that there is no "justiciable controversy." What does that mean? Who won? Is the ruling good news or bad news, and for whom?

Sometimes it's even hard to tell what is a fact. A presidential commission, after a year-long study, says there is no widespread hunger in America. Is the conclusion a fact? Or is the fact only that the commission said it? And how can you determine whether the commission is correct?

Daily journalism presents still more complications. Usually, as a reporter you have only a few hours, at most a few days, to try to learn as many facts as possible. Then, even in such a limited time, you may accumulate information enough for a story of 2,000 words, only to be told that there is space or time enough for 1,000 or fewer.

When you take into account all these realities and limitations, you can see that just to reach the best obtainable version of the truth is challenge enough for any journalist.

How can you tell when the goal has been reached? Seldom, if ever, is there a definitive answer. But there are two questions every responsible journalist should ask about every story before being satisfied: Is it accurate? Is it fair?

Accuracy is the most important characteristic of any story, great or small, long or short. Accuracy is essential in every detail. Every name must be spelled correctly; every quote must be just what was said; every set of numbers must add up. And that still isn't good enough. You can get the details right and still mislead unless you are accurate with context, too. The same statement may have widely different meanings depending on the circumstances in which it was uttered and the tone in which it was spoken. Circumstances and intent affect the meaning of actions, as well. You will never have the best obtainable version of the truth unless your version is built on accurate reporting of detail and context.

Nor can you approach the truth without being fair. Accuracy and fairness are related, but they are not the same. The relationship and the difference show clearly in this analogy from the world of sports:

The umpire in a baseball game is similar, in some ways, to a reporter. Each is supposed to be an impartial observer, calling developments as he or she sees them. (Of course, the umpire's job is to make judgments on those developments, while the reporter's is just to describe them.) Television has brought to sports the instant replay, in which a key development, say a close call at first base, can be examined again and again, often from an angle different from the umpire's view. Sometimes the replay shows an apparent outcome different from the one the umpire called. A runner who was ruled to be out may appear to have been safe instead. The difference may be due to human error on the umpire's part, or it may be due to the difference in angle, the difference in viewpoint. Umpires recognize this problem. They try to deal with it by obtaining the best possible view of every play and by conferring with their colleagues on some close calls. Still, every umpire knows that an occasional mistake will be made. That is unavoidable. What can, and must, be avoided is unfairness. Umpires must be fair, and both players and fans must believe they are fair. Otherwise, umpires' judgments will not be accepted; they will not be trusted.

There are no instant replays in news. There are, however, different viewpoints from which every event or issue can be observed. Each viewpoint may yield a different interpretation of what is occurring and of what it means. There is also, in journalism as in sport, the possibility of human error, even by the most careful reporters.

Fairness requires that you as a reporter try to find every viewpoint on a story. Hardly ever will there be just one; often there are more than two. Fairness requires that you allow ample opportunity for response to anyone who is being attacked or whose integrity is being questioned in a story. Fairness requires, above all, that you make every effort to avoid following your own biases in your reporting and your writing.

These rules that mainstream journalists follow in attempting to arrive at the best obtainable version of the truth are commonly summarized as objectivity. Objectivity has been and still is accepted as a working credo by many, perhaps most, American journalists, students and teachers of journalism. It has been exalted by leaders of the profession as an essential, if unattainable, ideal. Its critics, by contrast, have attacked objectivity as, in the phrase of sociologist Gaye Tuchman, a "strategic ritual" that conceals a multitude of professional sins while producing superficial and often misleading coverage.

Michael Schudson, in his classic "Discovering the News," traces the rise of objectivity to the post–World War I period, when scholars and journalists alike turned to the methods and the language of science in an attempt to make sense of a world that was being turned upside down by the influence of Freud and Marx, the emergence of new economic forces and the erosion of traditional values. Objectivity was a reliance on observable facts, but it was also a methodology for freeing factual reporting from the biases and values of source, writer or reader. It was itself a value, an ideal.

Schudson wrote, "Journalists came to believe in objectivity, to the extent that they did, because they wanted to, needed to, were forced by ordinary human aspiration to seek escape from their own deep convictions of doubt and drift."

Schudson and Robert Karl Manoff, editors of an important collection of essays, "Reading the News," describe the conflict between the ideal of journalistic objectivity and the way journalism really works:

# THE ATLANTA CONSTITUTION

For 122 Years the South's Standard Newspaper

Copyright © 1991 The Atlanta Constitution  THURSDAY, APRIL 11, 1991  ★★★★★

---

## The Shuttle's First Decade

Experts say the gap between promise and reality has made it NASA's institutional albatross

**Page A12**

### BUSINESS

**Bottom line**

CNN has fame — that's for sure. Now the trick is transforming that fame into fortune. **D1**

▶ Nintendo zapped by price-fixing accusation. **D1**

### SPORTS

**All business**

Nick Faldo is a golfer with a purpose — to win. **E1**

▶ NFL Commissioner rules out dealing during draft. **E1**
▶ 40,000 runners! Field full for Peachtree Road Race. **E1**

### PEOPLE

**Photo finish?**

This TV season is turning out to be the closest three-way ratings finish since "Bonanza" was No. 1 in 1965. **F1**

▶ Sex, lies part of White House gossip tradition. **F4**

### WEATHER

Expect increasing cloudiness today, with a high of 74 and a low of 56. **E24**

### INDEX

BUSINESS ........... SECTION D
FOOD ................ SECTION W
METRO/STATE ....... SECTION C
NATION/WORLD ...... SECTION A
PEOPLE ............. SECTION F
SPORTS ............. SECTION E

DIV, 123, NO. 20911 112 PAGES, 10 SECTIONS

ABBY        F2   EDITORIALS   A18
GAYFER      E2   HOROSCOPE    F7
BRADLEY     A3   JUMBLE       E19
BRIDGE      F7   MOVIES       F6
CATHY       F2   NEWSMAKERS   F2
CLASSIFIEDS E14  OBITUARIES   C6
COMICS      F6   PEOPLE       A19
CROSSWORD   E19  TELEVISION   F6

**TO SUBSCRIBE, CALL 522-4141**

This newspaper is printed in part on recycled paper and is recyclable. For the recycling coordinator nearest you, please phone 222-2000.

---

## A war on tobacco in sports?
### Health chief Sullivan suggesting a boycott

The New York Times

WASHINGTON — Health and Human Services Secretary Louis W. Sullivan on Wednesday asked sports fans and promoters to boycott sports events sponsored by tobacco companies.

He said Americans should send a message to those "who would encourage our children to use addictive substances which will ruin their health and send them to an early grave."

Dr. Sullivan did not use the word "boycott," but staff members said that was only because he feared it would sound "coercive."

He specifically asked that owners of public and private arenas and parks stop letting their complexes be used for sporting events sponsored by tobacco companies, and he asked sports promoters to stop accepting tobacco companies as sponsors.

A spokesman for the department, Campbell Gardett, said Dr. Sullivan believes that fans should "recognize that when a sporting event is sponsored by a tobacco company that it is being used to pro-

**Please see SMOKING, A12 ▶**

**Louis W. Sullivan**

---

### Cigarettes and sports

Tobacco companies have learned one way to reach the public is through sponsorship of sporting programs. Some of the premier events they sponsor include:

**AUTO RACING**
▶ Winston Cup Series
▶ Marlboro Grand Prix
▶ Camel GT Series
▶ Benson & Hedges International

**GOLF**
▶ Vantage Seniors Tour

**PLUS** ▶ Virginia Slims Women's Tennis Series

---

### SIGN OF SUPPORT
## Bring *on the* Braves!

Fans support Atlanta's Dave Justice, 1990 National League rookie of the year, at the Braves-Dodgers game Wednesday. Tuesday night's scheduled opener was rained out.

From Nemann Staff

**INSIDE** ▶ Atlanta loses opener to Dodgers 6-4  **E1**
▶ Braves on road to recapturing audience  **E1**

---

## U.S. to keep watch over Kurdish relief
### White House warns Iraqis not to attack in refugee zone

By Deborah Scroggins and Andrew Alexander

▶ Bases in S.C., Alabama on closing list  **A9**

WASHINGTON — In a major expansion of U.S. involvement in northern Iraq, the United States on Wednesday offered military protection for a massive international relief operation to aid Kurdish refugees.

The State Department told aid agencies that

U.S. forces will provide air cover for relief workers helping the refugees, and the White House said it has warned Iraq not to interfere.

White House press secretary Marlin Fitzwater said the United States warned Iraq last weekend not to engage in "any military activities" in areas of the country where Kurdish refugees are fleeing from Iraqi President Saddam Hussein's forces.

"We informed Iraq that the United States, the

**Please see RELIEF, A15 ▶**

---

## Soviets defy Gorbachev, hold strike

By T. Elaine Carey
Journal-Constitution correspondent

MOSCOW — Tens of thousands of Soviets on Wednesday ignored President Mikhail S. Gorbachev's call for a moratorium on protests and refused to work, despite his warning that the country is teetering on the edge of economic ruin.

The largest work stoppage was in Byelorussia, where that republic's leaders permitted strike organizers to read a strident anti-Communist statement during the republic's nightly television news program.

"The Communist Party of the Soviet Union is guilty of the collapse of the economy ... and annihilation of the peoples and their languages," strike committee member Georgi Mukhin said in the broadcast. "This party tries to preserve its dominance over us at our expense."

By one estimate, up to 200,000 workers participated in the stoppage in Byelorussia, which is in the western Soviet Union next to the Baltic republic of Lithuania.

The non-Communist government in the southern republic of Georgia, which is seeking independence from Moscow, told its workers Wednesday to skip work to protest Soviet rule.

The work stoppages have added to the economic chaos in the Soviet Union, where a 6-week-old nationwide walkout by

about 300,000 coal miners has threatened to sharply reduce industrial output. On Wednesday, some striking coal miners said they are now prepared to stop shipping coal to consumers.

The Byelorussia strike was the most dangerous escalation of industrial discontent for Mr. Gorbachev. The protesters crowding the center square in Minsk, a city of 1.5 million, shouted first for Mr. Gorbachev's resignation — as did strikers elsewhere — and secondly for better food supplies.

Byelorussia has been one of the republics most politically loyal to the Kremlin and the Communist Party. Until now, it has witnessed little of the anti-Moscow political upheaval experienced in other independence-minded republics.

---

☭ **THE SOVIET DILEMMA:**
Can Gorbachev survive?

A special Q & A
**PAGE A2**

---

## Some kindergartners to speak in foreign tongues this fall
### Georgia pilot program targets 5-year-olds

By Betsy White
Staff writer

Georgia will launch an aggressive new foreign language program this fall by targeting a group of people who haven't even mastered their own language yet — kindergartners.

Fifteen school systems will offer the youngsters daily lessons in Spanish, French, German or Japanese — whichever the school chooses.

With that step, Georgia will join a handful of states that have moved to teach foreign languages to 5-year-olds.

Under a plan approved Wednesday by the state Board of Education, Georgia will start the program this fall with 15 teachers in 15 districts throughout the state. Classes will expand a grade each year, through grade four, in the pilot systems, then go statewide in 1996.

"This is really exciting," said board member Richard Owens of Oscilla. He noted that Department of Education officials had asked the Legislature for years to fund a pilot program of elementary foreign language instruction, only to be turned down.

This year, with new leaders in many state posts — including a new lieutenant governor whose undergraduate major was French — the Legislature came through with $341,000.

School systems chosen to pilot the program will be those that demonstrate they want it the most, Mr. Duncan said. Lessons will last 30 minutes each day and will focus on learning numbers, colors, days of the week and other concepts that kindergartners also are studying in English, he said.

"Kids learn languages best at early ages," said Greg Duncan, state coordinator of foreign language instruction. "They just pick it up by osmosis. ... The are elementary students who can fare as well, if not better in some cases, as high school students after four years of instruction."

**Please see LANGUAGE, A17 ▶**

---

**River outing:** Philip Greer and Christi Lambert canoe along a section of the Etowah, where erosion has contributed to trees tipping over the waterway.

Michael A. Schwarz/Staff

## Etowah River rushes toward uncertain future

By McKay Jenkins and Bill Torpy
Staff writers

Great blue herons arc across the river canopy, drifting restlessly from tree to tree. In the underbrush, a red fox, suspicious, peers out at the cedar-strip canoe passing nearby. A wooden paddle, dipped too deep, taps an ancient stone fishing dam hidden just below the river's gurgling surface.

In sections, the Etowah River has changed little since Native Americans chose the pastoral plains of its shores for a temple to the sun 10

centuries ago. More recently, a Saudi prince, captivated by its lush beauty, planned to build an opulent manor along 7,700 acres of its virgin banks.

But in the last few decades, this North Georgia river also has been a sewer for chicken guts, human waste and toxic runoff from old farms and new development. Its lowlands soon may be used for a granite quarry and to stow the region's trash. To get more drinking water, Cherokee County wants to build another dam on the

**Please see ETOWAH, A14 ▶**

---

Figure A
Front Page of the Atlanta Constitution for April 11, 1991.

# THE WORLD IN A MINUTE

■ **The Stock Market** hit a peri; crash high yesterday, closing up 27 points at 8,627. This was the third time in the last two weeks that stocks soared past the previous high, set before the November, 1999 crash. *Champagne was flowing on Wall Street.*

■ **The 'Morning After Pill'** has gone on sale in supermarkets and drug stores in California, marking the first non-prescription use of the once controversial instant-abortion. Sales yesterday were reported brisk. *The pills are expected to be on counter tops in all 51 states by spring.*

■ **South African** Prime Minister Benjamin Tutu will make his first official visit to the United States and to the United Nations in February, the State Department announced today. *Tutu announced earlier that he would set the long-awaited visit after the inauguration of President-Elect Bradley.*

■ **The Challenger** space shuttle will blast off Wednesday morning from it's Cape Atlantic platform off Puerto Rico, with it's largest load of space waste to date. *Deposit site for the toxic wastes is a Jupiter moon.*

■ **The unusual heat** wave in the New England states has ski resort owners trying to find new ways to lure skiers. *At Stowe in Vermont an outdoor art exhibit was mounted on ski lifts as the curious basked in the 70° sunshine.*

■ **Syria and Israel** are expected to sign their long-awaited trade pact in ceremonies today in Jerusalem. Leaders of the two countries – once bitter enemies – linked arms and joked with reporters. *The pact is expected to be a model for other mid-east trade ventures.*

■ **President-Elect** Bill Bradley was at home in New Jersey, reportedly closing in on a decision for the two un-named members of his cabinet. *Much speculation and no information is available on his choices to head the offices of Education and Housing.*

**Turn to the Back Page for the national/ international report.**

# SUBURBAN SPOTLIGHT

**Cave-in and catacombs: How safe is Jackson Hole?**

After more than a year of traipsing from neighbors' homes to hotels, John Ketchum is back in his own bed. His was one of seven homes that disappeared when a 120-year-old mining shaft gave way. Jackson Hole today is a tree-lined suburban dream, except for the tunnels that spread like a dangerous spiderweb under its homes. *Experts say the cave-ins will happen again.* Story B1

**KETCHUM:** "It was a living nightmare"

# ECO-LOTTERY

***Scratch off** and match and win $50! proceeds go to Ocean Clean-Up Committee.*

January 14, 2001

# The Suburban STAR

# BIZ WRAP

DOW JONES

4,200.11

HOUSING STARTS

Down 1.2%

$800 $611 $125

PUBLISHED IN NEPTUNE, N.J. — 50 CENTS — CENTRAL NEW JERSEY EDITION

# EDITOR'S LIST

**From the desk of Jane Smith, Managing Editor**

It's hard to be terribly interested in world politics when you're sitting in traffic jams, and, unfortunately, *yesterday's fire that crippled I-78* is guaranteed to make already bearish commutes a real test of patience. ☞ And, as though to add insult to proverbial injury, the poor ol' Garden State commuter took yet another hit yesterday: the announcement by the Parkway folks that *we're going to have to shell out a dollar at each toll booth along the stretch.* The double whammy — a major east-west thoroughfare closed and a 25-cent per booth toll increase — makes one wonder just how long the patience of the Jersey commuter will hold out. We've been *pleading for monorails like California's for years,* but those deaf wheeler-dealers in Trenton don't seem to be paying attention. But maybe with Dollar **Bill Bradley** headed for the White House, we'll have that extra bit of clout in the Capitol — enough for a mass transit slam dunk. Nevertheless, there are still a few items of "good" news. ☞ Remember **Melissa Stern**, *the bubbly blonde Baby M whose infamous mother and dad make surrogate parents household words?* Well, Melissa, now a 14-year-old freshman at Ranney School in Tinton Falls, brought home straight A's on her first high school report card. *She's philosophical about her early notoriety and her natural mother* whom she calls "a great friend." Her story is on Page C1. ☞ And while we're mentioning school, I understand *the 12-month school year,* which celebrates its second anniversary this week, is actually doing what it was intended to do: teach kids to read and write. Seems to me we've finally gotten our state government to do something worthwhile — *and without taxing (no pun intended) our wallets.* ☞ And, just in case you're able to swing off the Parkway early this evening, drop by Brookdale Community College between 3-5 p.m. **ChemFood Inc.** will give you a taste of things to come: *chemically reproduced anchovies, Chinese dumplings and sushi.* All free — as well it should be. Chat tomorrow.

**TELEPHONE INFO-DIAL 908**

| | |
|---|---|
| Business Report | 922-7698 |
| Community air quality | 922-6640 |
| Commuter traffic report | 922-6927 |
| Legislative calendar | 922-6587 |
| Sportsline | 922-7868 |
| World Weather | 922-6748 |

**INSIDE**



# ASBURY PARK

## CITY'S TOURISM UP 200% FOR NEW COUNTRY HIGH

■ Gambling responsible for rise
■ Unemployment cut in half

By JOE ADELIZZI
Star gambling editor

**Gambling casinos** have been credited with the exceptional rise in tourism for the City of Asbury Park. It has become, in fact the biggest boom town in the U.S. Figures released by the U.S. Dept. of Commerce and Tourism put Asbury Park at the top of the list of growth cities.

The casino gambling — which has been in effect for two years — was the last gasp effort of Henry Vaccaro to save a city which had been in disarray since the early 70s. Since then, a boardwalk reconstruction in 1994 and the addition of two new gambling hotels in 1999 have tourists flocking back to the city.

Vaccaro began talks with Gov. John F. Russo three years ago in his attempts to bring gambling to the city. Before that, Atlantic City and Newark were the only places in the state of New Jersey where casinos were legal.

**Atlantic City's** casinos opened in 1978. Betting parlors for pro sporting events and also casino games were approved by voters in 1996 for Newark. Since then Newark has been able to expand its low-income housing and now has an unemployment rate of less than three percent.

Asbury Park had an unemployment level of 12 percent which has been halved.

# I-78 aflame; drivers sizzle

BUCKLED PORTION OF I-78 can be seen at left, as trooper checks damage.

MICHAEL RAFFERTY/Star Photograph

## Firefighters hospitalized

■ 35 admitted for observation
■ None injured seriously
■ Most inhaled toxic fumes

By MATTY RABAS
Star Reporter

**Choking firefighters were rushed** to four New Jersey hospitals as toxic fumes downed scores during the height of the I-78 fire last night. None of the injuries were described as serious by medical authorities, but 35 were admitted for treatment.

SITE OF ROAD CLOSING — Newark — Newark International Airport — Elizabeth

"For Monmouth and Ocean commuters, they'll probably meet with substantial additional traffic," Gagliano said. "I would recommend that if they're going to drive, they leave earlier."

"Route 78 traffic would affect 25,000 to 30,000 vehicles during rush hours," he said. "Those that drive will be taking different routes, affecting those people already on those routes."

Gagliano said motorists seeking alternatives through NJ Transit can call a hot line number: 201-507-1500.

The fire at Hub Recycling Co. began at 1:30 a.m., and quickly spread throughout a 25-foot-high, 400-yard-long pile of rubbish and construction debris directly under the road. The blaze, which was still burning last

Please see Page 4

## Road crippled until April

By STEVE CHAMBERS
Star Newark Bureau Chief

**A rubbish fire** beneath an elevated section of Interstate 78 yesterday destroyed a part of the road, forcing its indefinite closing and creating a potential nightmare for commuters who use several roads in the already congested transportation hub.

It could take six months to a year to replace sections of the heavily traveled, 12-lane highway, which links Newark International Airport with western New Jersey counties and Pennsylvania, state transportation officials said.

**But the fire's biggest effect** on Shore-area commuters will likely be traffic jams on north-south roads such as the Garden State Parkway, Routes 1 and 9, and New Jersey Turnpike interchanges as thousands of additional cars and trucks that would have used I-78 are forced onto other roads.

"This is the most serious traffic emergency in my memory," said Gov. Kean, who flew over the site. "It could not have occurred in a worse place."

Motorists traveling to the airport are being advised to leave themselves extra time to reach the facility because of increased traffic congestion. Several people reported missing scheduled flights yesterday because of heavy traffic on airport approach roads.

"It doesn't look too good," acknowledged state Department of Transportation spokesman Randy Linthurst. "It's a major artery."

Gov. Kean is considering asking that the site be declared a federal disaster area to obtain funds for the rebuilding.

# THE PARKWAY

## $1 GSP TOKEN TO HIT SPRING COMMUTERS

■ First toll increase in five years
■ Commuters organize protest

By HARRIS SIEGEL
Star transportation writer

**A buck a day each way** is what you'll be paying starting Jan 1, 2001 if you go through one toll booth on the Garden State Parkway.

At least that's the plan according to the Garden State Parkway Highway Authority, which yesterday approved the additional twenty-five cents for each toll plaza on the Parkway.

"We haven't raised our tolls in five years," said executive director George Buckwald Jr., a member of the Authority for the last 30 years.

"A dollar a toll is well within the toll structure of other area roadways. In fact, when you compare it to the $12 toll to use bridges and tunnels leading into New York, the Garden State Parkway remains one of the best buys among highways."

Local commuters didn't agree. The Commuters Against Ripoffs (CAR), formed when the toll was raised to fifty cents in 1992, now numbers 60,000 members. Nearly a thousand of them

Please see Page 4

# JACKSON'S ROSE

## ROSE JR. SMELLS LIKE A ROSE; HITS FOR NEW RECORD

■ NJ star squashes Dimaggio log
■ Stadium crowd goes wild
■ Police called to Jackson field

By JOE 'SULLY' SULLIVAN
Star Sports Editor

**A new century begins** with a record that historians say can't be broken. Pete Rose Jr. last night erased the name of Joe Dimaggio from the record book when he singled in the seventh inning to increase his hitting streak to 57 straight games.

Rose Jr.'s hit for the New Jersey Yankees came before a standing room only crowd of 46,425 at the Jackson Township Stadium and led the Denver Orioles to a 3-2 victory.

Pete Jr., whose father was banned from baseball in 1989 but returned five years later as manager of the Yankees when they moved from Yankee Stadium to their home here at Adelizzi Park, had passed his father's hitting streak of 44 games two weeks ago. Since than, Rose Sr. has been allowed to follow his sons progress by Yankee Owner George Steinbrenner.

**While Rose Jr.'s hit** erased the name of another Yankee from the record books it brought this Ocean County crowd to its feet with excitement. Rose had been struck out twice in the early going, both by veteran Al Leiter.

But when Rose Jr. came to the plate in the seventh inning to face the ageless Nolan Ryan the crowd was in a frenzy.

As he lashed out at a Ryan fastball and lined the ball to center field the crowd stood as one, in recognition of his accomplishment.

Dimaggio's streak had been thought of as the last unreachable record in the game since Cy Young's record of 511 victories was surpassed by Nolan Ryan. Cal Ripkin Jr. broke Lou Gehrig's consecutive game record in 1994. Both of those players were on hand for Rose Jr.'s dramatic hit yesterday.

Rose Jr. refused to attend a press conference after the game. He has not spoken to the press since his father's banishment from the game 11 years ago. When his father came back as the Yankees' manager, he was still silent.

# TODAY'S TIP

***First home-issued passes set for boarding today*** ■ Long awaited direct reservations for the Coastal SuperTram and all scheduled airlines can now be made from home computers. To access, type the name of the service or carrier. Your screen will display the 4-step process.

**Figure B**
**A Front Page Prototype for the Suburban Star, January 14, 2001.**

In 1989, Fred Savage was 13 and star of the TV hit, "The Wonder Years," but when the show went off the air in 1993, Savage seemed to disappear. Where is he now?

"I got tired of being famous," Savage, 24, says, "and I was ready for college. So I gave up acting to pursue my real interest: biology."

Today, it's Dr. Fred Savage.

He's head of testing at Revlon in Fontana, Calif., where he has spearheaded a movement away from animal testing. He created a computer program model on which to conduct experiments.

"I loved acting, but show business seems so shallow compared to this," says Savage. "But I still get a kick out of seeing the reruns."

Fred Savage: 1988 and 2000

# WE
## The Suburban Family
Gannett Westchester Newspapers/October 22, 2000

Sam and Sue Burban

## HOUR BY HOUR
with the Burbans

### How a family drives down Easy Street

This is the first in a series on how one suburban family manages its time. Reporter Wallis Winchell spent a full 24 hours with Sam and Sue Burban in their split-level ranch house on Easy Street in Tea Town for this report.

**By Wallis Winchell**

The digitized voice from the Burbans' alarm radio has stopped urging them to "please wake." The soft music that followed the voice has also ended when the cohabitants of the Burban bed failed to rise. The Burbans are 8 minutes late, and the three-alarm howl of their failsafe electronic system has awakened not only them, but 4-year-old son S.J. and dog Dodie.

Sam and Sue Burban make up for lost time with quickie showers in their matching stalls. Sam's shave takes 2 minutes 37 seconds.

Sue opens the automatic waiter door and pours coffee for both of them.

The microwave buzzes and breakfast is ready. "Insta-oats again?" S.J. whines.

S.J. is not in a good mood. "I don't want to go to school," he hollers. "But you love Pre-K." Sue tells him, escorting him to the bus stop where he will be picked up by the district bus and deposited back 12 hours later.

Sam and Sue head for work in their twin BMWs. S.J. boards the bus.

Traffic is barely moving on the expressway. Sam turns off the radio news and inserts a video disk. His boss, George, is detailing today's assignments, beginning with a videoconference at 8 a.m. with commodities brokers from Topeka, Oslo and Lima. A traffic bulletin activates the radio and directs him to swing to the outer lane, take exit 12A and Forest Street to the Cross-Suburban Expressway. It should get him to work by 8:25 — an hour and a half isn't bad, he mutters.

Sue's commute is much easier, just a short mile or so to the Lawyers Condo Park where she practices international patent law. The office could be anywhere in the world, she muses, since video courts have linked attorneys and judges worldwide.

Sue arrives and walks into her office. "An early arrival is still essential if you want to get ahead in this world," she tells the reporter a step behind her.

Sue Burban barks instructions to her computer: "Activate. Overnight patent filings in drawer 12, please. Last hour on arrears."

*Please see HOUR BY HOUR, S6*

---

FAMILY THERAPY

## Teen runaway heads for sun

**By Barbara Nachman**
Staff writer

Today WE visits with Dr. Fred and the Randall family of Rye. Sharon Randall, 45, is an account executive with Randall, Sharwick and Sheldon, a White Plains advertising agency. Todd Randall, 11, was adopted as an infant by Randall who has never been married. Also present is Sharon's fiance Julian Baker, 44, a micro-nutritionist with private practices in Rye and Manhattan. The wedding is scheduled in two months.

WE's visit with Dr. Fred and the Randall's reflects this newspaper's continuing effort to explore the changing face of the family in the 21st century.

**Dr. Fred:** (After an initial greeting) I understand you're experiencing difficulties. Who would like to begin?

**Sharon:** Well, last week Todd ran away. He was missing for 28 hours before we located him in Cape May, N.J. I think he was trying to get to Florida.

**Dr. Fred:** Todd, would you like to talk about this.

(Todd shakes his head.)

**Julian:** I was at the house when Todd left. I guess you could say we had an disagreement. He was blasting that electro-magnetic music of his on the CD recorder and I asked him, I thought politely, to lower the volume. He said "You're not my boss." Then he stormed out.

**Todd:** (mumbles) Well you're not.

**Fred:** What was that, Todd?

**Todd:** It's none of his business. He can't tell me what to do.

**Sharon:** (crying) The thing is that Todd and Julian were getting along so well. I mean they're both into these memorial armchair things and Julian even took him to a "Fry and Cry" concert at the County Center.

**Fred:** So Todd, what gives? (Todd doesn't answer.)

**Fred:** Why Florida?

**Todd:** I think I can answer that. Todd and I went to Florida, I think it was in 1998. We had a great time. Didn't we Todd?

**Todd:** (his voice cracking) Why does everything have to change? Why can't things just stay the same? I liked it the way it was. Mom's just ragging out by marrying him anyway.

**Fred:** Well Todd, I certainly can understand your apprehension. The unknown can be pretty scary. But change can also mean improvement.

**Sharon:** Look, I never would have even gotten engaged if I didn't think Todd was for it. Todd even helped me come up with the date.

**Fred:** But now that the date is getting closer...

**Todd:** Yeah, like now I'll have two people bossing me around.

**Sharon:** That's not the way it will be.

**Fred:** OK. Here's what I'd like you to do. In the next week I'd like each of you to write a few notes about how you'd like your new family to function. We'll create a family contract, a written agreement that sets down the rules for your new family. You can be as specific as stating the time of day Todd can listen to the CD or as general as who has the last word on family vacations. Because the rules will be on paper, there will be no surprises. And of course, if anyone violates the contract, they'll have to answer to me.

---

# TIME-SAVERS

*Time Tips is a weekly feature devoted to a universal pursuit: saving time.*

*If you have time-saving tips to offer, send them to Time Tips, Gannett Westchester Newspapers, 1 Gannett Drive, White Plains, N.Y. 10604.*

■ **CHRISTMAS SHOPPING:** The coming Christmas season got you down? No time to shop? No patience for the crowds? Then shop by mail, like an increasing number of Americans.

Just about any kind of merchandise can be had by mail, if you're willing to look hard enough. There are the old standbys, Spiegel and L.L. Bean catalogs.

But if you're not on anyone's mailing list and you don't know where to begin, send for "Shop By Mail Worldwide" by Anne Flato and Marilyn Schiff, a handy guide to mail-order shopping for anything your heart desires. This 300-page guide will take you from blankets to furniture to jewelry to linens to toys, and from Copenhagen to Manhattan.

The book, which points you specifically to stores that specialize in bargains, even includes a foreign currency exchange table, and tips on how to order.

"Shop by Mail Worldwide" is $9.95 and available in most book stores. If you can't find it, write to Random House, 201 East 50th St., New York, N.Y. 10022.

**Time spent:** About 60 mins. **Time saved:** several weekends of shopping.

■ **FAMILY DESSERT:** Next rainy day project: Oat clusters.

2 cups Quaker Oats
1 cup cooked microwave popcorn (plain)
1 cup dark Karo syrup
1 cup peanuts or cashews
½ cup melted margarine or butter

Mix all ingredients in a large bowl, using a wooden spoon. When mixture is thick, tell the kids to rub butter or margarine on their hands. Then they can reach into the mixture and make small cluster balls. Place the balls on a greased cookie sheet, then into the refrigerator for one hour to chill. This is a great recipe that will keep the kids busy for a solid hour, and does not require the use of a stove or oven. While they're "cooking," you can get some work done.

**Time spent:** 15 mins. **Time saved:** One hour to do other things.

■ **REMEMBERING FRIENDS:** Are your friends and family feeling neglected? By the time you get home, get the family settled and grab a couple of seconds for yourself, are you too tired to call or write a note? Did you forget half the important birthdays on your last list year, or rush to a store to send belated, apologetic notes a week too late? Why not build your important but distant people right into your schedule? Go through your birthday/anniversary list. Buy a year's worth of cards in one trip to the card shop, and address and stamp the envelopes. File card and envelope by month —events that fall the first week of the month should be filed in the previous month's folder.

On the first day of every month, sign the cards, write quick notes on them and mail them. Yours will be the first to be received, never the last.

**Time spent:** 90 mins. **Time saved:** Hours and hours of guilt each year.

■ **ON THE HIGHWAY:** Did you know that a recent study by the Bridge and Tunnel Authority of New York showed that drivers who go to the farthest right-hand tollbooth will get through a toll plaza about 90 seconds faster than the driver who chooses the farthest left-hand tollbooth? Remember that the next time you're on the Tappan Zee.

*Staff photos/Michael DelOrto*

*Staff artist/Martha Grashofer*

---

THE
# RETURN
OF THE
# FAMILY DINNER

Text by Marshall Fine

It wasn't a forgotten feeling or a foreign one — but it did trigger something distant and familiar in Stanley Estrin. His evening partners' meeting at his Manhattan law firm — Kravitz, Kalish and Karsh — had been canceled. By coincidence, so had his wife Donna's women's group. And his son David, who was supposed to be working at the library, had stayed home from school that day with a fever.

So they all sat down for dinner together that night at their home in Hartsdale "for the first time in ages," Estrin recalls, with a sense of amazement.

*Please see DINNER, S3*

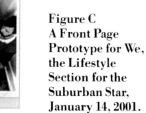

**TODAY'S MUST-READ**

**TOMORROW'S HOT TIPS, B4**

---

Figure C
A Front Page Prototype for We, the Lifestyle Section for the Suburban Star, January 14, 2001.

WN

**A happy kid** Most times a child's anger is a passing thing, but psychologists warn that sometimes an angry child needs professional help. Here are the signs to look for. Page 4.

**Preschool dilemma** With shrinking funds, fewer disadvantaged kids are getting a jump on life with free programs. Page 4.

**Sylvia** Prework anxieties—and one great early morning fantasy. Cartoon. Page 11

**Car care** Tips to help you stay sane through the worst the weather can do to your car. Page 13.

**Help for your life** Hints on coping with everything from infighting at the office to a plugged drain, plus an advertising guide to services that will make it all easier. Pages 9 and 10.

**African poet** Ugandan Mary Ubugu will come to Chicago Thursday to read from her award-winning works. Page 2.

**Anna Quindlen** Here's one working mom you don't have to feel sorry for. Page 3.

**Money talks** Pat Schroeder pushes for more money and more research into contraceptives and health issues. Page 12.

**Marital fidelity** Don't kid yourselves: Affairs don't just 'happen.' Page 11.

# WOMENEWS®

Prototype

Weekly News Report for Women on The Move

## INTERNATIONAL

**Well deserved** West Germany has awarded its Federal Cross of Merit First Class, to Miep Gies, 80, the Dutch woman who helped hide Anne Frank from the Nazis during World War II. Gies and her husband, Henk, smuggled food to the Frank family for two years, when the Nazis discovered their hiding place. Anne's diary was published after she died at 15 in a concentration camp.

**Poles to meet Dole** Labor Sec. Elizabeth is the only woman on a presidential commission that will visit Poland in a month to examine that country's economic plan and help target areas for American assistance.

**Entry Level** For the first time in Japan this year, more new female college graduates than male graduates found jobs. The proportion of females to males hired was 83 percent to 79 percent; this includes junior college graduates who go into clerical work. The proportion of male and female university grads is closer.

**Colonial conflict** British Prime Minister Margaret Thatcher's in trouble at home over her plan to grant full British citizenship to 225,000 Hong Kong residents before the colony reverts to China's control in 1997. Parliamentary opposition to the plan's enabling legislation includes 86 Conservatives.

## NATIONAL

**Ruling holds** The Supreme Court let stand one of the most far-reaching product-liability rulings ever issued by an American court. That ruling, by New York's highest court last April, made all manufacturers of the drug DES, a synthetic estrogen once widely prescribed in pregnancy and now linked to serious medical problems, potentially liable for damages in proportion to the share they had of the national market.

**Gender bias in court** A task force studying gender bias in Wisconsin's judicial system found it does exist. At the panel's first public hearing, a Milwaukee judge described insensitive judges and lawyers who asked sexual assault victims on the witness stand to detail their last sexual experience. Wisconsin is among 29 states examining court bias.

Bette Midler

**The inimitable Midler** Entertainer Bette Midler won a judgment against the Young & Rubicam advertising agency Monday in a suit contending the agency violated Midler's rights by imitating her voice in a 1986 TV commerical for the Ford Motor Co. Midler said she hoped the judgment would "contribute to higher ethical standards in advertising."

**Essence of heroism** Among seven black women to be honored by Essence magazine will be Bonnie Lee St. John, bronze medalist in the 1984 Handicapped Olympics. Susan L. Taylor, the magazine's editor, once was personally inspired by St. John: "I said to myself that if this woman with one leg can stand up and ski down a mountain, I can, too."

## LOCAL

**On her own** Attorney Cynthia Giacchetti and her partners, Patrick Tuite and David Mejia, have dissolved their law firm, Tuite, Mejia & Giacchetti, in favor of individual practices. Giacchetti, a former federal prosecutor, said she opted out to "develop a reputation of my own." She ends her five-year affiliation with Tuite on May 1, but will remain in Chicago to do federal and state criminal work as well as represent lawyers before the Attorney Registration and Disciplinary Commission, the state agency that investigates attorney misconduct.

**Performance artistry** Laurie Anderson, a Glen Ellyn native, came home from New York to wow a Chicago Theatre audience with her avante-garde multimedia show. Her two-hour solo, which mingled music with narrative and hundreds of slides projected on six screens, included excerpts from her "Strange Angels" album.

Photo by Steve Kagan

Georgette Watson

## $5,000 on her head

Community activist Georgette Watson directs Drop-a-Dime, a grassroots anti-drug hotline working from a constantly locked, unmarked office suite in one of Boston's most violent neighborhoods. She takes anonymous telephone tips about drug dealers and passes them on to the police. Watson, 46, is married and has three grown children and three grandchildren—and there is a street price of $5,000 on her head. Her story, page 12.

## Poverty level rising among elderly women

Unless working women make smart retirement plans now, poverty in the "golden years" could be as inevitable as aging, according to recent economic forecasts.

The current 15 percent poverty level among elderly women is expected to remain unchanged or increase over the next three decades, notes a Johns Hopkins University report. Conversely, poverty is expected to "virtually disappear" for elderly men and couples, according to the Commonwealth Fund study.

Women already account for three out of four of the nation's elderly poor who reside at home, reports Families United for Seniors in Action, a Washington-based lobbying group. Of those women, 75 percent squeeze by on less than $8,000 a year.

Hardest hit economically are elderly Hispanic and black women, many of whom have neither the skills nor the health to secure part-time work, notes Jeff Kirsch, organization spokesman.

Women are often less prepared financially for old age because years spent caretaking do not translate into pension dollars, notes Laura Loeb, director of public policy for the Older Women's League. ■

Maturity News Service

## Moonlighting

### Two jobs only way to fill wage gap

Amid the great wave of women sweeping into the U.S. labor force in recent years is a group whose numbers are increasing even faster: women who hold more than one job.

Government studies show that moonlighting among women is becoming as commonplace as it is among men, in both the percentage of working women and in absolute numbers.

The figures for men, by contrast, have changed little in decades.

The Bureau of Labor Statistics found in a sampling of the work force last May that the number of women with two or more jobs had quintupled, from 636,000 in 1970 to 3.1 million in May, while the number of moonlighting men rose much more slowly, from 3.4 million to 4.1 million.

Reasons for the surge among women are enmeshed in social and economic shifts of the 1970s and '80s, economists and government officials say.

With jobs opening that were once denied them, some women moonlight to gather experience for new careers, and some do extra work to build up savings or pay debts.

But as the last two decades have brought a record number of divorces and families maintained by single women, many of the women take two jobs because it is the only way to eke out a working-class life and stay above the poverty line.

Patricia Keammerer, 42, is a recently divorced mother of a 10-year-old girl who lives in Harrisburg, Pa. She gets no money from the child's father and holds three jobs.

She is an administrative assistant in the Harrisburg school system, works two nights a week and every other weekend at a fabric store, and from her home manages 41 homes that investors rent out.

She moonlights, she says, so her daughter, Sara, can live as she did before the divorce, in the same neighborhood and the same school.

The increase in moonlighting among women illustrates the larger role they are assuming in the economy.

"I put emphasis on the fact that women's contribution to families is increasing no matter how you measure it," said Heidi Hartmann, an economist who is the director of the Institute for Women's Policy Research in Washington.

For men and women, the incentive to moonlight has risen as it has become harder for people to manage on one paycheck, government statistics show. When increases in the cost of living are taken into account, hourly wages have slipped about 5 percent in 20 years.

Typically, a woman who moonlights has to work more than a moonlighting man to earn the same pay. The average woman working full time is paid 70 percent as much as the average man working full time. ■

N.Y. Times News Service

## Philadelphia cop wins discrimination case

PHILADELPHIA—A federal jury has awarded $2.44 million to the city's first female homicide detective and the four officers who supported her sex-discrimination complaint.

Carol Keenan, 38, alleged she was the victim of a pattern of discrimination, and her colleagues argued they were transferred out of the homicide unit merely because they supported her.

After two months of testimony, the U.S. District Court jury Wednesday awarded the five officers $640,000 in compensatory damages and $1.8 million in punitive damages.

The largest part went to Keenan.

"The next woman who makes this kind of complaint won't be ignored—they'll listen," she said.

The city planned to appeal. ■

Knight-Ridder Newspapers

Tribune Photo by John Dziekan

Lee Grant: Critical acclaim.

## Oscar competition gets serious

By Darlene G. Stevens

Male directors locked out their female colleagues in this year's 62nd Academy Awards race. However, Hollywood's handful of women filmmakers continue to strive for the honor and clout Oscar provides.

Susan Seidelman ("She-Devil"), Amy Heckerling ("Look Who's Talking") and Lee Grant ("Staying Together") are among the few women already being mentioned as possible candidates for Best Director nominees next year.

In 1987, the golden Oscar provided the Midas touch for director Lee Grant, who recently was honored for her documentary on homelessness, "Down and Out in America." Her fictionalized, made-for-television version, "No Place Like Home," starring Christine Lahti and Jeff Daniels, aired on CBS last fall.

Grant already was an Oscar, Tony and Emmy awarding-winning actress when she moved behind the camera more than a decade ago to begin a career as a director.

Since then she's crafted works that champion the disenfranchised and misunderstood. Equal rights for women, domestic violence and the plight of the mentally ill and handicapped—even transsexuals—have been among the topics she's tackled in her critically acclaimed documentaries.

"Eight-and-a-half years ago I left Hollywood

See Tribute, pg. 14

## Wife-battering shatters myth of French lovers

PARIS—The image of France as the cradle of romance still lingers abroad. But the government estimates that in 1 out of every 10 French households men beat, rape or otherwise molest their wives.

Estimating that there are at least two million battered women in France, the government recently launched the country's first-ever official campaign to expose their plight.

In doing so, it was prying open the door to a secret tightly guarded for generations.

Women's Rights Minister Michele Andre said: "If a man beats a dog on the street, someone will complain to the animal protection society. But if a man beats his wife in the street, no one moves."

Private support groups, like those in the United States and Britain, running hostels where women and their children can live for several months, say they cannot handle the number of women in need.

The government hopes to combat these gaps through a national campaign of TV advertisements, posters and films that will aggressively dramatize the problem and tell people where they can go for legal help. ■

Inside: Helping Hands—ideas to get the job done. A two-page pullout, pages 9 and 10.

**Figure D**
**A Front Page Prototype for Womenews.**

The reporter not only relates stories but makes them.

This, of course, is heresy within the world of journalism. You report, you do not manufacture. You ask your who, what, when, where, why, and how, get the answers; and come on home. But how . . . does the reporter know when to ask the basic journalistic questions, and who to ask them of? How does the reporter know when the questions have been answered? Who counts as a newsworthy "who"? What facts or events qualify as reportable responses to the question "what"? Even with the apparently simplest questions of all, "when" and "where," how does the reporter know if the answer is really sufficient? . . .

In short, the apparently simple commandment questions of journalism presuppose a platform for inquiry, a framework for interpreting answers, a set of rules about who to ask what about what. . . .

The best journalists keep in mind these questions and limitations, even if they are seldom articulated in news rooms. Ideally, your study of the craft will give you a critical understanding of its platform, framework and rules. You need to understand them whether in the end you choose to pursue the kind of mainstream, "objective" journalism practiced in most American news rooms or another of the many possible channels for expression.

In 1947 the Hutchins Commission on freedom of the press concluded that what a free society needs from journalists is "a truthful, comprehensive and intelligent account of the day's events in a context which gives them meaning." The goal of this chapter is to show you how the journalists of today and tomorrow understand that need, how they are trying to meet it, and the complexity of the task. The rest of the book will help you develop the skills you'll need to take up the challenge. There are few challenges so important or so rewarding.

# Suggested Readings

Gannett Center for Media Studies. The Media and the People. New York: The Gannett Center, 1985. A review of the research on press credibility.

Journalism Reviews: Any issue of the Columbia Journalism Review, the Washington Journalism Review, the Quill or the Bulletin of the American Society of Newspaper Editors offers reports and analyses of the most important issues of contemporary journalism.

Manoff, Robert Karl and Schudson, Michael, eds. "Reading the News." New York: Pantheon Books, 1986. A stimulating collection of essays that challenges the most important conventions of journalism.

Schudson, Michael. ''Discovering the News.'' New York: Basic Books, 1978. Subtitled ''A Social History of American Newspapers,'' this well-written study traces the development of objectivity in American journalism.

# Exercises

1. Get copies of today's issue of your local newspaper, a paper from a city at least 50 miles away and a paper of national circulation, such as USA Today or The Wall Street Journal. Analyze the front page according to the criteria discussed in this chapter.

   What can you tell about the editors' understanding of each paper's audience by looking at the selection of stories?

   If you find stories on the same topic on two or more front pages, determine if they are written differently for different audiences. Are there any attempts to localize national stories? Suggest any possibilities you can think of.

   On the basis of what you've learned in this chapter, do you agree or disagree with the editors' news judgments? Why?

2. Go to your library and look at both a recent issue of The New York Times and an issue from the same date 20 years ago. Describe the differences you find in subjects and sources of stories.

3. As a class project, visit or invite in the editor of your local paper and the news director of a local television station. Study their products ahead of time and interview them about how they decide the value of news stories, how they assess the reliability of sources and how they try to ensure accuracy.

# 2

# Newspapers
# and the
# News Room

Nicholas Negroponte, founder and director of the Media Lab at Massachusetts Institute of Technology, describes the newspaper of the 21st century as a home computer system that searches vast on-line data banks for news items at the subscriber's request, then displays the information on a computer screen or prints it in full color on the subscriber's laser printer (see Figure 2.1). "That newspaper will not only be personalized," Negroponte says, "but will come out, perhaps, on paper that is washable or changeable." So, rather than wrapping our garbage in yesterday's paper, in Negroponte's view readers will be environmentally responsible by reusing that paper.

Whether Negroponte's vision of the newspaper of the future will be realized remains to be seen. The landscape is littered with similar predictions that never came true. When radio arrived, its immediacy would kill newspapers, some predicted. When television arrived, even more joined the bandwagon. Yet newspapers endured, even prospered, in the heyday of television. They did so because they are, quite simply, better vehicles for the dissemination of vast amounts of information than the broadcast media. The print media excel in providing detail and explanation—in news as well as in advertising. Everything from detailed description and analysis to grocery and classified ads can be done better in print than on television. Just imagine someone trying to read classified ads on television.

That's not to say that broadcast news doesn't have its value. Most Americans, the polls show, are quite satisfied with the amount of news they get on television, and that medium clearly shines in times of major crisis. When the space shuttle Challenger exploded, television's coverage left little

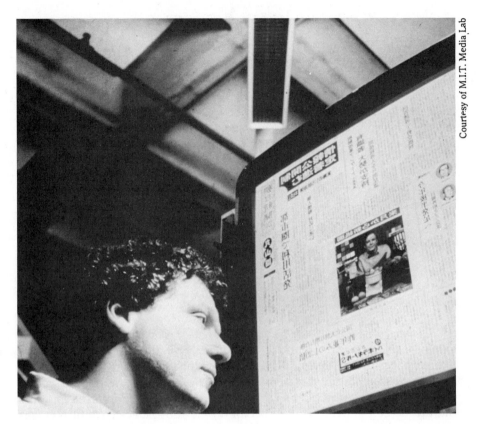

**Figure 2.1
Prototype
electronic
newspaper
developed as
M.I.T.'s Media Lab
dips into scores of
news sources to
meet subscribers'
specific requests.**

for the print media to add the next morning. Yet later in that unfolding story, the print media rebounded by ferreting out the story of faulty seals and warnings not to launch in cold weather because of the likelihood of failure. Those ignored warnings became the story behind the story, and newspapers, not television, led the way in telling it.

So, it's clear that both media have their strengths and weaknesses. Television has immediacy, the impact of motion and full color, and low distribution costs. Newspapers have the ability to carry large volumes of information, provide more detail and analysis, and have a permanency that television lacks.

Negroponte would argue, quite convincingly, that his vision of the future incorporates all of those advantages into one medium. His home-published electronic newspaper contains even more data than the traditional newspaper; allows the reader-viewer to see full-color, moving pictures of an event in which he or she is interested; provides permanency with its printout capability; and has the same low-cost distribution advantages as the broadcast media.

Such a medium would be a threat to newspapers. But it also would threaten television.

Does all this mean there is no future in newspapers? Or in television? Quite the contrary. Whether or not Negroponte's vision of the future comes true, it is clear that the information industry has a bright future in a society that consumes more and more information each year. Those who will prosper in the years ahead will be those who realize that they are in the business of providing information and are not wedded to a specific way of distributing their product.

Writer Joe Bernard, in an article on the future of newspapers, outlines the problem of newspapers this way:

> Confronted with a dazzling array of new communications technologies, with declining readership, with vastly altered lifestyles and with a generation weaned on microchips rather than typescript, the $40-billion newspaper industry faces a dilemma at century's end: change or perish. Since change is the only reasonable alternative to centuries of tradition—and since it is inevitable—all that remains to be answered is the degree of change and the direction it will take. The newspapers of tomorrow will unquestionably be different. But how?

## In this chapter you will learn:

1. Where newspapers stand today.

2. How the newspapers of today are organized and operated.

3. How copy is prepared.

4. How copy flows from one editor to the next at the typical newspaper.

5. What tools may be available to help you do your job.

# The Newspaper of Today

Nicholas Negroponte gives us plenty to think about as we try to envision the newspaper of the future. In the meantime, though, we must deal with the realities of today. What we find here is an industry that on the one hand is quite healthy; on the other hand, it is clear that the trends are not good.

A glance at some statistics belies the notion that newspapers are a dying art form. According to the American Newspaper Publishers Association:

- U.S. daily newspaper circulation stood at 62.5 million at the end of the 1980s, just short of the all-time high of 63 million recorded in 1984.

- Newspapers accounted for 26 percent of all the advertising dollars spent in the United States, the most of any medium (Figure 2.2). By comparison, television captured 21.8 percent, radio 6.7 percent and magazines 5.4 percent. Outdoor advertising, direct mail and other forms of advertising accounted for the rest.

- Newspaper employment reached 477,600 in 1990, ranking the industry as one of the nation's largest. Women employees continue to make gains; they now constitute 43.5 percent of the total newspaper work force. Minorities make up 16 percent of the newspaper work force but a lower percentage of the news room work force.

Although the preceding trends are encouraging, there are some negative ones as well:

- Though newspapers continue to be the largest advertising medium, their share is decreasing. As recently as 1985 newspapers captured more advertising revenue than radio and television combined. That no longer is true. Similarly, newspapers have been unable to stem a steady drift of national advertising dollars from newspapers to direct-mail marketing.

- Market penetration continues to decline. While circulation has generally held steady for the last two decades, the population has grown much

1988 and 1989 Sales and Percentage

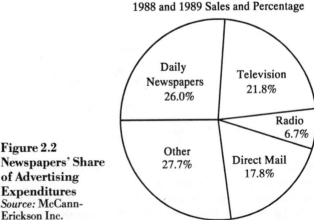

**Figure 2.2
Newspapers' Share
of Advertising
Expenditures**
*Source:* McCann-Erickson Inc.

faster. Thus, the percentage of homes subscribing to newspapers has declined. The impact is that only 64 percent of the adult population reads a newspaper on the average day, compared to 78 percent as recently as 1970. Surveys show that younger people, in particular, are reading less.

- The number of daily newspapers dropped from 1,745 in 1980 to 1,626 by the end of that decade. The number of weeklies also declined in the same period, from 7,954 to 7,550.

Statistics such as these have persuaded many editors that newspapers must change if they are to survive. This has led to some substantive changes in newspapers. Most notable is the attempt to modernize the appearance of newspapers. Spurred by a relatively new organization, the Society of Newspaper Design, newspapers nationwide adopted an ultramodern design concept often characterized by modular layout and increased use of color. Content, too, has changed. The old society sections have evolved into lifestyle sections more relevant to people's lives. Newspapers nationwide have created entertainment sections, business sections and children's pages designed to appeal to segments of the audience previously ignored or ill-served.

Unfortunately, none of the changes has had much impact on readership patterns. That reality led to the creation in the late 1980s of a journalism think tank called New Directions for News, based at the University of Missouri. The project, funded by almost all of the major newspaper groups in the United States, has, among other things, attempted an inventory of innovation at U.S. newspapers, sponsored creative research in a number of areas vital to the business and sponsored brainstorming sessions with some of the best minds in the industry.

The Gannett Media Center at New York's Columbia University also focuses on the need of the industry to change, sponsoring development of new ideas for the conduct of daily journalism. Another organization promoting change, the American Newspaper Publishers Association and its research labs, concentrates on improved methods of producing newspapers.

Thus some, at least, recognize that the newspaper industry is ripe for change.

# Newspaper Organization

To face the demands of a changing marketplace, newspapers also must change their internal organizations. New sections demand new staffing patterns. And the emphasis on design and appearance has prompted the creation of design desks at some newspapers and graphics departments at others.

Further, the changing economics of the newspaper business has had an impact on staffing. As the cost of newsprint has risen dramatically and other economic pressures have taken their toll, editors increasingly demand that new employees be well-trained and capable of making a significant contribution from the first days of their employment. This has led to demands that journalism schools increase the quality of their teaching.

Employers can afford to be picky. According to statistics compiled by the Dow Jones Newspaper Fund, only 15 percent of journalism graduates find their way into jobs in newspaper news rooms.

Chuck Haga, city editor of the Grand Forks (N.D.) Herald, wrote in the Bulletin of the American Society of Newspaper Editors:

> The managing editor and I were interviewing a job applicant, an earnest young man who wanted to be a reporter. "How would you go about covering city hall?" we asked him.
> "Well," the young man said, "first I'd find out where it is."

That young man undoubtedly did well in journalism; learning one's beat is important for a beginner. Also of importance is learning about the news room and the people who are part of it.

Strangely, news rooms often are places where communication leaves much to be desired. One editor of a small daily in the Midwest conducted a survey of new reporters and was told: "Operation (of the news room) could be improved considerably if communications were increased. Sometimes the standards differ from editor to editor."

One journalism graduate wrote a former professor and urged that in the future more time be spent discussing what the young reporter called "news room politics." He wrote:

> Human behavior is not a hands-off topic for classroom discussion. Reporters need to be taught that news room politics is not just a game of favoritism. If favoritism exists, it is earned.

The message was clear: Work hard, do a good job and sooner or later you will be rewarded with the best assignments. In the meantime, you can expect to be tested. You also can expect periodic evaluations of your performance. Traditionally, evaluations of newspaper reporters have been informal or nonexistent. At some papers, that's still true. A kind word for a job well-done or a harsh word for mistakes might be all you hear between annual evaluations for pay increases. Increasingly, editors are using guidelines to evaluate reporters such as those in Figure 2.3. You should welcome such evaluations; they

# The Seattle Times
# REPORTER
# PERFORMANCE REVIEW

Date _____

Employee _____

Job Title _____

Classification _____

Period Reviewed _____

Evaluated By _____

Department Manager Review _____

## PERFORMANCE-REVIEW
## GUIDELINES

Each employee is reviewed annually. This form is designed to help the supervisor assess the employee's performance over the past year and to help the supervisor and the employee set goals for growth and development over the next year. It is also an opportrunity for the employee to express his or her thoughts on the performance of the supervisor and of the newspaper, and to lay out longer-term career objectives.

The evaluation and self-evaluation sections of the review form should be filled out independently by the employee and the supervisor. After exchanging those sections, the employee and supervisor should together write the development plan. Each can also offer additional thoughts in the commentary section.

**Figure 2.3    Performance Review Guidelines.** These guidelines reflect the changing notions of the responsibilities and skills required of reporters.

# JOB DESCRIPTION: REPORTER

The following attributes and responsibilities are expected of every Seattle Times reporter. Additional responsibilities might be part of a specific job assignment. This list is meant as a guide and not as a grading grid; the employee and supervisor should decide which items deserve the most attention.

## PROFESSIONAL SKILLS:

- Seeks out and acts quickly on story opportunities.
- Aggressively follows through on stories.
- Gathers facts carefully and accurately.
- Seeks a variety of sources in covering a story, and effectively develops sources of continuing stories.
- Uses documents effectively.
- Handles a variety of stories and writing approaches.
- Writes clear, well-focused and well-organized stories.
- Writes effective, appropriate leads.
- Writes with authority based on clear understanding of the topic or beat.
- Produces stories that are fair and balanced.
- Self-edits for crisper, cleaner copy.
- Works well under pressure and meets deadlines.
- Maintains a steady flow of ideas and stories.

## WORK HABITS:

- Knows and effectively uses library and computer systems.
- Understands how the newsroom operates, and works effectively within it.
- Works effectively as a member of a team, including with other reporters, photographers, artists and editors.
- Responds well to direction, suggestions, criticism.
- Keeps appropriate people informed of schedules, work in progress, problems, changes.
- Works in a cooperative spirit in accepting, discussing or proposing changes in assignments.
- Keeps well-informed about news in general and assigned specialties by reading The Times and other publications.
- Organizes time well, and can work on more than one task at a time when necessary.
- Is punctual for staff meetings and time commitments.
- Maintains good staff communications and relationships.
- Shares knowledge and ideas with less-experienced workers.
- Seeks diversity in coverage.

## ENTERPRISE SKILLS:

- Demonstrates willingness to perform routine but necessary duties such as digest items, etc.
- Consistently suggests ideas for stories, photographs and illustrations.
- Produces enterprise stories.
- Seeks fresh ideas and approaches in reporting and writing.
- Stays ahead of stories by anticipating or uncovering developments.
- Is willing to travel, make calls from home and work unusual schedules when the coverage requires it.
- Is willing to take leadership of a story or project.
- Offers suggestions for improving the newspaper.
- Takes on new challenges.

**Figure 2.3 (continued)**

identify your strengths and weaknesses. Once your editors tell you what skills you need to improve, it's up to you to respond.

No one can describe the situation you will face in your first news room; no two are alike. Similarly, no two editors are alike. All have their likes and dislikes, their foibles and idiosyncrasies.

No two newspapers are organized exactly alike, either. Large dailies with large staffs obviously operate differently from small ones with small staffs. There are enough similarities, however, to make some observations about key personnel and their functions.

## TOP MANAGEMENT

*Publisher.*    This title often is assumed by the newspaper's owner, although some *chains* or *groups*—corporations that own two or more newspapers—designate as publisher the top-ranking local executive. The publisher presides over the entire newspaper operation but usually concentrates on financial matters and leaves editorial decisions to the editors. Unless you work at a weekly or small daily newspaper, as a reporter you seldom will see or work with the publisher.

*General Manager.*    Usually the general manager is responsible for advertising, circulation and production. In some chains, however, the general manager serves as the top-ranking local executive and may have a voice in editorial matters. As a reporter, you will have only limited contact with the general manager.

## THE EDITORIAL DEPARTMENT

*Editor.*    Most newspaper *editorial departments*, or *news rooms*, are headed by an editor in chief, often known simply as the editor. The editor is responsible for the editorial content of the newspaper, including everything from comics to news stories to editorials. Unless you begin work as a reporter at a weekly or small daily newspaper, you will have little contact with the editor. The editor's influence is exerted through those who report directly to that editor, usually the managing editor and the editorial page editor.

*Editorial Page Editor.*    This is the person charged with producing the editorial page, and, at large newspapers, an *op-ed page*. (The op-ed page draws its name from its position in the paper—opposite the editorial page.) Opinion—that of the newspaper, its columnists and its readers—usually is confined to these two pages. Traditionally the editorial function has been separated from news gathering to distinguish clearly between fact and opinion.

As a reporter you probably will have contact with the editorial page editor only when questioned about something you covered that will be the subject of an editorial. Reporters deal with fact, not opinion, although occasionally they may be asked to write analytical articles.

*Managing Editor.*    Primary responsibility for news-gathering operations is in the hands of the managing editor. The managing editor is the highest-ranking person who makes frequent appearances in the news room. Because of that, the managing editor is the highest-ranking editor with whom you, as a reporter, will have frequent contact.

The managing editor makes decisions about placement of major stories in the newspaper. Frequently the managing editor does the hiring, prepares the news room budget and makes most of the editorial department policy decisions (in consultation with the editor on major decisions). At larger newspapers the managing editor may have one or more assistants who share those responsibilities.

*News Editor.*    The news editor has supervisory control of the *copy desk*, where final editing of stories is done, pages are designed and headlines are written. Working for the news editor are *copy editors*, specialists who polish the wording of stories. They check verifiable information, including the spelling of names and the accuracy of addresses, and write headlines. They also may crop and size photographs and other artwork, lay out pages and work directly with the composing room to make sure that stories fit the space available.

At a small daily newspaper the news editor may serve as the copy desk chief, who designs pages and determines how stories are displayed. At a large newspaper he or she may direct the placement of stories, and a separate desk chief may carry out those instructions.

Some newspapers, mostly small ones, have universal copy desks to handle all news copy. Many large newspapers have separate desks that handle both the gathering and editing of various categories of news—city, state, national and international (see Figure 2.4). Others have a single desk to handle all such news but maintain specialized departments for sports, entertainment and lifestyle stories, each with its own copy editors.

Whatever the form, the copy desk plays an important role in the production of the newspaper. It is charged with enforcing deadlines so that the newspaper comes out on time. Deadlines affect everyone in the news room, including you, the reporter. Even so, you will have little direct contact with the copy desk. Deadline pressures are enforced through the city editor (see below). Only when a copy editor questions what you have written is there likely to be direct contact. Even then, the question may be channeled through the news editor to the city editor.

**Figure 2.4**
**The National Desk**
**at The New York**
**Times.** Large
newspapers, such as
The New York
Times, often have
separate desks
responsible for news
gathering and copy
editing.

Despite the infrequent contact, it is important for you to develop an appreciation of what the news editor and the copy desk crew accomplish. They polish writing and correct errors that if printed may embarrass you, particularly if your byline is on the story in question.

*Graphics Editor.*　The graphics editor is in charge of producing charts, maps and other graphics that go into the newspaper. This editor also reviews graphics produced by outside sources. Both major wire services and several of the supplemental services produce graphics that are transmitted electronically to client newspapers, much as wire copy is transmitted.

*City Editor.*　Known at some papers as the *metropolitan* or *metro editor*, the city editor supervises the reporters who gather local news. This editor directs the city desk, which may be shared with one or more assistant city editors. The city desk is the hub of the news room because of its importance; local news is the primary news product of most newspapers.

As a reporter you will work directly for the city editor and the assistant city editors. They will give you assignments and follow your progress from the time you begin to gather information until the story is written, edited and sent to the copy desk for final editing and a headline. The city editor often acts as devil's advocate, questioning you about the accuracy of your story and the way you have written it.

The city desk also serves as a primary link to the public because it answers inquiries about news stories. After the initial contact is made there, you may be assigned to act on a complaint or tip.

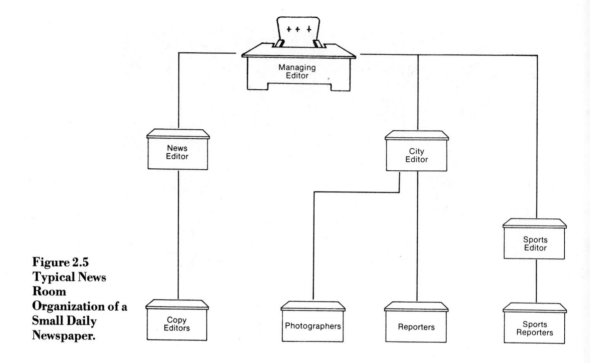

**Figure 2.5
Typical News
Room
Organization of a
Small Daily
Newspaper.**

The city desk maintains a *futures file,* a chronological collection of newspaper clippings, letters, public relations releases and notes to remind editors of upcoming events or stories that require follow-up. This file often is the source of stories you are assigned to cover. As a reporter you should keep a similar file of your own to remind you to follow stories you covered earlier. Never rely on the futures file for this purpose; notes and clippings can be misplaced easily.

Large newspapers may have editors whose jobs parallel that of the city editor but who deal with areas other than the city and its suburbs. State desks, national desks and international desks are examples. They are directed by editors who are charged with gathering, compiling and editing news in those areas. Feature editors, sports editors, business editors and Sunday editors may operate still other desks.

If, as a reporter, you are assigned to one of those desks, you will find that the editor in charge of that desk functions much like the city editor. Your job will be affected by the type of news you cover, but your relationship with the editor of your desk will be similar in any situation. Obviously, you will work most closely with the editor of your desk and his or her assistants. But you must understand the functions of the other editors who scrutinize your work.

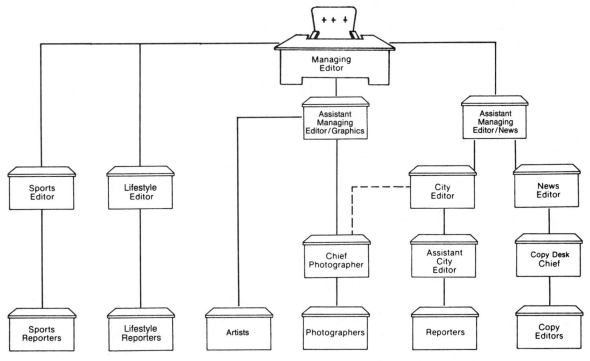

**Figure 2.6**    **Typical News Room Organization of a Medium-Sized Daily Newspaper.**

## OTHER DEPARTMENTS

You also should realize that the editorial department is but one of several departments that work as a team to produce the newspaper (sed Figure 2.7). Most newspapers have advertising, business, circulation and production departments. Some have separate departments to handle promotions, public relations and personnel matters as well.

The *advertising department* generates most of the newspaper's income, from which your salary is paid. Most advertising departments are divided into display and classified sections, which correspond to the two major forms of advertising. Large newspapers also may have advertising art and research sections, and they may separate display advertising into local and national sections.

The *business department* handles billing, accounting and related functions. It manages the payroll, group insurance plans and other benefits, and only in that capacity will you have frequent contact with it.

The *circulation department* is charged with distributing the newspaper

| Advertising | Business | Circulation | Editorial | Production |
|---|---|---|---|---|
| Local Display | Accounting | Mail Room | City Desk | Composing |
| Classified | Billing | Delivery | Copy Desk | Platemaking |
| National | Credit | Rural | Photography | Camera |
| Advertising Art | Payroll | City | Graphic/art | Data Processing |
| Ad Research | Credit Union | | Library | Maintenance |
| Ad Promotion | Labor Relations | | Sports | Press |
| Public Relations | | | Lifestyle | |
| Community Relations | | Carriers* | Other Desks | |
| | | Vendors* | | |

\* Outside contractors not employed by newspaper.

**Figure 2.7   Major Departments of a Typical Newspaper and Their Subsections.**

and is the second leading source of newspaper income. Only occasionally will the circulation department affect your job as a reporter. One such occasion is during periods of bad weather or on holidays, when the circulation manager asks for earlier news deadlines to allow more time for delivery of the newspaper.

The *production department*, as its name implies, is responsible for transforming the creative work of reporters, editors and advertising salespeople into the finished product—the newspaper. The composing room, where type is set and pages are assembled, the platemaking section and the pressroom are all parts of the production department.

Large newspapers may subdivide these departments further. Regardless of the newspaper's organization, all the functions mentioned are vital in producing a newspaper, from the nation's smallest weekly to its largest daily. As a reporter you play an important role in producing the newspaper. You are a part of a team.

It is important that you understand how that team works. Because most editors realize this, you can expect to be taken on a tour of the newspaper plant soon after you are hired. If no one offers such a tour, ask for it.

# Copy Flow

If learning how your newspaper is produced is important, so, too, is learning how the news room works. You should learn what happens to a story as it makes its way through the hands, or, more commonly, the *video display terminal queues*, of several editors.

## WORKING WITH THE EDITOR

At first glance, the flow of copy through an editorial department seems simple enough. You write your story and transfer it to the city desk queue, the electronic equivalent of an in-basket. There the city editor reads it and makes necessary changes. Then it is sent electronically to the copy desk, where it is edited again. The story is assigned a position in the newspaper, and a headline is written. Finally, an editor presses a key on the VDT keyboard to send your story to a typesetting machine in the composing room. This simple copy flow pattern exists at most newspapers, whether that newspaper uses VDTs or still does things the old-fashioned way with typewriters and paper copy. Indeed, electronic copy flow patterns in most cases merely duplicate the pre-computer copy flow patterns of newspapers. Despite the seeming simplicity of the pattern, many decisions can be made along the way that make the process much more complicated than it appears at first glance.

When the city editor receives your copy, that editor must read it and make some initial decisions: Is there missing information? Does the story need to be developed? Does it need more background? Are there enough quotes? Are the quotes worth using? Does the *lead*, or opening, need to be polished? Have you chosen the right lead or should another angle be emphasized? Is the story important? Is it useful, interesting or entertaining? Is there, in fact, some reason for publishing it? If it is important, should the managing editor and news editor be alerted that a Potential Page one story is forthcoming? Each time a city editor reads a story for the first time, these questions and more come up. The city editor is expected to answer them quickly; there is no time for delay.

After making those initial decisions, the city editor confers with you and gives directions on changes to be made. If the changes are minor ones, simply rewriting a section of the story or inserting additional information will suffice. If the changes are more substantial, involving additional interviews with sources or major rewriting, your job is more difficult.

When those changes are made, you resubmit your story to the city editor, who reads the revised version and edits it more carefully. Your work may be finished after you answer a few remaining minor questions. Or, if the city editor is still unhappy with it, another rewrite may be ordered.

You can expect frustration in the process. Often an assistant city editor reads your story first and gives instructions on how it is to be revised. When your rewrite is submitted, the city editor or another assistant may do the editing, resulting in the need for more changes and yet another rewrite. This can be discouraging, but such a system has its merits. Generally, a story is

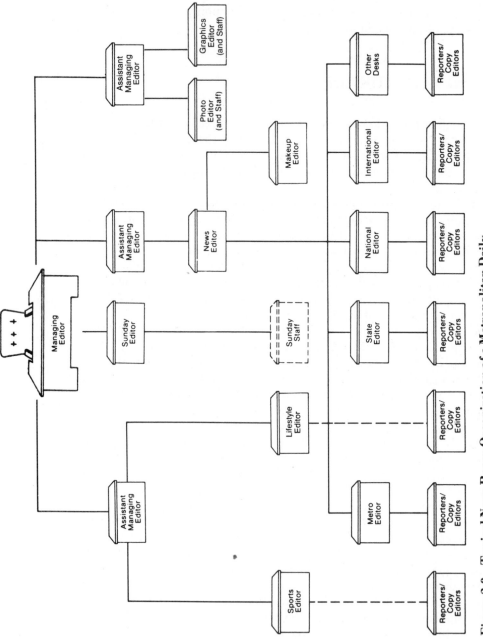

**Figure 2.8    Typical News Room Organization of a Metropolitan Daily Newspaper.**

improved when more than one editor handles it. Each sees gaps to be filled, and varied viewpoints usually lead to an improved story.

## USING PHOTOS AND GRAPHICS

At some point in the process, ideally at the outset, editors will decide whether to order a photograph to accompany your story. This once was done almost as an afterthought by editors, who considered photos mere decoration to break up the type of a newspaper page. Now, progressive newspapers realize that photos, artwork, charts and graphs are forms of communication with tremendous reader appeal. Photo editors and graphics editors, often with the authority of an assistant managing editor, work closely with the city editors to ensure that visual opportunities are not missed. Finding reporter-photographer teams assigned to a story from the outset is increasingly common.

It is important that you develop a good working relationship with the staff photographers. In recent years newspapers have become increasingly aware of the importance of making the photographer a full partner in the news-gathering process. Rather than shackle the photographer with precise instructions about how to take a picture to accompany your story, relate what the story is about and let the photographer make suggestions. Remember that your expertise is in written communication; the photographer's expertise is in visual communication.

When the story and photograph are ready, the city desk may submit them to the news editor, who decides where they are to be placed in the newspaper. Often this decision is made in consultation with the city editor, the managing editor or an assistant managing editor.

The story then may be handed to the copy desk chief, who designs the page on which the story and picture are to appear. That editor orders a headline for your story and transfers the package to a copy editor, still known at some newspapers by the antiquated term "copyreader."

## COPY EDITING

The copy editor asks many of the same questions about your story that the city editor asks. Have you selected the right lead? Does the writing need to be polished? Have you chosen the correct words? Primarily, though, the copy editor checks for misspelled words, adherence to style, grammatical errors, ambiguities and errors of fact. The copy editor reworks a phrase here or there to clarify your meaning but is expected to avoid major changes. If major changes are necessary, the copy editor calls that to the attention of the news

| Individual | Action |
|---|---|
| Reporter | Gathers facts, writes story, verifies its accuracy, forwards to city editor. |
| City Editor* | Edits story, returns to reporter for changes or additional detail (if necessary), forwards story to news editor. |
| News Editor* | Decides on placement of story in newspaper, forwards story to copy desk chief for implementation of instructions. |
| Copy Desk Chief | Prepares page dummy that determines story's length, setting and headline size, forwards to copy editor. At some large newspapers, a separate design desk may play this role. |
| Copy Editor | Polishes writing of story, checks for missing or inaccurate detail, writes headline, returns to copy desk chief for final check. |
| Copy Desk Chief | Verifies that story is trimmed as necessary and that correct headline is written, transmits story to typesetting machine. |

**Figure 2.9 Typical News Room Copy Flow Pattern.**

* Or assistant

*Note:* At any point in the process, a story may be returned to an earlier editor for clarification, amplification or rewriting.

editor. If the news editor agrees, the story is returned to the city editor, and perhaps to you, for yet another revision.

When the copy editor is satisfied with the story, work begins on the headline. The size of the headline ordered by the copy desk chief determines how many characters or letters can be used in writing it. Headline writing is an art. Those who are able to convey the meaning of a story in a limited number of words are valuable members of the staff. The quality of the copy editor's work can have a significant impact on the number of readers who will be attracted to your story. If the headline is dull and lifeless, few will; if it sparkles, the story's exposure will be increased.

The copy editor also may write the cutline, or caption, that accompanies the picture. At some newspapers, however, this is done by the photographer, the reporter or at the city desk. Large newspapers may have a photo desk to handle cutlines as well as picture cropping and sizing.

When finished, the copy editor transfers the story to the copy desk chief, who must approve the headline and may check the editing changes made by the copy editor. When the desk chief is satisfied, the story and headline are transferred to the composing room, where the creative effort of writers and editors is transformed into type. The picture is sent to another section of the production department for processing.

The size of the newspaper may alter this copy flow pattern substantially. At a small newspaper the jobs of news editor, copy desk chief and copy editor may be performed by one person. Some small dailies require the city editor or an assistant to perform all the tasks normally handled by the copy desk.

News room copy flow patterns have been designed with redundancy in mind. Built into the system is the goal of having not one editor, but several, check your work. Through repeated checking, editors hope to detect more errors—in fact and in writing style—to make the finished product a better one.

In this sense editors work as gatekeepers. They determine whether your work measures up to their standards. Only when it does is the gate opened, allowing your story to take the next step in the newspaper production process.

# Copy
# Preparation

Since 1970 remarkable changes have transformed the American news room from a citadel of 19th-century methods into a showcase of space-age technology. Manual typewriters have been replaced by video display terminals. Reporters and editors use VDTs to produce stories that subsequently are typeset with laser-driven typesetters at speeds of more than 1,000 lines per minute.

A few American reporters still use manual typewriters to produce copy that will be retyped by a compositor. Traditional copy preparation with a typewriter is most often used when a portable VDT is not available or when writing for a publication other than your own. Those who work in other fields, including broadcasting, public relations and advertising, are more likely to use traditional techniques.

The origins of modern newspaper technology can be traced to reductions in the American space program. When astronaut Neil Armstrong became the first man to walk on the moon on July 20, 1969, an American dream was realized and a 10-year obsession with accomplishing that feat ended. Subsequent reductions in the staff of the National Aeronautics and Space Administration forced many space-age computer technicians and engineers to find jobs in the private sector. As a result, space technology was used to benefit various industries, among them newspapers.

Those technicians realized that tremendous savings were possible in the newspaper industry if the reporter's typing effort could be used to operate typesetting machines. That would eliminate the redundant process of having another employee retype the story in the composing room.

VDTs, already used in other industries, were well suited for this task. They were first installed at newspapers in the early 1970s, and they brought about the most significant changes in newspaper production since the invention of Ottmar Mergenthaler's linecaster in the mid-1880s. No longer are reporters and editors involved in production only to the extent that they are required to meet deadlines. Reporters have become vital links in the production process because they have assumed the role of typing copy that ultimately will be used in typesetting.

The face of American news rooms has changed dramatically, and most reporters and editors have adapted well. They like the change to electronic editing because they have more control over what appears in the newspaper. The composing room is almost eliminated as a source of errors. Spurring the change, of course, is what the technicians realized from the outset: Money can be saved. Publishers have been able to reduce the number of composing room workers and to save thousands of dollars in labor costs.

A few of the more than 1,600 daily newspapers in this country are still in the process of converting to the new technology. The result is that you, as someone studying to become a journalist, must be familiar with both new and old methods.

## THE VDT PROCESS

Writing a story on a video display terminal can be a pleasure, and those who switch from the traditional method to VDTs seldom want to change back.

VDTs are keyboards with attached televisionlike screens that display information as it is typed. They are similar to the home computers now found in many North American households. Indeed, many small newspapers have begun to use personal computers with specially designed software, or computer programs, to produce their daily and weekly editions. The terminal screen substitutes for the paper copy produced by a typewriter. Corrections, deletions and insertions can be made easily and quickly, and the writer has the advantage of working with clean copy at all times. There are no strikeovers or handwritten insertions.

As you strike a key and the character appears on the VDT screen, it is stored on disk by a computer, called a controller, to which the VDT is attached by cable. The controller allows you to store your story for later retrieval or to send it to your editor.

Learning to operate a VDT is more complicated than learning to use a typewriter because there are more keys with which to contend. In addition to the standard typewriter keyboard layout, there are keys to control the *cursor*, a rectangle of light that indicates your position in the text. Still other keys control computer functions such as routing the story from desk to desk. Despite the extra keys, VDTs usually can be mastered in half a day. Newspapers often provide training for newcomers when they join the staff.

Once you master the keyboard and become accustomed to seeing your story on a VDT screen rather than on paper, the rest is simple. Mistakes can be corrected as you write simply by moving the cursor backward and striking over the incorrect letters. By striking the insert key, you can insert characters, words, sentences, paragraphs and even larger blocks of type at any point in the text. Sentences and paragraphs can be moved with similar ease.

Each terminal screen displays about 14 lines of text. As more space is needed, lines disappear from the screen but are stored in the memory of the computer. You simply depress a key to move forward or backward to any part of the story.

Once you are satisfied with your article, you can make a paper printout of it by depressing another key. The printout replaces the carbon copy produced in the traditional process and can be used for later reference.

With yet another key you transmit your article to the controller and assign it to the editor's queue. The editor can instruct the VDT to provide a *directory*, or index, of stories awaiting attention. When it is time to process your story, the editor simply strikes another key and the story appears on the screen for editing. The article moves from editor to editor in this way until finally it is sent electronically to the typesetter, much as a voice travels over telephone lines.

At some large newspapers, a copy of the story is filed in an electronic *morgue*, or reference library. When newspapers have such a system, reporters may be able to call to their VDT screens background information from earlier stories. That eliminates the need to go to the morgue for a search through old clippings.

## THE TRADITIONAL PROCESS

Few newspapers still use traditional copy-processing techniques, but failure to learn how to use such techniques would be a mistake. Whatever area of journalism you enter, you still will find occasion to edit on paper. Public relations practitioners, ad copy writers, broadcast reporters and editors, and book authors and editors all still use these procedures daily.

A writer using the traditional process produces stories on a typewriter with low-quality paper, often newsprint. The reporter using the traditional process usually makes at least two carbon copies. The reporter submits the original and one copy to the city desk. The original is edited and eventually finds its way to the composing room, where a compositor transforms it into type. The city desk and the reporter keep carbon copies in case the original is lost or they need to refer to the piece later. The assembled sheets of newsprint and carbon paper are known as *books*.

After inserting a book in the typewriter, you must type identifying information in the upper left-hand corner. The minimum information includes your name, the date and a story *slug*, an identifying word that will remain with the article throughout the production process. The slug should give some indication of the story's subject matter. An article about a city council meeting, for example, may use the slug ''Council.''

The first line of the article should appear no less than one-third down the page. This practice allows room at the top for the city editor or an assistant to insert your byline, if one is used. It also allows room for the city desk and copy desk editors to insert information such as typesetting instructions, headline specifications and, in some cases, the headline itself.

Articles are written on one side of the paper only and should be double- or triple-spaced, depending on the newspaper's practice. If there is insufficient space for the article on one sheet of paper—one *take* as it is commonly called—type ''more'' at the end of the last complete paragraph that will fit. A take should never end in the middle of a sentence or in the middle of a paragraph because that can complicate typesetting. Takes of an article often are set by different compositors and pieced together once the type is set. That task becomes difficult, if not impossible, if a take ends in mid-sentence.

The second take of copy should be treated similarly with these exceptions:

1. The date can be eliminated.

2. The slug should be followed by a dash and the words ''first add.'' A first add is equivalent to the second page of a manuscript. Some newspapers prefer to use numerical designations, so, depending on the practice at your newspaper, the second page would contain the slug ''council—first add'' or ''council—2.''

3. There is no need to leave the top third of the page blank.

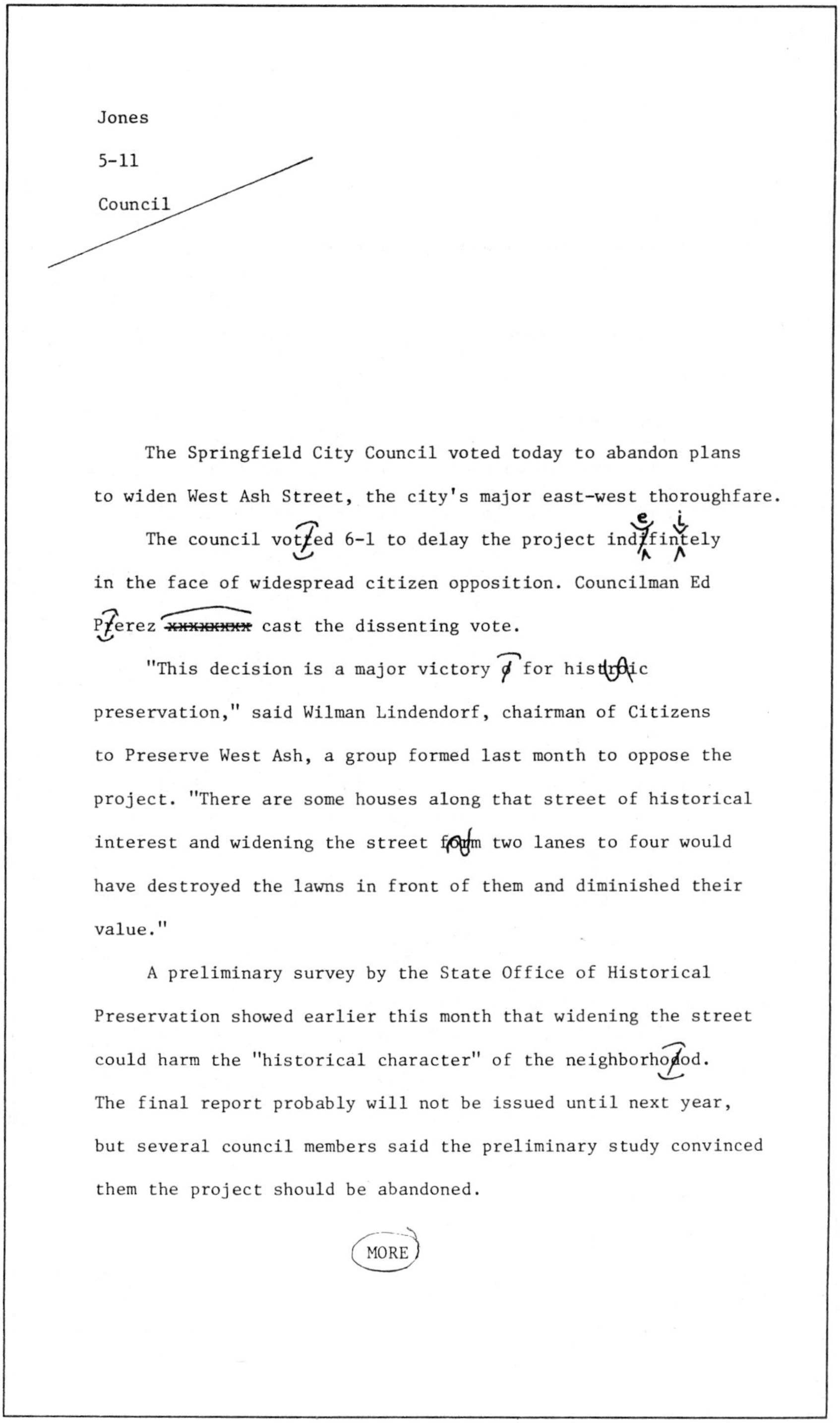

Jones

5-11

Council

 

The Springfield City Council voted today to abandon plans
to widen West Ash Street, the city's major east-west thoroughfare.

The council voted 6-1 to delay the project indefintely
in the face of widespread citizen opposition. Councilman Ed
Prerez ~~xxxxxxxx~~ cast the dissenting vote.

"This decision is a major victory for historic
preservation," said Wilman Lindendorf, chairman of Citizens
to Preserve West Ash, a group formed last month to oppose the
project. "There are some houses along that street of historical
interest and widening the street from two lanes to four would
have destroyed the lawns in front of them and diminished their
value."

A preliminary survey by the State Office of Historical
Preservation showed earlier this month that widening the street
could harm the "historical character" of the neighborhood.
The final report probably will not be issued until next year,
but several council members said the preliminary study convinced
them the project should be abandoned.

(MORE)

**Figure 2.10
First Take of a
Story.** The reporter
writes his or her
name, the date and
the story slug at the
top. The top third
of the page is left
blank for editing
instructions, and
"MORE" at the
bottom indicates
there are additional
takes.

COUNCIL -- first add

    Fifth Ward Councilwoman Jane Trevor said she was not convinced the city had studied alternatives to widening the street. "There is some indication that widening West Elm would be less disruptive," she said.

    Sixth Ward Councilman Giuseppi Grimaldi agreed. "We want to be certain we have the best solution to the east-west traffic problem, and I'm not convinced we know what that is."

-30-

**Figure 2.11
The Second and
Last Take of a
Story.** The slug and
"first add" at the
top identify the
piece, and "30"
indicates the end of
the story.

If the article is lengthy, you may need a "second add," "third add" and so forth. The end of the story should be marked by "30," "#" or "END." All information for editors and production personnel should be circled. That indicates the material is for information only and should not appear in print.

Writing an article this way is simple because perfect manuscripts are unnecessary. In fact, they are rare. The main requirement is that editors and compositors be able to read and understand what you have written. Because several people must read the copy, neatness is essential. For that reason, several rules governing copy preparation have evolved:

1. Never correct typing errors by backspacing and typing over a character. Instead, cross out the error with a pencil and retype, or strike over the entire word and retype.

2. Never use a hyphen at the end of a typewritten line. This leads to confusion because a compositor cannot be sure if the hyphen is to be inserted in the typeset copy.

3. Correct simple errors, such as transposed characters, with copy editing marks. These symbols differ from proofreading marks, which are used to mark corrections in typeset copy. (See Figures 2.12 and 2.13.)

4. If a section of an article is difficult to read because of numerous corrections, retype it. Corrected paragraphs, for example, can be pasted over difficult-to-read copy. Rubber cement is best for such pasting.

## Tools to Help You

A wise reporter wastes no time learning where the newspaper reference library—or morgue—is located. The library and the people who operate it can be of immense help to a reporter. Background information on literally thousands of people and topics will be available in a good one. Typically, libraries have subject files, biographical files and photo files. The librarian can show you how to use the library at your newspaper.

A good library will contain a variety of reference books that may be of great help to you. These may range from an encyclopedia to Bartlett's Familiar Quotations and from an almanac to Who's Who in America. Check to see what reference materials are available in your library. Then you will know where to turn for information that can enhance your story.

Many libraries are being converted to electronic data bases. With the best of the library storage and retrieval systems, a reporter can summon informa-

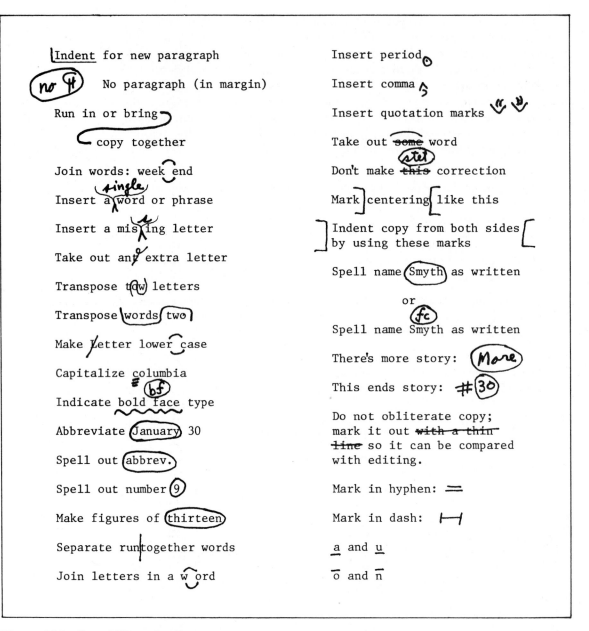

**Figure 2.12   Copy Editing Symbols.**

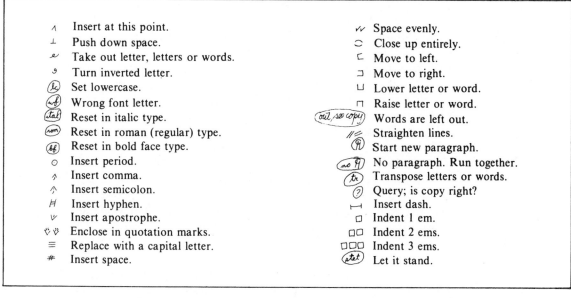

| | | | |
|---|---|---|---|
| ʌ | Insert at this point. | ⱽ⁄ | Space evenly. |
| ⊥ | Push down space. | ◡ | Close up entirely. |
| ℓ | Take out letter, letters or words. | ⊏ | Move to left. |
| ℈ | Turn inverted letter. | ⊐ | Move to right. |
| *(lc)* | Set lowercase. | ⊔ | Lower letter or word. |
| *(wf)* | Wrong font letter. | ⊓ | Raise letter or word. |
| *(ital)* | Reset in italic type. | *(out, see copy)* | Words are left out. |
| *(rom)* | Reset in roman (regular) type. | ∥= | Straighten lines. |
| *(bf)* | Reset in bold face type. | *(¶)* | Start new paragraph. |
| ⊙ | Insert period. | *(no ¶)* | No paragraph. Run together. |
| ⋏ | Insert comma. | *(tr)* | Transpose letters or words. |
| ⋏ | Insert semicolon. | *(?)* | Query; is copy right? |
| H | Insert hyphen. | ⊢ | Insert dash. |
| ⌵ | Insert apostrophe. | □ | Indent 1 em. |
| ⌵ ⌵ | Enclose in quotation marks. | □□ | Indent 2 ems. |
| ≡ | Replace with a capital letter. | □□□ | Indent 3 ems. |
| # | Insert space. | *(stet)* | Let it stand. |

**Figure 2.13   Proofreading Symbols.**

tion from the data base while sitting at a VDT in the news room. With other systems, it may be necessary to use a terminal in the library. Some newspapers have not yet converted their own libraries to electronic data bases but have purchased access to systems such as VuText, a data base that includes the libraries of more than 30 newspapers nationwide. Other data bases, available to the general public as well as to newspapers, include Dialog, the Source and CompuServe. The latter two carry the wires of United Press International and the Associated Press but do not serve as a form of archival storage of such information. Information from the wire services is retained in the data base for a matter of hours or days, then purged to make space for more up-to-date material. Other material available through Dialog, Dow Jones News Retrieval and VuText is more permanent and can be used to enhance your stories. Soon, the reporter who knows nothing about data bases will be at a distinct disadvantage in competing with more aggressive reporters. Relying on the librarian to conduct searches may not be good enough. More and more reporters are taking courses at their local libraries in data base searching techniques, and more and more journalism departments are including introductory information on searches in their curricula.

Data bases typically contain references to articles in newspapers and magazines. A reporter for the Columbus (Ohio) Dispatch, for example, found eight data base citations when researching reports that a doctor accused of income-tax evasion was connected to an offbeat religious order. At the Louisville (Ky.) Courier-Journal, reporters used several data bases to produce a 1,600-item bibliography that was useful in producing a 30-part series on toxic waste dumps. At the Providence (R.I.) Journal, a science reporter found data on herpes and the drug called Lysine by searching a data base called Medline. Such searches are both extraordinarily useful and increasingly common.

Another library system in use at newspapers employs computer-accessed microfiche. Articles are indexed by key words and then called to a viewing screen for review. Copies of the articles may be printed from the microfiche if the user desires. The advantage of this system is that it allows the user to see the article as it appeared in the newspaper. Electronic data base systems do not have that feature.

As a reporter you probably will have occasion to use portable VDTs. These permit you to transmit your story to the newspaper's computer system over telephone lines from almost any location. Some newspapers use terminals made specifically for newspapers, but others have found that portable personal computers are more useful; operators can use a variety of ready-made operating programs with them.

Personal computers are being used in newspaper offices, too. Some newspapers are using them to keep up with story assignments, and others are using them for news room budgeting. Still others are finding them useful to produce instant analyses of election results or to create maps and charts. The number of possibilities for using such devices in the news room is unlimited, and newspapers are just beginning to explore their potential.

Some reporters also have found themselves writing copy for various electronic publishing ventures in which their employers are involved. Many newspapers are now leasing cable television channels and programming local news on those channels.

In addition, some publishers are experimenting with videotex, audiotext and teletext. *Videotex* refers to a form of two-way communication with a data base. A videotex customer, for example, would be able to call to the television or computer screen the latest news and information such as theater listings and airline schedules. Videotex requires a connection with a central computer through cable television or telephone lines. *Audiotext* allows a subscriber to retrieve news via telephone by pressing keys on the telephone set. *Teletext* uses an unused part of a television signal, called the vertical blanking interval, to transmit digital information that can be unscrambled by a decoder and called to the TV screen. The information can be left there as long as the viewer desires. Most teletext systems can contain only about 200 screenfuls of information, so their capacity is severely limited. Teletext's advantage is that, unlike videotex, it does not depend on a cable connection to a remote computer. Because of that, it is a promising system in areas such as the American and Canadian West, where great distances separate communities and cable television lines are prohibitively expensive to install.

Newspaper publishers are experimenting with these technologies because they represent new markets for news and information material they

**Figure 2.14
Reporter at VDT.**
Reporters at many
newspapers now
write their stories
directly on video
display terminals
(VDTs).

**Figure 2.15
Closeup of VDT
Screen.** The
advantage of writing
and editing copy on
a VDT is that the
copy is always easy
to read. There is no
need to interpret
handwritten
insertions or
corrections.

already have paid to gather. Some experts believe that these technologies eventually will replace newspapers and magazines, which rely on costly distribution systems and consume vast amounts of expensive paper. Whether that prediction will come true is far from clear. It is clear that many publishers view reporters as information collectors and disseminators. If new methods of distributing information can be made profitable, reporters will be expected to adapt.

# Suggested Readings

Editors of the Harvard Post. "How to Produce a Small Newspaper." Port Washington, N.Y.: Harvard Common Press, 1983. A good discussion of the modern newspaper production process.

Fink, Conrad C. "Strategic Newspaper Management." New York: Random House, 1988. An up-to-date discussion of newspaper management.

Rucker, Frank W. and Williams, Herbert L. "Newspaper Organization and Management," Fifth Edition. Ames, Iowa: Iowa State University Press, 1978. This book details the structure of American newspapers and their operation.

# Exercises

1. Visit either your school newspaper or the local daily or weekly newspaper. Talk with staff members about how the staff is organized. Once you understand the system, draw an organizational chart for the news department.

2. Draw a copy-flow chart that shows how copy moves from the reporter to the typesetter at the newspaper you chose for exercise 1.

3. Talk with a newspaper librarian about the resources available in his or her library. If the newspaper does data-base searches for reporters, describe how one reporter's story was improved by using a search. If the newspaper does not use data-base searching, describe how that paper could benefit from investing in the equipment used for searches.

# PART TWO

# Basic Skills

# 3

## The Inverted Pyramid

**M**any people were surprised that USA Today, the most innovative newspaper ever marketed, primarily uses the *inverted pyramid*, a story form used by newspapers since the turn of the century. USA Today uses the inverted pyramid because it is the most space-efficient story form known. It permits writers to go on at great length, or, as is more often the case, to deliver the most important information in a paragraph or two. That attribute is what USA Today capitalizes on most; it is marketed as a paper you can read quickly. A national story that might be 10 paragraphs in your local newspaper will probably be five in USA Today. As the newspaper's circulation figures demonstrate, there is clearly an audience for that approach to the news.

The king in ''Alice in Wonderland'' would never succeed as an editor at USA Today. Asked where to start, he replied, ''Begin at the beginning and go on till you come to the end; then stop.'' Reporters often begin at the end.

Like the miner sifting through a million grains of sand for a speck of gold, the reporter pans the bits of information for the nugget that belongs in the lead, a statement of the most significant aspect of an event. That information—the climax of the event, the theme statement of a speech, the result of an investigation—is presented as simply and clearly as possible in the first paragraph. It sets the tone. It advertises what is coming in the rest of the story. It conveys the most important information in the story.

The lead sits atop a news-writing formula called the inverted pyramid, in which information is arranged in descending order of importance. These paragraphs explain and provide evidence to support the lead. Usually, each

Figure 3.1
USA Today, the
nation's most
innovative
newspaper, relies
on the inverted
pyramid for most
of its stories.

paragraph contains one idea. Newspapers developed this story formula for two important reasons:

1. Because the reader may stop reading at any time, you must provide the important news first. A person who reads as little as one paragraph gets the essential elements in the story.

2. Many newspaper stories are cut to fit a certain amount of space, and cutting is easier if information is presented in order of descending importance. The inverted pyramid format allows editors to cut stories from the bottom quickly without destroying the story.

The first is a necessary concession to a readership distracted by radio and television, by children and private concerns. On average, readers spend only 15 to 20 minutes a day with a newspaper. Many subscribers read only a few paragraphs of most stories. If a reporter were to write an account of a car accident by starting when the driver got into the car to begin a trip, many readers would never stay with the story long enough to find out that the driver was killed.

By the turn of the century, the inverted pyramid was fairly common. Before then, reporters were less direct. In 1869 The New York Herald sent Henry Morton Stanley to Africa to find the famous explorer-missionary David Livingstone. Stanley's famous account of the meeting began:

> Only two months gone, and what a change in my feelings! But two months ago, what a peevish, fretful soul was mine! What a hopeless prospect presented itself before your correspondent!

After several similar sentences, the writer reports, "And the only answer to it all is [that] Livingstone, the hero traveler, is alongside of me."

Stanley reported the most important information so casually that unless the headline reported the news, today's subscriber probably would not have read far enough into the story to learn that Livingstone had been found. Today's reporter would probably begin the story like this:

> Dr. David Livingstone, the missionary-explorer missing for six years, has been found working with natives in an African village on the shores of Lake Tanganyika.

The second function of the inverted pyramid—permitting editors to cut the story from the bottom—fulfills a mechanical requirement. If the story does not fit in the space allotted to it, an editor, working against a deadline, has to shorten the story quickly. If it is organized according to the inverted pyramid formula, the story can be shortened by eliminating paragraphs from the bottom. Because the most important information is contained in the first several paragraphs, the story will not be destroyed. But if an editor had cut Stanley's story from the bottom, we would never have had these now famous lines, which ended the story:

> "Dr. Livingstone, I presume?"
> And he says, "Yes."

William Caldwell, winner of a Pulitzer Prize in 1971, remembers the best lead he ever heard.

"One summer afternoon in 1922," Caldwell wrote for an Associated Press Managing Editors "Writing" report, "I was on my way home from school and my daily stint of work as editor of the village weekly, unhonored and unpaid. Like my father and two uncles, I was a newspaperman.

"My little brother came running to meet me at the foot of our street. He was white and crying. A telegram had come to my mother. 'Pa drowned this morning in Lake George,' he gasped, and I am ashamed to be remembering my inward response to that.

"Before I could begin to sense such elements as sorrow, despair, horror, loneliness, anger—before all the desolation of an abandoned kid would well up in me, I found myself observing that the sentence my brother had just uttered was the perfect lead. Noun, verb, predicate, period, and who-what-when-where to boot."

In Part Three, where basic story types are discussed, we shall see some examples of stories that are more effectively written in less traditional forms than the inverted pyramid, and in Chapter 17 we will discuss other ways to organize a news story. It may be that in the next several years, the inverted pyramid will become less important to newspapers. But if there is a change, it will be through evolution, not revolution.

The inverted pyramid will likely remain the backbone of radio journalism, and it may become even more important as new forms of electronic delivery are developed. Clients of specialized business news that is delivered to their computer or by fax want the facts fast. The inverted pyramid delivers.

Although the computer has made it easier for newspaper journalists to edit stories faster, the need to produce multiple editions with the same story running different lengths in each one makes it important that stories can be shortened quickly. The inverted pyramid serves that need well.

It does have some shortcomings. Although the inverted pyramid delivers the important news first, it does not encourage people to read the entire story. Stories stop; they don't end. There is no suspense. Newspapers and magazines, especially, look at the inverted pyramid as one of several ways to organize information.

The day when the inverted pyramid is relegated to journalism history books is not yet here and probably never will be. Perhaps 90 percent of the stories in today's newspapers are written in the style of the inverted pyramid. As long as newspaper and broadcast journalists continue to emphasize the quick, direct, simple approach to communications, and as long as millions of readers continue to accept it, the inverted pyramid will serve the journalist well, and every journalist should master its form. Those who do will have mastered the art of making news judgments. The inverted pyramid requires the journalist to identify and rank the most newsworthy elements in each story. That is important work. No matter what kind of stories you deal with—whether obituaries, accidents, speeches, press conferences, fires or meetings—you will be required to use the skills you learn here.

**In this chapter you will learn:**

1. How to write leads.

2. How to organize a story using the inverted pyramid.

# How to Write Leads

To write a lead—a simple, clear statement consisting of the first paragraph or two of a story—you first must recognize what goes into one. Journalists traditionally answer six questions. They are:

1. Who?

2. What?

3. When?

4. Where?

5. Why?

6. How?

The information from every event you witness and every story you hear can be reduced to answers to these six questions. Consider this example of an incoming call at fire headquarters:

>"Fire department," the dispatcher answers.
>
>"Hello. At about 10 o'clock, I was lying on my bed watching TV and smoking," the voice says. "I must have fallen asleep about 10:30 because that's when the football game was over. Anyway, I woke up just now and my bedroom is on fire. . . ."

That dialogue isn't very informative or convincing. More likely our sleepy television viewer awoke in a smoke-filled room, crawled to the telephone and dialed frantically. The conversation at headquarters would more likely have gone like this:

>"Fire department."
>"FIRE!" a voice at the other end yells.
>"Where?" the dispatcher asks.
>"At 1705 West Haven Street."

When fire is licking at their heels, even non-journalists know the lead. How the fire started is not important to the dispatcher; that a house is burning—and where that house is located—is.

The journalist must go through essentially the same process to determine the lead. Whereas the caller served himself and the fire department, reporters must serve their readers. What is most important to them?

After the fire is over, there is much information a reporter must gather. Among the questions a reporter would routinely ask are these:

- When did it start?

- When was it reported?

- Who reported it?

- How was it reported?

- How long did it take the fire department to respond?

- How long did it take to extinguish the fire?

- How many fires have been attributed to careless smoking this year?

- How does that compare to figures in previous years?

- Were there any injuries or deaths?

- What was the damage?

- Who owned the house?

- Did the occupant or owner have insurance on the house?

- Will charges be filed against the smoker?

- Was there anything unusual about this case?

With this information in hand, you can begin to write the story.

## WRITING THE LEAD

Start looking over your notes.

The who? The owner, a smoker, Henry Smith, 29. The age is important. Along with other personal information, such as address and occupation, it differentiates him from other Henry Smiths in the readership area.

What? Fire caused damage estimated by the fire chief at $2,500.

Where? 1705 W. Haven St.

When? The call was received at 10:55 p.m., Tuesday. Firefighters from Station 19 arrived at the scene at 11:04. The fire was extinguished at 11:30.

Why? The fire was started by carelessness on the part of Smith, according to Fire Chief Bill Malone.

How? Smith said he fell asleep in bed while he was smoking a cigarette.

If you had asked other questions, you might have also learned from the fire department that it was only the third fire this year caused by smoking in bed. At this time last year, there had been four such fires. Smith said he had insurance. The fire chief said no charges will be filed against Smith. It was the first fire at this house. Smith was not injured.

Assume your city editor has suggested you hold the story to about four paragraphs. Your first step is to rank the information in descending order of importance. There are lots of fires in this town, but only three this year have been caused by smoking in bed. Perhaps that's the most important thing about this story. You begin to type:

> A fire started by a careless smoker caused an estimated $2,500 in damage to a home.

Only 16 words. You should try to hold every lead to fewer than 35 words unless you use more than one sentence. Maybe it's too brief, though. Have you left anything out? Maybe you should include the time element—to give the story a sense of immediacy. You rewrite:

> A Tuesday night fire started by a careless smoker caused an estimated $2,500 in damage to a home at 1705 W. Haven St.

The reader would also want to know "where." Is it near my house? Is it someone I know? Besides, you still have only 23 words.

Just then the city editor walks by and glances over your shoulder. "Who said it was a careless smoker?" the editor asks. "Stay out of the story."

You realize you have committed a basic error in news writing: You have allowed an unattributed opinion to slip into the story. You have two choices. You can attribute the "careless smoker" information to the fire chief in the lead or you can rewrite. You choose to rewrite by using the chief's exact words. You also realize that your sentence emphasizes the damage instead of the cause. You write:

> Fire that caused an estimated $2,500 in damage to a home at 1705 W. Haven St. Tuesday night was caused by smoking in bed, Fire Chief Bill Malone said.

Now 29 words have answered the questions of "what" (a fire), "where" (1705 W. Haven St.), "when" (Tuesday night), and "how" (smoking in bed). And it is attributed. But you have not answered "who" and "why." You continue, still ranking the information in descending order of importance. Compare this fire story with the approach in Figure 3.2.

> The owner of the home, Henry Smith, 29, said he fell asleep in bed while smoking a cigarette. When he awoke about 30 minutes later, the room was filled with smoke.
>
> Firefighters arrived nine minutes after receiving the call. It took them 26 minutes to extinguish the fire, which was confined to the bedroom of the one-story house.
>
> According to Chief Malone, this is the third fire this year caused by careless smokers.
>
> Smith, who was not injured, said the house was insured.

You take the story to the city editor, who reads through the copy quickly. Then she checks the telephone book and the city directory.

As you watch, she crosses out "caused an estimated $2,500 in." She also specifies who was smoking. The lead now reads:

> Fire that damaged a home at 1705 W. Haven St. Tuesday night started when the occupant fell asleep while smoking in bed, Fire Chief Bill Malone said.

She is eliminating the less important to emphasize the most important aspects of the story. Besides, $2,500 isn't much money when you are talking about a house fire. Put it lower in the story.

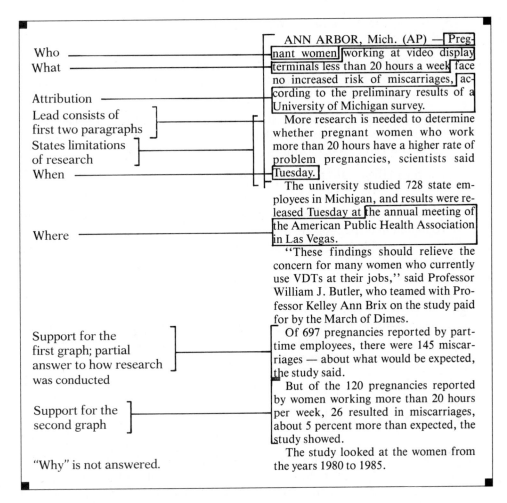

**Figure 3.2   The Anatomy of an Inverted Pyramid Story**

This time, though, you have an even more serious problem. Both the telephone book and the city directory list the man who lives at 1705 W. Haven St. as Henry Smyth. S-m-y-t-h.

Never put a name in a story without checking the spelling, even when the source tells you his name is Smith.

There are several lessons you can learn from this experience. They are:

1. *Always* check names.

2. Keep the lead short, usually fewer than 35 words unless you use two sentences.

3. Attribute opinion. (Smoking in bed is a fact. That it was careless is an opinion.)

4. Find out the who, what, where, when, why and how. However, if any of these elements have no bearing on the story, they might not have to be included.

5. Report information basic to the story even if it is routine. Not everything you learn is important enough to be reported, but you'll never know unless you gather the information.

6. Write to the length discussed with your editor.

The late Harry Stapler of the University of Florida studied stories in 12 metropolitan newspapers. He found that the number of words per sentence in the first paragraph was significantly longer than in the rest of the paragraphs. The average was 26.1 words per sentence for the first paragraph and 21.1 in the rest of the sentences. He also found that almost 84 percent of the first paragraphs had only one sentence while 54 percent of the rest of the paragraphs had two or more.

The lesson in this research is that writers are trying to cram too much into one sentence in the lead. Remember, there is no rule against using two sentences in your first paragraph.

## ALTERNATE LEADS

In the lead reporting the fire, the ''what'' (fire) is of secondary importance to how it started. A slightly different set of facts would affect the news value of the elements and, consequently, your lead. For instance, if Smyth turned out to have been a convicted arsonist, you probably would have emphasized that bizarre twist to the story:

A convicted arsonist awoke Tuesday night to find that his bedroom was filled with smoke. He escaped and later said that he had fallen asleep while smoking.
Henry Smyth, 29, who served a three-year term for . . .

That lead emphasizes the news value of novelty. If Smyth were the mayor, you would emphasize prominence:

Mayor Henry Smyth escaped injury Tuesday night when he awoke to find his bedroom filled with smoke. Smyth said he had fallen asleep while smoking in bed.

The preceding examples also illustrate the so-what factor in news. A $2,500 fire is not news to enough people in large communities where there are dozens of fires daily. Even if you crafted a tightly written story about it, your editor probably would not want to print or broadcast it.

In small communities the story would have more impact because a larger proportion of the community is likely to know the victim and because there are fewer fires. The so-what factor grows more important as you add other information. If the fire occurred during a fire-safety campaign, the so-what would have been an example of the need for fire safety in a community where awareness of the problem had already been heightened. If the fire involved a convicted arsonist or the mayor, the so-what would be even stronger. Oddity or well-known people increase the value of a story. If someone had been injured or the damage had been $250,000 instead of $2,500, the so-what factor might have pushed the story even into the metropolitan press. Remember that when you have answered all six of the basic questions, ask yourself what it means to the reader. The answer is your so-what factor.

No journalist relies on formulas to write inverted pyramid leads, but you may find it useful, especially in the beginning, to learn some typical types of leads. The labels that follow are arbitrary, but the approaches are not. Here are some types of leads that can help you write once you have decided what is most important:

1. Immediate-identification leads.

2. Delayed-identification leads.

3. Summary leads.

4. Multiple-element leads.

5. Leads with flair.

The news value or values you choose to emphasize determine the kind of lead you write. The first fire story has a summary lead that emphasizes "how." That lead uses the news value of novelty. However, because smoking in bed is not that unusual, the story is only worth a few paragraphs inside the paper. The next lead also emphasizes novelty. This time, however, it deals with an arsonist. That is more unusual, and the story is more interesting. As a result, the story probably would get better display in the paper. The third is an immediate-identification lead emphasing prominence.

Now let's look at each type of lead in more detail.

## Immediate-Identification Leads

In the *immediate-identification lead*, one of the most important facts is "who," or the prominence of the key actor. Reporters often use this approach when someone important or someone whose name is widely recognized is making news. Consider the following example:

> ORLANDO, Fla. (AP)—Freed journalist Nicholas Daniloff, in an emotional speech greeted with tears and applause, told fellow journalists yesterday they should not forget about a colleague held hostage in Lebanon.

At the time this story was written, Daniloff had been on the front page of most newspapers and on the television news every day for nearly two weeks. The Moscow correspondent for U.S. News & World Report, Daniloff had been imprisoned in Moscow on charges of spying. Daniloff was freed in exchange for a Russian the United States had accused of spying. A month earlier—and today—few readers would recognize his name.

Daniloff's case illustrates how fast names can become common currency in the media—and how fast they can disappear. Some names, such as those of the president, have staying power because of the office. You would rarely, if ever, see a story quoting Carter or Reagan begin, "A former president said . . ." Instead, the writer would begin, "Former President Reagan said . . ." Well-known names catch the reader's eye and interest.

Any action by a person in the public eye can merit an immediate identification:

> Bruce Springsteen has plunged into the 2 Live Crew controversy—at least symbolically—by allowing the melody from his anthem, "Born in the U.S.A.," to be used on the rappers' next single. Titled "Banned in the U.S.A.," it will be released July 4.

It would make no sense to delay the identification of someone as well-known as Springsteen. Names, as People magazine has shown, make news.

In any accident, the "who" may be important because it is someone well known by name or position:

> MADISON, Wis.—Mayor John Jones was killed today in a two-car collision two blocks from his home.

In small communities the "who" in an accident may always be in the lead. In larger communities names are not as recognizable. As a rule, if the name is well-known, it should appear in the lead.

## Delayed-Identification Leads

When a reporter uses a *delayed-identification lead*, usually it is because the person or persons involved have little name recognition among the readers. John Jones, the mayor, is well-known; John Jones, the carpenter, is not. Thus, in fairly large cities an accident is usually reported like this:

> MADISON, Wis.—A 39-year-old carpenter was killed today in a two-car collision two blocks from his home.
>
> Dead is William Domonske of 205 W. Oak St. Injured in the accident and taken to Mercy Hospital were Mary Craig, 21, of 204 Maple Ave., and Rebecca Roets, 12, of 207 Maple Ave.

There are two other occasions when the reporter may choose to delay identification of the person involved in the story until the second paragraph. They are:

1. When the person is not well-known but the person's position, occupation, title or achievements are important or interesting.

2. When the lead is becoming too wordy.

In the following examples, the occupations of those making news are common but the names are not:

> ATLANTA—Conservatives controlling the Southern Baptist Convention have demanded the resignations of the two top officials of Baptist Press, the denomination's news agency.
>
> Al Schackleford, director, and Dan Martin, news editor, were told to resign or "be dealt with harshly," Shackleford said Tuesday . . .

> WASHINGTON—A reputed crime kingpin in the nation's capital pleaded not guilty yesterday to taking part in an interstate gambling operation that included the distribution of counterfeit video games.
>
> The plea was entered in federal court by Joseph Nesline of Washington, D.C.

In both cases, the "what"—the resignations and the allegation—is more important than the "who." However, if you are writing for the journalists' hometown or even home-state newspaper or broadcast station, or if you are writing about Nesline in Washington, D.C., the "who" might be well-known enough to put in the lead. In that case, the stories might begin like this:

ATLANTA—Conservatives controlling the Southern Baptist Convention have demanded the resignations of Al Schackleford and Dan Martin, the two top officials of Baptist Press, the denomination's news agency.

WASHINGTON—Joseph Nesline, reputed crime kingpin in the Washington area, pleaded not guilty yesterday to taking part in an interstate gambling operation that included the distribution of counterfeit video games.

Some titles are bulky: "Chairman of the Federal Communications Commission" assures you of clutter even before you add the name. "United Nations ambassador" takes away many options from the writer. When dealing with these types of positions, writers often choose to use the title and delay introducing the name until the second or third paragraph. While the name often is shorter, it is more important that the title be introduced first. Many people would not recognize the name of the chair of the FCC or the ambassador to the United Nations. Thus, stories about them might open:

WASHINGTON—The U.S. ambassador to the United Nations today accused three Arab states of refusing to negotiate for peace "in good faith."

WASHINGTON—The chairman of the Federal Communications Commission said today that networks must decrease the amount of sex and violence shown on television.

In both examples, the title of the person who made the statements is more important than the name. The use of the title gives the story credibility. The exception occurs when an individual in one of those positions becomes well-known because he or she is popular or controversial. For instance, not many people outside the business community can name the president of your local chamber of commerce. But if the chamber president is the former mayor or is using the position to run for mayor, the name will be recognizable by itself.

## Summary Leads

Reporters dealing with several important elements may choose to sum up what happened in a *summary lead* rather than highlight a specific action. It is one of the few times that a general statement is preferable to specific action.

When Congress passed a bill providing family members with emergencies the right to unpaid leaves from work, the writer had to make a choice: Focus on the main provision or write a summary lead. The writer chose the latter:

A bill requiring employers to give workers up to three months unpaid

> leave in family emergencies won Sen-
> ate approval Thursday evening.

Several other provisions in the bill are explained later in the story: The unpaid leave can be for medical reasons or to care for a new child, employers would have to continue health insurance benefits and restore employees to their previous jobs or equivalent positions.

Likewise, if a city council rewrites the city ordinances, unless one of the changes is of overriding importance, most reporters will use a summary lead:

> MOLINE, Ill.—The City Council
> replaced the city's 75-year-old munici-
> pal code with a revised version Tues-
> day night.

The basic question the reporter must answer is whether the whole of the action is more important than any of its parts. If the answer is yes, a summary lead is in order.

## Multiple-Element Leads

In some stories, choosing one theme for the lead is too restrictive. In such cases the reporter can choose a *multiple-element lead* to work more information into the first paragraph. But such a lead must be written within the confines of a clear, simple sentence or sentences. Consider this example:

> PORTLAND, Wash.—The City
> Council Tuesday ordered three depart-
> ment heads fired, established an ad-
> ministrative review board and said it
> would begin to monitor the work
> habits of administrators.

Notice that not only the actions but also the construction of the verb phrases within the sentence are parallel. Parallel structure also characterizes the following news extract, which presents a visual picture of the scene of a tragedy:

> BAY CITY, Mich.—A flash fire
> that swept through a landmark down-
> town hotel Saturday killed at least 12
> persons, injured 60 more and forced
> scores of residents to leap from win-
> dows and the roof in near-zero cold.

In the last example, we are told where it happened, what happened, and how many were killed and injured.

Some multiple-element leads actually consist of two paragraphs. This occurs when the reporter decides that there are several elements that need prominent display. For example:

The Board of Education Tuesday night voted to lower the tax rate 12 cents per $100 valuation. Members then approved a budget of $150,000 less than last year's and instructed the superintendent to decrease the staff by 25 people.

The board also approved a set of student conduct rules, which include a provision that students with three or more unexcused absences a year will be suspended for a week.

Simpler leads are preferable. But a multiple-element lead is one of the reporter's options. Use it sparingly.

Many newspapers are using graphic devices to take the place of multiple-element leads in some cases. Summary boxes can be used to list other actions. Because the box appears under the headline in type larger than text, it serves as a graphic summary for the reader who is scanning the page. The box frees the writer from trying to jam too many details into the first few paragraphs. (See Figure 3.3.)

Another approach is to break the coverage of a single event into a main story and a shorter story or stories, called sidebars. This approach has the advantage of presenting the information in shorter, more palatable bites. It also allows the writer to elevate more actions into lead positions.

Both these methods of presentation have advantages over the more complicated multiple-element lead.

## Leads with Flair

Although the inverted pyramid is designed to tell readers the news first and fast, not all stories begin with the most important statement. When the news value you want to emphasize is novelty, often the lead is unusual.

When a group of suspected drug dealers was arrested at a wedding, the Associated Press account focused on the novelty:

NARRAGANSETT, R.I. (AP)— The wedding guests included drug suspects, the social coordinator was a narcotics agent, the justice of the peace was a police chief, and 52 officers were party crashers.

For the unsuspecting bride and groom, the ceremony Friday night was truly unforgettable—a sting operation set up by state and local police that led to 30 arrests.

> ## Other council action
> **In other action, the council:**
> √ **Voted to repave Broadway Ave.**
> √ **Rejected a new sign ordinance.**
> √ **Hired four school crossing guards.**
> √ **Expanded bus hours.**

**Figure 3.3**
A quick read.
Summary boxes
can take the place
of multiple-
element leads.

Not exactly your traditional wedding or your traditional lead. Yet, the essential information is contained within the first two paragraphs. A less imaginative writer would have written something like this:

> Thirty suspected drug dealers, including a couple about to be married, were arrested at a wedding Friday night.

That approach is like slapping a generic label on a Mercedes-Benz. The inverted pyramid approach is not so rigid that it doesn't permit fun and flair.

The difference between the two-paragraph, multiple-element lead on the Board of Education and the two-step lead on the wedding story is that in the first, the reporter was dealing with several significant actions. In the second, the reporter was dealing with only one, so she used the first paragraph to set up the surprise in the second.

## Story Organization

Like the theater marquee, the lead is an attention getter. Sometimes the movie doesn't fulfill the promises of the marquee; sometimes the story doesn't fulfill the promises of the lead. In either case the customer is dissatisfied.

The inverted pyramid is designed to help reporters put information in logical order. It forces the reporter to rank, in order of importance, the information to be presented.

Just as there is a checklist for writing the lead, there is also a checklist for assembling the rest of the inverted pyramid. Included on that checklist are the following:

1. Introduce additional important information you were not able to include in the lead.

2. If possible, indicate the significance or so-what factor.

3. Elaborate on the information presented in the lead.

4. Continue introducing new information in the order in which you have ranked it by importance.

5. Develop the ideas in the same order in which you have introduced them.

6. Generally, use only one new idea in each paragraph.

Let's see how the pros do it.

## ONE-SUBJECT STORIES

Most newspaper stories concentrate on a single subject. The following articles, the first from Cox News Service and the other from The New York Times News Service, show that there is no single way to construct a story successfully.

*Summary lead includes the notification requirement, the time element and the two states from which the cases came*

WASHINGTON—States may require that both parents be notified when their unmarried minor child seeks an abortion as long as a judge can waive the requirement in the child's interest, the Supreme Court ruled Monday in cases from Ohio and Minnesota.

*Specifics to support the lead; the states are named in the same order as in the lead*

In decisions that left many abortion questions still undecided, the justices:

—Voted 6-3 to uphold an Ohio law that requires one parent be notified unless a judge waives the mandate.

—Voted 5-4 to overturn a Minnesota measure that both parents be notified and did not contain a judicial waiver.

—Voted 5-4 to uphold a separate section of Minnesota law that contains the same notification requirement with a judicial-bypass provision that lets a judge waive the mandate. Nei-

*Introduces a new element*

*The so-what factor*

*Introduces a new element*

*Summary lead includes the ruling, the notification requirement and the time element*

*So-what factor*

*So-what factor continued*

*So-what factor continued as the writer explains the impact of the decisions*

*Background*

*Specifics to support the lead*

ther state requires a child to obtain parental permission.

Justice Sandra Day O'Connor—long considered the key vote in the high court's abortion decisions—switched sides to vote with the majority on both Minnesota questions.

Her actions highlighted the closeness of the court's abortion decisions, the uncertainty about the long-term status of the basic right to abortion and the many ways the court might decide to restrict it.

Advocates on both sides of the debate declared Monday's ruling victories for the anti-abortion movement.

WASHINGTON—The Supreme Court ruled Monday that states may require a teen-age girl to notify both parents before obtaining an abortion, as long as the law provides the alternative of a judicial hearing for pregnant teens who do not want to inform their parents of their decision.

The court addressed the parental-notification laws of two states Monday in decisions indicating continued turmoil among the justices over what approach to take toward abortion.

As in last year's ruling in Webster vs. Reproductive Health Services, it is evident that there is no longer a majority on the court that views abortion as a fundamental constitutional right, but the justices have still not settled on a standard for analyzing obstacles to abortion.

The two decisions, in cases from Minnesota and Ohio, are likely to provide road maps as legislatures try to fashion abortion laws that will win the Supreme Court's approval.

Thirty-two states now have laws requiring some form of parental involvement in teenagers' abortion decisions, and a number of other states are considering such legislation.

By a 6-to-3 vote, the court upheld an Ohio law requiring unmarried young women 18 years of age or under either to notify one parent or to get a judge's permission before terminating a pregnancy.

The decision, written by Justice Anthony M. Kennedy, overturned a ruling by a federal appeals court in Ohio. Justice John Paul Stevens, who has usually voted to strike down restrictions on abortion, expressed some reservations but joined the court's conservative majority.

*Specifics on another, related case*

By a 5-to-4 vote, the court ruled that Minnesota's requirements of notification to both parents—the strictest such law in the country—was constitutional only because the state provides the alternative of a judicial hearing. Like the Ohio law, the Minnesota requirement applies to unmarried young women 18 years of age or under. . . .

## MULTIPLE-ELEMENT STORIES

Earlier in this chapter, we discussed multiple-element leads. They occur most often when you are reporting on councils, boards, commissions, legislatures and even the U.S. Supreme Court. These bodies act on numerous subjects in one sitting. Frequently, their actions are unrelated, and more than one action is often important enough to merit attention in the lead. You have three options:

1. *You can write more than one story.* That, of course, depends on permission from your editor. There may not be enough space.

2. *You can write a summary box.* It would be displayed along with the story. In it you would list the major actions taken by the council or decisions issued by the court.

3. *You can write a multiple-element lead and story.* Let's go back to the one we used earlier when discussing leads:

The Board of Education Tuesday night voted to lower the tax rate 12 cents per $100 valuation. Members then approved a budget $150,000 less than last year's and instructed the superintendent to decrease the staff by 25 people.

The board also approved a set of student conduct rules, which include a provision that students with three or more unexcused absences a year will be suspended for a week.

There are four newsworthy actions in these two paragraphs: establishing a tax rate, approving a budget, cutting staff and adopting conduct rules. In this and all stories that deal with several important elements, the writer highlights the most important. Sometimes there are several that can be equated, as in the school board example. Most of the time, one action stands out above the rest. When it does, it is important to summarize other actions after the lead. For instance, if you and your editor judged that establishing the tax rate was more important than anything else that happened at the school board meeting, you would approach it like this:

| | |
|---|---|
| *Lead* | The Board of Education Tuesday night voted to lower the tax rate 12 cents per $100 valuation. |
| *Support for lead* | The new rate is $1.18 per $100 valuation. That means that if your property is assessed at $30,000, your school tax will be $354 next year. |
| *Summary of other action* | The board also approved a budget that is $150,000 less than last year's, instructed the superintendent to cut the staff by 25 and approved a set of rules governing student conduct. |

Notice that the lead is followed by a paragraph that supports and enlarges upon the information in it before the summary paragraph appears. Whether you need a support paragraph before summarizing other action depends on how complete you are able to make the lead.

In all multiple-element stories, the first two or three paragraphs determine the order of the rest of the story. To maintain coherence in your story, you must then provide the details of the actions in the order in which you have introduced them. We see this demonstrated in the Associated Press report of some Supreme Court decisions. Earlier, we showed you The New York Times and Cox News Service single-subject stories of the Supreme Court decisions. This is the AP roundup of the same action.

| | |
|---|---|
| *Multiple-element story with a lead that focuses on one of the actions* | WASHINGTON (AP)—Family members can be barred from ending the lives of persistently comatose relatives who have not made their wishes known conclusively, the Supreme Court ruled Monday in its first "right-to-die" decision. |
| *Specifics to support the lead* | By a 5-4 vote, the justices gave states broad power to keep such patients on life-support systems. Specifically, the court blocked the parents of a Missouri woman, Nancy Cruzan, from ordering removal of tubes that provide her with food and water. |

*Transition to the other action*

*Details to support this decision*

*Introduces the second case*

*Transition back to the subject introduced in the lead*

The court, clearing the way to end its term on Wednesday, decided another fundamental and emotional privacy issue by making it significantly more difficult for young girls to obtain legal abortions without first notifying their parents.

The court voted 6-3 to uphold an Ohio law that bans abortions for unmarried girls under 18 who are dependent on one or both parents unless one parent is notified.

And the court voted 5-4 to allow Minnesota to require notification of both parents as long as girls can avoid telling them by getting a judge's permission instead.

Monday's right-to-die ruling encourages supporters of "living will" laws because the court said the Constitution guarantees a competent person—as opposed to someone in a coma—a right to refuse medical treatment.

The most important thing to remember about multiple-element stories is to explain the elements in the same order in which they are introduced and to provide transitions out of and back into your items.

# Exercises

1. Identify the who, what, where, when, why and how, if they are present, in the following:

   The United Jewish Appeal is sponsoring its first ever walk-a-thon this morning in Springfield to raise money for The Soup Kitchen, a place where the hungry can eat free.

2. Here are four versions of the same lead. Which of the four leads answers more of the six questions basic to all stories? Which questions does it answer?

   a. What began 12 years ago with a federal staff investigation and led to hearings and a court fight culminates today with a Federal Trade Commission rule to prevent funeral home rip-offs.

   b. The nation's funeral home directors are required to offer detailed cost statements starting today, a service they say they are now ready to provide despite nearly a dozen years of debate over the idea.

   **c.** A new disclosure law going into effect today will make it easier for us to determine the cost of a funeral.

   **d.** Twelve years after first being proposed, a federal regulation goes into effect Monday to require funeral homes to provide an itemized list of services and materials they offer, along with the cost of each item, before a person agrees to any arrangements.

3. From the following facts, write a lead.
   *Who*:   a nuclear weapon with a yield equivalent to 150,000 tons of TNT
   *What*:   detonated
   *Where*: 40 miles from a meeting of pacifists and 2,000 feet beneath the surface of Pahute Mesa in the Nevada desert
   *When*:   Tuesday
   *Why*:   to test the weapon
   *How*:   not applicable
   Other information: Department of Energy officials are the source; 450 physicians and peace activists were gathered to protest continued nuclear testing by the United States

4. From the following facts, write the first two paragraphs of a news article.
   *Who*:   7-year-old boy missing for three years
   *What*:   found
   *Where*: in Brick Township, N.J.
   *When*:   Monday night
   *Why*:   not applicable
   *How*:   a neighbor recognized the child's picture when it was shown after the NBC movie ''Adam: The Song Continues'' and called police
   Other information: Police arrested the boy's mother, Ellen Lynn Conner, 27; she faces Alabama charges of kidnapping and interference with a custody warrant

5. From the following facts, write the first two paragraphs of a news article.
   *Who*:   40 passengers
   *What*:   evacuated from a Northwest Airlines jet, Flight 428
   *Where*: at the LaCrosse, Wis., Municipal Airport
   *Why*:   a landing tower employee spotted smoke near the wheels
   *When*:   Monday following a flight from Minneapolis to LaCrosse
   *How*:   not applicable
   Other information: There was no fire, the smoke was caused by hydraulic fluids leaking onto hot landing brakes, according to Bob Gibbons, a Northwest spokesman

6. Cut out six leads from newspapers. Identify what questions are answered (Who . . .). Identify what is not answered. Identify the kind of lead (Summary . . .).

# 4

# The
# Importance of
# Good Writing

Surveying news rooms full of reporters, many editors are asking: Where are the writers? The editor who picks up the paper and reads this lead has reason to ask.

> The Planning and Zoning Commission Thursday approved a petition to downzone land in the east-campus area from multifamily to two-family use.

But the editor who finds this account of the same meeting knows there is at least one writer on the staff:

There is "a time to be born, a time to die, a time to rezone," Mark Stevenson reminded the Planning and Zoning Commission Thursday night. And this is not the time, he argued, to rezone the neighborhood east of the university.

The commission, while not addressing the first two points, decided that the time to rezone, at least, had come.

The time also has come to re-emphasize the importance of good writing. Editors and readers are demanding it. Whenever organizations such as the

**Figure 4.1
Encouraging Good
Writing.**
Syndicated
columnist James
Kilpatrick urges
writers to take
greater care in
practicing their
craft.

Associated Press Managing Editors convene, there is talk of the need to stress writing skills. The editors once heard syndicated columnist James Kilpatrick, himself an expert writer, challenge them:

> If 99 percent of what we write is instantly blown away with the wind, well that is how the world is. I would suggest to you . . . if we write upon the sand, let us write as well as we can upon the sand before the waves come in.

If Kilpatrick's challenge to your pride is not enough, then the demands of the editors who are doing the hiring and of the readers who are doing the buying should be. One journalist whose prose is not being washed away with the sand is Rick Reilly, whose profile of Steve Garvey appeared in Sports Illustrated. This is how he opened the story:

Steve Garvey lines up his colognes by the amount unused. He arranges his Polo shirts by pastel. He'll keep vacuuming a clean carpet just to admire the parallel patterns he makes. His shirts are monogrammed. When he was a batboy, the bats rested trademarks out, knobs up, in the order of the day's starting lineup. He would save his allowance to buy Ban-Lon shirts. (He had 16 in varying colors.) He would sometimes reiron his mother's ironing, just to get it *exactly* right. As a player, he would sweep the dugout steps. When he joined the San Diego Padres, he suggested a reorganization of the bat and helmet racks. Much tidier. In his closet in his pink-and-pink house in Del Mar, Calif., all the shirts are on hangers, facing left. There are no blue jeans. On the floor, the shoes are treed and the toes all point outward. Muss his hair, go to jail. You can bounce a quarter off his bed.

So how come his life is such a mess?

The writer is as conscious of details as Garvey is. That example is from a profile. The next is from a news story written on the copy desk of the Chicago Tribune by editors working from versions received over Tribune wire services.

MIAMI—Elaine Yadwin had never flown a plane before. But her husband had just slumped, unconscious, over the controls of the Piper Cherokee, and she knew he needed help.

An hour later, with the help of radio directions from air-traffic controllers and a flight instructor, the 61-year-old woman brought the plane thumping down. It was a "miraculous" landing, but it was too late to save her husband.

Richard Yadwin, 66, was dead when he reached the hospital.

The ordeal began just before noon.

There was nothing special about this story for Chicago readers; it appeared in some editions two days after the accident. Still, someone cared enough to make it not only informative but also interesting. Good writing such as this is seen frequently these days, though not often enough by newspaper readers. Too much of what we put on newsprint is dull, awkward and pedestrian. As a result, many editors believe they need to improve the writing on their papers. The number of full-time writing coaches has multiplied in the last five years. A Pulitzer Prize is now given for writing. One result of this emphasis on quality of writing is that when an editor assigns an otherwise routine story, instead of a pedestrian piece, many of today's reporters try to give it punch. Reporters did just that in the following inverted pyramid stories:

The state's October floodwaters have receded, but the damage results are just beginning to pour in.

\* \* \* \* \* \*

NEW YORK—The friendly skies looked distinctly gray Wednesday as the British-American dogfight over trans-Atlantic air fares heated up again.

* * * * * *

For people faced with things so bad they wouldn't touch them with a 10-foot pole, Neiman-Marcus' Christmas gift catalogue has the perfect gift—an 11-foot pole.

Because dull writing is more common than writing that has vitality, editors are looking for those unusual people who can combine reporting and writing talents. The journalist whose prose jerks around the page like a mouse trapped in a room with a cat has no future in the business. The days when a reporter could hide behind the talents of a rewrite desk are over. To emphasize that point, the American Society of Newspaper Editors has made improved writing one of its principal long-range goals. Each year, in cooperation with the Poynter Institute of St. Petersburg, Fla., it awards $1,000 to the winners in several categories of the writing competition it sponsors. The winning entries are published annually by the institute in a book series titled ''Best Newspaper Writing.''

Many well-known writers—among them, Daniel Defoe, Mark Twain, Stephen Crane and Ernest Hemingway—began their careers as journalists. A more recent list would include the names John Hersey, Tom Wolfe and Gay Talese as well. The best-seller list is peppered with the names of journalists: Russell Baker, James J. Kilpatrick, William Safire, Ellen Goodman, George Will, Jimmy Breslin, Bob Greene. On newspapers around the country today, small but growing numbers of journalists are producing literature daily as they deal with everything from accidents to affairs of state. If you have a respect for the language, an artist's imagination and the dedication to learn how to combine them, you, too, may produce literature.

We should all attempt to bring quality writing, wit and knowledge to our work. If we succeed, newspapers will be not only informative, but also enjoyable; not only educational, but also entertaining; and not only bought, but also read.

## In this chapter you will learn:

1. Six characteristics of all good writing.

2. How the skills of reporting make good writing possible.

# Elements
# of Good Writing

Good writing has six characteristics:

1. It is precise.

2. It is clear.

3. It has a pace appropriate to the content.

4. It uses transitional devices that lead the reader from one thought to the next.

5. It appeals to the readers' senses.

6. It uses analogies.

Let's look at each of these characteristics.

## PRECISION

Words should be used precisely. They should mean exactly what you intend them to mean. You should never use "uninterested" when you mean "disinterested." Nor should you use "allude" for "refer," "presume" for "assume," "endeavor" for "try," "fewer" for "less," "farther" for "further." If you report that fire has destroyed a house, you mean it must be rebuilt, not repaired. If you say firefighters donned oxygen masks to enter a burning building, you are impugning either their intelligence or yours. Oxygen is dangerous around fire; firefighters use air tanks. You can make the mayor "say," "declare," "claim" or "growl"—but only one is accurate.

Even when used innocently, sexist and racist language, in addition to being offensive and discriminatory, also is imprecise. Doctors aren't always "he," nor are nurses always "she." Much of our language assumes people are male unless it is shown they are female. Precise writers avoid "policeman" (police officer), "adman" (advertising representative), "assemblyman" (assembly member) and "postman" (postal worker).

You have at least six ways to avoid sexism:

1. Use a generic term (flight attendant, firefighters).

**Figure 4.2 Early Newspaperman.** Mark Twain, known today to most people as a book author, began his career as a newspaper reporter and editor. He first gained national fame with his letters sent to newspapers while on a cruise in 1867.

**Figure 4.3 Journalist and Author.** Russell Baker began as a reporter and graduated to columnist for The New York Times. He is also a book author.

2. Participate in the movement to drop feminine endings (comedian, hero, poet).

3. Make the subject plural (Reporters must not form *their* judgments . . . ).

4. Drop the sexist pronoun and replace it with an article (A reporter must not form *a* judgment.).

5. Rewrite to eliminate the gender (A reporter must not judge . . .).

6. Write the sentence in the second person (*You* should not form *your* judgment . . .).

Our language is bursting with derogatory racial terminology. You should avoid using terms such as ''Chinaman,'' ''Jap,'' ''nigger'' and ''Indian giver'' not only because they are offensive but also because they are imprecise. They rain inaccurate stereotypes on a class of people. To be precise, use Asian-American, black or African-American, and American Indian or Native American.

Some words, perfectly precise when used correctly, are imprecise when used in the improper context. ''Boy'' is not interchangeable with ''young man,'' and ''girl'' is not interchangeable with ''young woman.'' A young Native American is not a ''young buck.'' All elderly women are not ''blue-haired,'' nor are all active retired persons ''spry.'' In that context, ''spry'' implies that the writer is surprised to find an elderly person who is active.

''Dumb'' as in ''deaf and dumb'' is imprecise and derogatory. To be accurate, use ''speech-impaired.'' When the terms are used in tandem, use ''hearing-impaired and speech-impaired'' for parallelism. Because alcoholism is a disease, use ''recovering alcoholic'' instead of ''reformed alcoholic.'' ''Handicapped'' is imprecise; ''disabled'' is precise.

Words are powerful weapons. They can define cultures, create second-class citizens and reveal stereotypical thinking. They also can change the way people think about and treat others. Writers have the freedom to choose precisely the right word. That freedom can be both exhilarating and dangerous.

Freedom in word choice is exhilarating when the result is a well-turned phrase. Barbara Yost turned several of them when writing about an old-fashioned roundup for the Phoenix Gazette.

Early in the morning, coyotes come out of the woods to howl. They sound like children at play. But by the time Mickey the cook wakes up Joe the wrangler at 4:30 a.m., and the smell of coffee wakes the other cowboys half an hour later, the chicken-livered coyotes have fled back into the trees.

They'll return later in the day when they smell cattle—coyote fast-food on the hoof.

And later in the story:

> When all the cowboys are mounted
> up, he gives a nod and they're off for
> work—no briefcases, no car pools or
> traffic jams, and the office covers
> 180,000 acres. Any smaller and you
> get to feeling a little itchy.

The writer informs and entertains. Reading about the beginning of the day is like sitting quietly at the side and watching it. The writer's sense of humor adds something to the scene that we might not even see. Her description of cattle as "coyote fast-food on the hoof" is both true and humorous. Her characterization of 180,000 acres as modest for these cowboys puts the size in perspective.

Freedom in word choice is dangerous when it results in nouns masquerading as verbs (prioritize, impact, maximize) or jargon masquerading as respectable English (input, output and throughput). Kilpatrick has a cure for this ailment:

> When your reporters feel the innovative impulse, suggest that they lie down until it goes away.

Precision, however, means more than knowing the etymology of a word; it means knowing precisely what you want to say. Instead of saying, "The City Council wants to locate the landfill three blocks from downtown," to be precise, you say, "Some members of the City Council . . ." Or better yet, "Five members of the City Council . . ."

Precision means writing in the conditional when discussing proposals:

> Incorrect: The bill *will* make it illegal . . .
> Correct: The bill *would* make it illegal . . .

The use of "will" is imprecise because the legislation has not been passed. By using "would," you are saying, "If the legislature passes the bill, it would . . ."

Precision means using the correct sentence structure to communicate explicitly what you mean. The following sentence is technically corrrect but imprecise:

> The City Council passed the ordi-
> nance, and the 250 supporters cheered.

It is imprecise because the compound sentence gives equal importance to the two thoughts expressed. To show cause and effect, the writer should have used a complex sentence:

> Because (or When) the City Council passed the ordinance, the 250 supporters cheered.

When you write implicitly, you force the reader to make inferences. Say what you are thinking.

## CLARITY

Before typing a single word, reporters should remind themselves of three simple guidelines:

1. Rely on simple sentences.

2. Use correct grammar and punctuation.

3. Think clearly.

The result will be clear writing.

### Simple Sentences

The readers of one newspaper once confronted the following one-sentence paragraph:

> "Paradoxically, cancer-causing mutations often result from the repair of a cell by error-prone enzymes and not the 'carcinogenic' substance's damage to the cell," Abe Eisenstark, director of biological sciences at the university, said at a meeting of the Ad Hoc Council of Environmental Carcinogenesis Wednesday night at the Cancer Research Center.

If there is a message in those 53 words, it would take a copy editor, a lexicologist and a Nobel Prize-winning scientist to decipher it. The message simply is not clear. Although the sentence is not typical of newspaper writing, it is not unusual either. Too much of what is written is mumbo jumbo. For instance:

> Approximately 2 billion tons of sediment from land erosion enter our nation's waters every year. While industrial waste and sewage treatment plants receive a great deal of attention, according to the Department of Agriculture the number one polluter of our waterways is ''non-point'' pollution.

The writer of that lead contributed some linguistic pollution of his own. The message may have been clear in his mind, but it is not clear in print.

One remedy for unclear writing is the simple sentence. The following has impact because the message is stated clearly in a simple sentence:

> NEW YORK—The moon may still be wobbling from a colossal meteorite impact 800 years ago.

That lead gets to the point. The next one drags the reader through some prickly underbrush full of prepositional phrases:

> NEW YORK—From measurements with high-precision laser beams bounced off reflectors left at three lunar sites by Apollo astronauts, plus one atop an unmanned Soviet lunar vehicle, scientists believe that the moon is still wobbling from a colossal meteorite impact 800 years ago.

Both of the preceding leads are simple sentences, but only the first says it simply.

## Grammar and Punctuation

Errors in grammar are far too common in newspaper writing, and because of them, meaning is obscured. Consider this example:

> The Senate Tuesday rejected another attempt to block adoption of a tax increase proposal by weighing it down with complicating amendments.

Because of the loose sentence structure, the reader cannot be sure whether the proponents or the opponents of the measure tried to defeat the tax increase by attaching the amendments. The phrase ''by weighing it down with complicating amendments'' incorrectly modifies ''The Senate.'' Because of its placement, some readers may assume it refers to the tax increase proposal. That assumption is also incorrect. The phrase is supposed to describe the action of ''opponents,'' but that term does not even appear in the sentence. The sentence could be rewritten this way:

> The Senate Tuesday rejected another attempt to stop adoption of legislation to raise taxes. Opponents had tried to block the increase by adding amendments.

No one who aspires to be a writer will succeed without knowing the rules of grammar. Dangling participles, split infinitives, noun-verb disagreements, pronoun-antecedent disagreements and misplaced modifiers are like enemy troops: They attack your sentences and destroy their meaning. The best defense is to construct tight, strong sentences.

The personnel director of an Inglewood, Calif., aerospace company had to fill out a government survey form that asked, among other things, ''How many employees do you have, broken down by sex?''

After considering the sentence for a few moments, she wrote, ''Liquor is more of a problem with us.''

Sentence modification was more of a problem with the writer of the survey. Here are some typical errors and ways to correct them:

| | |
|---|---|
| *Incorrect antecedent:* | Each of the boys brought *their* sleeping bags. |
| *Correct:* | Each of the boys brought *his* sleeping bag. |
| *Dangling participle:* | The mayor told the taxpayer to submit a claim to the clerk, *bringing it to her* before noon. |
| *Correct:* | The mayor told the taxpayer to submit a claim to the clerk before noon. |
| *Split infinitive:* | The mayor agreed *to* soon *submit* his resignation. |
| *Correct* | The mayor agreed *to submit* his resignation soon. |
| *Misplaced modifier:* | *Despite his size*, the coach said Jones would play forward. |
| *Correct:* | The coach said that Jones, *despite his size*, would play forward. |

Improper punctuation creates ambiguities at best and inaccuracies at worst. For instance:

Giving birth to Cynthia five years earlier had been difficult for Mrs. Davenport and the two parents decided they were content with the family they had.

Without the required comma before "and," the reader misses the pause and sees this: " . . . had been difficult for Mrs. Davenport and the two parents . . ." That's a lot of people in the delivery room.

## Clear Thinking

A story must have a beginning, middle and end. Put in a maze, rats make many mistakes before they find their way out. So do writers who start a sentence, a paragraph or a story without knowing where it will end. The problem is most obvious when the reporter is unsure of the lead. The result usually is a story that jumps from one idea to another without transitions and without supporting evidence for each idea introduced. When you are sure of your lead, the rest of the story often will fall into place. How that can happen is illustrated in the following example of an article about a city council meeting.

If you cover a meeting at which the city council votes on five ordinances, lead with the most important one. If the other votes are important enough to merit early mention, summarize them in the second paragraph. Support your lead, then pick up the rest of the action. For example:

| | |
|---|---|
| *Lead* | The Springfield City Council voted Tuesday to make four streets in the downtown area one-way. |
| *Summarize other action:* | The council also raised parking fines to $5, voted to buy two snowplows, ordered a study of downtown parking facilities and hired a firm to audit the city. |
| *Support lead:* | Effective March 1, the four streets that will be one-way are . . . |

Too many reporters would try to work several of the council actions into the lead and then would not know where to go in the second and third paragraphs. Rank the elements in the order of importance. Then take them one at a time.

You must guide your readers through the story. If *you* do not know the trail, your readers will certainly get lost.

## PACING

The untrained observer looking at a new car may see the glossy finish, flashy chrome and stylish lines. An engineer may see the hundreds of complicated working parts under the hood.

Like the untrained observer, the reader enjoys a story because of the message. Another writer will recognize the author's skillful use of techniques that make the story readable.

One of those rarely noticed but important techniques is pacing. Sentences, as much as the words themselves, give a story mood. Short sentences convey action, tension, movement. A series of long sentences conveys a more relaxed mood; long sentences slow down the reader.

Between these two extremes are sentences of varying lengths, and good writers use them all. Not all sentences should be long. Or short. Nor should they all be of medium length. An abrupt change in sentence length draws attention to the sentence. Try it sometime.

Giving precisely selected words the proper pace is a skill of the creative writer. Describing the assassination of President Kennedy, some writers used short, clipped sentences to convey the frantic atmosphere. The cadence of the sentences describing the funeral was slow, reflecting the rhythmic pace of the lone black horse as it led the slain president's bier down Pennsylvania Avenue.

The pace also was appropriately slow when Greta Tilley described her visit to the home of a 16-year-old high school girl who had committed suicide. Tilley, then a reporter for the Greensboro (N.C.) News and Record, relied on moderate to long sentences to describe the scene:

On this cold January morning, the bed is covered with school homework papers, letters, a directory of colleges, a family photo album and high school and junior high yearbooks, which Douglas Oxendine eagerly has taken from his daughter's closet and drawers to help open her life to a stranger.

Near the spot where the rifle once was lodged is a large cardboard box. Inside are nine manila envelopes, each tagged with a Greensboro Police Department label.

In the hours after Tonja's death, Detective Ken Brady was particularly interested in the single sheet of notebook paper marked "Evidence No. 12." In uneven, penciled script, lines of poetry are listed along with corresponding page numbers that show where the poems can be found in the 11th-grade literature book, "Encounters." Each poem is about death.

Although some of the sentences are long, there is variety. They range from five to 49 words. Rhythm does not mean sameness.

Some writers read their copy aloud to themselves. Their ear tells them if the story has the proper pace and variety. The beginning writer should count the number of words in each sentence. Look for variety.

Variety not only in length of consecutive sentences but also from one part of the story to another is what UPI's George Frank wrote into his account of the attempted assassination of Gerald Ford. Notice that in the opening section the pace is leisurely, as is the peaceful and relaxed scene in the park. When the would-be assassin lunges forward, the sentences become staccato:

|  |  |
|---|---|
| 22 | SACRAMENTO, Calif. (UPI)—The day was sunny and beautiful, and the tiny woman in red waited with other spectators for President Ford to walk by. |
| 10 | Most of the well-wishers wanted to shake Ford's hand. |
| 7 | The woman in red had a gun. |
| 31 | Lynette Alice Fromme, 27, known as ''Squeaky'' in the terrorist Charles Manson family to which she belongs, stood quietly behind the spectators on the grounds of the state capitol, eyewitnesses said. |
| 15 | ''Oh, what a beautiful day,'' she told a girl in the crowd, Karen Skelton, 14. |
| 8 | ''She looked like a gypsy,'' Karen said later. |
| 15/5 | Squeaky wore a long red gown and red turban, and carried a large, red purse. They matched her red hair. |
| 25 | On her forehead was a red ''X'' carved during the 1971 Los Angeles trial in which Manson and three women followers were convicted of murder. |
| 22 | Squeaky, who had moved to Sacramento in northern California to be closer to the imprisoned Manson, 41, waited patiently for President Ford. |
| 9 | In her purse was a loaded .45 caliber automatic. |
| 4/9 | The sun beat down. The spectators squirmed in the 90-plus-degree heat. |
| 6<br>20<br>5 | Then, suddenly, the crowd perked up. Ford had emerged from the Senator Hotel and was coming up a sidewalk through the park of the capitol grounds. Secret Service agents accompanied him. |
| 8 | He stopped to return greetings from the crowd. |
| 11 | The spectators, restrained by a rope, pressed forward to say hello. |
| 12 | He faced to his left and reached out for the extended hands. |
| 11 | ''Good morning,'' he said to the well-wishers, one after another. |
| 4 | Squeaky made her move. |
| 14 | She lunged forward from the rear of the spectators, splitting them away on both sides. |
| 17 | Now she was only two feet from the president, and, said police, aimed the gun at him. |
| 15 | Ford saw the revolver and ''the color went out of his face,'' said Karen Skelton. |

14

He looked "alarmed, frightened, and he hunched over," said another spectator, Roy Miller, 50.

18

At that moment, Secret Service Agent Larry Buendorf took the action that may have saved the president's life. Risking his own life, he lunged forward and threw himself between Squeaky and Ford.

14

12

He wrestled Squeaky to the ground, and he and police disarmed her.

6

Squeaky screamed, "He's not your servant."

9

Then she told the police, "Easy, guys, don't batter me. The gun didn't go off."

5

16

Four or five agents threw themselves around the president and pushed him away from the crowd.

---

# TRANSITIONS

Besides being well-paced, good writing also uses transitions to lead the reader imperceptibly from one thought to the next. Transitions assure the reader that the writer has a sense of direction. A transition is a bridge. It can be a word, a phrase, a sentence or a paragraph. The reference to "memory" transports us from the first to the second paragraph in this example:

Mr. and Mrs. Lester Einbender are using their memory to project life as it might have been.

That memory centers around a son named Michael, a rheumatic disease called lupus and a desire to honor one while conquering the other.

The word "That" in "That memory" is a demonstrative adjective. Its use is subtle, but its impact is dramatic. If you write "A memory," you are not linking the reader to the memory already mentioned; if you write "The memory," you are being more specific; if you write "That memory," you are pointing directly at the memory in the preceding paragraph. Because it is good only for general references, "a" is called an indefinite modifier; because it is more specific, "the" is called a definite modifier; because it is most specific, "that" is called a demonstrative adjective. It demonstrates precisely the word or phrase to which you are referring.

These linkages help you achieve coherence, the logical connection of ideas. The linkages transfer you from one sentence to the next, from one paragraph to the next. The different types of linkages are called *transitions*. Writers unfamiliar with transitions merely stack paragraphs, like wood, atop one another. Transitions keep the story, if not the woodpile, from falling apart.

Repeating a word or phrase is one way to keep the story from falling apart. In the preceding example, the writer uses both a demonstrative adjective (others include "this," "these" and "those") and also repeated a word.

Repetition of a phrase or of sentence construction, called *parallelism*, is another way to guide readers through a story. Writers frequently use parallelism to achieve coherence.

Writing about the complicated subject of nuclear-waste disposal in America, Donald Barlett and James Steele of The Philadelphia In-

14/5    Ford's knees, troubled in the past, buckled in the crush, and he almost stumbled. But he stood up quickly.

12/6    "The country is in a mess," shouted Squeaky as officers handcuffed her. "The man is not your president."

20    Moments later, as a police car drove her away, she had a faint smile on her face and appeared calm.

Before Frank reports that Fromme was carrying a gun in her purse, the average sentence length is 16 words. From that point, where the tension begins to build, until the last line, the average sentence length is only 10 words.

---

quirer relied on parallelism for coherence and emphasis:

This assessment may prove overly optimistic. For perhaps in no other area of modern technology have so many experts in the government, industry and science been so wrong so many times over so many years as have those involved in radioactive waste.

They said, repeatedly, that radioactive waste could be handled like any other industrial refuse. It cannot.

They said that science had most of the answers, and was on the verge of getting the few it did not have, for dealing with radioactive waste permanently. It did not, and it does not.

They said that some of it could be buried in the ground, like garbage in a landfill, and that it would pose no health hazard because it would never move. It moved.

They said that liquid radioactive waste could be put in storage tanks, and that rigorous safety systems would immediately detect any leaks.

The tanks leaked for weeks and no one noticed.

Chronology and references to time are other ways to tie a story together. Words and phrases such as "now," "since then," and "two days later," are invaluable in helping readers understand where they have been and where they are going. Chronology is important in everything from reports of automobile accidents (which car entered the intersection first?) to recaps of events that occurred over months or even years. For instance, Barlett and Steele's stories covered 35 years of efforts to store nuclear waste.

Transitions include but are not limited to "and," "but" and "however." A word, a phrase, a thought, like a road sign, leads the reader from one paragraph to the next. The linkages that make the following story coherent are shown by the connecting lines.

FREDERICKSBURG, VA. (AP)— The distinguished visiting professor with the patch over his right eye tugs at a tweed sleeve and bends an ear to his chiming wristwatch.

"Twenty-eight minutes past one," James Farmer announces in that resonant, mellifluous voice to a

## TRANSITIONS (*cont. from p. 87*)

hushed class of 40 juniors and seniors, leaning forward, pens poised over notebooks.

"As I was saying, those troopers were bellowing. 'Come on out, Farmer. We know you're in there.'

'I was meant to die that night. They were kicking open doors, beating up blacks in the streets, interrogating them with electric cattle prods. I got out alive in a hearse.''

It was a lovely spring day on the campus of predominantly white Mary Washington College, a state institution in historic Fredericksburg. Bright sunshine slanting through the budding trees gave a roseate glow to the white-columned Georgian brick buildings.

But the imposing black figure at the lecture desk in Monroe Hall was wrapped in the darkness of another time, in another Southern state.

He couldn't see the azaleas blushing at the windowsill or sniff the cherry blossoms just come into bloom around the fountain in the square. There was too much tear gas billowing through the busted windows of the Plymouth Rock Baptist Church in Plaquemine, La. And the splashing fountain brought back the swoosh of the fire hose washing hymn books and Bibles down the aisle as the mob smashed pews and ransacked the church.

"Scared spitless," Farmer says, recalling that violent summer night a quarter of a century ago.

One moment he's a terrified Freedom Rider pleading with the local telephone operator to put a call through "to the White House, the attorney general, the FBI in New Orleans.''

Now he's a redneck deputy, snarling through jowls chock full of chaw. "We know you're in there, Farmer.''

## SENSORY APPEAL

As you chauffeur the reader through the scenes in your story, you can drive down the road or over the green-laced, rolling hills of Kentucky. You can report that a car hit a skunk, or you can convey the nauseating smell. A word here, a phrase there and you hear the plane ripping the tin roof off the house; smell the acrid tires burning on a flaming car; feel the boxing glove's leather rasp against the skin. Good writing appeals to one or more of our five senses: sight, hearing, smell, taste and touch.

Whether he was reporting or writing a novel, Ernest Hemingway appealed to the reader's senses. Reporting for The New York Times from Madrid during the Spanish Civil War, he wrote:

Next he's the spunky lady operator of the funeral parlor down the street telling him to "play dead in the back of that hearse" and ordering the driver to take dirt roads known only to blacks since plantation days.

Then he's himself, the founder of CORE, the Congress of Racial Equality, wondering if that night in Louisiana less than a week after the march on Washington and Martin Luther King's "I Have a Dream" speech, would be his last on Earth.

"This guy is tremendous," says senior Rich Cooper, one of the students in Farmer's course, "The History of the Civil Rights Movement," a three-credit course in the history department. . . .

"Here is a man who has changed history. He's seen it all, and now the tragedy is he sees nothing."

But in the classroom the now totally blind champion of civil rights sees something he never saw before in his 70 years—a ray of hope: "just a glimmer."

"The hope for America is with these young people," he says, gathering up a bundle of their term papers. "Their minds are not closed. At the beginning of the semester, black kids and white kids alike find it difficult to grasp that this is the way things were here."

With Martin Luther King, Roy Wilkins and Whitney Young now dead, Farmer is the last of the Big Four of the civil rights movement. "We were the knights of the round table," he chuckles, counting the nine steps down to the taxi taking him home for a brief rest before facing an evening class of nearly 200 freshmen and sophomores. . . .

> There is a rifle fire all night long.
> The rifles go "tacrong, carong,
> craang, tacrong," and then a machine
> gun opens up. It has a bigger caliber
> and is much louder—"rong, cararibg,
> rong, rong."

Moving to another war and another writer, we get the same sense of detail. Reporting for the Chicago Daily News, Keyes Beech described his flight from Saigon during the panic of the American evacuation from that city in 1975:

> We were only men fighting for our
> lives, scratching, clawing, pushing

> ever closer to that wall. We were like
> animals. . . .
>     I lay on a tin roof gasping for
> breath like a landed fish, then
> dropped to the ground. God bless the
> Marines; I was one myself in the last
> of the just wars.

Through Hemingway's ears, we listen not just to gunfire but also to ''rong, cararibg, rong, rong.'' Through Beech's fingers we feel not just a roof but a tin roof, too.

Knowing when a detail enhances the story rather than just making it wordy is the skill of an accomplished writer. Some details are as out of place as white tennis shoes with a black business suit. If Beech had written, ''Wearing blue denim jeans, white sneakers and a torn blue shirt, I lay on a tin roof gasping for breath like a landed fish . . .'' we would laugh instead of marvel at the description. What he was wearing was not important.

But what country music singer Tammy Wynette was wearing was important in a profile of her, and reporter Leola Floren captured the scene this way:

> On stage, she is surrounded by musicians in green suits and cowboy boots. Stuck there in the middle, Tammy looks like one smooth pearl in a bucket of peas. Her wavy blond hair tumbles over bare shoulders to the middle of her back. Her black strapless gown is of the kind the slightly bad girls wore to the senior prom: slit up past the knees in the back, cut so low in front there isn't any decent place to pin a corsage. When she picks up her guitar, you think it ought to be a champagne glass, she looks so elegant.

Another writer gives the reader a visual picture of Johnny Cash on stage: ''He moves with the grace of a little boy who has to go to the bathroom.'' Physical description like this can be helpful in establishing the tone of a piece—in this case, a humorous tone. In other cases, though, it is distracting.

Assigned to cover a dress-up day at a local elementary school, a reporter produced a story that began this way:

> Denita Perrigo, 10, went to her fifth-grade class at New Bloomfield Elementary School Wednesday. Dressed as a hillbilly, she wore a *floppy straw hat* and her father's *oversized flannel shirt*, and she sported *Magic-marker freckles*.
>
> That might have been enough to prompt any self-respecting teacher to send Denita to the principal's office—except that the principal was wearing a *sheriff's uniform, circa 1910*, complete with a *tinfoil badge* on his chest.

The writing is better because the reporter wrote not just about what she was told but also about what she observed. The words in italics identify the reporting she did with her eyes.

What you don't see in the preceding example are such details as Denita's hair or eye color, her size or what she scored on the last math test. That's because those are inappropriate details *in this story*.

A reporter once wrote of a landlord and "his pregnant wife" who testified at a city council meeting against a proposed ordinance to license rental units. Because the fact that the landlord's wife was pregnant had no bearing on the story, it was deleted by the editor. If, while testifying, the landlord's wife had fainted, reporting her pregnancy would have been appropriate. The good writer must know when detail is appropriate.

## USING ANALOGIES

Good writers also know how to use another literary device called *analogy*. Analogies permit writers to show similarities and contrasts. Similes show similarities by using the word "like" or "as": "Tammy looks like one smooth pearl in a bucket of peas." Describing a long-distance runner, another writer used this simile: "Her legs, so rubbery they wobbled like jelly, shook and then surrendered."

The metaphor is the first cousin of the simile. Where the simile compares one thing to another, a metaphor says one thing is another: "Tammy is one smooth pearl in a bucket of peas." A metaphor is a stronger analogy than a simile. Sports columnist Jim Murray once described football coach John Robinson in metaphorical language: "He's the world's biggest Easter rabbit, a marshmallow sundae."

With similes and metaphors, writers draw word pictures. Reading about Tammy Wynette, you see white and green. You picture Robinson as pudgy, friendly, smiling. The techniques set the pages of a scrapbook of images turning in each reader's mind.

The technique of analogy is also important to every journalist trying to make dimensions and numbers meaningful. That's important whether you are writing about the national debt or the size of the offensive guard. You make numbers meaningful by translating them. Writing about the national debt, one college reporter pointed out it was enough to operate the university for decades. No number means much unless it is compared to something else.

Instead of writing that 75 percent of the people in the United States do not know that you are innocent until proven guilty, say that three of four people do not know. Trying to show the dimensions of a nuclear power plant, a writer pointed out that workers poured 15,500 cubic feet of concrete for the 430-foot-diameter base, "enough to build a two-lane highway 35 miles long."

All budget figures, all sizes, all speeds are enhanced by comparing them to something else. The $5 million city budget means more if you translate that to spending per resident. Reporting the price of a bushel of corn or of a stock means little to most readers until you give the number context. What was the price last week or last year?

Analogies are your film; use them to take word pictures.

# Good Writing Begins with Good Reporting

Without the proper ingredients, the best chef is no better than a short-order cook. Without the proper use of participant accounts, personal observation and detail, the best writer writes dull stories. Good writing begins with good reporting.

## INTERVIEWING PARTICIPANTS

A car-truck accident: Is it routine? That depends on the reporting. The writer of the story that follows gathered information only from lifeless police reports:

A 39-year-old St. Louis man whose car was run over this morning by a truck walked out of Columbia Regional Hospital in good condition and was transferred to a St. Louis hospital.

Wheel marks from a tractor-trailer hauling 25,000 pounds of meat could be seen from the rear of Frank Cramer's 1975 Cadillac along the roof to the front. The car was a total wreck, but Cramer walked away with only minor injuries, according to police reports.

The driver of the truck, Alan Charles Floyd, 24, of Dallas, Texas, was issued a summons for following Cramer's car too closely.

Floyd told police he was attempting to pass Cramer on Interstate 70 near the Business Loop 70 exit when he lost control of his truck. Floyd told police he didn't remember what happened after that.

A witness told police he saw Cramer's car disappear beneath the tractor-trailer.

Cramer said he was headed east in the right lane of I-70 when he saw headlights approaching him from behind. Then he felt a collision. Cramer's vehicle was pushed into a guardrail, then rolled into a ditch. The truck turned on its side.

Floyd was treated for injuries at the University of Missouri-Columbia Medical Center and was released, according to police reports.

Two passengers in the truck, Terry Grider from Rockwell City, Iowa, and Tom Garner from Dallas, Texas, received minor injuries.

A 42-year-old Chesterfield, Mo., man was a passenger in Cramer's vehicle. He also received minor injuries.

The details of an apparently remarkable accident are lost in this dull account.

Another reporter recognized the story's potential. Not only did he use the police report, he talked to both of the passengers in the car and obtained a comment from a police officer. Good reporting permitted the writer to insert the human angle into a terrifying experience.

Frank Cramer of St. Louis slowed his Cadillac Coupe de Ville late Tuesday night as he entered the construction area along Interstate 70, one-quarter mile west of the Business Loop 70 overpass.

In his rear-view mirror he saw two large headlights bearing down on him, the light reflecting off the rain-slick pavement. Then his car was hit.

Bruce Bynum of Chesterfield was a passenger in the car. "I looked behind us, and all I saw was one huge headlight shining in the rear window," he said. "Then it started up over the car and smashed in the glass."

"I can't get the guy off the top of the car!" Cramer yelled.

"Frank," Bynum said, "I think we've had it."

The story is true, and Columbia police say they are surprised that Cramer 39, and Bynum, 42, lived to tell it. Cramer's car was run over by a truck hauling 25,000 pounds of frozen meat and driven by Alan Floyd, 24, of Dallas, Texas.

The truck drove over the left side of the car, Bynum said, pinning it against the guardrail and sliding down the highway on top of it.

"I could hear the engine going over us," Bynum said. "It seemed to go on for ever and ever."

At the end of the guardrail the car flew off the road. Bynum said he remembers telling Cramer, "It's all over."

"Yeah," Cramer replied, "things aren't going too well."

The car came to rest in a field 50 feet from the highway.

"I busted my door open and pulled him out," Bynum said. "He was pinned under the roof—it was smashed to the seat." Bynum said that was when he saw the two tire tracks running over the car from trunk to hood.

Cramer and Bynum were taken to Columbia Regional Hospital. Bynum was treated and released, and Cramer transferred in good condition to a St. Louis hospital early Wednesday.

Floyd, 24, and his passenger, Tom Garner, also of Dallas, were treated at the University Medical Center and released.

"It's lucky for all of them that they got out of that one alive," said Columbia police Capt. Carl Antimi. "They shouldn't have."

Bynum, reached Wednesday afternoon at his home, agreed. "It's amazing. I don't know how we got out of it," he said. "I figure we had the 'Force' with us."

Floyd was summoned for careless and imprudent driving, and is scheduled to appear in Magistrate Court Nov. 22.

This version tells the story through the eyes of two of the participants. The detail—the view in the mirror, the reference to the rain-slicked pavement and the effective use of dialogue—puts the reader in the car with the victims.

## DIGGING FOR THE TELLING DETAIL

Specific detail gathered by observant and questioning reporters always wins over general description. One young reporter learned that the hard way. His assignment began when the city desk heard that an elderly victim of a crime committed a week earlier had died in the hospital that evening. The reporter was sent to interview the victim's neighbors, one of whom had seen a man carrying a television out of the victim's house the night she was injured. Suspicious, the neighbor had summoned police, who arrived in time to make the arrest. They found the beaten victim inside the house.

The reporter's first draft was a dry, straightforward account of the neighbor's reactions to the woman's death and the burglary. The story obviously deserved much more.

Did the victim live alone? What is the neighborhood like? Were there many break-ins in that area? Were the neighbors friendly to her? What was her house like? Nearly every question directed at the reporter required him to return to the scene. He had failed to do his reporting.

He wrote a second draft that the city editor was moments from approving. "By the way," the reporter mentioned, "did you know the television set that guy tried to steal didn't even work?" That's when he started writing this third version:

When 11-year-old Tracy Britt visited her neighbor Rose Shock in the small, one-story house just two doors off Providence Road, they just talked, mostly, because the television set was broken.

One week ago tonight, another neighbor, Al Zacher of 300 Wilkes Blvd., heard suspicious noises. Looking outside, he saw a man carrying the television set that didn't work from Mrs. Shock's home. As the man set the television down and headed for a green station wagon, Zacher called the police.

Inside lay Mrs. Shock, battered about the face.

Sunday in Springfield County Hospital, where she worked as a dietitian for many years before she retired in 1955, 85-year-old Rose Shock died.

If Mrs. Shock's relatives had their way, she would not have been living in the house with aluminum siding and paint peeling from its window frames at 302 Wilkes Blvd. After her house was burglarized last summer, her family tried to convince her to move.

"She didn't seem to be too alarmed to be living by herself," her sister, Ruth Tremaine of 306 Harley Court, said Monday. "She'd been living there 18 or 19 years and she was happier there than she would have been anywhere else. We wanted her to go, but she just wanted to stay in her own home."

Widowed since 1948, Mrs. Shock, cane in hand, would walk around the yard and talk to her neighbors. Gladys and Paul Ray of 410 Wilkes Blvd. lived near her for several years. To them, she was a "nice, gentle, kind person."

Ruth Britt, who lived around the corner at 804 N. Fourth St., had been to Mrs. Shock's home a few times with her children.

"I didn't even know her last name," she said. "We just always called her Rosie."

"My children loved her, and, as old as she was, she was always glad to see them."

Mrs. Shock's home is located in a neighborhood caught between a spreading downtown commercial district and Business Loop 70. Before and after school, the unkempt city streets and sidewalks teem with students from Jefferson Junior High School and Hickman High School. When Mrs. Shock bought the house, Springfield had a population of about 30,000, and Providence Road was just being expanded from two lanes to four lanes. In those postwar baby boom years, the seeds for a changing neighborhood were being planted.

Now residents of the neighborhood are afraid.

"When something like this happens close to you, you think about it more," said Mrs. Ray.

Some residents spoke bluntly about their fear of burglary and refused to give their names because they believed it increased their chances of being victimized. A woman who lives down the street from the Shock home says, "They ought to string a few of them up down at the courthouse. That might teach them a lesson."

Another neighbor also criticized the system.

"They're letting them get by too easy," said Dorothy Mustain of 304 Wilkes Blvd. "If they'd punish them more so they'd have to suffer like the ladies they're beating up, maybe that would put a stop to it."

David Herron, 45, of 207 Providence Walkway, is being held in lieu of $100,000 bond in connection with the incident. He is charged with assault with intent to kill, carrying a concealed weapon and first-degree robbery.

Prosecuting Attorney Milt Harper said Monday he will meet with the medical examiner Thursday before deciding whether to file additional charges. He is waiting for results of autopsy tests.

Monday night, flashing red lights atop Springfield police cars once again lit up the Wilkes Boulevard neighborhood. Police were investigating a report of a burglary at Zacher's house.

We see dirty streets, hear crowds of students walking down the sidewalk in front of Rose Shock's house, see the aluminum siding and feel the peeling paint. We learn that Mrs. Shock died in the hospital where she worked for many years. We know, too, the sad irony that she was killed over a broken television set.

Good writing does not require the talent of a Dickens or a Hemingway. Good reporting makes good writing possible.

# Suggested Readings

Barzun, Jacques. ''Simple and Direct.'' New York: Harper & Row, 1975. An excellent rhetoric book that explains many of the details of sentence construction.

Bernstein, Theodore. ''The Careful Writer.'' Boston: Atheneum, 1975. An excellent desk book for people concerned with both grammar and the precision of their language.

Brooks, Brian S. and Pinson, James L. ''Working with Words.'' New York: St. Martin's Press, 1989. Like Strunk and White's ''The Elements of Style,'' this is an excellent handbook for every writer. It covers everything from grammar and punctuation to racism and sexism in language.

Kilpatrick, James J. ''The Writer's Art.'' Kansas City: Andrews, McMeel & Parker, 1984. An informative and entertaining discussion of writing.

Strunk, William and White, E. B. ''The Elements of Style,'' Third Edition. New York: Macmillan, 1979. This little book practices what it preaches. For the beginner it is a good primer; for the pro it is a good review of writing rules and the meaning of words.

# Exercises

1. Choose precisely the right word:
   a. We need to (ensure, insure) a victory.
   b. Stop (aggravating, annoying) your friend.
   c. The attorney won because she (refuted, responded to) the allegations.
   d. The prisoner was able to produce (mitigating, militating) evidence.

2. Rewrite the following to take out the parallelism. Which version, the original or yours, is better and why?

This assessment may prove overly optimistic. For perhaps in no other area of modern technology have so many experts in the government, industry and science been so wrong so many times over so many years as have those involved in radioactive waste.

They said, repeatedly, that radioactive waste could be handled like any other industrial refuse. It cannot.

They said that science had most of the answers, and was on the verge of getting the few it did not have, for dealing with radioactive waste permanently. It did not, and it does not.

They said that some of it could be buried in the ground, like garbage in a landfill, and that it would pose no health hazard because it would never move. It moved.

They said that liquid radioactive waste could be put in storage tanks, and that rigorous safety systems would immediately detect any leaks. The tanks leaked for weeks and no one noticed.

3. Punctuate the following sentences:

   a. Government officials have come under a newly enacted censorship system and several foreign speakers have been denied permission to enter the country.

   b. It was a Monday night and for the next two days he teetered between life and death.

   c. The council approved the manager's proposals and rejected a tax increase.

4. Use an analogy to explain the following numbers:

   The student council's budget is $350,000. The university has 19,000 students. The local city budget is $3 million. The city has 70,000 residents.

5. In newspaper articles find examples of:

   a. Incorrect word usage. (Correct it.)

   b. Ambiguous wording. (Correct it.)

   c. Incorrect grammar. (Correct it.)

   d. Incorrect punctuation. (Correct it.)

   e. A nicely worded sentence or paragraph.

   f. Use of an analogy.

# 5

# Interviewing

David Hacker of the Kansas City (Mo.) Times knew it was a long shot. Just four days earlier, a balcony in the Hyatt Regency Hotel had collapsed and killed 111 people. Kansas City was awash in grief. He wanted to talk to some of the relatives of the victims.

But how? And who?

Hacker called a priest, whom he didn't even know. He described what he wanted, but told the priest that if he didn't think it would help the relatives and the community deal with the loss, he didn't want the priest to help. And he asked the priest not to answer then but to think about it and get back to him.

The priest not only got back to him but was able to convince a couple of the victims' spouses to talk to Hacker. With this commitment, Hacker asked a rabbi for the same favor. The rabbi also helped.

That much savvy and sensitivity was needed just to get to the interviews. Once there, Hacker needed all the experience and skill he had acquired during his years as a journalist, but he knew that if he didn't get his foot in the door, he'd never have a chance to ask questions.

Interviewing is the key to most stories you will write. Your ability to get people to talk to you is the difference between mediocre reporting and good reporting.

Although you already have experience interviewing someone, you probably haven't thought much about how or why you've been doing it. And you probably haven't had much experience trying to get information from someone who wants to withhold it. Those few times you've tried, you probably have been frustrated:

"Professor, why did I get a B in your course?"
"Because you didn't deserve an A."
"Why not?"
"Because."

Sooner or later, you stomp out of the office. Now you are a reporter and confronted by a similar situation:

"Mr. Mayor, why did you fire the police chief?"
"I don't want to discuss that because it's a personnel matter."

Because journalists should not go stomping out of the room when they are denied information, they must have other resources. The mayor may not want to discuss the firing; perhaps he never will. But a skillful questioner often can obtain information the source does not want to divulge or does not even realize he or she is giving. The reporter may ask, for instance, what qualities the mayor will be looking for in a new police chief. The answer may provide the clue to why he fired the last one.

Information is the merchandise of a journalist. While some of it is gathered from records and some from observation, most of it is gathered in person-to-person conversations. For that reason every journalist needs to develop interviewing skills.

Interviewing is an imperfect process. As in the city water-works system, there is plenty of leakage. When the city pumps a million gallons of water, not all of it reaches the customers. Some evaporates, some leaks through decaying pipes. Some people illegally siphon some of the water.

Information leaks out, too, as it is passed from source to interviewer to editor to reader. The source may not want you to know everything. The source may be telling you everything, but you may not understand the subject. Unrecognized differences in cultural and ethnic backgrounds can influence meaning. When someone says "blue" to you, a color flashes in your mind's eye. However, it may not be the same shade of blue that is in the mind's eye of the speaker. Shades of meaning often leak out of the information pipeline.

In such an imperfect system of information gathering and transfer, we can reduce—though not eliminate—the leaks. Consequently, you must work hard to refine your skills. You simultaneously ask questions, digest responses, record answers, cajole the source, gauge reactions and look for details. This is no work for the unprepared.

## In this chapter you will learn:

1. How to prepare for an interview.

2. How to phrase your questions.

3. How to establish rapport with a source.

4. How to ensure accuracy.

# Preparing for the Interview

A reporter was assigned to interview Vivien Leigh, who was attending the premiere of the reissue of "Gone With the Wind." When he opened the interview by asking her what part she played in the film, Miss Leigh, whose portrayal of Scarlett O'Hara is a classic, indignantly ended the conversation—with good reason. A reporter who begins an interview without the proper preparation is like a student taking a final exam without studying. Both may make it, but luck, rather than skill, may have more to do with it.

The success of the interview depends as much on what you do before you ask the first question as it does on the questioning and writing. You should research both the subject and your source. A.J. Liebling, a famous journalist, author and press critic, didn't know much about horse racing, but his first question in an interview with jockey Eddie Arcaro was, "How many holes longer do you keep your left stirrup than your right?" Arcaro responded enthusiastically to the knowledgeable question. Liebling's research gave him the key to open the interview. A source who thinks the reporter is knowledgeable about the subject of the interview is more likely to speak frankly and fully than one who must explain everything as the conversation progresses.

Liebling was able to overcome Arcaro's skepticism with a single question. Syl Jones had considerably more difficulty with William Shockley, who won a Nobel Prize for his work developing the transistor. Jones, however, wanted to talk to him for Playboy magazine about much more volatile topics: Shockley's theory of black genetic inferiority and his revelation that he had participated in a Nobel-laureate sperm bank. Burned many times by the press, Shockley was exceedingly cautious.

Shockley often turned down reporters' requests for interviews because he believed they didn't know enough about genetics. By phone, Shockley quizzed Jones, a science and medical writer, about genetics. The quizzes involved complicated mathematical analyses of statistics designed by Shockley in support of his theories. After a few weeks of grilling, he agreed that Jones was competent enough to interview him.

But first Shockley wanted even more information. He asked for personal information, everything from where Jones was born to where he went to school. Jones told the rest of the story in Playboy:

Long before this point in the process, most other reporters had written Shockley off as a kook and had given up. I was tempted to do the same. But something intrigued me: Never once did he ask my race or make any kind of racist remark, and he had no idea I was black. I didn't tell him, because I was hoping for a confrontation. . . .

When a white photographer and I showed up at Stanford for the interview, Shockley instinctively reached to shake the photographer's hand with the greeting, ''Hello, Mr. Jones.'' It was a wrong guess that seemed almost to stagger him. Obviously stunned by my blackness, he insisted that I submit to one final test, concocted on the spur of the moment, concerning the application of the Pythagorean theorem to some now long-forgotten part of his dysgenic thesis. Somehow, I came up with a satisfactory explanation, and Shockley had no choice but to grant me the interview.

Let's hope you never have to overcome those kinds of barriers.

## CONSIDERATION OF STORY TYPE

How you prepare for the interview depends in part on what kind of a story you intend to write. You may be doing a news story, a personality profile or an investigative piece. In each case you check the newspaper library and search the data bank, talk to other reporters and, if there's enough time, read magazine articles and books.

To prepare for a *news story*, you pay more attention to clips about the subject of the story than to those about the personality of the individual to be interviewed. To prepare for a *profile*, you look for personality quirks and the subject's interests, family, friends, travels and habits. To prepare for an *investigative piece*, you want to know both your subject matter and the person you are interviewing. In all these stories, do not overlook other reporters and editors who know something about the person or subject. Let's look at each of these three types of stories more closely.

### The News Story

One day Paul Leavitt made a routine telephone call to a law enforcement source. Leavitt, then assistant city editor for the Des Moines (Iowa) Register, was working on a story. He knew the source from his days as a county government and courts reporter for the Register.

He expected the story, and the interview, to be routine. Polk County was building a new jail. Leavitt wanted to find out about the progress on the new building. The source begged ignorance. He said, ''Oh, Leavitt, I don't know. I haven't had time to keep up on that, what with all these meetings on the pope's visit.''

Leavitt didn't say anything right away. A less astute reporter might have let the source know he was surprised. The pope in Des Moines? Are you kidding? Instead, Leavitt remembered a story he had read about an Iowan who had extended an invitation for John Paul II to stop in Iowa during his American visit. Leavitt didn't think the Iowan had much of a chance. When the Vatican had announced the pope's visit, people from every state were bartering for a chance to bask in the worldwide limelight.

Still, the source's slip of the tongue seemed genuine. Leavitt finally replied, "Oh, yeah, that's right. When's he coming, anyway?"

"October 4," the source said.

As the conversation progressed, Leavitt waved frantically to the Register's managing editor. A major story was brewing.

"I started asking him some more questions," Leavitt recalls, "then it dawned on him that he probably wasn't supposed to be talking about this. But it was clear from what he said that the pope was definitely coming to Iowa. He even had the hours."

Before the conversation ended, Leavitt had learned of a meeting among the Secret Service, the Vatican, the U.S. State Department and Iowa law enforcement officials to discuss the trip. He also had learned when the pope would arrive, where he would arrive, where he would celebrate Mass and when he would leave.

As a result, the Register stunned its readers the next morning with a copyright story saying the pope would speak in Des Moines on Oct. 4. The story was printed three weeks before the Vatican released its official itinerary of the visit. Other area reporters scoffed at the story. One newspaper even printed a story poking fun at the thought of John Paul II hobnobbing in an Iowa cornfield.

Leavitt and the Register were vindicated. As scheduled, the pope arrived Oct. 4—and celebrated Mass in an Iowa cornfield.

Remembering his conversation with the source, and how a routine question turned into a bona fide scoop, Leavitt said, "I don't even remember what the original question was."

Leavitt probably would not have gotten the story had he not remembered the earlier story about the invitation and known something else about interviewing: When a source unwittingly gives you a scoop, sometimes it is best to act as if you already know it. That may encourage the source to give you more information.

## The Profile

A reporter who decided to write a profile of a local free-lance writer prepared differently. Because the reporter had used the writer as a source in an earlier story, she knew something about the writer. But she needed to know more. So she looked in Contemporary Authors and found biographical information. She also asked the writer to send her copies of some of the articles she had written. Before the reporter went to see the free-lancer, she had read several of her articles. She also interviewed the editor at one of the magazines that bought the writer's material.

The reporter was prepared. Or so she thought. She had to pass one more test. The free-lance writer was an animal lover, and when the reporter arrived, she first had to make friends with a handful of dogs. Fortunately, she loved dogs. That immediately established rapport with the free-lancer. The resulting story was full of lively detail:

Joan Gilbert stretches lazily to soft sunbeams and chirping birds. She dresses casually in blue denim shorts and a plaid, short-sleeved blouse. She and her favorite work companions, five playful dogs, file out the door of her little white house to begin their day with a lazy walk in the surrounding woods. When she returns, she'll contentedly sit down at her typewriter. Such is work.

Joan Gilbert is a free-lance writer.

## The Investigative Piece

The casual atmosphere of the Gilbert interview is not always possible for the investigative reporter. Here, the adversary relationship determines both the preparation required and the atmosphere of the interview itself. An investigative reporter is like an attorney in a courtroom. Wise attorneys know what the answers to their questions will be. So do investigative reporters. Preparation is essential.

In the early stages of the investigation, you conduct some fishing-expedition interviews: Because you don't know how much the source knows, you cast around. Start with persons on the fringes. Gather as much as you can from them. Study the records. Only after you have most of the evidence do you confront your central character. You start with a large circle and gradually draw it smaller.

When Glenn Bunting, a reporter for the San Jose (Calif.) Mercury News, heard complaints about the low caliber of workers turned out by a government-funded training agency, he quietly did a little checking. Before he had gone too far, he had a friendly interview with the administrator, who did not know the real purpose of Bunting's inquiries.

Then Bunting went to work. He tracked the trail of money. He examined bank statements and canceled checks, government audit reports, purchase orders and weekly time cards—all public records because the agency got its money from the government. He interviewed counselors and job-training instructors, law officers and others who did business with the agency. By the time Bunting was ready to talk to the administrator again, he already had most of his story confirmed. This is how the story of the interview began:

Robert Bernal was getting angry.
Confronted with evidence of wrong-

doing in Project DARE, his face
turned red and his voice grew louder.

"Why are you attacking me?" he
asked. "You don't believe me, but
everthing I've told you is the truth. I
haven't told you any barefaced lies."

But he had.

Among other things, Bunting was able to show that Bernal had earned a
"degree" not from Stanford as he claimed, but from San Quentin Prison.
Confronted with the evidence, Bernal told Bunting, "You never lose the
stigma of being in prison. You have a tendency to build up a facade, a degree
of phoniness—even saying that you have a college degree."

Bunting was able to pierce the deceptions because he had drawn the
circle around Bernal tighter and tighter before he went into the interview.

## OTHER PREPARATORY
## CONSIDERATIONS

All this homework is important, but it may be something as trifling as your
appearance that determines whether you will have a successful interview. You
would hardly wear cutoff shorts into a corporation president's suite, and you
wouldn't wear a three-piece suit to talk to underground revolutionaries. It is
your right to wear your hair however you wish and to wear whatever clothes
you want, but it is the source's prerogative to refuse to talk to you. Most
reporters choose to blend in with the environment.

That environment, too, is important. Most interviews are conducted in
the source's office. Especially if the story is a profile or a feature, it usually is
better to get the source away from his or her work. If you are doing a story
about a rabbi's hobby of collecting butterflies, seek a setting appropriate to the
topic. Suggest meeting in the rabbi's den or even outside.

In some interviews, it would be to your advantage to get the source on
neutral territory. If you have some questions for the mayor or other public
official, suggest meeting in a coffee shop at a quiet time. A person has more
power in his or her official surroundings.

It is important, too, to let the source know how much time you need and
whether you expect to return for further information. And if you don't already
know how the source might react to a tape recorder, ask when you are making
the appointment.

You have now done the appropriate homework. You are properly attired.
You have made an appointment and told the source how much time you need.
Before you leave, you should write down a list of questions you want to ask.

They will guide you through the interview and prevent you from missing important topics altogether. The best way to encourage a spontaneous conversation is to have your questions prepared. You'll be more relaxed. Barbara Walters once told a reporter that she writes as many as 500 questions on index cards, then selects the best ones for use during the interview. The thinking you must do to write the questions will help prepare you for the interview. Having questions prepared relieves you of the need to be mentally searching for the next question as the source is answering the last one. If you are trying to think of the next question, you will not be paying close attention to what is being said, and you might miss the most important part of the interview.

Preparing the questions for an interview is hard work, even for a veteran like Isabel Hilton, European affairs editor of The Independent in London. She was promised an interview with Gen. Alfredo Stroessner, the dictator who fled Paraguay and was living in Brazil. Many had tried to interview Stroessner, but only Hilton had been invited. Writing about the experience later, Hilton recalled, ''I found myself worried. I imagined myself forgetting to ask the most obvious question, paralysed by the absurdity of the situation.'' She added, ''That night I went through my notebooks. I couldn't think of a single thing I could ask him that he would possibly want to tell me.''

While you may ask all of your prepared questions in some interviews, in most, you probably will use only some of them. Still, you have benefited from preparing the questions in two important ways. First, even when you don't use many, the work you did thinking of the questions helped prepare you for the interview. Second, your sources who see that you have a prepared list often are impressed with your seriousness.

On the basis of the information you have gathered already, you know *what* you want to ask. Now you must be careful about *how* you ask the questions.

# Phrasing the Question

Listen to an accomplished courtroom lawyer ask questions. How the question is structured often determines whether the lawyer will win the case. Journalists face the same challenge. Reporters have missed many stories because they didn't know how to ask questions. Quantitative researchers have shown how just a slight wording change affects the results of a survey. If you want to know whether citizens favor a city plan to beautify the downtown area, you can ask the question in several ways:

- Do you favor the city council's plan to beautify the downtown area?

- The city council plans to spend $3 million beautifying the downtown area. Are you in favor of this?

- Do you think the downtown area needs physical changes?

- Which of the following actions do you favor?
  —Building a traffic loop around the downtown area.
  —Prohibiting all automobile traffic in an area bounded by Providence Road, Ash Street, College Avenue and Elm Street.
  —Having all the downtown storefronts remodeled to carry out a single theme and putting in brick streets, shrubbery and benches.
  —None of the above.

How you structure that question may affect the survey results by several percentage points. Similarly, how you ask questions in an interview may affect the response.

By the phrasing of the question, many reporters signal the response they expect or prejudices they have. For instance, a reporter who says, "Don't you think that the city council should allocate more money to the parks and recreation department?" is not only asking a question but is also influencing the source or betraying bias. A neutral phrasing would be, "Do you think the city council should allocate more money to the parks and recreation department?" Another common way of asking a leading question is this: "Are you going to vote against this amendment like the other legislators I've talked to?"

Sometimes a reporter unwittingly blocks a response by the phrasing of the question. A reporter who was investigating possible job discrimination against Hispanics conducted several interviews before she told her city editor she didn't think the Hispanics with whom she talked were being frank with her. "When I ask them if they have ever been discriminated against, they always tell me no. But three times now during the course of the interviews, they have said things that indicate they have been. How do I get them to tell me about it?" she asks.

"Perhaps it's the way you are asking the question," the city editor replies. "When you ask someone whether they have ever been discriminated against, you are forcing them to answer yes or no. Don't be so blunt. Ask them if others with the same qualifications at work have been advanced faster than they have. Ask if they are paid the same amount as whites for the same work. Ask them what they think they would be doing today if they were white. Ask them if they know of any qualified Hispanics who were denied jobs."

The city editor was giving the reporter examples of both closed- and open-ended questions. Each has its specific strengths.

# OPEN-ENDED QUESTIONS

*Open-ended questions* allow the respondent some flexibility. Minorities may not respond frankly when asked whether they have ever been discriminated against. The question calls for a yes-no response. But an open-ended question such as ''What would you be doing today if you were white?'' is not so personal. It does not sound as threatening to the respondent. In response to an open-ended question, the source often reveals more than he or she realizes or intends to.

A sportswriter who was interviewing a pro scout at a college football game wanted to know who the scout was there to see. When the scout diplomatically declined to be specific, the reporter tried another approach. He asked a series of questions:

- ''What kind of qualities does a pro scout look for in an athlete?''

- ''Do you think any of the players here today have those talents?''

- ''Whom would you put into that category?''

The reporter worked from the general to the specific until he had the information he wanted. Open-ended questions are less direct and less threatening. They are more exploratory and more flexible. However, if you want to know a person's biographical data, don't ask ''Can you tell me about yourself?''

# CLOSED-ENDED QUESTIONS

Eventually the reporter needs to close in on a subject, to pin down details, to get the respondent to be specific. *Closed-ended questions* are designed to elicit specific responses.

Instead of asking the mayor, ''What did you think of the conference in Washington, D.C.?'' you ask, ''What did you learn in the session 'Funds You May Not Know Are Available'?'' Instead of asking a previous employee to appraise the chancellor-designate's managerial abilities, you ask, ''How well does Uehling listen to the people who work for her?'' ''Do the people who work for her have specific job duties?'' ''Does she explain her decisions?''

A vague question invites a vague answer. By asking a specific question, you are more likely to get a specific answer. You are also communicating to your source that you have done your homework and that you are looking for precise details.

**Figure 5.1**
Tad Bartimus, AP
regional reporter
for the Rocky
Mountains, has had
extensive experience
interviewing people.

Knowing exactly when to ask a closed-ended question or when to be less specific is not something you can plan ahead of time. The type of information you are seeking and the chemistry between the interviewer and the source are the determining factors. You must make on-the-spot decisions. The important thing is to keep rephrasing the question until the source answers it adequately.

# Establishing a Rapport

Tad Bartimus, AP's regional reporter for the Rocky Mountains, has interviewed hundreds of people, beginning with former President Harry S Truman while working for her hometown weekly at age 14. She approached the ex-president and said, ''Excuse me, sir, but I'm from the local paper. Could you please talk to me?''

''Well, young lady, what would you like to know?'' Truman responded.

Years later, Bartimus recalled, ''For the first time in my life, I was struck dumb. What *did* I want to know? What *was* I supposed to ask him? How do you *do* this interviewing stuff, anyway?''

Bartimus knows the answers to those questions now. One piece of advice

**Figure 5.2**   This reporter from WNYW in New York helps put the person being interviewed at ease by being relaxed and friendly.

she offered her colleagues in an article for AP World was to share and care. ''I try never to go to an interview as a hostile antagonist. I am merely a reporter asking questions, with no ax to grind. I am a person with a family, a home, an unbalanced checkbook, a weight problem and a car that goes 'thonka-thonka-thonka' when it's cold. Unless my interview subject is Ivana Trump or Meryl Streep or Richard Nixon, my life is probably, at least in one way or two ways, similar to the person of whom I'm asking the questions.''

Wariner urges reporters to reveal themselves as people. ''A little empathy goes a long way to defuse [the] fear and hostility that is so pervasive against the press,'' she says.

Rapport—the relationship between the reporter and the source—is crucial to the success of the interview. The relationship is sometimes relaxed, sometimes strained. Often it is somewhere in between. The type of relationship you try to establish with your source is determined by the kind of story you are doing. Several approaches are possible.

# Is It Betrayal?

Are all these techniques "morally indefensible," as author Janet Malcolm calls them in her book, "The Journalist and the Murderer." Malcolm says the journalist is "a kind of confidence man, preying on people's vanity, ignorance, or loneliness, gaining their trust and betraying them without remorse."

Malcolm was writing about the relationship between Joe McGinnis, a successful non-fiction author, and Jeffrey MacDonald, a doctor who was convicted of murdering his wife and two daughters. McGinnis had written permission to be party to all the discussions relating to MacDonald's defense before and during the trial as well as access to MacDonald's papers. In return, MacDonald was to share the income from the book.

MacDonald entered into the agreement to get a sympathetic hearing and to raise money for his defense. McGinnis, who lived with MacDonald for a time, showed him great empathy in conversations and letters, even after he had decided that MacDonald was guilty. In his book, "Fatal Vision," McGinnis described MacDonald as a "pathological narcissist."

MacDonald sued McGinnis for fraud. The trial ended with a hung jury, but five of six jurors favored MacDonald's position, according to Malcolm. The case later was settled with a $325,000 payment to MacDonald.

Malcolm's thesis—that not just McGinnis but all journalists betray their sources—started a firestorm of debate in the profession. In an article in Columbia Journalism Review, author Nora Ephron, for instance, said she was "astonished" that anyone took issue with Malcolm. Author David Halberstam accused Malcolm of going after the subject with a sledgehammer. "I think 'betrayal' is a very, very strong and ugly word," he said. Author J. Anthony Lukas described the reporter–source relationship as "mutually manipulative."

Two critical differences exist between the McGinnis–MacDonald relationship and those involving most journalists. First, McGinnis had a contract giving him access to the information. The legal relationship created a partnership, even though McGinnis protected his artistic rights in the contract. McGinnis was working with MacDonald and sharing the profits. Most journalists are working for their publications, not their sources. Second, the relationship lasted years, not hours or days as it does for most journalists. Beat reporting comes the closest to the long-term relationship between McGinnis and MacDonald. Even beat reporters, however, are not partners with their sources in the news-gathering effort. It is one thing to remain disinterested, as most journalists try to do; it is quite another to mislead a source, as Malcolm claims McGinnis did.

Still, journalists must be aware of the debate and adopt techniques that are defensible. Some techniques that are defensible for public officials who have betrayed their office may not be defensible with sources who are private citizens.

## INTERVIEW APPROACHES

For most news stories and personality profiles, the reporter has more to gain if the subject is at ease. Often that can be accomplished by starting off with small talk. Ask about a trophy, the plants or an engraved pen. Bring up

**Figure 5.3**
Did Joe McGinnis misrepresent himself to gain Jeffrey Mac-Donald's confidence when McGinnis was writing "Fatal Vision"? Janet Malcolm thinks so, and in a book about journalists, she charged that journalists prey on people.

something humorous you have found during your research. Ask about something you know the source will want to talk about. In other interviews, if you think the subject might be skeptical about your knowledge of the field, open with a question that demonstrates your knowledge.

Reporters who can show sources what they have in common also have more success getting information. When Janet Chusmir was a reporter for the Miami Herald, she was assigned to interview the parents of Bernardine Dohrn. Dohrn was a suspect in an anti-war protest bombing and a fugitive. Many reporters, including some from the Herald, had tried to talk to the parents. None had succeeded.

Chusmir went to their home and knocked on the door. She identified herself and told them why she was there. They said they didn't want to talk. She said she understood because she was a parent, too. She asked for a glass of water. They complied with her request. She edged into the house and sat down to drink the water. While she sat there, they chatted about, among other things, why the parents didn't want to be interviewed. Before she left, she had enough information for a story. Although the request for water bought the reporter some time, it was her ability to talk to them sympathetically parent-to-parent that made her successful.

On another occasion, Chusmir was among a group of reporters who showed up expecting to witness kidnappers return a mother's child. The kidnappers never showed up. The police slipped the mother into the back seat of a police car and edged through the crowd. As the car went by her, Chusmir tapped on the window. The mother rolled it down slightly, ''I hope you find your child,'' Chusmir said. The woman told her to call. Chusmir did and got an exclusive story.

One of the mistakes reporters make is not being empathetic, Chusmir says. ''I genuinely feel for these people. I think sources can sense that.''

Rapport also depends on where you conduct the interview. Many persons, especially those unaccustomed to being interviewed, feel more comfortable in their workplace. Go to them. Talk to the businessperson in the office, to the athlete in the locker room, to the conductor in the music room. In some cases, though, you may get a better interview elsewhere if the source cannot relax at the workplace or is frequently interrupted. Reporters have talked to politicians during car rides between campaign appearances. They've gone sailing with businesspeople and hunting with athletes. One reporter doing a feature on a police chief spent a weekend with the chief, who was painting his home. To do a profile, which requires more than one interview, vary the location. New surroundings can make a difference.

Scott Kraft of the Associated Press once did a story on a couple who for more than two years drove the streets of Los Angeles looking for the man who raped their 12-year-old daughter. The search was successful.

''When I knocked on their door in May, I wanted them to know that I would be careful and honest, and I wanted them to tell me everything, even though it would probably be difficult,'' he wrote in Editor & Publisher.

Kraft conducted interviews in three locations. The first was in the family's living room. The second was in a car as they revisited the places where the family searched. The third was by phone. Kraft said the mother talked more candidly on the phone after her children had gone to school.

There are times when the reporter would rather have the source edgy, nervous or even scared. When you are doing an investigation, you may want the key characters to feel uneasy. You may pretend you know more than you actually do. You want them to know that the material you have is substantive and serious. Seymour Hersh, a Pulitzer Prize-winning investigative reporter, uses this tactic. Time magazine once quoted a government official commenting on Hersh: ''He wheedles, cajoles, pleads, threatens, asks a leading question, uses little tidbits as if he knew the whole story. When he finishes you feel like a wet rag.''

In some cases, however, it is better even in an investigation to take a low-key approach. Let the source relax. Talk around the subject but gradually bring the discussion to the key issues. The surprise element may work to your favor.

So may the sympathetic approach. When the source is speaking, you may nod or punctuate the source's responses with comments such as ''That's interesting.'' Sources who think you are sympathetic are more likely to volunteer information. That was the key to Chusmir's success. Researchers have found, for instance, that a simple ''mm-hmmm'' affects the length of the answer interviewers get.

## OTHER PRACTICAL CONSIDERATIONS

Where you sit in relation to the person you are interviewing can be important. Unless you deliberately are trying to make those interviewed feel uncomfortable, do not sit directly in front of them. Permit your sources to establish eye contact if and when they wish.

Some people are even more disturbed by the way a reporter takes notes. A tape recorder ensures accuracy of quotes, but it makes many speakers self-conscious or nervous. If you have permission to use a tape recorder, place it in an inconspicuous spot and ignore it except to make sure it is working properly. Writing notes longhand may interfere with your ability to digest what is being said. But not taking any notes at all is risky. Only a few reporters can leave an interview and accurately write down what was said. Certainly no one can do it and reproduce direct quotes verbatim. You should learn shorthand or develop a system of your own.

# Techniques for Ensuring Accuracy

Accuracy is a major problem in all interviews. Both the question and the answer may be ambiguous. You may not understand what is said. You may record it incorrectly. You may not know the context of the remarks. Your biases may interfere with the message.

You have no control over some of the things that may affect the accuracy of the answers you receive in an interview. In 1946 two researchers conducted an experiment in which a group of people were asked, ''Do you think there are too many Jews holding government offices and jobs?'' The interviewers were divided into four groups: Jewish in appearance with a Jewish name; Jewish in appearance; non-Jewish in appearance; and non-Jewish in appearance with a non-Jewish name. Ten percent more people answered yes to the non-Jewish-appearing interviewer than they did to the Jewish-appearing interviewer with a Jewish name. Some respondents tailored their answer to what they believed the interviewer wanted to hear.

Some possibilities for making errors or introducing bias are unavoidable, but others are not. To ensure the most accurate and complete reporting possible, you should use all the techniques available to obtain a good interview, including observing, understanding what you hear and asking follow-up questions. Let's examine these and other techniques.

## OBSERVING

Some reporters look but do not see. The detail they miss may be the difference between a routine story and one that is a delight to read. Of course, it was not delightful to read about the flood damage in Hattiesburg, Miss., but reporter Sharon Wertz's observations as she listened to one of the victims brought the agony home to readers:

> "You know," Cheryl says, covering her anguished face with her hands, her shoulders shaking, "we canceled our flood insurance two months ago. The premiums went up. . . . Who would have thought this would happen?"
> She wipes her reddened eyes.
> "I'm sorry," she says, sniffing. "We're really lucky to be alive."

Gabriel Garcia Marquez, a Colombian writer and Nobel laureate, has experience on both sides of the interview. He, too, counsels the interviewer to listen and observe. "Today one has the impression that the interviewer is not listening to what you say, nor does he think it important, because he believes that the tape recorder hears everything. But he's wrong; it doesn't hear the beating of the heart, which is the most important part of the interview."

These same powers of observation serve the investigative reporter. Is the subject nervous? What kinds of questions are striking home? The mayor may deny that he is going to fire the police chief, but the reporter who notices the chief's personnel file sitting on an adjacent worktable may have reason to continue the investigation.

People communicate some messages non-verbally. Researchers have been able to correlate some gestures with meanings. For instance, folded arms often signal unapproachability; crossed ankles often signal tension. Many non-verbal messages, however, may not be the same for all ethnic and cultural groups. Reporters should read more about the subject.

## UNDERSTANDING

Understanding what you see is crucial to the news-gathering process. So is understanding what you hear. It is not enough merely to record what is being said; you must also digest it. The reporter who was investigating job discrimination was listening but not understanding. Her sources were telling her about incidents of discrimination, but all she heard were their denials.

Sometimes what you don't hear may be the message. The reporter who was trying to find out if the mayor was going to fire the police chief asked several questions about the chief's performance. What struck the reporter during the interview was the mayor's lack of enthusiasm for the chief. That unintentional tip kept the reporter working on the story until he confirmed it.

The Miami Herald's Chusmir listened, too. Once when she was interviewing Joan Fontaine, the actress, Chusmir mentioned that she had a daughter about the same age as Fontaine's. Fontaine asked, "Is she jealous of you?" Listening closely, Chusmir correctly deduced that Fontaine was revealing a problem of jealousy in the family, and the interview took an unexpected turn.

## ASKING FOLLOW-UP QUESTIONS

If you understand what the source is saying, you can ask meaningful follow-up questions. There is nothing worse than briefing your city editor on the interview and having the editor ask you, "Well, did you ask . . ." Having to say no is embarrassing.

Even if you go into an interview armed with a list of questions, the most important probably will be the ones you ask in response to an answer. A reporter who was doing a story on bidding procedures was interviewing the mayor. The reporter asked how bid specifications were written. In the course of his reply, the mayor mentioned that the president of a construction firm had assured him the last bid specifications were adequate. The alert reporter picked up on the statement:

"When did you talk to him?"
"About three weeks ago," the mayor said.
"That's before the specifications were published, wasn't it?"
"Yes, we asked him to look them over for us."
"Did he find anything wrong with the way they were written?"
"Oh, he changed a few minor things. Nothing important."
"Did officials of any other construction firms see the bid specifications before they were advertised?"
"No, he was the only one."

Gradually, on the basis of one offhand comment by the mayor, the reporter was able to piece together a solid story on the questionable relationship between the city and the construction firm.

## OTHER TECHNIQUES

Although most questions are designed to get information, some are asked as a delaying tactic. A reporter who is taking notes may fall behind. Emily Yoffe, a senior editor of Texas Monthly, will say, ''Hold on a second—let me get that'' or ''Say that again.'' Other questions are intended to encourage a longer response. ''Go on with that'' or ''Tell me more about that'' encourages the speaker to add more detail.

You don't have to be stalling for time to say you don't understand. Don't be embarrassed to admit you haven't grasped something. It is better to admit to one person you don't understand than to advertise your ignorance on newsprint in front of thousands. Once you have written the story, check with your sources. Check the facts. Check the concepts. Catch your errors before publication. You'll impress your editors, you will serve your readers better, your newspaper will have more credibility, and your sources will be happy to talk to you the next time.

Another device for making the source talk on is not a question at all; it is a pause. You are signaling the source that you expect more. But the lack of a response from you is much more ambiguous than ''Tell me more about that.'' It may indicate that you were skeptical of what was just said, that you didn't understand, that the answer was inadequate or several other possibilities. The source will be forced to react. The only problem with this, says the AP's special correspondent Saul Pett, ''is that it invites the dull to be dull at greater length.''

Many dull interviews become interesting after they end. There are two things you should always do when you finish your questions: Check key facts, figures and quotes and then put away your pen but keep your ears open. You are not breaching any ethical rule if you continue to ask questions after you have put away your pen or turned off the tape recorder. That's when some sources loosen up. Many reporters find they get their best material after the formal interview has ended and they are having a cup of coffee with the source.

Before you leave, ask if there's anything you forgot to ask. Put the burden on the source. You are also doing your subject a favor by giving the person a chance to contribute to the direction of the interview. You may have missed some important signals during the conversation, and now the source can be more explicit about what he or she wanted to say. Sometimes this technique leads to entirely new subjects.

Quickly review your notes and check facts, especially dates, numbers, quotes, spellings and titles. Besides helping you get it right, it shows the source you are careful. If necessary, arrange a time when you can call to check other parts of the story or clear up questions you may have as you are writing.

As a matter of courtesy, tell the source when the story might appear. You may even offer to send along an extra copy of the article when it's completed.

Remember that, although the interview may be over, your relationship to the source is not. When you have the story written, call the source and confirm the information. Better to discover your inaccuracies before you print than after.

# Suggested Readings

Brady, John. ''The Craft of Interviewing.'' Cincinnati: Writer's Digest, 1976. Full of anecdotes to illustrate interviewing techniques.

Burgoon, Judee K. and Saine, Thomas J. ''The Unspoken Dialogue: An Introduction to Nonverbal Communication.'' Boston: Houghton Mifflin, 1978. An excellent look at the subject for readers who are not acquainted with the field.

Gottlieb, Martin. ''Dangerous Liaisons.'' ''Columbia Journalism Review,'' July/Aug. 1989: 21–35. In this excellent debate over whether interviewers betray sources, Gottlieb interviews several authors.

Malcolm, Janet. ''The Journalist and the Murderer.'' New York: Knopf, 1990. Using the Joe McGinnis–Jeffrey MacDonald case, the author accuses all journalists of being ''confidence men'' who betray their sources.

Metzler, Ken. ''Creative Interviewing.'' Englewood Cliffs, N.J.: Prentice-Hall, 1977. An invaluable in-depth look at problems of interviewing.

# Exercises

1. Learn to background. Write a memo of up to two pages about your state's senior U.S. senator. Concentrate on those details that will allow you to focus on how the senator views the pro-life versus pro-choice issue. Indicate the sources of your information.

2. List five open-ended questions you would ask the senator.

3. List five closed-ended questions you would ask.

4. Interview a student also enrolled in this reporting class. Write a two- to three-page story. Be sure to focus on one aspect of the student's life. Ask your classmate to read the story and to mark errors of fact and perception. The instructor will read your story and the critique.

5. Your instructor will give you a news item. Prepare a list of questions you would ask to do a follow-up interview. As each question is read aloud in class, cross it off your list. See if you can come up with the most original and appropriate questions.

# 6

## Quotes
## and Attribution

"**A**nd you can quote me on that."

Many people who say these words don't expect to be quoted. They mean only that they are sure of what they are saying and are not afraid or ashamed to say it. Nonetheless, these are sweet words to a reporter.

Direct quotes add color and credibility to your story. By using direct quotes, you are telling readers you are putting them directly in touch with the speaker. Like a letter, direct quotes are personal. Quotation marks signal the reader that something special is coming. Direct quotes provide a story with a change of pace, a breath of air. They also loosen up a clump of dense type.

Not everything people say should be put into direct quotes. You need to learn what to quote directly, when to use partial quotes and when to paraphrase. You also must learn how and how often to attribute quotations and other information. Like a researcher, you must know when information must be tied to a source. However, attributing a remark or some information does not excuse you from a possible libel suit. And, of course, you want to be fair.

Being fair sometimes is difficult when sources do not want to be quoted. For that reason you also must learn how to deal with off-the-record quotes and background information.

### In this chapter you will learn:

1. What is worth quoting directly.

2. How and when to attribute direct and indirect quotes.

3. How to handle both on- and off-the-record information.

# What to Quote Directly

Crisp, succinct, meaningful quotes spice up any story. But you can overdo a good thing. You need direct quotes in your stories, and you also need to develop your skill in recognizing what is worth quoting. Here are some guidelines:

1. Use direct quotes when someone says something unique.

2. Use direct quotes when someone says something uniquely.

3. Use direct quotes when someone important says something important.

Let's look at these guidelines further.

## UNIQUE MATERIAL

When you can say, "Ah, I never heard that before," you can be quite sure your readers also would like to know exactly what the speaker said. Instead of quoting someone at length, look for the kernel. Sometimes it is something surprising, something neither you nor your readers would expect that person to say. For example, when Seattle Times columnist Eric Lacitis wrote about a Tukwila, Wash., couple who claimed to have had sex 500 times in nine months, the Tukwila City Council denounced the column. "We're tired of Tukwila being known as the Rodney Dangerfield of King County—we get no respect," said Councilman Clarence Moriwaki. And consider this unexpected statement by an 80-year-old man: "Dog food's not so bad when you're hungry."

Striking statements like these should be quoted, but there is no reason to place simple, factual material inside quotation marks. Here is a segment of copy from a story about the similarities in the careers of a father and his son that needed no quotes at all:

"My son was born on campus," says the elder Denney, 208 Westridge Drive, a professor in regional and community affairs.

"In fact, he was born in the same hospital that I met my wife," he says, explaining he was in Noyes Hospital with a fractured spine when she was a student nurse.

Since that time, he has earned his bachelor's degree "technically in agriculture with a major in biological science and conservation."

Although the quoted material is informative, it contains nothing particularly interesting, surprising, disturbing, new or even different. It should be written:

Denney, of 208 Westridge Drive, is a professor in regional and community affairs. While hospitalized in Noyes Hospital with a fractured spine, he met a student nurse who became his wife. Eight years later, his son was born at the same hospital.

The son has since earned a bachelor's degree in agriculture with a major in biological science and conservation.

The first version has 72 words; the second, with 60 words, is tighter and better.

Sometimes spoken material is unique not because of individual remarks that are surprising or new, but because of extended dialogue that can tell the story more effectively than writers can in their own words. The writer of the following story made excellent use of dialogue:

Lou Provancha pushed his wire-rimmed glasses up on his nose and leaned toward the man in the wheelchair.

"What is today, Jake?" he asked.

Jake twisted slightly and stared at the floor.

"Jake," Provancha said, "Jake, look up here."

A long silence filled the tiny, cluttered room on the sixth floor of the University Medical Center.

Provancha, a licensed practical nurse at the hospital, glanced at the reporter. "Jake was in a coma a week ago," he explained. "He couldn't talk."

Provancha pointed to a wooden board propped up on the table beside him.

"Jake, what is today? What does it say here? What is this word? I've got my finger pointed right at it."

Jake squinted at the word. With a sudden effort, like a man heaving a bag of cement mix onto a truck bed, he said: "Tuesday."

Provancha grinned. It was a small victory for both of them.

The shaggy-haired nurse was coaxing his patient step-by-step back into the world he had known before a car accident pitched him into a two-month-long coma, with its resulting disorientation and memory loss.

Here's another example of how dialogue can move the story along and "show" rather than "tell" about the characters in the story. The story is about the restoration of old cars. A father is passing on a rare technique to his son:

When the lead is smooth and the irregularities filled to his satisfaction, he reaches for his file.

"How long has it been since you've done this?" his son asks.

"It's been at least 20 years."

"How do you tin it so it won't melt and all run off on the floor?"

"Very carefully."

Before the lesson is finished, a customer and two other shop workers have joined the group watching Larry at work. This is a skill few people know.

"I don't like the way this lead melts," he says.

"That's what it does when there's not enough tin?" his son asks.

"Tin helps it stick."

"Why do you pull the file instead of pushing it?"

"So I can see better."

"I would already have the fiberglass on and be done by now."

"I know, but anything worthwhile you have to work for."

## THE UNIQUE EXPRESSION

When you as a listener can say, "Ah, I never heard it said *that* way before," you know you have something quotable. Be on the lookout for the clever, the colorful, the colloquial. For example, an elderly man talking about his organic garden said, "It's hard to tell people to watch what they eat. You eat health, you know."

A professor lecturing on graphic design said, "When you think it looks like a mistake, it is." The same professor once was explaining that elements in a design should not call attention to themselves: "You don't walk up to a beautiful painting in someone's home and say, 'That's a beautiful frame.'"

Sometimes something said uniquely is a colloquialism. Colloquialisms can add color and life to your copy. For example, a person from Louisiana may say: "I was just fixing to leave when the phone rang." A person from an area in Pennsylvania "makes the light out" when turning off the lights. And people in and around Fort Wayne, Ind., "redd up" the dishes after a meal, meaning that they wash them and put them where they belong.

## IMPORTANT QUOTES
## BY IMPORTANT PEOPLE

If citizen Joe Smith says, "Something must be done about this coal strike," you may or may not consider it worth quoting. But if the president of the United States says, "Something must be done about this coal strike," many papers would quote him. Generally reporters quote public officials or known personalities in their news stories (though not everything the famous say is worth quoting). Remember, prominence is an important property of news.

Quoting sources that readers are likely to know lends authority, credibility and interest to your story. Presumably, a meteorologist knows something about the weather, a doctor about health, a chemistry professor about chemicals. However, it is unlikely that a television star knows a great deal about cameras, even if he or she makes commercials about cameras.

### Verification

When someone important says something important, but perhaps false, just putting the material in quotes does not relieve you of the responsibility for the inaccuracies. Citizens, officials and candidates for office often say things that may be partially true or altogether untrue and perhaps even libelous. Quotations, like any other information you gather, need verification.

During the time of Sen. Joseph McCarthy, many newspapers, in the interest of strict objectivity, day after day quoted the Wisconsin senator's charges and countercharges. (It should be pointed out that some publishers did this because they agreed with his stance and because his remarks sold newspapers.) Few papers thought it was their responsibility to quote others who were pointing out the obvious errors and inconsistencies in the demagogue's remarks. Today, however, in the interest of balance, fairness and objectivity, many papers leave out, correct or point out the errors in some quotations. This may be done in the article itself or in an accompanying story.

If candidate Billy Joe Harkness says that his opponent Jimbo McGown is a member of the Ku Klux Klan, you should check before you print the charge. Good reporters don't stop looking and checking just because someone gives them some information. Look for yourself. Prisoners may have an altogether different account of a riot from the one the prison officials give you. Your story will not be complete unless you talk to all sides.

# Problems in Direct Quotation

## PARAPHRASING QUOTES

While some quotations need verification, others need clarification. Do not quote someone unless you are sure of what that person means. The reason (or excuse), ''But that's what the man said,'' is not a sufficient reason to use the quote. It is much better to skip a quotation altogether than to confuse the reader.

The best way to avoid confusing and unclear quotes or needlessly long and wordy quotes is to *paraphrase*. It is the meaning of the speaker that you must convey to the reader. As a reporter you must have confidence that at times you are able to convey that meaning in fewer words and in better language than the speaker did. You can save your editors a lot of work if you shorten quotes. Digesting, condensing and clarifying quotes take more effort than simply recording them word for word. You will not impress anyone with long quotations. On the contrary, you may be guilty of some lazy writing. Here is a quote that could be cut drastically:

> ''When I first started singing lessons I assumed I would be a public school teacher and maybe, if I was good enough, a voice teacher,'' he said. ''When I graduated from the university, I still thought I would be a teacher, and I wanted to teach.''

A rewrite conveys the meaning more succinctly:

> When he first started singing lessons, and even after he graduated from the university, he wanted to be a public school voice teacher.

## USING PARTIAL QUOTES

It is also much better to paraphrase or to use full quotes than to use fragmentary or partial quotes. Some editors would have you avoid ''orphan quotes'' almost altogether. Here is an example of the overuse of partial quotes:

> The mayor said citizens should ''turn off'' unnecessary lights and ''turn down'' thermostats ''to 65 degrees.''

The sentence would be better with no quotation marks at all.

If it is a particular phrase that has special significance or meaning, a partial quote may be justifiable. In his campaign for the presidency, George Bush spoke of ''a thousand points of light.'' He referred to that phrase again in his inaugural address. A reporter covering the address could hardly have used those words without putting them in quotes.

When you do use partial quotes, do not put quotation marks around something the speaker could not have said. Suppose a speaker told a student audience at a university, ''I am pleased and thrilled with your attendance here tonight.'' It would be incorrect to write:

The speaker said she was ''pleased and thrilled with the students' attendance.''

Partial quotes often contain an *ellipsis*—three spaced periods—to tell the reader that some of the words of the quote are missing. For example:

''I have come here tonight . . . and I have crossed state lines . . . to conspire against the government.''

This practice at times may be justifiable, but you should not keep the reader guessing and wondering what is missing. Sometimes the actual meaning of the speaker can even be distorted by dropping certain words. If a critic writes about a three-act play, ''A great hit—except for the first three acts,'' an ad that picks up only the first part of that quote is guilty of misrepresentation.

## CAPTURING DIALECT OR ACCENT

Using colorful or colloquial expressions helps the writer capture a person in a particular environment. The same is true when you write the way people talk:

''Are you gonna go?'' he asked.
''No, I ain't goin','' she replied.

In everyday speech hardly anyone enunciates perfectly. To do so would sound affected. In fiction, therefore, it is common to use spellings that match speech. But when conversation is written down in newspaper reporting, readers expect correct, full spellings. Not only is correct spelling easier to read, it is also less difficult to write. Capturing dialect is difficult, as these passages from a story about a Hollywood actress illustrate:

''Boy, it's hot out theah,'' she started, ''I could sure use a nice cold beer. How about it, uh? Wanta go get a couple beers?''

It seems strange that if she says, ''theah,'' she wouldn't also say ''beeah.'' Or perhaps she said, ''How 'bout it, uh?'' And if she said ''wanta,'' maybe she also said ''geta.''

In another passage, the author has the actress speaking "straight" English:

> "Would you believe I used to dress like that all the time? Dates didn't want to be seen with me. I was always being asked to change clothes before going out."

Then later in the story, she reverts to less formal speech:

> "I'm tired of pickin' up checks. I've never been ta college, so I'd like to take a coupla classes. I wanta take law so I can find out who's stealing the country. And I wanta take geology. The San Andreas Fault is my hobby, y'know? I think man can beat out nature."

First the actress wanted "a couple beers." Then she wanted to take "a coupla classes." In the same passage she is tired of "pickin'" up checks, but she wants to find out who's "stealing" the country. It is unlikely she is that inconsistent in her speech.

The writer of this story tried to show us something of the character of the actress. If he wanted to convey her speech patterns, he should either have been consistent or simply reported that she talked the same off the set as on it.

Sometimes when a newspaper attempts to quote someone saying something uniquely it betrays a bias. Years ago some Northern newspapers delighted in quoting Gov. George Wallace exactly, even trying to reproduce his Southern drawl. But some of these same newspapers did not try to reproduce the Boston accent of John F. Kennedy or of his brothers.

However, you should not make everyone's speech the same. Reporter Barbara King laments "our frequent inability to write other than insipid speech," and "our tendency to homogenize the day-to-day speech patterns of the heterogeneous people we write about." She acknowledges that writers worry about exposing to ridicule the immigrant's halting or perhaps unconventional speech while the broker's speech appears flawless.

But King calls the argument specious. Of course, people should not be exposed to ridicule through their speech. "The point here," she says, "is simply that when the writer's intention in writing dialects, quaint expressions, non-conventional grammar, flowery or showy speech, or the Queen's English is to make a person human, that intention is not only acceptable, it's desirable.''

The only way you can make people human is to *listen* to them. King says reporters and writers usually hear but rarely listen. She advises reporters to ''listen for expressions, turns of phrase, idiosyncratic talk'' and to work it into their stories.

USA Today reporter James Cox did that when he wrote about multi-millionaire Rose Blumkin and her Mrs. B's Warehouse in Omaha, Neb. Cox wrote that the 95-year-old proprietor rues the day she hired her grandsons, Ron and Irv Blumkin, to help her manage her furniture business, especially after she began to feel as if they were trying to go over her head.

> ''They don't have no character. They don't have no feelings,'' says Mrs. B. in her thick Russian accent. They told me I am too old, too cranky. . . . They don't know nothing. What I got in my finger they don't got in their whole heads.''
>
> Mrs. B. is wonderful with customers but has no use for the hired help. ''He's a dummy, my salesman. A stupe.''
>
> Says salesman Jerry Pearson, ''She's hell on the help but great with customers. She closes like a bear trap.''

Reporter Cox was listening that day, and he worked those quotes into his story with great effect.

## MIX-MATCHING QUESTIONS AND ANSWERS

Writers have other problems with quotes. They often agonize over whether they may use answers from one question to answer another question. Later on in an interview or in a trial, a person may say something that answers better or more fully a question posed earlier.

In the preceding Cox quotations of Mrs. B., notice the ellipsis in the quote about her sons. Mrs. B. probably did not say those words sequentially. The words after the ellipsis may have been said hours after the previous quote.

The only questions you must ask yourself in situations like this are: Am I being fair? Am I distorting the meaning? Am I putting quotes together that change what the speaker intended to say?

Sentences that logically go together, that logically enhance one another, that are clearly sequential can and often should be placed together.

## CORRECTING QUOTES

The quotes from Mrs. B. bring up another and perhaps the most perplexing problem tied to proper handling of direct quotations. The Russian immigrant uses incorrect grammar. When do you, or should you, correct grammatical errors in a direct quotation? Should you expect people in news conferences or during informal interviews to speak perfect English?

Although quotation marks mean you are capturing the exact language of a speaker, it is accepted practice at many newspapers to correct mistakes in grammar and to convey a person's remarks in complete sentences. None of us regularly speaks in perfect, grammatical sentences. But if we were instead writing down our remarks, presumably we would write in grammatically correct English.

Even the best reporters differ on when or even whether to do this. To More magazine's question, ''Do you fix quotes to make the person you're quoting sound grammatical?'' columnist James J. Kilpatrick replied:

Sure. It's elementary courtesy, and everyone does it. You don't change the substance of your subject's thought, of course. You could make anyone in politics look ridiculous if you qouted him verbatim all the time with all the ands, ifs, buts, and ors.

Jack Newfield, then senior editor for The Village Voice, said:

No, I don't. New York political leader Meade Esposito's colorfulness comes from his lack of grammar.

Sally Quinn, former reporter for The Washington Post, said:

If the person used bad grammar as a matter of course, I would never fix a quote. But if it's in the middle of a sentence—if he starts out using the plural and switches his train of thought and ends up using the singular—rather than put in the bad grammar, which really wouldn't be fair, I'll change it.

Finally, the AP Stylebook says:

Quotations normally should be corrected to avoid the errors in grammar and word usage that often occur unnoticed when someone is speaking but are embarrassing in print.

One final word about correcting quotations: Some argue that registered political candidates and elected officials should never be corrected; others say that consistency is important. If a reporter quotes a farmer using incorrect grammar, then should the same be done for the mayor or for the college professor?

A letter in The Washington Post scored the newspaper for quoting exactly a mother of 14 children who was annoyed at Mayor Barry's advice to stop having babies. The quote read: ''And your job is to open up all those houses that's boarded up.'' The writer then accused the Post of regularly stringing together quotes of the president to make him appear articulate. The writer concluded: ''I don't care whether the Post polishes quotes or not. I simply think that everyone—black or white, rich or poor, president or welfare mother—deserves equal treatment.''

## REMOVING REDUNDANCIES

Another question you must deal with as a reporter is whether to remove redundancies and other irrelevant material by using ellipses. Again, there is no agreement in the industry. News Editor Allan M. Siegal of The New York Times said in an article in the Washington Journalism Review that although cleaning up quotes is ''a form of lie,'' omitting words and even sentences from quotes without indicating the omission by an ellipsis is acceptable. Siegal says the Times does not use ellipses because they distract the reader and ''because typographically they make the paper look like chicken pox.'' Nor does the Times use brackets inside quotation marks.

By contrast, The Washington Post does use ellipses and brackets.

For most reporters and editors, the answer to the problem of correcting quotes is to take out the quotation marks and to paraphrase. However, David K. Shipler of The New York Times says that when you paraphrase, you lose a lot. The value of the quotes, he says, lies in their richness and uniqueness.

The one thing that most writers and editors agree on is that newspapers should have a policy about changing or not changing direct quotations. But some say even that is impossible because often it depends on who is doing the talking and in what situation or context. Does the practice change if a politician is speaking in casual conversation to a friend or colleague? Should private individuals always be treated differently from public officials? How about sports personalities, members of ethnic groups or people who use English as a second language?

One thing's for sure. Changing quotes affects your credibility and that of your newspaper. As former White House spokesman and syndicated columnist Jody Powell reminds us, if no one knows you changed a quote except the person quoted, you know someone has begun to question your credibility. One person is one too many.

Without question, you should know the policy of your news organization regarding the use of direct quotations. But equally without question, that policy should be that you place inside quotation marks only the exact words of the speaker. Make that your personal policy, and you can't go wrong.

## DELETING OBSCENITY

On most newspapers, *some* things people say are never permitted in print, even if they are said uniquely. Newspapers rarely print obscenities, profanities or even vulgarities unless they are essential to the story. In The Washington Post, for example, obscenities may be used only with the approval of a top editor. Even then, for "hard-core" obscenities referring to the body and sexual or excretory functions, the Post's stylebook calls for the use of the first letter followed by dashes.

## MAKING UP QUOTES

In 1989, by a 2-1 decision, the 9th U.S. Circuit Court of Appeals in Pasadena, Calif., ruled in Jeffrey M. Masson vs. The New Yorker Magazine that journalists can make up quotes by public figures without fearing a libel suit if the words fairly reflect what the person actually said.

Appellate Judge Arthur Alacron wrote in the majority opinion that malice can be inferred if the quotes are "wholly the product of the author's imagination." Nevertheless, he wrote: "Malice will not be inferred from evidence showing that the quoted language does not contain the exact words used by the plaintiff provided the fabricated quotations are either rational interpretations of ambiguous remarks made by the public figure . . . or do not alter the substantive content of unambiguous remarks actually made by the public figure."

In his dissenting opinion, Judge Alex Kozinski acknowledged that the courts have a grave responsibility under the First Amendment to safeguard freedom of the press, but the right to alter quotations deliberately is not included in that right. "To invoke the right to deliberately distort what someone else has said in print is to assert the right to lie in public."

Editor & Publisher magazine reported that libel lawyers reacting to the decision generally pointed out the distinction between what might be professionally ethical and what should determine the outcome of a libel suit. Harold W. Fuson Jr., vice president and general counsel of Copley Newspapers, said: "We are not talking about what's right. We are talking about what justifies a multimillion-dollar lawsuit."

Newspaper editors generally agreed. Gene Roberts, executive editor of the Philadelphia Inquirer, praised the ruling as "very good law." But he added, "That does not mean I think the practice of not getting quotes right is good journalism. It's very bad journalism." Similarly, James I. Houck, managing editor of the Baltimore Sun, said: "Any reporter who made up quotes wouldn't be a reporter here very long. I believe that when a newspaper puts quotation marks around a sentence, they warrant that is what the speaker literally spoke. If you make up quotes or alter them in any way, you are misleading readers." And Max Frankel, executive editor of The New York Times, summarized the newspaper's policy this way: "We think quotation marks are sacred. They represent our bond to the reader that the words inside the quotation marks were actually spoken in the way reported. Since the language and law leave us free to paraphrase and interpret at will, we tolerate no exceptions to that rule, period."

That's a policy you should live with.

# Attributing Direct and Indirect Quotes

## WHEN TO ATTRIBUTE

You should *always* attribute direct quotes. With rare exception, you should never allow a paragraph of direct quotes to stand without an attribution. However, at times when you are quoting from a speech, an interview or a press conference and no one else is mentioned in the story, putting an attribution in every paragraph of direct quotation may be excessive.

Ordinarily you should attribute indirect quotes. That is, you should usually have a source for the information you write, and when you do, attribute it to that source. The source can be a person or a written document.

However, there are exceptions. You do not have to attribute information to a source if one or more of the following is true:

1. The information is a matter of public record.

2. It is generally known.

3. It is available from several sources.

4. You are a witness.

5. It is easily verifiable.

6. It makes no assumptions.

7. It contains no opinions.

8. It is non-controversial.

If you are a witness to damages or injuries, do not name yourself as a source in the story. Attribute this information to the police or to other authorities. But if you are on the scene of an accident and can see that three people were involved, you do not have to write: " 'Three people were involved in the accident,' Officer Osbord said." If you are unsure of the information or if there are conclusions or generalities involved, your editor probably will want you to attribute the information to an official or witness. At other times when you are involved in the story as a witness, your editor may want you to write a first-person account.

In summary, though it is possible to attribute too often and though you do not always need to attribute, when you have doubts, go with the attribution.

## HOW TO ATTRIBUTE

In composition and creative writing classes, you may have been told to avoid repeating the same word. You probably picked up your thesaurus to look for a synonym for the word "say," a colorless word. Without much research you may have found a hundred or more substitutes. None of them is wrong. Indeed, writers may search long for the exact word they need to convey a particular nuance of meaning. For example:

A presidential candidate *announces* the choice of a running mate.
An arrested man *divulges* the names of his accomplices.
A judge *pronounces* sentence.

At other times, in the interest of precise and lively writing, you may write:

"I'll get you for that," she *whispered*.
"I object," he *shouted*.

Nevertheless, reporters and editors prefer forms of the verb "to say" in most instances, even if they are repeated throughout a story. And there are good reasons for doing so. "Said" is unobtrusive. Rather than appearing tiresome and repetitious, it hides in the news columns and calls no attention to itself. "Said" is also neutral. It has no connotations. To use the word "said" is to be objective.

Some of the synonyms for "said" sound innocent enough—but be careful. If you report a city official "claimed" or "maintained" or "contended," you are implying that you do not quite believe what the official said. The word "said" is the solution to your problem. If you have evidence that what the official is saying is incorrect, you should include the correct information or evidence in your story.

In some newspaper accounts of labor negotiations, company officials always "ask," while labor leaders always "demand." "Demanding" something sounds harsh and unreasonable, whereas "asking" for something is calm and reasonable. A reporter who uses these words in this context is taking an editorial stand—consciously or unconsciously.

Other words you may be tempted to use as a substitute for "say" are simply unacceptable because they represent improper usage. For example:

"You don't really mean that," he *winked*.
"Of course I do," she *grinned*.
"But what if someone heard you say that?" he *frowned*.
"Oh, you are a fool," she *laughed*.

You cannot "wink" a word. It is difficult, if not impossible, to "grin," "frown" or "laugh" words. But you may want to say this:

"Not again," he *said, moaning*.
"I'm afraid so," she *said with a grin*.

This usage is correct, but often it is not necessary or even helpful to add words like "moaning" or phrases like "with a grin." Sometimes, though, such words and phrases are needed to convey the meaning of the speaker.

Learning the correct words for attribution is the first step. Here are some other guidelines you should follow when attributing information:

1. *If a direct quote is more than one sentence long, place the attribution at the end of the first sentence.* For example:

"The car overturned at least three times," the police officer said. "None of the four passengers was hurt. Luckily, the car did not explode into flames."

That one attribution is adequate. It would be redundant to write:

"The car overturned at least three times," the police officer said. "None of the four passengers was hurt," he added. "Luckily, the car did not explode into flames," he continued.

Nor should you write:

"The car overturned at least three times. None of the four passengers was hurt. Luckily, the car did not explode into flames," the police officer said.

Although you should not keep the reader wondering who is being quoted, in most cases you should avoid placing the attribution at the beginning of a quote. Do not write:

The police officer said: "The car overturned at least three times. None of the four passengers was hurt. Luckily, the car did not explode into flames."

However, if direct quotes from two different speakers follow one another, you should start the second with the attribution to avoid confusion:

"The driver must have not seen the curve," an eyewitness said. "Once the car left the road, all I saw was a cloud of dust."
The police officer said: "The car overturned at least three times. None of the four passengers was hurt. Luckily, the car did not explode into flames."

Notice that when an attribution precedes a direct quotation that is more than one sentence long, wire service style requires that a colon follow the attribution.

2. *Do not follow a fragment of a quote with a continuing complete sentence of quotation.* Avoid constructions like this one:

The mayor said the time had come "to turn off some lights. We all must do something to conserve electricity."

The correct form is to separate partial quotes and complete quotes:

The time has come "to turn off some lights," the mayor said. "We all must do something to conserve electricity."

3. *The first time you attribute a direct or indirect quote, identify the speaker fully.* How fully depends on how well the speaker is known to the readers. In Springfield, Ill., it is sufficient to identify the mayor simply as Mayor John Johnston. But if a story in the Chicago Tribune referred to the mayor of Springfield, the first reference would have to be "John Johnston, mayor of Springfield"—unless, of course, the dateline for the story was Springfield.

4. *Do not attribute direct quotes to more than one person, as in the following*:

"Flames were shooting out everywhere," witnesses said. "Then electrical wires began falling, and voices were heard screaming."

All you have to do is eliminate the quotation marks, if indeed any witness made the statements.

Whatever you do, do not make up a source. Never attribute a statement to "a witness" unless your source is indeed that witness. At times you may ask a witness to confirm what you have seen, but never invent quotes for anonymous witnesses. Inventing witnesses and making up quotes is dishonest, inaccurate and inexcusable.

5. *In stories covering past news events, use the past tense in attributions, and use it throughout the story.* However, stories that do not report on news events, such as features, may be more effective if the attributions are consistently given in the present tense. In a feature story such as a personality profile, when it is safe to assume that what the person once said, he or she would still say, you may use the present tense. For example, when you write, " 'I like being mayor,' she says," you are indicating that she still enjoys it.

6. *Ordinarily, place the noun or pronoun before the verb in attributions*:

"Everything is under control," the sheriff said.

If you must identify a person by including a long title, it is better to begin the attribution with the verb:

"I enjoy the challenge," says Jack Berry, associate dean for graduate studies and research.

# Handling Both On- and Off-the-Record Information

## USING A SOURCE WHO DOES NOT WISH TO BE NAMED

Sometimes a speaker or source may not want to be quoted at all—directly or indirectly. Reporter Diana Dawson tells this story of her experience while working in Memphis:

I had been investigating the Memphis, Tenn., mental health system for about a month with Mike Mansur, Press-Scimitar medical writer, when we stumbled upon two doctors who were fed up with the system. Both worked with the state hospital in Bolivar, Tenn., on a consultant basis. And both were appalled by what they'd observed.

''You can't use our names or identify us in any way whatsoever,'' said one of the doctors. ''We have to maintain a working relationship with the staff there. It's important for the patients that we are able to go in, work with the docs and catch some of the things that are going wrong.''

The consultants told stories of a state hospital that served all of western Tennessee but had no certified psychiatrists. Some doctors had been treated for drug and alcohol problems. The one considered the most skilled had killed himself. There were extremely few doctors for the number of patients.

With that, we checked the state hospital personnel files and found that there were, indeed, no certified psychiatrists. We sat down with the medical chief and a staffing chart to determine the staff-patient ratios. We picked up a copy of the psychiatrist's autopsy report.

As our investigation continued, one of the sources led us to the records we needed to prove that the patients who were taken to the city hospital emergency room with mental problems were often released within a matter of hours. They were released even if they had proven themselves dangerous to the public.

The seven-part series that resulted won Tennessee's UPI grand prize for public service.

And well it should have. Here's how the first of that series began:

Human warehousing—the stashing away of society's insane stepchildren—theoretically ended in 1977.

But today, mental health professionals—including the superintendent of the Gothic asylum called Western Mental Health Institute in Bolivar—say the state psychiatric hospital's level of staffing remains suited only to human storage.

"This place is staffed for custodial care," said Dr. William Jennings, superintendent of Western.

Half the clinical staff consists of psychiatric technicians who have a high school education or less. As darkness falls on Bolivar, the technicians often become responsible for entire wards.

Western's more than 500 patients are seen by a staff of only six licensed physicians, which includes the superintendent and one doctor who has been on sick leave for more than two months.

The six physicians, each responsible for care of between 25 and 93 patients, work as many as 96 hours a week. The licensed doctors also are responsible for every move made by the eight unlicensed doctors, who have medical degrees but have not passed their state board examinations.

That is the kind of reporting that often results from talking to sources who refused to be named. You must learn to use sound professional judgment in handling them. If you agree to accept their information, you must honor their requests to remain off the record. Breaching that confidence destroys trust and credibility. But it is your obligation to take that information elsewhere to confirm it and get it on the record.

## GUIDELINES FOR CITING SOURCES

Bob Woodward and Carl Bernstein, who as Washington Post reporters helped uncover the Watergate scandal that eventually led to the resignation of President Richard M. Nixon, were criticized for citing "high-level sources" without identifying them. Even though Woodward and Bernstein say they did not use this technique unless two independent sources had given them the same information, anonymous sources should be used rarely.

Not naming sources is dangerous for two important reasons. First, such information lacks credibility and makes the reporter and the newspaper suspect. Second, the source may be lying. He or she may be out to discredit someone or may be floating a trial balloon to test public reaction on some issue or event. Skilled diplomats and politicians know how to use reporters to take the temperature of public opinion. If the public reacts negatively, the sources will not proceed with whatever plans they leaked to the press. In such cases the press has been used—and it has become less credible.

Some reporters make these distinctions regarding sources and attribution:

1. *Off the record:* You may not use the information.

2. *Not for attribution:* You may use the information but may not attribute it.

3. *Background:* You may use it with a general title for a source (for example, ''a White House aide said'').

4. *Deep background:* You may use the information, but you may not indicate any source.

By no means is there agreement on these terms. For most people ''off the record'' means not for attribution. For Richard Reeves, political reporter for New York magazine, it means that you cannot use the information in any way. For James Kilpatrick, ''off the record'' is not for quotation, and not for attribution means the same thing. Kilpatrick also thinks there is no difference between background and deep background. Sally Quinn agrees and thinks the term *deep background* is just a joke. Seymour Hersh, author and former reporter for The New York Times, says the terms are different for everyone.

Miles Beller, a reporter for the Los Angeles Herald-Examiner, agrees. Writing in Editor & Publisher, Beller says:

> Universally misunderstood and misread by journalists of every stripe, ''off the record'' suffers from more crude interpretations than does John Cleland's ''Fanny Hill.'' For some reporters, ''don't quote me.'' Others take it to mean ''use the information but peg it to a 'high ranking official,' 'a government spokesman,' 'a well-placed Western diplomat' or any other such 'fill-in-the-blank sources.''' Still others believe that the phrase has lost even the slightest vestige of meaning and should be taken as seriously as Have-a-Nice-Day slogans emblazoned on T-shirts.

Because there is little agreement among journalists, sources may be equally vague about the terms. Your obligation is to make sure you and your sources understand each other. Set the ground rules ahead of time. Clarify your terms.

Also be sure you know the policy of your paper in these matters. For example, many newspapers do not allow reporters to use unidentified sources unless an editor knows the source and approves the usage. Other news organizations such as The Associated Press will not carry opinions, whether positive or negative, expressed by an unidentified source. The news agency will cite statements of fact without attribution, but only if the story makes it clear that the person providing this material would do so only on the condition of anonymity. The New York Times has a policy of not allowing direct quotations of pejorative remarks by an unidentified source.

Again, know the policy of your paper.

In addition, you should be careful not to allow a speaker suddenly to claim something is off the record. Mike Feinsilber of The Associated Press tells this story about David Gergen, at the time director of communications for President Ronald Reagan, former director of communications for President Gerald Ford and former speech writer for President Richard Nixon. One day Gergen "forgot the ground rules."

> Tradition in Washington, and elsewhere, is that a public official cannot go off the record after he has said his piece. And that's the rule that Gergen forgot.
>
> One day last week, he was addressing 150 advertising executives attending the annual conference of the American Association of Advertising Agencies. It was late in the afternoon; the scene was a meeting room in a Washington hotel.
>
> In his half-hour speech, Gergen spoke with somewhat more candor than administration officials—especially those who brief reporters regularly—usually display.
>
> Then during a question-and-answer session, one of the advertising executives asked about the administration's efforts to reverse anti-nuclear sentiment among college students in Europe. He started to answer, then interrupted himself.
>
> "This is all off the record, isn't it?" he asked.
>
> From the back of the room, I shouted, "No."
>
> "Who are you with?"
>
> "The Associated Press."
>
> "Well, can we put this on background (not for attribution)?"
>
> "Nope."
>
> Gergen would up his remarks quickly. . . .
>
> The AP was the only news organization there. And it was on the record.

Nevertheless, if a city manager or police chief wishes to have a background session with you, unless it is against newspaper policy, you should not refuse. Often these officials are trying to be as open as they can under certain circumstances. Without such background sessions the task of reporting complex issues intelligently is nearly impossible. But you must be aware that you are hearing only one point of view and that the information may be self-serving.

Miles Beller gives this example:

> Several years ago a woman phoned this reporter and "wanted to go off the record" in regard to a Los Angeles official's "secret ownership of a Las Vegas radio station" and other questionable holdings tied to this public servant. Funny thing though, the caller plumb forgot to mention that she was working for another candidate. This bit of minutia probably just slipped her mind, what with her man trailing so badly and the election a few weeks away.

Some sources make a habit of saying everything is off the record and of giving commonplace information in background sessions. Although you should not quote a source who asks to remain off the record, you may use information if one or more of the following is true:

1. The information is a matter of public record.

2. It is generally known.

3. It is available from several sources.

4. You are a witness.

So as not to lose credibility with your source, it's a good idea to make it clear that you plan to use the information because of one or more of the preceding reasons.

Knowing when and how to attribute background information is an art you will have to give continuing, special care and attention to as a reporter. Remember these two important points:

1. When possible, set the ground rules with your sources ahead of time.

2. Know your newspaper's policy in these matters.

# Suggested Readings

Anderson, James. "The Background of Backgrounders." *UPI Reporter*, June 22, 1978. A defense and some warnings about background and off-the-record information.

Beller, Miles. "For and Off the Record." Editor & Publisher, Jan. 2, 1982, p. 56. Argues cogently against overuse of off-the-record information.

Callihan, E.L. "Grammar for Journalists," Revised Edition. Radnor, Pa.: Chilton Book Company, 1979. Good section on how to punctuate, attribute and handle quotations.

Davenport, Lucinda D. "News Story Quotes: Verbatim?" Paper delivered at the annual convention of the Mass Communication and Society Division, Association for Education in Journalism and Mass Communication, Norman, Okla., 1986. Discusses what students are taught from leading journalism texts about quoting verbatim.

Gibson, Martin L. "Red." "Attribution Sometimes Best Left Out." Missouri Press News, January 1989, p. 18. Argues not to attribute innocuous information.

King, Barbara. "There's Real Power in Common Speech." Ottaway News Extra, No. 137, Winter 1989, pp. 8, 16. Excellent discussion about using real quotes from real people.

Krohe, James Jr. "Fixing Quotes Cheats Public, Editor Says." Publisher's Auxiliary, April 30, 1979. Argues that quotes should never be changed.

Leslie, Jacques. "The Anonymous Source, Second Thoughts on 'Deep Throat.'" Washington Journalism Review, September 1986, pp. 33–35. A superb treatment of a complicated problem.

Leslie, Jacques. "The Pros and Cons of Cleaning Up Quotes." Washington Journalism Review, May 1986, pp. 44–46. Shows that there are no easy answers and no agreement on how to handle direct quotations.

Stein, M.L. "9th Circuit: It's OK to Make Up Quotes." Editor & Publisher, Aug. 12, 1989, pp. 16, 30. Reactions from the press and lawyers to the court decision allowing quotes that are not verbatim.

"Using Sources." ASNE Bulletin, September 1983, pp. 17–22. An excellent discussion by various experts: "Sources and Principles," by Peter J. Bridge; "Sourcerers Are Bad People," by Richard Smyser; "We Have Helped Create the Monster," by James I. Houck; and "How Really Protected Are We?" by Everette E. Dennis.

# Exercises

1. Rewrite the following story, paying special attention to the use of quotations and attribution. Note the sensitive nature of some of the quotations. Paraphrase when necessary.

Christopher O'Reilly is a remarkably happy young man, despite a bout with meningitis eight years ago that has left him paralyzed and brain damaged.

"I am happy," O'Reilly commented, as he puffed a cigarette.

He has much to be happy about. Physical therapy has hastened his recovery since the day he awoke from a 10-week-long coma. He has lived to celebrate his 26th birthday.

"I had a helluva birthday," he said, "I seen several friends. I had big cake," he added slowly.

He lives in a house with his mother and stepfather in the rolling, green countryside near Springfield.

O'Reilly's withered legs are curled beneath him now, and his right arm is mostly paralyzed, but he can do pull-ups with his left arm. He can see and hear.

"When he came back, he wasn't worth a damn," his mother said. "The hack doctors told me he would be a vegetable all his life,'' she claimed.

"He couldn't talk; he could only blink. And he drooled a lot,'' she smiled.

Now, Chris is able to respond in incomplete sentences to questions and can carry on slow communication. "He don't talk good, but he talks,'' his mother commented.

It all began when he stole a neighbor's Rototiller. His probation was revoked, and he found himself in the medium-security prison in Springfield. Then came "inadequate medical treatment'' in the prison system. O'Reilly's family argued that he received punishment beyond what the Eighth Amendment of the U.S. Constitution calls "cruel and unusual.''

"Those prison officials were vicious,'' they said.

As a result, he was awarded $250,000 from the state, the largest legal settlement in federal court in 10 years. "That sounds like a lot of money. But it really isn't, you know, when you consider what happened and when you consider the worth of a human life, and the way they treated him and all, we thought we should get at least a million,'' his mother remarked.

O'Reilly contracted the infection of the brain after sleeping "on the concrete floor'' of a confinement cell, his mother maintained. He had been placed in solitary confinement because he would not clean his cell. The disease went undiagnosed for eight days, leaving him paralyzed and brain-damaged, she said.

Now O'Reilly likes watching television. "I like TV,'' he grinned. "And smoking.''

His mother said she "never gives up hope'' that "one day'' her son will "come out of it.''

2. Here is part of a speech by Professor Richard L. Weaver II of the Department of Interpersonal and Public Communication at Bowling Green State University. It was delivered at the International Student Leadership Conference, Bowling Green, Ohio, Oct. 28, 1989. Assume the speech was given at your university and that you are writing for your school paper. Indicate the direct quotations you would use and why you would use them.

So I want to take a few moments this afternoon and look at this twofold problem that leaders face—building the proper foundation (your credibility) and motivating others. And did you know that the two are closely related? Your ability to motivate others is, according to the research, dependent *mostly* upon your credibility.

Let's just look briefly at what goes into credibility. Credibility is really the attitude others hold toward you at any given time. Sure, it has to do with the house *you* build, but as a leader you must realize that much more important than the house itself is the view that others have of the house that you build. Want to motivate others? Get your house in order first.

This might be a good self-test. Let me give you the top five components of credibility. You are all past, present, and/or future leaders. How do *you* measure up?

According to the research in the speech-communication discipline, the most important and first component of credibility is good, old-fashioned, *sociability*.

Are you the kind of person others think of as friendly, cheerful, good natured, warm, and pleasant? If not, why not? I've always thought that a sociable outlook had to do with the way one comes at life. Are you generally an optimist rather than a pessimist? Now, I know that most of you are optimists, but did you know that recent studies showed that those who look on the bright side tend to do better on achievement tests, have more job success, live longer, and have better health? The attitude of helplessness, typical of pessimists, is associated with the weakening of the immune systems' resistance to tumors and infection. Pessimists, according to these studies, tend to neglect themselves and tend to smoke and drink more than optimists. You see, there are actually substantial benefits for:

> Expecting things, in general, to work out well for you.
>
> Expecting your best effort to be successful.
>
> And, when looking at new situations, seeing potentials rather than road-blocks.

Beliefs in limits create limited people. Being sociable comes from an outlook on life. And such an outlook is contagious! Other people perceive it, and, what's more, they notice it quickly! If they like the outlook, they *do* respond!

The second characteristic of credibility is *competence*. There is no substitute for knowledge. You have to come off as knowing what you are doing. I'm not saying that you have to be the most intelligent, well-trained, informed, expert in your area. But I want you to know right up front, others appreciate those who have done their homework, who know what they are talking about, and who seem to have a grip on what needs to be known. You have to understand that good leaders don't waste other people's time!

The third characteristic of credibility is *extroversion*. Now, this does not mean that all leaders are bold and verbal, talkative and assertive, or animated and dynamic. But I will tell you this: it sure helps! Extroversion often comes across as enthusiasm. Knowledge is power, but enthusiasm pulls the switch! Think of the *extroverted* teachers you have had, and you often think of the *enthusiastic* teachers you have had. Why? Because the traits are similar. When a teacher says to you, "Fabulous job," or "I love it," these are bold, verbal qualities of extroversion. When teachers are highly nonverbal, using gestures, touch, and movement in front of the classroom, these are the animated and dynamic characteristics of both enthusiasm and extroversion. Just remember, the level of excitement in an organization often rises to the level of enthusiasm of the leader.

The fourth characteristic of credibility is *composure*. Credible people are often perceived as poised, in control, and self-confident. This quality helps keep the extroversion in perspective because a leader who is self-assured without being bombastic or overbearing instills confidence in others. Are you cool under pressure? Can you retain composure when you are threatened or when your leadership ability is under attack? Composure means being able to remain relaxed, calm, and cool in trying circumstances.

The fifth characteristic of credibility is *character*. Are you someone others view as virtuous (courageous), honest, unselfish, sympathetic, and trustworthy? In my experience, I have always related character with commitment and commitment with passion. How much do *you* care? There is no great success without great commitment. There is character in commitment. You look at successful people in *any* field, and you'll find they're not necessarily the best and the brightest or the fastest and strongest—they are, instead, the ones with the most commitment. Have you ever heard the acronym *WIT*?—Whatever It Takes! Successful people are willing to do whatever it takes to succeed. Are you one who sees difficulties in every opportunity or opportunities in every difficulty?

3. Attend a meeting, a press conference or a speech and tape-record it. While there, write down the quotes you would use if you were writing the story for your local newspaper. Then listen to the tape and check the accuracy of the quotations.

4. Interview at least two reporters, asking them about their policies on handling sources regarding the following:

   a. Off the record

   b. Not for attribution

   c. Background

   d. Deep background

   Write at least a 200-word essay on the subject.

# 7

## Sources
## and Searches

When reporters Lou Kilzer and Chris Ison started investigating a thriving industry suspected of profiting from arson and suspicious fires, they created a computer data base to help keep track of the data they had accumulated after pawing through 10,000 pages of government documents.

The data base they constructed cross-referenced each of 200 suspicious fires in St. Paul, Minn., over a 25-year period. Those fires, the reporters believed, in some way involved the fire chief, his brother, the public adjuster or their friends and associates. The data base helped make the connection clear, and the result was a 1990 Pulitzer Prize for Kilzer and Ison, reporters for the Star Tribune, the Newspaper of the Twin Cities, in Minneapolis-St. Paul.

With the help of their computer, Kilzer and Ison cross-referenced each fire with the address and property owner, the cause, the St. Paul Fire Department investigator, the amount of damage, the insurance claim, the adjuster and the repair contractor. As a result, the reporters were able to report that profits from suspicious fires flowed to people personally and professionally connected to Fire Chief Steve Conroy. They said Conroy tolerated shoddy fire investigations and allowed firefighters to moonlight for a firm that represented alleged arsonists in fire-insurance claims.

After the series was published, Conroy removed himself as fire chief pending an investigation. Subsequently, the mayor banned firefighters from working for fire-insurance adjusters in the city, and federal agencies began investigations.

With their success, Kilzer and Ison became part of a growing cadre of reporters who know how to use the computer as an effective tool for reporting. For all reporters, the computer is becoming as essential as the notepad. Although Kilzer and Ison used the computer to create their own data base, other reporters use it to tap the massive amount of data created by government agencies—federal, state and local.

A leader in computer-assisted reporting is Elliot Jaspin, a Pulitzer Prize winner and director of the Missouri Institute for Computer-Assisted Reporting at the University of Missouri. Jaspin's specialty is teaching student journalists and working reporters how to extract useful data from the mountain of information available in government data bases. Using techniques perfected by Jaspin, reporters nationwide are able to access government records for stories that previously would have taken years to research and extract.

Imagine, for example, being able to access a state's computer data bases for (1) school bus drivers and (2) persons convicted of drunken driving. Cross-referencing would make it possible to determine, quickly and accurately, if any school bus drivers had been convicted of drunken driving. To access the same information without the assistance of a computer would take months of sorting through thousands of records by hand.

The best reporters of the 1990s are likely to be those who know how to use the computer and other resources to their advantage. In addition to a knowledge of more traditional reference materials, you will need computer skills to pursue the stories of the future. But to do any story, of course, you first must come up with the idea for one.

### In this chapter you will learn:

1. Where reporters turn for sources of news.

2. How reference materials can be used to verify facts.

3. How computer data-base searches are improving the quality of reporting.

# Finding the Story

Readers bring some story ideas to the newspaper office. Most story ideas, though, are the result of an active imagination, a lively curiosity and a little help from friends. Journalists soon learn to recognize how stories written for other publications can be written for their own. They get in the habit of carrying a little notebook to jot down ideas when something somebody says strikes a responsive chord.

But even for good journalists, the wellspring of ideas sometimes dries up. Bank these 10 sources of story ideas, good for any time and any place, for the day that happens to you.

1. *Other people*. As a journalist you meet many persons. What are they talking about when they aren't talking business? What have they heard lately? Journalists have to listen, even when it means eavesdropping while having a cup of coffee. What interests people? There is no better source of story ideas than the people you meet while you are off-duty. They are, after all, your readers.

2. *Other publications*. Stories are recycled across the country. Read other newspapers, magazines, books, pamphlets and the magazines and newsletters of businesses and organizations.

Not all stories will work in every community. You have to know your readership. A story about urban renewal, for example, would attract more attention in New York than in Helena, Mont. The problems of water supply in the West could not be adapted to make a story on the East Coast. But a story about the federal government's hot-lunch program probably could be done in New York, Kansas and California.

When you are reading other publications for ideas, remember that you should not duplicate a story. You are looking for ideas. Think of a new angle.

3. *News releases*. Some news releases from public relations people are used, but many of them are not. Yet they can be a valuable source of story ideas. News that one company has posted increased profits may be worth one or two paragraphs; news that several companies in your community are prospering may be a front-page story. A handout stating that an employee received a 40-year pin may be worth a follow-up.

4. *A social services directory*. Many cities and counties have a composite listing of all agencies providing social services. Look beyond the pages. There are stories of people serving—or not serving—residents. Each of those agencies and their clients is a story.

5. *Government reports*. Flowing from Washington like flood waters are pages and pages of statistics. Behind every statistic, however, is a person. And every person can be a story. The census reports, for instance, list not only the number of people in a community but also their income and education, how many cars they own, whether they rent or own a house. They tell much more, too. Find out what, and you have a treasure chest of stories.

6. *Stories in your own newspaper*. Many a stream has yielded gold nuggets after the first wave of miners has left. Newspapers sometimes play hit-and-run journalism. Ask yourself if the human-interest angle has been reported adequately. When your newspaper is concentrating on the election winners, maybe you can get an interesting story by talking to the losers and their supporters. After the story of the two-car accident has been written, perhaps there is a feature on the victims whose lives have been changed. And when the unemployment statistics are reported in your paper, remember that behind each of those numbers is a person without a job.

News stories are not the only source of ideas. Read the records column: Can you spot a trend developing in the police report section or in the births or divorce listings? Is the divorce rate up? Have several crimes been committed in one neighborhood?

7. *Advertisements.* In the advertisements, particularly the classifieds, you may find everything from a come-on for an illegal massage parlor to an auction notice from a family losing its home. Look through the yellow pages, too. Your fingers might walk right up to a story.

8. *Wire copy.* Browse through the copy available from your wire services. Are there stories that can be localized? When a story comes across the wires describing the increase in the rate of inflation, you should ask how the people in your community will be affected. Or if a foundation reports that Johnny cannot read, you should talk to your local education officials. Can the Johnnys in your community read any better than the national average?

9. *Local news briefs.* Usually reports of local happenings are phoned in; sometimes they are brought in, written longhand on a piece of scratch paper. News of an upcoming family reunion may or may not be printed, but the enterprising reporter who notices in the information that five generations will attend the reunion probably has a story that will receive substantial play in the paper. A note that the Westside Neighborhood Association is planning its annual fund-raiser may result in a feature on how the neighbors plan to raise funds to upgrade recreational facilities in their area.

The local news brief as a source of stories is often overlooked. A city editor once received a call from a man who said he thought the paper might be interested in a story about his daughter coming to visit. The city editor tried to brush him off. Just before the man hung up, the editor heard, ''I haven't seen her in 32 years. I thought she was dead.''

10. *You.* In the final analysis you are the one who must be alert enough to look and listen to what is going on around you. Ask yourself why, as in, ''Why do people act the way they do?'' Ask yourself what, as in, ''What are people thinking about? What are their fears, their anxieties?'' Ask yourself when, as in, ''When that happened, what else was going on?'' And wonder about things, as in, ''I wonder if that's true in my town.''

Reporters who are attuned to people rather than institutions will find the world around them a rich source of human interest stories. Do not tune out.

## Checking the Facts

A wealth of information is available for the thorough reporter who wants to develop the sound habit of checking every verifiable fact that goes into a story. Some of that information can be found in the reference manuals maintained in most news rooms or in newspaper libraries. A good reporter will learn quickly what materials are available.

Here is a list of 20 commonly used references:

1. *Local and area telephone directories.* Used for verifying the spelling of names and addresses. These usually are reliable, but they are not infallible.

2. *City directories.* These can be found in most cities. They provide the same information as the telephone directory but also may provide information on the occupations of citizens and the owners or managers of businesses. Useful street indexes provide information on the names of next-door neighbors.

3. *State manuals.* Each state government publishes a directory that provides useful information on various government agencies. These directories sometimes list the salaries of all state employees.

4. *Maps* of the city, county, state, nation and world. Local maps usually are posted in the news room. Others may be found in atlases.

5. *Bartlett's Familiar Quotations* (Little, Brown).

6. *Congressional Directory* (Government Printing Office). Provides profiles of members of Congress.

7. *Congressional Record* (Government Printing Office). Complete proceedings of the U.S. House and Senate.

8. *Current Biography* (Wilson). Profiles of prominent persons, published monthly.

9. *Dictionary of American Biography* (Scribner's).

10. *Facts on File* (Facts on File Inc.). Weekly compilation of news from metropolitan newspapers.

11. *Guinness Book of World Records* (Guinness Superlatives). World records listed in countless categories.

12. *National Trade and Professional Associations of the United States* (Columbia Books, Washington, D.C.).

13. *Readers' Guide to Periodical Literature* (Wilson). Index to magazine articles on a host of subjects.

14. *Statistical Abstract of the United States* (Government Printing Office). Digest of data collected and published by all federal agencies.

15. *Webster's Biographical Dictionary* (Merriam).

16. *Webster's New World Dictionary of the American Language,* Second College Edition. Primary reference dictionary recommended by both The Associated Press and United Press International.

17. *Webster's Third New International Dictionary*. Unabridged dictionary recommended by AP and UPI.

18. *Who's Who* (St. Martins). World listings.

19. *Who's Who in America* (Marquis). Biennial publication.

20. *World Almanac and Book of Facts* (Newspaper Enterprise Association). Published annually.

These useful publications, and many others like them, enable reporters to verify data and to avoid the unnecessary embarrassment caused by errors in print.

A burgeoning new source of reference material now available to reporters is contained on CD-ROMs, compact disks accessed by computers. These include everything from complete encyclopedias to data on thousands of businesses worldwide. The usefulness of such data in a news room is obvious, and reporters and editors increasingly are making use of it.

## USING COMPUTER DATA BASES

At the beginning of this chapter, we outlined how two reporters created a computer data base to help make sense of a mountain of data. We also described how the computer can be used to analyze data bases created by government agencies. But those are just two of several ways that the computer is being used in news rooms today. The computer is also commonly used to search commercial data bases. And computer-assisted telephone interviewing, though still in its infancy in the newspaper industry, is likely to become important to reporters as well.

More than 100 U.S. daily newspapers now make their libraries available to the public and other newspapers through companies that specialize in selling data-base services. The most common, and perhaps the most useful to journalists, are Vu/Text Information Services and DataTimes. These data-base services provide the full text of newspaper libraries at dozens of newspapers dating back several years. Imagine how useful it can be to access by way of a computer the vast library of The Washington Post or the Los Angeles Times. Services such as Vu/Text and DataTimes have made that possible for any newspaper, and many have taken advantage of the ability to do so.

Dow Jones News Retrieval is another popular data-base service. It provides the full text of the Wall Street Journal and other Dow Jones publications. Somewhat less useful but still of value to journalists are the indexed services, such as Dialog Information Services, that provide a synopsis of stories rather than the full text. Add to that thousands of other data bases made available by government agencies, companies and non-profit corporations and the world of information available to the enterprising reporter is almost unlimited.

Finally, newspapers increasingly are using computers to conduct opinion surveys and to interpret the data obtained from those surveys. The St. Louis Post-Dispatch, among others, has employed a service bureau to conduct computerized telephone interviews. The results have been front-page stories predicting election results and other societal trends.


## COMPUTER-ASSISTED REPORTING


Conventional resources provide a wealth of information for the enterprising reporter, but electronic data bases have unlocked doors that many never thought would be opened. Because of the tight deadlines under which reporters operate, there seldom is time to trek to the local library to research a story. So, while a great deal of information may be there, the opportunity to tap that resource may not be available. Electronic data bases, however, are as close as the nearest modem-equipped computer and telephone line.

In the United States and Canada, thousands of data bases offer uncountable tidbits of information. The reporter who learns to use them will be able to produce many stories that would have been impossible to do in past years. For example, while it would take a reporter using conventional means thousands of hours to search through all the nation's medical journals for information on a particular disease, a well-trained librarian could find the same information in a data base in a matter of minutes or seconds. Of course, not everything is available on data bases, but each day more and more material is.

One newspaper has been a leader in using data bases—and computers in general—to assist the reporter: the Star Tribune, Newspaper of the Twin Cities, in Minneapolis-St. Paul. John Ullmann, formerly assistant managing editor and now a consultant to the newspaper, says computers have helped to elevate the quality of journalism practiced at the Tribune. As an example, he cites investigation by reporters Tom Hamburger and Joe Rigert that uncovered abuses in minority contracting programs. The use of computers made it possible for them to achieve an unusual depth. Instead of simply citing a litany of problems in contracting programs, computers enabled the reporters to find patterns, provide context and indict an entire system rather than just individuals and companies within that system.

Hamburger and Rigert found that front firms for big contractors had captured more than 25 percent of the $179 million awarded to Minnesota companies supposedly controlled by women and minorities in the early 1980s. They also found that two-thirds of the money earmarked for highway-construction companies run by women actually went to firms owned by relatives of well-established male contractors.

Ullmann details how the computer helped:

**Figure 7.1
Data Base
Searches.**
Computer data
bases provide
reporters and editors
with a wealth of
information at the
touch of a button.

1. *Background information.* Through a data-base search conducted by the newspaper's library staff, Hamburger and Rigert obtained articles on abuses and investigations involving similar programs in other states. They also got information on states that appeared to be running model operations. From this search, they were able to determine that reporters and government specialists had completed few investigations of minority contracting programs. A legislative data base gave the reporters a comprehensive history of federal votes and committee hearings on the subject and identified key critics of the program.

2. *Organization and retrieval.* In their newspaper's computer system, the reporters established a filing system with an index of subjects and lists of documents and sources. By referring to their subject-matter index, which was cross-referenced to documents and interviews, they were able to manage the large volumes of information they collected, establish a chronology of events, prepare for interviews and organize for the writing phase. They also were able to use the computer's search function to pick out references to specific companies or individuals.

3. *Polling and tabulation.* Working with the newspaper's poll division, Hamburger and Rigert devised a census survey of all minority contractors certified in Minneapolis. The results were placed in a computer to speed up

the tabulation of findings and provide breakdowns of responses from various groups. The survey found that women and minority contractors thought competition from front companies was hurting their businesses and that the government wasn't helping. The poll, in effect, confirmed what Hamburger and Rigert already had learned.

Rigert showed how effectively computers can be used on deadline while reporting on the crash near Reno, Nev., of a plane chartered by Minnesotans. A data-base search revealed that the type of plane that had crashed, a Lockheed Electra, had the worst fatal-accident rate of any aircraft in common use.

With that report, other data from the search and information obtained on the telephone, Rigert was able to report in the next edition that 10 percent of Electras had been involved in fatal crashes, that the airplanes had the worst fatal-accident rate on record and that Electras had a history of mechanical problems. He also was able to produce a chart of each fatal crash dating back to 1959. The chart included the cause of each crash and the number of fatalities.

Also in Minneapolis, a challenger in the political race for prosecuting attorney accused the incumbent of being a weak plea-bargainer. Under plea bargaining, a person charged with crimes agrees to plead guilty to a lesser offense than the one with which he or she was originally charged. The state thus saves the time and expense of a trial and the accused often draws a lighter sentence. The Minneapolis incumbent, of course, disagreed with his opponent. Star Tribune reporter Eric Black decided to reduce the rhetoric to statistics to see which candidate was correct.

Black found a state agency that maintained highly detailed statistics on criminal justice matters. But before he sought the data for which he was looking, he interviewed both candidates. He asked the challenger, "If you're right about your opponent's weak plea bargaining, how would that show up statistically and with whom would it be reasonable to compare him?" Black asked the incumbent, "If you're right and you have a strong record on plea bargaining, how would that show up statistically?"

Plea bargaining can be complicated, and the story that eventually was written contained caveats about the risks of a statistical approach in such a complex area. But Black was able to devise a valid plan of measurement that both candidates agreed in advance would be a fair measure of the incumbent's record.

The analysis showed that in comparison with prosecuting attorneys in neighboring counties, the incumbent's record was strong.

Black found other interesting material in the statistics that shed considerable light on the overall performance of Minnesota's judges and prosecutors. In fact, half of those who came into the criminal justice system facing prison terms were able to avoid incarceration because of plea bargaining or leniency of judges. The chief justice of the Supreme Court, the chairman of the state Sentencing Guidelines Commission and legislators were disturbed by the article's findings.

Both stories appeared on Page One of the Star Tribune. The first allowed readers to go beyond the campaign rhetoric. The second allowed them to pierce the veil surrounding the criminal justice system.

The key, though, is the reporter's ability to learn how to make technology work in his or her favor. Black's study may have been useless had he not managed to get the candidates to agree on a valid means of measurement.

Such inventive uses of the computer are not limited to Minneapolis, of course. Although large metropolitan newspapers have been leaders in the field, smaller newspapers are beginning to realize the importance of tapping into the wealth of information available through data bases. The reporter who fails to learn what data bases can do soon will be outclassed.

## SAMPLING OF AVAILABLE MATERIAL

Most data bases contain bibliographies annotated and cross-indexed by subject matter. A major vendor is Dialog Information Services, a Palo Alto, Calif., company owned by Lockheed. Dialog contains literally hundreds of data bases, each with a wealth of information. Users are charged for the service according to the length of time their computer is connected to the data base. To give you an idea of what is available through Dialog, just one of many database services, here are descriptions of a few of its data bases:

1. *ASI (American Statistics Index)*: From 1973 to present, monthly updates (Congressional Information Service, Inc., Washington, D.C.). ASI is a comprehensive index of the statistical publications from more than 400 central or regional issuing agencies of the U.S. government. ASI provides abstracts and indexing of all federal statistical publications, including non-Government Printing Office publications, which contain social, economic, demographic or natural resources data. It also covers a selection of publications with scientific and technical data. All types of publications are covered, including periodicals, as special, one-time reports; as items within a larger continuing report series; or as annual or biennial reports. Types of statistical data found in ASI include population and economic censuses; foreign trade data; Consumer Price Index reports; unemployment statistics; agricultural data on production, yield, prices, and so on; vital statistics; educational data; and much more.

2. *Congressional Record Abstracts*: From 1976 to present, weekly updates (Capitol Services International, Washington, D.C.). This data base provides comprehensive abstracts covering each issue of the Congressional Record, the official journal of the proceedings of the U.S. Congress. Coverage includes

congressional activities regarding bills and resolutions, committee and sub-committee reports, public laws, executive communications and speeches, and inserted materials. Records include data on bills, members of Congress, roll-call votes, reference to floor debates and specific issues. Abstracts are included.

3. *Foundations Grants Index*: from 1972 to present, bimonthly updates (The Foundation Center, New York). This data base contains information on grants awarded by more than 400 major American philanthropic foundations, representing all records from the Foundations Grants Index section of the bimonthly Foundation News. Information on grants given by foundations is useful in determining types and amounts of grants awarded because foundations seldom announce the availability of funds for specific purposes. Each foundation conforms to the description of a "nongovernmental nonprofit organization, with funds and program managed by its own trustees or directors, and established to maintain or aid social, common educational, charitable, religious or other activities serving the common welfare, primarily through the making of grants," as defined in the Foundation Directory, Edition 5. Approximately 20,000 grant records are added to the file each year. Grants are given primarily in the fields of education, health, welfare, sciences, international activities, humanities and religion, with education as the most-favored field for foundation giving. Grants to individuals and grants of less than $5,000 are not included.

4. *Legal Resource Index*: From 1980 to present, monthly updates (Information Access Corp., Menlo Park, Calif.). This data base provides cover-to-cover indexing of more than 660 key law journals and five law newspapers plus legal monographs and government publications from the Library of Congress data base. It comprehensively indexes articles, book reviews, case notes, president's pages, columns, letters to the editor, obituaries, transcripts, biographical pieces and editorials, providing access to valuable secondary information for the legal profession and others. Relevant articles from Magazine Index (File 47) and National Newspaper Index (File 111) are also included.

5. *Magazine Index*: From 1976 to present, monthly updates (Information Access Corp., Menlo Park, Calif.). This data base was the first on-line data base to offer truly broad coverage of general magazines. It was created especially for general reference librarians who must handle a constant flow of diverse requests for information from the mundane to the scholarly to the lighthearted. It covers more than 370 popular magazines and provides extensive coverage of current affairs, leisure-time activities, home-centered arts, sports, recreation and travel, the performing arts, business, science and technology, consumer product evaluations, and other areas. In addition to being a valuable tool for the public and academic library information desks, it also serves business and government libraries with information not available on any other on-line data base. In particular, libraries serving patrons in the fields of market research, public relations, government relations, journalism, food and nutrition, and the social sciences find it to be a significant resource.

6. *Newsearch*: Current month only, daily updates (Information Access Corp., Los Altos, Calif.). This data base is a daily index of more than 2,000 news stories, information articles and book reviews from over 1,400 of the most important newspapers, magazines and periodicals. Every working day the previous day's news stories are indexed and added to Newsearch to provide current information on product reviews; executive and corporation news; current events; book, record and theater reviews; and much more. At the end of each month, the magazine article data are transferred to the Magazine Index data base; the newspaper indexing data are transferred to the National Newspaper Index data base. Daily indexing from Legal Resource Index, Management Contents, and Trade and Industry Index is also transferred at the end of each month.

7. *Standard and Poor's News*: September 1979 to present, weekly updates (Standard and Poor's Corp., New York). This data base offers both general news and financial information on more than 10,000 publicly owned U.S. corporations. It covers interim earnings, management changes, contract awards, mergers, acquisitions, bond descriptions and corporate background, including subsidiaries, litigation and officers. It is the most up-to-date and comprehensive on-line source of annual reports, interim earnings reports and statistical data of U.S. companies. It is a major source of financial information for competitive analysis and investing and is the equivalent of the printed Standard and Poor's Corp. Records Daily News and Cumulative News.

Remember that these are merely a few of the hundreds of data bases available through just one source, Dialog. The information now available to reporters through such services is invaluable. Your college or local library may offer a class in data-base search techniques.

## EXAMPLE OF A SEARCH

Searching a commercial data base for information isn't difficult if you have some idea of what you want to find and where it may have appeared. Most commercial vendors allow you to search the entire data base using key words, but such searches can be costly and ineffective; usually, they result in more articles than you can use.

To illustrate the wealth of material available on one narrow topic, the authors searched Vu/Text for all articles in the Miami Herald regarding the visit of South African activist Nelson Mandela to Miami. First, we limited the search to 1990, when the visit occurred. Then we decided to search for the key words "Mandela," "blacks," and "Miami." Our intent was to obtain background information on the visit and the furor that resulted in the black community there after Cuban-American community leaders snubbed Mandela because of favorable statements he had made about Fidel Castro.

We could have limited our search even more by adding key words or asking the computer not to give us articles that contained certain words. Our search produced 28 articles that ranged from the actual news coverage and analyses to columns and letters to the editor. Asterisks in the text mark the key words we used in the search. Here is a sampling of the results:

```
RANK   28 OF    28,   PAGE    1 OF    5,  DB MHO,  DOCUMENT  12247
  THU  FEB  08  1990 ED:   FINAL
  SECTION:  NEIGHBORS CT  PAGE:  3    LENGTH:   23.78" MEDIUM
  ILLUST:
  SOURCE:  Herald Staff
  DATELINE:
  MEMO:
. . . . . . . . . . . . . . . . . . . . . . . . . . . . . . . . . . . . . . . .
                 BROAD SPECTRUM
                OF EVENTS HONORS
                 BLACK HISTORY
     A multitude of events from ethnic food tasting to spiritual
singing and special children's programs are among the highlights
of Black History Month to take place in the Coral Gables,
Kendall and South Dade area throughout February.
     Among participants featuring special events and programs
are the Metro-Dade Department of Human Resources' Neighborhood
Service Centers; *Miami-Dade*Community College and the*Miami-
Dade*Public Library System.
     WDNA-FM 88.9 community radio is offering a number of
special programs including:  Malcolm X:  A Retrospective, 9 a.m.
Tuesday; Nelson*Mandela:* Noblest Son of Africa, 10:30 a.m.
Tuesday, Wednesday, Feb. 15 and 16; and Equal Rights Under the
Law:  Desegregation in America, 10:30 a.m. Feb. 19 to 23, Feb.
26 to 28 and March 1. . .
```

Obviously, this was not the information we were looking for, which is one of the problems associated with data base searches. Sometimes you access material that is not quite what you are trying to find.

Another article, though, proved to be more useful:

```
RANK   26 OF    28,   PAGE    1 OF    3,  DB MHO,  DOCUMENT  12609
  MON FEB 12 1990    ED:   FINAL
  SECTION:  FRONT      PAGE:  17A   LENGTH:   12.83" MEDIUM
  ILLUST:  photo:  William GIBSON
  SOURCE:   SANDRA DIBBLE And CARLOS HARRISON Herald Staff
  Writers
  DATELINE:
  MEMO:  FREEDOM DAY
. . . . . . . . . . . . . . . . . . . . . . . . . . . . . . . . . . . . . . . .
        S. FLORIDA GUARDEDLY HOPES FOR MORE CHANGE
     Word of Nelson*Mandela's*release Sunday -- after 27 years
behind bars for opposing apartheid in South Africa --
```

reverberated in South Florida, bringing cautious optimism that
his struggle for equality will not be overlooked here.

''It is a signal, it's an inspiration for black Americans
to believe and understand that there are some problems here that
can be solved just as well,'' Dr. William Gibson, chairman of
the National Association for the Advancement of Colored People,
said at the New Shiloh Missionary Baptist Church in*Miami.*

''I think it shows that a commitment, a determination, a
sense of will and belief for what you think is right and what
you stand for, a willingness to endure 27 years in jail, can
change a lot of things,'' Gibson said before the start of the
service honoring the 81st anniversary of the NAACP. . . .

While this still was not exactly what we sought to find, it was useful
material as we researched the background of the visit.

The following article, which explained the controversy, was right on
target:

RANK   14 OF   28,   PAGE 1 OF   5,  DB MHO,  DOCUMENT   43636
WED JUN 27 1990      ED: FINAL
SECTION: LOCAL      PAGE:  1B    LENGTH:    23.47" MEDIUM
ILLUST:  photo: Johnnie McMILLIAM
SOURCE:  CARL  GOLDFARB  Herald  Staff  Writer
DATELINE:
MEMO:
. . . . . . . . . . . . . . . . . . . . . . . . . . . . . . . . . . . . . . . . .
                 *BLACKS*REJECT SUAREZ'S
               OLIVE BRANCH ON*MANDELA*
    The day after rebuking Nelson*Mandela,*Miami*Mayor Xavier
Suarez moderated his tone, but black leaders Tuesday said the
mayor's actions were too little, too late.

    Suarez was the lone Hispanic official to attend a meeting
called by Metro Commissioner Barbara Carey in support
of*Mandela,*but he received a chilly welcome from some.

    ''I think it would have been a good idea if he didn't show
up,'' said the Rev. Victor Curry, who accused the mayor of
trying to straddle the black-Cuban divide over*Mandela's*visit.

    So it went Tuesday, the day before*Mandela*is to arrive
in*Miami,*as efforts to ease racial tensions and find common
ground fell short in three meetings held by different segments
of the black community.

    Black leaders demanded a worthy welcome for*Mandela,*while
Cuban exile groups announced plans to protest outside
the*Miami*Beach Convention Center where*Mandela*is to speak
Thursday morning.

    The controversy -- the latest rift between*Miami's*black
and Cuban communities -- continued to dominate Spanish-language
and black-oriented radio stations. . . .

The story that chronicled the visit also was useful:

```
RANK    8 OF    28,    PAGE   1 OF    7,  DB MHO,   DOCUMENT 44310
  FRI JUN 29 1990            ED:  FINAL
  SECTION:  FRONT          PAGE:  1A    LENGTH:  51.05" LONG
  ILLUST:  color photo: Nelson and Winnie*MANDELA*in*Miami*Beach,
  H. T. Smith embraces*MANDELA;*photo:  Verne Crosky at Gwen
  Cherry Park*(MANDELA*TRIP U.S.), confrontation outside
  Convention Center*(MANDELA*)*
  SOURCE:  KIMBERLY CROCKETT, ELINOR BURKETT and KAREN BRANCH
  Herald Staff Writers
  DATELINE:
  MEMO:  *MANDELA*IN SOUTH FLORIDA; see related stories
```
. . . . . . . . . . . . . . . . . . . . . . . . . . . . . . . . . . . . . . . . . . . . . . . .
```
                 UNOFFICIALLY,*MANDELA*DAY
                   GRASS-ROOTS WELCOME
                  COUNTERS OFFICIAL SNUB
     Elected officials might have turned their backs, but grass-
  roots*Miami*Thursday enveloped Nelson*Mandela* in a warm
  embrace.
     The numbers and rousing welcome didn't rival New York's.
  The cast of characters was not a Who's Who of politics and
  entertainment -- as it was in Washington and Atlanta.
     But*Miami,*ordinary*Miami* -- the teachers and technicians,
  homemakers and health-care workers -- streamed across the
  causeways and bridges wearing*Mandela* T-shirts and the red,
  black and green of the pan-African movement to welcome the
  deputy president of the African National Congress.
     As*Mandela*emerged onto the podium before the 29th
  international convention of the American Federation of State,
  County and Municipal Employees, he waved and a gentle smile
  creased his face.  His wife, Winnie, raised a victorious
  clenched fist.
     ''Sisters and brothers,'' he greeted the 6,000 delegates
  and guests at the*Miami*Beach Convention Center.  They erupted
  into cheers of*''Mandela,*yes. Apartheid, no.''
     ''To be welcomed by those who hold the reins of power in
  this area . . . to be warmly received by residents of*Miami,*is
  a source of great inspiration to us,''*Mandela*said. . . .
```

Finally, several columns and analyses were also useful:

```
RANK    6 OF    28,    PAGE   1 OF    9,  DB MHO,   DOCUMENT  44537
  SUN JUL 01 1990            ED:  FINAL
  SECTION:  LOCAL      PAGE:  1B     LENGTH:  49.14" LONG
  ILLUST:  photo:  Nelson*MANDELA*
  SOURCE:  CARL GOLDFARB Herald Staff Writer
  DATELINE:
  MEMO:  NEWS ANALYSIS
```
. . . . . . . . . . . . . . . . . . . . . . . . . . . . . . . . . . . . . . . . . . . . . . . .
```
                 *MANDELA'S*VISIT PROMPTS
                RERUN OF OLD ETHNIC BATTLES
     When Nelson*Mandela*came to town,*Miami's*politicians and
  activists replayed their parts from past ethnic controversies,
```

```
like wooden horses on a merry-go-round, unable to escape their
ideological harnesses.
     Again, it was*blacks*against Hispanics, with precious
little middle ground.
     As*Miami*lurched toward*Mandela's*arrival Wednesday, the
voices of moderation were few, political leaders mostly silent
or divided along racial and ethnic lines, community activists
increasingly vocal.
     To*blacks,*Mandela*is a symbol of the fight against racism
in South Africa and their own struggle for equality in this
country. To Cubans, all else pales beside*Mandela's*embrace of
Cuban President Fidel Castro, who has sundered so many families,
jailed so many dissidents.
     Each side felt righteously indignant -- one because its
hero was attacked, the other because its devil was praised. Both
sides felt misunderstood. . . .
```

Although only a mere sampling of the wealth of material derived from our search, the preceding selections illustrate how useful such background information can be. A reporter who had read this material would be much better prepared to write a story on the subject.

Finally, we offer one word of caution. The material available through data bases is copyrighted, so it cannot be copied without the permission of the publication in which it originally appeared.

## MAJOR DATA-BASE VENDORS

Here is a list of major data-base vendors of interest to journalists:

BRS/After Dark
1200 Route 7
Latham, N.Y. 12110
(518) 783-1161

CompuServe
P.O. Box 20212
5000 Arlington
Centre Blvd.
Columbus, Ohio
43220
(800) 848-8199

DataTimes
818 N.W. 63rd St.
Oklahoma City,
Okla. 73116
(800) 642-2525

Dialog Information
Services
3460 Hillview Ave.,
Dept. 79
Palo Alto, Calif.
94304
(800) 334-2564

Dow Jones News
Retrieval
P.O. Box 300
Princeton, N.J. 08540
(609) 520-4000

News Net
945 Haverford Road
Bryn Mawr, Pa.,
19010
(215) 527-8030

Vu/Text Information
Services
1211 Chestnut St.
Philadelphia, Pa.
19107
(800) 258-8080

# Suggested Reading

Brand, Stewart. "The Media Lab: Inventing the Future at MIT." New York: Viking, 1987. An examination of Nicolas Negroponte's Media Lab.

# Exercises

1. Choose any story in your local newspaper, and tell how that story could have been improved with a data-base search.

2. If you were interested in determining where Apple Computers Inc. is located and the name of its president, where would you look? What other sources of information might be available?

3. Write a one-page biographical sketch of each of your two U.S. senators based on information you retrieve from your library or a data base.

# PART THREE

## Basic Stories

# 8

## Obituaries

Fortunately for The Associated Press, Mark Twain had a sense of humor about himself as well as the world around him. When the AP carried the news in 1897 that Twain had died, the author cabled the news agency from London. ''The reports of my death,'' he observed dryly, ''are greatly exaggerated.''

The Associated Press was certainly not the first nor will it be the last to report someone's death mistakenly. Many newspapers ran Ernest Hemingway's obituary in 1953 when it was thought he had died in an airplane crash in Africa. Some, like Twain and Hemingway, are amused by these mistakes. Others are not. The Mainichi Daily News, an English-language daily in Tokyo, prematurely announced the death of Emperor Hirohito in late 1988. The newspaper published an apology at the top of Page One. The general manager and editor-in-chief were dismissed.

Most people read the obituaries, or ''obits'' as they are known in the trade, with great interest. Friends, co-workers, neighbors, former classmates, creditors, casual acquaintances—all are interested. Everybody knows somebody.

And obituaries are read critically. If the deceased was an Odd Fellow, you'd better not say he was an Elk. If she belonged to the Shiloh Baptist Church, count on a phone call if you say it was Bethany Baptist. Michael Davies, then editor of the Kansas City (Mo.) Star and Times, once told of a call from an owner of a funeral home. The caller was complaining about inaccuracies in obituaries. Skeptical, Davies checked all the next day's obits. He was shocked to find an error of some kind in nearly every one. ''If we can't get obits right, how can we expect readers to believe the Page One stories?'' he asked. For many people an obituary is the only story the paper ever carries about them. You are summing up a life in a few paragraphs. That's important work.

Despite this importance many newspapers do not publish a news obituary unless the person who dies is well-known. At those papers the advertising department handles obituaries as paid notices. Many metropolitan papers have adopted this policy because to publish obits on everyone who died in the area would require a substantial amount of space. At papers where obits are handled as advertising, the skill and creativity a reporter brings to the reporting and writing of the story are missing.

Still, there are many reporters who wish their papers would handle obits as advertising matter. These are the reporters who look at obits as a tedious exercise in formula writing. Often that attitude is fostered by editors who assign the obits only to new reporters.

Other papers have a different philosophy. They give the assignment to anyone and everyone in the news room. Deborah Howell, former executive editor of the St. Paul (Minn.) Pioneer Press, says, "I constantly remind assignment editors to search for reasons to do an obit, rather than reasons not to write one." Some papers have reporters who specialize in writing this type of story. The New York Times has a reporter interview important public figures to write advance obits. The wire services and most large newspapers write obits in advance about famous people. When these people die, the newspaper or wire service can move quickly not only to report the death but also to provide complete biographical information on the individual. They understand that they are writing about life, not death.

Even if you work at a paper where most obituaries are run as paid notices, when a prominent person dies, the news department will want a story. Knowing how to report and write an obit is important to you because you may make your first impression on a city editor by the way you handle the assignment. The city editor will examine your work critically. Is the information correct? Is it complete? Did you check additional sources? Did you follow newspaper style? Did you follow newspaper policy? This chapter examines such questions.

### In this chapter you will learn:

1. How to write an obituary and what information you will need.

2. Where to get interesting material.

3. What policies newspapers may follow in printing controversial information.

# Basic
# Obituary Information
# and Style

An obituary is a news story. You should apply the same standards to crafting a lead and building the body of an obituary as you do to other stories.

## CRAFTING A LEAD

You begin by answering the same questions you would in any news story: who (Michael Kelly, 57, of 1234 West St.), what (died), where (at Regional Hospital), when (Tuesday night), why (heart attack) and how (suffered while jogging). With this information, you are ready to start the story.

The fact that Kelly died of a heart attack suffered while jogging may well be the lead, but the reporter does not know until the rest of the information essential to every obituary is gathered. You also must know:

1. Time and place of funeral services.

2. Time and burial place.

3. Visitation time (if any).

4. Survivors.

5. Date and place of birth.

6. Achievements.

7. Occupation.

8. Memberships.

Any of these items can yield the nugget that will appear in the lead. However, if none of these categories yields notable information, the obituary probably will start like this:

Michael Kelly, 57, of 1234 West St., died Tuesday night at Regional Hospital.

Another standard approach used later in the news cycle would be:

Funeral services for Michael Kelly, 57, of 1234 West St., will be at 2 p.m. Thursday at the First Baptist Church.

However, good reporters often find distinguishing characteristics of a person's life. It may be volunteer service, an unusual or important job, service in public office or even just having a name of historical significance. Whatever distinguishes a person can be the lead of the obituary. The Associated Press demonstrates the techniques in these examples:

Pauline Frederick, a veteran broadcaster who began by interviewing the wives of diplomats and rose to a distinguished career in network journalism that paved the way for other women, died Wednesday of a heart attack at age 84.

Lotte Jacobi, a photographer known for her candid portraits of such figures as Albert Einstein and Eleanor Roosevelt, died Sunday at age 93.

Madeline Ball Wright, a pioneering woman reporter, died Thursday at age 101.

Writing approaches can be as varied for obituaries as for any other news story. For instance, the following story emphasizes the personal reactions of those who knew the deceased:

Few persons knew her name, but nearly everyone knew her face.

For 43 years, Mary Jones, the city's cheerful cashier, made paying your utility bills a little easier.

Tuesday morning after she failed to report to work, two fellow employees found her dead in her home at 432 East St., where she apparently suffered a heart attack. She was 66.

By Tuesday afternoon, employees had placed a simple sign on the counter where Miss Jones had worked.

"We regret to inform you that your favorite cashier, Mary Jones, died this morning. We all miss her."

"She had a smile and a quip for everybody who came in here," said June Foster, a bookkeeper in the office.

"She even made people who were mad about their bills go away laughing."

## BUILDING THE STORY BODY

Most of the obituary information is provided by the mortuary on a standard form. When the obituary is written straight from the form, this is usually what results:

Michael Kelly, 57, of 1234 West St., died Tuesday night at Regional Hospital. Kelly collapsed while jogging and died apparently of a heart attack.

Services will be at 2 p.m. Thursday at the First Baptist Church. The Rev. Sherman Mitchell will officiate. Burial will be at Glendale Memorial Gardens in Springfield.

Friends may visit at the Fenton Funeral Chapel from 7 to 9 p.m. Wednesday.

Born Dec. 20, 1935, in Boston to Nathan and Sarah Kelly, Kelly was a member of the First Baptist Church and a U.S. Navy veteran of World War II. He had been an independent insurance agent for the last 25 years.

He married Pauline Virginia Hatfield in Boston on May 5, 1950.

Survivors include his wife; a son, Kevin of Charlotte, N.C., and a daughter, Mary, who is a student at the University of North Carolina at Chapel Hill.

Also surviving are a brother, John of Milwaukee, Wis. and a sister, Margaret Carter, Asheville, N.C.

The Kelly obituary is a dry biography, not a story of his life. There is no hint of his impact on friends, family or community. Good reporting produces stories of life, such as this one:

Jyles Robert Whittler, a World War I veteran and son of a former slave, died Monday at Truman Veterans Hospital. He was 94.

Mr. Whittler helped build the Missouri United Methodist Church in Springfield and served as its janitor for 55 years. In 1986, the church's basement social hall was christened the Jyles Whittler Fellowship Hall in his honor.

''He's a legend in Springfield and rightfully so,'' said his friend Roy Smith. ''He labored hard and lived well. He's in heaven.''

The more traditional biographical information, along with information about visitation and funeral services, appears later in the story.

Here is another example built on good reporting:

Ila Watson Portwood died Sunday at the Candlelight Care Center of complications stemming from a stroke she suffered about two weeks earlier. She was 89.

She was born on Aug. 30, 1903, in Boone County. She graduated from Howard-Payne School in Howard County and attended the University of Michigan.

She was the former owner and operator of the Gem Drug Company. She and her late husband, Carl, started as employees in 1925 and bought the business in 1952. They retired in 1971 and sold the company to Harold Earnest.

''She was a total lady,'' Earnest said. ''I've never seen her mistreat anyone. Just the sweetest lady anyone can meet.''

Mrs. Portwood volunteered from 1974 to 1980 at the Cancer Research Center's Women's Cancer Control Program and was named volunteer of the year in 1977.

"She was a people person," said Rosetta Miller, program coordinator. "Her caring personalized her commitment to the staff and patients. . . ."

Whittler and Portwood are ordinary people whose lives affected people. An obituary should celebrate that life rather than merely note the passing.

Because much of the information in any obituary comes directly from the family, it generally is accurate. But you still should check the spelling of all names, addresses and the deceased's age against the birth date. You should also never print an obituary based on information obtained by phone from someone purporting to be a funeral home representative. Too many newspapers have been the victims of hoaxes. Always call the funeral home to confirm the call.

## CHOOSING YOUR WORDS

Avoid much of the language found on mortuary forms and in obituaries prepared by morticians. The phrasing often is more fitting for a eulogy than a newspaper story.

Because of the sensitivity of the subject matter, euphemisms have crept into the vocabulary of obituary writers. "Loved ones," "passed away," "our dearly beloved brother and father," "the departed" and "remains" may be fine for eulogies, but such terms are out of place in a news story.

Watch your language, too, when you report the cause and circumstances of a death. Unless the doctor is at fault, a person usually dies not "as a result of an operation" but "following" or "after" one. Also, a person dies "unexpectedly" but not "suddenly." All deaths are sudden. Note, too, that a person dies "apparently of a heart attack" but not of "an apparent heart attack." And a person dies of injuries "suffered," not "received."

Be careful with religious terms. Catholics "celebrate" Mass; some Jews worship in "temples," others in "synagogues." An Episcopal priest who heads a parish is a "rector," not a "pastor." Followers of Mohammed are called "Moslems," although there is an organization known as the "Black Muslims."

Consult your wire service stylebook when you have a question.

The stylebook prescribes usage in another instance, too. A man is survived by his wife, not his widow, and a woman is survived by her husband, not her widower. In fact, you will need to consult the stylebook often when you are writing an obit. Do you use titles such as Mr. and Mrs.? Do you identify pallbearers? Do you say when memorial contributions are requested?

Once you have checked the spelling and corrected the language, it is time to begin gathering additional information.

# Sources of Information

## MORTUARY FORMS

For many newspapers the standard form from the mortuary mentioned previously is the primary source of information. The mortuary can be of further help if more information is needed. Does your city editor want a picture of the deceased? Call the mortuary. It usually can obtain one quickly from the family. Is there some conflicting or unclear information on the form? Call the mortuary.

But writing obituaries from the mortuary's information alone is a clerk's work. As a reporter you should go beyond the form. Sometimes, what the obituary form doesn't tell you is as important as what it does say.

For the writer of the following obit, the first clue that the death notice was unusual was the age. The deceased was 12. That alone was enough for the reporter to start asking questions. The result was an obituary that moved from the records column to the front page:

Sherrill Ann Grimes, 12, lost her lifetime struggle against a mysterious muscle ailment Wednesday night. The day she died was the first day she had ever been admitted as a hospital inpatient.

Although they knew it was coming, the end came suddenly for Sherrill's family and school friends, said her father, Lester, of 1912 Jackson St.

Just last Friday, she attended special classes at the Parkdale School. "She loved it there," Grimes said. "Like at recess, when the sixth graders would come in and read to her. She always wanted to be the center of attention."

"Bright as a silver dollar" was the way one of Sherrill's early teachers described her. In fact, no one will ever know. Sherrill couldn't talk.

"We didn't know what she knew or didn't know," her father said. Sherrill's only communication with the world around her came in the form of smiles and frowns—her symbols for yes and no.

"There were times when I'd come around the corner and kind of stick my head around and say 'boo,'" her father recalled. "She smiled. She liked that."

The care and attention Sherrill demanded makes the loss particularly hard for her family to accept, Grimes said. "I can't really put it into words. You cope with it the best you can, keep her comfortable and happy. We always took her with us."

Sherrill came down with bronchitis Friday. Complications forced her to be admitted Wednesday to Boone

County Hospital, where she died later that night.

Sherrill's fight for life was uphill all the way. It started simply enough when she was four months old. Her mother, Bonnie, noticed she "wasn't holding up her head" like her other children.

Although her ailment was never nailed down, doctors found Sherrill's muscles held only half the tissues and fibers in a normal child's body. The diagnosis: a type of cerebral palsy. The prognosis: Sherrill had little chance to live past the age of 2. Medical knowledge offered little help.

Sherrill was born in Columbia on Jan. 15, 1980. She is survived by her parents; one brother, Michael Eugene Grimes; one sister, Terrie Lynn Grimes, both of the home; and her grandparents, Gordon Grimes of Seale, Ala., and Mrs. Carrie Harris of Phoenix, Ariz.

Services will be at 3:30 p.m. today at the Memorial Funeral Chapel with the Rev. Jack Gleason conducting. Burial will follow at the Memorial Park Cemetery.

The family will receive friends at the Memorial Funeral Home until time for the service.

The reporter who wrote this obituary obviously did a great deal of research beyond what was on the mortuary form. Because the girl was not a public figure, the reporter could not consult a reference work such as Who's Who in America or a national publication. But the reporter did have access to the newspaper library and could interview the girl's family and friends. These are the sources that can help make interesting copy.

One way to irritate the source and fail to get interesting copy is to ask people who are grieving, "How do you feel?" It's a question asked often by television reporters at the scene of a disaster when people are waiting to hear about their relatives or friends. As one editor commented, "How the hell should they feel? Newspapers are not in the business of measuring the degree of grief. . . ."

## THE NEWSPAPER

Another good source is the paid funeral notices in the newspaper. One that appeared in the St. Paul (Minn.) Pioneer Press mentioned that there would be a party after the funeral. With the permission of the family, the reporter attended. His story began:

The ladies sat in a circle of lawn chairs in the neatly clipped backyard, between the pea patch on the right and the tomatoes and cucumbers on the left, sipping their gentle scotches and bourbons and beers, while the mos-

quitoes buzzed around their ears, and
the evening slowly faded without pain
into the night.

The story goes on to describe how the deceased had asked that her friends
gather to remember the good times rather than mourn her passing.

A reporter in Columbus, Ind., spotted another good story when he
realized that an obituary notice from a funeral home was for the city's "broom
man." The resulting story, which appeared on Page One, began this way:

You probably knew him.

Notice of his death Christmas day
almost seemed to fade among the others published Thursday. Ernest W.
Ferrenburg, 75, of 1210 California
died at 2:50 p.m. Wednesday at Bar-
tholomew County Hospital, the notice
said.

"Nobody knew him by his name.
He was just the old broom salesman,"
said one of his six daughters, Irene
Michaelis of Greenwood.

Workers and shoppers probably
can recall seeing Ferrenburg standing
on a street corner downtown on
Washington Street, holding a generous
stock of brooms of various shapes and
sizes. The thin white cane he carried
told passersby he had lost his sight.
That happened in a gun accident when
he was 19.

The story ends this way:

Ferrenburg never considered himself handicapped.

"I can hear birds sing. I can hear
little children," Mrs. Michaelis said
her father replied when asked whether
he would rather see than hear. "I'd
rather be blind anytime than deaf."

Hartford Courant reporter Leonard Bernstein wrote about another remarkable life after the obituary notice had already been published. It began
this way:

For as long as anyone can remember, David Lowery had two dreams: to
buy his own home and raise his own
children.

For 23 years, he worked—often two
jobs at a time—and finally, on Sept.
1, 1983, he bought a house in Hartford.

Within nine months, the second
dream was fulfilled: On June 11, Lowery became a single father, bringing
home two brothers from Massachusetts who had been seeking a
family for two years.

And then it ended.

On July 8, a cool Sunday evening,

Lowery was driving his new family home from church in Middletown when he pulled to the side of I-91 and told the boys he was sick. The 10-year-old flagged down a passing car; the 13-year-old climbed in to go for help.

Seven hours later, David Lowery, 44, was dead of a cerebral hemorrhage.

His death did not make the head-lines. No famous people spoke at the funeral.

But David Lowery—a Big Brother for 14 years in Hartford, a member of Shiloh Baptist Church in Middletown where he sang and formed a youth choir, a regular visitor to people whom others had forgotten—was loved by many, and they still mourn.

Each of the last two stories could have been run as a combination obituary and death story if someone had pursued the obituary information when it came to the city room.

## THE NEWSPAPER LIBRARY

In the newspaper library, you may find an interview with the deceased, an interesting feature story or clips indicating activities not included on the obituary form. In an interview or feature story the person may have made a statement about a philosophy of life that would be appropriate to include in the obituary. The subject also may have indicated his or her goals in life, against which later accomplishments can be measured. The names of friends and co-workers can be found in the clips as well. These persons are often the source of rich anecdotes and comments about the deceased.

A reporter assigned to do the obituary of a local man, Harold Riback, hit pay dirt in the newspaper morgue. There he found the names of two associates, Pauline Yost and Viva Spiers, from whom he was able to secure some interesting details:

When Harold Riback was a student at the university, he drove a salvage truck to St. Louis at night for his father's business. He always took his books so he could study when he stopped to rest.

"Even when he was young, he was very ambitious," said Pauline Yost, the secretary for the Boone County Democratic party, while reminiscing about Riback, 66, who died Monday morning at Boone County Hospital.

"When he agreed to a project, you didn't have just a name, you had a completely involved person," said Viva Spiers, the Sixth Ward Democratic committeewoman.

Those same files also yielded another interesting quote from Riback himself:

> Mr. Riback once said, "I've always had a strong community commitment. My dad used to say, 'Whenever you've enjoyed the fruits of the harvest, you have to save a little bit of the seed for the next year's crop.' When you benefit from the community, you have to give it back. This philosophy has had a strong bearing on my life."

That is the type of statement a newspaper obtains if it has a regular program of interviewing public figures for their obituaries in advance of their death. Because most newspapers do not, looking through the library is the next best thing.

## INTERVIEWING FAMILY AND FRIENDS

Papers treat public figures in more detail not only because they are newsworthy but also because reporters know more about them. Even though private citizens usually are less newsworthy, many good stories about them are never written because the reporter did not—or was afraid to—do the reporting. The fear is usually unfounded. William Buchanan, who has written many obituaries for the Boston Globe, said his calls are almost always welcomed: "The person I called appreciated that someone cared enough to want to know more about a loved one."

That's true even in the worst of circumstances, such as a suicide. Karen Ball, a former reporter for the Columbia Missourian, learned that lesson when she was assigned to do a story on Robert Somers, a university professor who had committed suicide. Ball didn't look forward to calling Mrs. Somers. First, Ball talked to students, Somers' colleagues and university staff members. She obtained a copy of his resume.

"By knowing a lot about him—where he'd studied, what his interests were and where he worked—I knew that I could go into an interview with a bereaved relative and at least have something to talk about," she says.

Ball approached Mrs. Somers in person and explained that her husband was respected and liked. Mrs. Somers agreed to talk. To get her to elaborate on his personality and what he was like away from school, Ball prodded her with questions about their children, where they had lived before and other family matters. She also talked to Somers' mother. Ball told her some of the positive things that students and faculty had said about her son. That helped the mother vent her sorrow and helped Ball write her story. It began:

Miko Somers sat at her kitchen table folding and unfolding her youngest daughter's bib as she talked about her husband.

"He could never do anything halfway," Mrs. Somers says. "He set such a high standard for himself. Whatever he did had to be the very best, and he pushed himself to make it that way."

Today Mrs. Somers buries her husband. Monday, Robert Somers, 40, her husband for 17 years, the father of their four daughters and an associate professor in the University's history department, took his life by driving his car head-on into a tree.

Not all calls to the family of the deceased go so smoothly. A reporter working for a Memphis paper during the Vietnam War had the assignment to call the parents of a soldier killed in action. The news of his death was reported by the Pentagon and had been distributed by the wire services. The news of the death, however, had not reached the mother. The reporter found herself in the position of unwittingly being the first to tell her; the Pentagon mistakenly had released the name before the family was notified.

The embarrassed reporter apologized. The shocked mother regained her composure enough to give the reporter the information she needed. And the newspaper angrily notified the Pentagon.

**Figure 8.1 Start at the Newspaper Library.** Good reporting for obituaries and all other news stories begins at the newspaper library, also called the morgue. Newspaper libraries generally contain clippings, photographs, and reference materials. Many libraries now have electronic data bases.

# Newspaper Policy

Newspaper policy often dictates what will—and will not—be included in an obituary. Those newspapers that do have written policies may prescribe how to handle everything from addresses to suicides.

Some newspapers, for instance, prohibit a statement such as, "In lieu of flowers, the family requests donations be made to the county humane society." This prohibition is in response to lobbying from florists.

Because of threats to the safety of property and the individuals involved, in some cities even information essential to the obituary no longer appears in the paper. Some newspapers specifically tell reporters not to include the address.

Criminals have used information taken from the obituary columns to prey on widows. Knowing the time of the funeral and the address of the deceased makes it easy to plan a break-in at the empty residence during the services. Therefore, this information also may be withheld.

Two other kinds of information newspapers may have restrictive policies on are the cause of death and potentially embarrassing information.

## CAUSE OF DEATH

If the person who dies is not a public figure and the family does not wish to divulge the cause of death, some newspapers will agree. That is questionable news judgment. The reader wants to know what caused the death. A reporter should call the mortuary, the family, the attending physician and the appropriate medical officer. Only if none of these sources will talk should the newspaper leave out the cause of death. The Des Moines (Iowa) Register and Tribune will refuse to run an obituary without the cause of death.

A death certificate must be filed for each death, but obtaining it often takes days, and some states do not make the cause of death public record. Even if the state lists the cause of death and the reporter has timely access to the death certificate, the information is often vague.

If the death is caused by cancer or a heart attack or is the result of an accident, most families do not object to including the cause in the obituary. But if the cause is cirrhosis of the liver brought on by heavy drinking, many families do object, and most papers do not insist on printing the cause.

If the deceased was a public figure or a young person, most newspapers insist on the cause of death.

If the death is the result of suicide or foul play, reporters can obtain the information from the police or the medical examiner. Some newspapers include suicide as a cause of death in the obituary, others print it in a separate news story, and still others ignore it altogether. This is one way to report it:

> Services for Gary O'Neal, 34, a local carpenters' union officer, will be at 9 a.m. Thursday in the First Baptist Church.
> Coroner Mike Pardee ruled that Mr. O'Neal died Tuesday of a self-inflicted gunshot wound.

## EMBARRASSING INFORMATION

Another newspaper policy affecting obituaries concerns embarrassing information. When the St. Louis Post-Dispatch reported in an obituary that the deceased had been disbarred and that he had been a key witness in a bribe scandal involving a well-known politician 13 years earlier, several callers complained.

Sue Ann Woods, who wrote the Reader's Advocate column, defended including that history in the obituary with this comment in her column:

> One who called to complain about the obit told me it reminded her of the quotation from Shakespeare's "Julius Caesar," about how the good a man does is often buried with him and forgotten.
>
> Yes, I said, and the first part of that quotation could be paraphrased to say that the news a man makes often lives after him.

When author W. Somerset Maugham died, The New York Times reported that he was a homosexual even though the subject generally had not been discussed in public before. When public figures die, newspapers sometimes make the first public mention of drinking problems in their obituaries. Acquired immune deficiency syndrome (AIDS) is the latest cause of death to trouble editors. The death of actor Rock Hudson brought AIDS to the attention of many who had never heard of the disease before. Many newspapers agonized over whether to say that Hudson had AIDS. As other public figures died of AIDS, it became almost routine to report the cause of death. Because society still regards AIDS negatively, some spokespeople go out of their way to give the cause of death to make certain people don't think it was AIDS. When Muppet creator Jim Hensen died, the AP originally reported that he died of a ''massive bacterial infection.'' That aroused suspicions. A few hours later, journalists were informed that Hensen died of pneumonia, and the AP used this quote from a doctor: ''Categorically, he did not have AIDS.''

The more AIDS is reported as a cause of death, the more accepted it will become. Cancer once had a similar stigma. One professor who has studied AIDS coverage suggests that obituary writers ought not to soften the language or use euphemisms when reporting AIDS-related deaths; should refer to AIDS patients, rather than victims; and should try to reach the family for information and confirmation.

The crucial factor in determinng the extent to which you should report details of an individual's private life is whether the deceased was a public or private person. A *public figure* is one who has been in the public eye. An officeholder, a participant in civic or social activities, a person who spoke out at public meetings or through the mass media, a performer, an author, a speaker—these all may be public figures.

## POLICY OPTIONS

Whether the subject is a public figure or private citizen, the decisions newspapers must make when dealing with the obituary are sensitive and complicated. These are the options your newspaper has:

1. Run an obituary that ignores any embarrassing information and, if necessary, leave out the cause of death. If circumstances surrounding the death warrant a news story, run it separate from the obituary.

2. Insist on including embarrassing details and the cause of death in the obituary.

3. Insist on including embarrassing details and the cause of death in the obituary only for public figures.

4. Put a limit on how far back in the person's life to use derogatory information such as a conviction.

5. Print everything newsworthy that is learned about a public figure but not about private figures.

6. Print everything thought newsworthy about public and private figures.

7. Decide each case as it comes up.

It is the reporter's obligation to be aware of the newspaper's policy. In the absence of a clear policy statement, the reporter should consult the city editor.

# Suggested Readings

Casella, Peter A. ''Media Mistakes Can Be Devastating.''*The Bulletin*, ASNE, Sept.–Oct. 1986, p. 40. Casella, a journalist, tells about the time the broadcast media mistakenly reported that his wife had been killed in a helicopter crash.

Hart, Jack and Johnson, Janis. ''A Clash Between the Public's Right to Know and a Family's Need for Privacy.'' *The Quill*, May 1979, pp. 19–24. An account of the backlash against a newspaper that printed a syndicated story of how the daughter of a locally prominent family had died a big-city prostitute.

Hipple, John and Wells, Richard. ''Media Can Reduce Risks in Suicide Stories.'' *E&P*, Oct. 14, 1989, p. 72. A counselor who specializes in treating suicidal young people and a journalist combine to offer suggestions on handling stories involving suicide.

''Why Do We Handle Obits in Such Deadly Fashion?'' *The Bulletin*, ASNE, July–Aug. 1982, pp. 7–13. Various editors describe their attitudes toward obituaries and tell about their experiences handling obits.

# Exercises

1. Which elements are missing from the following obituary information?

    a. John Peterson died Saturday at University Hospital. Funeral services will be at 1:30 p.m. Tuesday. Friends may call at the Black Funeral Home, 2222 Broadway Ave., from 6 to 9 p.m. Monday. The Rev. William Thomas will officiate at services in the First Baptist Church. Burial will be at City Cemetery.

    b. Richard G. Tindall, a retired U.S. Army brigadier general, died at his daughter's home in Summit, N.J. Graveside services will be at 2 p.m. July 3 at Arlington National Cemetery in Arlington, Va.

2. Write a lead for an obituary from the following information:

    Martha Sattiewhite, born July 2, 1965, to Don and Mattie Sattiewhite, in Norman, Okla. Martha was killed in a car accident June 30, 1985. Funeral services will be July 2. She was president of her high school class and of the sophomore class at the University of Oklahoma.

3. An obituary notice comes from a local funeral home. It contains the basic information, but under achievements it lists only "former member of Lion's Club." Your city editor tells you to find out more about the deceased. Whom would you call and why?

4. If George Thomas, private citizen, committed suicide while alone in his home, would you include that in his obituary? Why or why not?

5. Write a two-page advance obituary of one of the following: Ronald Reagan, Abe Rosenthal, Mother Theresa, Madonna. At the end, list your sources.

# 9

## News Releases

**R**eporters do not go out and dig up all the stories they write. Many stories come to them. They are mailed, telephoned, telexed or hand-delivered by people who want to get something in the paper. They come from people or offices with different titles: public relations departments, public information offices, community relations bureaus, press agents, press secretaries, publicity offices. The people who write them call their stories *news releases*; other journalists are more apt to call them *handouts*.

Because good publicity is so important, private individuals, corporations and government agencies spend a great deal of money to obtain it. Much of the money goes for the salaries of skilled and experienced personnel, many of whom have worked in the news business. Part of their job is to write news releases that newspapers will use.

Skilled public relations or public information practitioners know how to write news, and they apply all the principles of good newswriting in their news releases. A good news release meets the criteria of a good news story.

Nevertheless, as two of the best professionals, Carole Howard of Reader's Digest and Wilma Mathews of AT&T, tell us, news releases are never intended to take the place of reporters. News releases, they write in "On Deadline, Managing Media Relations," simply acquaint an editor with the basic facts of potential stories. Those who write them come to accept that their carefully crafted sentences will be rewritten by reporters.

As a reporter, you must recognize that news releases are both a help and hindrance to a newspaper. They help because without them, newspapers would need many more reporters. They are a hindrance because they sometimes contain incomplete or even incorrect information. Most of the time, in one way or another, they are self-serving and, unlike objective journalism, start with a point of a view.

Nevertheless, wise editors do not discard news releases without reading them. These editors often give them to reporters, often the newest ones, to check out for possible rewrite.

When your editor hands you a news release, you are expected to know what to do with it. You must be able to recognize the news in the release, applying all that you have learned about news values. The release may lead you to a good story. Your resourcefulness may improve your chances of being assigned to bigger things.

**In this chapter you will learn:**

1. What types of news releases there are.

2. How to handle the news release.

# Types of News Releases

After you have read a number of news releases, you will notice that generally they fall into three categories:

1. Announcements of coming events or of personnel matters—hiring, promoting, retiring and the like.

2. Information regarding a cause.

3. Information that is meant to build someone's or some organization's image.

Recognizing the types and purposes of news releases (and that some are hybrids and serve more than one purpose) will help you know how to rewrite them.

## ANNOUNCEMENTS

Organizations use the newspaper to tell their members and the public about coming events. For example:

The Camera Club will have a special meeting at Wyatt's Cafeteria at 7 p.m. on Wednesday, March 22. Marvin Miller will present a slide program on "Yellowstone in Winter." All interested persons are invited to attend.

Although the release promotes the Camera Club, it also serves as a public-service announcement. Newspapers that print such announcements are serving their readers. Here is another example:

The first reception of the new season of the Springfield Art League will be on Sunday, Sept. 11, 3 to 5 p.m. in the Fine Arts Building.

Included in the exhibition will be paintings, serigraphs, sculpture, batiks, weaving, pottery, jewelry, all created by Art League members, who throughout the summer have been preparing works for this opening exhibit of the season.

The event also will feature local member-artists' State Fair entries, thus giving all who could not get to the fair the opportunity to see these works.

The exhibition continues to Friday, Sept. 16. All gallery events and exhibitions are free.

Other news release announcements concern appointments, promotions, hiring and retiring. The announcement of an appointment may read like this:

James McAlester, internationally known rural sociologist at Mannheim University, has been appointed to the board of directors of Bread for the World, according to James Coburn, executive director of the humanitarian organization.

McAlester attended his first board meeting Jan. 22 in New York City. He has been on the university faculty since 1985. Prior to that, he served as the Ford Foundation representative in India for 17 years.

The 19,000-member Bread for the World organization is a "broad-based interdenominational movement of Christian citizens who advocate government policies that address the basic causes of hunger in the world," says Coburn.

The occasion for this release is the appointment of McAlester. But the release also describes the purpose of the Bread for the World organization. By educating readers regarding the organization's purpose, the writer hoped to promote its cause.

Companies often send releases when an employee has been promoted. For example:

James B. Withers Jr. was named senior vice president in charge of sales of the J.B. Withers Company, it was announced Tuesday.

Withers, who has been with the company in the sales division for two years, will head a sales force of 23 persons.

''We are sure Jim can do the job,'' James B. Withers Sr., company president, said. ''He brings youth, intelligence and enthusiasm to the job. We're pleased he has decided to stay with the company.''

Founded in 1936, the J.B. Withers Company is the country's second-largest manufacturer of dog and cat collars.

A release like this one is an attempt by the company to get its name before the public and to create employee good will. Written in the form of an announcement, it is an attempt at free publicity.

## CAUSE-PROMOTING RELEASES

The second category of news releases seeks to further a cause. Some of these releases come from worthwhile causes in need of funds or of volunteers. For example, the letter reprinted here is from a county chairman of the American Heart Association to the editor of a newspaper. It is not written in the form of a release, but its effect is meant to be the same:

The alumnae and collegiate members of the Alpha Phi Sorority have just completed their annual Alpha Phi ''Helping Hearts'' lollipop sale. This year Valerie Knight, project chairwoman, led sorority members to achieve record-breaking sales. The lollipop sale is a national project of the Alpha Phi Sorority.

Sunday, March 5, Valerie Knight presented a check for $1,800 to the American Heart Association, Shelby County Unit. The contribution was presented during a reception at the Alpha Phi house. This contribution is an important part of the annual fund-raising campaign of the American Heart Association.

I wish to extend special thanks to the members of Alpha Phi and in particular to Valerie Knight for this outstanding project. In addition, I wish to thank the many merchants who participated in the project by selling lollipops in their businesses.

Heads of organizations such as this attempt to alert the public to their messages in any way they can. Any release, notice or letter they can get printed without paying for it leaves money for the cause that they represent. Sometimes the cause is a local private college:

Libbi Given, director of the Adelphos College community campaign, has named 17 division chairpersons for the fund drive that will begin Sept. 21.

The division heads met Sept. 9 to organize for the campaign, which has a $100,000 goal, an increase of $22,000 over last year's local gift support.

The college has developed a four-year gift support plan to raise $8.5 million.

Included in the amount is $4.5 million in Annual Fund gifts to provide assistance with the operating expenses of the college, as it plans almost to double its endowment base and renovate existing on- and off-campus facilities.

Again, the cause is a good one. The college needs money, and to raise money it must publicize its fund drive.

## IMAGE-BUILDING RELEASES

Another kind of news release serves to build up someone's or some organization's image. Politicians seek to be elected or to be re-elected. They desire as much *free* publicity as they can get. For example:

James M. Merlin, honorary chairman of the board and director of Merlin Corporation, has been named honorary chairman of the Finance Committee, which will seek statewide financial support for the campaign to elect William C. Candace as U.S. senator from Maine.

Merlin, a nationally recognized civic leader and philanthropist, termed the election of Candace ''one of the most important and far-reaching decisions the voters of Maine will ever make. The nation's financial crisis can only be solved through the kind of economic leadership Candace has demonstrated.''

The appointment of Merlin as honorary chairman serves only to promote the image of the senator. The quote is self-serving.

Organizations and government agencies at all levels often try to build their public image. Many of them have local mayors proclaim a day or a week of recognition, as in the following:

Mayor James Lampert has proclaimed Saturday, May 6, as Fire Service Recognition Day. The Springfield Fire Department in conjunction with the University Fire Service Training Division is sponsoring a demonstration of fire apparatus and equipment at the Springfield Fire Training Center. The displays are from 10 a.m. to 5 p.m. at 700 Bear Blvd. All citizens are urged to attend the display or visit their neighborhood fire station on May 6.

Our PRODUCT is your SAFETY.

If an editor hands you a release such as this, he or she probably has decided that it is worth using in some form. The rest is up to you.

# Handling the News Release

Regardless of the type of news release, be sure to read the information that appears on the top. Here is an example:

NEWS FROM SUNSET
Contact: Sheila Gretchen
Office of Public Information
Sunset Community College
Springfield
Phone (315) 555-2231 Ext. 695

Betty S. Snead
Director of Public Information

IMMEDIATE RELEASE
November 8, 1991

Most news releases begin with the following information:

1. The place or institution involved.

2. The address and phone number.

3. The name of the director of information.

4. The release date, or the date on which the announcement should be printed, which is often "immediate."

5. The date on which the release was sent.

6. The name of the contact person from whom you may secure further information.

Although all of that information may be useful to you, many news releases leave unanswered questions. You probably will want to contact people other than the director of information or even the contact person if you have serious doubts about some of the data given. But for routine accuracy checks, the persons listed on the release can do the job. They may lead you to other helpful sources, too. Sometimes you may have sources of your own. And sometimes you may uncover the real story only from people who are neither connected to nor recommended by the director of information.

You may have to consult your editor regarding the release date. As a courtesy most newspapers honor release dates. However, sometimes a morning or evening paper will publish the release early because waiting until the following day would render the information useless. Also, once a release is public knowledge, editors feel justified in publishing whatever information it contains, even prior to the suggested release date. A release date is broken for all when it is broken by one.

## REWRITING THE ANNOUNCEMENT RELEASE

Sometimes directors of information want nothing more than a listing on the record or calendar page of a newspaper. Here is an example:

> FOR THE CALENDAR
> Elisabeth Bertke, quiltmaker and designer from Salem, Massachusetts, will discuss her work at 7:00 o'clock P.M. Tues., February 7, in Charters Auditorium, Hampton College. Two quilts designed and constructed by Bertke are included in the exhibit ''The New American Quilt,'' currently on display at the Smith Art Gallery.
> ''This is an exciting display,'' Betty Martin, president of the Smith Art Gallery board of directors, said. ''You simply can't afford to miss it.''

This simple release may go directly to the copy desk or to a special calendar editor. If given to you, rewrite it. Some newspapers insist that you rewrite every news release if for no other reason than to avoid the embarrassment of running the same story as a competing newspaper. For some it is a matter of integrity and professionalism.

First note all the violations of AP style in the preceding example:

- ''Massachusetts'' should be abbreviated *Mass.*
- ''7:00 o'clock P.M. should be *7 p.m.*
- Tues. should be spelled out *Tuesday.*
- ''February'' should be abbreviated *Feb.*
- A hyphen should be inserted in *quilt-maker.*

Avoid relying on the copy desk to do your work if the rewrite is given to you.
You should check other points as well. Determine the spelling of Bertke's name, and see if there is an apostrophe in Charters Auditorium. The Smith Art Gallery may or may not be on the Hampton campus. Ask how long the exhibit will be at the gallery. Are quilts made by local people included in the

exhibit? Perhaps your questions will lead to a feature story on local quilt-making.

In your rewrite, you will drop the quotation of Betty Martin. But you may insert better, less self-serving and less promotional quotes.

Here is another example:

> Mr. Richard G. Henderson has been selected as the Outstanding Biology Teacher of Nevada of the year by the National Association of Biology Teachers. He was previously selected as Nevada Science Educator of the year.
>
> As an outstanding representative of good high-school biology teaching Henderson will receive a certificate and a series 50 binocular microscope with an engraved citation. Henderson has been teaching at Hickman High School since 1980.

The story is far from earthshaking, but the honor is statewide. On large newspapers the release may not get much play. A small community newspaper, however, will use it and perhaps enlarge upon it.

A first reading of the release tells you it is wordy and that it leaves many questions unanswered. Henderson may be an interesting fellow, but the release tells us little about him. You should approach this release in the same way you approach any news release: Finish the reporting, and then rewrite it. News style demands a new lead to the release:

> A Hickman High School science teacher has been named Outstanding Biology Teacher of the year by the National Association of Biology Teachers.
>
> Richard G. Henderson, a Hickman teacher since 1980, will receive a certificate and a series 50 binocular microscope with an engraved citation.
>
> Previously selected as Nevada Science Educator of the year, Henderson . . .

Here the story runs out of information. You need to ask the following questions:

- Age?
- Degrees from where?
- Local address?
- Spouse, family?
- Annual award? One teacher selected from each state?
- Any previous Hickman winners? Or from local high schools?
- Year he received Nevada Science Educator award?

- Nominated for the award by whom?
- Date and place of bestowal? Public ceremony?
- Value of series 50 binocular microscope?

Then call Henderson and find out how he feels about the award. Talk to the principal, to fellow teachers and to some of Henderson's students. Good quotations will spice up your story.

## REWRITING THE CAUSE RELEASE

Newspapers generally cooperate with causes that are community-oriented. News releases like the following get attention:

A free tax clinic for low-income persons and senior citizens will be held on Feb. 9 and 10 in Springfield.

The clinic is sponsored by the Central State Counties' Human Development Corporation in cooperation with the Mannheim University School of Accountancy.

Senior and graduate accounting students under the direct supervision of accounting faculty members will work with each taxpayer to help that taxpayer complete accurately his or her tax return.

The Human Development Corporation encourages persons especially to use the clinic who may be eligible for senior citizens' credits or other credits.

This is the fifth year the clinic has operated in Shelby County. Last year more than 275 persons in the eight counties served were assisted.

For information regarding location of the clinics and to make an appointment, contact the Shelby County Human Development Corporation, 600 E. Broadway, Room 103, Springfield, 555-8376.

Again, you need more information. To begin with, you need to know more about the Human Development Corporation. A background paragraph on its origins, where it gets its money and its other areas of concern will put the story into context.

The release is unclear about who is eligible. What must your income be? How old must you be? Also, you must find out the exact locations of the clinics.

Once you have all your questions answered, dig for some human interest. Talk to a participating faculty member and to students who have helped before and will help again. Then talk to some people who have been helped in the past and to some who will come for help. Obviously, you must talk to those in charge of the joint effort.

Because efforts like these are in the public interest, newspapers will give them space. They will be more critical with releases that are merely self-serving.

## REWRITING THE IMAGE-BUILDING RELEASE

The following is a typical release from a politician:

> Sen. John C. Smith said today that nearly $400,000 in grants have been given final approval by two departments of the federal government for interlocking improvements in Springfield and Shelby County.
>
> Smith said, ''This is something I have been working for this past year. It is a chance to show that federal agencies are interested in communities. It also demonstrates that two agencies can work together to produce a coordinated, workable solution to improve a blighted area in Springfield.''
>
> The grants, Smith said, come from the Federal Bureau of Outdoor Recreation -- $247,000 for purchasing Baltimore and Ohio railroad rights of way and developing a strip park, and the Department of Housing and Urban Development -- $150,000 for planning the Flat Branch area. The second grant also stipulates that part of the money be used to coordinate the two projects, the B&O strip park and the Flat Branch redevelopment.
>
> ''I think residents of Springfield and Shelby County will have a chance to help out in the planning of these two facilities. I hope this means the entire community will express opinions and come to a conclusion that will see these projects become a reality in the next two years.''

The first four words of the release indicate who is being served by the release. A Springfield reporter might write the lead this way to serve the reader:

> Springfield and Shelby County will receive nearly $400,000 in federal grants to fund the B&O strip park and the Flat Branch redevelopment project, Sen. John C. Smith said today.

The second paragraph of the release is a long and newsless quote from the senator. Probably he did not say those words at all; they were written by his press agent. You should eliminate them, or if you want a quote from the senator, call him and talk to him yourself.

The second paragraph of the story should indicate the source of the funding:

> The grants come from two federal agencies. The Federal Bureau of Outdoor Recreation granted $247,000 for purchasing the Baltimore & Ohio Railroad rights of way and for developing a strip park, and the Department of Housing and Urban Development granted $150,000 for planning the Flat Branch area. The second grant also stipulates that part of the money be used to coordinate the two projects.

Smith's last quote could be handled this way:

> Smith said he hoped Springfield and Shelby County residents will have a chance to help plan the two facilities. "I hope this means the entire community will express opinions and come to a conclusion that will see these projects become a reality in the next two years."

Like many news releases of this kind, this announcement would trigger other news stories in the local papers. This story would call for local reactions from city and county officials and from local residents. The editor might assign several stories on the matter.

## Rewriting an Organization's Image-Building Release

Releases from organizations can also be self-serving—and sometimes misleading. Suppose you were given this news release to rewrite:

> Springfield -- Dogcatchers in Springfield make a higher beginning salary than Springfield teachers, as discovered in a recent survey by the Springfield Community Teachers Association. According to their research, a beginning teacher in the Springfield public school system makes $16,300 while a dogcatcher starts at $16,830 or $530 more than a beginning teacher. "This is a shameful situation for an educational community," said Tom Monnin, Springfield SCTA Salary Committee chairman.
>
> The statistics gathered by the Springfield SCTA Salary Committee indicate that police with a bachelor's degree make $20,130, while a beginning teacher with a bacherlor's degree makes $16,300. This is a $3,830 gap in beginning salaries for public employees with comparable education. Following is a com-

parison of beginning salaries of some Springfield city employees and of public school teachers for the school year:

| Occupation | Beginning Salary |
| --- | --- |
| Police with B.S. | $20,130 |
| Firefighter with B.S. | 19,988 |
| Meter Reader | 16,830 |
| Animal Control Officer | 16,830 |
| Bus Operator | 16,387 |
| Teacher with B.S. | 16,300 |

"Springfield teachers do not think city employees are overpaid but that teachers are underpaid," Monnin said.

Even though teachers work under a 9¼-month contract, the workweek is not 40 hours. When the hours for preparing and grading, attending sports events, musical concerts, dances, other after-school activities, and PTA meetings are considered, a teacher's workweek is much longer than 40 hours. Summer break is used by many teachers for advanced preparation at the university, at their own expense.

The Springfield SCTA Salary Committee will present their salary proposal at the next meeting of the Springfield Board of Education.

The Springfield SCTA represents approximately 523 members in the public school system.

For additional information contact Tom Monnin, Springfield SCTA Salary Committee Chairman, at 555-6794 (Central High School) or 555-2975 (home).

Your first task is to read the release carefully. The lead cleverly suggests that dogcatchers make as much money as teachers do, although it speaks only of "beginning" salaries. The more you read the release, the more uncomfortable you should feel with it. No one can blame teachers for wanting more money, but there are other compensations to consider. What about working conditions? Teachers in Springfield's schools hardly have to put their lives on the line the way police officers and firefighters do. Most people do not want to spend their lives chasing stray dogs.

The fact that teachers work for a little more than nine months a year is down in the fourth paragraph. The release fails to mention a two-week break over Christmas and a week off in the spring semester. Most dogcatchers get two weeks off all year.

Is the release trying to suggest that because teachers actually spend more than 40 hours a week working, they should not have to work more than 9¼ months? Not all teachers spend all their lives going to summer school. You probably know several who have summer jobs.

Before you turn in a rewrite of the release, you have a lot of checking to do.

One reporter began by calling Animal Control. He told Tom Merell, the officer who answered his call, that he had a news release saying that animal control officers start with higher salaries than Springfield's schoolteachers.

"Could be," Merell replied. "But I sure wish I got summers off like those teachers. I got nothing against teachers. But most of them make more money than I'll ever make."

The reporter asked him to explain.

"Look," Merell said, "the most money any animal control officer can make is $18,757, and it will take him quite a few years to make that. I know some teachers who are making more than $22,000. Besides, students don't bite many teachers."

The reporter knew he was on to something. Comparing beginning salaries was one thing. But how much could a person eventually earn in a position?

The reporter then called the city of Springfield's office of personnel. "Yes," the director of personnel said, "$20,130 is the beginning salary for a police officer with a B.S. degree."

The reporter then asked whether anyone could get hired at that salary if he or she had a B.S. degree.

"Most people wouldn't stand a chance of being hired," he said. "We have more than 100 applicants for every position, so we can be quite choosy. Unless a person has had some real experience as a police officer, I don't think he would make it."

Further questioning revealed that a top salary for a police officer was $23,125 after 4½ years of service. When asked about the $19,988 beginning salary of a firefighter, the personnel officer replied:

"You wouldn't begin at that salary. Everyone is hired at $17,944 for a trial period of at least six months. If you work out OK, you might jump up to $19,988. Again, there are a lot of other considerations besides the college degree."

Further checking revealed that the news release did indeed contain inaccurate information about the beginning salaries of firefighters. The reporter then called a high school teacher. He asked her if she had to put in more than 40 hours a week at her job.

"Oh, yes," she said. "I teach a section of English composition, and I have a lot of papers to grade. I used to spend a lot of evenings preparing for classes, but once you've taught a course, it gets easier. And then I have to go to all those football games and basketball games."

The reporter then found out that she was indeed required to attend, but only because she was in charge of the cheerleaders. When he expressed sympathy, the teacher replied, "No, I really don't mind. After all, I get $1,200 a year extra for being in charge of the cheerleaders."

The reporter then learned from someone at the Springfield School Board personnel office that quite a few teachers received compensation for after-school activities—coaching, directing plays, directing musical activities, chaperoning dances. Teachers sponsoring class and club activities could earn from $500 to $1,200; a sponsor of the pep squad could earn up to $1,200. The top teacher's salary without any of these extras was $23,272.

Now the reporter was ready to call Tom Monnin, the man whose name was on the release for additional information. He asked if it was fair to compare a beginning teacher's salary with a beginning dogcatcher's salary when the top pay for a dogcatcher was $18,757 and the top teacher's salary was $23,272. Monnin explained that it took 16 years for a teacher with a master's degree plus 60 hours to reach that top salary. A teacher with a bachelor's degree could make $19,620 after 11 years of teaching. When the reporter asked about the summer off and other vacations, Monnin replied, "I figure I work a 60-hour week. That means I work 51¾, 40-hour weeks a year."

Monnin acknowledged that many teachers got paid extra for extracurricular activities. "But not all of them do," he said. "And there are many activities we do feel the responsibility to attend."

When asked about the argument that teachers do not have to put their lives on the line the way police and fire officials and even dogcatchers do, Monnin replied:

"It's debatable who has to put their lives on the line. We're not as bad off as some schools, but we often have to restrain students physically."

Only now was the reporter ready to write the story. Here's what he wrote:

The Springfield Community Teachers Association said Tuesday that beginning dogcatchers earn more than beginning teachers.

What the teachers did not say was that a teacher eventually can earn nearly $5,000 more a year than a dogcatcher can earn.

The SCTA statement was included with a survey that lists starting teachers' salaries at $16,300 and a Springfield dogcatcher's starting salary at $16,830. Other figures listed as beginning salaries are: police with a bachelor's degree, $20,130; firefighters with a bachelor's degree, $19,988; meter reader, $16,830; bus operator, $16,387.

"This is a shameful situation for an educational community," said Tom Monnin, the Springfield SCTA Salary Committee chairman. "Springfield teachers do not think city employees are overpaid but that teachers are underpaid."

The association officers said that even though teachers work under a 9¼-month contract, extracurricular activities extend the workweek beyond 40 hours. Summer break, they said, is used for advanced study at the teachers' own expense.

"I figure I work a 60-hour week," Monnin said in an interview. "That means I work 51¼, 40-hour weeks a year."

Some extracurricular activities, such as coaching, directing plays and supervising cheerleaders, earn extra compensation.

Teachers are not compelled to attend after-school functions, but "we do feel the responsibility to attend," Monnin said.

Teachers also feel compelled to continue their education. Top pay for a teacher with only a bachelor's degree is $19,620 after 11 years of teaching. A teacher with a master's degree plus 60 hours of classes can earn $23,272 after 16 years of teaching.

A police officer with a bachelor's degree can reach a top salary of $23,125 after 4½ years of police work. But a person with a bachelor's degree and no police work experience is not likely to be hired, said Phil James, the Springfield director of personnel. James also said all firefighters are hired at $17,944. If a person has a bachelor's degree and stays on, he or she could make $19,988 after a six-month trial period.

Top pay for a dogcatcher is $18,757. "I sure wish I got summers off like those teachers," Tom Merell, an animal control officer, said. "I got nothing against teachers. But most of them make more money than I'll ever make. . . . Besides, students don't bite many teachers."

The SCTA Salary Committee will present its salary proposal at the next meeting of the Springfield Board of Education.

The reporter did with this news release what should be done with many of them. He was not satisfied with the way it was written, nor with the information it contained. By asking some important questions, he was able to put together an informative and more accurate story. Without saying that the news release was dishonest or misleading, the reporter corrected or clarified some of the information contained in it. The plight of the teacher is told clearly and objectively, but it is placed in a much better perspective than was found in the news release.

Like many news releases, this one was the basis for a story the newspaper otherwise would not have had. That is why editors pay attention to them and why reporters look for the real story. Remember:

1. Read the information that appears on the top of the release form.

2. Check the news style. Ask questions about missing information. Verify any spellings or information you have doubts about.

3. Take for granted you are to do a rewrite. Fill in missing information. Tighten the copy.

4. Watch for self-serving quotations and information. Look for news. Write the news.

5. Look for other news stories—local angles, reactions and the like—triggered by the release.

# Suggested Readings

Cutlip, Scott M., Center, Allen H. and Broom, Glen M. ''Effective Public Relations,'' Sixth Edition. Englewood Cliffs, N.J.: Prentice-Hall, 1985. This has become the standard college text on the subject. It treats all aspects of public relations.

Howard, Carole and Mathews, Wilma. ''On Deadline, Managing Media Relations.'' Prospect Heights, Ill.: Waveland Press, 1988. A practical book on how organizations should deal with the news media.

Reeves, Richard. ''Our National Flacks.'' *Esquire*, Dec. 1977, pp. 68, 70. Reeves talked with 16 reporters and editors holding public relations jobs with the Carter administration, who said that press coverage was accurate generally, but that the media should work harder to ferret out governmental news.

# Exercises

1. Read each of the following news releases. First, correct all departures from Associated Press style rules. Second, indicate the type of news release it is. Third, list questions you would have if you were to rewrite it, including the facts you would check and the sources you would turn to for the answers.

   **a.** NEWS RELEASE

   The 1991 Sheep Knowledge awards will be made on the basis of a comprehensive test over knowledge in the book, Raising Sheep the Modern Way, by Paula Simmons. Information concerning availability of this book may be obtained from libraries, bookstores, or university agriculture departments.

   The test will be developed, administered, and scored by nationally known livestock specialists. The contest is being announced early to give students adequate time for preparation. The test will be given in Springfield at 8:00 P.M. on September 5. The contest will be open to any person who is not yet eighteen, on that day.

   The four top winners will receive trophies and divide ten commercial ewes as follows: First - 4 ewes, Second - 3 ewes, Third - 2 ewes, Fourth - 1 ewe.

**b.** NEWS RELEASE

Plaza Frontenac will be filled with floral displays from 10:00 A.M. to 9:00 P.M. on Friday October 31 and 10:00 A.M. to 4:00 P.M. on Saturday November 1 as the East Central District of the Federated Garden Clubs of America, Inc. presents ''Challenge'', a flower show of artistic flower arrangements and outstanding horticultural specimens on both levels of the plaza.

Hundreds of entries, including table settings, arrangements featuring fresh flowers, evergreens and dried plants will offer decorating ideas for special occasions. Educational exhibits on state birds, the propagation and growing of African violets, and a patio garden of perennials designed by Doug and Cindy Gilberg of Gilberg Perennial Farms.

General co-chairmen for the event are Wilma Stortz and Kay Schaefer. In 1989 the group staged a major flower show at Plaza Frontenac and won a national award.

The show is free and open to the public. Plaza Frontenac is located on the corner of South Main and Hamilton. Shopping hours are 10:00 A.M. to 9:00 P.M. Monday through Friday.

**c.** NEWS RELEASE

The teaching faculty, administration and staff of The South Shore Country Day School formally began the school year Friday, August 30, with an all day workshop on curriculum planning.

This year, the School will be involved in a year long task of self evaluation. All aspects of the School's curriculum and student life will be considered and a new five year, long range plan for the curriculum will be written. The School's last major plan was constructed in 1988.

The evaluation process is designed to keep curriculum consistent with the School's educational philosophy and statement of mission. It will identify problems, strengths, and opportunities for expansion. At various stages of the process, all constituencies of the School will have an opportunity to express concerns and opinions. By the end of the school year, a new plan will be ready for integration and implementation by the School's administration.

William R. Bring, Chairman of the School's Board of Trustees, spoke to the faculty about the upcoming project and the need to change. ''We will attempt to make the current school better; we will not be creating a new school,'' he said.

Thomas B. Lang, the School's headmaster, emphasized the importance of total faculty participation in the formulation and execution of the mission statement. ''We're all in this together,'' Lang said. ''Curriculum is the sum of all the parts. No one teaches in a vacuum.''

Among topics discussed at the workshop were: the importance of academic excellence; student social service; a need for diversity within the student body; the importance of educating the whole child; providing increased opportunity for students to participate in a variety of academic and non-academic projects; and the ethical considerations in the School.

**2.** Assume you are a reporter for the Springfield paper. Your instructor will be your news source for any questions you have. Rewrite each of the following releases:

**a.** NEWS RELEASE

Nearly 11,000 seat belt violation warnings were issued to motorists by the State Highway Patrol during the first month the new seat belt law was in effect.

Colonel Howard J. Hoffman, Superintendent of the State Highway Patrol, reported today that 10,808 warnings were issued to motorists in passenger vehicles for not wearing their seat belts as required by State law.

Colonel Hoffman also noted that during this same reporting period, 50 persons were killed in traffic accidents investigated by the Highway Patrol. Only two of the persons killed in these mishaps were found to be wearing seat belts.

"The value of wearing a seat belt cannot be overemphasized," Hoffman said. "We don't know how many of these investigated traffic deaths could have been avoided by the use of seat belts. It is known, however, that seat belts have saved lives and prevented serious injuries to others. We will continue to vigorously enforce the State seat belt law and hopefully more and more motorists will make it a habit to buckle their seat belts."

**b.** NEWS RELEASE

The Better Business Bureau serving the tri-state area has launched a fundraising drive to finance the installation of a 24-hour computerized telephone service called Tel-Tips.

James C. Schmitt, President, said Tel-Tips is a unique consumer information and education system designed to give quick useful information about specific goods and services. Consumers would be provided with a number to call and the system will put the caller in contact with a selected pre-recorded message.

A goal of $20,000 has been established to finance installation of Tel-Tips and the physical expansion of the BBB's office.

"Despite efficient telephone communications and computer system, we expect to lose nearly 24,000 calls this year," said Schmitt. "Our operators are trained to limit time given to each caller to avoid losing callers, while at the same time attempting to provide complete information."

The Bureau is unable to respond to inquiries before and after business hours and on weekends, times many customers need BBB services.

Tel-Tips is a computerized information center that allows 114 consumer tip messages to be made instantly available to callers. This system answers incoming calls with a pre-recorded message and instructs the caller to dial the number of the message he or she wants to hear. This unit operates automatically with the use of a touch-tone telephone, 12 hours a day. A rotary dial telephone may be used during regular business hours with the assistance of an operator.

**c.** NEWS RELEASE

"Chest Pains," a film in the HEALTHSCOPE series produced by the American College of Physicians, will be shown from 7-8:30 p.m., Wednesday, Oct. 22, at St. Mary's Health Center. Springfield internist, Dr. Harold Kanagawa, will host a question-and-answer period following the film.

Although most people assume that chest pains signify a heart attack, the public is less aware that other conditions -- hiatal hernia, ulcers, viral infections of the heart's membranes -- can also cause pains that require prompt diagnosis and appropriate medical treatment. Designed to help increase awareness of these symptoms and their possible significance, ''Chest Pains'' features an internist and actual patients as they work together to resolve underlying medical problems.

Through a human-interest style of presentation, each 25-minute documentary encourages people to take an increased responsibility for their own well-being by establishing healthy habits and assuming a more active role in disease prevention.

The HEALTHSCOPE series is produced under an educational grant from The Upjohn Company of Kalamazoo, Mich. Other films in the series cover ''Aches, Pains and Arthritis,'' ''Diabetes,'' and ''Abdominal Discomfort.''

Dr. Kanagawa, a specialist in internal medicine, is one of 50,000 members of the American College of Physicians. Founded in 1915, the College is the largest medical specialty society in the United States. It represents doctors of internal medicine, related non-surgical specialists, and physicians-in-training.

To register or for more information, contact the Women's Life Center.

3. Your professor will give you a local news release. Using local sources and resources, report and rewrite the story.

# 10

## Speeches, News Conferences and Meetings

$\mathbf{Y}$ou can be quite sure that in your first year or so of general-assignment reporting you will be assigned to cover many speeches, news conferences and meetings. They are sometimes routine, sometimes of great importance. Communities often elect and re-elect their leaders on the basis of their performance at these events. Communities are rallied to causes and nations to wars.

For example, before President Lyndon B. Johnson's televised address on the Gulf of Tonkin incident in 1964, a Harris Survey showed that less than half of the electorate approved of the president's Vietnam policy. After his address, a second poll indicated that 70 percent approved. Before President Richard M. Nixon addressed the nation to attempt to justify the invasion of Cambodia in 1970, a Harris Survey showed that only 7 percent of the public supported the decision. Following Nixon's television address, more than 50 percent approved of the president's action.

Some argue that it was President Kennedy's display of intelligence and wit at news conferences that got him elected and earned him respect as president. President Nixon, however, had little flair for give and take, and less love for reporters. Consequently, his performance at news conferences added little to his popularity. President Ronald Reagan felt at home in front of cameras, and although he disliked news conferences, his televised speeches helped boost his image tremendously.

Because speeches, news conferences, and meetings are similar, all three are examined in this chapter. But the distinguishing characteristics of these three forms should be kept in mind as well.

A *speech* is a public talk. Someone stands and speaks to an audience in person or on radio or television. Regardless of the medium, the nature of a speech is the same: It is a one-way communication; the speaker speaks, and the audience listens.

Speakers usually are invited and sometimes paid to address an audience. That is not the case with those who hold a *news conference*. People "call" a news conference. They do not send invitations to the general public, but they do alert members of the various news media. The media respond because of the importance of the person calling the news conference and because that person may have something newsworthy to say. The person holding the news conference often begins with an opening statement and then usually accepts questions from reporters. A news conference is meant to be a two-way communication.

Unlike speeches and news conferences, *meetings* are not held with an audience in mind, even though an audience may be present and allowed to participate. A meeting is primarily for communication among the members of a group or organization, whether a local parent-teacher association or the Congress of the United States. If reporters are permitted to witness a meeting, they are there to report to the public what is of interest and importance. This task of the news media is especially important if the meeting is of a governmental body that deals with the public's money collected through taxes.

You can be sure that you will spend a great deal of your time as a reporter covering speeches, news conferences and meetings. For that reason you will want to learn all you can about covering them well.

### In this chapter you will learn:

**1.** How to prepare to cover speeches, news conferences and meetings.

**2.** What is involved in covering these events.

**3.** How to structure and write stories about them.

# Preparation

The professional reporter knows that preparation makes covering a story much easier. In all cases reporters should do their homework. You prepare for the speech, news conference or meeting story in much the same way. Let's begin with a speech story.

# PREPARING FOR THE SPEECH STORY

Not every speech you are assigned to cover will demand a great deal of research. Many speakers and speeches will be dry and routine. The person giving it will be someone you know or someone you have covered before. At other times you may be given an assignment on short notice and may be forced to find background information after you have heard the speech. But never take the speaker or the topic for granted. A failure to get enough background on the speaker and on the speech nearly guarantees failure at writing a comprehensive speech story.

When one reporter was assigned to cover a speech by Kenneth Clark, she presumed that this was the Kenneth Clark who had done so much on culture and civilization on public television. When she called the information service at the public library, she discovered two famous Kenneth Clarks. One, Kenneth Mackenzie Clark, was indeed an expert on civilization and the arts. The other, Kenneth Bancroft Clark, was a psychiatrist and author, most famous for writing ''Dark Ghetto,'' the study of the effects of the ghetto on Harlem children. It was the psychiatrist who was giving a speech.

The first step in your research is to get the right person. Middle initials are important; sometimes they are not enough. Sometimes checking the address is not enough. One reporter wrote about the wrong person because he did not know that a father and son shared the same name at the same address.

Before doing research on the speaker, contact the group sponsoring the speech and ask for the topic. You might find you need some reading to prepare you to understand the subject better. If you are lucky, you may get a copy of the speech ahead of time. Also check your newspaper library to see what your paper has done on the speaker. If you have access to a data bank, use it. If the assignment calls for it, visit your local library and check the references noted on pages 149–150 in Chapter 7.

If the speech is important enough, you might want to contact the speaker ahead of time for a brief interview. If he or she is from out of town, you might plan for a meeting at the airport. You might also arrange ahead of time to interview the speaker after the speech. You may have some questions and some points to clarify.

Again, not every speech will demand this much effort. But even the routine speech assignment needs preparation. It may seem obvious, for instance, that the reason Gene Martin, the director of the local library, is addressing the state Writer's Guild is to tell members how to use the library to write better stories. Not so. Gene Martin also is a successful ''true confessions'' writer. He has been published dozens of times in such magazines as True Confessions, True Romance and others. He may be addressing the guild on how he does it.

Sooner or later you may be called on to cover speeches of major political candidates, perhaps even of the president of the United States. For this task, too, you need background—lots of it. It demands that you read the news and that you know what is going on. You *must* keep up with current events.

## PREPARING FOR THE NEWS CONFERENCE STORY

Preparing for a news conference is like preparing for speeches. You need to know the up-to-date background of the person giving the news conference, and you must learn why the news conference is being held.

Often the person holding the news conference has an announcement or an opening statement. Unless that statement is leaked to the press, you will not know its content ahead of time. But you can do some educated guessing. Check out any rumors. Call the person's associates, friends, secretary. The more prepared you are, the better chance you have of coming away with a coherent, readable story.

A problem you will encounter at news conferences is that every reporter there has a line of questions to pursue. Your editor may want certain information, and other editors may want something else. You will not have time to think out your questions once you are there: The job of recording the responses to other reporters' questions will keep you too busy.

It may be impossible, as well, to arrange an interview before or after the news conference. If the person holding the news conference wanted to grant individual reporters interviews, he or she probably would not have called the news conference. But you can give it a try. You never know, and you may end up with some exclusive information.

## PREPARING FOR THE MEETING STORY

You never know just what to expect at a meeting, either. But again, you must do your best to prepare for it. Who are the people holding the meeting? What kind of an organization is it? Who are the key figures? Again, the morgue is your first stop.

Contact some of the key figures. See if you can find out what the meeting is about. Perhaps the president or the secretary has a written agenda for the meeting. If you know the main subject to be discussed at the meeting, you will be able to study and investigate the issues before arriving. Knowing what to expect and being familiar with the issues will make covering the meeting much easier.

A reporter with a regular *beat*—an assigned area of responsibility—usually covers the meetings of more important organizations and of groups like the city council, the school board or the county board. (Beat reporting is discussed in detail in Chapter 14.) A beat reporter has a continuing familiarity with the organization and with the issues involved. Often the meetings of important organizations are preceded by an *advance*—a report outlining the subjects and issues to be dealt with in the upcoming meeting.

In summary, then, to cover speeches, news conferences and meetings well, you must arm yourself with information concerning the people involved and the issues to be discussed. Do your homework.

# Covering Speeches, News Conferences and Meetings

The story is often told of the reporter who prepared well for a speech assignment, contacted the speaker, got a copy of the speech, wrote the story and spent the evening in a bar. He didn't know until after the speech story was handed in that the speech had been canceled.

And then there's the yarn about the reporter who was assigned to cover a meeting and came back to tell the city editor there was no story.

"Why not?" the city editor asked.

"Because the meeting was canceled."

"Why was that?"

"Well," replied the young reporter, "when the meeting started, some of the board members got in this big argument. Finally, three of them walked out. The president then canceled the meeting because there was no quorum."

The reporter had been sent to cover a meeting. But the canceled meeting and the circumstances surrounding its cancellation probably were of more interest to readers than the meeting itself would have been.

Preparing to cover events is only the beginning. Knowing what to do when you get there is the next step. Remember this: Covering the *content* of a speech, news conference or meeting often is only half of the job—and sometimes the less important half. You must cover the entire *event*—the time, place, circumstances, number of people involved and possible consequences of what was said or of the actions taken.

To achieve total coverage, of content and event, you must remember to:

1. Get the content correct. Tape recorders can be helpful, but *always* take good notes. Quote people exactly and in context.

2. Note the background, personal characteristics and mannerisms of the main participants.

3. Cover the event. Look around the edges—at the audience (size, reactions) and sometimes at what is happening outside the building.

4. Get there early, position yourself and hang around afterward.

Let's take a closer look at each of these.

## GETTING THE CONTENT CORRECT

You may find the tape recorder useful in covering the content of speeches, news conferences and meetings. Tape recorders often scare newspaper people, but they need not. As with anything else, you must practice using a tape recorder. You must use it again and again to become completely familiar with its idiosyncracies. In other words, learning to operate tape recorders is not enough. You need to be comfortable with the one you are using. For example, you must be sure just how sensitive the microphone is. It is sound you want, and sound you must get.

The most frequent complaint you may hear about tape recorders is that it takes too long to listen to the entire recording. You may have to listen to a whole speech again just to find a certain quote that you want to check. But you may avoid this problem if you have a tape recorder with a digital counter. At any point in a speech or a meeting when something of importance is said, you need only to note the number on the counter. Finding it later will then be no problem.

But there is one thing you *must* do even when you tape-record an event: You must take notes in exactly the same way that you would if you were not tape-recording. The truth of the matter is, you may *not* be. Malfunctions can occur with the best machines at the most inopportune times.

So, with or without a tape recorder, you must become a proficient note taker. Many veteran reporters wish they had taken a shorthand or speedwriting course early in their careers. You may find it useful to buy a speedwriting manual and become used to certain symbols. Every reporter sooner or later adopts or creates some shortcuts in note taking. You will have to do the same.

You may be one of those fortunate people with a fantastic memory. Some reporters develop an incredible knack of re-creating whole conversations with complete accuracy without taking a note. But you may be one of those who takes reams of notes. If you are, take them as neatly as you can. Many of us cannot read our own handwriting at times—a nuisance, particularly when a proper name is involved.

Taking notes is most crucial when you wish to record direct quotes. Putting someone's words in quotation marks means only one thing: You are quoting the person word for word, exactly as the person spoke. Speeches, news conferences and meetings all demand that you be able to record direct quotes. Your stories will be lifeless and lack credibility without them. A speech story, for example, should contain many direct quotes.

Whether covering a speech, news conference or meeting, you must be careful to quote people in context. For example, if a speaker gives supportive evidence for an argument, you would be unfair not to report it. Quotes can be misleading if you carelessly or deliberately juxtapose them. Combining quotes with no indication that something was said in between them can lead to inaccuracies and to charges of unfairness. Suppose, for example, someone said:

> "Cutting down fuel costs can be an easy thing. If you have easy access to wood, you should invest in a good wood-burning stove. With little effort, you can cut your fuel bills in half."

If a reporter omitted the middle sentence of that quote, the speaker would be made to look ridiculous:

> "Cutting down fuel costs can be an easy thing. With little effort, you can cut your fuel bills in half."

But there is more to the speaker than the words he or she is saying. Quoting the speaker at length or printing a speech in its entirety may at times be justified. But when you quote a whole speech, you are recording it, not reporting it. The overall content of the speech may or may not be news. Sometimes the news may be what a speaker left unsaid. You must decide what is newsworthy.

## DESCRIBING THE PARTICIPANTS

In addition to listening to what a speaker says, you must watch for other things. A tape recording misses the facial expressions and the gestures of a speaker. These sometimes are more important than the words themselves.

For example, you may have heard the story of how Soviet Premier Nikita Khrushchev pounded the table with his shoe in the United Nations General Assembly on Sept. 20, 1960. But you probably are unsure about what he was saying or what he was protesting. Similarly, many remember the setting of President Franklin D. Roosevelt's fireside chats, but few remember the content.

Simply recording the words of a speaker (or of the person holding a news conference or participating at a meeting) does not indicate volume and tone of voice, inflections, pauses, emphases, and reactions to and from those in attendance. You may note that a speaker very deliberately winked while reading a sentence. Or you may notice an unmistakable sarcasm in the speaker's voice.

Regardless of who the speaker is or where the speech is taking place, you always must note the speaker's background. A person's words often must be measured against that individual's background. For example, if an ex-Communist is speaking on communism, this fact may have a bearing on what is said. If a former CIA agent speaks about corruption in the CIA, the message would not be adequately reported if the person's background were not mentioned.

Sometimes purely physical facts about the speaker are essential to the story. A blind man pleading for funds to educate the blind, a one-armed veteran speaking about the hell of war, a gray-haired woman speaking about care for the elderly—these speakers must be described physically for the story to be accurate and understandable.

You also should note what the person who introduces a speaker says. This may help you understand the significance of the speaker and the importance of what he or she has to say.

## COVERING THE EVENT

At all these events keep an eye on the audience and on what's happening around the edges. You need to measure the mood of the audience by noting the tone of the questions. Are they sharply worded? Is there much laughter or applause? Perhaps members of the audience boo. Does the speaker or the person holding the news conference or the person presiding over the meeting remain calm and in control at all times? Is there a casual bantering or joking with the audience? Is the audience stacked with supporters or detractors?

Sometimes the real action is taking place outside in the form of a picket line or protest of some kind. Sometimes it is right in front of you.

In the 1960s, civil rights and anti-war activists made many a speech and meeting interesting and newsworthy. When John Howard Griffin, author of "Black Like Me," spoke in a college auditorium in Milwaukee, the audience and reporters noted the number of police officers who were continually clearing the aisles of the crowded hall. Not too unusual—just enforcing the fire code, the officers said. But some were puzzled by the fact that Griffin left immediately after his speech without giving the audience any chance for questions and discussion. It was all the more surprising because Griffin is a warm and generous man, and he had an urgent anti-racist message he wished to share.

One enterprising reporter found out someone had threatened Griffin's life. Though Griffin insisted on delivering the speech, police whisked him away immediately after he finished. Obviously, this, rather than anything Griffin said that night, was the lead for the story.

Most speeches do not involve threats on the speaker's life. But don't overlook the obvious. For example, you should note the size of the audience. Reporting a ''full house'' means little unless you indicate the house capacity. One way to estimate attendance is to count how many people are sitting in a row or in a typical section. Then you simply multiply that number by the number of rows or sections in the hall.


## ARRIVING, POSITIONING YOURSELF AND STAYING ON

Most reporters arrive early. At some events they have special seating, but you should probably not count on it unless you know for sure. At a speech, for example, sitting in the first row is not necessarily the best thing to do. Perhaps you should be in a position that enables you to see the reaction of the audience. If there is a question-and-answer period, you may want to be able to see the questioner. And you certainly want to be in a good position to ask questions yourself.

At a news conference the position you're in may help you get the attention of the person holding the conference. You should have your questions prepared, but preparing them is not enough. You have seen presidential news conferences on television, and you know how difficult it is to get the president's attention. Though on a smaller scale, any news conference presents the reporter with the same difficulties. You have seen how difficult it is for reporters to follow up on their own questions. At some news conferences you will not be called on twice.

But you must do more than try to get your own questions answered. You must listen to others' questions and be able to recognize the making of a good story. Too often a good question is dropped without follow-up because reporters are not listening carefully or are too intent on pursuing their own questions. Listen for what is newsworthy and pursue it. Sticking with an important subject will make the job of writing the story easier. Remember, when the news conference is finished, you will have a story to write. Piecing together notes on dozens of unrelated topics can be difficult, if not impossible.

At a meeting you should be in a position to see and hear the main participants. Ordinarily, a board or council will sit facing the audience. Before the meeting starts you should know which members are sitting where. You may want to assign each participant a number so that you do not have to write the person's name each time he or she speaks. You also can draw a sketch of where they are sitting. In this way you will be able to quote someone by number, even if you do not know the name until later. Know who the officers are. The president or the secretary may have some handouts before the meeting. After a meeting, sometimes the secretary can help you fill in missing words or information.

As a general rule, when the speech, news conference or meeting is over, do not rush off (unless you are on deadline). Hang around awhile. Some of the best stories happen afterward. You should have some questions to ask. You may want some clarifications, or you may arrange to interview a key spokesperson. Listen for reactions from those in attendance. If you are covering a night meeting for an afternoon paper, you may be able to raise some questions and answer others that were not brought up or clarified at the meeting.

**Figure 10.1 Covering News Conferences.** Reporters at news conferences, especially those called by presidents, often have difficulty getting the speaker's attention.

# Structuring and Writing Your Story

Writing the lead for the speech, news conference or meeting story is no different from writing a lead for any story. All of the qualities of the lead discussed in Chapter 3 are important here as well.

You must be careful not to emphasize something about the event that is of great interest or curiosity but that does not lead into the rest of your story. It is tempting, for example, to lead with a striking quote. But rarely does a speaker or someone holding a news conference highlight the content or the main point in a single, quotable sentence. As always, there are exceptions. As a lead for one of Dr. Martin Luther King Jr.'s addresses, a good reporter might have begun with, "I have a dream."

Because of the nature of the inverted pyramid news story, rarely should you follow the chronology of the event you are covering. But the flow of your story may demand some attention to chronology. If you pay no attention to chronology, you may distort, or cause readers to misinterpret, the meaning of the event.

## WRITING THE SPEECH STORY

Let's look at how the pros reported President George Bush's first State of the Union address on Jan. 31, 1990. Here are the opening paragraphs of Ann Devroy's front-page story in The Washington Post:

President Bush, calling the dramatic changes in Eastern Europe "the beginning of a new era in the world's affairs," last night proposed deep cuts in the level of U.S. and Soviet combat forces in Europe.

Delivering his first State of the Union address before a joint session of Congress, Bush made the surprise proposal as he described the cataclysmic changes of 1989 that produced what he called a "singular moment in history." That moment, he said, required the United States to lead the spread of democracy around the globe and to improve democracy at home by curbing drug use, bettering education and increasing American competitiveness.

Notice how Devroy, in the last sentence of paragraph two, summarizes much of what the president discussed. In the following paragraph (not shown here) she returns to the subject of her lead by giving the numbers involved in the proposed reduction of troops and by showing the decline in number from an earlier proposal of the president. The next paragraph continues to give background and interpretation to Bush's speech:

> Until last night, Bush had said he would not support the deeper cuts being called for by key Democrats, European allies and Soviet officials until completion of the talks on his original troop-cuts proposal in Vienna. But a senior U.S. official said yesterday that events in Eastern Europe are ''running ahead of the negotiations.''

Devroy sometimes inserts others' opinions about the president's proposals. She writes:

> The claim that Bush's budget would reduce the deficit to 1 percent of GNP in 1991 is based on what many economists view as overly optimistic assumptions.

Devroy ends her story by summarizing the president's opening comments:

> The president opened his speech with a pledge to bring all American troops, except those normally stationed there, home from Panama by mid-February.

Even though the president apparently thought this bit of news was significant enough to open his speech, an experienced newswriter put it at the end of her story. When you cover a speech, you need not write about it sequentially. Your job is to put the most newsworthy items first.

Similarly, reporter R.W. Apple, Jr., of The New York Times, did not mention the return of U.S. troops from Panama until the 15th paragraph of his 23-paragraph story. Apple says Bush ''announced'' the withdrawal, but the reporter does not mention that the president opened his speech with the announcement.

Apple, too, inserts some observation into his story:

> Often a lackluster orator, he some-
> times seems to rise to the big occasion,
> and tonight he was clearly conscious
> of speaking at an important mo-
> ment—one of the ''singular moments
> in world history'' of which he spoke.

In addition, Apple included the Democratic reaction to the speech by quoting Sen. Claiborne Pell, who heads the Senate Foreign Relations Committee.

Writing in The Wall Street Journal, Michel McQueen and Gerald F. Seib began their story this way:

> President Bush, in a relentlessly
> upbeat State of the Union message,
> called for larger cuts in U.S. and So-
> viet forces in Europe than he proposed
> previously. He also said the U.S. inva-
> sion force in Panama will be with-
> drawn by the end of this month.

Although McQueen and Seib chose to put the news about the Panama troops in the lead, they did not mention that the president said this before he talked about the reduction of troops in Europe.

Different writers, somewhat different stories, same speech. Remember, even when covering a speech, look for the news. The news may not be what the speaker begins with or even what the speaker spends the most time on.

## WRITING THE NEWS CONFERENCE STORY

Writing the news conference story may be a bit more challenging than a speech story. Because you will come to the conference with different questions in mind than your fellow reporters, you may come away with a different story. At least your lead may be different from those of other reporters.

A news conference often covers a gamut of topics. Often it begins with a statement from the person who called the conference.

For example, when the mayor of Springfield holds a news conference to announce his candidacy for a second term, you can be sure that he will begin with a statement to that effect. Although his candidacy might be news to some people, you may want to ask him questions about the location of a new landfill that the city is rumored to be planning. Most citizens will admit the need for landfills, but their location is always controversial. And then there's that tip you heard about the possibility of the city manager resigning to take a job in a large city.

Other reporters will come with other questions. Will there be further cuts in the city budget? Will the cuts mean that some city employees will lose their jobs? Whatever happened to the plans to expand the city jail?

After you come away from a news conference that covered many topics, you have the job of organizing the material in some logical, coherent order. Usually you will treat the most newsworthy subject first and deal with the other subjects in the order of their importance. Rarely would you report on them in the chronological order in which they were discussed.

Suppose you decided the location of the landfill was the most important item of the news conference—especially if the mayor revealed the location for the first time. You may begin your story this way:

> The city will construct its new landfill near the intersection of State Route 53 and Route E, four miles north of Springfield, Mayor Lance B. Randolph said today.
>
> "After nearly a year of discussion and the best advice we could obtain, we are certain the Route E location is best for all concerned," Randolph said at a news conference.
>
> The mayor admitted there would be continued opposition to the site by citizens living in the general area, especially those in the Valley High Trailer Court. "No location will please everyone," Randolph said.
>
> Randolph called the news conference to make the expected announcement of his candidacy for a second term.

Now you have to find a way to treat the other topics of the conference. You may want to list them first in a series of bullets in this way:

> In other matters, Randolph said:
> - City Manager Mannie Conners will not be resigning to take another post.
> - Budget constraints will not permit any new construction on the city jail this year.
> - Budget cuts will not cost any city employees their jobs. However, positions vacated by retiring personnel will not be filled.

After this list, you will either come back to your lead, giving more background and citing citizens or other city officials on the subject, or go on to treat, one at a time, the matters you listed. Pay particular attention to making proper transitions from paragraph to paragraph so that your story is coherent. "On other subjects, the mayor said . . ." "The mayor defended his position on . . ." "Again he stressed . . ."

If one of the subjects is of special interest, you may want to write a sidebar, a shorter piece to go with your main story. For this story, you may want to do a sidebar on the mayor's candidacy, his record, his possible opponents, and so on.

With a longer or more complicated story, you may want to make a summary list of all the main topics covered and place them in a box or sidebar.

Remember, your job is to give readers the news, as simply and clearly as possible. Remember, too, to cover the event as well as the content. Perhaps only three reporters turned up for the news conference, or perhaps some pickets protested the mayor's remarks about a local abortion clinic. Sometimes what happens at a news conference is more newsworthy than anything the person holding the conference says. What happens there might well be the lead of your main story, or you may want to place it in a sidebar.

## WRITING THE MEETING STORY

Readers also want you to take their place at the meeting you are covering. Let's look at a simple meeting story—in this case a meeting of a local school board:

The decision of three national corporations to protest a formula used to compute their property taxes is causing more than $264,000 to be withheld from the Walnut School District's operating budget for the 1990–91 school year.

Superintendent Ralph Thompson said at Monday's school board meeting that International Business Machines Corp., NCR Corp. and Xerox are protesting that the method used in computing their 1989 property taxes was no longer valid. Nine California counties are involved in similar disputes.

The taxes, totaling $264,688, are being held in escrow by the county until the matter is resolved. Some or all of the money eventually may be returned to the district, but the administration cannot determine when or how much.

"If we take a quarter million dollars out of our program at this time, it could have a devastating effect," Thompson said. "Once you've built that money into your budget and you lose it, you've lost a major source of income."

Mike Harper, the county prosecuting attorney, and Larry Woods, the school district attorney, advised board members to take a "wait-and-see attitude," Thompson said. He said that one alternative would be to challenge the corporations in court. A final decision will be made later.

The board also delayed action on repayment of $80,000 to IBM in a separate tax dispute. The corporation claims the district owes it for overpaid 1976 property taxes. The county commission has ruled the claim is legitimate and must be repaid.

A possible source of additional income, however, could be House Bill 1002, Thompson said. If passed, this appropriations bill would provide an additional $46 million for state education, approximately $250,000 of which could go to the Walnut School District.

Charles Campbell, the district architect, said plans for the area's new vocational technical school to be built on the Rock Bridge High School campus will be given to contractors in February. Bids will be presented at the March 13 board meeting.

The board voted to have classes on Presidents Day, Feb. 20, to make up for time missed because of the teachers' strike.

The issue of the meeting was money problems—a subject that concerns every taxpayer. The writer jumped right into the subject in the lead and then in the second paragraph gave us the who, when and where. The reporter then dealt with specifics, naming names and citing figures, and quoted the key person at the meeting. In the last two paragraphs the writer dealt with other matters discussed in the meeting.

Even meetings on complicated subjects need not begin with heavy, ponderous prose. A story about how cancer can be caused by enzymes that normally are supposed to repair cells, started with the lead, ''Even enzymes make mistakes.'' Though the subject was heavy, the lead was great.

Remember, you are allowed to use your imagination. And you are expected to write well—even for an everyday event like a speech, news conference or meeting.

# Suggested Reading

Rivers, William L. ''Finding Facts.'' Englewood Cliffs, N.J.: Prentice-Hall, 1975. Chapter 6, ''Central Sources,'' is particularly helpful, but other chapters also are useful.

# Exercises

1. Journalist Bill Moyers is coming to town to speak on the current U.S. president's relationship with the press. Prepare to cover the speech. Record the steps you will take to prepare for the speech and the information you have gathered on Moyers.

2. You learn that actor Dennis Weaver is holding a news conference before speaking to a local group about environmental issues. You also learn that Weaver has spoken on this topic to other groups in recent months. Record the steps you will take to prepare for the news conference and the information you have gathered on Weaver.

3. Find out when the Faculty Council or similar faculty representative group is having its next meeting. Record the steps you will take to prepare for the meeting and the information you have gathered for it.

4. Following is the speech by Charles B. Reed, Chancellor of the State University System of Florida, delivered to the NCAA Presidents' Commission National Forum in San Francisco on Jan. 9, 1989. Write a speech story of three takes, concentrating on the content of Reed's speech.

### Education Is What It Is All About

Good afternoon. To begin my comments, I want to borrow a line from Governor Mario Cuomo of New York. He recently told an audience in Washington that, back when he was considering running for president, late one night, the devil came to him and offered him a deal.

Governor Cuomo said, "He offered me the presidency in exchange for my soul. So I said: What's the catch?"

I think we need to think about the report of American Institutes for Research in this light, and ask the question: If we are going to have big-time intercollegiate athletics in an environment of academic excellence, what's the catch?

That catch is, I think, not that we're trying to do two things that are totally incompatible, but that we've lost our sense of proportion and our sense of priority.

We often hear conversations within the NCAA that come to the conclusion that we "must not kill the golden goose"—meaning television contracts. Well, I think the golden goose really isn't broadcast revenues, but American higher education itself.

Our sense of proportion should tell us that. Anyone who has trouble deciding whether education or athletics is more important should recognize that we could easily have higher education without athletics.

Ask yourself: What would we do differently if tomorrow there were no such thing as intercollegiate athletics?

We'd still teach every course in the college catalogue. That wouldn't change one bit. We'd still conduct research at the same pace. We'd still perform public service.

What we wouldn't be doing in American higher education is bending or breaking the recruiting rules, stealing players and coaches from each other, struggling to keep our more rabid and fanatical boosters under control and trying to prevent the academic reputations of our institutions from being mocked or disgraced by our athletic programs.

Ask yourself another question: Is there another single reason why more university presidents have had to resign, or have been dismissed, than problems with athletics?

And finally, ask yourself this one:

What's more important in the life of a student-athlete—winning, or graduating?

I say, graduating is more important. And I think the real values of our universities are not merely what we say they are. Our real values are reflected not in words, but in the way we conduct ourselves. No institution is value-free. We either live up to high standards, or we don't.

Sometimes the recognition of our own imperfections prompts us to consider abandoning all pretense of amateurism and declaring the tradition of the scholar-athlete an unattainable myth. Some say we should openly pay our athletes, not require them to make progress toward a degree, and create a semi-professional feeder system for professional sports.

I disagree. I think the way to avoid hypocrisy is not to abandon our ideals, but to make a greater effort to live up to them.

And so we return to the issue of setting a priority. I think that priority ought to be graduating—on time—and at the same rate, if not at a higher rate, than students as a whole. Notre Dame, Penn State and Georgetown show us clearly that this is possible.

I know this can be done because I've seen it happen time after time. And frankly, I would not be here today as Chancellor of the State University System of Florida were it not for the athletic scholarship that made it possible for me to attend George Washington University, where I ultimately earned all three of my degrees.

I think we have to set graduation rates—not the score of the game or the won-loss record—as the priority, for three reasons.

First, it gives the student athlete a chance at life after college.

Second, it sends the right message to younger students.

Third, it preserves the values of our society and of our universities.

Let's look at these three points one at a time.

The first point is the future of our student athletes. Our system today throws up the photos of—to name two athletes from my own system—Deion Sanders and Sammy Smith, off to the National Football League without degrees, to make millions of dollars.

Those two students will make enough money that, with some good advice, they'll be set for life even without degrees. But if they'd finished college, they'd be in a better position to evaluate the financial advice they'll get, and also have the basis for a second career after their knees give out. But they are two in a million.

Most of our student athletes never get a shot at professional sports. Most who do don't last long enough to have what could reasonably be called "a career" as a professional athlete. What about those people who, having been exploited, now compete in the job market with former students who earned their diplomas?

Ask yourself this question: Which applicant would you rather hire—someone whose academic focus was on remaining eligible for sports, or on graduating? Someone who barely passed a freshman algebra course, or someone who majored in computer science?

Second, we need to send a message to the younger students in the junior high schools and high schools of the nation that goes beyond the message of Proposition 48. We need to tell them that sports can be a meaningful part of life, but that hardly anybody makes a living in sports. Your odds of becoming a rock star or an astronaut are about the same as starting for the New York Knicks.

So we need to tell the next generation of student athletes that, if they are unprepared academically to do college work, they can forget about playing college sports. In my experience, there are few better motivators for athletes than threatening to withhold participation in sports. Make it stick and you'll make it work.

Third, making academic success the true focus of intercollegiate athletics keeps us true to the purpose of our universities. Education is what it's all about—not touchdowns, skyhooks or home runs.

So let me make the following modest proposal:

1. Abolish spring training for football. This report tells us that athletes spend less time on the books than they do on sports. Let's cut back on some of the athletic distractions.

2. Reduce eligibility from four years to three. Let our freshmen find out where the library is and experience a degree of academic success first.

3. Report annually our graduation rates by institution, by sport, and by gender. We've started doing this in Florida, and we're beginning to see the results. Until now, only the coaching staff has been held accountable, because we don't keep score in the academic area.

Let's start keeping score—and compete with Notre Dame and Penn State and Georgetown not just on the field, but on Commencement Day.

4. Finally, let's extend the score-keeping to junior high and high schools, by making it clear that we do not recruit and will not accept as athletes students whose grades and test scores predict academic failure.

I realize not everyone is going to agree with everything I say here today. That's fine. But I think one thing we can all agree on is this:

Education is what it's all about. And if we make graduating the priority of every student athlete, we'll be dealing honestly with our student-athletes, we'll set a positive example for younger students coming up, and we'll be true to the values that our institutions are supposed to embody.

Otherwise, when the devil offers us a bowl bid in exchange for our souls, we'll ask—what's the catch?

Thank you.

5. Prepare for, cover and write:

   **a.** A speech story.

   **b.** A news conference story.

   **c.** A meeting story.

   Then compare your stories to those appearing in the local paper.

# 11

# Accidents, Fires and Disasters

$S$tories about accidents, fires and disasters have been a principal ingredient of newspapers for many years. There's a good reason for that. In a nationwide survey prepared for the American Newspaper Publishers Association and the Newspaper Readership Council, news of crime and accidents ranked behind only government news and military news in reader interest. That study confirmed what editors have known for years: When people hear sirens, they want to know what happened and, perhaps more important, whether their friends or acquaintances were involved.

Newspapers also cover these events in their capacity as watchdog for the public over government agencies. If the police are slow in responding to an accident, is it because there are not enough officers or because they are poorly supervised? Did someone die needlessly because police, fire or ambulance personnel were slow, poorly trained or inefficient? To ask these questions on behalf of their readers, reporters must observe public officials as they perform their duties.

In news rooms and newspaper bureaus throughout the country, editors and reporters stay tuned to the police and fire radio frequencies on monitors provided for that purpose. When they hear something out of the ordinary, reporters and photographers are dispatched to the scene.

Editors have varying ideas about which accident, fire and disaster stories are worth reporting at all and which are worth developing into major articles. Perhaps the most important factor in that decision is the size of the city and its newspaper. An apartment fire in which nobody was hurt may be routine in New York City and merit only one or two paragraphs, if any space at all. But in Cedar City, Utah, a similar fire may be unusual enough to warrant more extensive coverage.

**Figure 11.1-11.3 The Importance of Good Photographs.** These Pulitzer Prize-winning photographs had tremendous impact on readers and served to attract them to the accompanying stories about a truck accident, a fire and an airplane crash. Good photographs always help communicate the drama of such events.

As a beginning reporter you almost certainly will be assigned to cover an accident or fire. You even may become part of a team of reporters and photographers assigned to cover a disaster. Consequently, you need to know what to expect and how to get the information you need.

In many ways covering accidents, fires and disasters is the simplest form of reporting. The subject matter lends itself to the classic inverted pyramid writing style. But you also can produce far more interesting accounts of the pain and suffering—and often the remarkable strength—of people who have encountered crisis.

As a reporter assigned to cover an accident, fire or disaster, you must report the effects of the event on the victims. Only then can you write a story that tells the event in terms of the human experience. This chapter addresses the reporting of both the event and its personal aftermaths.

### In this chapter you will learn:

1. How to cover the scene of an accident, fire or disaster.

2. How to complete the reporting.

# Covering the Scene

Whether you are assigned to cover an accident, fire or disaster, many of the facts and all of the color are gathered at the scene. By being there, you will have a better picture of what happened. Too many reporters, however, cover accidents and fires as purely passive observers. You must observe. But you also must actively solicit information from those who are there. Many of them, including those directly involved, you may never be able to find again. With that advice in mind, let us turn to the techniques you should employ to secure that information at each of the scenes you will cover.

## THE SCENE OF AN ACCIDENT

When dispatched to the scene of an accident, you first must concentrate on gathering the facts. Move as quickly as possible to collect this information:

1. The names, ages, addresses and conditions of the victims.

2. Accounts of witnesses or police reconstructions of what happened.

3. When the accident occurred.

4. Where it occurred.

5. Why or how it happened or who was at fault, as determined by officials in charge of the investigation.

If that list sounds familiar, it should. You could simplify it to read "who, what, when, where and why." As in any news story, that information is essential. You must gather such information as quickly as possible after being assigned to the story. If the accident has just taken place, a visit to the scene is essential. Just as important is knowing what to do when you get there. These suggestions will help:

1. *Question the person in charge of the investigation.* This individual will attempt to gather much of the same information you want. A police officer, for example, needs to know who was involved, what happened, when it happened and who was at fault. If you are able to establish a good relationship with the investigator, you may be able to secure much of the information you need from this one source, though single-source stories usually are inadequate.

Remember that the spellings of names, addresses and similar facts must be verified later. Any veteran reporter can tell you that police officers and other public officials are notoriously bad spellers and often make errors in recording names of the victims. To avoid such errors, call relatives of the victims or consult the city directory, telephone book or other sources to check your information.

2. *Try to find and interview witnesses.* Police and other investigators may lead you directly to the best witnesses. The most accurate account of what happened usually comes from witnesses, and the investigators will try to find them. You should, too. A good way to do that is to watch the investigators. Listen in as they interview a witness, or corner the witness after they are finished. If there is time, of course, try to find your own witnesses. You cannot and should not always rely on investigators to do your work for you.

3. *Try to find friends or relatives of the victims.* These sources are helpful in piecing together information about the victims. Through them you often get tips about even better stories.

4. *If possible, interview the victims.* Survivors of an accident may be badly shaken, but if they are able to talk, they can provide firsthand detail that an official report never could. Make every attempt to interview those involved.

5. *Talk with others at the scene.* If someone has died at the scene of the accident, an ambulance paramedic or the medical examiner may be able to

give you some indication of what caused the death. At the least you can learn from them where the bodies or the injured will be taken. That may help, because later the mortician or hospital officials may be able to provide information you need for your story.

6. *Be sensitive to victims and their families.* You have a job to do, and you must do it. That does not mean, however, that you can be insensitive to those involved in an accident.

Of course, your deadline will have a major impact on the amount of information you are able to gather. If you must meet a deadline soon after arriving at the scene, you probably will be forced to stick to the basics of who, what, when, where, why and how. Thus it is important to gather that information first. Then, if you have time, you can concentrate on more detailed and vivid information to make the story highly readable.

The following account of a tractor-trailer accident was produced in a race against the clock by the staff of an afternoon newspaper:

A truck driver was killed and a woman was injured this morning when a tractor-trailer believed to be hauling gasoline overturned and exploded on Interstate 70, turning the highway into a conflagration.

Both lanes of I-70 were backed up for miles after an eastbound car glanced off a pickup truck, hurdled the concrete median and collided with a tanker truck heading west.

The explosion was immediate, witnesses said. Residents along Texas Avenue reported the initial fireball reached the north side of the street, which is about 300 yards from the scene of the accident. A wooded area was scorched, but no houses were damaged.

Police evacuated the 600 block of Texas Avenue for fear that the fire would spread, but residents were returning to their homes at 12:35 p.m., about an hour after the collision. Authorities also unsuccessfully attempted to hold back the onlookers who gravitated to a nearby shopping center parking lot to view the blaze.

Police did not identify the driver of the truck, which was owned by a Tulsa, Okla., firm named Transport Delivery Co. "Apparently it was gasoline," said Steve Paulsell, chief of the County Fire Protection District. "That's what it smelled like." Other officials reported the truck may have been hauling fuel oil or diesel fuel.

For an afternoon newspaper with an early afternoon deadline, such a story presents major problems, particularly when it occurs, as this one did, at about 11:30 a.m. Four reporters were dispatched to the scene; all of them called in information to a writer back at the office. There was little time to interview eyewitnesses. Because of the pressing deadline, the reporters were forced to gather most of their information from fire and police officials at the scene.

Writers for the morning newspaper, by comparison, had plenty of time to gather rich detail to tell the story in human terms. Much of the breaking news value was diminished by the next morning because of intense coverage by the afternoon newspaper, radio and television. It was time to tell the story of a hero:

Witnesses credited an off-duty fireman with saving a woman's life Monday following a spectacular four-vehicle collision on Interstate 70 just east of its intersection with Business Loop 70.

The driver of a gasoline truck involved in the fiery crash was not so lucky. Bill Borgmeyer, 62, of Jefferson City died in the cab of his rig, which jackknifed, overturned and exploded in flames when he swerved in a futile attempt to avoid hitting a car driven by Leta Hanes, 33, of Nelson, Mo.

Mrs. Hanes, who was thrown from her auto by the impact, was lying unconscious within 10 feet of the blazing fuel when firefighter Richard Walden arrived at the crash scene.

"I knew what was going on," Walden recalled, "and I knew I had to get her away from there." Despite the intense heat, Walden dragged the woman to safety.

"She had some scrapes, a cut on her knee and was beat around a little bit," Walden said. "Other than that, she was fine."

Mrs. Hanes was taken to Boone Hospital Center, where she was reported in satisfactory condition Monday night.

Smoke billowing from the accident scene reportedly was visible 30 miles away. Westbound interstate traffic was backed up as far as five miles. Several city streets became snarled for several hours when traffic was diverted to Business Loop 70. The eastbound lane of I-70 was reopened about 2 p.m.; the westbound lane was not reopened until 3 p.m. . . .

The story added detail and eyewitness accounts from several other people:

"It was a big red fireball," said Don Morgan of Clear Spring, Mo., who was driving about 100 yards behind the Borgmeyer rig when the crash occurred. "It exploded right away, as soon as it rolled over on its side."

Doug McConnell, 23, was in the kitchen of his nearby home at 606 Texas Ave. when the house shook.

"I heard a boom, and all of a sudden there was fire," he said. "It looked like a firecracker or something."

The richness of detail in the second account and the eyewitness descriptions of what happened make the story more interesting. The importance of adding such detail is apparent.

## THE SCENE OF A FIRE

Accidents and fires present similar problems for the reporter, but at a fire of any size you can expect more confusion than at the scene of an accident. One major difference, then, is that the officer in charge will be busier. At the scene of an accident the damage has been done and the authorities usually are free to concentrate on their investigation. At a fire the officer in charge is busy directing firefighters and probably will be unable to talk with you. The investigation will not even begin until the fire is extinguished. In many cases the cause of the fire will not be known for hours, days or weeks. In fact, it may never be known. Seldom is that the case in an accident, except perhaps for air accidents.

Another problem is that you may not have access to the immediate area of the fire. Barriers often are erected to keep the public—and representatives of the news media—from coming too close to a burning structure. The obvious reason is safety, but such barriers may hamper your reporting. You may not be able to come close enough to firefighters to learn about the problems they are having or to obtain the quotes you need to improve your story.

These problems usually make covering a fire more difficult than covering an accident. Despite the difficulties, you cover a fire in much the same way, interviewing officials and witnesses at the scene. You also should try to interview the owner. Moreover, because the official investigation will not have begun, you must conduct your own. When covering any fire, you must learn:

1. The location of the fire.

2. The names, ages and addresses of those killed, injured or missing.

3. The name of the building's owner or, in the case of a grass fire or forest fire, the name of the landowner.

4. The value of the building and its contents or the value of the land.

5. Whether the building and contents were insured for fire damage. (Open land seldom is.)

6. The time the fire started, who reported it and how many firefighters and pieces of equipment were called to the scene.

7. What caused the fire, if known.

As in any story, the basics are who, what, when, where, why and how. But the nature of the fire will raise other questions that must be answered. Of primary importance is whether life is endangered. If not, the amount of property damage becomes the major emphasis of the story. Was arson involved? Was the building insured for its full value? Was there an earlier fire there? Did the building comply with the fire codes? Were any rare or extremely valuable objects inside? Were there explosives inside that complicated fighting the fire and posed an even greater threat than the fire itself?

Your job is to answer these questions for the newspaper's readers. You will be able to obtain some of that information later on from the official fire reports if they are ready before your story deadline (see Figure 11.4). But most

PAGE    OF                          **CASUALTY REPORT**                                    FD-500

CHANGE 2 ☐
(74)
DELETE 3 ☐

INCIDENT NO.    EXP
8 | 0 | 9 | 0 | 5 | 1 | 3 |
1   2 3                7 8   9

NAME
S|A|N|D|O|Z|A| |M|A|N|U|E|L| |R| | | | | | |        AGE 3|2    Time of Injury 0|9|4|5    MONTH 0|2    DAY 0|8    YEAR 9|1
LAST, FIRST MIDDLE                                        33 34 35 36                    39 40                45

HOME ADDRESS                                                              TELEPHONE
307 Banning Ave., Apt. 3                                                  555-9088

| 46 SEX | 47 CASUALTY TYPE | 48 SEVERITY | 49 AFFILIATION |
|--------|-----------------|-------------|----------------|
| 1 ☒ Male | 1 ☒ Fire Casualty | 1 ☒ Injury | 1 ☐ Fire Service |
| 2 ☐ Female | 2 ☐ Action Casualty | 2 ☐ Death | 2 ☐ Other Emergency Personnel |
|  | 3 ☐ EMS Casualty |  | 3 ☒ Civilian |

| FAMILIARITY WITH STRUCTURE | LOCATION AT IGNITION | CONDITION BEFORE INJURY |
|---|---|---|
| Occupant            50 | Unknown            51 | Unknown            52 |
| CONDITION PREVENTING ESCAPE | ACTIVITY AT TIME OF INJURY | CAUSE OF INJURY |
| N/A                 53 | Leaving building   54 | Falling debris     55 |
| NATURE OF INJURY | PART OF BODY INJURED | DISPOSITION |
| Broken leg          56 | Leg                57 | Hospitalized       58 |

REMARKS:
Occupant was leaving burning structure when burning eave fell and struck his leg.

By _#31_       Ambulance  to   _General_        Hospital

---

NAME
| | | | | | | | | | | | | | | | | | | |        AGE    Time of Injury    MONTH    DAY    YEAR
LAST, FIRST MIDDLE                                        33 34 35 36                    39 40                45

HOME ADDRESS                                                              TELEPHONE

| 46 SEX | 47 CASUALTY TYPE | 48 SEVERITY | 49 AFFILIATION |
|--------|-----------------|-------------|----------------|
| 1 ☐ Male | 1 ☐ Fire Casualty | 1 ☐ Injury | 1 ☐ Fire Service |
| 2 ☐ Female | 2 ☐ Action Casualty | 2 ☐ Death | 2 ☐ Other Emergency Personnel |
|  | 3 ☐ EMS Casualty |  | 3 ☐ Civilian |

| FAMILIARITY WITH STRUCTURE | LOCATION AT IGNITION | CONDITION BEFORE INJURY |
|---|---|---|
|                     50 |                    51 |                    52 |
| CONDITION PREVENTING ESCAPE | ACTIVITY AT TIME OF INJURY | CAUSE OF INJURY |
|                     53 |                    54 |                    55 |
| NATURE OF INJURY | PART OF BODY INJURED | DISPOSITION |
|                     56 |                    57 |                    58 |

REMARKS:

By        Ambulance   to                   Hospital

*Nelson Riley*
Supervisor*
*Injury reports for fire personnel,
Immediate supervisor to sign here.

SIGNATURE of person completing form/DATE
*John R. Sanders.*

Printed in U.S.A

**Figure 11.4    Fire Report.** This casualty report is typical of the types of reports available to
reporters at most fire stations.

of it will come from interviews conducted at the scene with the best available sources. Finding your sources may not be easy, but you can begin by looking for the highest-ranking fire official.

Another important source in covering fire stories is the fire marshal, whose job is to determine the cause of the fire and, if arson is involved, to bring charges against the arsonist. You should make every effort to talk with the fire marshal at the scene, if he or she is available. In most cases, though, the marshal will be the primary source of a second-day story.

As in covering any *spot news* story—a story in which news is breaking quickly—deadlines will determine how much you can do at the scene of a fire. If your deadline is hours away, you can concentrate on the event and those connected with it. You will have time to find the little boy whose puppy was killed in the fire or interview the firefighter who first entered the building. But if you have only minutes until your deadline, you may have to press the fire official in charge for as much information as possible. You may have to coax from that person every tidbit, even making a nuisance of yourself, to gather the information you need. Through it all, you can expect confusion. There is little order to be found in the chaos of a fire.

## THE SCENE OF A DISASTER

Disasters present special problems for reporters. Even the investigators may have difficulty determining where to begin. For example, when tornadoes slice through cities, efforts may be concentrated on finding those trapped in the rubble of buildings. No one may know for certain who is trapped or where they are, or, in fact, whether anyone is trapped at all.

The confusion at the scene of a disaster makes your job more difficult. Officials often are caught up in the turmoil of the moment and overestimate the number of people killed or the amount of damage. In some instances you may find yourself in the unusual position of being ahead of the investigators. You may be in a better position to determine the death toll or estimate the damage. At least you will be able to make an informed judgment about the accuracy of what you are told. American newspaper history is filled with incidents of reporters' quoting inflated estimates of deaths and damage. Failure to make informed judgments about the accuracy of those estimates leaves your newspaper open to charges of irresponsibility.

In addition to confusion you may well encounter hazards to your personal safety as a reporter at the scene of a disaster. After a tornado, for example, electric wires may lie on the ground for hours until repair crews are able to reach them. At the scene of an earthquake you may be frighteningly close to a wall about to collapse. Or, in the aftermath of that earthquake, decaying bodies may present serious health hazards, as reporters found when covering the Mexico City earthquake of 1985. As you go about your work, you must avoid all such hazards; you will be of little value to your newspaper in a hospital bed. Further, what little information you can learn by being that close probably is not worth the risk. Nevertheless, there will be times when you will be forced into dangerous situations.

At the scene of a disaster, you can expect the unexpected. One beginning reporter for a Memphis, Tenn., newspaper learned this when dispatched to the scene of a tornado in Forrest City, Ark., about 60 miles from the office. He gathered information about the disaster for a few hours, then decided to call his editor for further instructions. He found that all the telephone lines to Memphis were down because of the storm. After a few minutes of indecision, he remembered having driven by a telephone company service office earlier in the evening. He went there, and when a few lines were re-established, his call to Memphis was one of the first out of Forrest City after the tornado. Presence of mind like that is important in such situations.

Fortunately, when disasters strike, you may not have to shoulder the entire reporting load. In such cases editors usually mobilize their reporting staffs to gather as much information as quickly as possible. You probably will be assigned a specific responsibility, such as interviewing witnesses or survivors. You may then be asked to write a *sidebar*, a secondary story that runs with the major story and usually captures the personal side of an event. Other reporters may focus on the damage involved and compile lists of the dead and injured.

# Completing the Reporting

In reporting almost any account of an accident, fire or disaster, your work at the scene will be merely the beginning. When you return to the office and sort through your notes, you probably will find that many questions remain unanswered. You must check with other sources.

## SOURCES TO CHECK

When a disaster occurs, the follow-up stories often are as dramatic, important and significant as the story of the event itself. When the space shuttle Challenger exploded in January 1986, reporters began prying into records of the National Aeronautics and Space Administration and found massive evidence of inadequate concern for safety. The defective hard-rubber seals blamed for the explosion of the shuttle shortly after takeoff had been a cause of concern to safety experts for years. But even though the seals were known to be susceptible to failure in cold weather, NASA officials authorized launch of the shuttle in near-freezing conditions. Good secondary reporting led to a major story that prompted an investigation by a presidential panel.

An industrial accident should prompt calls to company executives or a corporate safety officer and may require you to check with local, state and

## DETAIL IMPORTANT IN DISASTER STORIES

Editors agree almost universally that when a disaster occurs, it is a time for a newspaper to pull out all the stops. Dozens of reporters and photographers may be dispatched to gather as much detail as possible. It then falls on one or two reporters back at the office to mold it all into an article that makes sense.

What follows is the main story from the San Francisco Chronicle on the day following the disastrous Bay Area earthquake in October 1989. As you read the story, notice its richness of detail. Also try to list the likely sources of the material the story contains. The number of sources it includes is staggering.

### HUNDREDS DEAD IN HUGE QUAKE OAKLAND FREEWAY COLLAPSES— BAY BRIDGE FAILS

By Randy Shilts and Susan Sward
Chronicle Staff Writers

A terrifying earthquake ripped through Northern California late yesterday afternoon, killing at least 211, injuring hundreds more, setting buildings ablaze and destroying sections of the Bay Bridge.

The quake was the strongest since the devastation of the great 1906 shock. Yesterday's tremor measured 7.0 on the Richter scale and shook the state from Lake Tahoe to Los Angeles.

The temblor erupted from the treacherous San Andreas fault and was centered in sparsely populated mountains 10 miles north of Santa Cruz.

Late last night, Lt. Gov. Leo McCarthy estimated damage at "well over $1 billion" and predicted, "It will climb much higher in the light of day."

McCarthy said he had talked with White House Chief of Staff John Sununu, who had activated 20 federal agencies to provide emergency relief.

The earthquake struck just as hundreds of thousands of people were leaving work for the afternoon commute, jamming freeways, filling mass-transit systems and crowding city streets throughout the Bay Area.

Meanwhile, the eyes of the nation were already riveted on San Francisco, where the third game in the World Series was just 30 minutes away from the first pitch at Candlestick Park. The game was abruptly canceled.

The heaviest fatalities came about two miles south of the San Francisco-

federal regulatory agencies. If a worker is severely burned by a toxic chemical, you may have to call the federal government's Occupational Safety and Health Administration to learn what safety precautions are mandated for the use of the chemical. Only then will you be able to determine if there is reason to suspect the company—or the worker—of violating OSHA restrictions designed to ensure safety in the workplace.

Airplane crashes require a check with the Federal Aviation Administration, which investigates all of them, regardless of their severity. FAA inves-

Oakland Bay Bridge when the upper deck of a mile-long section of two-tiered Interstate 880 collapsed onto the lower deck.

An estimated 200 people were crushed to death amid the cascade of tumbling concrete and automobiles from the upper deck, according to the state Office of Emergency Services.

"But," added Alameda County Sheriff Charles Plummer, "we have an awful lot of concrete to be picked up."

At 11 p.m., however, rescue operations were suspended until dawn because of the lack of light.

At a makeshift morgue at the Ralph Bunch School a few blocks from the freeway collapse, Red Cross volunteers escorted sobbing family members to identify bodies.

Another 400 people were thought to be injured at the site near the Cypress Street exit.

"We heard people screaming like hell everywhere," said Thomas Stevens, a neighborhood resident. "The people on top we could help, but there was nothing we could do about the people underneath." At least two motorists leaped from the top tier of the crumpled upper deck and were rushed to the hospital.

Meanwhile, on the bridge itself, a

50-foot section of the upper span fell, puncturing a hole in the lower level. It was not known whether there were any fatalities on the bridge.

The U.S. Coast Guard dispatched two 41-foot vessels to search for cars or people who may have plummeted into the bay while stunned motorists abandoned their cars on the bridge to walk back to solid ground.

At the approaches to the bridge's toll plazas, black mud from the bay oozed through fissures in the roadway that snaked for hundreds of yards.

Three people were confirmed dead and one report said as many as 12 may have died in Santa Cruz when fire roared through entire city blocks.

In San Francisco, at least five people were confirmed killed when the quake tore off two sides of a six-story brick building at 175 Bluxome St. in the South of Market warehouse district.

The causes of death ranged from decapitation to severe blood loss. Most of the victims were in their cars, leaving work when caught in the avalanche of falling bricks and mortar from the building.

"They never knew what hit them," said a police officer.

(*continued*)

# Detail Important in Disaster Stories

(*cont. from p. 231*)

The worst fires broke out in San Francisco's Marina District, where at least three people were killed in frightening scenes reminiscent of the devastation of the 1906 quake.

Among the dead was a 9-month-old infant who died after a four-story building collapsed. Firefighters battled flames in 12 apartment buildings in the comfortable residential neighborhood, nestled on the northern edge of the city.

Water mains burst, and the smell of gas hung over the streets.

Witnesses said the streets echoed with the screams of terrified bystanders and the sirens of emergency vehicles speeding the injured to hospitals. Men with chain saws worked furiously to break into collapsed buildings to search for survivors.

"It seemed impossible not to have more deaths—it's good it happened before more people were home from work and lots of people would have been killed," said eyewitness Thomas Murray.

"When it hit, it was so scary I thought I was having an acid flashback," Murray said.

Diego Reiwald, a Swiss tourist, said mothers clutched children as they surveyed the damage.

"There wasn't a building that wasn't cracked or slanted," he said.

Within moments of the quake, power went out for all of San Francisco, abruptly halting the BART system and San Francisco's Municipal Railway.

Up to one million Bay Area residents were left without power as a result of the quake, and gas leaks were reported throughout the region.

A PGE spokesman said police ordered the utility to keep the power off until reports of gas leaks could be checked out. The spokesman could not predict when power would be restored, saying the utility "would bring the power up very slowly and see if the system holds together."

Geologists said they were not surprised by the earthquake, which erupted along a section of the San Andreas fault in the Santa Cruz Mountains. Last year, a U.S. geological survey reported that there was a 30 percent chance of the fault rupturing within 30 years. The 1906 jolt probably measured between 7.9 and 8.3 on the Richter scale, though no such measuring device existed at that time.

Geologists said they won't know immediately how severe the quake was, though they said they expected to find that the displacement along the fault could be as much as five feet.

Thomas McEvilly of the seismographic station at the University of California at Berkeley said, "We can expect a major aftershock sequence for weeks or months," but none are likely to be as large as yesterday's quake. Geological survey instruments recorded continuous earth-shaking that lasted 15 minutes, geologists said.

The intensity of the quake even frightened the veteran geologists. "This is the first time I've seen seismologists climbing under the desk," said Linda Seekins, an earthquake researcher in Menlo Park.

From the moment the quake hit, the Bay Area was awash with dramatic scenes of destruction.

In Richmond, the temblor ruptured a 400,000-gallon Union Oil gasoline tank, sending its unleaded gasoline gushing across the ground.

Late last night, Richmond firefighting crews struggled to pump the gasoline into an adjacent tank without triggering an explosion.

In San Francisco, firefighters treated numerous [people who suffered] heart attacks throughout the city.

At San Francisco International Airport, authorities evacuated between 20,000 and 25,000 air travelers after many were hit by falling ceiling tiles in the terminal lobbies.

Officials estimated it may be three days before the airport is in full operation again.

In the Financial District, dazed office workers abandoned public transportation to pick their way home through shattered glass and fallen bricks that littered the streets.

The elegantly appointed windows of I. Magnin's department store disintegrated into a shower of flying glass. Bloody shards lay on the streets around the fashionable Union Square shopping district.

At St. Patrick's Church, one of the only downtown buildings that survived the 1906 earthquake, a man was injured by falling debris as he prayed.

"Everything everywhere is almost totally damaged," said Zain Azzahayer, as he stood among thousands of broken bottles in Zain Li-

quors on Third Street near Market. "We're fine; that's the main thing."

At the foot of Market Street, the damaged flag pole on the Ferry Building tilted off at an eerie angle as darkness fell over the early evening sky.

Throughout San Francisco, people clustered around transistor radios and cars to listen to the latest reports on the quake's damage.

In the midst of all the destruction, an eerie calm prevailed on some streets. Motorists politely waved each other through intersections while volunteers directed traffic through the busiest corners.

There were reports of lootings, muggings and beatings. At the city housing projects on Army Street, police broke up a gang of 150 youths who were attacking local residents.

As night plunged the city into the darkness, the only lights in the city came from car headlights.

In the aftermath of the quake elsewhere in the Bay Area, authorities reported several buildings collapsed, including a K mart in San Jose and an engineering building on the Stanford University campus. There were numerous power outages and road closures throughout the region. In San Mateo County, scores were injured. Several floors of the Amfac Hotel collapsed in Burlingame. In Marin and Contra Costa counties, no major injuries were reported.

As hospital emergency rooms filled up with the wounded, hospital executives appealed for all employees to come to work.

The Office of Emergency Services announced that the entire 27,000-

*(continued)*

## Detail Important in Disaster Stories

(*cont. from p. 233*)

member California National Guard was put on standby for possible mobilization.

In a press conference at the Emergency Services Command Center in the Western Addition last night, San Francisco Mayor Art Agnos appealed to all San Franciscans to stay home from work today. All schools would be closed, he said.

Vice President Dan Quayle will come to San Francisco to inspect the damage today, a spokesman said last night.

Gov. George Deukmejian cut short a trade mission to West Germany and said he would fly back to California on a military transport, spokesman Kevin Brett said.

Throughout Northern California, many residents were shaken but still relieved to have survived unscathed.

Outside a delicatessen in the Castro District, Kevin Waldron, 25, poured champagne into paper cups for his friends and said, "This is an earthquake celebration, because we're still alive."

Most editors would consider the Chronicle's story a good piece of work completed under extremely difficult circumstances. Yet the newspaper was criticized for overestimating what was perhaps the single most important fact—the number of dead. Largely caused by Oakland authorities' overestimates of the number of dead in the Oakland freeway collapse, the newspaper took the heat. Thus, this is a good example of why it is so important to question the information provided by police or other public officials. At the time of a disaster, no one may know the exact number of dead until much later. The wise reporter reports only the number of confirmed dead. If estimates of further deaths are appropriate, they should be well-attributed to the source.

The Chronicle could have avoided the criticism it took in this case by qualifying the number of dead in the lead. Other than that, the story is an excellent one, full of the rich detail that such an event demands.

tigators usually cooperate with reporters by revealing likely causes of crashes. Try to get such information because FAA investigations routinely last several months, and by then the cause of the crash may have little news value.

When you cover a drowning you may want to check with local authorities to find out if swimming is permitted where the drowning occurred. State water-patrol officials may help when you are reporting boating accidents.

In our well-regulated society there are government regulatory agencies at all levels that can provide details to help you focus on the problem. City agencies that deal with such matters can be found at city hall; similar county agencies probably will be located at the courthouse or county office building. State regulatory agencies are located in your state capital; regional offices of federal agencies usually are located in a nearby large city. Take advantage of their expertise.

This also is the time to call relatives of victims and to verify information gathered at the scene that can be checked with other sources. The nature and extent of such checks is dictated by the circumstances.

## FOLLOW-UP STORIES

Most editors expect their reporters to initiate follows to major stories of accidents, fires and disasters. Sometimes, the follows are as good as or better than the original stories. Several months after a series of fires blamed on an arsonist resulted in the loss of several businesses and gained national attention, Jill Young Miller, formerly of the Columbia (Mo.) Daily Tribune, decided to see what had become of the companies affected:

Anne Moore remembers all too well the call that shook her from her sleep last spring and summoned her to the corner of 10th Street and Broadway. A silver bowl and a faded floor plan are her only mementos of the D&M Sound Systems Inc. store that flames destroyed May 27.

D&M President Moore keeps both treasures in her new store at 700 Fay St. She and other local entrepreneurs have spent the past several months piecing together their businesses destroyed during the city's arson plague last spring.

No one has been charged with setting the Stephens Endowment Building fire that devastated D&M, the Columbia Art League, the French Room Hairdressing Salon, Spinning Wheel Realty, The Copy Center and Orlanco Financial Corp. Nor has the culprit been identified in the 10 other blazes investigators say were deliberately set last spring.

An intergovernmental arson task force folded in July after arson charges were filed against two men in unrelated fires—one in Rocheport and the other at the former Brown Derby Liquors, 120 S. Ninth St. Those two fires preceded the rash of blazes that struck fear into the business com-

munity for six weeks.

Orlanco, which owned the turn-of-the-century building housing the businesses, has not decided whether to rebuild or to sell the property. Orlanco President Chris Kelly, Moore's brother, says several people have offered to buy the property, which he declined to tag with a value.

"It's worth quite a bit," he says, considering the property is "right in the very core of the retail district."

Options for the land include retail stores, offices or a combination of both, Kelly says. "We think it can be made into the dominant corner in downtown Columbia."

In the meantime, all of the businesses but The Copy Center have found new quarters.

There was not nearly enough insurance to replace what was lost, says Mildred Grissum, who owned the business at 14 N. 10th St. for five years. Grissum, now a secretary in the U.S. Department of Commerce's local office, harbors no hope of reopening her business. "At my age, I wasn't ready to start again."

Columbia Fire Chief Girard Wren estimates damages from last spring's spate of fires at $5 million. . . .

Too often, reporters fail to produce such retrospective articles, perhaps because of the press of newer, more timely events. Those who avoid that temptation can find good articles that not only will please editors but also will interest readers.

# THE STORY OF A CRASH AND ITS FOLLOW-UP

The importance of pursuing every angle of a major story is well illustrated by the San Jose (Calif.) Mercury's coverage of a tragedy that almost became a disaster. A small airplane with four people aboard lost power after takeoff and crashed into an elementary school parking lot. First- and second-grade students on recess were on a playground only 50 feet from the crash site.

When editors at the Mercury learned of the crash, they sent reporters and photographers to the scene. One concentrated on the main news story, which was to become the *lead story* for the day—the one most prominently displayed on the front page. This was the result:

A light plane crashed into an elementary school parking lot near 150 children on noontime recess in East San Jose Wednesday, killing three of the four persons aboard.

No one on the ground was injured, although the plane exploded and burned within 50 feet of first- and second-graders on the playground at Katherine Smith School, 2025 Clarice Drive.

Among the dead was the plane's pilot, Francis K. Allen, who had 13 years of flying experience—but who never before had flown the type of plane that he died in Wednesday, his daughter, Debbie Schlict, said.

Allen, 51, lived at 1398 Cerro Verde Lane, San Jose.

He was being checked out in the plane, a single-engine Bellanca, by an 18-year-old licensed instructor, who also was killed. The instructor was identified as Ralph G. Anello, 1681 The Alameda, Apt. 31, San Jose, who also served as co-pilot.

A Federal Aviation Administration spokesman said it is not uncommon for an 18-year-old to be an instructor. "As long as you're certified, there are no restrictions," he said.

The third victim was Ila Diane Cooper, 32, of 390 Bluefield Drive, San Jose.

The survivor, who scrambled clear of the wreck, is Lawrence Allen Herbst, 32, of 5870 Christ Drive, also San Jose. He was in stable condition at Alexian Brothers Hospital Wednesday night with first- and second-degree burns on his face, hands and elbows.

The plane apparently lost power on takeoff at 12:13 p.m. from Reid-Hillview Airport, circled south and plunged into the parking lot at the front of the school after a flight of only one minute.

Alerted by two playground aides, the children saw the faltering aircraft heading for them and ran, screaming, for the shelter of a nearby classroom wing, a witness said.

The craft overturned one car, and it

and four other vehicles were bathed in flames as the plane's gas tank exploded.

Witnesses said it appeared the pilot may have nosed the craft into the ground at the last moment to avoid hitting the playground, which was in direct line with the plane's final course.

The youngest victim, Anello, is the son of Superior Judge Peter Anello, who is on vacation in Italy.

Mrs. Cooper, an employee at IBM, is survived by her husband, Donald, and two children.

Allen also was an employee at IBM.

The victims died of extensive burns, not crash injuries, the coroner's office reported.

Authorities said the plane had been rented from Western Aviation Flight Center Inc. at Reid-Hillview.

One of the first on the scene and one who helped lead Herbst away from the burning craft was Trellis Walker of San Jose, a special investigator for the Department of Defense.

"I arrived about 30 seconds after the plane hit," said Walker. "The man was staggering away from the plane, screaming, 'Oh, my God! Oh, my God! There are three others in there. Get them out!'"

"The engine was making so much noise that everyone heard the plane coming," said David Bess, a custodian at the school who was walking on the sidewalk beside the parking lot when the plane hit. . . .

The reporter who wrote that story tells concisely what happened, reports the names, ages and addresses of the victims and quickly anticipates a question that readers are likely to ask: Isn't it unusual for an 18-year-old man to be a flight instructor? A spokesman for the FAA said it is not. The reporter then identifies the survivor of the crash, who understandably was not available for an interview, and tells the reader that the crash was caused by an apparent loss of power. He describes the scene, works in other details about those involved and quotes witnesses.

All the information except that from the FAA spokesman was gathered at the scene. The story is as complete as possible with the information available. There are other ways this story could have been written, but the plan chosen by this reporter worked well.

Colleagues, meanwhile, were working on related stories. Because the school was so near the airport, San Jose school officials had anticipated the possibility of something similar happening. This story emphasized that angle:

"Sure, we've thought something like this might happen someday," said James Smith. "But what could we possibly do to prepare for it?"

Smith, superintendent of the Evergreen School District, was at Katherine Smith School within half an hour Wednesday after a small airplane crashed into the parking lot.

"We have emergency procedures for things like this, and they were followed," he said. "In this case, they were the same procedures we would use for a fire drill. All the children were evacuated immediately to the back play yard, a great distance away from the crash."

The school staff responded immediately. As Principal Jennie Collett ordered the evacuation, custodian Dave Bess ran out to the flaming plane with a fire extinguisher.

"I saw the crash through the window (of the school office)," said school nurse Laura Everett. "I ran to the front door to see if I could help. But just as I got there, an aide came in and shouted for someone to call the Fire Department. I saw there was nobody else in the office, so I called for the Fire Department and an ambulance.

"Then I ran outside, but by that time the fire was great, and I didn't attempt to get near the plane."

The Evergreen District has only two school nurses. The other nurse rushed to Smith School as soon as she heard about the crash, Mrs. Everett said.

Editors of the Mercury knew that many of their readers have children of elementary school age. They knew that readers would cringe at the thought of their children playing within 50 feet of a plane crash site and would wonder if the school system's emergency procedures were adequate. The response of this school's staff could be indicative. In reporting this story the Mercury was fulfilling its responsibility of serving as a watchdog over a government agency—in this case the school system.

Other sidebars in the Mercury that day provided profiles of two of the victims, the pilot and his young instructor, and an overview of the airport from which the plane took off. That story answered questions readers may have had about traffic and previous crashes at the airport, and about what other facilities were nearby.

Reporters for the Mercury continued to work on the story, and the next day this appeared:

Shortly after noon Wednesday, Mrs. Carmen Eros, a playground aide at Katherine Smith Elementary School, heard a loud grating noise, looked up and saw a plane heading straight for the kindergarten building where her grandson is a pupil.

At first, Mrs. Eros was so panicked she was unable to move and could think of nothing but her grandson, Adam. The she heard the pupils, who were on their lunch recess, begin screaming.

"Without thinking I grabbed three little kids near me and covered their eyes so they wouldn't see," Mrs. Eros said. "Then I yelled to the other aide to get the kids to the building. The kids were crying and screaming, just like us."

Seconds later Mrs. Eros heard an explosion, stopped running and turned around.

"The plane now was heading right towards us and white smoke was coming from its tail," she said, motioning with her hands. "Then all of a sudden, the nose of the plane headed to the ground and it looked like the pilot crash-landed to avoid hitting us.

"I saw a man fly out of the plane, land on the sidewalk and roll over and over. Then I heard someone from the plane yell, 'Help the others! Help the others!'"

After hearing the explosion, the teachers ran outside and helped the aides gather the children inside the building. Mrs. Eros was dizzy and in shock, she said. As soon as the children were safe in the building, she went into the nurse's office and passed out.

Wednesday night she could not sleep at all, she said, and Thursday she was so nervous she made an appointment to see a doctor about getting some medication to relax. All day at work Thursday, when she was on the playground, she got chills whenever she glanced at the spot where the plane crashed.

Killed in the crash were Ralph Anello, 18; F. Kempton Allen, 51; and Ila Diane Cooper, 32.

"When you see something like that, it's hard to just forget about it. I'm still real shaken up. I wish I could sleep or at least relax. I hate to think how close all the children and my grandson came to disaster. Thank God nothing happened to the kids.''

In an effort to determine the cause of the crash, federal inspectors tore down the engine of the Bellanca aircraft Thursday afternoon, but preliminary examination failed to disclose anything significant.

Jerry Jamison of the National Transportation Safety Board and Chuck Burns, coordinator of the Federal Aviation Administration, spent the day inspecting engine debris and the flight control system.

Burns said he did not think the plane ran out of fuel because of the fire that erupted after the crash.

It may be weeks before the final determination of why the plane crashed is made, the officials said.

In this story the writer looks at the crash through the eyes of a witness and follows up on the investigation of the crash.

That kind of reporting and writing makes stories of accidents, fires and disasters more readable and more meaningful. It allows the reader to know what it was like to be there. As in most good reporting, the human element is entwined with the news.

# Exercises

1. Find an accident story in a local newspaper. List all the obvious sources the reporter used in obtaining information for the story. List additional sources you would have checked.

2. Talk with a firefighter in your local fire department about the department's media policy at fire scenes. Based on what you learn, write instructions for your fellow reporters on what to expect at fires in your city or town.

3. Using your library or a data base, compare the coverage of the same disaster in two daily newspapers. In your analysis, explain which story had the more effective coverage and why.

# 12

# Crime and the Courts

**E**ver since Benjamin Day borrowed an idea from London newspapers and began publishing police court reports in his New York Sun, crime news has played an important role in American journalism. The Sun's humorous accounts of drunkenness, thefts and streetwalking were a hit with the citizens of New York in 1838, and they soon made that newspaper New York's largest daily. Today's newspaper accounts of crime probably are less humorous and more responsible, and there can be little doubt that court reporting is more subdued. Now few editors seriously consider peddling crime news as a means of building circulation.

That does not mean, however, crime and court reports are any less important to today's editors than they were in making the Sun an overnight success. Indeed, such reports are so common in American newspapers that a reporter's first assignment may well involve one or the other.

Why is there such an emphasis on crime? Editors answer in part that the public *needs* to know about it. A public not alerted to a series of murders, for example, may be easy prey for the murderer. Police officials reinforce this view by insisting that public awareness is the key to controlling the nation's soaring crime rate. Editors often add that the public *wants* to know about crime. Readers may not subscribe to newspapers because they contain crime news, but they still are fascinated by it and interested in it. The public also needs to know whether the justice system is performing well.

Because of the emphasis on crime, almost every reporter eventually is called on to cover a crime or a court hearing. Such stories are not covered exclusively by reporters who have police and court beats. The general-assignment reporter often is dispatched to the scene of a crime or to a courtroom when beat reporters are occupied elsewhere.

The reporter who covers a crime or follows it through the courts walks squarely into the middle of the free press–fair trial controversy. Because of past abuses by the press, real or perceived, in recent years judges and trial lawyers have sought to prevent the publication of evidence or details of a crime that in their view may make it difficult to impanel an impartial jury. A judge's attempt to protect a defendant's Sixth Amendment right to an impartial jury seemingly may conflict with the reporter's responsibility to inform the public. But almost invariably that apparent conflict is resolved by the judge invoking the power to order a change of venue or to sequester the jury. A change of venue means that the trial is moved to a location where pretrial news coverage may have been less extensive. When a judge sequesters a jury, jurors are not allowed to go home, read newspapers, listen to radio or watch television during the trial.

The media are vital in transmitting crime and court news. The public wants to have such news, editors are eager to provide it, and judges and lawyers often are determined to limit it. As a reporter who almost certainly will cover crime and the courts, you must know how to meet the expectations of the public and your editors without trampling on the rights of the accused.

**In this chapter you will learn:**

1. How crime news is covered and written.

2. How court news involving crime is covered and written.

3. How questions of taste and responsibility affect crime and court reporting.

# Gathering and
# Writing Crime News

## SOURCES OF INFORMATION

The last thing Tom Wicker expected to write on Nov. 22, 1963, was a crime story. Wicker, then White House correspondent for The New York Times, was accompanying President John F. Kennedy on a goodwill visit to Texas. Kennedy was trying to re-establish good relations with the southern wing of the Democratic Party, and Wicker expected little more than to cover a few speeches and to interview some of the key figures.

The rest is history. An assassin's bullet hit Kennedy as his motorcade passed through Dallas' Dealey Plaza. Soon afterward the president died at Parkland Hospital, and Wicker found himself asking some of the same questions any reporter who covers a murder must ask. How many times was the victim hit? From where were the shots fired? What kind of weapon was used? What is the name of the accused? The list of such questions was endless, and many of them have not been answered to everyone's satisfaction. Wicker later wrote:

> At first no one knew what happened, or how, or where, much less why. Gradually, bits and pieces began to fall together, and within two hours a reasonably coherent version of the story began to be possible. Even now, however, I know no reporter who was there who has a clear and orderly picture of that surrealistic afternoon; it is still a matter of bits and pieces thrown hastily into something like a whole.

The example, of course, is an extreme one. Few reporters are likely to cover a presidential assassination. But the incident illustrates how difficult it is to piece together an account of a crime, even when, as in this case, there are thousands of witnesses.

Most information comes from three major sources:

1. Police officials and their reports.

2. The victim or victims.

3. The witness or witnesses.

The circumstances of the crime may determine which of these three sources is most important, which should be checked first or whether they should be checked at all. If the victim is available, as a reporter you should make every effort to get an interview. But if the victim and witnesses are unavailable, the police and their report become primary sources.

*When* your editor assigns you to a crime story is important. If you are dispatched to the scene of the crime as it happens or soon afterward, you probably will interview the victim and witnesses first. The police report can wait. But if you are assigned to write about a crime that occurred the night before, the police report is the starting point.

**BURGLARY**

| 1 OFFENSE | | 2 CASE # |
|---|---|---|
| Burglary | | 32701 |

| 3 OCCURRED AT (ADDRESS) | 4 DATE/TIME OCCURRED | 5 DATE/TIME REPORTED | 6 DATE/TIME REPORT WRITTEN |
|---|---|---|---|
| 308 Maple St. | 0100 - 0800 | 0830 | 0945 - 11 March |

| 7 PERSON REPORTING | RAC | SEX | DOB | ADDRESS | HOME PHONE | BUS. PHONE |
|---|---|---|---|---|---|---|
| Linda L. Mellotti | W | F | 9-11-45 | 308 Maple St. | 372-1124 | 372-9988 |

| 8 OWNER OF BUILDING | | | | ADDRESS | HOME PHONE | BUS. PHONE |
|---|---|---|---|---|---|---|

| 9 WITNESS | RAC | SEX | DOB | ADDRESS | HOME PHONE | BUS. PHONE |
|---|---|---|---|---|---|---|
| NONE | | | | | | |

| 10 VICTIM (FIRM OR INDIVIDUAL) | RAC | SEX | DOB | ADDRESS | HOME PHONE | BUS. PHONE |
|---|---|---|---|---|---|---|
| VICTIM | | | | | | |

11 RESIDENCE ☒  NONRESIDENCE ☐  12 FORCE ☒ NO FORCE ☐  13 DAY ☐ NIGHT ☒  14 TYPE OF BUSINESS  UNKNOWN ☐

15 POINT OF ENTRY  Back door

16 HOW WAS ENTRY GAINED  Glass broken to unlock door

17 TYPE OF LOCK OR STRUCTURE DEFEATED  Type A

18 DAMAGE CAUSED BY ENTRY  Broken window glass

19 WHO SECURED BLDG  Occupant

| 20 QUAN | 21 TYPE | 22 BRAND | 23 SERIAL # | 24 PHYSICAL DESCRIPTION | 25 VALUE | 26 DATE ENTERED | BY | 27 DATE CLEARED | BY |
|---|---|---|---|---|---|---|---|---|---|
| STOLEN PROP | | | | | | | | | |
| A | 1 | Console | GE | Unknown | TV set | $300 | | | |

| 28 SUSPECT NAME | RAC | SEX | DOB | ADDRESS | HOME PHONE | BUS. PHONE |
|---|---|---|---|---|---|---|
| NONE | | | | | | |

| HT. | WT. | EYES | HAIR | BUILD | FACIAL HAIR | HAT | COAT | SHIRT | TROUSERS | SHOES |
|---|---|---|---|---|---|---|---|---|---|---|

UNUSUAL IDENTIFIERS

MARKS SCARS & TATTOOS

| SUSPECT VEHICLE COLOR | YEAR | MAKE | MODEL | STYLE | VIN | LIC YR | LIC STATE | LIC TYPE | LIC NUMBER |
|---|---|---|---|---|---|---|---|---|---|

29 INVESTIGATING OFFICER   DEPT   30. APPROVED BY   31. EVIDENCE COLLECTED BY   32. PHOTOGRAPHY BY   PHOTO OBTAINED   33. REASSIGNED TO   BY

34. NARRATIVE:

Victim works night shift at Milan Hospital. Residence
entered while she was working. TV set only item
known missing.

**WORK SHEET**

Figure 12.1   Police Report. This burglary report is typical of the types of reports available to reporters at most police stations.

243

## Police and Police Reports

A police officer investigating a crime covers much of the same ground you do. The officer is interested in who was involved, what happened, when, where, why and how. Those details are needed to complete the official report of the incident, and you need them for your story.

When you write about crime, the police report always should be checked. It is often the source of such basic information as:

1. A description of what happened.

2. The location of the incident.

3. The name, age and address of the victim.

4. The name, age and address of the suspect, if any.

5. The offense police believe the suspect has committed.

6. The extent of injuries, if any.

7. The names, ages and addresses of the witnesses.

The reporter who arrives at the scene of a crime as it takes place or immediately afterward has the advantage of being able to gather much of that information firsthand. When timely coverage is impossible, however, the police report allows the reporter to catch up quickly. The names of those with knowledge of the incident usually appear on the report, and the reporter uses that information to learn the story.

Crime stories often are written from the police report alone. In the case of routine stories, some editors view such reporting as sufficient. Good newspapers, however, demand much more because police reports frequently are inaccurate. Most experienced reporters have read reports in which the names of those involved are misspelled, ages are wrongly stated and other basic information is inaccurate. Sometimes such errors are a result of sloppy reporting by the investigating officer or mistakes in transcribing notes into a formal report. Occasionally the officer may lie in an attempt to cover up shortcomings in the investigation or misconduct at the scene of the crime. Whatever the reason, good reporters do their own reporting and do not depend solely on a police officer's account.

Robert Snyder, a former history professor at Princeton University, studied U.S. crime reporting while a research fellow at the Gannett Center for Media Studies in New York. He was alarmed by what he found. Crime stories, he discovered, still rely heavily on one police source. That, Snyder insists, is a dangerous and seemingly irresponsible practice because one of journalism's founding principles is that a story's credibility is built on the number of sources used. Thus, while the quality of other kinds of reporting has advanced significantly thanks to innovative techniques or editors' insistence on plain old hard work, crime reporting lags behind. Indeed, it clings too often to the single-source practices of the 19th century.

Another concern Snyder expresses is that minorities tend to be covered mainly in the context of crime news. Crime reporting is a staple of urban news, and urban areas are where minorities are concentrated. In cities such as New York, some areas make news only because of crime. This gives readers a skewed impression of what life in those areas is like. As it is reported now, Snyder says, crime is almost always a conversation about race. He concludes that if the media are to change that perception, they must cover minorities more broadly and sympathetically. Crime reporters must help readers understand that crime afflicts all races. The real story of crime, Snyder says, should be the story of the "breaking down of communities and the real weakening of the social structure."

## The Victim

The difficulty of obtaining information about a crime often is caused by the confusion that accompanies such events. The victim may be unavailable for interviews. Even if the victim is available, the trauma of the event may have prompted enough hysteria to preclude reconstruction of the event.

That does not mean, however, that the victim's words necessarily are useless. One young reporter sent to cover a bank robbery returned to the office and announced to her editor, "I couldn't get a thing from the teller. As the cops took her away, she just kept mumbling, 'That big black gun! That big black gun!'" The editor smiled, leaned back in his chair and said, "That's your lead." He realized that the shocked teller's repetition of that phrase said more about the terror of the moment than the reporter could have conveyed in several paragraphs.

Not always, of course, is the victim's account of the story incoherent. One young reporter discovered that fact his first day on the job while filling in for the ailing police-beat reporter. In checking through a pile of offense reports, the reporter noticed that the police had captured a man armed with a rifle who had forced a cab driver to drive around town for an hour at gunpoint. The reporter called the cab driver, who by then was off duty, and produced an interesting story about a quick-thinking cabbie who worked his way out of a sticky situation.

"I just kept flippin' the button on the microphone (of the cab's two-way radio)," the driver said.

The cab company dispatcher grew curious and asked the driver if his cab was still occupied.

"I told him it was. He must have realized I was nervous and called the police."

Moments later, a police officer spotted the cab. The man with the rifle jumped from the back seat and fled, but the police officer caught him. The story itself was not important, but the account of the quick-witted cabbie and an alert dispatcher made it interesting. In most cases the victim's account adds immeasurably to a crime story.

### Witnesses

Frequently the account of a witness is more accurate and vivid than the account of the victim. And frequently a witness will be available for an interview when a victim is not. If the victim has been taken to a hospital or is huddled with the police giving them details of what happened, you are effectively cut off from a major source.

Witnesses, like police officers and the victim, can provide vivid detail and direct quotes to make the story more readable. In addition, witnesses can provide a new view of what happened. Only after interviewing them can you determine if that view will be a useful addition to your story.

Conflicting accounts of an incident sometimes surface when you interview several sources. Such conflicts may be difficult, if not impossible, to resolve. A victim, for example, may describe an incident one way and a witness another. Presumably the victim is in the best position to know what really happened, but, because of the stress the victim encountered, the account of the witness may be more accurate. In contrast, a cool-headed victim is certainly more reliable than a distressed witness. Seldom can the reporter resolve conflicting reports, so the best solution in this case may be to acknowledge the conflict and to publish both versions of the story.

### Other Possible Sources

Although police reports, victims and witnesses are the most important sources, crime reporting does not depend solely on them. In most cases there are other sources, perhaps including relatives, friends, and neighbors of the victim; the victim's doctor; the medical examiner; the prosecuting attorney; and the suspect's lawyer. A good reporter quickly pieces together an account of the crime and uses that information to determine the best sources of information.

## WRITING THE STORY

There is no magic formula for writing crime news. Solid reporting techniques pay off just as they do in other types of reporting. Then it is a matter of writing the story as the facts demand.

Sometimes the events of a crime are most effectively told in chronological order, particularly when the story is complex (this story approach is discussed in more detail in Chapter 17). More often a traditional inverted pyramid style is best. How much time the reporter has to file the story also influences the approach. Let's take a look at how the newspaper accounts of two crimes were developed over time and why different writing styles seemed appropriate for each.

## The Chronologically Ordered Story

Gathering facts from the many sources available and sorting through conflicting information can be time-consuming tasks. Sometimes the reporter may have to write the story before all the facts are gathered. The result is a bare-bones account written to meet a deadline. Such circumstances often lead to crime stories written like this:

A Highway Patrol marksman shot and killed a Kansas man in a rural area south of Springfield this morning after the victim threatened to blow off the head of his apparent hostage.

A hitchhiker reportedly told police earlier this morning that his "ride" had plans to rob a service station on Interstate 70. That tip apparently followed an earlier report of a van leaving a station at the Millersburg exit of I-70 without paying for gasoline.

An ensuing hour-long chase ended at 9:30 a.m. in an isolated meadow in the Pierpont area when Capt. N.E. Tinnin fired a single shot into the stomach of the suspect, identified as Jim Phipps of Kansas City, Kan.

Phipps, armed with a sawed-off shotgun, and his "hostage," identified as Anthony Curtis Lilly, 17, also of Kansas City, Kan., eluded police by fleeing into a rugged, wooded area at the end of Bennett Lane, a dead-end gravel road off Route 163.

Tinnin said he fired the shot with a .253-caliber sniper rifle when it appeared Phipps was going to shoot Lilly. Two troopers' efforts to persuade Phipps to throw down his weapon and surrender were unsuccessful, Tinnin said.

Note that even in this bare-bones account, the available facts of this particular story dictate a chronological approach after a summary lead.

The reporter who produced that story for an afternoon newspaper did a good job of collecting information following a puzzling incident. Still, several words and phrases (the *apparent* hostage, a hitchhiker *reportedly* told police, a tip *apparently* followed) provide tip-offs that the series of events was not entirely clear.

With more time to learn the full story, a reporter for the city's morning newspaper resolved many of those conflicts. As a result, readers got a more complete account of what occurred:

James Phipps and Anthony Lilly, a pair of 17-year-olds from Kansas City, Kan., were heading west on Interstate 70 at 7:30 a.m. Friday, returning from a trip to Arkansas.

Within the next hour and a half, Phipps had used a sawed-off shotgun stolen in Arkansas to take Lilly hostage, and, after holding that shotgun to Lilly's head, was shot and killed by a Highway Patrol captain on the edge of a rugged wooded area south of Springfield.

As the episode ended, local officials had only begun to piece together a bizarre tragedy that involved a high-speed chase, airplane and helicopter surveillance, a march through a wooded ravine and the evacuation of several frightened citizens from their country homes.

As police reconstructed the incident, Phipps and Lilly decided to stop for gas at the Millersburg exit east of Springfield at about 7:30 a.m. With them in the van was Robert Paul Hudson Jr., a San Francisco-bound hitchhiker.

Hudson was not present at the shooting. He had fled Lilly's van at the Millersburg exit after he first suspected trouble.

The trouble began when Lilly and Phipps openly plotted to steal some gasoline at Millersburg, Hudson told police. He said the pair had agreed to display the shotgun if trouble arose with station attendants.

Hudson said he persuaded Phipps to drop him off before they stopped for gas. He then caught a ride to Springfield and told his driver of the robbery plans he had overheard. After dropping Hudson off near the Providence Road exit, the driver called Springfield police, who picked up Hudson.

Meanwhile, Phipps and Lilly put $5.90 worth of gas in the van and drove off without paying. The station attendant notified authorities.

As he approached Springfield, Phipps turned onto U.S. 63 South, where he was spotted by Highway Patrol troopers Tom Halford and Greg Overfelt. They began a high-speed chase, which ended on a dead-end gravel road near Pierpont.

During the chase, which included a U-turn near Ashland, Phipps bumped the Highway Patrol car twice, forcing Halford to run into the highway's median.

Upon reaching the dead end, the suspects abandoned the van and ran into a nearby barn. At that point, Phipps, who Highway Patrol officers said was wanted in Kansas for escaping from a detention center, turned the shotgun on Lilly.

When Halford and Overfelt tried to talk with Phipps from outside the barn, they were met with obscenities. Phipps threatened to "blow (Lilly's) head off," and vowed not to be captured alive.

Phipps then left the barn and walked into a wooded area, pressing the gun against Lilly's head. Halford and Overfelt followed at a safe distance but were close enough to speak with Phipps.

While other officers from the Highway Patrol, the Boone County Sheriff's Department and Springfield police arrived at the scene, residents in the area were warned to evacuate their homes. A Highway Patrol plane and helicopter flew low over the woods, following the suspects and the troopers through the woods.

The four walked through a deep and densely wooded ravine. Upon seeing a partially constructed house in a nearby clearing, Phipps demanded of officers waiting in the clearing that his van be driven around to the house, at which time he would release his hostage.

Halford said, "They disappeared up over the ridge. I heard some shouting (Phipps' demands), and then I heard the shot."

After entering the clearing from the woods, Phipps apparently had been briefly confused by the officers on either side of him and had lowered his gun for a moment.

That was long enough for Highway Patrol Capt. N.E. Tinnin to shoot Phipps in the abdomen with a high-powered rifle. It was about 8:45 a.m. Phipps was taken to Boone County Hospital, where he soon died.

The story is as complete as possible under the circumstances. The reporter who wrote it decided to describe the chain of events in chronological order both because of the complexity of the story and because the drama of the actual events is most vividly communicated in a chronological story form.

The story is also made effective by its wealth of detail, including the names of the troopers involved, details of the chase and much, much more. The reporter had to talk with many witnesses to piece together this account. The hard work paid off, however, in the form of an informative, readable story.

Notice how the third paragraph sets the scene and provides a transition into the chronological account. Such attention to the details of good writing helps the reader understand the story with a minimum of effort.

*The Sidebar Story.* If a number of people witnessed or were affected by a crime, the main story may be supplemented by a sidebar story that deals with the personal impact of the crime. The writer of the preceding chronological account also decided to write a separate story on nearby residents, who had little to add to the main story but became a part of the situation nonetheless:

In the grass at the edge of a woods near Pierpont Friday afternoon, the only remaining signs of James Phipps were a six-inch circle of blood, a doctor's syringe, a blood-stained button and the imprints in the mud where Phipps fell after he was shot by a Highway Patrol officer.

Elsewhere in the area, it was a quiet, sunny, spring day in a countryside dotted by farms and houses. But inside some of those houses, dwellers still were shaken by the morning's events that had forced a police order for them to evacuate their homes.

Mrs. James G. Thorne lives on Cheavens Road across the clearing from where Phipps was shot. Mrs. Thorne had not heard the evacuation notice, so when she saw area officers crouching with guns at the end of her driveway, she decided to investigate.

"I was the surprise they weren't expecting," she told a Highway Patrol officer Friday afternoon. "I walked out just before the excitement."

When the officers saw Mrs. Thorne "they were obviously very upset and shouted for me to get out of here," she said. "I was here alone and asked them how I was supposed to leave. All they said was 'Just get out of here!'"

Down the road, Clarence Stallman had been warned of the situation by officers and noticed the circling airplane and helicopter. "I said, 'Are they headed this way soon?' and they said, 'They're here,'" said Stallman.

After Stallman notified his neighbors, he picked up Mrs. Thorne at her home and left the area just before the shooting.

On the next street over, Ronald Nichols had no intention of running.

"I didn't know what was happening," Nichols said. "The wife was scared to death and didn't know what to do. I grabbed my gun and looked for them."

Another neighbor, Mrs. Charles Emmons, first was alerted by the sound of the surveillance plane. "The plane was flying so low I thought it was going to come into the house," she said. "I was frightened. This is something you think will never happen to you."

Then Mrs. Emmons flashed a relieved smile. "It's been quite a morning," she said.

## The Inverted Pyramid Account

The techniques of writing in chronological order and separating the accounts of witnesses from the main story worked well in the preceding case. More often, however, crime stories are written in the classic inverted pyramid style:

A masked robber took $1,056 from a clerk at Gibson's Liquor Store Friday night, then eluded police in a chase through nearby alleys.

The clerk, Robert Simpson, 42, of 206 Fourth St. said a man wearing a red ski mask entered the store at about 7:35 p.m. The man demanded that Simpson empty the contents of the cash register into a brown grocery bag.

Simpson obeyed but managed to trigger a silent alarm button under the counter.

The robber ordered Simpson into a storage room in the rear of the building at 411 Fourth St.

Officer J.O. Holton, responding to the alarm, arrived at the store as the suspect left the building and fled south on foot.

Holton chased the man south on Fourth Street until he turned west into an alley near the corner of Olson Street. Holton said he followed the suspect for about four blocks until he lost sight of him.

Simpson said receipts showed that $1,056 was missing from the cash register. He described the robber as about 5 feet 11 inches with a bandage on his right thumb. He was wearing blue jeans and a black leather coat.

Police have no suspects.

Such an account is adequate and can be written directly from the police report. An enterprising reporter can add much to a story of this sort by taking the time to interview the clerk and police officer.

After filing this story for the first edition, the reporter found time to call the police officer. He had little to add. Then the reporter contacted the clerk, who had plenty to say. This was the result:

"I'm tired of being robbed and I'm afraid of being shot," says Robert Simpson. "So I told the owner I quit." Simpson, 42, of 206 Fourth St. quit his job as night clerk at Gibson's Liquor Store today after being robbed for the fourth time in three weeks Friday night.

Simpson said a man wearing a red ski mask entered the store at 411 Fourth St. at about 7:35 p.m. and demanded money. Simpson emptied $1,056 into a grocery bag the robber carried and was ordered into a storage room at the rear of the building.

"He said he'd blow off my head if I didn't cooperate, so I did exactly what he told me," Simpson said. "But I managed to set off the alarm button under the counter while I was emptying the cash register."

Officer J.O. Holton responded to the alarm and arrived as the robber left the store, but lost him as he fled through nearby alleys on foot.

"We keep asking the cops to set up a stakeout, but they don't do any-thing," Simpson said. "I know they've got a lot of problems, but that place is always getting hit."

Police records revealed that Gibson's was robbed of $502 Sept. 10, $732 Sept. 14 and $221 Sept. 24. Simpson was the clerk each time.

"This may have been the same guy who robbed me last time," Simpson said, "but I can't be sure because of that mask. Last time he had a different one."

Police Chief Ralph Marshall said he has ordered patrol cars to check the vicinity of the liquor store more often and is considering the owner's request for a stakeout.

"That's just great," Simpson said. "But they can let someone else be the goat. I quit."

Simpson described the robber as a heavyset man about 5 feet 11 inches tall. He was wearing blue jeans and a black leather jacket and had a bandage on his right thumb.

Police have no suspects.

The reporter took the time to get a good interview, and the direct quotes add to the readability of the story. The reporter also recognized and brought out the best angle: the personal fear and frustration experienced by people in high-crime areas. The result is a much more imaginative use of the basic inverted pyramid formula and a much more interesting story.

The clerk, in the course of his remarks, supplied an important tip about repeated robberies at the store. Two weeks later, police arrested a man as he tried to rob the store. The earlier report was used for background, and a complete story resulted.

# Court Organization
# and Procedure

When a suspect is apprehended and charged with a crime, the reporter's job is not finished. Indeed, it has only begun. Because the public wants and needs to know whether the suspect is guilty and, if so, what punishment is imposed, the media devote much time and space to court coverage of criminal charges.

At first glance reporting court news appears to be simple. You listen to the judicial proceeding, ask a few questions afterward and write a story. It may be that simple if you have a thorough knowledge of criminal law and court procedure. If not, it can be extremely confusing. No journalism textbook or class can prepare you to deal with all the intricacies of criminal law. That is a subject better suited for law schools. You should learn the basics of law, court organization and procedure, however. With this foundation you will be prepared to cover court proceedings with at least some understanding of what is happening. This knowledge can be supplemented by asking questions of the judge and attorneys involved.

## COURT ORGANIZATION

In the United States there are two primary court systems, federal and state. Each state has a unique system, but there are many similarities. The average citizen has the most contact with the city or municipal courts, which have jurisdiction over traffic or other minor offenses involving city ordinances. News from these courts is handled as a matter of record in many newspapers.

Cases involving violations of state statutes usually are handled in the state trial courts that can be found in most counties. These courts of general jurisdiction (often called *circuit* or *superior courts*) handle cases ranging from domestic relations matters to murder. General jurisdiction is an important designation. It means these courts can and do try more cases of more varieties than any other type of court, including federal district (trial) courts.

Federal district courts have jurisdiction over cases involving violations of federal crime statutes, interpretation of the U.S. Constitution, civil rights, election disputes, commerce and antitrust matters, postal regulations, federal tax laws and similar issues. Federal trial courts also have jurisdiction in actions between citizens of different states when the amount in controversy exceeds $50,000.

# COURT PROCEDURE

Crimes are categorized under state statutes according to their seriousness. The two primary categories of crimes are *misdemeanors* and *felonies*. Under modern statutes, the distinction between felonies and misdemeanors involves whether the offense is punishable by imprisonment in a state penitentiary or a county jail. Thus, most state statutes describe a misdemeanor as an offense punishable by a fine or a county jail term not to exceed one year or both. Felonies are punishable by a fine, a prison sentence of more than one year or death.

## Pretrial Proceedings in Criminal Cases

A person arrested in connection with a crime usually is taken to a police station for fingerprinting, photographing and perhaps a sobriety test or a lineup. Statements may be taken and used in evidence only after the person arrested has been informed of and waives what police and lawyers call *Miranda rights,* so named because the requirement was imposed in a Supreme Court case involving a defendant named Miranda. Usually within 24 hours a charge must be filed or the person must be released. The time limit may vary from state to state, but all have some limitation to prevent unreasonable detention.

## Initial Appearance

If, after consulting with police and reviewing the evidence, the *prosecuting* (or *state* or *circuit*) *attorney* decides to file charges, the defendant usually is brought before a judge and is informed of the charges, the right to have an attorney (either hired by the defendant or appointed by the court if the defendant is indigent) and the right to remain silent. *Bail* usually is set at this time.

If the charge is a misdemeanor and the defendant pleads guilty, the case usually is disposed of immediately, and a sentence is imposed or a fine is levied. If the plea is not guilty, a trial date usually is set.

If the crime is a felony, the defendant does not enter a plea. The judge will set a date for a *preliminary hearing,* unless the defendant waives the right to such a hearing. If the defendant waives this hearing, he or she is bound over to the general jurisdiction trial court. The process of being bound over means simply that the records of the case will be sent to the trial court.

A preliminary hearing in felony cases usually is held before a magistrate or lower-level judge in state court systems. The prosecutor presents evidence

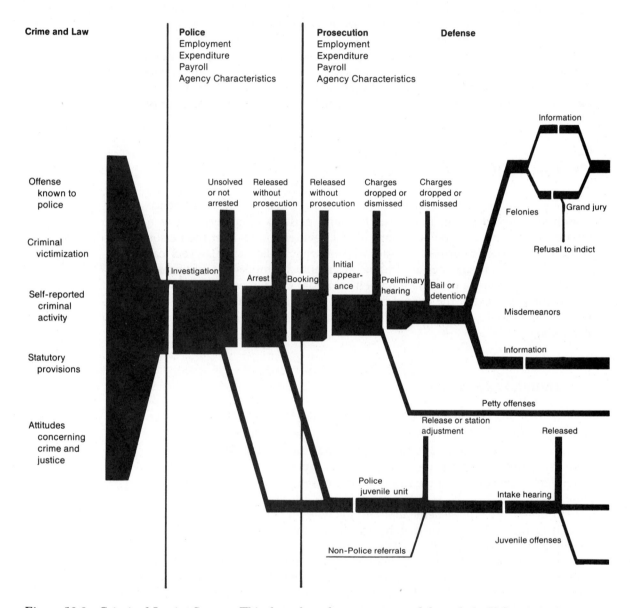

**Figure 12.2    Criminal Justice System.** This chart shows how cases proceed through the U.S. criminal justice system.

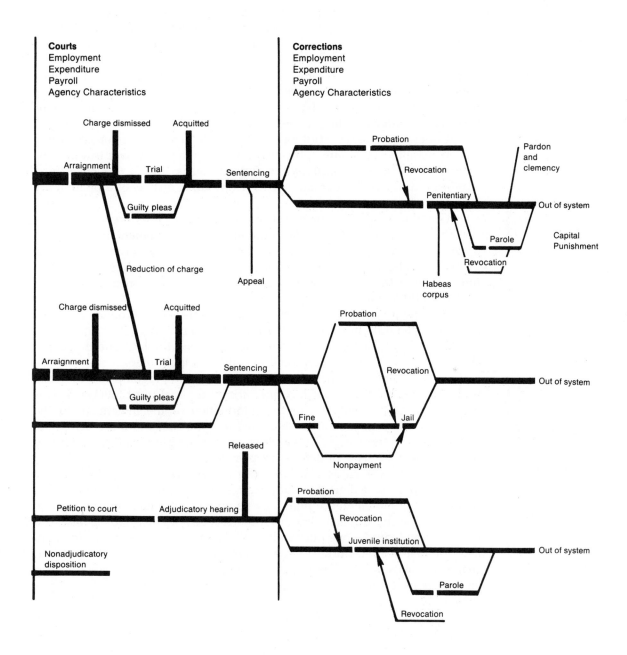

to try to convince the judge there is *probable cause* to believe that a crime has been committed and that the defendant committed it.

The defendant has the right to cross-examine the state's witnesses and the defendant may present evidence, but this normally is not done. Thus, because stories about preliminary hearings often are one-sided, care must be exercised in writing a story that is well-balanced. If the judge does find that there is probable cause, the prosecuting attorney then must file what is called an *information* within a short period of time (usually 10 days) after the judge has ordered the defendant bound over for trial. This information must be based on the judge's findings of probable cause.

Under most state constitutions, it is possible to bring a person accused in a felony case to trial in one of two ways. One is the preliminary hearing; the other is a *grand jury indictment*. In federal courts, the U.S. Constitution requires indictment by a grand jury in felony cases instead of a preliminary hearing.

Grand jury hearings are secret. Jurors are sworn not to reveal information about what takes place in the grand jury room, and potential defendants are not allowed to be present when testimony is given concerning them. The prosecuting attorney presents evidence to the grand jury, which must determine whether there is probable cause to prosecute. The prosecutor acts as adviser to the grand jury.

A grand jury returns a *true bill* when probable cause is found. A *no true bill* is returned if no probable cause is found. When a grand jury finds probable cause, an indictment is signed by the grand jury foreman and the prosecuting attorney. It then is presented in court to a trial judge.

If the defendant is not already in custody, the judge orders an arrest warrant issued for the accused. *Arraignment* in the trial court follows. This is the first formal presentation of the information or the indictment to the defendant. The arraignment is conducted in open court, and the defendant enters a plea to the charge. Three pleas—guilty, not guilty and not guilty by reason of mental disease or defect—are possible.

A process known as *plea bargaining* sometimes is used at this point. Under this process, a defendant may change a plea from not guilty to guilty in return for a lighter sentence than may be imposed if a jury returns a guilty verdict. Typically, in such circumstances the defendant pleads guilty to a lesser charge than the one outstanding. A defendant charged with premeditated or first-degree murder, for example, may plead guilty to a reduced charge of manslaughter. The prosecutor often is willing to go along with such an arrangement if the time and expense of a trial can be saved and if justice is served.

If a guilty plea is entered, the judge may impose a sentence immediately, or a presentencing investigation of the defendant's background may be ordered to help the judge set punishment. Many jurisdictions require presentencing investigations, at least in felony cases. If sentencing is delayed for that purpose, a sentencing date usually is set to allow ample time for completion of the report. If a not-guilty plea is entered, the judge sets a trial date. Most jurisdictions have statutes or court rules requiring speedy trials in criminal cases and setting time limits from the date of the charge being filed to the date of the trial.

As the prosecutor and defense attorney prepare for trial, *motions* may be filed for disclosure of evidence, suppression of evidence and similar rulings. Journalists will have a special interest if a defense attorney files a motion for a change of venue, which allows the trial to be conducted in a county other than the one in which the crime occurred. Requests for venue changes often result from pretrial stories in the local media that may prejudice potential jurors.

## The Trial

The trial starts as a jury, usually made up of 12 members and at least one alternate, is selected from a group of citizens called for jury duty. During the selection process (called *voir dire*) the prosecutor and defense attorney question the prospective jurors to identify jurors that each side hopes will be sympathetic to its position. In the federal system the judge often asks questions, but the prosecutor and defense attorneys may suggest questions for the judge to ask potential jurors.

Each attorney is allowed to eliminate a certain number of individuals from consideration as jurors without having to state a reason. Thus, a prospective juror believed to be prejudiced against the attorney's view can be dismissed. Elimination of a prospective juror for cause (if, for example, he or she is related to the accused) also is permitted. An unlimited number of challenges for cause is allowed each attorney. Once 12 jurors and one or more alternates are chosen and sworn, the prosecutor makes an *opening statement*. The opening statement outlines how the prosecutor, acting on behalf of the state, expects to prove each of the elements of the crime. The defense attorney may follow with an outline of the defense or may wait until after the prosecution has introduced its evidence. The defense also may waive an opening statement.

To establish what happened and to link the defendant to the crime, witnesses for the state are called to the stand. During this procedure the prosecutor asks questions, and the witness responds. The defense attorney then has an opportunity to *cross-examine* the witness. Frequently, one attorney will object to questions posed by the other, and the judge must rule on the objection. When the defense attorney finishes cross-examination, the prosecutor conducts *re-direct examination* to try to clarify points for the jury that may have become confused during cross-examination and to bolster the credibility of a witness whose credibility may have been damaged on cross-examination. Then the defense attorney may conduct another cross-examination, and the prosecutor may conduct another re-direct examination. This process can continue until both sides have exhausted all questions they want to ask the witness. After all the prosecution witnesses have testified and the state rests its case, the defense almost always makes a *motion for acquittal*, in which it argues that the state has failed to prove its case beyond a reasonable doubt. Almost as routinely as such motions are made, they are denied.

The defense then calls witnesses to support its case, and the prosecutor is allowed to cross-examine them. Finally, when all witnesses have testified, the defense rests. The prosecutor then calls *rebuttal witnesses* in an attempt to discredit testimony of the defense witnesses. The defense then has the right to present even more witnesses, called *surrebuttal witnesses*. After the various rebuttal witnesses have testified, the judge presents to the jury instructions— what verdicts it can return and points of law that are key to the case. The prosecutor then makes his or her closing argument, usually an impassioned plea for a guilty verdict addressed directly to the jury. The defense attorney follows with a similar argument, and the prosecutor is allowed a final rebuttal. In the federal system, closing arguments precede jury instructions. The jury then retires to deliberate. Because unanimous verdicts are required for acquittal or conviction in a criminal trial, deliberations often are protracted. If the jury fails to reach a unanimous verdict (*a hung jury*) after a reasonable period of time, the judge may order a *mistrial*, in which event the entire case will be retried from the beginning of jury selection.

If a verdict is reached, the jury returns to the courtroom, where the verdict is read. In some states juries are permitted to recommend sentences when guilty verdicts are reached. Sometimes a second stage of trial occurs when the jury must decide, for example, whether to recommend life imprisonment or death. But the final decision always is made by the judge unless a crime carries a mandatory sentence. Sentencing may be done immediately, but more likely a presentencing report will be ordered and a sentencing date set.

The defense often files a motion asking that a guilty verdict be set aside. Such motions usually are denied. A motion for a new trial usually brings similar results. However, in most jurisdictions a motion for a new trial and a denial are prerequisites to the filing of an appeal. Appeals often follow guilty verdicts, so a verdict seldom is final in that sense. Except in extreme circumstances involving serious crimes, judges often permit the defendant to be released on bail pending the outcome of appeals.

# Writing Court
# Stories

Throughout the court procedure, a reporter has opportunities to write stories. The extent to which the reporter does so, of course, depends on the importance of the case and the amount of local interest in it. In a major case the filing of every motion may prompt a story; in other cases only the verdict may be important. As in any type of reporting, news value is the determining factor.

Also, as in any form of reporting, accuracy is important. Perhaps no other area of writing requires as much caution as the reporting of crime and court news. The potential for libel is great.

## AVOIDING LIBELOUS STATEMENTS

*Libel* is damage to a person's reputation caused by a written statement that brings the person into hatred, contempt or ridicule, or that injures his or her business or occupational pursuits (see Chapter 21). Reporters must be extremely careful about what they write.

One of the greatest dangers is the possibility of writing that someone is charged with a crime more serious than is the case. After checking clippings in the newspaper library, for example, one reporter wrote:

> The rape trial of John L. Duncan, 25, of 3925 Oak St. has been set for Dec. 10 in Jefferson County Circuit Court.
> Duncan is charged in connection with the June 6 rape of a Melton High School girl near Fletcher Park.

Duncan had been charged with rape following his arrest, but the prosecutor later determined the evidence was insufficient to win a rape conviction. The charge had been reduced to assault, and the newspaper had to print a correction.

In any story involving arrests, caution flags must be raised. The reporter must have a sound working knowledge of libel law and what can and cannot be written about an incident. The reporter who writes the following, for example, is asking for trouble:

> John R. Milton, 35, of 206 East St. was arrested Monday on a charge of assaulting a police officer.

Only a prosecutor, not a police officer, may file charges. In many cases, a police officer may arrest a person with the intent of asking the prosecutor to file a certain charge. Then, when the prosecutor examines the evidence, the evidence may warrant only a lesser charge. For that reason, most newspaper editors prefer to print the name of an arrested person only after the charge has been filed. Unfortunately, deadline constraints sometimes make that impossible, and many newspapers publish the names of those arrested before the charge is filed. A decision to publish a name in such circumstances requires extreme caution. If an individual were arrested in connection with a rape and the newspaper printed that information, only to learn later that the prosecutor had filed a charge of assault, a libel suit could result. Many states, however, give journalists a qualified privilege to write fair and accurate news stories based on police reports. Once the charge is filed, the lead should be written like this:

> John R. Milton, 35, of 206 East St. was charged Monday with assaulting a police officer.
> Prosecutor Steve Scott said . . .

By writing the lead this way, the reporter shows that Milton not only has been arrested but also has been charged with a crime by the prosecutor. Carelessness leads not only to libel suits but also to attacks on a suspect's reputation.

Reporters who cover court news encounter many such pitfalls. They are not trained as attorneys, and it takes time to develop a sound working knowledge of legal proceedings. The only recourse is to ask as many questions as necessary when a point of law is not clear. It is far better to display ignorance of the law openly than to commit a serious error that harms the reputation of the accused and opens the newspaper to costly libel litigation.

However, it is also important to know that anything said in open court is fair game for reporters. If, in an opening statement, a prosecutor says the defendant is "nothing but scum, a smut peddler bent on polluting the mind of every child in the city," then by all means report it in context in your story. But if a spectator makes that same statement in the hallway during a recess, you probably would not report it. Courts do not extend the qualified privilege to report court proceedings beyond the context of the official proceeding.

## CONTINUING COVERAGE OF THE PROSECUTION

With the preceding points in mind, let's trace a criminal case from the time of arrest through the trial to show how a newspaper might report each step. Here is a typical first story:

> An unemployed carpenter was arrested today and charged with the Aug. 6 murder of Springfield resident Anne Compton.
> Lester L. Rivers, 32, of 209 E. Dillow Lane was charged with first-degree murder, Prosecuting Attorney Mel Singleton said.
> Chief of Detectives E.L. Hall said Rivers was arrested on a warrant after

a three-month investigation by a team of three detectives. He declined to comment on what led investigators to Rivers.

Miss Compton's body was found in the Peabody River by two fishermen on the morning of Aug. 7. She had been beaten to death with a blunt instrument, according to Dr. Ronald R. Miller, the county medical examiner.

This straightforward account of the arrest was filed on deadline. Later, the reporter would interview neighbors about Rivers' personality and write an improved story for other editions. This bare-bones story, however, provides a glimpse of several key points in covering arrest stories.

Notice that the reporter carefully chose the words "arrested and charged with" rather than "arrested for," a phrase that may carry a connotation of guilt.

Another important element of all crime and court coverage is the *tie-back sentence*. This sentence relates a story to events covered in a previous story—in this case, the report of the crime itself. It is important to state clearly—and near the beginning of the story—which crime is involved and to provide enough information about it so that the reader recognizes it. Clarification of the crime is important even in major stories with ready identification in the community. This story does that by recounting when and where Miss Compton's body was found and by whom. It also tells that she died after being hit with a blunt instrument.

The following morning the suspect was taken to Magistrate Court for his initial court appearance. Here is a part of the story that resulted:

Lester L. Rivers appeared in Magistrate Court today charged with first-degree murder in connection with the Aug. 6 beating death of Springfield resident Anne Compton.

Judge Harold L. Robbins scheduled a preliminary hearing for Nov. 10 and set bail at $10,000.

Robbins assigned Public Defender Ogden Ball to represent Rivers, 32, of 209 E. Dillow Lane.

Rivers said nothing during the 10-minute session as the judge informed him of his right to remain silent and his right to an attorney. Ball asked Robbins to set the bail at a "reasonable amount for a man who is unemployed." Rivers is a carpenter who was fired from his last job in June.

Despite the seriousness of the charge, it is essential that Rivers be free to help prepare his defense, Ball said.

Police have said nothing about a possible connection between Rivers and Miss Compton, whose body was found in the Peabody River by two fishermen on the morning of Aug. 7. She had been beaten to death.

The reporter clearly outlined the exact charge and reported on key points of the brief hearing. Again, the link to the crime is important to inform the reader of which murder is involved.

Next came the preliminary hearing, where the first evidence linking the defendant to the crime was revealed:

Lester L. Rivers will be tried in Jefferson County Circuit Court for the Aug. 6 murder of Springfield resident Anne Compton.

Magistrate Judge Harold L. Robbins ruled today that there is probable cause to believe that a crime was committed and probable cause that Rivers did it. Rivers was bound over for trial in Circuit Court.

Rivers, 32, of 209 E. Dillow Lane is being held in Jefferson County Jail. He has been unable to post bail of $10,000.

At today's preliminary hearing, Medical Examiner Ronald L. Miller testified that a tire tool recovered from Rivers' car at the time of his arrest "could have been used in the beating death of Miss Compton." Her body was found floating in the Peabody River Aug. 7.

James L. Mullaney, a lab technician for the FBI crime laboratory in Washington, D.C., testified that "traces of blood on the tire tool matched Miss Compton's blood type."

In reporting such testimony, the reporter was careful to use direct quotes and not to overstate the facts. The medical examiner testified that the tire tool *could have been used* in the murder. If he had said it *was used*, a stronger lead would have been needed.

Defense attorneys usually use such hearings to learn about the evidence against their clients and do not present any witnesses. This apparently was the motive here, because neither the police nor the prosecutor had made a public statement on evidence in the case. They probably were being careful not to release prejudicial information that could be grounds for a new trial.

The prosecutor then filed an *information*, as state law required. The defendant was arraigned in Circuit Court, and the result was a routine story that began as follows:

Circuit Judge John L. Lee refused today to reduce the bail of Lester L. Rivers, who is charged with first-degree murder in the Aug. 6 death of Springfield resident Anne Compton.

Rivers pleaded not guilty.

Repeating a request he made earlier in Magistrate Court, Public Defender Ogden Ball urged that Rivers' bail be reduced from $10,000 so he could be freed to assist in preparing his defense.

The not-guilty plea was expected, so the reporter concentrated on a more interesting aspect of the hearing—the renewed request for reduced bail. Finally, after a series of motions was reported routinely, the trial began:

Jury selection began today in the first-degree murder trial of Lester L. Rivers, who is charged with the Aug. 6 beating death of Springfield resident Anne Compton.

Public Defender Ogden Ball, Rivers' attorney, and Prosecuting Attorney Mel Singleton both expect jury selection to be complete by 5 p.m.

The selection process started after court convened at 10 a.m. The only incident occurred just before the lunch break as Singleton was questioning prospective juror Jerome L. Tinker, 33, of 408 Woodland Terrace.

"I went to school with that guy," said Tinker, pointing to Rivers, who was seated in the courtroom. "He wouldn't hurt nobody."

Singleton immediately asked that Tinker be removed from the jury panel, and Circuit Judge John L. Lee agreed.

Rivers smiled as Tinker made his statement, but otherwise sat quietly, occasionally conferring with Ball.

The testimony is about to begin, so the reporter set the stage here, describing the courtroom scene. Jury selection often is routine and becomes newsworthy only in important or interesting cases.

Trial coverage can be tedious, but when the case is an interesting one, the stories are easy to write. The reporter picks the most interesting testimony for leads as the trial progresses:

A service station owner testified today that Lester L. Rivers offered a ride to Springfield resident Anne Compton less than an hour before she was beaten to death Aug. 6.

Ralph R. Eagle, the station owner, was a witness at the first-degree murder trial of Rivers in Jefferson County Circuit Court.

"I told her I'd call a cab," Eagle testified, "but Rivers offered her a ride to her boyfriend's house." Miss Compton had gone to the service station after her car broke down nearby.

Under cross-examination, Public Defender Ogden Ball, Rivers' attorney questioned whether Rivers was the man who offered the ride.

"If it wasn't him, it was his twin brother," Eagle said.

"Then you're not really sure it was Mr. Rivers, are you?" Ball asked.

"I sure am," Eagle replied.

"You think you're sure, Mr. Eagle, but you really didn't get a good look at him, did you?"

"I sold him some gas and got a good look at him when I took the money."

"But it was night, wasn't it, Mr. Eagle?" Ball asked.

"That place doesn't have the best lighting in the world, but I saw him all right."

The reporter focused on the key testimony of the trial by capturing it in the words of the participants. Good note-taking ability becomes important here, because trial coverage is greatly enhanced with direct quotation of key exchanges. Long exchanges may necessitate the use of the question-and-answer format:

Ball: In fact, a lot of the lights above those gas pumps are out, aren't they, Mr. Eagle?

Eagle: Yes, but I stood right by him.

Q. I have no doubt you thought you saw Mr. Rivers, but there's always the possibility it could have been someone else. Isn't that true?

A. No, it looked just like him.

Q. It appeared to be him, but it may not have been because you really couldn't see him that well, could you?

A. Well, it was kind of dark out there.

Finally, there is the verdict story, which usually is one of the easiest to write:

Lester L. Rivers was found guilty of first-degree murder today in the Aug. 6 beating death of Springfield resident Anne Compton.

Rivers stood motionless in Jefferson County Circuit Court as the jury foreman returned the verdict. Judge John L. Lee set sentencing for Dec. 10.

Rivers, 32, of 209 E. Dillow Lane could be sentenced to death in the electric chair or life imprisonment in the State Penitentiary.

Public Defender Ogden Ball, Rivers' attorney, said he will appeal.

After the verdict was announced, Mr. and Mrs. Lilborn L. Compton, the victim's parents, were escorted from the courtroom by friends. Both refused to talk with reporters.

Many other types of stories could have been written about such a trial. Lengthy jury deliberations, for example, might prompt stories about the anxiety of the defendant and attorneys and their speculations about the cause of the delay.

Covering court news requires care and good reporting. As in any kind of reporting, you must be well-prepared. If you understand the language of the courts and how they are organized, your job is simplified.

# Taste and Responsibility

Some of the darkest moments in the history of the American press have involved coverage of crime and the courts. Certainly the sensational treatment of crime news was a hallmark of the yellow journalism era at the turn of the century. In the late 1890s, for example, William Randolph Hearst's New York

Journal scored a major success in building circulation with its reports of the "Guldensuppe mystery." The torso of a man was found in the East River, and Hearst's Journal printed every gory detail as one part of the body after another was found in various boroughs of New York. Few would charge that the press of today is that tasteless, but much of the criticism newspapers receive still is centered on crime reporting.

## THE FREE PRESS–FAIR TRIAL CONTROVERSY

Criticism of the press and its coverage of crime often is traced to the 1954 murder trial of Dr. Samuel Sheppard in Cleveland (see Figure 12.3). Sheppard, an osteopath, was accused of murdering his wife. News coverage in the Cleveland newspapers, which included front-page editorials, was intense. In 1966, the Supreme Court said the trial judge did not fulfill his duty to protect the jury from the news coverage that saturated the community and to control disruptive influences in the courtroom.

That case more than any other ignited what is known as the *free press–fair trial controversy*. It continued throughout the 1960s. Lawyers charged that the press ignored the Sixth Amendment right of the accused to an impartial jury, and the press countered with charges that lawyers ignored the First Amendment.

Editors realize that coverage of a crime can make it difficult to impanel an impartial jury, but they argue that courts have available many remedies other than restricting the flow of information. In the Sheppard case, for example, the Supreme Court justices said a change of venue, which moves the trial to a location where publicity is not as intense, could have been ordered. Other remedies suggested by the court in such cases are to continue (delay) the trial, to grant a new trial or to head off possible outside influences during the trial by sequestering the jury. Editors also argue that acquittals have been won in some of the most publicized cases in recent years.

Despite the remedies the Supreme Court offered in the Sheppard case, trial judges continued to be concerned about impaneling impartial juries. Judges issued hundreds of gag orders in the wake of the Sheppard case. Finally, in 1976, in the landmark case of Nebraska Press Association vs. Stuart, the Supreme Court ruled that a gag order was an unconstitutional prior restraint that violated the First Amendment to the Constitution. The justices did not go so far as to rule that all gag orders are invalid. But in each case, the trial judge has to prove that an order restraining publication would protect the rights of the accused and that there are no other alternatives that would be less damaging to First Amendment rights.

That, of course, did not end the concerns of trial judges. Rather than issue gag orders restricting the press from reporting court proceedings, some

**Figure 12.3   The Free Press-Fair Trial Controversy.** The Sam Sheppard murder trial in 1954 raised questions about how much reporters should be allowed to write during judicial proceedings. The carnival atmosphere of the trial fostered sensationalism, and reporters covering it rushed to the courthouse press room, shown here, to report every detail to their editors.

attempted to close their courtrooms. In the first such case to reach the Supreme Court, Gannett vs. DePasquale, the press and public suffered a severe but temporary blow. On July 2, 1979, in a highly controversial decision, the justices said, ''We hold that members of the public have no constitutional right under the Sixth and Fourteenth amendments to attend criminal trials.'' The case itself had involved only a pretrial hearing.

As a result of the decision and the confusion that followed, the Supreme Court of Virginia sanctioned the closing of an entire criminal trial. The accused was acquitted during the second day of the secret trial. The U.S.

Supreme Court agreed to hear the appeal of the trial judge's action in a case known as Richmond Newspapers vs. Virginia. On July 2, 1980, the court said that under the First Amendment "the trial of a criminal case must be open to the public." Only a court finding of an "overriding interest," which was not defined, would be grounds for closing a criminal trial.

In Massachusetts, a judge excluded the public and press from the entire trial of a man accused of raping three teen-agers. A Massachusetts law provided for the mandatory closing of trials involving specific sex offenses against minors. The U.S. Supreme Court held in 1982 in Globe Newspaper Co. vs. Superior Court that the mandatory closure law violated the First Amendment right of access to criminal trials established in the Richmond Newspapers case. The justices ruled that when a state attempts to deny the right of access in an effort to inhibit the disclosure of sensitive information, it must show that the denial "is necessitated by a compelling governmental interest." The court indicated in the opinion that in some cases *in-camera* proceedings for youthful witnesses may be appropriate. In-camera proceedings are those that take place in a judge's chambers outside the view of the press and public.

In Press-Enterprise vs. Riverside County Superior Court, the Supreme Court ruled in 1984 that a court order closing the jury-selection process in a rape-murder case was invalid. The court ruled that jury selection has been a public process with exceptions only for good cause. In a second Press-Enterprise vs. Riverside County Superior Court case, the Supreme Court said in 1986 that preliminary hearings should be open to the public unless there is a "substantial probability" that the resulting publicity would prevent a fair trial and there are no "reasonable alternatives to closure."

These cases appeared to uphold the right of the press and public to have access to criminal proceedings. Judges, however, have a duty to protect the rights of the accused, and similar situations may arise in the future. The Supreme Court of the State of Washington, in Federated Publications vs. Swedberg, held in 1981 that press access to pretrial hearings may be conditioned on the agreement of reporters to abide by voluntary press-bar guidelines that exist in some states. The decision involved a preliminary hearing in a Bellingham, Wash., murder case tied to the "Hillside strangler" murders in the Los Angeles area. The state Supreme Court ruled that the lower court order was "a good-faith attempt to accommodate the interests of both defendant and press." The lower court had required reporters covering the hearing to sign a document in which the reporters agreed to abide by press-bar guidelines. The state Supreme Court said the document should be taken as a moral commitment on the part of the reporters, not as a legally enforceable document.

The U.S. Supreme Court in 1982 refused to hear an appeal of that case. Fortunately, many states have statutes to the effect that "the setting of every court shall be public, and every person may freely attend the same." When such statutes are in place, the closed courtroom controversy appears to be moot. In states that have no such statute, the result seems to be:

1. That a criminal trial must be open unless there is an ''overriding interest'' that requires some part of it to be closed.

2. That judges must find some overriding interest before closing pretrial hearings.

One effect of the Washington decision is that many media groups are withdrawing from state press-bar agreements in the few states that have such guidelines. Their reasoning is that the voluntary guidelines in effect could become mandatory.

The fact remains that there are many ways for judges to protect the rights of the accused without trampling on the right of the press and public to attend trials and pretrial hearings. Indeed, most editors are sensitive to the rights of the accused. Most exercise self-restraint when publishing information about a crime. Most have attempted to establish written policy on such matters, though others insist that individual cases must be judged on their merits.

## DISPUTED ISSUES

Some of the major issues involving taste and responsibility in crime and court reporting are these:

1. When should newspapers publish details of how a murder or another crime was committed?

2. When should newspapers publish details about sex crimes or print the names of sex-crime victims?

3. When should newspapers publish a suspect's confession or even the fact that the suspect has confessed?

4. When should newspapers write about a defendant's prior criminal record?

5. When should newspapers print the names of juveniles charged with crimes?

None of these questions can be answered to everyone's satisfaction, and it is doubtful whether rules can be established to apply in all such situations. There have been charges that when newspapers print details of a murder, some people employ the techniques outlined to commit more murders. This charge is directed more frequently at television, but newspapers have not been immune.

The reporting of sex crimes also causes controversy. Most editors think of their publications as family newspapers and are properly hesitant about reporting the lurid details of sex crimes. What began as an interesting murder case in one college town turned into grist for the scandal mill. A college professor murdered one of his students who had asked for after-hours tutoring. When police unraveled the morbid tale of the professor, a homosexual necrophiliac, knowing what to write for the family newspaper became a major problem for the reporter. The newspaper provided information to the public on what had happened but deliberately avoided sensationalism. Even during the trial, specifics were avoided in favor of testimony that revealed the nature of the case in general terms:

> "He lived in a world of fantasies,"
> the doctor said. "He spent much of
> his time daydreaming about homosex-
> ual, necrophilic, homicidal, suicidal
> and cannibalistic fantasies."

To have been more specific would have been revolting to many of the newspaper's readers.

A related problem is the question of how to handle rape reports. Too often, rapes are not reported to police because victims are unwilling to appear in court to testify against the suspects. Defense attorneys sometimes use such occasions to attack the victim's morals and imply that she consented to sexual relations. Many victims decline to press charges because of fear that their names will be made public in newspapers and on radio and television. There is, after all, still a lingering tendency to attach a social stigma to the rape victim, despite increasing public awareness of the nature of the crime.

In some states "rape shield" statutes have been passed to prohibit a defendant's attorney from delving into the rape victim's prior sexual activity unless some connection can be shown with the circumstances of the rape charged.

Many editors will not publish details of a suspect's confession in an effort to protect the suspect's rights. Publication of such information blocks the way for a fair trial perhaps more easily than anything else a newspaper can do. Some newspapers, however, continue to publish assertions by police or prosecutors that a confession has been signed. Many question whether such information isn't just as prejudicial as the confession statement itself.

Occasionally, the question arises of whether to publish or to suppress an unsolicited confession. After a youth was charged with a series of robberies and was certified to stand trial as an adult, a newspaper reporter phoned the youthful defendant, who was free on bail, for an interview. The result was interesting:

> Ricketts said he and two others took money from the service station "because we was broke at the time and needed the money, and we was ignorant."
>
> He said they had "no idea we'd ever get caught. It wasn't worth it."

The defendant went on to admit to two other robberies in what amounted to a confession to the newspaper and its readers. The editor, who would not have printed a simple statement by police that the defendant had confessed to the crime, printed this one. Why? The editor reasoned that information about a confession to police amounts to secondhand, hearsay information. The confession to a reporter, however, was firsthand information obtained by the newspaper directly from the accused.

Lawyers also view as prejudicial the publication of a defendant's prior criminal record. Even if authorities refuse to divulge that information, much of it may be in the newspaper morgue. Should it be published? Most editors believe it should, particularly if a prior conviction was for a similar offense. Most attorneys disagree.

Whether to use the names of juveniles charged with crimes is a troublesome issue as well. Most states prohibit law enforcement officers and court officials from releasing the names of juveniles. The reasoning of those who oppose releasing juveniles' names is that the publicity marks them for life as criminals. Those who hold this view argue that there is ample opportunity for these individuals to change their ways and become good citizens—if the newspaper does not stamp them as criminals. Others argue that juveniles who commit serious offenses, such as rape and armed robbery, should be treated as adults.

Questions such as these elicit divergent views from editors, some of whom regularly seek the advice of their newspapers' lawyers. Little guidance for the reporter can be offered here. Because the decision to publish or not to publish is the editor's, not the reporter's, consultation is necessary. Each case must be decided on its merits.

# Suggested Readings

Buchanan, Edna. "The Corpse Had a Familiar Face." New York: Random House, 1987. An excellent description of covering crime in Miami by one of the nation's most respected crime reporters.

Franklin, Marc A. "The First Amendment and the Fourth Estate." Mineola, N.Y.: The Foundation Press, 1985. A good explanation of the law of the press.

Nelson, Harold L. and Teeter, Dwight L., Jr. "Law of Mass Communication." Mineola, N.Y.: The Foundation Press, 1986. An excellent compilation of law as it affects the working reporter.

# Exercises

1. Cover a session of your local municipal court. Write a story based on the most interesting case of the day.

2. You have just been named managing editor of a newspaper. Write a policy for your staff on withholding the names of rape and sexual-assault victims.

3. Find a court story in a local newspaper. Determine what sources the reporter used in the story, and tell how the story could have been improved.

# 13

## Follows

**D**etails of the first Watergate story on June 17, 1972, were phoned in by Alfred E. Lewis, a Washington Post police reporter for 35 years. The first front-page Watergate story carried his byline. It was the work of eight reporters, one named Bob Woodward. The same paper carried a story by Carl Bernstein about the suspects. As Woodward and Bernstein wrote later in "All the President's Men," city editor Barry Sussman asked them to return to the office that Sunday morning to "follow up." Thus began one of the most intensely followed events in the history of newspapers. By reporting it, Woodward and Bernstein led The Washington Post to a Pulitzer Prize and became millionaires.

After the National Guard shot and killed four students at Kent State University in Ohio in 1970, the Akron Beacon Journal sent a team of reporters to the campus to try to re-create the events. The result was a massive report that challenged the official version of the tragedy. For following up a story, the Akron Beacon Journal group, like The Washington Post, won a Pulitzer Prize.

What follows a news story may be as important or interesting as the original story. After people ask what happened, they usually ask, what happened next? Because newspapers cannot wait to go to press until a story is complete, follow-up stories (or simply, follows) are common.

A *follow* may tell readers what happened next, or it may catch up with or complete a story broken by another paper. It may keep readers posted about a story that is breaking or continuing. Or a follow may deal with something that happened months ago and report developments since then.

Follows are part of every news medium and are the major portion of most news magazines. Some papers and magazines offer regular columns or sections of follows. Sometimes they are the most-looked-for and the most-read items a publication has to offer.

Because you will be assigned to follow stories, you must learn the proper techniques for writing them.

**In this chapter you will learn to report and write:**

1. *The second-cycle story,* a second version of a story already published, also called a *second-day story.*

2. *The developing story,* a story in which newsworthy events occur over several days or weeks.

3. *The update,* a story that reports on a development related to an earlier story.

# The Second-Cycle Story

Even the best newspapers sometimes get scooped on a story. The same is true of broadcast news operations, radio or television. Competition is not a thing of the past. Newspapers try to get stories before they appear on television and vice versa. Also competing are vigorous suburban dailies and weeklies, weekly news magazines, and newspapers from other areas, including the national newspapers The New York Times, The Wall Street Journal and USA Today.

Sometimes one medium gets the story first because of when the news breaks. In rare cities that still have competing morning and afternoon papers, an afternoon paper will have news that occurred after the morning paper has gone to press and vice versa. A news organization should never use exactly the same story as its competitor, but neither can it ignore a story that is newsworthy.

A *second-cycle story* provides a fresh slant. By writing such a story, reporters allow readers and listeners to catch up with or follow a story that has already broken. To give a fresh slant to second-cycle stories, reporters can:

1. Supply information not available when the first story was written.

2. Use enterprise to uncover information not contained in the original.

3. Supply fresh details, color and background, even when nothing of substance is new.

4. Respond to the news of the first story with analysis, possible developments or the reactions of people whom the news would affect.

5. Gather local reactions to a national or international story.

Let's look at each of these approaches.

## SUPPLYING PREVIOUSLY UNAVAILABLE INFORMATION

When you are asked to do a rewrite of a story appearing in a competing news medium, you are expected to make your story as dissimilar as possible without distorting the facts. Read the story carefully. Verify all the information yourself. Then discover whether you can add any new information or report any developments since your competitor wrote the story. For example, here is a part of a morning newspaper's story:

Police called to a northside residence Wednesday found the body of a teen-age boy lying between a toolshed and a garage.

Police said the victim had been tentatively identified as a 14-year-old Springfield youth. However, authorities withheld his name until relatives could make a positive identification.

Lt. Richard Moses and Dr. Erwin Busiek, the medical examiner, said the victim had received several large wounds, one in his head and another on his chest. Authorities said a large rock was found near the body, but they had not determined if he had been beaten, stabbed or shot to death.

An autopsy was scheduled for later Wednesday at St. John's Hospital.

A reporter rewriting the story for the afternoon paper called the police station and found that more information had become available. His story began:

A 14-year-old boy, whose body was found Wednesday near a northside residence, has been identified as Maurice Comstock of Springfield, police said.

Dr. Erwin Busiek, the medical examiner, said Comstock died from a skull fracture. A large rock near the body could have been the murder weapon, police said.

The second reporter was able to identify the victim and to give the cause of death. In this case the new information was readily available from routine sources.

## UNCOVERING NEW INFORMATION

Many times you may have to do some digging to find additional information. An enterprising reporter sometimes wins bigger play with a recycled story than with the original. For example, when one newspaper reported that a man, James Wiley, had been arrested on a driving-while-intoxicated charge, a reporter from the competing newspaper asked the police a few questions and looked at police records. What was at first a routine item on the records page became a front-page story, which began this way:

> For the third time in the last six months, James Wiley, of 403 W. Third St., has been arrested on a driving-while-intoxicated charge.
>
> Springfield police said Wiley, whose driver's license had been suspended, was using his brother-in-law's license last night.

You show enterprise when, through your own initiative, you uncover previously unknown information or add up known information to come up with a new result.

## SUPPLYING DETAILS, COLOR AND BACKGROUND

When a story appears to cover all bases and no new developments have occurred, you still can dig for more details. Here is an example of how a reporter who followed a story made it worth reading a second time. The story first appeared like this:

A 20-year-old Mercer County man drowned while swimming with friends yesterday afternoon at Finger Lakes State Park.

Arthur James Frazier, of 164 Crescent Meadows Trailer Court, drowned at about 5:10 p.m., said Maj. Jim White of the Mercer County Sheriff's Department.

Frazier's body was recovered about seven hours later by divers and a rescue squad from the Mercer County Volunteer Fire Protection District.

White said Frazier swam across the lake with Stanley Shenski, 20, of Springsdale, and apparently tired on his way back.

Shenski said he attempted to carry the youth after he became tired but said Frazier struggled away from him and went under about 15 feet from shore. Shenski and other friends dived for Frazier but could not find him.

Here is the second-cycle story:

Just 20 feet from life.

"I got him within 20 feet of shore. Then he said he could make it. But he couldn't. When I got back to him, he pulled me under."

A dejected Stanley Shenski, 20, of Springsdale, was on the verge of tears. Perhaps it was anger, frustration—how could it happen that a good, strong swimmer could not swim just 20 more feet?

Yet, his friend Arthur James Frazier, 20, of 164 Crescent Meadows Trailer Park, had drowned at Finger Lakes State Park. His body was recovered early this morning.

"He told me he was tired, so we rested a while before swimming back," Shenski said. "It was only 50 feet across."

Shenski was also angry about something else. Other swimmers, as many as 10 or 12 of them, were enjoying the lake that sunny Thursday afternoon. Shenski said he and Frazier did a lot of shouting for help.

But apparently no one heard them.

By interviewing the survivor and digging for details, the reporter was able to keep the story on the front page. The more-engaging lead sets the scene before telling the story.

Here is another example of how a reporter recycled a news story into a news feature. The morning paper's account began like this:

Charles W. Moreland of Jacksonville, Fla., has been appointed administrator of Myron Barnes State Cancer Hospital by Dr. Whitney Cole, director of the State Division of Health.

Moreland, 54, succeeds Warren Mills, who retired last week after nine years as director. At a news conference, Cole praised Mills for "outstanding leadership" and cited the multimillion dollar building program completed during Mills' tenure as an example of his achievements.

A reporter for the competing afternoon paper wrote it this way:

At 5:30 this morning, employees at Myron Barnes State Cancer Hospital caught their first bleary-eyed glimpse of the hospital's new administrator—he was roaming the halls.

But Charles W. Moreland's motive for the early morning stroll wasn't secret. He didn't expect to find someone taking one too many coffee breaks. Instead, he says, "I just wanted to meet the people who work here."

The 54-year-old Moreland will meet a host of people in the next few days. He was named administrator of Myron Barnes by Dr. Whitney Cole, health director in the State Department of Social Services.

Moreland succeeds Warren Mills, 67, who retired after nine years as administrator.

The writer of the second story chose to tell us something more than the news of the naming of a new administrator. We learn something *about* the new administrator. By doing this, the reporter tempted even those who had read the morning paper's version to look at the story again.

Here's another example. First, the morning paper's version:

Susan Teller, Fourth Ward councilwoman since 1983, announced her resignation, effective Sept. 1, at Monday night's City Council meeting.

Ms. Teller will move with her three daughters, Melanie, Betty and Diana, to Ann Arbor, Mich., to work for the University of Michigan as an instructor in city planning. She said she would remain with the council through August to help choose a new city manager and to formulate the new city budget.

"I'd like to stay with the city manager search, since I've been through it before," she said.

Ms. Teller was a council member when George Billing was chosen in 1985 as Springfield's city manager.

The story of the same resignation appeared this way in the city's competing afternoon newspaper:

Fourth Ward Councilwoman Susan Teller, in her characteristically quiet way, waited her turn when it came time for general comments by Springfield City Council members at the end of last night's meeting.

Then she said, "At the end of the summer, I will be moving to Ann Arbor, Mich., to become an instructor in city planning at the University of Michigan."

Just like that. No dramatics. Teller was resigning the council seat she had been elected to three times and had held 7½ years.

She had kept her decision to herself. Even Sam Jasper, the Sixth Ward representative who is her closest friend on the council, learned the news only last weekend.

Mayor James Burd, clearly unprepared, said, "This is a surprise," and then mustered his wits for a short tribute to Teller, although he noted there would be time for more comments later.

"Susan has demonstrated an outstanding ability to take care of her constituents' needs," Burd said.

Teller said she would continue to serve on the council through August, giving her a hand in the selection of the new city manager and in the preparation of next year's city budget.

The morning newspaper carried a straight news lead. The writer of the follow wrote a more reflective feature lead. Then she allowed the councilwoman herself to tell the news by means of a direct quote. The third paragraph continues the feature style with its use of sentence fragments. The reporter had nothing new to report, but she recycled the story in an entertaining and informative manner.

## RESPONDING WITH ANALYSIS, POSSIBLE DEVELOPMENTS AND REACTIONS

Although a news medium can choose to recycle the same information as its competitor, it has several other choices, some of them better.

1. Lead with an analytical approach:

   The resignation of Councilwoman Susan Teller gives the conservatives an opportunity for the first time in six years to control the City Council.

2. Lead with possible developments:

   John James, the conservative candidate defeated by Susan Teller in the 1988 elections, appears to be the favorite to replace her.

3. Lead with reaction:

   Mayor James Burd said he was stunned to learn that Councilwoman Susan Teller would be leaving the council in August.

Often news media follow or recycle their own stories in the three ways mentioned above. For example, after a story appeared saying that supporters of a proposed right-to-work state constitutional amendment had obtained enough signatures to put their measure on the next ballot, the newspaper followed with this reaction story:

An opponent of the right-to-work amendment, Democratic auditor candidate Warren Jones, says the proposal to prohibit mandatory union membership would pass if the vote were taken now.

The amendment was certified for the Nov. 7 ballot Friday by Secretary of State James Gilmore. The proposal received sufficient signatures in eight of the 10 congressional districts.

Having the measure on the November ballot, Jones said, also will divert money away from himself and other candidates.

Both Jones and his opponent—Republican John Hagan—doubted the right-to-work issue would directly affect the auditor's race, the only state-wide office on the ballot.

"The only bearing—the only question I have is how many votes is it going to bring out," Jones said. "Without it, you would have around a million. With it, I have no idea."

The story gives readers a different perspective on the news that the right-to-work issue would be on the ballot. Note the second paragraph. Its first sentence ties the lead to a previous story announcing that the amendment would be on the ballot. The second sentence reports spot news. Then the third paragraph picks up on the lead and discusses the issue's relevance to the election of the next state auditor.

## GATHERING LOCAL REACTIONS TO A NON-LOCAL STORY

Often a newspaper follows a national or international story by seeking local reactions. Remember, proximity is one of the characteristics of news. How has a declining or low inflation rate affected the buying habits of local consumers? How have cuts in Medicare affected a local nursing home?

A week after Greyhound filed for Chapter 11 bankruptcy, a reporter from a small college town thought to call the local Greyhound station. He was surprised by what he found:

More people than usual are riding in and out of town on Greyhound buses.

That's after a three-month-old strike and after Greyhound filed for Chapter 11 bankruptcy.

"I simply can't explain it," said Nora Lipscomb, an agent here for Greyhound for the past six years. "This is a college town, but the students are all gone home. But we still have more passengers than usual."

Not only are there more passengers, but there are more Greyhound buses. No routes have been stricken from the schedule, and an extra eastbound and westbound have been added, Lipscomb said.

Greyhound has said it will continue service while trying to reorganize its finances under bankruptcy laws. Greyhound also says it is continuing to run buses to communities that provided 98 percent of its revenue last year.

"I don't know if we are one of those communities or not," Lipscomb said. "I don't care why we have more passengers. I just hope they keep coming."

This follow brings the story home. It shows the community how local people are affected by an event.

# The Developing Story

As events unfold, a newspaper reports the latest developments to its readers. Often there is a story on the following day, and sometimes a story continues to develop over weeks or months.

The *developing story* begins with the new information in the lead. In the second or third paragraph you write a tie-back to the previous story. A tie-back, you may recall, is a brief review of the previous story. Remember, some readers may not have read the previous story, and you must fill them in. But be careful not to become bogged down in too many details in the tie-back paragraph. If you spend too much on it, the reader is likely to forget what the present story is about. After this background, you need a good transition back to the new information. The usual organization of the developing story, then, is:

1. New lead

2. Tie-back

3. Transition

4. Return to the story

For example, when U.S. hostage Frank Reed was released, a developing story that appeared two days later began this way:

| | |
|---|---|
| *Lead* | WIESBADEN, West Germany (AP)—Former U.S. hostage Frank Reed revealed Wednesday he was held for months with two other American captives in Lebanon and said he was angry and embarrassed that they have not been freed. |
| *Tie-back*<br>*Transition* | Reed, who was released Monday after 42 months in captivity, said he also was held with two British hostages. Reed was flown Tuesday to Wiesbaden for a battery of medical exams and questioning at the U.S. Air Force hospital. |
| *Return to story* | "I have not seen Tom and Terry for a while, and I don't know where they are," Reed said, referring to Terry Anderson, The Associated Press chief Middle East correspondent, and Thomas Sutherland, an American educator. |
| | "For God's sake, it's nearly the sixth year for these men. I'm absolutely embarrassed I'm out before they are." |
| | Reed, in his first comments to reporters since arriving in Wiesbaden, said he spent "the good part of two years with Tom and Terry." |

Most developing stories are of three kinds. They may:

1. Follow the natural course of events.

2. Affect the course of events through enterprising reporting.

3. Both follow and affect the course of events.

# FOLLOWING THE COURSE OF EVENTS

Some follows result from events taking their natural course. In stories of trials or weather disasters, for example, all the reporter has to do is keep up with them.

In the following sequence of stories a community was about to lose its city manager. Its newspaper kept its citizens informed about the developments. Note especially the leads and tie-backs in the stories following the initial story. The initial story began:

Springfield City Manager Jim Thompson has applied for a job as city manager of Peoria, Ill.

The Peoria Chronicle said Thursday Thompson is among 12 finalists for the city manager's job there.

Peoria's Mayor Ron Myer declined to say whether that's so. Myer did say, however, that there were 87 applicants for the job.

Two weeks later:

| | |
|---|---|
| *Lead* | Springfield City Manager Jim Thompson still is in the running for the job of city manager in Peoria, Ill. |
| *Tie-back* | Thompson, city manager here for 5½ years, was one of 87 applicants for the job in Peoria. City officials there and Thompson here refuse to discuss the matter. |
| *Transition* | But the Peoria Chronicle has reported that Thompson is now among five finalists for the position. |
| *Return to story* | The finalists were asked to submit names of references by today. The council may narrow the field further before flying candidates to Peoria for interviews later this month. |

Three weeks later:

| | |
|---|---|
| *Lead* | Though not the front-runner, Springfield City Manager Jim Thompson has survived another screening for the city manager's job in Peoria, Ill. |
| *Tie-back* | The Peoria City Council, in a closed session Thursday, named Thompson as one of three finalists for the position. One of 87 initial applicants, Thompson earlier survived two other screening steps. He should learn within a month whether the job is his. |
| *Transition* | But Thompson is not first in line. |
| | The Peoria Chronicle said that Thompson's remaining rivals are Glen Yale, 56, Peoria's acting city manager, and Gerald R. Dale, 45, city manager of Vallejo, Calif. |
| *Return to story* | Yale is considered the front-runner. |

# Following and Affecting the Course of Events

Many times a developing story will both keep up with events as they happen and affect the course of events through enterprising reporting. Such was the case, for example, in The New York Times coverage of the tragic fire in the Happy Land Social Club in the Bronx on May 25, 1990. Following are a few excerpts from some of the dozens of stories from that continuing coverage.

May 26:

*Course of events*

Eighty-seven people, crammed into an illegal Bronx social club, were asphyxiated or burned to death within minutes in a flashfire early yesterday morning. The police later arrested a man who they said had set the blaze with gasoline after a quarrel there.

Same day:

*Enterprise*

The social club where 87 people died early yesterday was ordered closed at least once in the last 16 months because it was a fire hazard, Mayor David N. Dinkins said last evening.

But neighbors said the nightclub had reopened and appeared to have been operating with impunity in recent months, just as it had on and off since it opened more than two years ago.

For many Hondurans in the East Tremont section of the Bronx, the Happy Land Social Club was an after-hours discotheque where they could dance to the beat of salsa or reggae, drink a Honduran beer or Jamaican rum and socialize with others from their homeland. Many who went there said they knew it was illegal but did not care.

Same day:

*Enterprise*

The crackdown on illegal social clubs announced yesterday by Mayor David N. Dinkins is only the most recent in a long list of attempts to close the establishments, which spring up almost overnight, typically in dark basements and shabby buildings across New York City.

March 27:

*Enterprise*

A centerpiece of the Koch administration's promised crackdown on New York City social clubs—a bill to require owners of clubs closed for safety violations to post a large bond before reopening—died in a City Council committee last year after members said it might penalize innocent landlords.

The measure would have provided for civil penalties of up to $1 million for safety violations that resulted in death or serious injury and would have forced clubs closed for safety violations to carry $1 million in liability insurance before reopening.

Same day:

*Course of events*

Police teams sent into the field by Mayor David N. Dinkins to crack down on illegal social clubs yesterday found 14 clubs operating despite orders to close.

The 14 clubs were issued 15 summonses for 33 violations of fire and building codes. The sweep continued this morning, but the police said no new figures would be available until later.

March 30:

The economic ladder in the social club business spans the gap between street-smart entrepreneurs in New York City's poorest neighborhoods and wealthy, established real-estate operators—and along the way, everyone seems to make money.

*Enterprise*

Club operators—like the owner of the Happy Land Social Club in the Bronx who died in a fire that killed 87 people—generally pay no taxes, buy and sell liquor illegally, take in up to thousands of dollars a night, and occasionally cut corners when it comes to health and safety.

. . . A review of hundreds of building records from the last few years . . . shows that many are owned by long-established real-estate investors, with the City of New York the largest owner of all.

Same day:

A landlord of the Bronx social club where 87 people died in a fire early Sunday was told last year that a "vacate order" had been issued for safety violations, according to one of many documents released yesterday by the New York City Fire Department.

*Course of events*

April 1:

The city notice posted on the door of the Manhattan storefront said, "Vacate." Still, a sign promised "good times" inside the Wanda Social Club, and through the windows, tables and chairs and a bar seemed to await a crowd.

*Enterprise*

But on Friday night, this illegal club and scores of others like it remained shuttered, its operators either put out of business or lying low since the Happy Land Social Club fire in the Bronx.

Clubs like the Wanda are particularly embarrassing to the city, because the city is the landlord.

April 3:

A warrant was issued last year for the arrest of the owner of the building that housed the Happy Land Social Club after he failed to show up in court to answer complaints about safety conditions in the club, city records show.

*Enterprise*

But the owner of the Bronx building, Alex DiLorenzo 3d., a realty investor who owns more than 200 buildings in the city, was never arrested, the police said, because the arrest warrant had a low priority.

April 19:

The lawyer who filed the papers incorporating the Bronx social club at which 87 people died in an arson fire last month is a New York City police lieutenant who was moonlighting from his job in the Police Department's prosecutor's office, the department said yesterday.

*Course of events*

When the embers of the social club fire cooled, The New York Times did not leave the story. Other papers in other cities reported the Bronx fire and then went on to look at unlicensed clubs in their own cities. The follows produced are good examples of a combination of developing stories and enterprise.

Three weeks later:

| | |
|---|---|
| *Lead* | In a surprising turnabout, Springfield City Manager Jim Thompson reportedly has emerged the front-runner for the city manager's job in Peoria, Ill. |
| *Tie-back* | Thompson, now one of two finalists, was considered second choice after Glen Yale, Peoria's acting city manager. The Peoria City Council eliminated Gerald R. Dale as a contender. |
| *Transition* | The job may now go to Thompson. |
| *Return to story* | At a closed meeting Thursday night, the council's consensus was 4 to 3 in favor of Thompson, according to the Peoria Chronicle. The final selection should come within two or three days. |

Three days later:

| | |
|---|---|
| *Lead* | Weeks of speculation ended last night when Springfield City Manager Jim Thompson announced he has resigned to take the city manager's job in Peoria, Ill. |
| *Tie-back* | Thompson, Springfield's city manager for the past 5½ years, was chosen from among 87 applicants for the job. His top contender was Glen Yale, Peoria's acting city manager, who until recent days was considered the front-runner. |
| *Transition* | Thompson's announcement came in the middle of the Springfield City Council meeting. |
| *Return to story* | His resignation is effective July 1, and he will begin work in Peoria July 5. The job will mean an $8,150 raise for Thompson. |

In each instance the lead gives the new information, the tie-back puts the story into context, and the transition moves the story back to support the lead.

To write the developing story, you must establish reliable sources and consult with them regularly. Don't count on the people involved to keep you informed. Look for others with a stake in the story. In this case the reporter needed sources in Springfield and in Peoria. No source should be ignored, even if it is another newspaper. It is better, though, to do your own reporting in order to be sure your story is right.

## USING ENTERPRISE

Good reporters do more than keep up with events as they happen. Some stories would die unless reporters found information on their own initiative that otherwise would not be known. Reporters sometimes make the story happen.

When the city of Wichita, Kan., became involved with the Panhandle Eastern Pipeline Co. in a $1.25 billion coal gasification project, the Eagle-Beacon became interested in the project. In a long series of articles the newspaper exposed the city's secret dealing. For example, reporters discovered that members of the city's project team were so anxious to avoid detection that they made certain they did not fly on the same plane to meetings with Panhandle Eastern officials. The newspaper then detailed the significant risks the city would be taking if it continued to become involved in this massive, unproven technology.

Because of the newness and complexity of the subject, reporters had to study and learn from the few experts around the country who could discuss the technology involved. Because of their diligence and persistence, the citizens of Wichita were told what city officials were not telling them. As a result, citizens voted down a multimillion dollar bond issue that was to fund the coal gasification plant, and the Eagle-Beacon won numerous awards for its coverage.

Good reporters are enterprising; they are full of energy and initiative. They are curious, inquisitive and skeptical. They ask the readers' questions: Why? What next? How does this affect me? What is this going to cost me? Virtually every news event has unanswered questions. Answer them.

# The Update

A third type of follow is the *update*. After a story about a person or a situation has been published, a later book may result in another story, possibly of major significance. Newspapers often have been criticized for hit-and-run reporting, for arousing the curiosity or the ire of citizens and then dropping the matter. Because of that criticism and because of reader interest, some newspapers have begun regular sections of update stories.

A good example of a simple update began with this routine story:

The Springfield police will continue spot-checks, which have helped reduce the number of Springfield vehicles without city license stickers.

The spot-checks, like Tuesday's of 300 vehicles, 17 of which were cited for failure to possess a city sticker, have helped enforce the city's vehicle tax law, Police Maj. Bill Smith said. The checks are not aimed at catching any particular violation but are general inspections of the car and its driver.

At about the time of the spot-checks "the lines seem to start forming" at the city cashier's window, said W.J.

McGee of the city business license office, but there are still many vehicle owners who neglect the vehicle-tax law because "it's still too hard to enforce."

McGee said about 16,000 stickers were sold in September 1985, but that now there may be 5,000 vehicles in the city without stickers. The permits are valid for a year, from October to October, and can be bought at any time.

A week later a check on the sale of city stickers resulted in the following update story:

If the response to last week's vehicle spot-checks by Springfield police is any indication, the average Springfield citizen's sense of civic responsibility may need an occasional nudge.

The nudge this time came in the form of news that motorists without their required $10 city-tax stickers were prime targets of vehicle inspectors. That bit of information brought a deluge of sticker buyers to the city cashier's office.

Police Maj. Bill Smith said the spot-checks were not directed specifically against any particular violation. Still, their effect on sticker purchases has been marked. Seventeen drivers were cited for sticker violation in last Tuesday's check of 300 cars.

"When it came out in the paper, we had them lined up" to buy stickers, a city cashier said Monday. "All three (cashiers) sell maybe 10 to 20 stickers on a normal day," she said, "but last Thursday and Friday definitely were not normal. I would guess I alone had at least 100 the first day."

The lead of the update story refers immediately to the news of the week before. The quote in the fourth paragraph talks about the effects of the newspaper story. An enterprising reporter suspected that the first story might cause some motorists to buy stickers. He was right.

If the story has not come to the readers' attention for a long period of time, you must help by giving more background information on the original story. Nearly a year after a series of articles about a missing girl, for example, a reporter wrote this update:

Mary Dorset never arrived at work that Saturday, Aug. 7, 1989.

Her sister Betty found her apartment open, her unfed cat outside the front door. All her clothing was there. Even her shoes were in the apartment. Betty said she must have left barefooted.

Mary Dorset, who was 23 when she disappeared, was living in Springfield after dropping out as an education major at the university.

In the 13 months since her disappearance, police have traced dozens of separate leads in trying to locate her. Nothing has been successful.

Maj. Will Jones of the Springfield police, the man who led the search for Mary Dorset, says the case has been a puzzling one from the start.

"It's peculiar we couldn't trace her movements better than we did," Jones says. "People who should have known something didn't know at all. It was just strange."

The story then reviewed the leads police had followed in trying to find Mary Dorset. The piece concluded:

> Yet Jones says he is not ready to give up. "I haven't closed the case out yet. I'm still hunting her. I'm not going to quit on her yet.
>
> "It gnaws at you," he says. "Her picture is still hanging in there on the bulletin board."

Although the story is not a happy one, readers have had a question answered that may have bothered them from time to time: Did they ever find Mary Dorset?

Other good examples of updates are stories measuring a politician's campaign promises against his or her performance one or two years later, or those checking whether a law has been effective in correcting the abuses the legislators intended it to correct. Sometimes an update has nostalgic appeal: Whatever happened to . . . ?

If a story is worth writing in the first place, it probably is worth following—a day, a week, a month, a year later. Readers are interested. It's up to you to satisfy that interest.

# Exercises

1. The morning paper has run this story:

> A 7-year-old Springfield girl was molested Tuesday evening near the intersection of Broadway and Rockhill Road.
>
> Springfield police said that at about 5:30 p.m. a man grabbed the girl by the throat and pushed her into a ravine where he then molested her.
>
> Police estimate the man was alone with the victim for only about one or two minutes. The victim was fighting her assailant the whole time they were alone, said Sgt. Jack Phillip of the Springfield Police Department.
>
> The molester apparently was scared off when two friends the girl had been playing with began calling for her, he said.
>
> The assailant is described as a white male with a scar above his right eye, about 6 feet tall. He was last seen wearing an orange short-sleeved shirt with black-and-white checkered pants.
>
> Phillip said there is no suspect in the case and that there have been no similar incidents in the area recently.

You learn that a second minor, an 8-year-old boy, has told police that he had been molested by a person with the same description the day before the incident with the 7-year-old, and in the same vicinity.

That's all the information available. Write the story.

2. An earlier edition of your newspaper ran this story:

Springfield police described the 36-year-old victim of an apparent pistol whipping and robbery as bloodied and in "a daze with his head split wide open" when he was picked up Friday morning at the corner of Tenth Street and Broadway.

Police responded to a call after a citizen reported a man was "walking around downtown disoriented and possibly injured."

The victim, whose name is being withheld by police, related to officials that he had been approached by three men and robbed of his wallet and wristwatch. Police report that a small-caliber handgun was employed in the robbery and used to strike the victim several times about the head.

He was taken to the Springfield Hospital emergency room and treated for cuts, scrapes and lacerations about the face and cranium. He was released Friday morning.

Springfield Police Sgt. Jack Cron said an investigation of the armed robbery is under way, but as yet it hasn't turned up many solid details. He blamed the lack of detailed information concerning the identities of the assailants on the severely intoxicated condition of the victim at the time of the assault.

"He had a blood-alcohol count of .43 percent," Cron said, "and according to the Missouri State Highway Patrol a count of .35 percent to .50 percent can kill you."

Cron said the department has learned that the victim drank in a downtown bar until closing and evidently was attacked shortly thereafter.

Your professor will play the role of any persons you need to investigate the story further. Get the information and write the story.

3. You are told to write a follow to this story:

WASHINGTON (AP)—Physicians need to act more aggressively on the initial complaints of women—especially younger women—who find lumps in their breasts, a study of breast cancer malpractice claims and lawsuits indicates.

The study of the Physician Insurers Association of America found that in 69 percent of cases where claims were paid because breast cancer diagnosis was delayed, the patient had discovered the lump.

"The physician needs to be impressed by such findings and order follow-up studies," said the report.

"This study indicates that self-discovery often may be ignored, especially in younger women where the incidence of malignancy is thought to be less than in older women" and is more difficult to detect, the study said.

The study reviewed 2,373 paid claims reported by 21 member companies of the association.

Discuss a possible follow story, and list the sources you would contact to write it.

4. A competing news medium has reported this story:

The state attorney general Thursday alerted citizens that letters sent by a man soliciting money for his totally disabled wife prey upon the people's sympathy as well as upon their pocketbooks.

About 10,000 letters requesting from $200 to $1,000 each have been mailed by an Oregon man requesting a "loan" so he can build a "small but comfortable" home. The man explains that he refused to put his wife in a nursing home and that her needs have kept him from working for the past five years.

The letters claim that the lender will earn 10 percent interest and be paid back within 10 years.

Attorney General William Turner said complaints registered at the Oregon attorney general's office claim the wife's health is falsely represented. Reports indicate that she has worked as a hotel maid, is capable of driving a car and even delivered the letters to the post office to be mailed.

Fund-raising efforts for private individuals usually are organized through a local church, business or other organization. He advises checking whether any of these efforts are under way before making any donations.

Describe at least three different ways to recycle this story and the steps you would take for each.

5. Find a copy of your local paper that is at least six months old. Look for a story that is worthy of an update, do the necessary reporting, and write a follow story.

6. Read a current issue of your local newspaper. Find a national report or international story that you can localize. Report and write the story.

# PART FOUR

# Beat Reporting

# 14

## Covering
## a Beat

When Jeff Leen was a young reporter for the Miami Herald, he covered the police beat in Palm Beach County. An investment of time and effort paid off in a front-page story. Let Leen tell you how:

I was still visiting every day, talking as often about a sergeant's new white German shepherd puppy or a corporal's unpublished police novel as I was about the latest breaking and entering or the upcoming drug sweeps.

One day, over the phone, a tip came.

"You may be interested in this," an officer said. "The State Attorney's office dropped the charges on a guy we arrested for rape last fall."

A 72-year-old senile woman, a tourist from Ohio who thought she was in California, had wandered 15 blocks into a ghetto bar. She was the only white woman there, and when she met and danced with a 36-year-old ex-convict, no one interceded. He took her to the back seat of a car and had sex with her. The police caught them in the act, but the prosecutors said the woman's senility prevented her from testifying, so the charges had to be dropped. The felon walked.

"I just thought it might be something that you'd be interested in," the officer said.

Some time after the story ran, I was sitting in the police station, making my rounds. The sergeant chatted amiably about the lack of news and the trouble he was having house-training his puppy. His phone rang. It was my competition calling.

"I don't know how Jeff Leen always gets these stories," the sergeant said, smiling at me. "No, we don't favor any one newspaper. Well, you see, Jeff drops in here every day and . . ."

Beat reporting is the backbone of any newspaper's coverage of its community. The reporter who covers a beat keeps the paper's readers abreast of what government, business or some other powerful institution is doing, what it is about to do and what the effects are of what it has done in the past.

The principles of good reporting apply to the coverage of any beat, though the beats themselves are changing as journalists change their definition of the news that is most important to audiences. The traditional "big three" local beats—cops, courts and city hall—long since have expanded to include education, business, science and other topics. Increasingly, assignments are being made more on the basis of issues and less on the basis of institutions.

The environment, for example, is now an important beat that may include government, education, industry, politics and lifestyle stories—with a range of sources to match. Social issues such as abortion, poverty and crime are non-institutional beats at some newspapers. Even mass media themselves are a beat at The Wall Street Journal, the Los Angeles Times and other papers.

Still, beat reporting is likely to remain an important part of most reporters' careers. Such a career typically begins with an assignment like Jeff Leen's to cover the police. From there, more specialized beats may follow. The scene may change to the state capital or Washington, D.C., where the prime institutional beats remain the White House and Congress but where issue beats also are increasingly important.

The skills of beat reporting are readily transferable. In Jeff Leen's case, success as a beat reporter led to a promotion to the Herald's investigative reporting team. That, in turn, led to his co-authorship of a best-selling book on the Colombian drug cartel.

**Figure 14.1
Be There.** Miami Herald reporter Jeff Leen was successful on the police beat largely because of his frequent visits to the police station.

**In this chapter you will learn:**

1. Some basic principles for covering a beat.

2. How to apply those principles in covering the most common beats.

# Principles for Reporters on a Beat

Whether the beat you cover is the public library or the Pentagon, the county courthouse or the White House, the principles of covering it are the same. If you want to succeed as a reporter on that beat, you must:

1. Be prepared.

2. Be alert.

3. Be persistent.

4. Be there.

5. Be wary.

That checklist will help you win the trust of your sources, keep up with important developments on your beat and avoid the trap of writing for your sources instead of your readers. Let's take a closer look at what each of those rules means in practice.

## BE PREPARED

Where should preparation begin? For you, it has already begun. To work effectively, any journalist needs a basic understanding of the workings of society and its various governments. You need to know at least the rudiments of psychology, economics and history. That is why the best education for a journalist is a broad-based one, providing exposure to the widest possible sampling of human knowledge. But that exposure will not be enough when you face an important source on your first beat. You will need more specific information, which you can acquire by familiarizing yourself with written accounts or records or by talking to sources.

## Reading for Background

In preparing to cover a beat, any beat, your first stop is the newspaper library. Read the clips. Make notes of what appear to be continuing issues, questions left dangling in previous stories or possible ideas for stories to come. Go back three or four years in your research. History may not repeat itself, but a knowledge of it helps you assess the significance of current events and provides clues to what you can expect in the future.

The morgue is only the start of your preparation, however. You must become familiar with the laws governing the institution you cover. Find the state statutes or the city charter that created the agencies you will be covering. Learn what the powers, the duties, the limitations are of each official. You may be surprised to discover that someone is failing to do all that the law requires. Someone else may be doing more than the law allows.

In one Missouri town a reporter discovered that the county auditor was supposed to be checking the books of every agency every year. He wasn't doing it. After dozens of stories and two grand jury investigations, two members of the county court and the county clerk pleaded guilty to misconduct in office. The auditor resigned. The books now are checked regularly.

Look at your state's open meetings and open record laws, too. Every state has such laws, though they vary widely in scope and effectiveness. Knowing what information is open to the public by law can be a valuable tool for a reporter dealing with officials who may find it more convenient to govern privately.

## Talking to Sources

Now you're ready to start talking to people. Your first interviews should be conducted in the news room, with your predecessor on the beat, your city editor and any veterans who can shed some light on the kinds of things that rarely appear in statute books or even newspaper stories. Who have been good sources in the past? Who will lie to you? Who drinks to excess? Who seems to be living extravagantly? Whose friends are big land developers? Who wants to run for national office? Remember that you are hearing gossip, filtered through the biases of those relating it. Be a little skeptical.

Some understanding of the workings of your own news room won't hurt, either. Has your predecessor on the beat been promoted, or transferred because he or she was unsatisfactory? Will an introduction from your predecessor help you or hurt you with your sources? And what are your city editor's expectations? Is yours a paper of record, trying to report virtually every activity of government, or will you have time to do some investigative work and analysis? Trying to live up to your boss's expectations is easier if you know in advance what they are.

Only after gaining as much background as possible are you ready to face the people you will be covering. A quick handshake and a superficial question or two may be all you have time for in the first encounter, but within a week you should arrange for sit-down conversations with your most important sources. These are get-acquainted sessions. You are trying to get to know the sources, but don't forget that they need to know you, too, if they are going to respect and trust you.

You may have noticed that the preparation for covering a beat is similar to the preparation for an interview or for a single-story assignment. The important difference is that preparing for a beat is more detailed and requires more time and work. Instead of just preparing for a short-term task, you are laying the foundation for an important part of your career. A beat assignment nearly always lasts at least six months and often two years or more. That understanding helps shape your first round of meetings with sources.

A story may emerge from those first interviews, but their purpose is much broader. You are trying to establish a relationship, trying to convert strangers into helpful partners in news gathering. To do that, you demonstrate an interest in the sources as people as well as officials. Ask about their families, their interests, their philosophy, their goals. Make clear with your questions that you are interested rather than ignorant. (Don't ask if the source is married. You should already know that. Say, "I understand your daughter is in law school. Is she going into politics, too?" Similarly, don't ask if your source has any hobbies. Find that out beforehand. Say, "So you collect pornographic comic books. Sure takes your mind off the budget, doesn't it?")

And be prepared to give something of yourself. If you both like to fish, or you both went to Vassar, or you both have children about the same age, seize on those ties. All of us feel more comfortable with people who have something in common with us. This is the time, too, to let the source know that you know something about the office and that you're interested in it.

Was she elected as a reformer? Ask about the opposition she is encountering. Is it budget time? Let him know you're aware of the problems with last year's budget. Has he complained that he lacks the statutory power to do a satisfactory job? Ask if he's lobbying to change the law. Nothing does so much to create a warm reporter–source relationship as the reporter's demonstrated knowledge of and interest in the beat.

Solid preparation will help you avoid asking stupid questions. More important, it will help you make sure you ask the right questions. And because you have taken the trouble to get to know your sources, you are more likely to come away with responsive answers to the questions you ask.

## BE ALERT

The germ of a good story is hidden in many a routine one. Consider these possibilities:

- A veteran detective who is also president of the police officers' association is being transferred to the patrol division. It's a routine transfer, says a spokesman for the chief of police, a normal part of the detective's career pattern. The managing editor of the paper knows better. A former police reporter who has kept up her contacts, she knows a bitter struggle for control of the department is being waged behind the scenes. The new police chief is on one side, and the detective leads the opposition. The chief won't talk, but the detective and his colleagues are eager to tell their side. The public is let in on at least one version of a significant development in city affairs.

- The United Fund, the non-profit organization that solicits money to support all sorts of voluntary agencies, announces with regret that, once again, it has not met its fund-raising goal. One paper in town prints the announcement. The reporter who covers the beat for the other paper, however, has heard rumblings that all is not well within the organization. He visits a trusted source on the board of directors. Yes, he is told, there is a problem—the executive director. He just isn't competent. That's off the record, of course. The reporter talks with several other board members, who tell the same story. All are worried about the agency's image and hope the reporter won't use the information. The reporter goes outside the board to other community leaders and the heads of funded organizations. He finds a few who are fed up enough to talk on the record and others who refuse to have their names used. The story runs. The executive director retires. Under a new director, the fund reaches its goal for the first time in years.

- On the list of rezoning requests up for approval by the city council, the city hall reporter spots one that looks odd. It is for a change from agricultural to apartment zoning at an address she hasn't heard of. The planning department recommends approval. The reporter drops in on a friend in the assessor's office whose job requires him to be familiar with land deals, since he has to keep the property tax roll up to date. "Oh, yeah," he says. "That land's way out. Those streets aren't built yet." He lowers his voice. "It might be interesting to see who holds the mortgage." After a visit to the recorder of deeds' office, a call to the state capital to find out the names of the officers of two corporations and an interview with a real estate agent, the reporter uncovers an interesting fact. The newly elected mayor, formerly chairman of the planning commission, sold that land to a developer and held the mortgage himself.

The real estate salesman, thinking he is about to be featured in a business-page piece on the planned development, recalls that the mayor had assured the buyer that rezoning is no problem. The problem has turned out to be the mayor's.

Important stories are seldom labeled as such. In many cases the people involved may not realize the significance of what they are doing. Probably more often they realize it but hope nobody else will. The motivation for secrecy may be dishonesty, the desire to protect an image or a conviction that the public will misunderstand.

As a reporter on a beat you will find that many public officials and public employees think they know more about what is good for the public than the public does. The theory of democratic government is that an informed citizenry can make decisions or elect representatives to make those decisions in its own best interests. If you are the reporter assigned to city hall, the school board or the courthouse, you carry a heavy responsibility for helping your readers put that theory into practice. To discharge that responsibility, you must probe beneath the surface of events in search of the "why's" and "how's" that lead to understanding.

When you are presented with a press release or hear an announcement or cover a vote, ask yourself these questions before passing the event off in a few paragraphs:

1. *Who will benefit from this, and who will be hurt?* If the tentative answer to the first part suggests private interests, or the answer to the second part is the public, some digging is in order.

2. *How important is this?* In the zoning example cited earlier the importance lay in the possibility of wrongdoing. In the United Fund example the importance lay in the fund's role as collector of several hundred thousand dollars and as supporter of widely used social agencies. An event that is likely to affect many people for good or ill usually deserves more explanation than one affecting only a handful.

3. *Who is for this, and who is against it?* Answers to these questions often are obvious or at least easy to figure out. When you know them, the answers to the first two questions usually become clearer.

4. *How much will this activity cost, and who will pay?* An architect's design for renovating downtown may look less attractive when the price tag is attached. The chamber of commerce's drive to lure new industry may require taxpayers to pay for new roads, sewers, fire protection, even schools and other services for an increased population.

Once you have asked the questions and gotten answers, the story may turn out to be about no more than it appeared to be on the surface. But if you don't ask them, you—and your readers—may find out too late that more was there than met the eye. The answers allow you to judge that most important element of news value—impact.

## BE PERSISTENT

Persistence means two things to a reporter on a beat. First, it means that when you ask a question, you cannot give up until you get an answer. Second, it means that you must keep track of slow-developing projects or problems.

### Insisting on a Responsive Answer

One of the most common faults of beginning reporters is that they give up too easily. They settle for answers that are unresponsive to their questions, or they return to the news room not sure they understand what they were told. In either case the result is an incomplete, confusing story.

"Why is it that our fourth-graders score below average on these reading tests?" you ask the school superintendent.

He may reply, "Let me first conceptualize the parameters of the socioeconomic context for you."

The real answer probably is, "I only wish I knew."

Your job is to cut through the jargon and the evasions in search of substance. Often, that is not an easy task. Many experts, or people who want to be regarded as experts, are so caught up in the technical language of their special field that they find it almost impossible to communicate clearly. Many others seek refuge in gobbledygook or resort to evasion when they don't know an answer or find the answer embarrassing. Educators and laywers are particularly adept at such tactics.

Listen politely for a few minutes while the school superintendent conceptualizes his parameters. Then, when he finishes or pauses for breath, lead him back toward where you want to go. One way is to say, "It sounds to me as if you're saying . . ." and rephrase what he has told you in simple language. At those times when you simply are in the dark—and that may be often—just confess your puzzlement and ask for a translation. And keep coming back to the point: "But how does all that affect reading scores?" "How can the problem be solved?" "What are you doing about it?"

The techniques you have learned for preparing for interviews and conducting them will help you. Your preparation for the beat will help, too. Probably most helpful, though, are the questions you keep asking yourself rather than your source: "Does that make sense to me?" "Can I make it make sense to my readers?" Don't quit until the answer is yes. You should not be obnoxious, but you do have to be persistent.

**Figure 14.2    Be Persistent.** Reporters are required to track down the famous and the infamous in search of the quotes that breathe life into stories. When hotel magnate Leona Helmsley ran afoul of the Internal Revenue Service, journalists' questions changed; but the persistence required to get the answers was the same.

## Following Up Slow Developments

Persistence is also required when you are following the course of slow-developing events. Gardeners do not sit and watch a seed germinate. Their eyes would glaze over long before any change was apparent. Gardeners do, however, check every few days, looking for the green shoots that indicate the process is taking place as it should. If the shoots are late, they dig in to investigate.

Beat reporting works much the same way. A downtown redevelopment plan, say, or a revision in a school's curriculum is announced. The story covers the plans and the hoped-for benefits. The seed is planted. If it is planted on your beat, make a note to yourself to check on it in a week or two. And a week or two after that. And a month after that. Start a file of reminders so you won't forget. Such a file often is called a *tickler* because it serves to tickle your memory.

Like seeds, important projects of government or business take time to develop. Often what happens during that long, out-of-public-view development is more important than the announcements at the occasional news conferences or the promises of the promotional brochures. Compromises are made. Original plans turn out to be impractical or politically unpalatable. Consultants are hired. Contracts are signed. Public money is spent. The public interest may be served, or it may not.

Sometimes the story is that nothing is happening. At other times the story may be that the wrong things are happening. Consulting contracts may go to cronies of the mayor. Redevelopment may enhance the property values of big downtown landowners. Curriculum revisions may be shaped by some influential pressure groups.

Even if nothing improper is taking place, the persistent reporter will give the readers an occasional update. At stake, after all, is the public's money and welfare.

## BE THERE

In beat reporting there is no substitute for personal contact. Trying to do it by telephone just won't work. The only way to cover a beat is to be there—every day, if possible. Joking with the secretaries, talking politics with council members and lawyers, worrying over the budget or trading gossip with the professional staff, you must make yourself seem to be a part of the community you are covering.

Lisa Hoffman prefers to think of her beat as a sort of extended family:

> To become part of the family, you must convince your sources that you're a human being and that you're interested in them as people, too. I take them out to lunch or for drinks. I ask about their spouses and children and tell them about the fight I had with my boyfriend and the movie I saw Saturday night. I bitch about my editors and grumble about the play of a story. Many have only a ''Front Page'' perspective of the news business, and most are fascinated by how the process really works.

When Hoffman was first assigned to cover federal courts for the Miami Herald, she cultivated her sources diligently. She tells how:

> I check each morning with the secretaries who answer the phones, open the mail, prepare the dockets. Like most mothers, they're the ones who keep the household running. They also know first what's going on.
>
> Then I check in with the law clerks to the various judges. These folks, usually young, opinionated, bright and swelled with ego, have the ear of the judge, do their research and often write decisions for them.

**Figure 14.3 Cultivate Sources.** Reporter Lisa Hoffman contacted people at many levels of the criminal justice system while covering the court beat.

I pay my respects a few times a week to the judges themselves, father figures if ever there were any.

I've found that U.S. marshals, like bailiffs in state courts, can be the nosy, neglected aunts. They know who the good lawyers and judges are, but no one ever asks. They know when the grand jury meets and usually can identify the prominent folks who come to testify.

One of my best sources now is the guy who runs the courthouse coffee shop.

Later, she was able to apply the same techniques to covering other federal offices in Washington for the Dallas Times-Herald.

Remember that the sources who are most important to you probably are in great demand by others, too. They have jobs to do. Maneuver to get as much of their time as you need, but don't demand too much. Do your homework first. Don't expect a school superintendent to explain basic concepts of education. You can learn that information from an aide or from reading. What you need to learn from the superintendent is how he or she intends to apply those concepts, or why they seem to be inapplicable here. Find out what a "Class I felony" is before asking the police chief why they are increasing. You will get the time you need more readily if busy sources know their time will not be wasted.

There are other simple techniques you can use to build and maintain good relationships with the people on your beat. Here are some of them:

1. *Do a favor when you can.* As a reporter you spend much of your time asking other people to do favors for you—giving you their time, sharing information they need not share, looking up records and figures. If a source needs a favor in return, don't refuse unless it would be unethical. The favors asked usually are small things, such as getting a daughter's engagement picture or a club announcement in the paper, procuring a print of a picture taken with the governor to decorate the official's wall, bringing in a few copies of a favorable feature you wrote.

2. *Don't shun good news.* One ill-founded but common complaint is that newspapers print nothing but bad news. Admittedly, there is usually no story when people are doing what they are supposed to do. Sometimes there should be, if they do their duty uncommonly well or have done it for a very long time or do it under the burden of some handicap. Sources like these ''good news'' stories and so do readers.

3. *Protect your sources.* Many people in government—politicians and bureaucrats alike—are willing to tell a reporter things they are not willing to have their names attached to in print or otherwise. Sometimes, such would-be anonymous sources are trying to use you to enhance their own positions. You have to protect yourself and your readers against that possibility. Confer with an editor if you have doubts. Most papers are properly wary of relying on unnamed sources. Sometimes, though, the requests for anonymity are valid, necessary to protect the source's career. Once you have agreed to protect a source, you must do it. Don't tell anyone but your editor. An inability to keep your mouth shut can cost you more than a source. It can cost you your reputation. (The protection of sources has legal as well as ethical implications. So-called *shield laws* in some states offer limited exemptions for journalists from legal requirements to disclose sources. But there are no blanket exemptions. In one effort to resolve such problems, some news organizations try to negotiate written agreements obligating a source to come forward if continued secrecy might cost a reporter a jail term or the newspaper a loss in a lawsuit.)

4. *Above all, be accurate.* Inaccurate reporting leads first to loss of respect from sources, then to loss of the sources themselves, and finally to loss of the job. If you are a good, tough reporter, not everybody on your beat will love you. But if you are an accurate reporter, they will respect you.

The best way to assure accuracy is to check and doublecheck. Many of the stories you will write are likely to be complicated. You will be expected to digest budgets, master plans, legal opinions and complicated discussions, and to translate these into language your readers can understand. When in doubt, ask somebody. If you are unclear about the city manager's explanation of the budget before the council, arrange a meeting afterward and go over it. If the school board's brief in a legal case has you confused, call the lawyer who wrote it. If the new master land-use plan strikes you as vague, consult with the planner. If you are writing a story on a subject you feel tentative about, arrange to read it back to the sources when it is complete. Not all experts relish being asked to translate their jargon into English, so in some cases you will have to insist, politely. The best persuader is the assurance that it is far better for your sources to take a few minutes to explain now than to see themselves misrepresented in print.

Remember, beat reporting is a lot like gardening. Both require you to be in the field every day, cultivating. And in both the amount of the harvest is directly proportional to the amount of labor invested.

## BE WARY

The point of all this effort—the preparation, perceptiveness, persistence and personal contact—is to keep your readers informed. That is an obvious statement, but it needs to be made because every reporter on a beat is under pressures that can obscure the readers' importance. You must be wary of this problem.

You will have little to do with 99.9 percent of your readers. They will not write you notes when you have done a story they like or call you when they dislike what you have written. They will not offer to buy you a cup of coffee or lunch, or stop you in the hall to urge you to see things their way. But your sources will.

### The Source Trap

If you write that city council members are thinking about raising the property-tax rate, you probably will hear complaints from council members about premature disclosure. If you write that the police department is wracked by dissension, expect a less-than-friendly reaction from the chief. If you write that the school superintendent is looking for a new job, the chances are that he or she will deny it even though the story is true.

All sources have points of view, programs to sell, careers to advance, opponents to undercut. It is likely and legitimate that they will try to persuade you of the merit of their viewpoint, try to sell their programs through the columns of your newspaper, try to shape the news to help their careers.

Be wary of sources' efforts to use you. You can lose the critical distance a reporter must maintain from those being covered. When that happens, you start thinking like a participant rather than an observer. You begin writing for your sources rather than your audience. This is a real danger. No one can spend as much time as a reporter on a beat does with sources or devote as much effort to understanding them without becoming sympathetic. You may forget that you are writing for the outsiders when you associate so closely with the insiders.

Many veteran police reporters, for example, begin thinking like those they cover, some of them even adopting the common police officer's suspicion of journalists. The police reporter for one big-city radio station first took to carrying a gun, then quit reporting altogether to do public relations work for the sheriff's department.

One eastern newspaper had a veteran reporter covering the courts for years. A tall, dignified man with an impressive potbelly, he was called "Judge" by many of his sources, including some who were judges. He knew more law than some prosecutors and more about courthouse politics than many politicians. The trouble was that he thought, and wrote, more like a lawyer than a reporter. When he used the first-person plural pronoun in conversation, he often was referring to the attorney general's office instead of to himself and his colleagues on the paper. His writing was full of writs, dicta and other untranslated language of the law. It had become his language. Like too many diligent reporters assigned a beat, he had become part of the beat rather than an observer of it.

# Covering the Most Important Local Beats

Your political science courses will introduce you to the structure of government, but from a reporter's viewpoint, function is usually even more important than structure. You must learn who holds the real power, who has the most influence on the power holders and who are the most likely sources of accurate information. The specifics vary from city to city, but there are some general principles that will help you in covering any form of state or local institution.

1. *Information is power.* The holder of information may be a professional administrator—the city manager, school superintendent, police chief or court clerk—or it may be an elected official—the mayor, chair of the county commission or chair of the school board. The job title is unimportant. Find the person who knows in detail how any organization really works, where the money goes and how decisions are made. Get to know that person because he or she will be the most important person on your beat.

2. *The budget is the blueprint.* This principle is a corollary of the first. Just

# WRITING FOR READERS

What does it mean to write for your readers instead of your sources? It means that you must follow several important guidelines:

1. *Translate.* The language of bureaucrats, educators or lawyers is not the same language most people speak. You need to learn the jargon of your sources, but you also need to learn how to translate it into standard English for your readers. The city planning consultant might say, "Preliminarily, the concept appeared to permit attainment of all our criteria; but, when we cost it out, we have to question its economic viability." Your lead could translate that to:

> The proposed plan for downtown redevelopment looks good on paper, but it may cost too much, the city's planning consultant said today.

2. *Make your writing human.* In big government and big business, humanity often gets lost in numbers. Your readers want and need to know the impact of those numbers on real people. How many people will be displaced by a new highway? And who are they? Who will be affected by a school closing or a welfare cut? When a police report announced that burglaries were up by 35 percent in the last two months, an enterprising reporter told the story through the eyes of a victim. It began this way:

> Viola Patterson picked her way through the shattered glass from her front door, passed the table where her television used to sit, and stopped before the cabinet that had held her family silver.
> She wept.
> Mrs. Patterson, 72, is one of the more than 75 people victimized by burglars in the last two months.

3. *Think of the public pocketbook.* If the tax rate is going up 14 cents, how much will it cost the average homeowner? If city employees are seeking a 10 percent raise, how much will that cost in all? And what do they make now? If garbage collection fees are about to be increased, how do they compare to fees in comparable cities?

The city manager proposed "adjusting" the price of electricity to lower the cost to industrial customers and raise rates to private homes. The city hall reporter did a quick survey of comparable cities around the state. Then she wrote:

> City residents, who already pay more for their electricity than residents of eight similar-sized cities around the state, would be charged an average of $4 per month more under a proposal announced Tuesday by City Manager Barry Kovac.
> Industrial users, whose rate now is about average among the nine cities, would enjoy the second-lowest rate under Kovac's proposal.
> Kovac defended his plan as "equitable and necessary to ensure continued economic growth for the city."

4. *Get out of the office.* City council votes are important, but far more people will have personal contact with government in the form of a police officer, a clerk or a bus driver than with a council member. Go to where government meets its constituents. Ride a bus. Visit a classroom. Patrol with a police officer. Not only will you get a reader's-eye view of your beat, but you may also find some unexpected stories.

5. *Ask the reader's questions.* "Why?" "How much will it cost me?" "What will I get out of it?" You are the public's ombudsman.

Remember, a good beat reporter has to be prepared, be alert, be persistent and be there. If you keep in mind, too, who you are writing for, you'll keep the customers—and the editors—satisfied.

as detailed knowledge of how an organization works is the key to controlling that organization works. A budget is the blueprint for the organization's activities. The budget tells where the money comes from and where it goes. It tells how many people are on the payroll and how much they are paid. It tells what programs are planned for the year and how much they will cost. Over several years' time, the budget tells where the budget makers' priorities are, what they see as their organization's role in the community.

So, find copies of the last two or three years' budgets for your beat. Try to decipher them. Learn all you can from your predecessor and from newspaper clips. Then find the architect who drew up this blueprint—the budget director or the clerk or the assistant superintendent—and get a translation. Ask all the questions you can think of. Write down the answers.

When budget-making time arrives, follow every step. Attend every public hearing and every private discussion session you can. In those dollar figures are some of the most important stories you will write—stories of how much your readers will be paying for schools and roads and garbage pickup, stories of what they will get for their money. You'll find a guide to understanding budgets at the end of this chapter.

3. *Distributing power and money is politics.* While looking for your beat's power centers and unraveling its budget mysteries, you will be absorbing as well the most interesting part of beat reporting—politics.

At any organizational level in any form, power and money go hand-in-hand with politics. Politics provides the mechanisms through which limited resources are allocated among many competing groups. Neither elections nor political parties are necessary for politics. You will have to learn to spot more subtle forms of political maneuvering.

If you are covering city hall, for example, pay close attention as the city budget is being drafted. You may find the mayor's pet project being written in by the city manager. Nobody elects the city manager, but it is good politics for him or her to keep the mayor happy. Are the builders influential in town? If so, you will probably find plenty of road and sewer projects in the budget. Are the city employees unionized? Look for healthy wage and benefit increases if they are. Is there a vocal retirees' organization? That may account for the proposed senior citizens' center. None of those projects is necessarily bad just because it is political. But you and your readers ought to know who is getting what and why.

Now suppose an election is coming up, and the builders' campaign contributions will be heavy. A councilman who is running for mayor switches his vote from money for parks to money for new roads. Has a deal been made? Has a vote been sold? That's politics, too. Some digging is in order.

Power, money and politics are the crucial factors to watch in any beat reporting. With this in mind, let's take a closer look at the most important local beats.

# CITY AND COUNTY GOVERNMENT

Most medium-sized cities have council-manager governments. The mayor and council members hire a professional administrator to manage the day-to-day affairs of the city. The manager, in turn, hires the police and fire chiefs, the public works director and other department heads. Under the city charter the council is supposed to make policy and leave its implementation to the manager. Council members usually are forbidden to meddle in the affairs of any department.

Some small towns and a decreasing number of big cities have governments in which the mayor serves as chief administrator. Chicago under the late boss Richard Daley was probably the best-known example. Whatever the structure, you will have a range of good sources to draw on.

*Subordinate Administrators.*   They know details of budgets, planning and zoning, and personnel matters. They are seldom in the spotlight, so many of them welcome a reporter's attention so long as the reporter does not get them into trouble. Many are bright and ambitious, willing to second-guess their superiors and gossip about politics, again providing you can assure them the risk is low.

*Council Members.*   Politicians, as a rule, love to talk. What they say is not always believable, and you have to be wary of their attempts to use you, but they will talk. Like most of us, politicians are more likely to tell someone else's secret or expose the other guy's deal. So, ask one council member about the political forces behind another member's pet project while asking the other about the first's mayoral ambitions. That way you probably will learn all there is to know.

*Pressure Groups.*   You can get an expert view of the city's land-use policies from land developers and a different view from conservationists. The manager or the personnel director will tell one side of the labor–management story. The head of the employees' union tells the other. How about the school board's record in hiring minorities? Get to know the head of the NAACP or of the Urban League chapter. Public officials respond to pressure. As a reporter you need to understand those pressures and who applies them.

*Public Citizens.*   Consumer advocate Ralph Nader made the term *public citizens* popular, but every town has people—lawyers, homemakers, business executives, retirees—who serve on charter commissions, head bond campaigns, work in elections and advise behind the scenes. Such people can be sources of sound background information and useful assessments of officeholders.

*Opponents.*    The best way to find out the weaknesses of any person or program is to talk with an opponent. Seek out the board member who wants to fire the school superintendent. Look up the police captain demoted by the new chief. Chat with the leader of the opposition to the new hospital. There are at least two sides to every public question and every public figure. Your job is to explore them all.

Once you have found the sources, keep looking, listening and asking for tips, for explanations, for reactions, for stories. The fun is just starting.

Covering a city is very much like covering a county government. In both cases you deal with politicians, with administrators, with budgets, with problems. The similarities may be obscured by differences in structure and style, however.

Cities are more likely to have professional administrators, for example. The administration of county governments is more likely to be in the hands of elected commissioners, supervisors or judges. Counties, too, are more likely to have a multitude of elected officials, from the sheriff to the recorder of deeds. City governments are more likely to be bureaucracies. One way to generalize about the differences is to say that city governments often are more efficient and county governments are more responsive.

These differences frequently mean, for a reporter, that county government is easier to cover. More elected officials mean more politicians. That, in turn, can mean more talkative sources, more open conflict, more points at which constituents and reporters alike can gain access to the governmental structure.

The principles and the problems of reporting are the same. The budget remains the blueprint whether it is drafted by a professional administrator or an elected officeholder. Knowledge is power whether it is the city manager or the elected county clerk who knows where the money goes. Politics is politics.

## THE SCHOOLS

No institution is more important to any community than its schools. None is worse covered. And none is more demanding of or rewarding to a reporter. The issues that arise on the school beat are among the most important in our society. If it is your beat, be prepared to write about racial tensions, drug abuse, obscenity versus free speech, religious conflict, crime, labor-management disputes, politics, sex—and yes, education.

The process of learning and teaching can be obscured by the furor arising from the more dramatic issues. Even when everyone else seems to have forgotten, though, you must not forget that all those are only side issues. The most important part of the school beat is what goes on in the classroom.

The classroom is not an easy place to cover. You may have trouble getting into one. Administrators frequently turn down such requests on the ground that a reporter's presence would be disruptive. It would, at first. But a good teacher and an unobtrusive reporter can overcome that drawback easily. Many papers, at the start of the school year, assign a reporter to an elementary school classroom. He or she visits frequently, gets to know the teacher and pupils, becomes part of the furniture. And that reporter captures for readers much of the sight and sound and feeling of education.

There are other ways, too, of letting readers in on how well—or how badly—the schools are doing their job. Every school system administers some kind of standard tests designed to measure how well its students compare either to a set standard or to other students. The results of such tests are or ought to be public information. Insist on learning about them. Test scores are an inadequate measure of school quality, but they are good indicators. When you base a story on them, be sure you understand what is really being compared and what factors outside the schools may affect the scores.

Be alert to other indicators of school quality. You can find out how many graduates of your school system go to college, how many win scholarships and what colleges they attend. You can find out how your school system measures up to the standards of the state department of education. Does it hold the highest classification? If not, why not? National organizations of teachers, librarians and administrators also publish standards they think schools should meet. How close do your schools come?

In education, as in anything, you get what you pay for. How does the pay of teachers in your district compare to similar-sized districts? How does the tax rate compare? What is the turnover among teachers?

You also should get to know as many teachers, administrators and students as possible. You can learn to pick out the teachers who really care about children and learning. One way to do that is to encourage them to talk about their jobs. A good teacher's warmth will come through.

One reason schools are covered poorly is that the beat often does not produce the obvious, easy stories of politics, personalities and conflict that the city hall or police beats yield. School board meetings usually produce a spark only when a side issue intrudes. Most school board members are more comfortable talking about issues other than education itself, which often is left to the professionals.

As a reporter dealing with professional educators, seeking to learn the substance of their work, your skills of translation will be tested as seldom before. The jargon of education can be virtually unintelligible. ''The traditional reading, writing and arithmetic'' are now described as ''conceptualizing, verbal expression and computational skills.'' A person who is certified to teach is ''certificated.'' The school library has become the ''learning resource center.'' English may be ''language arts.''

Educators sometimes resist, but your job demands that their language be translated into that of your readers. Don't be dazzled by it. Much of the jargon is a disguise for the fact that teaching remains an art rather than the science many educators would like it to be.

The politics and the budgets of schools are very much like those of other institutions. The uniquely important things about the school are the classroom and what happens inside it. Your reporting will suffer if you forget that fact. So will your readers.

## THE POLICE BEAT

The police beat probably produces more good, readable stories per hour of reporter time than any other beat. It also produces some of the worst, laziest reporting and generates many of our most serious legal and ethical problems. It is the beat many cub reporters start on and the beat many veterans stay on until they have become almost part of the force. It offers great frustration and great opportunity. All these contradictions arise from the nature of police work and of reporting.

If you are going to be a police reporter—and nearly every reporter is, at least briefly—the first thing you have to understand is what police officers are and what they do. We hire police officers to protect us from each other. We require them to deal every day with the dregs of society. Abuse and danger are parts of the job, as is boredom. We pay police officers mediocre wages and accord them little status. We ask them to be brave but compassionate, stern but tolerant. What we get very often is less what we ask for than what we should expect. Police work seldom attracts saints. Police officers are frequently cynical, often prejudiced, occasionally dishonest.

When you walk into a police station as a reporter for the first time, expect to be met with some suspicion, even hostility. Young reporters often are perceived by police as being radical, unkempt, anti-authority. How closely does that description fit you or your classmates? And how many of you are pro-cop?

Police departments are quasi-military organizations, with strict chains of command and strong discipline. Their members are sworn to uphold the status quo. The reasons that police and young reporters are mutually suspicious should be clear by now.

Then how do you cover these people? You do so by using the same tricks of the trade you ply at city hall or in the schools. You should:

1. *Prepare yourself.* Take a course in law enforcement, if you can, or take a course in constitutional law. You also might read Joseph Wambaugh's novels for a realistic portrait of the police.

2. *Try to fit in.* Get a haircut, dress conservatively and learn the language. Remember that police officers, like the rest of us, usually are quicker to trust people who look and act like they do.

3. *Lend a sympathetic ear.* You enjoy talking about yourself to somebody who seems to be interested; so do most police officers. They know they have a tough job, and they like to be appreciated. Open your mind, and try to understand points of view with which you may disagree strongly.

4. *Encourage gossip.* Police officers may gossip even more than reporters do. Encourage such talk over a cup of coffee at the station, while tagging along in a patrol car or over a beer after the shift. The stories will be one-sided and exaggerated, but you may learn a lot. Those war stories are fascinating, besides. Just don't print anything you haven't verified.

5. *Talk with other police-watchers.* Lawyers can be good sources, especially the prosecutors and public defenders who associate every day with the police. Other law enforcement sources are good, too. Sheriff's deputies, for example, may be eager to talk about dishonesty or inefficiency in the city police department, and city police may be eager to reciprocate.

One important reason for all this work is that little of the information you need and want as a police reporter is material you are entitled to under public records laws. By law you are entitled to see only the arrest sheet (also called the *arrest log*, or the *blotter*). This record tells you only the identity of the person arrested, the charge and when the arrest took place. You are *not* entitled by law to see the arrest report or to interview the officers involved.

Writing a story depends on securing more than the bare-bones information. Finding out details depends on the good will you have generated with the desk sergeant, the shift commander and the officers on the case. The dangers—of being unfair, of damaging your and your paper's reputation—are ever-present. Good reporting requires that you know what the dangers are and how to try to avoid them.

The greatest danger arises from the one-sidedness and frequent inaccuracy of police reports. At best, the reports represent the officer's viewpoint. Particularly in cases involving violence, danger, confusion or possible repercussions, there may be plausible viewpoints different from that of the police officer. Conflicting interpretations of the same situation lead many times to the dropping of charges.

To protect yourself, and to be fair to the accused, always be skeptical. Attribute any accusatory statement to the officer who made it. If the room for doubt is great enough, talk to the accused, his or her relatives or lawyer, and any witnesses you can find. The result is almost sure to be a fairer, more complete story.

Sometimes, the story is that the police officers themselves are misbehaving. When the Bakersfield Californian received three letters in the same week alleging police brutality, reporter Tom Maurer decided to take a closer look. Over the next year, in his spare time and after hours, he examined records of lawsuits and police reports, interviewed victims and officers and studied medical files, including autopsy reports.

He learned that more than 20 police officers had been sued at least three times each for brutality, more than 80 suits in five years. He also learned that internal police disciplinary procedures weren't working. Only 3 percent of the more than 80 complaints were found valid by the department, compared to nearly 20 percent statewide. The results were not dramatic. No reform campaign was launched. Three officers, however, were forced to retire. Maurer's only reward was the knowledge of a job well done.

Edna Buchanan, however, became one of the best-known police reporters in America in 1986 when she won the Pulitzer Prize for general news reporting. Here are a couple of samples from her work:

Bad things happen to the husbands of the Widow Elkin.

Someone murdered husband No. 4, Cecil Elkin, apparently smashing his head with a frying pan as he watched "Family Feud" on TV.

Husband No. 3, Samuel Smilich, drowned in a weedy South Dade canal.

Husband No. 2, Lawrence Myers, cannot be found, though Metro-Dade homicide detectives, the FBI and the Air Force have searched for him.

Husband No. 1, Wayne Wise, was divorced about 25 years ago. He is alive and well. . . .

And this:

"My baby was trapped in a dead body," Charles Griffith said Saturday from the Dade County jail cell where he is stripped naked and charged with first-degree murder.

"I didn't go to the hospital thinking I was going to kill my daughter," said Griffith, 25. "I told the nurse to go call the police, I think, before it

happened. It is almost like a dream."

At 10:50 p.m. Friday, Griffith, a projectionist in a porno movie house, fired two bullets into the heart of his comatose 3-year-old daughter, Joy, as she lay in her crib in the special care nursery at Miami Children's Hospital. . . .

In the letter nominating Buchanan, who covered the police beat for the Miami Herald for 16 years, her editors made a comment to the Pulitzer Board that sums up the importance and the attraction of the police beat: "In truth, Edna Buchanan doesn't write about cops. She writes about people."

# THE COURTS

One way to begin trying to understand the American judicial system is to think of it as a kind of game. The opposing players in a criminal case are the state, which is the accuser, and the defendant, who is the accused. In a civil case the opponents are the plaintiff and the defendant. Each player is represented by a lawyer, who does everything possible to win for his or her client. The judge referees the contest, insisting that all players abide by the rules. At the end, the judge (sometimes with a jury) decides who won.

Such an irreverent description grossly oversimplifies a system that, because of its independence and usual honesty, stands second only to a free press in protecting the liberty of Americans. But it may help in demystifying a system that also can overawe a beginning reporter.

There is a great deal in courts and the law to inspire awe. Black-robed judges and learned attorneys speak a language full of Latin phrases and highly specialized terms. Written motions, arguments and decisions are laden with convoluted sentences and references unintelligible to the uninitiated. A court can deprive you of your money or your freedom.

You can hardly cover the courts aggressively while standing awestruck, though, so here are some tips that may help restore your working skepticism:

1. *Never trust a lawyer unless you know him or her very well.* Although most lawyers are honest, every lawyer is an advocate. Consequently, everything he or she writes or says must be interpreted as being designed to help the client and hurt the opponent. That is true whether the lawyer represents the defense or prosecution in a criminal case or represents either side in a civil lawsuit. Bar association codes of ethics forbid it, but many lawyers will try to use reporters to win some advantage. Be suspicious.

2. *A judge's word may be law, but it isn't gospel.* Not every judge is a legal scholar. Most judges are, or have been, politicians. All judges are human. They are subject to error, capable of prejudice. Some are even dishonest. Otto Kerner was a judge of a federal appeals court when he was convicted of corruption that occurred while he was governor of Illinois. Abe Fortas was a justice of the U.S. Supreme Court, a close adviser of President Lyndon B. Johnson, and Johnson's nominee for chief justice when a reporter disclosed he was receiving regular payments from a man convicted of violating federal law. Fortas resigned from the court.

3. *Truth and justice do not always prevail.* Prosecutors sometimes conceal evidence favorable to the defense. Defense lawyers sometimes seize on technicalities or rely on witnesses they know to be unreliable in order to win acquittals. Judges sometimes misinterpret the rules or ignore them. Innocent people do go to jail, and guilty ones go free. Courts are no more perfect than

are newspapers. The two combined can produce frightening scenes, such as the one in Cleveland in 1954 when the newspapers screamed for blood and a political judge denied Dr. Sam Sheppard the most basic rights before convicting him of murdering his wife. The Supreme Court decision overturning that conviction became a landmark in spelling out proper trial procedures. In other cases, the press has helped correct miscarriages of justice. Reporter Gene Miller has won two Pulitzer Prizes for winning freedom for persons wrongfully imprisoned after unjust murder convictions.

The judicial system is not exempt from honest and critical reporting. And the sources of that reporting—just as in city hall or the police station—are records and people. First, a few words about court records, where to find them and how to use them.

## Court Records

Whenever a case is filed in court—whether it is a criminal charge or a civil lawsuit—the court clerk assigns it a number. It also has a title. In the case of a criminal charge, the title will be State vs. Joe Doakes, or something similar. (The ''vs.'' is short for ''versus,'' the Latin word meaning ''against.'') A civil case—a lawsuit seeking damages, for example—could be Joe Doakes vs. John Doe. Doakes would be the plaintiff, the party filing the suit. Doe would be the defendant. In order to secure the records from the clerk, you must know the case number or its title, which lawyers also call the ''style'' of the case.

We saw in Chapter 12, on crime and the courts, how criminal cases work their way through the court system. You can follow those cases, of course, by checking the file. At least in the more important criminal cases, however, you usually keep track by checking with the prosecutor and defense lawyers.

Once a civil suit has been filed, the defense files a reply. The plaintiff may file a motion seeking information. The defense may file a motion to dismiss the suit, which the plaintiff will answer. The judge rules on each motion. You can follow it all by checking the file regularly. Except in rare cases, all motions and information filed with the court become public records. Often, information from lawsuits can provide you with interesting insights into the otherwise private affairs of prominent persons or businesses.

Many lawsuits never go to trial before judge or jury. It is common procedure for lawyers to struggle for advantage over a period of months, filing motions and countermotions to gain the best position or to sound out the other side's strength. Then, after a trial date has been set, one side or the other will propose a settlement, which is negotiated. The case is dropped. One reason for that course of action is that the details of an out-of-court settlement need not be made public, unlike the outcome of a trial.

### Human Sources

If a case goes to trial, you cover civil and criminal proceedings in much the same way. You must listen to testimony and, during breaks, corner lawyers for each side to seek explanation and elaboration, while filling in the background from court records and your morgue. Your personal contacts are important sources of information during this process.

***Lawyers.*** The best sources on the court beat are likely to be lawyers. Every courthouse reporter needs to win the confidence and good will of the prosecutor and his or her staff. Not only can they keep you abreast of developments in criminal prosecution, they often can—because assistant prosecutors generally are young, political and ambitious—keep you tuned in to all

**Figure 14.4    Human sources.** Most beat reporters, whether they cover the courthouse or the Supreme Court, rely mainly on human sources. Thurgood Marshall, who drew a crowd of journalists on his retirement from the high court, remained reticent to the end.

sorts of interesting and useful courthouse gossip. They are good sources for tips on who the best and worst judges are, which local officials may be on the take, which defense lawyers are less than upright. Like all gossip, such tips need careful handling and thorough checking. But the raw material is often there.

Lawyers in private practice can be grouped, from a reporter's viewpoint, into two classes—those who will talk and those who won't. The former class usually includes young lawyers, politically ambitious lawyers and criminal defense lawyers, all of whom often find publicity helpful. Cultivate them. Lawyers have egos only slightly smaller than those of reporters. Feed those egos. Encourage them to talk about themselves, their triumphs, their ambitions. You will reap story possibilities, background information and gossip to trade with other sources.

*Judges.*    Don't ignore judges as sources, either. Some are so conscious of their dignity and their images that they have no time for reporters. Remember, though, that most judges in most states are elected to their jobs. That makes them politicians, and it is a rare politician who slams the door on a friendly reporter. Even many federal judges, who are appointed by the president, have done a stint in politics and still have their taste for newspaper ink. Judges' egos may be even bigger than reporters'. Treat every judge accordingly.

*Other Court Sources.*    Many other court functionaries can be helpful sources. Police officers and sheriff's deputies or U.S. marshals assigned to court duty often are underworked and glad of a chance to talk about whatever they know, which may turn out to be good backstage stuff. The bailiffs who shout for order in court and help the judge on with a robe may be retired police officers or small-time politicians and also talkative. And secretaries, as everywhere, are good to know and even better to have know you.

You cover the courts, then, as you cover any other beat. You learn the language, figure out the records and develop your sources.

## RELIGION

National surveys show that Americans take religion seriously. Two-thirds say they are members of a church or synagogue; three-quarters consider themselves religious. That is far more than the number who take part in politics or organized sports. Yet religion attracts far less attention from journalists. A Los Angeles Times study found that fewer than 200 newspapers even have religion reporters.

There are signs that journalism is catching up. The number of papers devoting more than 100 column inches a week to news of religion doubled between the early 1970s and the early 1980s. It's not hard to see why. Just consider some of the continuing stories in which religion plays a central or at least a major part: The rise of the New Right and the Moral Majority; the issues of abortion, euthanasia and capital punishment; the drive for a constitutional amendment to allow prayer in schools; the anti-nuclear-weapons movement; civil war in Northern Ireland, India and the Middle East; the election of two consecutive U.S. presidents who were self-proclaimed born-again Christians.

Like any other beat, religion has a variety of specialized sources and specialized problems. Read as widely as you can. The best coverage of religion and related issues can be found in such magazines as Christianity Today, the National Catholic Reporter, Christian Century, Cross Currents, Worldview, U.S. Catholic, Commonweal and Commentary. Don't overlook the denominational publications that may serve your area.

For theological expertise and local comment on major stories about religion, consult theology professors at the nearest university or seminary. But beware of their possible bias. Knowing the local religious activists, both in the clergy and outside it, may be useful, too. Who are the rebels criticizing their co-religionists for lack of concern about civil rights, poverty or other social issues? Who are the powers behind the pulpit quietly raising money, directing its spending and guiding the institution?

Because churches are also businesses, public records can be useful sources. Records in the tax assessor's office can tell you how much property the church or synagogue owns and give you at least some idea of its worth. Many churches own business buildings, parking lots, rental housing. They pay no income taxes, but their economic impact is great. Another source for checking on that economic impact can be Form 990, which churches must file with the Internal Revenue Service to maintain their tax-exempt status. Those forms are public records. A check of such sources led the Kansas City (Mo.) Times to this church-as-business story, which ran on the front page:

Millions of tax dollars are going unpaid every year because many church-operated schools quietly launder tuition payments through church collection plates and deduct them as charitable contributions.

With 17,000 students in the Roman Catholic schools of the Kansas City-St. Joseph Diocese alone, no one knows exactly how much tax money slips through the collection plate loophole. Certainly not all churches or the schools they operate offer a tuition laundry, but a survey by the Times reveals the practice is widespread throughout the country and apparently growing in popularity.

Other stories are waiting to be found. One reason more are not found is that religious institutions and individuals too often escape the critical scrutiny that politicians and businesspeople must undergo. Religious leaders are human. They are often good, sometimes devious, occasionally rascally. Be respectful, but remember that a member of the clergy who demands deferential treatment just might be hiding something behind that ecclesiastical smile.

Another special problem in covering religion is the emotional intensity with which many people hold to their beliefs. If you do serious reporting, you will not be able to avoid arousing somebody's wrath. You can avoid arousing it needlessly, however, by doing your homework.

Do not confuse a Southern Baptist with an American Baptist, or a Lutheran of the Missouri Synod with a Lutheran of the American Lutheran Church. You will not get very far interviewing a Jesuit if you ask him what denomination he belongs to. But not every Roman Catholic priest is a Jesuit. Don't attribute the same beliefs to Orthodox and Reform Jews. And remember that Jews and Christians, though they dominate American religious life, are only a fraction of the world's religious believers.

Some stories about religion are uplifting. They tell of selfless service to the poor, the sick, the forgotten and abandoned. They illustrate values other than money or power. They describe the courage of people who put lives and property on the line for human rights or in opposition to war. Others are not so uplifting. Parishes run up huge debts. Parochial schools hire badly trained, poorly paid teachers. Blacks are refused admission. Women are refused ordination.

Stained-glass windows are no barrier to politics. Religious issues, such as abortion, homosexuality and capital punishment, are often also political issues. Churches may use their economic clout to combat injustice or to support it. Belief can be blind.

Whatever side of religion it explores, a good story about religion will wind up on the front page along with the best of the city hall or medical stories. The techniques for getting those stories are no different, either.

## SCIENCE, MEDICINE AND THE ENVIRONMENT

If you start work on a small or medium-sized newspaper, you may find that nobody is assigned full time to cover science, medicine or environmental issues. You may have a chance to stake out one or more of these interesting and important areas for yourself. On big papers such beats usually are covered by specialists, perhaps with some academic training in the area and certainly with several years of experience. Big paper or small, you will need some basic courses in the physical and biological sciences. And you will need an introduction to the special problems and sources encountered in this area.

On these beats there will be fewer meetings to attend or offices to visit than on a city hall or school beat. More of the stories here are likely to be generated by your own enterprise or by applying the local touch to a national story. You can find out what a new pesticide ban will mean to local farmers, for instance. Of you can determine whether local doctors are using a new arthritis treatment, or what a researcher at the state university is learning about the effects of alcohol on rats.

Where can you look for story ideas? Specialized publications are good places to start. Read the Journal of the American Medical Association, the New England Journal of Medicine, and Medical World. New developments and issues in medicine are covered in news stories. Scientific American and Science News are informed but readable sources of ideas in all the sciences. For environmental issues, read Natural History magazine. Your state's conservation department may put out a publication. Get on the mailing lists of the National Wildlife Federation, the Sierra Club, the Audubon Society and Friends of the Earth.

Nearly every community has human sources, too. In medicine these include members of the local medical association, the administrator of the hospital and public health officials. In the sciences, look for local school or college faculty, employees of government agencies such as extension or research centers, even interested amateurs such as those in astronomy societies. In the area of environment there usually is no shortage of advocacy groups or of industries that want to defend their interests. State and federal regulatory and research agencies are helpful, too.

The special problems posed by scientific beats begin with the language your sources use. It is a language full of Latin phrases, technical terms and numbers. You will have to learn enough of it both to ask intelligent questions and to translate the answers for your readers. A good medical dictionary and science dictionary are invaluable. Use them, and continue asking for explanations until you are sure you understand.

Another problem may be convincing scientists and physicians to talk to you in any language. Many of them have had little contact with reporters. Much of the contact they have had probably has been unpleasant, either because it arose from some controversy or because the reporter was unprepared. Reluctant sources are much more likely to cooperate if you demonstrate that you have done your homework, so you have at least some idea of what they are talking about. Promise to check your story with the sources. Accuracy is as much your goal as theirs.

In medicine a concern for privacy may deter some sources from talking freely. A physician's allegiance is, and should be, to the patient. As a reporter you have no legal right to know a patient's condition or ailment. That is true even if the patient is a public official. In fact, most information about a person's medical history and condition is protected by law from disclosure by governmental record keepers. When the mayor goes to the hospital, then, and you want to know why, your only tools are your persuasiveness and the good will you have built up with hospital officials, the attending physician or the mayor's family.

Sources also may be guarded in comments about their work. Most researchers in medicine and science are cautious in making any claims about the signficance or certainty of their work. Some are not so cautious. You must be. Check and doublecheck, with the researcher involved and others knowledgeable in the field, before describing any development as "important" or "dramatic" or "frightening." Overstatement will damage your credibility with sources and readers.

Sometimes a researcher will be reluctant to discuss his or her work until it has been published in a professional journal or reported at a convention. Such presentation may be more important to the scientist than any newspaper publicity. An agreement to give you first notice when he or she is ready to go public may be the best you can do in this circumstance.

Despite difficulties, the coverage of science, medicine or the environment offers great challenges and rewards. The challenge is discovering and explaining developments and issues that are important to your readers. The rewards, as in all other areas of reporting, can be prizes, pay raises or—most important—recognition by your sources and peers of a job well done. The key to success in covering these beats is the same as for any other beat: Be prepared, be alert, be persistent, be there and be wary.

# Making Sense of Budgets

Because the budget is the blueprint that guides the operation of any governmental agency, a reporter must learn to read it, just as a carpenter must learn to read an architect's blueprint. In either case, that isn't as difficult as it appears at first glance.

Every budget, whether it's your personal budget or the budget of the U.S. government, has two basic parts—revenues (income) and expenditures (outgo). Government revenues come from sources like taxes, fees and service charges, and payments from other agencies (such as state aid to schools). The budget usually shows, in dollar figures and percentages, the sources of the agency's money. Expenditures go for such things as staff salaries, purchase of supplies, payment of utility bills, construction and maintenance of facilities, and insurance. Expenditures usually are listed either by line or by program. The difference is this: A *line item budget* shows a separate line for each expenditure, such as "Salary of police chief—$50,000." A *program budget* provides less detail but shows more clearly what each activity of the agency costs; for example, "Burglary prevention program—$25,000."

Now let's see what kinds of stories budgets may yield and where to look for those stories. Take a minute to scan Figure 14.5, a summary page from the annual budget of a small city.

The most important budget stories usually deal with changes, trends and comparisons. Budget figures change, of course, every year. As costs increase, so do budgets. But look in our sample budget at the line for the Parks and Recreation Department. There's a decrease between Fiscal Year (FY) 1991 and 1992. Why? The summary page doesn't tell you, so you'll have to look behind it, at the detail pages. There, you'll discover that the drop results from a proposal by the city staff to halt funding of a summer employment program for teen-agers. That's a story.

Another change that may be newsworthy is the sharp increase in the Police Department budget. You'd better find out the reasons for that, too. In this case, the detail pages of the budget show that most of the increase is going to pay for an administrative reorganization that is adding several new posi-

## GENERAL FUND—SUMMARY

### PURPOSE

The General Fund is used to finance and account for a large portion of the current operation expenditures and capital outlays of city government. The General Fund is one of the largest and most important of the city's funds because most governmental programs (Police, Fire, Public Works, Parks and Recreation, and so on) are generally financed wholly or partially from it. The General Fund has a greater number and variety of revenue sources than any other fund, and its resources normally finance a wider range of activities.

### APPROPRIATIONS

|  | Actual Fiscal Year 1990 | Budget Fiscal Year 1991 | Revised Fiscal Year 1991 | Adopted Fiscal Year 1992 |
|---|---|---|---|---|
| Personnel services | $ 9,500,353 | $ 11,306,619 | $ 11,245,394 | $ 12,212,336 |
| Materials and supplies | 1,490,573 | 1,787,220 | 1,794,362 | 1,986,551 |
| Training and schools | 93,942 | 150,517 | 170,475 | 219,455 |
| Utilities | 606,125 | 649,606 | 652,094 | 722,785 |
| Services | 1,618,525 | 1,865,283 | 1,933,300 | 2,254,983 |
| Insurance and miscellaneous | 1,792,366 | 1,556,911 | 1,783,700 | 1,614,265 |
| Total operating | 15,101,884 | 17,316,156 | 17,579,325 | 19,010,375 |
| Capital additions | 561,145 | 1,123,543 | 875,238 | 460,143 |
| Total operating and capital | 15,663,029 | 18,439,699 | 18,454,563 | 19,470,518 |
| Contingency | —— | 200,000 | 200,000 | 100,000 |
| Total | $15,663,029 | $ 18,639,699 | $ 18,654,563 | $ 19,570,518 |

Figure 14.5 Summary Page of a Typical City Budget.

**Figure 14.5**
**(continued)**

**GENERAL FUND—SUMMARY**

### DEPARTMENT EXPENDITURES

| | Actual Fiscal Year 1990 | Budget Fiscal Year 1991 | Revised Fiscal Year 1991 | Adopted Fiscal Year 1992 |
|---|---|---|---|---|
| City Council | $    75,144 | $    105,207 | $    90,457 | $    84,235 |
| City Clerk | 61,281 | 70,778 | 74,444 | 91,867 |
| City Manager | 155,992 | 181,219 | 179,125 | 192,900 |
| Municipal Court | 164,631 | 196,389 | 175,019 | 181,462 |
| Personnel | 143,366 | 197,844 | 186,247 | 203,020 |
| Law Department | 198,296 | 266,819 | 248,170 | 288,550 |
| Planning & Community Development | 295,509 | 377,126 | 360,272 | 405,870 |
| Finance Department | 893,344 | 940,450 | 983,342 | 1,212,234 |
| Fire Department | 2,837,744 | 3,421,112 | 3,257,356 | 3,694,333 |
| Police Department | 3,300,472 | 4,007,593 | 4,139,085 | 4,375,336 |
| Health | 1,033,188 | 1,179,243 | 1,157,607 | 1,293,362 |
| Community Services | 50,882 | 74,952 | 74,758 | 78,673 |
| Energy Management | —— | —— | 54,925 | 66,191 |
| Public Works | 2,838,605 | 3,374,152 | 3,381,044 | 3,509,979 |
| Parks and Recreation | 1,218,221 | 1,367,143 | 1,400,334 | 1,337,682 |
| Communications & Info. Services | 532,153 | 730,129 | 742,835 | 715,324 |
| City General | 1,864,200 | 1,949,543 | 1,949,543 | 1,739,500 |
| Total Department Expenditures | 15,663,028 | 18,439,699 | 18,454,563 | 19,470,518 |
| Contingency | —— | 200,000 | 200,000 | 100,000 |
| Total | $15,663,028 | $ 18,639,699 | $ 18,654,563 | $ 19,570,518 |

tions at the top of the department. The patrol division is actually being reduced. Another story.

Look again at that Police Department line. Follow it back to FY 1990 and you'll see that the increase last year was even bigger. In two years, the budget for police has increased by nearly one-third. That's an interesting trend. The same pattern holds for the Fire Department. Some more checking is in order. With copies of previous budgets, you can see how far back the growth trend runs. You can also get from the departments the statistics on crimes and fires. Are the budget makers responding to a demonstrated need for more protection, or is something else at work behind the scenes?

More generally, you can trace patterns in the growth of city services and city taxes, and you can compare those with changes in population. Are the rates of change comparable? Is population growth outstripping growth in services? Are residents paying more per capita for city services than five or 10 years ago? More good story possibilities.

Another kind of comparison can be useful to your readers, too. How does your city government compare in cost and services to the governments of comparable cities? A few phone calls can add perspective to budget figures. Some professional organizations have recommended levels of service, such as number of police or firefighters per 1,000 inhabitants, that can help you help your readers assess how well they're being governed.

The same guidelines can be applied to the analysis of any budget. The numbers will be different, as will the department names, but the structures will be much the same. Whether you're covering the school board or the statehouse, look for changes, trends and comparisons.

Another document that is vital to understanding the finances of local government is the annual financial report. The financial report may be a few pages or it may be a book. In any case, its purpose is relatively simple. As its name suggests, the report is an explanation of the organization's financial status at the end of a fiscal year, which often is not the same as the end of the calendar year. Here you will find an accounting of all the income the organization received during the year from taxes, fees, state and federal grants, and other sources. You'll also find status reports on all the organization's operating funds, such as its capital improvement fund, its debt-service fund and its general fund.

Making sense of the financial report, like the budget, isn't as hard as it may look. For one thing, usually the financial officer includes a narrative that highlights the most important points, at least from his or her viewpoint. But you should dig beyond the narrative and examine the numbers for yourself. The single most important section of the report is the statement of revenues, expenditures and changes in fund balance, which provides important measures of the organization's financial health. Depending on the comprehensiveness of the statement, you may have to refer to the budget document as well. You can check:

1. Revenues actually received compared to budgeted revenues.

2. Actual spending compared to budgeted spending.

3. Actual spending compared to actual revenue.

4. Changes in fund balances available for spending in years to come.

Look, for example, at Figure 14.6. This combined statement gives a picture of a city in good financial health. How can you tell? Look first at the

### ALL GOVERNMENTAL FUND TYPES AND EXPENDABLE TRUST
### FUNDS FOR THE YEAR ENDED SEPTEMBER 30, 1991

|  | GOVERNMENTAL FUND TYPES | | |
|---|---|---|---|
|  | General Fund | Special Revenue Funds | Debt Service Funds |
| **REVENUES** | | | |
| General property taxes | $    663,932 | $    530,713 | $192,104 |
| Sales tax | 3,967,138 | 3,367,510 | —— |
| Other local taxes | 3,138,904 | 228,718 | —— |
| Licenses and permits | 253,287 | 5,146 | —— |
| Fines | 378,207 | —— | —— |
| Fees and service charges | 244,356 | —— | —— |
| Special assessments authorized | —— | —— | —— |
| Intragovernmental | 4,139,690 | —— | —— |
| Revenue from other | | | |
| governmental units | 796,292 | 1,164,482 | —— |
| Building rentals | —— | —— | —— |
| Interest | 1,314,130 | 196,612 | 6,228 |
| Miscellaneous | 53,548 | —— | —— |
| TOTAL REVENUES | 14,949,484 | 5,493,181 | 198,332 |
| **EXPENDITURES** | | | |
| Current: | | | |
| Policy development and | | | |
| administration | 2,328,546 | 291,493 | —— |
| Public safety | 8,403,851 | —— | —— |
| Transportation | 2,387,534 | —— | —— |
| Health and environment | 1,617,146 | —— | —— |
| Personal development | 1,915,376 | 622,065 | —— |
| Public buildings | —— | —— | —— |
| Miscellaneous non-programmed | | | |
| activities: | | | |
| Interest expense | 273,195 | —— | —— |
| Other | 34,975 | —— | —— |
| Capital outlay | —— | —— | —— |
| Debt service: | | | |
| Redemption of serial bonds | —— | —— | 175,000 |
| Interest | —— | —— | 278,488 |
| Fiscal agent fees | —— | —— | 758 |
| TOTAL EXPENDITURES | 16,960,623 | 913,558 | 454,246 |
| EXCESS (DEFICIENCY) | | | |
| OF REVENUES OVER | | | |
| EXPENDITURES | (2,011,139) | 4,579,623 | (255,914) |

**Figure 14.6 Combined Statement of Revenues, Expenditures and Changes in Fund Balance**

| | GOVERNMENTAL FUND TYPES | | FIDUCIARY FUND TYPE | TOTAL (MEMORANDUM ONLY) | |
| --- | --- | --- | --- | --- | --- |
| | Capital Projects Fund | Special Assessment Funds | Expendable Trust Funds | 1991 | 1990 |
| $ | — | $    — | $    — | $    1,386,749 | $    1,961,851 |
| | — | — | — | 7,334,648 | 4,967,691 |
| | — | — | — | 3,367,622 | 2,923,775 |
| | — | — | — | 258,433 | 247,608 |
| | — | — | — | 378,207 | 346,224 |
| | — | — | 1,129,784 | 1,374,140 | 328,185 |
| | — | 490,159 | — | 490,159 | 359,862 |
| | — | — | — | 4,139,690 | 3,911,418 |
| | 154,919 | — | 901,815 | 3,017,508 | 3,087,431 |
| | — | — | 172,766 | 172,766 | 175,479 |
| | 23,282 | — | 88,428 | 1,628,680 | 1,869,874 |
| | 29,226 | — | — | 82,774 | 97,593 |
| | 207,427 | 490,159 | 2,292,793 | 23,631,376 | 20,276,991 |
| | — | — | 3,338 | 2,623,377 | 2,285,509 |
| | — | — | — | 8,403,851 | 6,998,232 |
| | — | — | — | 2,387,534 | 1,996,520 |
| | — | — | 1,080,811 | 2,697,957 | 1,652,809 |
| | — | — | — | 2,537,441 | 2,084,648 |
| | — | — | 371,942 | 371,942 | 336,204 |
| | — | — | — | 273,195 | 486,031 |
| | — | — | — | 34,975 | 4,296 |
| | 1,287,520 | 2,357,784 | — | 3,645,304 | 1,990,648 |
| | — | — | — | 175,000 | 155,000 |
| | — | — | — | 278,488 | 32,435 |
| | — | — | — | 758 | 285 |
| | 1,287,520 | 2,357,784 | 1,456,091 | 23,429,822 | 18,022,617 |
| | (1,080,093) | (1,867,625) | 836,702 | 201,554 | 2,254,374 |

**Figure 14.6**
**(continued)**

| | GOVERNMENTAL FUND TYPES | | |
| --- | --- | --- | --- |
| | General Fund | Special Revenue Funds | Debt Service Funds |
| OTHER FINANCING SOURCES (USES): | | | |
| Proceeds of general obligation bonds | --- | --- | --- |
| Operating transfers from other funds | 3,011,358 | 62,974 | 266,711 |
| Operating transfers to other funds | (1,292,723) | (3,348,303) | --- |
| TOTAL OTHER FINANCING SOURCES (USES) | 1,718,635 | (3,285,329) | 266,711 |
| EXCESS (DEFICIENCY) OF REVENUES AND OTHER FINANCING SOURCES OVER EXPENDITURES AND OTHER FINANCING USES | (292,504) | 1,294,294 | 10,797 |
| FUND BALANCES BEGINNING OF YEAR | 4,195,912 | 3,004,533 | 43,645 |
| Equity transfer to Recreation Services Fund | --- | --- | --- |
| Contribution to Water & Electric Utility Fund | --- | --- | --- |
| Contribution to Sanitary Sewer Utility Fund | --- | --- | --- |
| Contribution to Regional Airport Fund | (200,000) | --- | --- |
| Contribution to Public Transportation Fund | --- | --- | --- |
| Contribution to Parking Facilities Fund | --- | --- | --- |
| Contribution to Recreation Services Fund | --- | (152,000) | --- |
| FUND BALANCES, END OF YEAR | $ 3,703,408 | $ 4,146,827 | $    54,442 |

| GOVERNMENTAL FUND TYPES | | FIDUCIARY FUND TYPE | TOTAL (MEMORANDUM ONLY) | |
|---|---|---|---|---|
| Capital Projects Fund | Special Assessment Funds | Expendable Trust Funds | 1991 | 1990 |
| 5,681,633 | 1,134,261 | —— | 6,815,894 | —— |
| 415,038 | 469,865 | —— | 4,225,946 | 3,466,261 |
| —— | (99,667) | (527,506) | (5,268,199) | (4,401,847) |
| 6,096,671 | 1,504,459 | (527,506) | 5,773,641 | (935,586) |
| 5,016,578 | (363,166) | 309,196 | 5,975,195 | 1,318,788 |
| 628,856 | 781,248 | 514,378 | 9,168,572 | 8,489,184 |
| —— | —— | (1,532) | (1,532) | (292,958) |
| —— | —— | —— | —— | (30,395) |
| —— | —— | —— | —— | (71,367) |
| —— | —— | —— | (200,000) | (160,191) |
| —— | —— | —— | —— | (4,000) |
| —— | —— | —— | —— | (15,489) |
| —— | —— | —— | (152,000) | (65,000) |
| $ 5,645,434 | $ 418,082 | $ 822,042 | $ 14,790,235 | $ 9,168,572 |

bottom line. All of the end-of-year fund balances are positive. (Negative balances, or deficits, are shown in parentheses.) Now look at the totals in the far right-hand columns. They show an increase of more than $5 million in total funds available at the end of FY 1991 as compared to FY 1990. That seems a phenomenal increase, more than 50 percent. Better look more closely.

Run your eyes up those "total" columns. The explanation for the increase is about halfway up. In 1991, you see, the city sold general obligation bonds and received $6.8 million in extra income. Those bonds, of course, will have to be repaid over a period of years. In fact, then, the city has taken on a major new obligation rather than having reaped a windfall. If that hasn't already been reported, it should be now.

This statement also shows you what is happening from one year to the next in each of the city's major revenue sources. Sales tax revenue is up dramatically, while property tax revenue is down. That's good news for owners of homes and businesses. It suggests that the tax rate on real estate has been reduced. It also suggests that economic activity has picked up significantly. With a little more reporting, you may be onto another good story or two.

There are other clues that may lead to other stories. As in these examples, they'll require more reporting and more explanation than any reporter can pull from the numbers by themselves. Document in hand, head for the budget officer. The guidelines offered here should help you shape your questions and understand the answers. With financial statements, as with budgets, look for changes, trends and comparisons. And always look hard at those numbers in parentheses.

# Suggested Readings

Royko, Mike. "Boss." New York: New American Library, 1971. A classic, brilliantly written study of urban machine politics.

Ullmann, John and Colbert, Jan, eds. "The Reporter's Handbook," Second Edition. New York: St. Martin's Press, 1990. The first comprehensive guide to using public records and documents, written by members of Investigative Reporters and Editors. A must for serious reporters. See also the readings after the Investigative Reporting chapter. They'll be useful in beat reporting, too.

# Exercises

1. You've been assigned to cover city government. Do some background reading in your local newspaper and the other sources described in this chapter. Then write a memo describing what you expect to be the most important issues on your new beat and who you expect to be your most important human sources.

2. In the library or in a computer data base, look up three recent national or international stories about a religious issue. Write a memo explaining how you would localize each story for your city. Include possible sources.

3. Look at the budget document on page 324 headed "Department Expenditures." From the figures listed there, propose at least two story ideas. Suggest possible sources for the stories.

4. Get a copy of your city or town's current budget and come up with 10 questions a reporter should ask about the changes, patterns and trends the budget suggests.

# 15

## Business and Consumer News

Not so long ago, business news was regarded by many reporters and editors as that dreary stuff full of numbers and unfathomable terms that separated the stock market tables from the ads somewhere in the back of the paper. Those days are gone. Business has become big news. Newspapers in recent years have expanded both the quantity and the quality of their coverage of economic activities. Investigative and analytical stories, reports on community efforts to lure new industries or bolster old ones, and profiles of corporate decision makers now turn up on the front page as well as the business page. Most newspapers now give business its own daily section front and many have added a weekly "business extra."

Likewise, newspapers today devote much more attention to stories aimed at the consumers of what business sells. In front-page stories and feature-page columns, newspapers are telling readers how to do everything from buying insurance to reducing energy use. Other consumer stories may expose frauds or report on the efforts of lobbying groups.

The surge in popularity—among journalists and readers alike—of these two closely related types of stories reflects a growing awareness of how economics, politics and everyday life are linked. Inflation affects tax policies, which affect paychecks. International alliances affect tariff rates, which in turn affect imports, prices and jobs, and even election outcomes. Virtually any story can be a business story. And nearly any business story can be a consumer story.

Business news and consumer news are among the major beats of many newspapers. Increasingly, the reporters who cover these beats are emerging from business journalism programs at such schools as the University of Missouri and American University. Many other business reporters have had their skills sharpened at mid-career programs offered by Missouri, Columbia University and the Wharton School at the University of Pennsylvania. But you don't have to be a specialist to do good work in either field. You do need an understanding of basic economics, a working knowledge of the language of business, and the skills of any reporter on a beat. You also need an awareness of the special sources and special problems of these beats, which are examined here.

## In this chapter you will learn:

1. How to prepare to cover business news.

2. Where to find business news.

3. How to understand the numbers of business.

4. How to find and report consumer news.

# Preparing to Cover Business News

The range of business stories can be as broad as the range of business itself. A business story may be about promotions and retirements. It may concentrate on a company's potential profits, of interest to investors and potential investors in that company. It can be a story about a new kind of instant camera that would interest not just shareholders of the company but potential buyers as well. It may deal with a drought in Kansas that affects the price farmers in Michigan will get for their wheat and the price homemakers in Florida will pay for English muffins. It can be a personality profile of a corporate executive that gives some insight into the way business is conducted. It may be about a new industrial plant that could affect people looking for jobs. Or about owners of stores that sell goods to people with jobs. Or it can focus on the style of dress in New York offices—trends that may indicate how readers elsewhere may soon dress.

These stories have obvious local angles. Sometimes, though, the local angle is not that obvious. The story about a decision by the Federal Reserve Board's Open Market Committee to expand or tighten the money supply may seem esoteric. But that decision can affect your readers' ability to get a loan for a new car or house and the rate they pay for that loan. Or it can affect them in how it adds to or subtracts from inflation. News of a sizable trade deficit for the United States may weaken the value of the dollar and increase the price of a Sony TV, a Volkswagen or a bottle of Cutty Sark Scotch whisky.

Although most major corporate and economic decisions that affect us all are made in Washington, New York, Chicago and a few other major metropolitan centers, those cities do not have a monopoly on the creation and coverage of business news. Even in towns of a few thousand residents, businesses will be opening or closing, manufacturing plants will be increasing or decreasing production, hiring or firing employees. And those residents will be spending money for houses or cars, ski trips or Harris tweeds, or socking it away in the town's banks or savings and loan associations. There is a business story in every such development.

Business stories can be as bright and as interesting as any story in any other section of the paper. That is demonstrated regularly in such publications as The Wall Street Journal, The New York Times, the Chicago Tribune, Business Week and Fortune magazine. Here, for example, is the beginning of a Boston Globe story about fraud in the commodity futures trading business:

The town of Vina, Ala. (pop. 366), will never be the same.

Chuck LeMieux went down there in the spring of 1973 and they're still talking about him. And looking for him.

It started when he bought the Vina Packing Co. Just walked in, courted the bankers, got some cash and bought it. Bought it with 10 years of unpaid debt behind him, his pingpong ball company—Tennex—going bust in Connecticut, his two radio stations—WELM and WKOP—on the brink of receivership in New York, City National Bank of Bridgeport about to foreclose on his mortgages, and dunning letters coming from all over the world.

But the hundreds of thousands of dollars owed up North didn't stop him from acting like a Rockefeller down South.

You don't have to be from Vina to want to read on.

## HOW TO REPORT BUSINESS STORIES

What separates a business story from a soccer story—or, for that matter, a soccer story from a story about atomic particles—is the knowledge and language required to ask the right questions, to recognize the newsworthy answers and to write the story in a way that the reader without specialized knowledge will understand. A reporter who understands the subject can explain what the jargon means.

For example, the term ''prime rate'' by itself may be meaningless to a majority of newspaper readers. If the reporter explains that the prime rate is a benchmark interest rate banks quote to their customers and that it is a somewhat negotiable figure, readers can see that an increase of one percentage point in the prime rate could result in a higher rate of interest on a car loan or home mortgage.

But beware of writing in such simplistic terms that you tell your readers nothing useful. Besides failing your readers, you will damage respect for your newspaper in the business community. The Wall Street Journal avoids both traps by shunning jargon as much as possible and explaining any technical terms essential to the story. In one story, for example, the Journal explained the terms ''Federal Open Market Committee,'' ''federal funds rate,'' ''M1,'' ''M2'' and ''free-reserve position.'' The sophisticated reader might know what those terms mean, but no doubt many of the paper's readers would not. The Boston Globe series mentioned earlier on the highly complicated problem of commodity options included a glossary of terms and an explanation of the mechanics of the business.

Former presidential economic adviser Gardner Ackley once said he would like to see two things in people covering economics and business news: first, that they had taken a course in economics, and second, that they had passed it. Financial journalist Louis Rukeyser urges newspapers to enlarge their ''coverage of the nation's economic scene: reporting, analysis and commentary of the highest order, adequately and prominently displayed. . . . We need more bright young journalists educated and trained, able and willing to operate on that broad frontier where politics and economics meet—and confuse each other.''

Most journalism schools and departments require students to take at least one course in economics, but too often that course is regarded in the same light as dental surgery or a hangover. If we hold our breath and dull our senses, time will take care of the pain.

Much of the animosity—and there is real animosity—between the press and business arises because too many practitioners of each neither understand nor want to understand what the other is trying to accomplish. Many reporters regard profits as some kind of social disease. Reporters and editors often see their own work as a noble demonstration of the freedom guaranteed by the Constitution but look on business and businesspeople as, at best, necessary evils. Many business managers view reporters and editors with a similar lack of respect or understanding.

You need not approve of everything business does, but to condemn it for trying to do what it is supposed to do—earn a profit—is like complaining about apples because they don't taste like oranges. Even Jane Fonda, activist and actress turned entrepreneur, says her exposure to business has changed her attitudes. "I am much more sensitive to the bottom line, and I must live with the tensions and contradictions that that brings," she told Fortune magazine. Business executives must realize that it is not the job of the press to make them look good and that reporters who ask tough questions or refuse to swallow every news release are not attacking the foundations of the free enterprise system.

The mistrust that many businesspeople have of the press can make it difficult to cover stories adequately, even when it would be in their interest to see that the story is told. Or, if executives are willing to talk, they may become angry if the reporter quotes an opposing point of view or points out a wart on the corporate visage.

The best antidote a reporter can use against this animosity is to report fairly and accurately what a business is doing and saying. By always being fair, you usually can win the trust and confidence of businesspeople, even if the latter reserve admiration for someone who can squeeze a few more cents of per-share profits out of the third quarter.

As in covering any other beat, the main precaution to take in covering the business beat is to guard against becoming so close to or biased toward your sources that you start to think more like them than like a reporter. This has become a greater danger in recent years with the emergence of glamorous executives like Lee Iacocca and T. Boone Pickens. Being conscious of that danger usually is enough to prevent its happening, but another way is to switch beats occasionally so you can deal with new people and new sets of circumstances.

Since business executives tend to be cautious when it comes to talking with reporters, it may help you to dress more like a business manager than a social protestor. That does not mean that you have to think like a manager, but appearances do count, and businesspeople, like reporters, plumbers, generals and linebackers, feel more comfortable with their own kind.

The more you can demonstrate that you understand their business, the more likely you are to generate the trust that will draw out the information you seek. "Understanding" is not synonymous with "sympathy," but ignorance usually means a reporter is apt to misinterpret what is said. When the Columbia Missourian put together a package on "Who Owns Main Street?" sources spent hours talking with the reporters because they felt comfortable with the reporters' extensive knowledge of the complicated subject.

Although public relations people often are helpful in providing background information and directing you to the executives who can provide other comment and information, you should try to get to know as many company officials as you can. Sometimes you can do this best through a "harmless" background interview, one not generated by a crisis but intended simply to learn about what the company is doing. Perhaps you can arrange to have lunch, to see what the officials are thinking about and to give them a chance to see you are probably not the demon they may have thought you to be.

Always remember that a company, government agency or pressure group may be trying to use you to plant stories that serve some special interest. Companies want a story to make them look promising to investors with the hope of driving up the price of the stock or to make them attractive merger partners. If you are suspicious, do some more digging; talk to competitors and analysts, and ask detailed questions. Just because a company or some other group is pushing a story does not mean you have to write it. The best place for some interview notes is the wastebasket.

In short, a business reporter should be all the things a good reporter is— honest, fair, alert to possible new stories and to new angles on old stories. Business writing can be rewarding, both financially (because specialists usually earn premium pay) and intellectually.

# WHERE TO FIND BUSINESS NEWS

The starting point in writing a business story is similar to the first step in reporting any story—understanding the subject you're writing about. For the business reporter, that almost always means some basic research into the subject. For openers, check your paper's library to learn what's been written locally about your topic or company.

Then move on to other secondary sources. The good business reporter knows how to use the Readers' Guide to Periodical Literature, the Business Periodicals Index, The New York Times Index, The Wall Street Journal Index and perhaps the National Newspaper Index (which indexes the Times, the Journal, The Los Angeles Times, The Washington Post and the Christian Science Monitor). These indexes will tell you where to find stories about your business or industry.

Another valuable secondary source for business reporters is Predicasts' F & S Index of Corporations and Industries, considered by many the best index for company and industry information. Predicasts indexes a broad range of business, financial and industrial periodicals, plus a few reports by brokerage houses. For information on foreign companies, see Predicasts' F & S Index International. The Public Affairs Information Service Bulletin is a less inclusive index from the areas of economics, social conditions, public administration and international relations.

Of growing importance are computer searches of data bases that provide lists and summaries of stories published on a broad range of subjects. Newsearch, Standard & Poor's, Predicasts, Dow Jones and Disclosure Inc. are some of the companies providing these data.

## Records and Reports

Here are some good sources of information that you will find invaluable when writing business stories.

*Corporate data.*    Basic information on corporations can be found in three directories published annually. Your university or public library probably has all three. Dun & Bradstreet's Million Dollar Directory includes almost 40,000 U.S. companies worth $1 million or more. It lists officers and directors, products or services, sales, number of employees and addresses and telephone numbers. The Middle Market Directory profiles companies worth $500,000 to $999,999. The three-volume Standard & Poor's Register of Corporations, Directors and Executives provides similar information for some 36,000 U.S. and Canadian companies. Volume 2 lists executives and directors with brief biographies. The third directory is the Thomas Register of American Manufacturers and Thomas Register Catalog File. The 11 volumes are more comprehensive than the other two directories.

*Investment data.*    To get specific information about the financial performance of a company or an industry, check reports prepared by Standard & Poor's (especially valuable is S&P's Compustat Services Inc.), Moody's, Dun & Bradstreet or Value Line Investment Survey. These reports also discuss company prospects and major trends. Also helpful are annual corporate scoreboards prepared by Fortune, Business Week and Forbes magazines. Business Week uses S&P's Compustat to prepare its scoreboard. You would be wise to purchase and file these issues for future reference.

*Financial ratios.*    To assess a company's financial picture and management, you should compare your subject's financial ratios with the averages for other firms in the same industry. Industry ratios and averages can be found in reports prepared by Dun & Bradstreet, Moody's and S&P's Compustat and in a number of trade journals.

*Company filings.*    For years the Securities and Exchange Commission operated under the guiding principle that companies should make available a maximum amount of information so that stockholders could make the most informed decision regarding management's performance. The SEC preferred to keep out of corporate affairs and let the stockholders provide necessary discipline. Much of that information was made public through SEC filings. In recent years, the SEC has required less information, but corporate filings remain a valuable source of information for reporters. The novice should start with the annual report, the 10-K and the proxy statement, all of which generally can be obtained from the company simply by asking. The annual report and 10-K give you an overview of the company's operations and finances. The proxy statement, which goes to shareholders before the annual meeting or other important meetings, provides an outline of issues to be voted on.

The proxy also can contain genuine news nuggets about the company's dealings. When Seafirst Corp. asked shareholders to approve its merger with a subsidiary of BankAmerica Corp. in May 1983, the company disclosed on page 35 of the 244-page document that the SEC was conducting an informal investigation into whether Seafirst had violated federal laws on financial disclosure. The 1982 CBS proxy statement noted that former anchorman Walter Cronkite had a contract that would pay him $1 million annually for seven years for acting as special correspondent and consultant and for various "special assignments." Interesting nuggets are found under mundane headings like "other matters" or "legal proceedings." Always read anything pertaining to lawsuits. That can, in turn, lead you to public documents regarding a particular suit.

Another valuable SEC document is the prospectus, which is filed when new stock is being offered. The prospectus gives an overview of the company's operation and finances, what it owns and controls, and how it plans to use the proceeds of the stock sale. Also worth noting are the 8-K, the 10-Q and the 13-D. The 8-K, or current update, must be filed within 15 days after any significant changes occur, including changed control of the company, major purchases or the hiring of new auditors. The 10-Q is the unaudited quarterly update of the 10-K. The 13-D must be filed by persons or companies buying more than 5 percent of most publicly held companies. With the proliferation of takeover attempts, reporters also have had to become familiar with 14-D1 and 14-D9 filings, which describe the takeover offer and the target company's response.

Many companies are quite willing to send you their annual report, 10-K and proxy statement. They may even send you the other documents outlined above. To keep up with SEC filings, you may want to follow the SEC News Digest at your local library. To obtain specific filings, you can contact an organization such as Disclosure Inc., which, for a fee, will provide copies of reports filed with the SEC by public companies.

*Trade press.*    Beyond the newspapers and magazines you all know and read is another segment of journalism known as the *trade press*. In these journals and house organs you will find grocers talking with grocers, undertakers talking with undertakers and bankers talking with bankers. You will learn the important issues in a field, how an industry markets its products and services, and what legislation it fears and favors. Interested in health care and physicians? Try Medical Economics, where investigative reporter Jessica Mitford predicts you will find "many a crass and wonderfully quotable appeal to the avarice of the practitioners of the healing arts." When Chris Welles wrote a piece on the health hazards of modern cosmetics, much of his best information came from trade magazines. He found the specific periodicals by looking in the Drug & Cosmetics Periodicals Index and the F & S Index of Corporations and Industries.

A number of trade publications are independent and objective. Among them are Advertising Age, Aviation Week & Space Technology, Institutional Investor, Oil & Gas Journal, American Banker, Medical World News and

Variety. Many more, however, are virtual industry public relations organs. Even these can be valuable for learning about current issues, marketing and lobbying strategies, and even market shares. To find trade publications, consult the Standard Periodical Directory, Ulrich's International Periodicals Directory, Standard Rate & Data Service: Business Publication Rates and Data, and Gale Directory of Publications and Broadcast Media.

*Newsletters.*   Newsletters have become an important source of inside information in recent years. Some are purely ideological, but others can be valuable. Among the best are Energy Daily, Nucleonics Week, Education Daily, Higher Education Daily and the Washington Report on Medicine. To find newsletters, consult The Newsletter Yearbook Directory.

*Associations.*   Although trade associations clearly represent the interests of their members, they can provide expert commentary on current issues or give explanations from the perspective of the industry. When The New York Times reported on the revival of the moving industry, the Household Goods Carriers Bureau, a major trade group, proved to be an important source. The Wall Street Journal found the National Association of Realtors a valuable source for a story on housing costs. To find trade associations, look in the Encyclopedia of Associations or the National Trade and Professional Associations of the United States.

*Directories.*   Directories can be an invaluable tool in seeking information on companies, organizations or individuals. You can use them to learn who makes a certain product, to identify company officers or directors, or to find an expert source for an interview. Basic directories include Who's Who, Directory of Directories, Guide to American Directories, Consultants and Consulting Organizations Directory, Directory of Special Libraries & Information Centers, Research Centers Directory, Consumer Sourcebook, Statistical Sources and Directory of Industrial Data Sources. To contact companies by phone or mail, look in the National Directory of Addresses and Telephone Numbers, published by Concord Reference Books Inc.

*Court records.*   Most companies disclose only information required by the SEC. But when a corporation sues or is sued, an extensive amount of material becomes available. In preparing her story on Jim Walter Corp. for the Jackson (Miss.) Clarion-Ledger, Maria Halkias found court records of great value. ''A complicated lawsuit filed by consumers, subcontractors or former employees can tell a lot about a company's personality that doesn't always come out of the interviews,'' she said. ''The discovery period often makes public exhibits that would be difficult for a reporter to get his hands on, such as contracts, memos, correspondence, working papers, etc. Also, depositions can reveal company practices or intentions that would probably be denied in an interview." Check courts of all levels, including bankruptcy and divorce court.

*Local regulators.*    Frequently businesses want to enlarge their facilities or expand into new markets. To do so, a business may seek funds from an industrial revenue bond authority, which helps the company obtain large sums of money at below-market rates. Or when an institution such as a hospital wants to expand its services, often it must make a case for the expansion before a regional or local agency. In either case, documents filed to support the requests may be revealing and may put into the public record information that previously was unobtainable.

*Others.*    The preceding items are certainly not exhaustive. Other relevant materials may be found at local tax and record-keeping offices, as well as in filings with the Federal Trade Commission, the Federal Communications Commission, the Food and Drug Administration, the Interstate Commerce Commission, the Labor Department and various state agencies. Crain's Chicago Business used Census Bureau figures as the basis of a story on retail sales trends. The U.S. Government Manual lists and describes government agencies, including their functions and programs. And a number of private firms specialize in economic analysis, such as the WEFA Group and Data Resources Inc. In writing about the benefits OPEC could reap from the oil company mergers, The Wall Street Journal cited figures generated by WEFA.

Don't overlook documents and testimony from congressional hearings. Chris Welles drew much of the best material for his book on the ending of fixed brokerage commissions, "The Last Days of the Club," from the 29 volumes of hearings and reports that came out of several years of investigations by two congressional subcommittees. The best indication of the vast array of materials available is found in the preface to "Empire," the extensive examination of the Howard Hughes empire by Donald L. Barlett and James B. Steele. They cite as their sources:

> thousands of Hughes' handwritten and dictated memoranda, family letters, CIA memoranda, FBI reports, contracts with nearly a dozen departments and agencies of the federal government, loan agreements, corporate charters, census reports, college records, federal income-tax returns, Oral History transcripts, partnership agreements, autopsy reports, birth and death records, marriage license applications, divorce records, naturalization petitions, bankruptcy records, corporation annual reports, stock offering circulars, real estate assessment records, notary public commissions, applications for pilot certificates, powers of attorney, minutes of board meetings of Hughes' companies, police records, transcripts of Securities and Exchange Commission proceedings, annual assessment work affidavits, transcripts of Civil Aeronautics Board proceedings, the daily logs of Hughes' activities, hearings and reports of committees of the House of Representatives and Senate, transcripts of Federal Communications Commission proceedings, wills, estates records, grand jury testimony, trial transcripts, civil and criminal court records.

For guidance through the maze of documents, directories and other reference books, several sources are particularly valuable. They are "Business Information Sources," Revised Edition, by Lorna M. Daniells, published by University of California Press; "The Reporter's Handbook: An Investigator's Guide to Documents and Techniques," Second Edition, edited by John Ullmann and Jan Colbert, published by St. Martin's Press; "Manual of Corporate Investigation," published by the AFL-CIO; "Building Corporate Profiles: Sources & Strategies for Investigative Reporters," by Alan Guggenheim, published by Salem Press; "Where to Find Business Information," by David M. Brownstone and Gorton Carruth, published by John Wiley & Sons; and "The Encyclopedia of Business Information Sources," published by Gale Research Co.

## Human Sources

Who are the people you should talk to on the business beat? Here are some who are important sources of information.

*Company officials.*    Although many public relations people can be helpful, the most valuable information probably will come from the head of the corporation or its divisions. Chief executive officers are powerful people, either out front or behind the scenes, in your community. They are often interesting, usually well informed. Not all of them will be glad to see you, though in recent years companies and top executives have started to realize the importance of communicating their point of view to the public. Don't automatically assume the public relations person is trying to block your path. Many people working in corporate communications are truly professional and can be of assistance.

*Analysts.*    To learn what the experts think about specific companies, many business reporters contact securities analysts. Analysts can be valuable if they are not overused and if you get information on the company from other sources as well. Don't assume, however, that analysts are all-knowing, infallible seers. Remember, too, that a broker is selling stock and is not the same as an analyst. When it wrote about the possibility that broadcasting and entertainment companies could become takeover targets, The Wall Street Journal strengthened its story with a quote from an analyst with Donaldson Lufkin & Jenrette Securities. To find the appropriate analyst, consult Investment Decisions Directory of Wall Street Research, also called Nelson's Directory, which is a must for any business department's library.

Other analysts and researchers, frequently economists, are employed by banks, trade groups, Chambers of Commerce and local businesses. They often are willing to talk because the exposure is good for their organizations. In its story on the oil mergers, the Journal also spoke with former Energy

Secretary James R. Schlesinger, senior adviser to the investment firm of Shearson Lehman American Express.

*Academic experts.*   Your college or university will have faculty members with training and experience in varying areas of business and economics. Often they are good sources of local reaction to national developments or analysis of economic trends. They are usually happy to cooperate. Many university public information offices prepare lists of their nationally or regionally known experts and their phone numbers. The lists are available for the asking.

*Chamber of Commerce officials.*   Their bias is clearly pro-business, and they will seldom make an on-the-record negative comment about business, but they usually know who is who and what is what in the business community. The chamber may be involved in such projects as downtown revitalization and industry recruiting.

*Former employees.*   The best business reporters say that frequently their most valuable sources are former employees of the company they're profiling. Writes Welles, ''Nobody knows more about a corporation than someone who has actually worked there.'' He warns, ''Many, probably most, have axes to grind, especially if they were fired; indeed, the more willing they are to talk, the more biased they are likely to be.'' The good reporter will show care in using materials thus gained.

*Labor leaders.*   For the other side of many business stories and for pieces on working conditions, upcoming contracts and politics, get to know local union officials. The workings, legal and otherwise, of unions make good stories, too.

*Others.*   Don't overlook the value of a company's customers, suppliers and competitors. You also may want to consult with local bankers, legislators, legislative staff members, law enforcement agencies and regulators, board members, oversight committee members and the like.

## Announcements and Meetings

The source of much business news, and the *starting point* for many good stories, is the announcement by a company of a new product or the firm's reaction to some action by a government agency. Such announcements should be treated like any news release. The same standards apply to judging newsworthiness, and the same reporting techniques come into play.

The news may come in a news conference, which may be called to respond to a general situation such as a strike or takeover attempt. Or it may be called to try to add some glitter to a corporate announcement the company feels will be ignored if done by news releases alone. You can almost tell how newsworthy something is going to be by the amount of paraphernalia on hand in the news conference room. The more charts, graphs, enlarged photos, projectors and screens in the room, the more likely you are to be dazzled instead of enlightened. They should not be ignored, however, because you can never be sure in advance that something newsworthy will *not* be said.

If you work in a city where one or more corporations are based, you may have the opportunity to cover an annual meeting, which invariably produces some news. Although some are more lively and more newsworthy than others, all say something about the state of the company's business and provide an opportunity for shareholders to ask management questions about the company's performance. A typical story on an annual meeting might begin:

Executives of Condor Airlines assured stockholders Monday that, despite last year's loss of $1.8 million, the company is in no danger of collapse or takeover.

Company president Karen Sherman told the annual meeting that passenger numbers are climbing and so is revenue.

"If the government would just lift some of its silly and unneeded so-called safety requirements, we would be in the black in no time," she said.

In answer to a question from the floor, Sherman defended the 10 percent salary raises given the company's top executives.

"If you want top people, you've got to pay top salaries," she said. Sherman's salary went up last year from $500,000 to $550,000.

## Reporter Enterprise

As in other areas of journalism, often the best business news stories are generated by a reporter's own initiative, sparked by a hunch or a tip passed along by an editor, a shareholder or a disgruntled employee or customer. Sometimes, a self-promoting source can lead to a good story. When the president of a commodity options firm called the Boston Globe to suggest a story on her company, reporter Susan Trausch was dispatched. It was a new company and headed by a woman. But the reporter quickly became suspicious of some things she saw and was told. The investigation that followed produced a series on abuses in an unregulated industry and won several national prizes. The original caller got her name in the paper, all right, but hardly as she had expected.

In other cases a news release may raise questions that turn into stories. For example, a routine announcement of an executive appointment may lead a curious reporter to a story about the financial problems that produced the changes in leadership. A stockholder's question may result in a story about a new trend in corporate financing or a shift in emphasis on operations within the company. Sometimes, an offhand comment at lunch about what one executive has heard about another company will lead to a front-page story after you do some digging. Or a former employee's call that a company is quietly laying off workers may produce a story about the firm's declining fortunes.

A discussion by Chicago Tribune writers and editors about how to explain the impact of world trade on Illinois residents led to a six-part series that won the University of Missouri's business journalism award. The series began by focusing on one worker's plight (a writing technique discussed in Chapter 17):

"You work for a joint 22 years. Then they tell you one day that it's all over. Where do you go? For me, it's all over. I'll sell my excess junk and go on welfare. If that's what they want, that's what they'll get."

Steve Soltis is 47. Last September, his job as a steel shearer vanished when Youngstown Sheet & Tube Co. closed part of its ancient mill beside the Mahoning River in Youngstown, Ohio, and laid off 5,000 workers. . . .

Steve Soltis is a casualty in one of the battles in a threatening world trade war.

Most major business stories are developed like this one, by using a combination of human and documentary sources. The techniques are no different from those of covering city hall, sports or science.

## LOOKING AT THE NUMBERS

Although most reporters find accounting about as appealing as quantum physics or microbiology, an understanding of the numbers business generates is essential to any intelligent analysis of a company or industry. The most complete summary of the financial picture of a business is found in the annual report and the 10-K.

An annual report may be viewed as a statement of the image a company wants to project. Some companies print their reports on the highest-quality paper and fill them with big, bright color pictures; others try to project an image of dignity. Occasionally an annual report's presentation will reflect the financial health or illness of a company. The 1980 Chrysler Corp. report remains a classic; the company reported a net loss of $1.7 billion in a black-and-white report that was 32 pages long, on plain paper stock and without a single photograph. The next year it reported a loss of "only" $475 million in a report on heavier paper, and with 16 color pictures of its best-selling products. In 1982 Chrysler touted a profit of $170 million in a splashy, multicolored report that included a color portrait of Chairman Lee Iacocca.

More than 100 million copies of annual reports are pumped out each year at a cost of $1 to $6 each. Before its breakup, AT&T printed more than 4.5 million copies annually. Reports are sent to shareholders, prospective investors, investment analysts, employees, customers, public affairs officers, corporate sales divisions, journalists and professors.

Annual reports can be a valuable tool, but you should realize that they are not written to be read like a magazine. Rather, annual reports should be approached by sections with specific goals in mind. Accountants suggest that readers skim sections and move from point to point. They note that it is less like reading than a process of digging out information.

Most veteran reporters start with the auditor's report, which is generally located near the back of the annual report together with basic financial data, explanations of footnotes and supplementary financial information. The basic auditor's report, ranging from one long paragraph to three or four paragraphs, states that the material conforms to generally accepted auditing standards and that it fairly presents the financial condition of the company.

Until recently, an auditor's report longer than two paragraphs indicated trouble. Now, however, reporters must read the entire report closely because auditors tuck warnings of trouble in the middle of turgid boilerplate. For example, the 1987 auditor's report on Alamco Inc. was five paragraphs long when two were the standard—a red flag for reporters. The 1988 auditor's report was four paragraphs and referred to litigations that, "if resolved unfavorably, could have a material adverse affect [sic] on the" company—a powerful warning given the basic conservative nature of accountants.

Next, move on to the footnotes, where the seeds of many fascinating stories may be germinating among the innocuous prose and numbers that follow and supplement the company's basic financial data. The J.C. Nichols Co. annual report for 1989 showed that the company's financial condition had improved dramatically from the previous year. But Chris Lester and Charles R.T. Crumpley of the Kansas City Star developed a page-one story around a lengthy footnote explaining that the Nichols Co. had disregarded generally accepted accounting principles (GAAP) in stating its financial condition. Under GAAP rules, the company's net worth would have been $100 million less than Nichols claimed. The unusual accounting gimmick also earned the company a "qualified" auditor's report.

Now flip back to the front of the annual report and find the report from the chairman or chairwoman. It is usually addressed "To our shareholders" and should give an overview of company performance. Although most of these reports tout the glories of the company's management team, an occasional report will be disarmingly frank. Pan Am Corp. Thomas G. Plaskett, chairman and chief executive officer, addressed the December 1988 bombing of Pan Am flight 103, which killed 270 people, in the second paragraph of his letter: "While the magnitude of such human losses is incalculable, the financial impact on the corporation is enormous."

Warren Buffett, chairman of Berkshire Hathaway Inc., is legendary for his straightforward assessment of company performance. Buffett's letters to shareholders can run to 20 pages, include references to investment guru Ben

Graham, Adam Smith and Karl Marx, and offer lessons in investment theory. His letters have been compiled and make fascinating reading.

Next take a few minutes to examine the company's operating divisions to get an idea of its different products. You should look for areas that will help the company in the future. Perhaps a new product has been developed or another company has been acquired that will boost profits.

After that you're ready to look at the numbers. Here are a few things to watch for:

- *Balance sheet*—This is a snapshot of the company on one day, generally the last day of the fiscal year. The left side of the balance sheet lists the assets, or what the company owns. On the right side are the liabilities, or what the company owes, and the shareholders' equity, or the dollar value of what stockholders own. The two sides must balance, so the balance sheet can be summarized as assets equal liabilities plus shareholders' equity. The balance sheet shows how the year in question compares with the previous year. Reporters should note any significant changes worth exploring for a possible story.

- *Income statement*—This report, also referred to as an *earnings statement* or *statement of profit and loss*, answers the key question: How much money did the company make for the year? Look first at net sales or operating revenues and determine if they went up or down. If they increased, did they increase faster than last year and faster than the rate of inflation? If sales lagged behind inflation, the company could have serious problems.

- *Return on sales*—Company management and financial analysts calculate a number of ratios to gain better insights into the financial health of an organization. One important test of earnings is the relation of net income to sales, which is obtained by dividing net income by sales. This will tell you how much profit after taxes was produced by each dollar of sales. The figure varies by industry, but the 1990 Business Week 1000 issue (1000 largest companies ranked by stock-market valuation) composite return on sales was 5.2 percent in 1989, a decline from 5.9 percent the year before. Reporters should remember that percentages can vary widely by industry.

- *Return on equity*—This ratio, which shows how effectively a company's invested capital is working, is obtained by dividing net income minus preferred dividends by the common stockholders' equity for the previous year. The 1990 Business Week 1000 composite return on equity was 13.2 percent.

- *Dividends*—These are declared quarterly and generally are prominently noted in the annual report. Dividends are an inducement to shareholders to invest in the company. Because companies want to see dividends rise each quarter, they sometimes go so far as to change their accounting or pension assumptions so enough funds will be available to increase dividends. Other companies, such as Berkshire Hathaway Inc., declare no dividends because they prefer to reinvest profits internally.

Now that you have an idea of how to examine an annual report and its numbers, it is time for some important words of caution. First, the numbers in an annual report, though certified by an auditor and presented in accordance with Securities and Exchange Commission regulations, are not definite because they are a function of the accounting assumptions used in their preparation. That leads to the second and third points: A company's numbers should be looked at in the context of both its industry and several years' performance. To understand how well a firm is performing, the numbers must be examined along with those of other firms in the same industry. For example, the debt-equity ratios of utilities are much higher than those of most manufacturing companies, such as auto manufacturers. Look at how the company has performed for the last five to 10 years. Then you will discern trends, instead of basing your conclusions on a year's performance, which may be atypical.

The next caution: Don't think reading this section or passing an accounting course makes you qualified to analyze a company's finances. Rather, use the knowledge gained in this chapter to reach some preliminary conclusions that you should pursue with the experts and then with company officials. Only the best reporters are qualified to draw conclusions from company financial data and only after years of study and practice.

To develop a better understanding of company finances, many reporters attend mid-career workshops on accounting and financial analysis. You can develop a better understanding of this complex subject by reading several booklets, including ''Understanding Wall Street,'' published by the New York Stock Exchange, and ''How to Read a Financial Report,'' published by Merrill Lynch. More extensive books include ''How to Read a Financial Report,'' by John A. Tracy (John Wiley & Sons, Second Edition), and ''Quality of Earnings,'' by Thornton O'Glove (The Free Press).

A number of companies prepare supplements to their annual reports to make them easier to understand. Figgie International Inc. even prepares an annual report for children called ''Ump's Fwat.''

# Consumer News

The phrase ''consumer news'' is in its broadest sense arbitrary and redundant. All news is, directly or indirectly, about consumers. And many business stories could just as easily be called consumer stories. A story about the stock market may affect or be of interest to "consumers" of stocks and bonds even though those items aren't "consumed" in the same sense as corn flakes. A story about OPEC raising the price of crude oil affects consumers of gasoline and many other products refined from crude oil. A story about a drought that may drive up the price of wheat has an impact on consumers of hamburger buns. And a story that beef prices are increasing affects the consumer of the hamburger that goes with the bun. The person who has purchased the newspaper in which your stories run is a consumer of newspapers.

Consumer news deals with events or ideas that affect readers in their role as buyers of goods and services in the marketplace. Although news of

**Figure 15.1 Consumer Advocacy.** Ralph Nader popularized the role of the "public citizen" as a force for change and as a source for consumer reporters.

that kind has existed for as long as there have been newspapers and was spread by word of mouth long before that, its development as a conscious area of coverage generally began in the mid-1960s with the development of vocal consumer groups. The consumer movement was helped along immeasurably by Ralph Nader's book "Unsafe at Any Speed," an attack on the Chevrolet Corvair. General Motors Corp.'s subsequent attempts to spy on him and the ensuing publicity when the matter went before Congress also generated interest.

In many ways consumerism is as much a political as an economic movement. The wave of federal, state and local regulations promulgated in the 1960s and '70s attests to that fact. Such legislation has affected producers of goods not only in the area of safety, but also in the realms of finance, labeling and pricing.

The media have played such a major role in publicizing crusaders such as Nader and their causes that in many respects the consumer movement is a creature of the media. Those who espouse consumer causes recognize the power public exposure can bring them. This means to you as a reporter that, while consumer groups may be friendlier than businesspeople, they too will try to use you to their advantage.

## WHERE TO FIND CONSUMER NEWS

Sources of consumer news fall into three general categories: government agencies, quasi-public consumer groups, and private businesses. Let's consider each of these groups.

### Government Agencies

Many municipalities, especially large cities, have a public consumer advocate who reports to the mayor and calls public attention to problems that affect consumers. Most county prosecuting attorneys' offices also have someone—or even a whole department—to challenge business practices of questionable legality. Cases of consumer fraud—in which people pay for something they do not receive or pay for something of a certain quality and receive something less—are handled by these offices.

At the state level most states have a consumer affairs office to investigate consumer problems and to order or recommend solutions. In addition, state attorneys general investigate and prosecute cases of consumer fraud. Most states also have regulatory commissions that represent the public in a variety of areas. The most common commissions regulate insurance rates and practices, rates and levels of service of utilities and transportation companies, and practices of banks and savings and loan associations.

At the federal level, the government regulatory agencies involved in consumer affairs have the power to make rules and to enforce them. Among these are:

- The Federal Trade Commission, which oversees matters related to advertising and product safety.

- The Food and Drug Administration, which watches over prices and safety rules for drugs, foods and a variety of other health-related items.

- The Securities and Exchange Commission, which oversees the registration of securities for corporations and regulates the exchange, or trading, of those securities.

- The Interstate Commerce Commission, which regulates prices and levels of service provided by surface-transportation companies in interstate commerce.

- The Federal Power Commission, which regulates the rates and levels of service provided by interstate energy companies.

Virtually every other federal cabinet office or agency deals with some form of consumer protection, ranging from banking and finance to education to housing to highway and vehicle safety. These agencies are useful to reporters in several ways. First, they are good sources of background information and data of almost every conceivable form. Second, they are good sources of "hard" information such as the results of investigations, cautionary orders and the status of legislation affecting their area of expertise. Also, public information officers of these offices, regulatory agencies and even members of Congress usually are accessible and helpful in ferreting out information for reporters. You may have to make several calls to Washington to get plugged into the right office, but that can be done easily and quite quickly. Many federal agencies have regional offices in major cities.

## Quasi-Public Consumer Groups

Quasi-public consumer groups are composed of private citizens who say they represent the consumer's interest. They, too, are often good sources of background information or comment.

Consumers Union, which publishes the popular Consumer Reports, and Common Cause, which lobbies for federal and state legislation, are general in nature. Many states have public interest research groups. Other organizations are specialists, such as the Sierra Club, which concentrates on environmental matters. Still other groups may be more local in scope. They may try to enact such legislation as returnable-bottle ordinances or to fight what they perceive

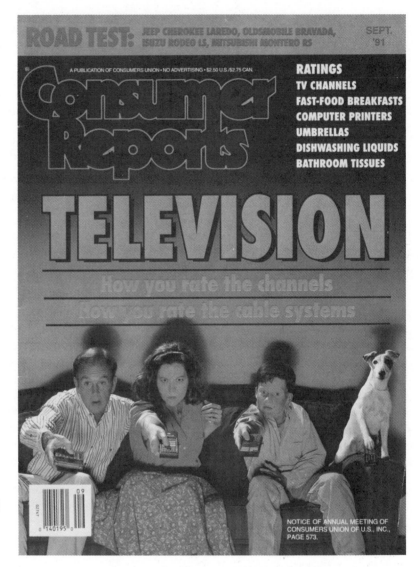

**Figure 15.2 Consumer Reporting.** Consumer Reports is a good source of story ideas and information on product quality and other issues important to nearly every reader.

as discrimination in the way housing loans are made by banks and savings and loan associations.

These groups, through their ability to attract the attention of the media and to find sympathetic ears in Washington and the state capitals, have a greater impact on legislation and news coverage than their numbers would suggest. It is always a good idea to try to determine just who a particular group represents and how broad its support is, especially in cases where the group has not already established its legitimacy. The group may be an association with many members or merely a self-appointed committee with little or no general support. One person, under the guise of an association or committee, can rent a hotel meeting room and call a news conference to say almost anything. Such is the nature of the media that in most cases at least one reporter will attend the news conference and write something about it. The broader a group's support, the greater the impact of its statement. If Consumer Reports says an auto model is dangerous, that judgment is national news. If an individual says the same thing, nobody pays any attention.

### Businesses

Virtually all large corporations and many smaller ones have public relations departments. They try to present their company in the most favorable light and to mask the scars as well as possible when the company is attacked from the outside, whether by the press, the government or a consumer group.

Because of the successes of the consumer movement, a number of companies have taken the offensive and have instituted programs they deem to be in the public interest. We see oil companies telling drivers how to economize on gasoline, the electric utility telling homeowners how to keep their electric bills at a minimum, banks suggesting ways to manage money better, and the telephone company pointing out the times it is least expensive to make long-distance calls.

Corporate public relations people can be valuable sources for a variety of stories by providing background information or comments and reactions to events affecting their company. Also, they may help a reporter place an event in perspective, as it affects a company or industry, for example. Sometimes they are good primary sources for feature stories about products or personalities.

## HOW TO REPORT CONSUMER STORIES

Consumer stories may be "exposés," bringing to light a practice relating to consumers that is dangerous or that increases the price of a product or service. Research for such stories can be simple and inexpensive to conduct, and the findings may arouse intense reader interest. The project can be something as simple as buying hamburger at every supermarket in town to see if all purchases weigh what they are marked. Or it may be something that takes more time and work, such as surveying auto repair shops to see how much unnecessary repair work is done or how much necessary repair work is not diagnosed. Thomas P. Lee of the Tucson (Ariz.) Citizen explored how consumers paid $5 million more for natural gas than necessary, demonstrating that stories can be both business- and consumer-oriented.

Consumer stories also may be informational, intended to help readers make wiser or less expensive purchases. For example, if beef prices are rising, you may suggest protein substitutes that will be as healthful and less expensive. Or you may want to discuss the advantages and disadvantages of buying a late-model used car instead of a new one. Or you can point out the advantages and disadvantages of buying term life insurance instead of whole life insurance.

Other consumer stories may be cautionary, warning readers of impending price increases for products, quality problems with products or questionable practices of business or consumer groups. Such stories can have great impact. The Knight-Ridder chain's revelation that the Firestone radial tires suspected of repeated failures had not passed some of the company's own quality tests helped force a recall that cost the company millions of dollars. Ralph Nader's exposé of the Corvair led to the discontinuance of the model.

Sometimes the newspaper can act as a surrogate for consumers. The best example of this is the ''Action Line'' kind of question-and-answer column published in many newspapers. A column like this has the power of the paper behind questions to companies and thus often is more successful than an individual in reaching satisfactory settlements on questions of refunds, undelivered purchases and other reader complaints.

Consumer and business news stories can provide valuable services not only to readers who are consumers but to readers who are producers and financiers and regulators as well. But they must be carefully reported and compellingly written.

One especially valuable source of information for consumer stories is the Consumer Sourcebook, published by Gale Research Co. The two-volume book describes more than 135 federal and 800 state and local agencies and bureaus that provide aid or information dealing with consumers.

# Suggested Readings

Barlett, Donald L. and Steele, James B. ''Empire: The Life, Legend and Madness of Howard Hughes.'' New York: Norton Press, 1979. Massive study of Hughes' empire showing diversity of documentary sources authors used in their research.

MacDougall, A. Kent. ''Ninety Seconds to Tell It All: Big Business and the News Media.'' Homewood, Ill.: Dow Jones–Irwin, 1981. Examination of the business–press relationship.

Mitford, Jessica. ''Poison Penmanship: The Gentle Art of Muckraking.'' New York: Vintage Books, 1957. Classic introduction on sources, especially the trade press, and then 17 investigative pieces with commentary on the reporting techniques.

Morgan, Dan. ''Merchants of Grain.'' New York: The Viking Press, 1979. Excellent use of sources in analysis of the international grain trade. Especially impressive because the companies are privately held.

Rukeyser, Louis. ''What's Ahead for the Economy: The Challenge and the Chance.'' New York: Simon & Schuster, 1983. Overview and commentary on major economic issues of the 1980s from a free-market perspective.

Schmertz, Herbert. ''Good-bye to the Low Profile: The Art of Creative Confrontation.'' Boston: Little, Brown, 1986. Mobil executive touts the merits of public relations hardball.

Ullmann, John and Colbert, Jan. ''The Reporter's Handbook: An Investigator's Guide to Documents and Techniques,'' Second Edition. New York: St. Martin's Press, 1990. See Chapter 11, ''Business,'' for a close look at the records and documents available.

# Exercises

1. Arrange for a local stockbroker to take the class through the ''purchase'' of 100 shares of a stock of local relevance. Ask the broker to talk about the company, why it's a good or bad buy, how he or she decides on companies to recommend to investors, and so on.

2. Invite an accounting professor to take the class through the New York Stock Exchange's ''Understanding Wall Street'' or Merrill Lynch's ''How to Read a Financial Report.''

3. Invite an economics professor to discuss strengths and weaknesses he or she sees in business reporting in your local newspaper.

4. Obtain a copy of an industrial revenue bond filing and examine it in class.

5. Obtain the Educational Issue of The Wall Street Journal and review it with the class.

# 16

## Sports

This may be the most famous lead ever written for a newspaper story:

Outlined against a blue-gray October sky, the Four Horsemen rode again. In dramatic lore, they are known as Famine, Pestilence, Destruction and Death. These are only aliases. Their real names are Stuhldreher, Miller, Crowley and Layden. They formed the crest of the South Bend cyclone before which another fighting Army football team was swept over the precipice at the Polo Grounds yesterday afternoon as 55,000 spectators peered down on the bewildering panorama spread on the green plain below.

Sportswriting, like the rest of the world, has changed since Grantland Rice crafted those flowery phrases to begin his account of the 1924 Notre Dame–Army game. Styles are less ornate. Subject matter is more diverse. Some reporters, at least, have begun to explore the business and sociology of sports.

In many ways, though, Grantland Rice would feel at home in today's sports departments. Most sports reporters still are sports fans. Critical, probing reporting still is the exception rather than the rule. Writers trying to be colorful still spew out copy that is full of clichés instead.

Readers deserve better. Even if sports were only the toy department of life, sportswriting—like toys—should be entertaining and educational. But sports in America is more than that. The heroes and the language of sports are woven into our politics and our literature. Sports itself is big business. Any institution so pervasive and influential demands solid coverage. Sports offers a reporter all the elements of which good stories are made—triumph, heartbreak, courage, skulduggery, comedy, artistry, even love and hate.

Some of America's best-known writers and journalists began as sportswriters. Ernest Hemingway, Damon Runyon, Heywood Broun, Paul Gallico and Ring Lardner were among them. New York Times columnist James Reston not only wrote sports, but spent some time as traveling secretary for the Cincinnati Reds baseball team before turning to political reporting. Jim Murray and the late Red Smith never left the sports pages but won the Pulitzer Prize for their columns. David Halberstam and George Will, in contrast, won national reputations writing on politics. Both have also produced critically acclaimed books on baseball.

## In this chapter you will learn:

1. How to apply the techniques of beat reporting to the special challenges of sports.

2. How to cover a sports event.

3. How to avoid the trap of clichés in writing sports.

# Covering the
# Sports Beat

A sportswriter for The Washington Post once wrote a column describing a typical colleague. He concluded:

> He lives in a beautiful world where it's always game time and yesterday's tragedies fade like the ripples on a lake. He's the eternal juvenile who would not change places with a king. He's Pagliacci, the Pied Piper, Walter Mitty, Peter Pan, and Jack Armstrong, the All-American Boy.

That description hardly fits a good reporter. Can you imagine an aggressive city hall reporter "living in a beautiful world where it's always council meeting time"?

Another writer, Leonard Schecter, was even harsher. He characterized most sports reporters as "so droolingly grateful for the opportunity to make their living as non-paying fans at sporting events that they devoted much of their energy to stepping on no toes."

Few reporters in other areas are fans of the subjects they cover. Reporters who cover education don't go to school board meetings for fun. Medical writers don't spend their days off watching operations. Many sports reporters, though, were sports fans first. The sports editor of one Florida newspaper so worshipped the New York Yankees that he named his firstborn son after Mickey Mantle.

Many sports reporters, of course, do not fit Schecter's description. The best—and those who are trying to emulate the best—bring to their work the same critical eyes and probing questions that good reporters on any other beat do. They have to. You will have to, as well, if you want to do more than the "consistently bland and hero worshipful" coverage Schecter sees from too many of his colleagues.

In Chapter 14, we discussed the techniques employed by successful reporters. Review them. They apply to coverage of sports as well as to politics or education or science. Now we will see how they can help you meet the special challenges of reporting sports.

## BEING PREPARED

Before you even thought about sports reporting, the chances are that you were reading, watching, playing sports. In that sense, at least, preparing to be a sports reporter is easier than preparing to cover city hall. Nobody grows up reading budgets. But there is more to preparation than immersing yourself in sports. Competition pushes people to their limits, bringing out their best and worst. So you need to know some psychology. Sports has played a major role in the struggles of blacks and women for equality. So you need to know some sociology and history. Sports, professional and amateur, is big business. So you need a background in economics. Some of our greatest writers have portrayed life through sports. So you need to explore literature.

Grantland Rice, the most famous American sportswriter in the first half of this century, graduated Phi Beta Kappa from Vanderbilt University. He majored in Latin and Greek. His prose may have been overblown by today's standards, but he wrote some memorable poetry, too. And he knew who the Four Horsemen of the Apocalypse were.

## BEING ALERT AND PERSISTENT

When editors at the Lexington (Ky.) Herald-Leader learned that another paper was investigating ticket policies in the University of Kentucky's basketball program, two young reporters were assigned to do some checking of their own. Jeffrey Marx and Michael York didn't find any substance to that tip, but they began picking up hints that even more serious problems surrounded the nationally known team. Over the next seven months, the reporters interviewed more than 200 people, including 33 former players, and used the state's freedom of information law to pry loose expense account and ticket records.

The series they produced, titled "Playing Above the Rules," documented widespread cash payments and other gifts to players at Kentucky, and quoted some of the country's most talented high school players about the improper inducements offered by many universities in athletic recruiting. The series began with this lead:

For years, ordinary fans have rewarded University of Kentucky basketball players with a loyalty that is nationally known. What is less known is that a small group of boosters has been giving the players something extra: a steady stream of cash.

The cash has come in various amounts—as little as $20 and as much as $4,000 or more—and it has come often.

UK players have received what they call "hundred-dollar handshakes" in the Rupp Arena locker room after games. They have visited the offices and homes of boosters to receive gifts of up to $500 at a time. They have sold their free season tickets for $1,000 each or more, and they have pocketed excessive payments for public appearances and speeches.

The payments and other benefits directly violated the rules of the National Collegiate Athletic Association. . . .

The stories were published on the newspaper's front page. They generated fierce reaction. Hundreds of subscriptions were canceled. A bomb scare led to evacuation of the newspaper building. Marx, York and their editor were threatened with violence. Local television stations attacked the paper for damaging the university's reputation. But there was other reaction, too. The university launched an investigation and tightened its rules. The NCAA began its own investigation. The coach at another university whose recruiting tactics were revealed in the series announced his resignation.

Perhaps most important, "The series also prompted an impassioned debate in the community over the ethics of under-the-table payments to players and over the relative emphasis placed on academics and athletics at the state's principal university." That summary comes from the letter accompanying the series when it was entered in the Pulitzer Prize competition. It was also entered in the national competition of Investigative Reporters and Editors and in the annual Best Sports Stories contest. It won all three.

The judge's commentary accompanying the article, reprinted in "Best Sports Stories 1986," captured the importance of serious reporting on a subject often treated frivolously: "By exposing the seamy side of the sport so that it could be cleaned up, they demonstrated that they are bigger fans of sports than the boosters who were paying money under the table."

Being alert to a good sports story, however, doesn't always mean examining the seamy side. One reason for the eternal appeal of sports and of sportswriting is that, at their best, both are full of life. Here, for example, are excerpts from a piece Bob Verdi wrote in the Sporting News about the Special Olympics:

These are all athletes who gladly would sign autographs, if they all could.

These are all athletes who would submit to up-close-and-personal interviews, but sometimes their words fail.

These are all athletes who would dearly give back to sports what sports has given them, if only they were agile enough. . . .

Mind you, Donna Sue Montgomery, 37, from Kentucky, came to win the 25-meter walk. But when the first-place time was announced, as 6.7 sec-

onds and hers was 1 minute, 41 seconds, it didn't seem to matter. She got into her wheelchair with a smile and headed over to receive her medal or ribbon—it didn't matter which. They all earn something, including David Diekow of Alaska, who had to be propped up by a volunteer—on vacation time—to accept his prize for fourth, a red rose, which the youngster held high in a quivering hand. . . .

Indeed, you wonder exactly who is handicapped here? Them or us?

Here are a few tips to help you find stories that are different from—and better than—the ones everyone is writing:

1. *Look for the losers.* Losing may not—as football coaches and other philosophers like to assert—build character, but it certainly bares character. Winners are likely to be full of confidence, champagne and clichés. Losers are likely to be full of self-doubt, second-guessing and surliness. Winners' dressing rooms are magnets for sportswriters, but you usually can tell your readers more about the game and those who play it by seeking out the losers.

2. *Look for the bench warmers.* If you follow the reporting crowd, you'll end up in front of your local version of Joe Montana or Steffi Graf every time. Head in the other direction. Talk to the would-be football player who has spent four years practicing but never gets into a game. Talk to the woman who dreams of being a professional golfer but is not yet good enough. Talk to the baseball player who is growing old in the minor leagues. If you do, you may find people who both love their sport more and understand it better than do the stars. You may find less press agentry and more humanity.

3. *Look beyond the crowds.* Some of the best, and most important, sports stories draw neither crowds of reporters nor crowds of fans. The recent and rapid growth of women's sports is one example. Under the pressure of federal law—the "Title IX" you read and hear about—the traditional male dominance of facilities and money in school and college athletics is giving way slowly to equal treatment for women. From junior high schools to major universities, women's teams now compete in virtually every sport except football. With

better coaching and more incentive, the quality of performance is increasing, too. The results of this revolution are likely to be felt far beyond the playing fields, just as the earlier admission of blacks to athletic equality advanced blacks' standing in other areas. Male-run sports departments, like male-run athletic departments, can no longer overlook women athletes.

The so-called "minor" sports and "participant" sports are other largely untapped sources of good stories. More Americans watch birds than play football. More hunt or fish than play basketball. More watch stock-car races than watch track meets. But those and similar sports are usually covered—if at all—by the newest or least talented reporter on the staff. Get out of the press box. Drop by a bowling alley, a skeet-shooting range, the local college's Frisbee-throwing tournament. Anywhere you find people competing—against each other, against nature, against their own limits—you can find good stories. Once you have found them, persist with follow-up questions and close observation until you have enough to satisfy your readers' desire to know the hows and whys.

## BEING THERE AND DEVELOPING CONTACTS

Being there, of course, is half the fun of sports reporting. You're there at the big games, matches and meets. You're there in the locker rooms, on team buses and planes, with an inside view of athletics and athletes that few fans ever get. And you should be there, most of the time. If you are to answer your readers' questions, if you are to provide insight and anecdote, you must be there, most of the time.

Sometimes you should try being where the fans are. Plunk down $10 (of the newspaper's money) for an end-zone seat and write about a football game from the average fan's point of view. Cover a baseball game from the bleachers. Cold hot dogs and warm beer are as much a part of the event as is a double play. Watch one of those weekend sports shows on television and compare the way a track meet or a fishing trip is presented to the way it is in person. Join a city league softball team or a bowling league for a different kind of inside view.

A sports reporter must develop and cherish sources just as a city hall reporter must. You look for the same kinds of sources on both beats. Players, coaches and administrators—like city council members and city managers— are obvious sources. Go beyond them. Trainers and equipment managers have insiders' views and sometimes lack the fierce protectiveness that often keeps players, for example, from talking candidly. Alumni can be excellent sources for high school and college sports stories. If a coach is about to be fired or a new fund drive is being planned, important alumni are sure to be involved. You can find out who they are by checking with the alumni association or by examining the list of major contributors that every college proudly compiles. The business managers and secretaries who handle the money can be invaluable for much-needed but seldom-done stories about the finances of sport at all levels. Former players sometimes will talk more candidly than those who are still involved in a program. As on any beat, look for people who may be disgruntled—a fired assistant coach, a benched star, a big contributor to a losing team. And when you find good sources, cherish them. Keep in contact, flatter them, protect them. They are your lifeline.

Unfortunately, being where a reporter needs to be isn't always easy or pleasant. Just ask Lisa Olson. A young reporter for the Boston Herald, Olson was doing her job, interviewing a New England Patriot football player in the locker room, when several other players began harassing her. At least one player made sexually suggestive comments and gestures while he stood nude beside her. After a complaint, and after much national publicity, players and the team owner were fined and reprimanded by the National Football League. Many other women, and some men, have found themselves victims of harassment by athletes, coaches or fans. Life in the toy department isn't always fun. Sports reporters, especially women, may find their professionalism tested in ways—and in surroundings—seldom encountered by colleagues on beats that usually are considered more serious.

## BEING WARY AND DIGGING FOR THE REAL STORY

It is even harder for a sports reporter than it is for a political or police reporter to maintain a critical distance from the beat. The most obvious reason is that most of the people who become sports reporters do so because they are sports fans. To be a fan is precisely the opposite of being a dispassionate, critical observer. In addition, athletics—especially big-time athletics—is glamorous and exciting. The sports reporter associates daily with the stars and the coaches whom others, including cynical city hall reporters and hard-bitten managing editors, pay to admire at a distance. Finally, sports figures ranging from high school coaches to owners of professional baseball teams deliberately and persistently seek to buy the favor of the reporters who cover their sports.

We are taught from childhood that it is disgraceful to bite the hand that feeds you. Professional, and many college, teams routinely feed reporters. (One Missouri newspaper created a minor furor when it disclosed that a lobbyist in the state capital took political reporters to St. Louis for baseball games. But it creates no furor at all for the same baseball team to give free admission, free food and free beer to the reporters covering those games.) Major-league baseball teams even pay reporters to serve as official scorers for the game. In one embarrassing incident the reporter-scorer made a controversial decision that preserved a no-hit game for a hometown pitcher. His story of the game made little mention of his official role. The reporter for the opposition paper wrote that if it had been *his* turn to be scorer, he would have ruled the other way.

Sports journalism used to be even more parasitic on the teams it covered than is the case now. At one time reporters routinely traveled with a team at the team's expense. Good newspapers pay their own way today.

Even today, however, many reporters find it rewarding monetarily as well as psychologically to stay in favor with the teams and athletes they cover. Many teams pay reporters to write promotional pieces for game programs. And writing personality profiles or "inside" accounts for the dozens of sports magazines can be a profitable sideline.

Most sports reporters, and the editors who permit such activities, argue that they are not corrupted by what they are given. Most surely are not. But temptation is there for those who would succumb. Beyond that, any writer who takes more than information from those he or she covers is also likely to receive pressure, however subtle, from the givers.

Every sports reporter is given a great deal by high school and college coaches or publicity agents, who feed reporters sheets of statistics, arrange interviews, provide space on the team bus or plane, and allow access to practice fields and locker rooms. And what do they want in return? They expect nothing more than an unbroken series of favorable stories. Too often, they get just that. Only the names have been changed in this excerpt from a metropolitan newspaper:

The State U. troops reported today to begin three weeks' tune-up before the Fighting Beagles invade Western State.

Offensive commander Pug Stanley had some thoughts available Thursday before some 90-odd players arrived.

"We really made some strides this year," Stanley declared. . . . Charlie Walker, he said, is no longer feeling his way around at quarterback. The Beagle pass catchers are hardly old men, but the top four targets are two juniors and two sophomores rather than two sophomores and two freshmen.

State U.'s heaviest artillery is located behind Charlie Walker. Beagle runners ranged from good to outstanding a year ago. Most are back, with a season's more experience.

"Our runners keep on getting better," commented their attack boss. "Our backfield has to be our biggest plus. We're going to burn some people with it this year."

The story did not mention that State U., which had managed only a 6-5 record the previous year against weak opposition, was universally picked to finish in the second division of its second-rate conference. That's not only bad writing, but bad reporting.

Anywhere athletics is taken seriously, from the high schools of Texas to the stadiums of the National Football League, athletes and coaches are used to being given special treatment. Many think of themselves as being somehow different from and better than ordinary people. Many fans agree. Good reporters, though, regard sports as a beat, not a love affair. Tom Tuley, executive sports editor of the Cincinnati Post, wrote:

> Slowly, but ever so surely, is vanishing the notion that the sports department's job is to cover the games and perpetuate the image that sports are pure, its participants are All-American boys, and its pages places simply to report the game and what was said after it was over.
>
> And who knows, maybe someday we'll even achieve equal status in job title. Through the years, it has always been "reporter" on the news side, sports "writer" in my world.
> I'm beginning to discover more sports reporters.

Those sports reporters maintain their distance from the people they cover, just as reporters on other beats do, by keeping their readers in mind. Readers want to know who won, and how. But they also want to know about other sides of sports, sides that may require some digging to expose. Readers' questions about sports financing and the story behind the story too often go unanswered.

**Money.**    Accountants have become as essential to sports as are athletes and trainers. Readers have a legitimate interest in everything from ticket prices to the impact of money on the actual contests.

**The Real "Why."**    When a key player is traded, as much as when a city manager is fired, readers want to know why. When athletes leave school without graduating, find out why. When the public is asked to pay for expansion of a stadium, tell the public why. One of the attractions of sports is that when the contest is over, the spectators can see who won and how. Often that is not true of struggles in government or business. The "whys" of sports, however, frequently are as hard to discover as they are in any other area.

**The Real "Who."**    Sports figures often appear to their fans, and sometimes to reporters, to be larger than life. In fact, athletics is an intensely human activity. Its participants have greater physical skills, and larger bank accounts, than most other people, but they are people. Probably the best two descriptions of what it is really like to be a major-league athlete were written by athletes—"Ball Four" by Jim Bouton and the novel "North Dallas Forty" by Pete Gent. Still, some of the best sportswriting results from the continuing effort by reporters to capture the humanity of games. Roger Kahn, in perhaps the finest baseball book ever written, "The Boys of Summer," needed only two inches of type to reveal Carl Erskine, the old Dodger pitcher, in this scene with his wife and mongoloid son:

Jimmy Erskine, nine, came forward at Betty's tug. He had the flat features and pinched nostrils of Mongolism.

"Say, 'Hello, Roger,'" Betty said. Jimmy shook his head and sniffed.

"Come on," Carl said.

"Hosh-uh," Jimmy said. "Hosh-uh. Hosh-uh."

"He's proud," Carl said, beaming. "He's been practicing to say your name all week, and he's proud as he can be." The father's strong right hand found Jimmy's neck. He hugged the little boy against his hip.

As Tom Tuley observed, sports reporting is much more than covering the contests and perpetuating the myths.

# Covering the Contests

A major part of any sports reporter's job, however, is covering the games, matches or meets. That task is harder than it might seem. You have the same problems you would have in covering any event, from a city council meeting to a riot. You must decide what to put in your lead, capture the most interesting and significant developments, find some good quotes, answer as many of your readers' probable questions as you can and meet your deadline. But a reporter covering a football game, for instance, has a major concern that a reporter writing about a council meeting does not have. Most of the readers of your football story already know a great deal about the game. Many were there. Others saw it on television or listened on radio. They know *what* happened. They expect you to tell them *why* and *how*.

A story like this one, though it may be easy to produce, falls far short of meeting that demand:

Jefferson High turned two fumble recoveries into touchdowns and shut out Oakland High, 16-0, Monday night at Hickley Field.

The Cyclones, who held Oakland to minus 32 yards rushing in the game,

scored their points on consecutive possessions in the second quarter.

The scoring started when Jefferson recovered a fumble at the Eagle 42-yard line and marched in for the score.

The reporter is adding little to what most fans already know. The only two quotes in the story, just two paragraphs from the end, could have been pulled from a list of coaches' stock comments, suitable for all occasions:

"We didn't make the mistakes we did last week against West," said Cyclones Coach David Carlson.

Oakland Coach Lyle Wheeler praised his defense after the game. "I thought they played real well. They were on the field the whole game."

Too many games are reported just as that one was, without probing the hows and whys. The reporter sits in the press box, has three-quarters of a story written before the game is over, breezes through each dressing room just long enough to ask, "Any comment, Coach?" and applies the finishing touches to the story on the way to the telephone or back to the office. But that is recording, not reporting.

Suppose, instead, that the reporter had done a little homework. Some digging would have revealed that this was Oakland's third loss of the season, with no victories. It would have shown that Coach Wheeler had predicted before the season a winning record, possibly a conference championship. And it would have shown that the player counted on to be the star of the team had been dropped from the squad just before the first game for "disciplinary reasons."

Suppose the reporter had gotten to know the players and supporters of the team. He or she would have learned that the black athletes and many of their parents believed the suspension of the star, who was black, was a case of racial discrimination by the white coach. And if the reporter had gotten out of the press box, there might have been more revealing comments from players and fans, some explanation of what was seen on the field. The story might have read:

From the top row of the Hickley Field Stadium, Gary Thomas watched in agony as his former teammates at Oakland High lost their third game of the season, 16-0, to archrival Jefferson High.

He groaned each time an Oakland ball carrier was dropped for a loss. He cursed each of Oakland's four lost fumbles.

"Cut left," he muttered as halfback David Oldham ran head-on into four Jefferson tacklers. "Hold the ball, damn it," as Oldham fumbled.

The outcome of Friday's game would have been different, Thomas believes, if he had been on the field displaying the skills that made him the leading rusher in the conference last year as a junior.

But he is spending his senior season in the stands, suspended from the team for what Coach Lyle Wheeler calls "disciplinary reasons" after a fight with a white student in a school rest room. Thomas thinks he was discriminated against.

"The dude just don't like blacks," he said of Wheeler.

Black and white teammates agreed

as they wearily dressed after the game that they want Thomas back in uniform.

"We ain't got a prayer without him," said Oldham, who is white.

Linebacker Chris Pannell, who is black, added. "He's the heart of this team. Without him, we got no heart."

Coach Wheeler, asked about the effect of Thomas' absence, responded by praising his defense. "I thought they played real well. They were on the field the whole game."

Jefferson ran 62 offensive plays to only 42 for Oakland. But, had it not been for the fumbles, which put Jefferson in easy scoring range three times, Oakland might have escaped with a scoreless tie.

That story tells its readers not only what happened, but how it happened and at least part of why it happened. It combines solid reporting with deft writing to add something that was new and interesting even for those who had seen or heard the game.

Notice first the form of the story. In sportswriting, as elsewhere in journalism, the inverted pyramid structure has given way in many cases to an alternate approach. (You will learn about these alternatives in Chapter 17.) In this story the reporter starts by setting the scene and introducing the most important character, while also providing essential information about the game. Your goals for the opening of any story about a sports event should be twofold:

1. *Focus on the unique element.* No sporting event is quite like any other. A perceptive reporter picks out what made this game different and shares it with the reader. The unique element may be a single play, a questionable ruling by an official, an untimely injury. Or it may be, as in this case, the missing player. Find that unique element and you have found the key to your story. Your lead may be a quote, the description of a scene, an analysis by some expert observer or your own summary of the contest's high point. Whatever opening device you choose, be sure the facts support it. A summary or analysis based on fact is permissible in a news story. Reliance on your own opinion is not.

2. *Tell the reader who won.* No description is so compelling and no analysis so astute that a reader will forgive you if you forget to say at the start what the outcome of the event was. The basic who, what and where must never be left out or buried in the body of your story. The story is, after all, about the contest.

As in the story on Oakland High, the body of your story should develop the unique angle brought out in the lead. This writing technique gives a unified focus and maintains the reader's interest. In the course of the story, you should also meet three other objectives:

1. *Describe what happened.* In addition to knowing the outcome, your audience will want to read at least the highlights of *how* it was reached, if only to savor them again. Analysis and background are hollow without the solid descriptive core of what happened. In the Oakland High story, that description begins in the second and third paragraphs and resumes in the last paragraph of the excerpt.

2. *Answer readers' questions.* The story should supply the explanation—or part of it, at least—of *why* the game turned out as it did. It should tell its readers something they could not have discovered easily for themselves. The reporter of the Oakland High story accomplished that by taking the trouble to learn the background of the event, and then by seeking out the right sources. Rarely should you have to rely on your own expertise to answer the questions of why and how. Experts abound at virtually every sports event. Assistant coaches or scouts sit in the press box. The coaches and players directly involved are available after the game. Alumni, supporters, former players can be found if you will just go looking. The most important question for you to ask as a reporter is what your readers will want to know. Then try to find the answers for them.

3. *Get the competitors into the story by using good quotes.* Readers usually want to know what the competitors think about what they have done. When winners exult, when losers cry, put your readers in the scene. That is part of the attraction of sports. The hours spent getting to know them pay off when the athletes share with you—and your readers—what the contest was really like.

The preparation and techniques of interviewing are essentially the same in a locker room as in a politician's office, though you seldom have occasion to interview a mayor who is dressing or undressing. The reward for a good job in either situation is the same, too. You get, as in the preceding story, lively quotes that provide some insight.

Remember, you produce a good game story by:

1. Doing your homework before the game.

2. Spotting the unique element and building the story on it.

3. Telling your readers who won and how.

4. Answering readers' questions.

5. Getting the participants into the story.

Those guidelines will serve you and your readers well, whether the event is a professional football game or the semifinals of the Sunday night bowling league.

# Writing about
# Sports

Many sports journalists think of themselves more as writers than reporters. This chapter is intended to help you become a sports reporter. But good writing is an important part of any top reporter's skills, and sports offers abundant material for good writing.

Good writing is precise, conveying what the author means to say and nothing else. It is descriptive, re-creating for the reader the sights, the sounds, the smells of the event. It is suited in pace and in tone to the story—lively for an exciting game, somber for the reflections of a loser.

Here's Jere Longman's view of Temple University basketball coach John Chaney:

If you are sitting in your seat at a Temple game, it is a safe bet that John Chaney is not sitting in his. He stalks the sideline, snarling—barking, he calls it—tie loosened, arms flailing, veins straining in his neck, screaming at his players, haranguing the referees, sometimes even challenging other coaches.

"He's not a drinking man, but he's got that whiskey voice," said Clarence (Bighouse) Gaines, the legendary coach at Winston-Salem who tried to recruit Chaney out of Ben Franklin High. "And he's got those eyes. Gray, cat eyes. Strange-looking eyes."

John Chaney never howls at his players when they are behind. He sits, eyes wide, face transfixed in a death stare. "I'm afraid to say anything when we're behind," he said. "I'm too worried we're going to lose."

It's when Temple is ahead that Chaney does his best Mount St. Helens impersonation. His most infamous explosion took place on February 22, 1984, during halftime of a game Temple won over George Washington, 93-77. To Chaney, it seemed as if the George Washington center, Mike Brown, was throwing left hooks instead of hook shots inside. Chaney brought the point up in a courteous debate with George Washington Coach Gerry Gimelstob and made his point by grabbing Gimelstob around the neck.

As the debate continued, Chaney pointed a finger in Gimelstob's face and said, "I'll knock you out and you know it."

Soon, the fighters were dispatched to neutral corners, and later Gimelstob and Chaney shook hands. . . .

The image so precisely sketched in the first paragraph—"tie loosened, arms flailing, veins straining"—is supported by the testimony of another coach and then by a graphic example. Notice the specifics ("Gray, cat eyes"), the volcano allusion ("Mount St. Helens impersonation"), the repetition ("left hooks instead of hook shots''), the comic understatement (''courteous debate . . . made his point by grabbing Gimelstob around the neck''). Here is a writer in firm control of both material and tools.

Franz Lidz gave readers an equally compelling look at less triumphant athletes in a piece on boxing's professional sparring partners. Here he describes a Larry Holmes training session:

Next up was Phil Brown, famed for a strong jab and weak chin. About the only fighter he hasn't worked with is Norman Mailer. Brown was here so Holmes could hone his techniques. Bathed in the disco light, Brown stood still, calm and quiet awaiting Holmes' first punch.

"Stick, stick, stick," Ballard shouted instructions to Brown. "Work your jab up and down like a yo-yo. . . .''

Holmes ripped combinations into Brown's stomach. Brown's head sagged. He was throwing punches, but they were not connecting.

"Touch him and get out. . . .''

Holmes slapped Brown back into a corner. Brown's brow crooked. His eyelids dropped. He was too pined-in to parry.

"Step around, step around. . . .''

Holmes straightened Brown with a left and tagged him with a right cross. Brown answered with weak uppercuts.

"Flick, flick, flick. . . .''

Holmes doubled up on his hooks. Brown's body slumped, twisted.

"Come on Phil, this ain't no tappin' contest.''

Holmes let loose a big right. Brown's back arched and his knees buckled. The bell sounded. Brown later said, "If Larry's got a clear shot, he'll take it. I've been shooken up and dazed, but it's all part of what he's paying me for.''

Old-time writers called it the sweet science, but Lidz shows boxing's sweaty, bloody, brutal back rooms. Notice the scene-setting, with its introduction of the protagonist, literary allusion, explanation and contrast to the impending violence. Then the pace quickens. The sentences shorten, the verbs harden. Notice the alternation of the manager's instructions with the description of the overmatched fighter's failure to carry them out. Then, in this brief scene, just as in a full-blown drama, the action builds up to its crunching climax. And, finally, Phil Brown, having played his role, reflects on it.

Lidz, in simpler sentences than Mailer would have used, has applied the novelist's storytelling technique to the reporter's job of describing a fragment of life. The same kind of detailed observation, precise description and varied pacing will help you tell almost any sports story.

Perhaps the best contemporary sports reporter and writer is Thomas Boswell of The Washington Post. He has won the Best Newspaper Writing award of the American Society of Newspaper Editors. His work regularly heads the list of best sports stories published annually by the Sporting News. Here are a few samples. First, the opening of a story about aging baseball players:

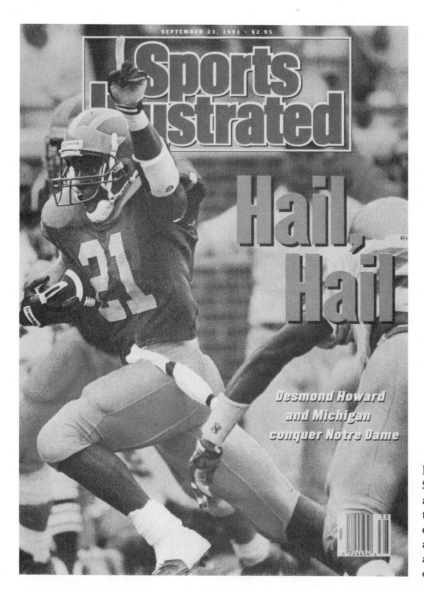

**Figure 16.1 Sports Reporting at Its Best.** Much of the best sports coverage—reporting and writing— appears in the pages of Sports Illustrated.

The cleanup crews come at midnight, creeping into the ghostly quarter-light of empty ballparks with their slow-sweeping brooms and languorous, sluicing hoses. All season, they remove the inanimate refuse of a game. Now, in the dwindling days of September and October, they come to collect baseball souls.

Age is the sweeper, injury his broom.

Mixed among the burst beer cups

and the mustard-smeared wrappers headed for the trash heap, we find old friends who are being consigned to the dust bin of baseball's history. If a night breeze blows a back page of the Sporting News down in the stadium aisle, pick it up and squint at the one-time headline names now just fine print at the very bottom of a column of averages.

Notice the imagery, as gloomy as the subject matter. Notice the pacing, with long, complex sentences slowing the eye to match the mood of sadness. Notice the metaphor, age as the sweeper, injury the broom. But notice, too, the sharp-eyed description that must ring true to anyone who has ever seen or thought about the debris cast aside by a baseball crowd.

A little later in the same story:

"I like a look of Agony," wrote Emily Dickinson, "because I know it's true." For those with a taste for a true look, a glimpse beneath the mask, even if it be a glimpse of agony, then this is the proper time of year. Spring training is for hope; autumn is for reality. At every stop on the late-season baseball trail, we see that look of agony, although it hides behind many expressions.

Familiarity with the classics of literature did not die with Grantland Rice. Boswell not only can find the line, he can make it work.

**Figure 16.2 Craftsman at Work.** Thomas Boswell of The Washington Post sets a high standard for excellence in sports reporting and writing.

From another story, this one about a championship boxing match, comes a short paragraph that is equally powerful but sharply different in tone:

> Boxing is about pain. It is a night
> out for the carnivore in us, the hidden
> beast who is hungry.

Later in that story, Boswell returns to the theme:

> But boxing never changes. One central truth lies at its heart and it never alters: Pain is the most powerful and tangible force in life.
>
> The threat of torture, for instance, is stronger than the threat of death. Execution can be faced, but pain is corrosive, like an acid eating at the personality.
>
> Pain, as anyone with a toothache knows, drives out all other emotions and sensations before it. Pain is priority. It may even be man's strongest and most undeniable reality.
>
> And that is why the fight game stirs us, even as it repels us.

From the poetry of aging to the brutality of pain, Boswell matches his images, his pace, his word choice to the subject matter. The principles of careful observation and clear writing cover all occasions.

There is one thing that sets a writer like Boswell apart from many lesser writers. It is his attitude toward his readers. That may be worth copying, too. After winning the ASNE award, he told an interviewer:

> We vastly underestimate our audience in newspapers. In 11 years I have never had one letter from anybody saying, "What's all this highfalutin talk?" I get the most touching letters from people who seem semi-literate but who really appreciate what you're doing. I think the fact that people are capable of understanding the Bible, or sensing the emotion in Shakespeare, just proves how far they are above our expectations.

# Suggested Readings

Feinstein, John. "A Season on the Brink." New York: Macmillan, 1986. This chronicle of a year with Indiana basketball coach Bobby Knight entertains while explaining much about the high-pressure world of big-time college sports.

Flood, Curt. ''The Way It Is.'' New York: Trident Press, 1971. The first-person story of the baseball player whose challenge to the reserve clause revolutionized professional sports in America. Also noteworthy are the caustic comments on sportswriters.

Kahn, Roger. ''The Boys of Summer.'' New York: New American Library, 1973. One of the best sports books ever written.

''Sports Illustrated.'' Features the best continuing examples of how sports should be reported.

Wolff, Alexander and Keteyian, Armen. ''Raw Recruits.'' New York: Pocket Books, 1990. A hard look at college basketball recruiting written by two veterans of Sports Illustrated.

# Exercises

1. You have been assigned to cover your college's men's basketball team. Write a memo describing at least five likely sources and listing at least five story ideas.

2. Now do the same for the women's basketball team. Compare facilities, funding, fan interest and actual coverage. Be prepared to discuss your findings.

3. Select a ''minor'' sports event, such as a wrestling meet or a volleyball game. Prepare for and cover the event. Write the story.

4. Choose one of the story ideas in Exercise 1 or 2. Report and write it.

5. Compare the coverage of a major event in your local newspaper and in Sports Illustrated. Which seems better written? Why?

# PART FIVE

## Advanced Techniques

# 17

# Alternatives to the Inverted Pyramid

$\mathbf{F}$or all its strengths, the inverted pyramid has a telling weakness: It cannot maintain, let alone build, reader interest as the story progresses. After the first three paragraphs, it is not going to get any better.

Storytelling doesn't have to be done that way. Good writing and alternative story forms have always been available to journalists to tell stories. Whether it is for spot news or a personality profile, the information can be handled in a variety of ways that will meet reader's needs. The best writers recognize that. As a result, occasionally readers are treated to the exception:

> Friday night they had double-dated to the movies in Independence. Saturday they had driven to a friend's party in Sibley. Sunday they were all dead.
>
> Four Independence teen-agers, two still in high school and two friends since kindergarten, were killed late Saturday night.

Even though these two paragraphs open a spot news story, the traditional who, what, when, where, why and how are not answered until after the first paragraph.

Alternative approaches such as this have been used for some time for other kinds of stories. These include:

1. *Backgrounders*, which explain and update the news.

2. *Investigative pieces*, which reveal information and make news.

3. *Profiles*, which explain people and organizations.

4. *Human-interest stories*, which describe people.

5. *Brighteners*, which bring a smile to the reader.

Profiles, human-interest pieces and brighteners traditionally are lumped under the heading "Features." What they have in common is the lack of a spot news event. The stories are not event-oriented.

Many textbooks have chapters on feature writing. This one does not because the authors believe that the literary techniques of good writing belong in any story, and that any story, event-oriented or not, can be told in a form other than the inverted pyramid. Because deadline pressure sometimes prevents the reporter from gathering anything beyond the basic facts, alternative story structures are not used as often on spot news. Space, too, is a consideration. The inverted pyramid requires the fewest words because the most important information comes first. The narrative story form takes longer to get to the point. Detail, and the literary devices used to weave it in, also take precious space.

But when the time and space are available, take advantage of them. Whether you are writing about a car accident, the Boy Scouts, the health-care system, corruption in government or the 8-year-old running the corner lemonade stand, writing the story will be easier if you know some of the alternatives to the inverted pyramid. None of the alternative story forms has attained the widespread use or recognition of the inverted pyramid, and none is as detailed a formula as the inverted pyramid. All, however, help you organize your story and attract readership. And attracting the reader's attention is, after all, part of our job.

### In this chapter you will learn:

1. How to write a story using the focus structure.

2. Two variations of the focus structure.

3. How to write a story using extended dialogue.

4. How to write a story that is organized chronologically.

5. When to use first-person accounts and how to do so effectively.

# The Focus Structure

For centuries, writers have used the literary device of telling a story through the eyes of one person or by examining part of the whole. The device makes large institutions, complex issues and seven-digit numbers meaningful. Few of us can comprehend the size of the U.S. budget, but we can understand the numbers on our own paycheck. Not many of us can explain the marketing system for wheat, but we could if we followed a bushel of wheat from the time it was planted until a consumer picked up a loaf of bread in the supermarket.

Even though Joseph Stalin was hardly talking about literary approaches, he summed up the impact of focusing on a part of the whole when he said, "Ten million deaths are a statistic; one death is a tragedy."

Individual newspaper journalists have used the technique often, but no

**Figure 17.1    Making It Readable.** In its daily column-one story, The Wall Street Journal has perfected an organizational formula that permits the reporter to describe large institutions and complex issues in understandable terms.

newspaper has seized upon it like The Wall Street Journal. In its daily column-one feature examining national and international issues, the Journal routinely and expertly puts a literary magnifying glass on the individual involved in an issue or institution. Readers who find little to interest them in a story about IBM, for example, may read about it as told through the eyes of a rising young executive. Those to whom unemployment rates are meaningless may eagerly follow a story about the jobless as told through the eyes of a factory worker who was laid off because the company shut down rather than comply with anti-pollution standards.

This alternative approach, called the *focus structure*, combines the best of the inverted pyramid and the narrative forms, and is widely used in newspapers and magazines throughout the country. Andrew Pollack used it for a story in The New York Times about a new business venture that some consider illegal. In his lead, he focused on one person:

> SAN FRANCISCO—George Burditt of Santa Barbara, Calif., won $1 million recently by being the first person to punch in, using the buttons on his telephone, the correct numerical answers to seven questions. He was the first winner of a new national contest that people enter by dialing a ''900'' telephone number, paying $2.99 for the call.

With that story told, Pollack moves to the news in his second paragraph:

> The contest, called the Game, features such questions as ''How many eggs are in three dozen?''—the query Mr. Burditt answered to win $1 million. But not everyone is playing along. Representative Bart Gordon, Democrat of Tennessee, has asked the Attorney General to investigate the contest, saying it appears to be an illegal lottery. The organizer of the contest, a Los Angeles company called 900 Million Productions, maintains that the Game involves skill and is therefore not gambling.

From there, the reporter moves to the so-what factor:

> That issue is but one part of a growing debate among regulators and businesses about ''900'' telephone numbers and how they are used. Other issues. . . .

The story is about abstract issues, but the example is concrete.

By comparison, the inverted pyramid lead that follows gets the news to the reader quicker, but probably won't attract readers' interest in the same way:

Legislators and legal officials are discussing how "900" numbers can be used for charitable and political fundraising, whether the cost of making "900" calls is disclosed clearly enough to consumers and even whether a game that gives away millions to "900" callers is gambling.

Writers should use real people to connect readers to issues. When there is no one for readers to touch, they may not read at all. One newspaper mistakenly separated the human touch from the main story, which began this way:

Roots—they become more important with each passing decade. They are the ties to family, friends, home and community. Roots make the past tangible, the present understandable, and the uncertainty of the future bearable.

But in our increasingly mobile society, families tend to scatter. Senior citizens, often widowed, find it financially or physically difficult to maintain their homes. Many of their friends are in the same situation. Reluctantly, they sell their homes and move to communities where housing and transportation are more affordable.

So the roots get severed.

But not always. Through a shared housing program now offered by the Eden Council of Hope and Opportunity. . . .

The sidebar, a second story dealing with the same topic, began this way:

If you ask Helen Velasques and Esther Stobeck what they value most about the new lives they have built for themselves, "independence" would be the response.

They are two senior citizens who have benefited from a concept known as "shared housing." Through the Fremont office of the Eden Council of Hope and Opportunity. . . .

The writer would have used less space and gotten better results if she had combined the stories and put the women in the opening.

Reporters working on local stories have just as many opportunities to apply this approach as those writing national and international stories. For example, instead of being preoccupied with the thousands of dollars your United Way is raising for its campaign organization, you could focus on the people who benefit—or fail to benefit—from the campaign. If the streets in your city are bad, write about the problem from the point of view of a driver. Or if Dutch elm disease is killing the trees in your city, concentrate on a homeowner who has lost several. The focus structure offers the writer a powerful method of reducing institutions, statistics and cosmic issues to a level readers can relate to and appreciate.

Advertising agencies use the technique, too. That's why instead of being solicited for money to help the poor and starving in a foreign country, you are asked to support one child or one family for only pennies a day. The advertising gives poverty and hunger a face. Millions starving are a statistic; one child starving is a tragedy.

## STEPS IN APPLYING THE FOCUS STRUCTURE

The focus structure is applied through an established sequence of steps (see Figure 17.2). Focusing on the individual is the first and most important. Three more steps follow:

— Providing a transition to the larger issue.

— Reporting on the issue or institution.

— Providing a strong finish that returns to the subject of your focus or carries a summary statement.

Let's look at each of these steps.

### The Transition

Transitions ease the reader from the personalized openings to the issues being reported. In the story about the ''900'' telephone lines, Pollack moved from a description of the Game to the issue of whether it was legal. From there, he connected the inquiry to other questions about ''900'' numbers.

The transition connects the opening to what some writers call the *nut paragraph*. Here the reader learns the reason for the story. The paragraph usually includes most of the information found in the lead of an inverted pyramid story. When The Wall Street Journal reported on changes in bidding procedures at the Pentagon, for three paragraphs it discussed how money could be saved by changing the bid requirements for Worcestershire sauce. The theme paragraph put the relatively unimportant Worcestershire sauce in context:

The savings of less than four cents a bottle is pint-sized next to the $49 billion the Defense Department will spend this year to arm and supply the military. But Pentagon officials hope to realize more savings on vast numbers of other purchases by dropping specifications for thousands of products and purchasing commercial items instead.

Here the transitional sentence begins with the sauce and ends with the $49 billion the department will spend. This transition from the specific to the general comes in the fourth paragraph. In other stories, it might be in the second, third or fifth. The transition always should come near the top of the story.

### Exposition of the Larger Issue

After the transition you begin the exposition of your story. Reporting on this larger issue or institution is your reason for writing. You have left Game winner George Burditt behind. You have left the Worcestershire sauce at the Pentagon. Now you must construct the body of your story.

Constructing the body of a story using the focus structure is similar to writing the inverted pyramid story. Until the ending, you arrange the material in descending order of importance. Your success at maintaining readers'

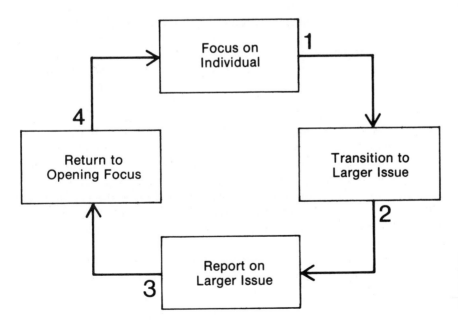

**Figure 17.2
Steps in Applying
the Focus
Structure.**

interest throughout the story, however, will depend on the content and your writing skills.

One way to maintain interest is to refer to the spotlighted individual or subject in the body of the story. Another is to lace the informational material with anecdotes and colorful description. For example, in the story about Pentagon bidding procedures, we find this anecdote deep in the story:

Federal purchase specifications have long been a symbol of bureaucratic bedlam. Several years ago Sen. Lawton Chiles disclosed that someone trying to sell mousetraps to the military would have to comply with about 500 pages of specifications. The requirements included one for "wire, steel, carbon (high carbon, round, for mechanical springs, general purpose)." The Florida Democrat concluded that the detailed standards were so stultifying that "if you build a better mousetrap, don't try to sell it to the federal government."

Embarrassed, the government trimmed its mousetrap standard to less than a page.

Anecdotes help, but the most important elements of all are focus, detail and transitions. These three elements are important whether you are writing a human-interest feature about a former teacher on his or her 100th birthday or a profile of a professional athlete. Nearly any story can be told using the focus structure. But they all need to have focus, detail and transitions.

Focus requires you to be clear about your objectives from the beginning. For example, if you have decided the most interesting aspect of the athlete is his personality, focus on the traits that make him the way he is. What and who influenced him? What is his philosophy? If he happens to hunt deer for recreation, don't include that fact unless it is germane to the story. It might, for instance, be an example of how competitive he is.

Focus requires a goal not only when you write but also when you ask questions. Sometimes you can identify the focus when you are preparing yourself for the interview. Other times you will not know until during the interview what your focus will be.

Look for detail. Don't tell; show. Instead of reporting simply that Karen Goldberg, corporate president, is a competitive, combative, single-minded individual, provide concrete examples. How does she treat her secretary? Her vice presidents? Can people who work for her—and who used to work for her—give you anecdotes about how she treats them? Maybe the person who sold her a car recently has the same impression of her as one of the corporate officers. Detail combined with focus makes the story easier to write and more interesting for others to read.

Miles Corwin of the Los Angeles Times used detail to show, not tell, when he wrote a profile of a killer that contained this passage:

Then Barbara Harris noticed his eyes, and she began to shudder. She

always had admired Robert's eyes.
They are pale gray with blue flecks
and are accentuated by long black
lashes. But on this Fourth of July, Barbara saw only coldness and an absence
of life in his eyes.

Interest, of course, depends not just on detail but also on the care you've taken to construct the story so that it flows from one thought to the next. The transitions you build into your story often will determine whether readers move on to something else in the paper or continue reading your story.

This focus-detail-transition test is crucial to good writing. Pass this test, and your story will evoke a reaction from your readers: humor, anger, frustration, sympathy. When you win that kind of commitment from your readers, you have successfully written the story.

## The Finish

One characteristic of a well-written story is a strong finish, the last step in the focus structure. Unlike the inverted pyramid, in which the importance of the material diminishes as the story concludes, this story structure requires a strong finish.

A good technique is to return to the person, thing, event or theme introduced at the beginning. This technique, called a *tie-back*, is one of the significant differences between the inverted pyramid and focus structure approaches. The inverted pyramid story diminishes in importance and interest so that it can be cut from the end, but the focus structure has an ending. Walt Harrington of The Washington Post opened his profile of syndicated columnist Jack Anderson with an anecdote illustrating the relationship between Jack and his dad. (The story is printed in its entirety at the end of this chapter.) As Anderson toured his childhood home, Harrington listened to him describe how life used to be. Anderson said his father had bought a home so big that they couldn't afford to maintain it. They rented the main part of the house and lived in the basement. The opening anecdote ends this way:

He thinks of his father, and, once
again, his voice goes hollow and distant . . .
"He was a weird guy."

Having developed the tense relationship between father and son throughout the profile, Harrington concludes with another anecdote about that relationship.

Jack stands at the door, and his father sits in a chair across the room. Only yesterday Jack saw his father cry for the first time, only the day before he heard him say for the first time that he was proud of his son. Jack is uncomfortable with emotional goodbyes, and with a strained cheerfulness, he says, well, gotta go, gotta catch a plane. His father is quiet for a long, awkward moment, until he says, "You're the most generous son a father could have." He then drops his head, covers his eyes and sobs. Jack hesitates, looks plaintively to his right, shrugs, walks over and hugs his father, pats him softly on the back. "It's all right," he says quietly. "It's all right."

Then Jack falls silent, fighting back his own deep tears.

That anecdote not only provides a tie-back but also closes the circle that has been drawn throughout the profile. The story doesn't just run out; it ends.

# Variations of the Focus Structure

The focus structure, the primary alternative to the inverted pyramid, allows you to tell the general story by focusing on an individual or smaller part of the story and delaying the traditional "lead" information. We see two variations of this alternative approach:

1. Scenic leads.

2. Anecdotal leads.

In both the scenic and the anecdotal approaches only the openings differ from the basic formula. The rest of the story's structure—transition, account of an issue or institution and ending—is the same.

## SCENIC LEADS

Using a *scenic lead* is an effective way to attract the reader's attention. In this approach the writer re-creates a scene, with or without the leading characters, that is relevant to the point of the story. In an article about the Amish preparing for winter, a writer for the Columbia (Mo.) Daily Tribune opened with this scene:

The countryside was in pause, between days of bountiful harvest and those that would be stern, stingy and cold.

Cornstalks, tied together by hand, pointed to a sky laden with low gray clouds pushing in from the west. Brown leaves clung stubbornly to tall trees that looked gaunt and stark as, in undress, they girded for the winter. Tawny grasses waved stiffly in the chilly wind.

Most of the land looked drab. But in some fields winter wheat was getting a toehold, and its green beginnings hinted at yet another genesis in the spring.

Overhead, no power or telephone lines cluttered the scenery. Along gravel lanes, riders with horses and buggies traveled unhurriedly. Numerous signs told of homemade candies, sorghum and peanut brittle for sale.

This is a country where Amish people live. And if the land was preparing to rest, the people living on it and from it were not. On every farm, in barnyard and in field, people labored. It is their way to work hard, and most of the work is done by horse or by hand. "It's been that way a long time, and God made it that way, and we feel to keep it," one farmer explained.

The opening scene slips into the transition in the last paragraph of the excerpt. From there, the writer describes how the Amish go about the fall harvest.

In the scenic approach you can take any of several directions after the opening, but generally you continue to use detailed descriptions to back up the general points being made. The distinctive characteristic of this type of story is a focus on relevant descriptive scenes.

## ANECDOTAL LEADS

The other variation is the *anecdotal lead*. It opens with an anecdote—a short recreation of an event or narrative of an incident that is interesting or amusing. Larry Van Dyne used the technique when he opened a story in The Washingtonian magazine on the controlling owner of The Washington Post:

The old letter that Katharine Graham holds in her hands is so private that she normally keeps it locked in an office safe. She wrote it nearly half a century ago, on December 10, 1937, when she was a senior at the University of Chicago. Its nine typewritten pages—intended only for the eyes of an older sister—divulge some of the big plans and secret longings that occupy a person at the age of twenty.

Leafing now through its pages, as she sits on a sofa in her office at The Washington Post, Graham skims the text in search of a particular passage. It's where she told her sister that she couldn't imagine working for her father, Eugene Meyer, owner of the Post.

"Ah, here it is," she says, pointing to the top of page six. The passage reads:

"What I am most interested in doing is labor reporting, possibly working up to political reporting later. As you can see, that is no help to Dad. He wants and needs someone who is willing to go through the whole mill, from reporting, to circulation management, to editorial writing, and eventually to be his assistant.

"This presents the payoff in problems. I detest beyond description advertising and circulation, and that is what a newspaper executive spends most of his time worrying about . . . I (also) doubt my ability to carry a load like The Washington Post, and . . . I damn well think it would be a first-class dog's life."

The scene completed, the writer moves into the transition and the nut paragraph, which explains what the story is about:

Appreciative of irony, Graham smiles. How odd those sentiments of youth sound when you consider that she is in her 23rd year in the executive suite of The Washington Post Company. She not only has long since brushed aside her adolescent distaste for the business of advertising and circulation, but has grown accustomed to days crowded with the concerns of corporate management. Strategic planning, profit-margin targets, marketing, labor relations, executive-compensation plans, financing, stock prices—such are the challenges she now faces daily as the controlling owner and chief executive officer of one of the nation's largest companies.

Your job is to tell a story. Often you can do it best by telling little stories within larger ones. Anecdotes make the readers' journey through your story much easier and more pleasant.

# Extended-Dialogue Stories

Occasionally, the reporter comes upon a person so quotable or an event so dramatic that it is better to step aside and let the subjects speak for themselves at length in an extended-dialogue story. When either of these conditions is met, you may disregard the rules of when to quote people as detailed in Chapter 6.

You still must provide an opening, a close and transitions within the body of the story. In the opening you may use any of the approaches discussed thus far in this chapter—or even a more traditional opening that contains the standard "lead" information. But the emphasis thereafter is on the speech of the persons involved. Remember, too, that it is nearly impossible to write an extended-dialogue story if you have failed to tape-record the interviews.

Edna Buchanan of the Miami Herald used dialogue when she wrote about a disc jockey who was assaulted while working alone early one morning. At the point in the story where the disc jockey, James T., encounters his visitor, Buchanan moves from straight attribution to dialogue:

James T. put the caller on hold. He always urges listeners to "Have a great day! You are in control of your day." He answered the door—and his day went out of control.

There stood a young man in a red shirt. James T. likes young people. Only the day before he had spoken to fifth- and sixth-graders at Sunset Elementary School and to students and parents at Arcola Junior High, hoping to inspire and motivate them.

"Can I go on the air and say something to somebody?" the man in the red shirt asked.

"I'm sorry, you can't, but if you'd like to make a dedication or want me to play something for you, I will," James T. replied.

"You mean it's Saturday morning and I can't say something on the air?"

James T. felt a twinge of alarm, since it was Wednesday morning.

"If you'd like me to say hello to someone, tell me who, and I'll do that, but you have to hurry, I have only a couple of seconds."

"C'est la Vie," the extended seven-minute, four-second version, was almost over. The man in the red shirt thought for a moment, then pulled a gun . . .

In that interplay, the journalist let the participants talk to each other.

Author Pat Conroy used the extended-dialogue technique in relating a story about a conversation with his mother:

"I'd like to ask you a favor in the new book, Pat. Don't write about me like this. Make me beautiful. Make me beautiful again."

I knelt beside my mother's bed and said in a voice that I barely recognized, "I'll make you so beautiful, Mama. You made me a writer and I'm going to lift you out of this bed and set you singing and dancing across the pages of my book forever."

"And after you write about my death," my mother said with a smile, "I'd like Meryl Streep to play the role in the movie."

Remember these important points about extended dialogue:

1. Don't try writing it unless you have used a tape recorder. You are being less than honest if you think you can reproduce large blocks of dialogue verbatim with no aid. An expert at shorthand might be able to reproduce dialogue but not dialect.

2. Don't use the approach as an excuse for emptying your notebook—or tape recorder—into the newspaper's columns. That is laziness.

3. Do use extended dialogue sparingly.

# The Chronological Approach

In addition to the focus structure, variations of that structure and the extended-dialogue story, journalists have another alternative to the inverted pyramid—the *chronological approach*. Oddly enough, it is not necessary to begin at the beginning to use this approach. Often writers open with a scene from the story they are reporting, provide a paragraph or two to put the scene in context, and then pick up the chronological report at the beginning.

Alice Hartmann of the Kansas City (Mo.) Times used this approach when she returned to the scene of a hotel fire two months later:

> It is just after 3 o'clock on a bitterly cold Saturday morning in January. The sky is clear. A west wind blows haltingly, pumping more cold on deserted downtown streets.

**Figure 17.3 Prize-Winning Writing.** Edna Buchanan, who won a Pulitzer Prize for her work at The Miami Herald as a police reporter, uses the full range of literary techniques in her stories.

For firefighters it is four more hours before quitting time.
. . .

*Setting the scene*

And at 1005 Broadway, the place tenants call "the House" is, in its noisy way, quiet. Some residents sleep in the rooms lining five floors of the long, wide hallways. Others lie sleepless, waiting for dawn.

In the lobby of the massive hotel, Carl Kendall, the night desk clerk, bickers with Mrs. Martha Donovan over change for a dollar. . . .

On the third floor, Mrs. Margaret Nichols has almost dropped off to sleep when the racket begins over her head. It sounds like a fight. . . .

*Transition and theme paragraph*

Different people, playing different roles in different parts of the sleeping city. . . . But that Jan. 28 morning they will be thrown together in a nightmare they will never forget: The Coates House fire. The worst fire in Kansas City history.

*Chronological approach*

3:50 a.m.—Working the night shift at the Estille Hotel at 1018 Broadway, Joseph Patrick Hoyle sits behind the front desk making out occupancy reports. He hears a scream outside. From the street Hoyle sees smoke coming from the top floor of the Coates House.

The minute-by-minute report that follows covers the critical next two hours of the fire. The fire and deaths certainly were not news to Kansas City residents because the event had been reported when it happened. But Hartmann's reporting uncovered many anecdotes and ironies. The chronological approach permitted her to bring together people from all over the city in a cohesive and compelling account.

Even when writers do begin at the beginning, they usually provide a transition to the background paragraphs and then return to the narrative. This alternate approach differs only in the lead. The writer starts the clock ticking in the opening scene, then provides a context for the story before continuing with the narrative. Here, for example, is the story of a kidnapping:

*Beginning at the beginning*

Banker Henry Venski kissed his wife, Margaret, and his 3-year-old daughter, Kathy, and climbed into his Lincoln Continental for the 20-minute drive to work Tuesday. In his mind, he already was going over some of the problems he would encounter that day.

*Transition*

As he swung the car out on the business loop, Venski had no idea that business problems would be of no importance that day, for 10 minutes after he arrived at work, he would receive a call telling him that his daughter had been kidnapped. For the next five hours, the bank was the furthest thing from his mind. Forty-eight hours after the ordeal was over, Venski and his wife reconstructed the minute-by-minute events that saw their daughter returned safely. Two men were charged with the kidnapping. This is the Venskis' story:

*Picking up the chronological approach*      8:10 a.m. Venski had just reached his desk when his secretary told him his wife was calling.

Sometimes, however, the essential information is so important that delaying it even until the third or fourth paragraph is too late. Yet a straight inverted pyramid approach is not the most effective way to maintain readers' interest beyond the first several paragraphs.

One solution, proposed by Roy Peter Clark, director of The Writing Center at the Poynter Institute for Media Studies, is to use the inverted pyramid opening and then switch to chronology. The structure lends itself primarily to events that have inherent drama, such as crimes, fires, rescues, sporting events and some trials. Using this approach, the Venski kidnapping could be handled this way:

Police today rescued a banker's 3-year-old daughter after she had been held captive for five hours by kidnappers.

Two men, John H. Johnson, 25, and Andrew McKinney, 36, both of 221 W. Cornell St., are being held without bond in Springfield County Jail. Police recovered the $50,000 ransom that Henry Venski, president of First National Bank, offered for his daughter, Kathy. She was unharmed.

Police and the Venskis said this is what happened:

Ten minutes after he arrived at work, Venski received a call from the kidnappers . . .

The structure has two important advantages: It permits the writer (1) to give the most important information first and (2) to tell the rest of the story in chronological order. That should encourage some readers to stay with the story longer without irritating others who want to know what happened quickly.

An anecdotal lead works well with chronological stories, too. When the Kansas City (Mo.) Star received a story about a man who killed a pet deer, the paper could have written the traditional news lead:

August John Scherer, 28, Brownwood, was fined $400 Wednesday after he was found guilty of killing a pet fawn.

Instead, the Star chose an anecdotal approach and left the punch until the end:

AQUILLA, Mo.—Three years ago Harold Merick, who runs Angus cattle on a 240-acre farm near this southeast Missouri community, found a fawn tangled in his wire fence.

The fawn, a doe, had struggled in the wire. She was bloody, half-crazed with fear and, most of all, alone. So Merick, his wife, Mary, and their daughter, Sandra, who was then 8, adopted the doe. They managed to dress the wounds and in time, with softness and tenderness, to wipe the film of fear from the doe's eyes.

The fawn survived, and they named her Joanie.

Joanie grew. She grazed with the Mericks' cattle, occasionally being bossed around by a calfless cow in need of company—no matter how odd-looking.

Mrs. Merick remembers Joanie was a joy.

"We'd get school buses filled with kids who came to look," she said. "So did people just driving by, fascinated at this deer in among the cattle. Everybody around here knew her. Most people knew her name, too."

Although Joanie grew to be a fine, strong doe, she never went near the Mericks' fences, which she could have bounded over easily. She apparently was content being a deer in a herd of cattle.

On April 13 an early-rising neighbor heard three shots, looked out and saw Joanie staggering around the pasture. Down near a gravel road was a man with a rifle. The neighbor called the Mericks.

Merick arrived in time to confront a man by the road with a small, yellow pickup truck. He remembered later there was a farm strike sticker in the rear window. Asked what he was doing, the man said he was just "watching the deer."

Merick went off to see whether he could help Joanie. He couldn't. A veterinary report later said the animal was hit by two bullets, one piercing the heart.

By the time Merick returned, the man was gone. But Merick remembered the truck.

Don May, a Missouri Conservation Commission agent, found 14 trucks fitting the same general description within a five-mile area. None belonged to the man Merick described.

But just as he was about to give up, May saw the 15th. In it was a man who two hours after he was arrested made a statement about killing the deer.

And in Stoddard County Magistrate Court here Wednesday, 28-year-old August John Scherer, a Brownwood, Mo., liquor store owner, was found guilty of discharging a firearm from a public highway and of hunting out of season. Scherer was fined $400—the largest fine ever levied in the county for such an offense.

Asked why he shot Joanie, Scherer replied:

"Just for fun."

When the question "what happened?" is not answered until the end, as in the preceding example, the story is commonly called a *suspended-interest account*. The only difference between this and the approach used in the kidnapping story is that instead of providing a transition into the news near the top, the writer structures the entire story chronologically.

# First-Person Stories

In all its variations, the focus structure is also appropriate for *first-person stories*. Some follow the basic structure; others rely on dialogue; still others are chronological.

Although the organization is flexible, the subject matter is not. Such stories are most effective when the personal, first-person viewpoint adds a special dimension to the story that no other writing approach could capture. A daughter describing her father's battle with terminal cancer would be remiss not to use "I." Readers can empathize with the special father–daughter relationship.

One of the most effective uses of a first-person story is when the reporter is involved in an unusual event. For instance, when an off-duty reporter for the Columbia Missourian became a participant in a suicide, the situation clearly called for a first-person story:

It looks so easy on "Kojak," and it always works. Someone teeters on a ledge. A cop says, "Let's talk about it." There are a few minutes of tense silence, portentous music, and the person staggers in through the window. Case closed; problem solved.

It isn't like that in real life.

If I hadn't wrecked my car Sunday night, I wouldn't have been walking along Broadway at College Avenue Monday morning when a young man ended his life from the Stephens College overpass at Broadway and College. But I was, and I tried to help. I did all the right things—I had someone call campus security, followed the man, kept a few feet away from him, asked if he wanted to "talk about it."

He jumped anyhow.

So infrequently would a reporter ever be involved in a suicide that the first-person approach is warranted. The account permits the reader to share not only the event, but also the emotions of the participant who tried to stop the suicide.

Most first-person stories involve participatory journalism (see pages 512–14). Reporters take the reader on the court with the athletes, backstage with the stars, into the fields with the migrants, into the mental hospital with the inmates. When the reporter participates rather than watching others do something, there may be a first-person story worth writing. But use the approach sparingly. It too easily becomes an ego trip or a subterfuge for lazy reporters.

# Putting It Together

We have talked about alternative openings, transitions, theme paragraphs, anecdotes and tie-backs. Walt Harrington of The Washington Post Magazine demonstrates expert use of all these techniques in his profile of syndicated columnist Jack Anderson. The profile, reprinted in its entirety here, is an example of good reporting, good writing and an alternative story structure.

The house is empty and the front door is unlocked. The man, an old man now with white hair and a watermelon belly and a grandfather's amble, hesitates a moment, glances around at the overgrown and untended yard where as a boy he watered row upon row of his father's carrots and beans and strawberries. *God, he hated that job!* But he never complained, choosing instead the captive laborer's silent revenge: He refused to enjoy his work. He looks to the east. "See that peak?" he asks, pointing to Utah's Mount Olympus, which towers in the mist only a few miles away. "I've hiked to that peak. I didn't want to. My father did. He won." The man then lets out a kind of chuckle, or perhaps it is a sigh. In the last 45 years, he has never been inside his boyhood home—a huge, elegant Tudor on several beautifully wooded acres in Salt Lake City's affluent Cottonwood suburb. In the last 45 years, the only times he has even driven past were when his kids insisted.

Always aggressive, quick to step across the little boundaries that deter other men, the man walks right through the front doorway of what is now someone else's home. The house is being renovated—its wallpaper is stripped, its patched plaster is unsanded, its doors are off their hinges. And for an instant, everything seems wrong. But wait, that crystal chandelier, it was here 45 years ago. He points to it with a kind of excitement, and it seems that nostalgia might sweep over him, but it passes, and he continues to walk slowly from room to room, commenting in the deadpan tone of a bored tour guide: "These were a couple of bedrooms. This was the kitchen." Then he stops, turns to his right and looks down a narrow, darkened stairway to the basement. His voice goes hollow and distant . . .

"And this is where *we* lived."

In fine Cottonwood, on these fine manicured grounds, in this fine Tudor home, Jack Anderson—the famed "Washington Merry-Go-Round" columnist, the scourge of the pols, the Pulitzer Prize winner, the pricey speechmaking pundit, the TV celeb— lived in the basement. Jack, his two younger brothers and his parents all slept in the same room and bathed in the laundry tub. Upstairs, a man who would later become chaplain of the U.S. Senate lived with his family. Only with their rent could Jack's father, on his $200-a-month postal clerk salary, afford this magnificent house. Upstairs, the future chaplain of the Senate had a flush toilet. Outside, Jack's family had an outhouse—over there, Jack points, across the back yard, where that brown house sits today.

"We had the only crapper in the whole valley," he says, a slight smile finally cracking a granite face. "I would be a little embarrassed to escort my friends to the crapper. We were the Cinderellas. I think Mother was annoyed with Dad for buying a house we couldn't afford to live in." He thinks of his father, and, once again, his voice goes hollow and distant . . .

"He was a weird guy."

Jack Anderson, one of America's most famous reporters, isn't really a reporter anymore, at least not like he used to be. He doesn't put it exactly that way. As he does with so much in his life, he gives it a grander, nobler face. He describes himself as the "publisher" of the "Merry-Go-Round" column, which is produced by a staff of 10 editors, reporters and interns who are led by the column's co-author, Dale Van Atta. Anderson consults with the staff, slips them story tips and writes a few columns a month.

But it has come to this: Jack Anderson has little to do with Jack Anderson's column anymore. There are many reasons, but one stands out starkly: For about the last decade, Jack Anderson has been busy trans-

forming himself from working reporter to working celebrity—too busy to spend long hours reporting, as he once did.

Anderson is still busy—giving 50 speeches a year around the country for $250,000, which is his personal income. The $200,000 a year he earns from his other operations—his UPI radio broadcasts, his "Insiders" TV show on the Financial News Network and his Washington newsletter—is all pumped back into the "Merry-Go-Round." Anderson's support for the column is substantial, but not entirely altruistic. The visibility he gains from the "Merry-Go-Round" helps maintain his popularity on the national speaking circuit.

Now 67, Anderson has been a Washington institution for four decades. He broke some of the biggest stories of his generation—the Sherman Adams scandals of the '50s, the Sen. Thomas Dodd scandals of the '60s and the ITT-Dita Beard scandals of the '70s. He had hundreds of other exposés that, in their season, commanded headlines. He put men in jail, drove one man to suicide. He cajoled and manipulated confessions from some of the most powerful and savvy politicians in the nation. He unmasked the CIA's plans to kill Fidel Castro.

But he also had less grandiose scoops: He revealed that Indiana Sen. Vance Hartke had bad breath, that Georgia Sen. Herman Talmadge spat tobacco juice onto the floor of the Senate, and that FBI Director J. Edgar Hoover calmed his stomach with Gelusil. Anderson reported such trivialities, he said, to deflate the images and egos of men made arrogant and pompous by power, to prove they were no better than anybody else. That sentiment runs deep in Anderson.

Today he is still feared on Capitol

Hill, although his influence has waned. He's not universally respected by his journalistic colleagues, who, despite his thousands of genuine scoops, have often seen his reporting as petulant and petty, holier-than-thou. The number of newspapers carrying his column has dropped from about 1,000 in 1975 to about 650 today. While a smattering of big-city papers, The Washington Post among them, carry Anderson's column, it runs mostly in the little towns of heartland America. Again, Anderson gives this a noble face: The "Merry-Go-Round" reaches the *real* America. Says one respected investigative reporter in Washington: "The guy's outta gas. He's been outta gas for 15 years."

That is the temptation: to judge Jack Anderson harshly because he has judged so many others harshly. The temptation is to say he's "outta gas," he ain't what he used to be. But the truth is, although Anderson isn't reporting much anymore, he still *is* what he used to be: layer upon layer of complicated motivations—some so deeply rooted they seem more instinct than motive, more personality than morality. Like so many other American heartlanders drawn to Washington, Jack Anderson eventually achieved power, prominence and glory. Over the years, he came to see his work as a heroic candle lit against the darkness of political corruption, greed and arrogance. About this he is undeniably sincere. But deep inside Jack Anderson—in the intimate, painful place where boundless ambition must reside—a little machine also runs constantly, always has, propelling him ahead in private rebellion and indignation.

Les Whitten, Jack's friend and former "Merry-Go-Round" co-author, recalls a time years ago when Jack

asked him this question: "If we didn't have this column, who would we be?"

"Stop here, stop at this bridge," Jack says, as the car crosses a little bridge on narrow Fardown Avenue within sight of his childhood home outside Salt Lake City. "This is a very momentous bridge." He is joking now, enjoying himself, recalling an event that, five decades after the fact, still seems eerily prophetic. Jack's friend, Ray Fritsch, the only man Jack has remained close to from his youth, slows his blue Cadillac but doesn't stop. "Oh, this is *the* bridge," Ray says, with the mocking deference of friends who show affection and respect by never saying a nice word to each other. If the achievements of a lifetime can have an actual beginning, this bridge is where it began for Jack Anderson, Investigative Reporter. When he was 12, covering local news for the suburban Murray Eagle for $7 a week, a car ran a bicycling boy off this bridge, then only a single lane. The boy was badly bruised, and the public outrage that resulted from young Jack's story in the Eagle ended with a new, wider, safer bridge.

Jack had changed the world. And it was a taste of real power—used, indisputably, for good. If young Jack was impressed with himself, though, he certainly didn't say so. His father wouldn't have allowed that. Jack doesn't know how it first began, but when Jack was just a boy, his father became convinced that Jack was, well, too big for his britches. Jack was a smart kid. His mother says he knew the alphabet at age 1. But Orlando Anderson was wary of Jack's precociousness.

In Orlando—and the Mormon faith he held so deeply—there was a strong vein of egalitarianism that discouraged showiness or flamboyance, getting too far ahead of the pack, which Jack always did and which he always seemed to relish. The phrase "no one is better than anyone else" was a kind of religious-cultural mantra in Jack's childhood. For the ambitious, confident and proud, there was always this cut-you-down-to-size question: "Just who do you think you are?"

It started early. Orlando believed Jack's grandparents doted on him while ignoring his two younger brothers. Orlando wouldn't have said it this way in the 1930s, but, looking back, he feared the other boys would get an inferiority complex. His way of handling this was to remind Jack that he was not as smart as his brothers. Orlando, sitting with his wife talking about Jack's childhood on the weekend of his son's visit to the old family home, still seems miffed when he recalls Jack's confident reply: "That doesn't worry me." With an edge in his voice, Orlando says, "He was very much for himself. I thought Jack was a little uppity-up and would rather be in a job, any job, that would give him a boost. He built himself up. I thought he should have been more common."

"He wanted to be tops," says Jack's 90-year-old mother, Agnes.

"He wanted to be in the limelight," retorts Orlando.

Jack's father was a mercurial man, with a quick temper and an opinion about everything. He loved to argue. He loved to be righteously indignant. Jack believes his father even liked being poor. "He had a martyr complex," Jack says, "and it suited him to glory in his poverty." Orlando remembers that the happiest time of his life was when the boys weren't yet teens and he had built them a sandbox and swing set in the back yard, where they all played. Without a hint of emotion, Jack says, "Yes, that's when he could run us."

Orlando Anderson was a stern man who could explode at the most minor provocation. "He would erupt like Vesuvius," says Jack, who tried not to stoke the volcano. But that wasn't always possible. Jack's boyhood friend Darwin Knudsen remembers a time when one of Jack's brothers said something that irritated Orlando, and he reached out and squeezed the boy's nose until tears rolled down his cheeks. Darwin remembers looking at Jack and thinking that he was embarrassed by his father.

"He knew what was right," Jack says of his dad. "And even if he was wrong, he was right." Jack doesn't say this with rancor. He says it with a touch of humor, perhaps with a tone of forgiveness. But most of all, he seems to say it with almost no feeling at all. He says, "I understood that Dad's fulminations were meant well."

Over the years, Jack developed a strategy for dealing with his dad: He dealt with him as little as possible. He stayed constantly busy, and out of the house. When his dad barked orders, Jack usually listened intently—and then paid no attention to what his father had said. When his father would sit down with a pencil and paper and figure out to the penny how much money Jack would need for some outing, Jack would take the coins—and then go to his mother, who'd slip him a dollar.

"Don't tell Dad," was her constant refrain.

Agnes Anderson, a serene woman who never lost her composure, played counterpoint to Orlando. With her connivance, Jack maneuvered around the slumbering bear. In personality, he grew to resemble his mom—friendly, well-liked and gentle. In character, he resembled his dad—self-righteous, certain, opinionated. "I don't think he really enjoyed his childhood," Jack's daughter Laurie Anderson-Bruch says of her father. "He just wanted to get away. My father worked really hard to get away from being raised poor and to show his dad."

Nothing seemed to slow Jack down. His father rode him, and he lived in a basement and wore shabby clothes, but he was president of his junior high and high schools and editor of their newspapers. A lean, handsome, dishwater-blond kid, he got along with everybody. He was an Eagle Scout. When Jack was 12, Orlando got him a summer job thinning sugar beets. Orlando had thinned sugar beets as a boy. But the job was not for Jack, who hated working on his knees in the dirt, under the hot sun. He quit and got his first job with the Murray Eagle. "I think Jack psychologically escaped from his father when he took that job," says Darwin Knudsen, who's known Jack since grade school. "It was obvious that Jack would not kowtow to him."

Jack went on to become editor of the Boy Scout page for the Deseret News, and, while still in high school, the youngest reporter on the Salt Lake City Tribune. Yet at the same time, he was runner-up to the class valedictorian. Orlando didn't attend his son's graduation.

"He thought I was getting too many honors," Jack says.

Soon after, while working as a reporter, Jack angered his father like never before—and demonstrated just how far he'd go in pursuit of a story. When Jack discovered that a cousin of his belonged to a polygamist cult, he decided to infiltrate it. Polygamy—condoned by the Mormon Church in the 19th century but banned for decades—still flourished secretly in the 1930s, and Jack hoped the Saturday Evening Post would buy an exposé. So he went to his cousin—without revealing he was working on a story—and feigned interest in polygamy. The cousin fell for the ruse and got Jack into the select fold. Still without revealing his reporter's intent, Jack began attending the cult's social gatherings.

But he wasn't alone in his curiosity. A detective hired by the Mormon Church to spy on the polygamists took the license number of Jack's car—which was, unfortunately, Orlando's car. Vesuvius exploded. "Steam, fire, brimstone!" says Jack, laughing at the memory. It turned out that Orlando had been called before church officials and questioned about his seeming involvement in the cult. Says Jack, "I don't think he ever forgave me."

Jack reluctantly abandoned the story before heading off to begin his Mormon missionary work in Alabama, leaving the day Pearl Harbor was bombed. Jack would eventually become deeply absorbed in his faith, and Mormonism—with its call for the forces of good to constantly fight the forces of evil—would come to provide a justification for his often ruthless muckraking. But he wasn't particularly religious as a youth—didn't want to go on a mission, didn't want to get off the Tribune's career ladder. Still, he went, to make his parents happy, and on his door-to-door visits discovered what every reporter eventually learns: People will tell their deepest secrets to a perfect stranger, if only he strikes a sympathetic pose.

Relentlessly charming and competent, Jack was promoted to a good administrative job in the mission's regional office. At the same time, he reinforced his image as a man apart. "Jack is an abiding psychological enigma," says Darwin Knudsen. "In a way, Jack was estranged. Everybody regarded Jack as a friend, but not a buddy. He was just too self-centered or self-occupied." Darwin was also a Mormon missionary, in a different state, and he recalls a time Jack visited him for a few days. Darwin was living in the house of a poor family with several daughters and one bathroom. But Jack, used to the privy out back and the washtub in the basement, spent forever each morning "primping" in the bathroom, Darwin says, while the girls waited politely for him to finish. "Jack made no apology for this," he says, still amazed. "It was just his nature. He didn't realize this was an imposition."

For years after Jack left Salt Lake City, Darwin and another old friend of Jack's often talked about how they'd write Jack letters and how rarely he wrote back. "It hurt my feelings that he wouldn't write," Darwin says. "Why wouldn't he sit down and scratch out a note? It says to me that he's so self-contained, happy with his menu, that he doesn't need the friendship. Jack is still the loner, standing against the crowd. But, you understand, that's how he was from the beginning. The Bible refers to people being on the Lord's errands. Jack was always on his own errand."

When Jack finished his missionary stint and returned to Salt Lake City, World War II was raging. He avoided the draft legally by joining the Merchant Marines. He had no conscientious objections to war. He simply didn't want to fight for his country in the infantry, didn't want to fight hand-to-hand. "Cowardice," he calls it today. The Merchant Marines made Jack an officer, which angered Orlando, who figured he should have started at the bottom. But the job was short-lived, because after eight months at sea, Jack wangled war correspondent credentials from the Deseret News. He quit the Merchant Marines and went to China, where the draft finally caught up with him, and he was assigned to the military newspaper Stars and Stripes. It was in China, sitting around with the older, seasoned reporters, that Jack first remembers hearing of the "Washington Merry-Go-Round" and its feisty, moralistic, crusading, liberal creator, Drew Pearson. That, Jack decided, was the job for him. Soon after his return to Salt Lake City, he headed off to Washington with little more than ambition and an inflated résumé.

As ever, Jack's father was skeptical.

Jack's friend Ray Fritsch will never forget the day he and Orlando dropped Jack off at the bus station when Jack was first heading out for the Merchant Marines. After Jack had ridden off, Orlando turned to him and said angrily, "All these high ambitions he's got. He'll be slapped back, because he's not that smart." Ray's wife Ella, who was with them that day, could see Ray's ire rising. Ray and Jack, it turned out, shared a mysterious bond. Almost half a century later, Ray still remembers the day clearly: "I was thinking about my own father. Orlando was just like my dad. My dad always told me I'd never amount to anything. He never told me he was proud of me. When I was making more money in a day than he made in a year, you know what he said? He said I was a spoiled brat." That day, Ray blew up.

"Why don't you just quit downgrading Jack?" he raged at Orlando. "You have no right to say these things about your own son!"

When Jack hit town in 1947, he was like a character out of Frank Capra's "Mr. Smith Goes to Washington."

Jimmy Stewart does journalism. In 1947, Jack really *believed* his high school civics lessons: great statesmen struggling in marble halls to serve *The People*. Well, Jack, from his basement home in Utah, was *The People*, or about as close to them as you can get. He'd been raised in a strict Mormon home—no drinking or smoking. But perhaps more important, he hadn't shared the birthright of children born to power and privilege: the firsthand knowledge that Great Men really are "just like everybody else." That idea had been pounded into Jack as a philosophy of life, but from the basement, from the bottom of the social ladder, that egalitarian notion was also a kind of populist scream, a little man's cry for self-respect. The absolute truth of the philosophy was a shock.

At 24, Jack was without what novelist John O'Hara called the "unearned cynicism" of the prematurely sophisticated. So he was amazed—at the booze drinking, great volumes of booze drinking! At the skirt-chasing, wrinkled codgers pursuing sweet young things! At the lying, incompetence, nepotism, corruption, laziness, ruthlessness, stupidity, greed, selfishness, pettiness of his Great Men! It was a naivete that fueled Jack's rebellious indignation, the same kind of naivete that today fuels the indignation of the "Washington Merry-Go-Round's" young reporters, most of whom hail from average American families in average American places like Montana. It's not that Anderson isn't happy to get an application from some Ivy League genius, but he doesn't get many. Somehow, the "Merry-Go-Round" speaks more to State U grads used to seeing power from the bottom up.

Most are like Anderson's current co-columnist, Dale Van Atta, who as a young reporter exposed a police ticketing scam and was called before angry policemen to defend his story. He was terrified, but quickly realized the police were even more terrified. "To have them all in fear of me when I'm usually in fear of them," Van Atta recalls with delight. "It was a great moment."

The tale of how Jack Anderson—despite his father's dire predictions—came to Washington and went on to fame and fortune after landing a job with Drew Pearson is today a piece of journalism folklore. Pearson, who headed the "Merry-Go-Round" from 1932 until he died in 1969, was the most influential muckraker of his day. Sending his message into hamlets all across America, he portrayed Washington as a corrupt place inhabited by pooh-bahs, bigwigs and brass hats bent on feathering their nests by promoting big business at the expense of the little people. The view fit Jack like his BVDs. In the next few years, he helped Pearson assault and depose conservative Republican senators Joseph McCarthy and Owen Brewster, as well as Defense Secretary James Forrestal.

Jack had one personality trait that made him a great reporter: He could genuinely like a man, but still be hard as nails when reporting about him. He could later look that man in the eye and convince him again that he liked him personally, that unpleasant reporting was simply his job. This wasn't phoniness on Jack's part. It was at the heart of his nature. He had a way of disarming folks, of outmaneuvering them with his genuine sincerity. He wasn't troubled by the ethics of this.

He once convinced Connecticut Rep. Robert Giaimo that he doubted rumors linking Giaimo to a known gambler, and if Giaimo would only let Jack go through his files, Jack would straighten it out. Giaimo did—and

Anderson cited the files as alleged proof of the accusations, although the Justice Department later declined to take any action against Giaimo based on Anderson's information. Anderson once asked Vice President Hubert Humphrey for a letter of introduction when he was going to Iraq. Anderson presented it to the U.S. Embassy there, failed to say he was a reporter and asked to go through the files. It was days before they asked if he worked for the vice president. "No," Jack said. They turned white. Anderson bluffed California Sen. George Murphy into confessing that he was on a cash retainer to Technicolor Inc. by saying, after Murphy denied the allegation, "Now, Senator, you and I have been friends for a long time. I don't think you want to be quoted as denying this whole thing. So, because we've been friends, I'll forget what you said before and give you another chance, in fairness." Murphy cracked and confessed. Says Anderson's former co-columnist Les Whitten, "He was just a wonderful con man."

Jack was a curiosity in Washington—a city that breeds, even demands, an arching self-importance and arrogance. In contrast, young Jack was refreshingly unpretentious and open-faced. But as his old friends and his father had sensed, as his hours in the bathroom had hinted, Jack could be pretty self-absorbed, even if his charm hid the trait. Then, as a kind of antidote, Jack met Olivia Farley, one of the more amazing and fortunate discoveries of his life.

Libby, as Jack calls her, was from a coal-mining family in West Virginia, and she worked as a clerk at the FBI. If Jack's father was militant in his efforts to keep Jack humble, Libby, also a Mormon, extended that militancy to everyone. Not in Orlando's way, but in her own. She once arrived

to meet Jack in President Lyndon Johnson's hotel room—where the Duke and Duchess of Windsor also were guests—wearing slacks and beat-up shoes. "My God, Libby!" Jack moaned. She once took her daughter Cheri with her to buy an evening gown for a night at the Kennedy White House—and they went to Korvettes, where Libby pulled one of about 30 identical gowns off the rack. Her daughter was appalled. "No," Libby said, reassuring her, "I'll be the only one there with this dress."

Over the years, Jack Anderson has made a big thing about how he has refused to be part of the Washington social set because he never wanted to be tainted by friendships with the powerful. "What's wrong is that these reporters adopted the views of the people they're writing about," he once said. "They've become a part of the Establishment they cover." That would never happen to Jack. A noble view, as always. But it wasn't only Jack's idealism that put the kibosh on the Washington party circuit. It was also Libby's down-home militancy. "A lot of it was my mother," says the Anderson's daughter Cheri Loveless. She says her dad would have gone to parties to help his career, but her mother refused. To Libby—with her plain beauty, a lingering West Virginia twang and nouns and verbs that don't always match—the Washington soiree scene consisted of people putting on airs and wasting a lot of money doing it.

From their first date, she performed a familiar role: She kept Jack's massive ego in its place. "He was trying to impress me and took me to a French restaurant on Vermont, where they played violins at your table," Libby says. "And then he took me to a nightclub in Baltimore, and Jackie Gleason was playing. He was trying to impress me, but I didn't care about those things. After he stopped trying to be debonair and I brought him back to earth, he was all right."

They had nine kids.

Orlando Anderson was once a hefty, strong man. Now he is thin and frail and fragile, George Burns without the cigar. At 92, he has the look of a man curling inward upon himself. The less the old curmudgeon complains and gripes about everything and everybody, the less ornery he is, the more people worry about him. Agnes is his reverse image. She never interrupts. She's quiet and sweet and radiant. Ninety years old and using a walker, she still moves gracefully. Orlando pounds out "Rock of Ages" on the piano. She smiles warmly. All this morning, Orlando has insisted, loudly, that Agnes' 90th birthday party is tomorrow. No, she says, it's today. When the grandkids finally come to pick them up at the nursing home to take them off to the party this afternoon, Orlando says nothing about his mistake.

"Where should I sit?" he grumbles as he gets to the car.

"Put him in the trunk," says Agnes, sweetly.

Jack is in Salt Lake City for his mother's birthday party. Jack's son Kevin, who lives there and organized the party, has invited dozens of his grandparents' old friends, and it's like a scene from "This Is Your Life." It will turn out to be the last big gathering of friends and family while Agnes is alive, because in only a few weeks she will suffer a fatal stroke. But today at her birthday party, she glows with delight. Orlando, the tough old coot, is overcome: He's so touched by seeing his old friends and family that when people walk up to him in the

kitchen, where he is leaning with his left hand on his cane, Orlando looks at them without expression, drops his head, puts his right hand over his eyes and sobs. People smile, put an arm around his shoulders and say, "Oh, oh, that's okay." Posted at the buffet nearby, Jack watches: "It's the first time I ever saw my father cry."

Orlando is trying. Just the day before, Jack visited his folks, and his father seemed, in his own way, to be struggling to reach out to his son. "We're proud of you, Jack," he said out of the blue. "You know that." Well, yes, Jack knew that, somehow he knew that, but in his entire life he couldn't recall hearing his father ever say it. Just like Ray Fritsch. Not once. Later, Jack chuckled and said wryly, "I guess you get to be 90 and you repent."

That same day, Orlando also mentioned Jack's first newspaper job with the Murray Eagle. "Remember that, Jack?" he asked proudly. Pleasantly, Jack said, "Yes, I remember you wanted me to thin beets." Orlando said nothing, looked down at his lap. Did he comprehend? Recognize that even now, at the end, his son could not let him off the hook completely?

Orlando: "Jack, did I ever tell you that you were a hard birth?"

Jack, cheerfully: "I heard it all before."

This time, Orlando didn't drop his head. And when Jack left the room, Orlando's voice went hard and angry: "Did you hear what he said? He said, 'I heard it all before!' That's what he said." Yes, Orlando comprehended. He talked of a time when Jack was just a toddler and he got a bladder blockage and was in excruciating pain. Orlando, who didn't own a car, carried Jack all the way to the hospital. "He was so little," Orlando said. "I felt so sorry for him." Later, he said,

"He was obedient to me. He was obedient to me. But he didn't like it. I could tell."

At Drew Pearson's death in 1969, the "Washington Merry-Go-Round" seemed destined for the dustbin. But Jack Anderson bought the column from Pearson's widow and worked like a madman, night and day. He eventually hired his own staff of hungry novice reporters who came and went, and he hired a handful of crackerjack investigative reporters. In those days, Jack did half the columns himself, rewrote the others and oversaw the whole operation. After 20 years in Washington, he had the place wired. By this time, Jack had come to see his journalism as a sword for the little people in their epic struggle against greed and corruption in government. But these heroic motivations aside, at age 46, Jack also wanted the recognition that had eluded him in the shadow of Drew Pearson.

Les Whitten, who was for years Jack's heir apparent, once asked when he could start sharing Jack's byline on the "Merry-Go-Round." Without hesitation, Jack said, "When I'm as famous as Drew."

That happened almost overnight. In the early '70s, Anderson's flame burned so brightly that it would have taken a waterfall to douse it. President Richard Nixon despised Anderson, who with Pearson had revealed during Nixon's unsuccessful 1960 presidential race that Nixon's brother Donald had received a secret $205,000 loan from billionaire Howard Hughes. Anderson's name adorned Nixon's infamous "Enemies List." Future Watergate felons and then-White House operatives G. Gordon Liddy and Howard Hunt talked of killing him. The CIA gave him a 24-hour tail. When Anderson discovered his CIA shadow, he dispatched his own nine children—his "Katzenjammer *paparazzi*"—to tail the tailers. It was high, mocking theater, and Anderson won the publicity war hands down. But at the time, there was no guarantee he would win his battles with the Powers That Be, and Anderson showed real nerve, even bravery, in his zealous crusades against the outrages of Nixon and his minions.

For his crowning coup, Anderson revealed that Nixon and national security adviser Henry Kissinger, while denying it in public, were privately tilting toward Pakistan in its 1971 war with India. The exposé won him a 1972 Pulitzer Prize—and the cover of Time. In a Playboy interview, at the peak of his power, Anderson said: "Too many bureaucrats in Washington have developed an elitist attitude. They are our servants and they want to become our masters. I just want to deflate them a little, remind them of their proper place."

Orlando and Libby must have smiled.

In three years, Jack Anderson had eclipsed the fame of his mentor. But if this tale is mythic, then the hero—made prideful and overly certain by his rise—undid himself. The same year he won the Pulitzer, Anderson reported on one of his radio broadcasts that he had located documented evidence that Missouri Sen. Thomas Eagleton, the Democratic vice presidential candidate, had been arrested for drunk driving. But Anderson didn't have documented evidence in his hands. He had relied on sources, who then didn't deliver the goods. After days of stubbornly refusing to retract his story, Anderson was forced to admit that he had no proof after all. He had been deflated, reminded of his proper place. And he had done it to himself.

It's hard not to wonder: Did Orlando smile again?

The director of the nursing home where Jack's folks live is bluntly solicitous when the famous investigative reporter visits: "I said, 'We better have this place up to snuff if Jack Anderson's coming.'" So he ordered the staff to clean and scrub and shine the whole place. Jack chuckles, having gotten used to such royal treatment. His son Kevin seems more impressed. He whispers, "They kiss our ass." When Jack arrives at his parents' room, Orlando must be helped out of his chair, but as soon as he's up, he starts complaining that too many of the old people in the home stink of body odor.

"He's feeling fine," says Jack, laughing. "He's more mellow now."

Funny, so is Jack. He was always a great boss, easy to work for, demanding as hell but never harsh or rude. As a father, he was very unlike his own dad. Jack rarely even raised his voice with the kids, almost never disciplined them. He didn't spend much time, say, tossing around the old football, but he was always "available," say his children. He'd always stop whatever he was doing when a child entered his office at home, where he often worked. He once put President Kennedy on hold. Less driven today, Jack sees his two dozen grandkids a lot more than he did his own children. Daughter Tanya Neider says that three years ago was the first time her dad ever went on a family vacation when he didn't work. She thinks that's great. But this new mellowness—and the implication that at age 67 he's slowing down—isn't something Jack is quick to admit. He says he could yet win another Pulitzer. "No reason I shouldn't," he says grandly. "I've got the sources."

His wife, Libby, knows it's hard for a workaholic like Jack to retire, but she'd at least like him to cut back, sell the big house in Bethesda (it's worth about $1.5 million, she says) and buy a little place in the Virginia countryside. That would mean Jack could afford to do only 25 speeches a year instead of 50. But Jack says he can't retire, that he needs the money, that he has a daughter with a permanent debilitating disease, children with their own kids who occasionally need financial help, huge medical bills from Libby's successful treatment for cancer last year. No, he *can't* retire.

But, never one to abandon the moral high ground for long, he also says the "Merry-Go-Round" is too important, that Drew Pearson's legacy is too historic, that somebody has got to ferret out wrongdoing and defend the little guy, the milkman in Kansas City, that even though he doesn't report much for the "Merry-Go-Round" anymore, his fame is important to its existence. Jack acknowledges that without the "Merry-Go-Round" his demand as a well-paid speaker would diminish, but it's also true that without the money from Jack's radio and TV contracts, the "Merry-Go-Round" couldn't stay afloat. No, he *can't* retire.

Yet there were times in the '80s when Jack considered it. He'd become a kind of folk hero by the mid-1970s, and when TV knocked at his door, he answered. For almost a decade he appeared on "Good Morning America," bringing in up to $550,000 a year. "My folks were finally impressed when I was on television," Jack says. With the huge TV income, all of which Jack poured into the "Merry-Go-Round," the staff burgeoned. But Jack Anderson was less and less a part of the daily operation. He came to think of himself as the column's "publisher." Staffers were less subtle: They called him a "figurehead," a "front," a "public relations man." There was a strong feeling among column staffers that it wasn't only Jack's parents but Jack himself who was impressed with the fame that television brought to him.

"He loved it," says one former staffer who worked with Jack for many years. When somebody walked up on the street and said, "Aren't you Jack Anderson?," the man says, Jack "flared up like a peacock." Even some of Jack's children, his good friends and loyal allies lovingly chuckle at what they see as his fascination with fame. "It inevitably went to his head," says Jack's daughter Laurie Anderson-Bruch. "There was a time we had to bring him down. He was just full of himself." For a while, she says, it even seemed to her that getting another TV show was more important to her dad than his Mormon faith. Jack once confided to Les Whitten that when he gets on a plane and is recognized, he hates it because he has to talk to the guy for the whole flight. But, Jack said, if he gets on a plane and nobody recognizes him, he then worries about why nobody has recognized him. When Whitten told Jack he was leaving the column to write novels, Jack asked, "How can you give up this fame?"

"I have a visceral love for the column and Jack," says a reporter who worked for him for several years. "But I'm angry at him. I've been angry at him for years because he betrayed the ideal. It started with 'Good Morning America.' He stopped being a reporter and started being a celebrity. It was a big mistake because he was a great reporter. He had this Everyman quality that was really corrupted by his ego." Says another former staffer, "We always joked on the staff that he'd give up the column for a weekly TV show." Says another, "He craves being on television." Says another, "This is one story where you don't follow the money. You follow the fame." Says still another, "He really wanted to be famous, a household word."

Jack doesn't see it this way. In his mind, his motives were heroic: He could reach tens of millions of people through his column, but he could reach many millions more through TV. It wasn't his name that needed to be a household word, but his message—the message that people must be constantly diligent in policing their public officials. His only interest in fame, he says, was its "market value"—the power it gave him to reach a wider audience. He says that his question to Whitten—"How can you give up this fame?"—was meant only to suggest that Whitten might find it harder to make a living without the public visibility of the "Merry-Go-Round." "Reveling in fame?" he asks, "I'm surprised anyone would say that. It's not true."

Says Whitten, "Fame meant a lot to him."

In the late '70s and early '80s, Jack entered a variety of business deals that brought him the kind of press he was used to giving instead of getting. He held an interest in a bank, for instance, that turned out to have links to the Rev. Sun Myung Moon. Increasingly, questions were raised about his use of poorly paid young reporters to produce his column while he was earning a six-figure income on the speaking circuit. Libby says she and Jack got tired of the criticism and talked about his retiring, maybe teaching at Brigham Young University. But Jack gave up the idea, two of his children say, after experiencing personal religious insights from which he concluded he should continue his work. Says Jack's son Rodney, "He has received guidance from the heavenly father."

Whatever the reason, in the '80s Jack Anderson began putting his fame and credibility behind what he considered to be "good causes." He told his partner, Dale Van Atta, that he was going to be more involved in policy issues than in the past. It was a kind of warning, Van Atta says, because Jack knew his activities would be controversial. Jack asked President Ronald Reagan to support his idea for a Young Astronaut Council to promote interest in math and science in the nation's schools. Jack became its chairman, and Reagan made many public appearances for the group. Jack also became co-chairman of Citizens Against Government Waste with corporate executive J. Peter Grace. The group backed controversial proposals for reducing the deficit. Jack also helped his son Randy launch a Hollywood anti-drug organization aimed at putting pressure on moviemakers to stop glamorizing drug use. He advised Randy to begin his group in Washington by first winning the backing of key politicians, because that would pressure Hollywood to fall in line. It worked nicely. Nancy Reagan was honored at one of the group's early fund-raisers.

At the column office, they grumbled. The deficit recommendations of Citizens Against Government Waste were off limits, says "Merry-Go-Round" economics reporter Mike Binstein. So was any hint that a tax increase—Reagan's worst bogyman—might be necessary to fight the federal budget deficit. Jack was plugging the Young Astronauts often, and some staffers believed critical stories on Reagan were increasingly hard to get in print. Other staffers deny this. But

Jack's son Randy remembers hearing Van Atta himself once ask, "Who's the sacred cow this week, Jack?" There was much armchair analysis about what had happened to the tough Jack Anderson.

"Jack has a deep need for acceptance," says Joseph Spear, who worked with Jack on the "Merry-Go-Round" for 20 years, but who knows nothing of Jack's childhood. "He was between the devil and the deep blue sea, because there was no way he could write the stories he did and be accepted in this town. It was a fundamental conflict in his personality—the need to be accepted at the same time he did things that kept him from being accepted."

Jack's friend Lee Roderick, a journalist and fellow Mormon, says Jack was attacked from all sides so often that he got sick of it: Journalists demeaned him, politicians despised him, and even Mormons, with their strain of political conservatism, often criticized him for supposedly tearing down America rather than building it up. "I definitely think he was tired of it," says Roderick, who agrees with those who say Jack was enamored of fame. "Everything about him tells me the guy lives for it, but I think that in recent years what he craves more than fame is acceptance." Says Jack's son Kevin, "He liked Reagan and he liked that Reagan was interested in helping him. It just didn't fit the image I had of Dad from the Watergate days."

Again, Jack sees it differently. "I just decided that at this point in my life, I'd do it, be a good citizen." Drew Pearson had often thrown his public clout behind worthwhile causes, he says, and he decided to do the same.

It is Jack's son Randy who is left to frame his father's heroic role, which he does in the context of his father's religion: The Book of Mormon says that righteous societies can be undermined by evil forces, Randy says, and his father believes that the three greatest threats to America are its eroding educational system, the deficit and illegal drugs. His dad's three causes—Young Astronauts, Citizens Against Government Waste and his anti-drug work—are all aimed at battling these great threats to the nation. "To put it bluntly, individuals are used to further the work of the Lord, as vessels and instruments," says Randy, who adds that he and his father have talked about this before. "I think he feels there's more to it than just being a journalist."

Jack is asked how his recent involvement with these interest groups squares with the remark he made years ago, soon after winning his Pulitzer: "What's wrong," he said then, "is that these reporters adopted the views of the people they're writing about. They've become a part of the Establishment they cover."

Says Jack now, "I believe these are good causes."

Jack is visiting his father for the last time on this trip to Salt Lake City. And at his father's age, Jack can never be sure if it will be the last time he sees him alive, although he believes beyond a doubt that he will see him in Heaven someday. Yet on this Earth, on this trip, it has become clear that the life-long struggle between the father who tried to humble his son and the son who chafed and rebelled is near its end. The son has won. Strange, how that troubled bond between them set the stage for Jack's remarkable life, as if in trying to restrain his son's ambition Orlando unleashed it a hundred-fold.

Jack stands at the door, and his father sits in a chair across the room. Only yesterday Jack saw his father cry for the first time, only the day before he heard him say for the first time that he was proud of his son. Jack is uncomfortable with emotional good-byes, and with a strained cheerfulness, he says, well, gotta go, gotta catch a plane. His father is quiet for a long, awkward moment, until he says, "You're the most generous son a father could have." He then drops his head, covers his eyes and sobs. Jack hesitates, looks plaintively to his right, shrugs, walks over and hugs his father, pats him softly on the back. "It's all right," he says quietly. "It's all right."

Then Jack falls silent, fighting back his own deep tears.

# Suggested Readings

Clark, Roy Peter. "A New Shape for the News," Washington Journalism Review, March 1984, pp. 46–47. Clark describes how to combine the inverted pyramid and the narrative story forms.

Clark, Roy Peter and Fry, Donald, eds. ''Best Newspaper Writing: 1990.'' St. Petersburg, Fla.: The Poynter Institute, 1990. Each year the winning entries in the American Society of Newspaper Editors writing contest are published in this book, which also contains interviews with the writers.

Sims, Norman, ed. ''The Literary Journalists.'' New York: Ballantine Books, 1984. With an introductory essay defining literary journalism, this book offers reprints from the best of the bunch.

Snyder, Louis L. and Morris, Richard B., eds. ''A Treasury of Great Reporting,'' Second Edition. New York: Simon & Schuster, 1971. The reader can trace the evolution of several writing styles in American journalism.

Zinsser, William. ''On Writing Well,'' Third Edition. New York: Harper & Row, 1985. An entertaining narrative on the art of writing.

# Exercises

1. Write four to eight paragraphs about how you and your classmates learned to be reporters. Pick a scene from one of your classes and re-create it. Provide the transition into the body of the story and then stop.

2. Interview a student in your reporting class. Ask questions that elicit anecdotes. Write an anecdotal introduction to a story about the person. Continue through the transitional paragraph.

3. Using the chronological approach, write about eight paragraphs of a story about some aspect of your experience in the reporting class.

4. Choose a personal experience that is worth telling in a first-person story. Write two to three pages using the first-person approach.

5. Identify the anecdotes in Harrington's profile of Jack Anderson. Are they pertinent? Informative and entertaining? Do the transitions flow into and out of the anecdotes well? Explain your answers.

# 18

# Social Science Reporting

Increasing numbers of journalists are practicing a type of reporting that is likely to become routine by the turn of the century. Some call it *scientific* or *social science reporting*; others use no special label. This reporting method employs the techniques of the social sciences to help in telling stories that would be difficult or impossible to report in other ways. As the world about which journalists write increases in complexity, the number and importance of such stories will increase, too. Here are a few examples:

The Anchorage (Alaska) Daily News wanted to describe the devastating impact of modern culture—especially its drugs—on native Alaskan peoples. So the paper combined traditional reporting with information-gathering techniques developed by anthropologists and added extensive computer analyses of data, including death records and tax receipts. The result, a series called "A People in Peril," led to heightened public awareness and governmental reforms. It also won for the newspaper journalism's highest awards.

The Atlanta Constitution analyzed by computer the lending records of the city's financial institutions for a less exotic but no less significant report on discrimination in home loans. "The Color of Money," as the report was titled, also produced reforms and won national awards.

Associated Press reporter Michael Graczyk didn't just interview or observe Houston, Texas, police officers as they practiced when to use—and when not to use—their pistols. He went through the course himself. It was a harrowing experience. His lead was, "A New York Times photographer is dead because I shot him by mistake. So is at least one Houston police officer." The deaths were faked, of course, but the emotion was not.

Other AP reporters checked on the efficiency of the U.S. Postal Service by mailing dozens of letters between AP bureaus.

Cooperating in an intensely competitive business, The Washington Post and ABC conduct national public opinion polls jointly. So do The New York Times and CBS. Dozens of newspapers do their own local polling.

All these examples show the tools of the social sciences in the hands of journalists. In all these cases, the tools were used responsibly. There can be problems, though, even when proper care is taken. When pseudoscience creeps in, the problems for audiences and practitioners become greater.

What is a news organization to do, for example, when its public opinion poll shows sharply different results from another, taken from the same population and covering the same topics? That can, and does, happen. As Leo Bogart, one of the most respected newspaper researchers, notes, ''Even the best polls are estimates, not facts.'' The solution, then, is to explain to readers how the estimates are made and how differences can occur. Remember, your readers are growing increasingly sophisticated—and increasingly skeptical— about such surveys.

Despite the leadership of such journalists and social scientists as Bogart, Phil Meyer, Maxwell McCombs and others, too many reporters and editors continue to use worn-out techniques such as call-ins or ''people-in-the-street polls'' to produce stories. It is a trap for journalists and audiences alike because the results look as if they're scientific and reliable when they actually are not.

Both the possibilities and the problems of using social science techniques show why it is important for today's journalists and those of the 21st century to possess more quantitative skills and better backgrounds in statistics than did the generation of their teachers.

### In this chapter you will learn:

1. When and how to use four popular social science techniques.

2. What to look out for when using or writing about any of them.

3. Detailed guidelines for the most common technique—public opinion polling.

# Participant Observation

When Al Pagel walked into the state psychiatric hospital, he carried neither a notebook nor a tape recorder. He did not identify himself as a reporter. As far as hospital officials or patients knew, he was just another attendant. Eight hours a day for two weeks, Pagel participated in the life of the people he was observing. He was verbally abused, physically attacked, smeared with human excrement. He was overworked, underpaid and untrained. His experiences, coupled with interviewing and background reading, helped him compile for the Miami Herald a story that probably could not have been told if he had relied on conventional reporting alone.

Pagel, like AP reporter Graczyk, was engaging in *participant observation*, a technique in which reporters disguise themselves to obtain inside stories. Subjects ranging from school teaching to vegetable picking have been explored using this technique. Sociologists and psychologists also use participant observation in their research, for the same reasons reporters do. Participant observers get firsthand, close-up pictures of their subjects not obtainable by studying statistics or by formal interviewing. Facts and feelings can be captured that otherwise would remain unknown.

Along with its unique advantages, participant observation also poses some unique problems. These problems may have no clear solutions, but you and your editors need at least to consider them before you set out to become an ambulance attendant or a migrant worker.

***The Problem of Invasion of Privacy.***    Unless you identify yourself as a reporter, you are, in effect, spying on the lives of people who are not aware they are being observed—an ethically questionable activity. But if you do identify yourself, the advantages of the technique can be lost. Sensitivity is essential, especially when the people you write about may be embarrassed or have their jobs placed in jeopardy.

***The Problem of Involvement.***    There are two things to watch out for here. First, do not become so involved that you change the course of the events you are observing. You may be on stage, but you are not a star performer. Second, do not assume that the people you are observing feel the same way you do. No matter how hard you work at fitting in, you remain an outsider, a visitor. The view from inside a migrant workers' camp or a psychiatric hospital is different when you know you will be there two weeks instead of two years or a lifetime.

***The Problem of Generalizing.***    Scientists know well the danger of generalizing on the basis of limited observation. Reporters don't always know that or sometimes forget it. Keep in mind that, although participant observation yields a detailed picture of a specific situation, it tells you nothing reliable about any other situation. Pagel could not assume that what he found in one ward of one hospital would be true of other wards in other hospitals. Participant observation is a good tool, but it is a limited one. It usually works best as a supplement to the standard techniques of interviewing and examining documents.

# Systematic Study
# of Records

Nina Bernstein of the Milwaukee Journal spent two months sifting through court documents, analyzing payment records and supervising a computer analysis of House of Correction records on 899 inmates. She discovered that thousands of people—most of them poor and black—were being routinely sent to jail in the city for up to six months for non-payment of fines for offenses as minor as jaywalking or disorderly conduct.

In a series that won a gold medal from the national organization Investigative Reporters and Editors, Bernstein revealed the plight of those she termed "the losers in a system of 'cash register justice,' as one judge called it, a mushrooming municipal legal system where the bottom line is pay or be locked up, and where the final balance is routinely tallied by a computer, not a court."

Political scientists, historians and other scholars long have used such *systematic study of records* in their research. Its use by reporters is still limited but growing. The advantage of detailed analysis of court records, budgets, voting records and other documents is that it permits reporters and readers to draw conclusions based on solid information. No amount of interviewing or courtroom observation could have produced the indisputable facts that Bernstein turned up or that Bill Dedman of the Atlanta Constitution found in his analysis of mortgage lenders. Studies like theirs would have been nearly impossible without the use of a computer, but nearly every newspaper now has a computer or access to one. The programs needed for this kind of study are relatively simple. So the systematic study of records is within the reach of many newspapers.

The main obstacles to such study are shortages of time and money. Philadelphia Inquirer projects often require months of work by one or more reporters. On small papers, especially, you may have trouble freeing yourself for even several days. And reporters' time and computer time both cost money. Editors and publishers must be convinced that the return will be worth the investment before they will approve. You probably should have at least some clues that wrongdoing, injustice or inefficiency exists before launching a systematic study.

Once you have begun a study, you should make sure that it is in fact systematic. You must either examine all the pertinent records or choose the ones you examine in such a way that they will be truly representative of the rest. Be sure you are asking the right questions and recording the information necessary to answer them. A computer can perform complicated analyses very quickly, but it cannot analyze facts that have not been fed into it. People who use computers have a word for that problem: *GIGO*, an acronym for "Garbage In, Garbage Out."

Don't set out on a systematic study without assurances of time and money, a clear idea of what you're looking for and expert technical advice. If the expertise is unavailable at your newspaper, look to the nearest college.

# Field Experiments

Instead of just asking questions about mail service, The Associated Press tested it. Letters were mailed from one bureau to another, some with ZIP codes and some without, some by air mail and some by regular first-class mail. A scientist conducting the same kind of test would call it a *field experiment*. In all such experiments researchers take some action in order to observe the effects.

Reporters rarely think of themselves as scientists, but they conduct a great many experiments. The mailing experiment is a common one. Another frequent test is to examine the honesty of auto mechanics by taking a car in perfect condition to several shops and reporting what each finds "wrong" with it. Consumer reporters also commonly check weights and measures: Does a "pound" of hamburger really weigh a pound? Or they test for discrimination by having a male and a female reporter apply for insurance policies or mortgages.

If they are to be successful, reporters' field experiments must follow the same guidelines—and avoid the same pitfalls—that scientists' experiments must. A little scientific jargon is necessary here. It is fairly straightforward, though, and it will be useful if you ever have the opportunity to set up an experiment.

## BASIC EXPERIMENTAL METHODS AND TERMINOLOGY

Your field experiment must have a *hypothesis*, a statement of what you expect to find. Your hypothesis must be stated clearly and simply. When it is, it will help focus your attention on the two elements of the experiment—the independent variable and the dependent variable. The *variables*, just as their name implies, are the things that change during the experiment. The independent variable is what you think may be a cause. You change it and observe what happens to the dependent variable, the effect.

Let's take an example. Suppose you think bankers in your town are discriminating against women by demanding more collateral for loans from them than from men. Form a hypothesis: "Women are forced to put up more collateral to secure loans than men are.'' The variables are the gender of the borrower and the amount of collateral demanded. Gender is the independent variable, the suspected cause. For your experiment, then, you will have applicants of each gender seek a bank loan. You will be looking for any change in the dependent variable—the collateral demanded.

There are two other steps you must take to assure a successful experiment. First you must *control* the experiment. Every aspect of the experiment must be carefully structured to make sure that any change you observe is caused only by the independent variable you want to test. For example, your male and female loan applicants must be as much alike as possible in the financial details they provide, the way they dress, their race and their age. Otherwise, any differences in the responses by the loan officer might be due to something other than gender, the variable you are interested in. Also, the applicants should visit the same bank or banks and speak to the same officials. Without careful control of the experiment, you may end up unable to say with certainty that you have proved or disproved your hypothesis. Then you've got no story.

The other step is called *randomization*, or *random selection*. In a small town you could run your experiment at every bank. But in a big city that would be impossible. So, if you want to be reasonably sure that the results of the experiment apply to all the banks in town, you must choose at random the ones to approach. Randomization allows you to assume that what you select— 10 banks, for instance—is representative of the whole—the total number of banks in the city.

Choosing a bank or anything else, such as a name, at random simply means that you employ a method for choosing that gives every bank or every name an equal chance of being picked. The procedure for making a random selection is beyond the scope of an introductory reporting text. The Suggested Readings at the end of the chapter include several books in which you can find that and other material relating to the concepts introduced here. Much of that other material deals with statistics. Many experiments require statistical analysis to ensure that what you have found is significant. Most polls and surveys require some statistical analysis, too. Explanations of the fairly simple math involved also can be found in the books listed in Suggested Readings.

# Public Opinion Polls

Public opinion polling has become an important tool of journalists. Many news organizations now go beyond reporting the findings of such national polling firms as the Gallup and Louis Harris organizations to conducting or commissioning their own surveys. Several journalism schools—including those at the universities of Alabama, Florida, North Carolina and Missouri—have developed scientific polling operations staffed by faculty and students to serve newspapers and broadcasters in their regions.

The Media Research Bureau at the University of Missouri, for example, conducts for newspaper and broadcast clients regular polls of Missouri residents to sample their opinions on such subjects as drug testing, a new state lottery and tax reform. Each survey involves telephone calls to at least 500 people, selected at random to be representative of the adult population of the nine-county central Missouri region.

When polls are conducted properly and reported carefully, they can be both interesting and useful, telling people something they could not know otherwise and perhaps even helping to produce wiser public policies. But when they are badly done or sloppily reported, polls can be bad news for journalists and readers alike.

The chances are good that sometime in your reporting career you will want to conduct an opinion poll or at least help with one your newspaper is conducting. The Suggested Readings listed at the end of the chapter will tell you much of what you need to know for that. Even if you never work on one, you almost certainly will be called on to write about the results of polls. What follows will help you understand what you are given and help you make sure your readers understand it, too.

## REQUIREMENTS FOR SOUND POLLING

The Associated Press Managing Editors Association prepared a checklist of the information you should have and should share with your readers about any poll on which you are reporting. Included on that list were the following:

1. The identity of the sponsor of the survey.

2. The exact wording of the questions asked.

3. A definition of the population sampled.

4. The sample size and, where the survey design makes it relevant, the response rate.

5. Some indication of the allowance that should be made for sampling error.

6. Which results are based on only part of the sample (for example, probable voters, those who have heard of the candidate, or other subdivisions).

7. How the interviews were collected—in person, in homes, by phone, by mail, on street corners, or wherever.

8. When the interviews were collected.

Several of those points require some explanation.

The identity of the survey's sponsor is important to you and your readers because it gives some clues to possible bias. Most people would put more trust in a Gallup or Harris poll's report that, for instance, Smith is far ahead of Jones in the presidential campaign than they would in a poll sponsored by the Smith for President organization.

The exact wording of the questions is important because the answer received often depends at least in part on how the question was asked. (See Chapter 5 on interviewing for more detail.) The answer might well be different, for example, if a pollster asked, "Who do you favor for president, Jones or Smith?" rather than "Wouldn't Jones make a better president than Smith?"

In the third point on the checklist, the word "population" is another bit of jargon. Most of us use the word to mean the number of people living in the town, state or country. In science, however, *population* means the total number of people—or documents or milkweed plants or giraffes—in the group being studied. For an opinion survey the population might be all registered voters in the state, black males under 25 or female cigarette smokers. To understand what the results of a poll mean, you must know what population was studied. The word "sampled" simply refers to the procedure discussed earlier in which a small number—or *sample*—of persons is picked at random so as to be representative of the population.

The sample size is important because—all other things being equal—the larger the sample, the more reliable the survey results should be. The response rate is especially important in surveys conducted by mail, in which a low rate of response may invalidate the poll.

The *sampling error* of any survey is the allowance that must be made for the possibility that the opinion of the sample may not be exactly the same as the opinion of the whole population. A simpler name for it is *margin of error*. The margin of error depends mainly on the size of the sample. For instance, all other things being equal, a sample of 400 would have a margin of error of 5 percent while a sample of 1,500 would have a margin of error of 3 percent. If, with a sample of 1,500, the poll shows Jones with 60 percent and Smith with 40 percent, you can be confident that Jones actually has between 57 and 63 percent while Smith actually has between 37 and 43 percent. The laws of probability say that the chances are 19 to 1 that the actual percentages fall in that range. Those odds make the information good enough to publish.

The existence of sampling error helps explain why it is important to know which results may be based on only part of the sample. The smaller that part, the greater the margin of error. In political polls it is always important to know whether the results include responses from all eligible voters or just those likely to vote. The opinions of the likely voters are more important than the others.

When the interviews were collected may be of critical importance in interpreting the poll, especially during campaigns when the candidates themselves and other events may cause preferences to change significantly within a few days. A week-old poll may be meaningless if something dramatic has happened since it was taken. Candidates have been known to use such outdated results to make themselves appear to be doing better than they really are, or their opponents worse. Be on guard.

When the poll is your newspaper's, the obligation remains to let your readers know how it was taken. It is also incumbent on the paper to reveal how reliable the poll is.

## THE NEED FOR CAUTION IN INTERPRETING POLLS

Whether you are helping to conduct a survey or just reporting on one produced by someone else, you must exercise caution. You should be on guard for the following potential problems:

1. *The people interviewed must be selected in a truly random fashion if you want to generalize from their responses to the whole population.* If they are not, you have no assurance that the interview subjects are really representative. The old-fashioned people-in-the-street interview is practically worthless as an indicator of public opinion for this reason. The man or woman in the street probably differs in important ways from all those men and women who are not in the street when the questioner is.

Also invalid are such "polls" as the questionnaires members of Congress mail to their constituents. Only strongly opinionated—and therefore unrepresentative—people are likely to return them. For the same reason the "question-of-the-day" feature some newspapers and broadcast stations carry tells you nothing about the opinions of the great mass of people who do not respond.

2. *The closer the results, the harder it is to say anything definitive.* Look again at the example of the Smith–Jones campaign. Suppose the poll showed Smith with 52 percent and Jones with 48 percent of the vote. Smith may or may not be ahead. With the 3 percent margin of error, Smith could actually have only 49 percent, and Jones could have 51 percent. All that you could report safely about those results is that the race is too close to call. Many reporters—and pollsters—are simply not careful enough when the outcome is unclear.

3. *Beware of polls that claim to measure opinion on sensitive, complicated issues.* Many questions of morality, or social issues such as race relations, do not lend themselves to simple answers. Opinions on such matters can be measured, but only by highly skilled researchers using carefully designed questions. Anything less can be dangerously oversimplified and highly misleading.

Surveying, like field experiments, systematic analysis and participant observation, can help you as a reporter solve problems you could not handle as well by other techniques. But these are only tools. How effectively they are used—or how clumsily they are misused—depends on you.

# Suggested Readings

Campbell, Donald and Stanley, Julian. ''Experimental and Quasi-Experimental Designs for Research.'' Skokie, Ill.: Rand McNally, 1966. A classic guide to field experimentation that is also useful in providing a better understanding of scientific research.

Demers, David Pearce and Nichols, Suzanne. ''Precision Journalism: A Practical Guide.'' Newbury Park, Calif.: Sage Publications, 1987. A primer for students and journalists, simply written and complete with examples.

McCombs, Maxwell, Shaw, Donald L. and Grey, David. ''Handbook of Reporting Methods.'' Boston: Houghton Mifflin, 1976. Offers examples of real-life uses of social science methods in journalism, but does not provide enough on statistics to serve as a guide in employing the methods.

Meyer, Philip. ''Precision Journalism.'' Bloomington, Ind.: Indiana University Press, 1979. A detailed introduction to surveying, conducting field experiments and using statistics to analyze the results by a reporter who pioneered the use of these methods in journalism. The theoretical justification of the techniques is included as well.

Meyer, Philip. ''The Newspaper Survival Book: An Editor's Guide to Marketing Research.'' Bloomington, Ind.: Indiana University Press, 1985. A concise, clearly written explanation of basic research methods and how to interpret their results.

Williams, Frederick. ''Reasoning with Statistics.'' New York: Holt, Rinehart and Winston, 1979. A non-intimidating but sufficiently complex guide to using mathematical tools.

# Exercises

1. Find a newspaper story that reports on the results of a public opinion survey. Analyze the story using the guidelines discussed in this chapter.

2. Using the techique described by Philip Meyer in "Precision Journalism" (see the Suggested Readings), design a simple survey. Write a memo outlining your plan.

3. Design a field experiment: State your hypothesis, identify the dependent and independent variables, and describe the controls you will use.

4. As a class project, carry out one of the surveys a class member designed in Exercise 2.

# 19

## Investigative Reporting

Investigative reporting is the most glamorous form of journalism. It may well be the most important form. Its practitioners are more likely than other reporters to win Pulitzer Prizes, to write best-selling books, to become heroes to their peers and, occasionally, to the public. But the work of investigating is hard, often dull, sometimes risky. Days may be spent tracking down leads that prove fruitless. Weeks of effort may yield a story that goes unnoticed or may yield no story at all. Pressures and even threats are common.

Investigative reporting by Betty Gray and Mike Voss of the Washington (N.C.) Daily News showed residents of that small town that—contrary to assurances issued by public officials—their drinking water was unsafe, possibly even cancer-causing. The reporters uncovered ignored health reports, learned the language of water chemistry and endured the resistance and outright opposition of the city officials whose dereliction of duty they exposed.

Investigative reporting by a team of 10 reporters at the Lexington (Ky.) Herald-Leader uncovered a statewide pattern of undertaxation and political interference that was, in the title of the series, "Cheating Our Children." The reporters interviewed hundreds of school and other public officials, used computers to analyze millions of records and compiled stories so compelling that seven other papers in the state agreed to distribute reprints to their readers. During the interviewing, one reporter was punched in the face when he requested tax records at the office of a local assessor.

Investigative reporting by four reporters for the Anchorage Daily News showed how both industry and government regulators failed to enforce safeguards adequate to prevent the massive oil spill from an Exxon tanker in Alaskan waters.

**Figure 19.1 Original Muckraker.** Ida Tarbell's early 20th-century work in examining Standard Oil helped set the pattern for modern investigative reporters.

Such stories, and hundreds like them, are the payoffs for the long hours, the frustrations and the expense of investigative reporting. They make the investment worthwhile for journalists and readers alike. These examples also show that serious reporting, including the analysis of systems such as public education in Kentucky, is not the exclusive province of the biggest newspapers or the television networks. Imagination, skill and courage—not size and wealth—are the prerequisites for investigative reporting. They always have been.

Investigative reporting has a rich tradition in the history of American journalism. The fiercely partisan editors of the Revolutionary era dug for facts as well as the mud they hurled at their opponents. In the early 20th century investigative reporting flowered with the ''muckrakers,'' a title bestowed with anger by Theodore Roosevelt and worn with pride by the reporters. Lincoln Steffens dissected America's cities, one by one, laying bare the corrupt combinations of businessmen and politicians that ran them. Ida Tarbell exposed the economic stranglehold of the oil monopoly. Theodore Dreiser, Upton Sinclair and Frank Norris revealed the horrors of working life in factories and packing plants.

The complexities of big government, big business and big society in the 1990s will require even more widespread—and more sophisticated—investigative reporting if the press is to fulfill its role of keeping a free people fully informed.

Few editors assign beginning reporters to investigative work. It is the most demanding kind of reporting. Still, you need to know what it is and how to do it so that you will be ready when your chance comes. Many of the techniques of investigative reporting also can be used to produce good stories from what otherwise would be routine assignments.

## In this chapter you will learn:

1. The process of investigative reporting.

2. How to find and use sources and records.

3. What kinds of obstacles you will face as an investigative reporter.

# The Process

## BEGINNING THE INVESTIGATION

Most investigations start with a hunch or a *tip* that something or someone deserves a close look. No good reporter sets out on an investigation unless there is some basis for suspicion. That basis may be a grand jury report that leaves something untold or a tip that some public official is on the take. It may be a sudden upsurge in drug overdoses or it may be long-festering problems in the schools. Without some idea of what you're looking for, investigation is too likely to turn into wild goose chasing.

Based on the tip or suspicion, together with whatever background material you have, you form a hypothesis. Reporters hardly ever use that term, but it is a useful one, because it shows the similarity between the processes of investigative reporting and scientific investigation. In both, the *hypothesis* is the statement of what you think is true. Your hypothesis may be, ''The mayor is a crook,'' or, ''The school system is being run incompetently.'' It is a good idea to state clearly your hypothesis when you start an investigation. By doing so, you focus on the heart of the problem and cut down on the possibility of any misunderstanding with your editor or other reporters who may be working with you.

Once the hypothesis is stated, the reporter—like the scientist—sets out to prove or disprove it. You should be open to the possibility of disproof. Reporters—like scientists—are not advocates. They are seekers of truth. No good reporter ignores or downplays evidence just because it contradicts his or her assumptions. In journalism as in science, the truth about a situation is often sharply different from what is expected. An open mind is an essential quality of a good investigative reporter. Remember, too, that you may have a good story even if your hypothesis is disproved.

## CARRYING OUT THE INVESTIGATION

The actual investigative work usually proceeds in two stages. The first is what Robert W. Greene, Pulitzer Prize-winning reporter and editor for Newsday of Long Island, N.Y., calls the *sniff*. In this stage you sniff around in search of a trail worth following. If you find one, the second stage, the serious investigation, begins.

The preliminary checking should take no more than a day or two. Its purpose is not to prove the hypothesis but to find out the chances of proving it. You make that effort by talking with the most promising source or sources, skimming the most available records, consulting knowledgeable people in your news room. The two questions you are trying to answer at this stage are: (1) "Is there a story here?" and (2) "Am I going to be able to get it?" If the answer to either question is no, there is little point in pursuing the investigation.

When the answer to both questions is yes, however, the real work begins. It begins with organization. Your hypothesis tells you where you want to go. Now you must figure out how to get there. Careful organization keeps you on the right track and prevents you from overlooking anything important as you go. Many reporters take a kind of perverse pride in their illegible notebooks and cluttered desks. As an investigative reporter you may have a messy desk, but you should arrange your files of information clearly and coherently. Begin organizing by asking yourself these questions:

1. Who are my most promising sources? Who am I going to have trouble with? Who should I go to first? Second? Last?

2. What records do I need? Where are they? Which are public? How can I get to the ones that are not readily accessible?

3. What is the most I can hope to prove? What is the least that will still yield a story? How long should the investigation take?

Now draw up a plan of action. Experienced reporters often do this mentally. But when you are a beginner, it's a good idea to write out a plan and then to go over it with your editor. The editor may spot some holes in your planning or have something to add. And an editor is more likely to give you enough time if he or she has a clear idea of what has to be done.

Carry out your plan, allowing flexibility for the unexpected twists most investigations take. During your first round of interviews, keep asking who else you should talk to. While you are checking records, look for references to other files or other persons.

Be methodical. Many investigative reporters spend an hour or so at the end of every day adding up the score, going through their notes and searching their memories to analyze what they have learned and what they need next. Some develop elaborate, cross-indexed files of names, organizations, incidents. Others are less formal. Virtually all, however, use a code to disguise names of confidential sources so that those sources will remain secret even if the files are subpoenaed. The method you use isn't important, as long as you understand it. What is vitally important is that you have a method and use it consistently. If you fail to keep careful track of where you're going, you may go in the wrong direction, or in circles.

## An Example

Steve Woodward was less than a year out of journalism school when, as a reporter in a suburban bureau of the Kansas City (Mo.) Star, he first heard the name of Frank Morgan. Over the next few months, the name kept popping up. Morgan, it appeared, owned a great deal of land. He was rumored to have an interest in several banks and to be the behind-the-scenes financier of important business developments. He won concessions from the zoning board and the tax assessor. He associated with important politicians. But despite all the activity, little was known about the man himself. He refused to be interviewed and forbade his associates to talk to reporters.

Woodward, intrigued, decided to investigate. In months of part-time work, while he kept up with his regular assignments, Woodward was able to put together from public records and interviews a word portrait of one of the city's most important but least-known businessmen. He traced Morgan's holdings in shopping centers, banks and apartment buildings in five states and found them to be worth nearly half a billion dollars. The reporter also produced a biographical sketch of Morgan, an account of his political connections and a look at Morgan's use of a ''straw party''—a person apparently unconnnected to him—to conceal ownership of real estate.

In a modest summary of his work, Woodward said, ''No laws were broken by the persons named in the stories, and no one went to jail because of them. The stories were meant only to demonstrate how power really works.''

Here's how he did it:

He began with the clippings in the newspaper morgue. He doublechecked every name he could come up with that had a possible Morgan connection. Some seemingly unrelated individuals and corporations were linked by material from other records.

Then Woodward went to the courthouse. There, depositions taken in the divorce case of a Morgan associate revealed numerous land transactions and yielded other names to check. The indexes showed a great number of lawsuits filed against Morgan and associates. These contained still more names of corporations and business properties.

Corporation records kept by the secretaries of state of Kansas and Missouri showed names and addresses of officers and directors and when the corporations were formed. For business partnerships that were not incorporated, much the same information came from the fictitious name files, also calld *d.b.a.* (for ''doing business as'') files, also in the secretary of state's office. A pattern of connections was beginning to emerge.

Most banking records are secret, but Woodward put to good use a federal form (FFIEC 003) that has been required since 1979 and that details the principal owners of the bank and any loans the bank has made to its owners. Depending on whether the bank has a national or state charter, the form can be obtained from the U.S. Comptroller of the Currency, the Federal Reserve Bank or the Federal Deposit Insurance Corp.

City planning commission records included minutes of meetings, staff reports and other details of developments such as shopping centers. County collectors' records showed who paid the property taxes on various parcels. County recorders' offices produced details of land ownership and of the financing of purchases.

City directories, birth certificates, school and military records, all public, helped Woodward trace Morgan's life from the beginning. Marriage records in the county courthouse showed not only his wife's maiden name but even which synagogue he attended.

Campaign finance reports—local, state and federal—revealed support for some politicians whose later actions benefited Morgan.

Even some of Morgan's federal income-tax records, closed by law, were opened to inspection when they were entered as evidence in a suit in the U.S. Tax Court. Woodward got them with a request under the Freedom of Information Act.

Finally, Woodward said, ''I talked with dozens of real estate developers, city planners, politicians, bankers, appraisers—you name it. Many of their names I got from the clips. Others I got from lawsuits. Records gave me a start in tracking down the people who could fill in the gaps in my stories and demonstrated how documents and human sources can complement each other.''

The result was a series of stories rich in detail that told Kansas Citians a great deal about a man who had been secretly shaping their city.

The importance of accuracy in investigative reporting cannot be over-stated. It is the most essential element in good journalism of any kind. In investigative reporting especially, inaccuracy leads to embarrassment, to ruined reputations and, sometimes, to lawsuits. The reputations ruined often are those of the careless reporter and newspaper. Most investigative stories have the effect of accusing somebody of wrongdoing or incompetence. Even if the target is a public official whose chances of suing successfully for libel are slim, fairness and decency require that you be sure of your facts before you put them in print.

The Washington Post, during its famous Watergate investigation, fol-lowed the policy of requiring verification from two independent sources before an allegation could be published. That is a good rule to follow. People make mistakes. They lie. Their memories fail. Documents can be misleading or confusing. Check and doublecheck. There is no good excuse for an error.

## WRITING THE STORY

Most investigative stories require consultation with the newspaper's lawyer before publication. As a reporter you will have little or nothing to say about the choice of your paper's lawyer. That lawyer, though, will be an important part of your investigative career. The lawyer advises on what you can print safely and what you cannot. Most editors heed their lawyer's advice. If you are lucky, your paper's lawyer will understand and sympathize with good, ag-gressive journalism. If he or she does not, you may find yourself forced to argue for your story. You will be better equipped for such an argument—and few reporters go through a career without several—if you understand at least the basics of the laws of libel and privacy. Chapter 21 outlines those laws, and several good books on law for journalists are listed in the Suggested Readings at the end of that chapter.

The last step before your investigation goes public is the writing and rewriting. After days or weeks of intense reporting effort, the writing strikes some investigative reporters as a chore—necessary but unimportant. That attitude is disastrous. The best reporting in the world is wasted unless it is read. Your hard-won exposé or painstaking analysis will disappear without a trace unless the writing attracts readers and maintains their interest. Most reporters and newspapers that are serious about investigative reporting rec-ognize this. They stress good writing almost as much as solid reporting. The Chicago Tribune, for example, assigns an especially skilled writer to its Pulitzer Prize-winning investigative task force as it nears the completion of each project. The writer's sole job is to present months of reporting work as clearly and dramatically as possible. Other newspapers prefer to let their reporters do their own writing.

How do you write the results of a complicated investigation? The general answer is, as simply as you can. One approach is to use a *hard lead*, displaying your key findings in the first few paragraphs. Another approach, often used, is to adopt one of the alternative story structures discussed in Chapter 17.

For three months, six Miami Herald reporters examined every aspect of two counties' failing school systems. Their findings ran in an eight-part series, which began by focusing on a single student:

At 17, Frank Smith seems more harried than a high school student ought to be.

Up at 6 a.m., due in class by 7, he endures five hours of lessons with less than 18 minutes for lunch. Building a romance, holding down a full-time job, he rushes from one responsibility to another in a car that is both his burden and his pride.

Frank Smith, an 11th grader at Miami Killian High, is typical of thousands of youngsters in today's public schools.

Shaken by his parents' divorce when he was 9, forced to fend for himself when his mother and step-father were busy at work, Frank turned out like so many other kids: sometimes mischievous, usually affable, rarely diligent, but always on the move.

Described by his teachers as an "average" student, Frank fits neatly into an educational system plagued by problems.

A big, complicated story is introduced in simple, human terms. Readers who might have been put off by the mass of evidence the reporters had assembled were instead lured in by the plight of one real person.

Instead of a single blockbuster story, the material was presented in a series of shorter, less-complex pieces. There were stories on incompetent teachers and principals, a story on the money shortage, another on the politics of school finance, stories on curriculum, one on bureaucracy and several sidebars on schools and individuals doing something right.

The Philadelphia Inquirer spent six months investigating the scandalous nursing home business in New Jersey. Here is the beginning of one of the resulting series of stories:

For most of her 98 years, Alberta Senior was an inconspicuous domestic worker who earned little money, never married and had only a few friends.

Her death on March 22 was equally anonymous. Her funeral and burial in a pauper's grave were paid for by the Monmouth County Welfare Department.

Only in the last few weeks of her life, when she was finally taken to a hospital from a boarding home, did Miss Senior attract the attention of some of the influential persons who had overlooked her, and others like her, for so long. By then, the plodding bureaucracy had proved itself incapable of acting swiftly enough to help this woman who had spent nearly a century in society's shadows.

The writing here is of a quality not matched in many stories. The combination of good writing with careful, extensive reporting produced a story that was read widely.

Writing an investigative story so that it will be read takes the same attention to organization and to detail as does any good writing. Here are a few tips that apply to all types of writing but especially to investigative stories:

1. *Get people into the story.* Any investigation worth doing involves people in some way. Make them come alive with descriptive detail, the kind we learned of in Frank Smith's and Alberta Senior's cases.

2. *Keep it simple.* Look for ways to clarify and explain complicated situations. When you have a mass of information, consider spreading it over more than one story—in a series or in a main story with a sidebar. Think about how charts, graphs or lists can be used to present key facts clearly. Don't try to print everything you know. Enough to support your conclusions is sufficient; more than that is too much.

3. *Tell the reader what your research means.* A great temptation in investigative reporting is to lay out the facts and let the reader draw the conclusions. That is unfair to you and your reader. Lay out the facts, of course, but tell the reader what they add up to. A reporter who had spent weeks investigating the deplorable conditions in his state's juvenile corrections facilities wrote this lead:

> Florida treats her delinquent children as if she hated them.

If the facts are there, drawing the obvious conclusions is not editorializing. It is good and helpful writing.

4. *Organize.* Careful organization is as important in writing the investigative story as in reporting it. The job will be easier if you have been organized all along. When you are ready to write, examine your notes again. Make an outline. Pick out your best quotes and anecdotes. Some reporters, if they are writing more than one story, separate their material into individual folders, one for each story. However you do it, know what you are going to say before you start to write.

5. *Suggest solutions.* Polls have shown that readers prefer investigative stories that show how to correct the problems described in the stories. Many of today's best newspapers are satisfying readers' demands by going beyond exposure in search of solutions. Are new laws needed? Better enforcement of present laws? More resources? Better training? Remember that the early 20th-century Progressive movement of which the original muckrakers were a part produced reforms, not just good stories.

Think of writing as the climax of a process that begins with a hypothesis, tests that hypothesis through careful investigation, checks and doublechecks every fact, and satisfies the concerns of newspaper editors and lawyers. Every step in that process is vital to the success of any investigative story.

# The Sources

Investigative reporters—like other reporters—get their information from people or documents. The perfect source would be a person who had the pertinent documents and was eager to tell you what those documents mean. Don't count on finding the perfect source. Instead, count on having to piece together the information you need from a variety of people and records—some of the people not at all eager to talk to you and some of the records difficult to understand. Let's consider human sources first.

## HUMAN SOURCES

Suppose you get a tip that the mayor received campaign contributions under the table from the engineering firm that just got a big city contract. Who might talk?

*Enemies.* A person's enemies usually are the best sources when you are trying to find out anything bad about him or her. More often than not, the enemies of a prominent person will have made it their business to find out as much as possible about that person's misdeeds and shortcomings. Frequently, they will share what they know with a friendly reporter.

*Friends.* Surprisingly, friends are sometimes nearly as revealing as enemies. In trying to explain and defend a friend's actions, they may tell you more than you knew before. Occasionally you may find that someone your target regards as a friend is not much of a friend after all.

*Losers.* Like enemies, losers often carry a grudge. Seek out the loser in the last election, the losing contender for the contract, the loser in a power struggle. Bad losers make good sources.

*Victims.* If you are investigating a failing school system, talk with its students and their parents. If your story is about nursing home abuses, talk with some patients and their relatives. The honest and hard-working employees caught in a corrupt or incompetent system are victims, too. They can give you specific examples and anecdotes. Their case histories can help you write the story.

*Experts.*    Early in many investigations, there will be a great deal you may not understand. You may need someone to explain how the campaign finance laws could be circumvented, someone to interpret a contract, or someone to decipher a set of bid specifications. Lawyers, accountants, engineers or professors can help you understand technical jargon or complicated transactions. If they refuse to comment on your specific case, fit the facts you have into a hypothetical situation.

*Police.*    Investigative reporters and law enforcement agents often work the same territory. If you are wise, you will make friends with carefully selected agents. They can—and frequently will—be of great help. Their files may not be gold mines, but they have investigative tools and contacts you lack. When they get to know and trust you, they will share. Most police like seeing their own and their organization's names in the paper. They know, too, that you can do some things they cannot. It takes less proof for you to be able to print that the mayor is a crook than it may take to convince a jury. Most police investigators want to corner wrongdoers any way they can. You can use that attitude to your advantage.

*People in Trouble.*    Police use this source and so can you, although you cannot promise immunity or a lesser charge, as the police can. A classic case is the Watergate affair. Once the Nixon administration started to come unraveled, officials trying to save their careers and images began falling all over each other to give their self-serving versions of events. People will react similarly in lesser cases.

## Managing Human Sources

As an investigative reporter, you cultivate sources in the same ways a reporter on a beat does. You just do it more quickly. One excellent tactic is to play on their self-interest. Losers and enemies want to get the so-and-so, and thus you have a common aim. (But don't go overboard. Your words could come back to haunt you.) Friends want their buddy's side of the story to be explained. So do you. If you keep in mind that, no matter how corrupt your target may be, he or she is still a human being, it may be easier to deal sympathetically with that person's friends. That attitude may help ensure that you treat the target fairly, as well.

Experts just want to explain the problem as you present it. And you just want to understand. People in trouble want sympathy and some assurance that they still merit respect. No reporter should have trouble conveying either attitude.

Another way to win and keep sources is to protect them. Occasionally, a reporter faces jail unless he or she reveals a source. Even jail is not too great a price to pay in order to keep a promise of confidentiality. More often, the threats to confidentiality are less dramatic. Other sources, or the target of the investigation, may casually ask, "Where'd you hear that?" Other reporters, over coffee or a beer, may ask the same question. Hold your tongue. The only person to whom a confidential source should ever be revealed is your editor.

Human sources pose problems as well as solving them. They may lie to you. To get at an enemy or protect a friend, to make themselves look better or someone else look worse—and sometimes just for fun—people lie to reporters. No reporter is safe and no source is above suspicion. They may use you, too, just as you are using them. The only reason most people involved on any side of a suspicious situation will talk about it is to enhance their own position. That is neither illegal nor immoral, but it can trip up a reporter who fails to take every self-serving statement with the appropriate grain of salt.

Sources may change their stories as well. People forget. Recollections and situations change. Pressures can be applied. Fear or love or ambition or greed can intrude. A source may deny tomorrow—or in court—what he or she told you today.

Finally, sources will seldom want to be identified. Even the enemies of a powerful person often are reluctant to see their names attached to their criticisms in print. So are friends. Experts, while willing to provide background information, often cite their codes of ethics when you ask them to go on the record. Police usually will cooperate fully only if you promise them anonymity—since they are not supposed to prosecute people in the newspaper. Stories without identifiable sources have less credibility with readers, with editors, even with colleagues.

## WRITTEN SOURCES

Fortunately, not all sources are human. Records and documents neither lie nor change their stories, they have no axes to grind at your expense and they can be identified in print. Many useful documents are public records, available to you or any other citizen on request. Others are non-public but still may be available through your human sources.

### Public Records

As Steve Woodward's work shows, a great deal can be learned about individuals and organizations through records that are available for the asking, if you know where to ask. Let's take a look at some of the most valuable public records and where they can be found.

*Property Records.*    Many investigations center on land—who owns it, who buys it, how it is zoned, how it is taxed. You can find out all that information and more from public records. Your county recorder's office (or its equivalent) has on file the ownership of every piece of land in the county as well as the history of past owners. Most such offices have their files cross-indexed so that you can find out the owner of the land if you know its location, or the location and size of the property if you know the owner. Those files also will tell you who holds a mortgage on the land. The city or county tax assessor's office has on file the assessed valuation of the land, the basis for property taxes. Either the assessor or the local zoning agency can tell you for what use the property is zoned. All requests for rezoning are public information, too.

*Corporation Records.*    Every corporation must file with the secretary of state a document showing the officers and principal agent of the company. The document must be filed with every state in which the company does business. The officers listed may be only "dummies," stand-ins for the real owners. Even if that is the case, you can find out at least who the stand-ins are. But that is only the beginning. Publicly held corporations must file annual reports with the Securities and Exchange Commission in Washington. The reports list officers, major stockholders, financial statements and any business dealing with other companies owned by the corporation. Non-profit corporations—such as foundations and charities—must file with the Internal Revenue Service an even more revealing statement, Form 990, showing how much money came in and where it went (see Figure 19.2). Similar statements must be filed with the attorneys general of many states. Corporations often are regulated by state or federal agencies as well. They file regular reports with the regulating agency. Insurance companies, for instance, are regulated by state insurance commissioners. Nursing homes are regulated by various state agencies. Broadcasters are overseen by the Federal Communications Commission, truckers by the Interstate Commerce Commission. Labor unions must file detailed statements showing assets, officers' salaries, loans and other financial information with the U.S. Department of Labor. Those statements are called "5500 Forms."

Once you have such corporation records, you must interpret them. Your public library has books that tell you how. Or your newspaper's own business experts may be willing to help.

*Court Records.*    Few people active in politics or business go through life without some involvement in court actions. Check the offices of the state and federal court clerks for records of lawsuits. The written arguments, sworn statements and answers to questions (interrogatories) may contain valuable

Form **990**

**Return of Organization Exempt From Income Tax**

Under section 501(c) of the Internal Revenue Code (except black lung benefit trust or private foundation) or section 4947(a)(1) charitable trust

Department of the Treasury
Internal Revenue Service

Note: You may have to use a copy of this return to satisfy state reporting requirements. See instruction E.

OMB No. 1545-0047

19**90**

For the calendar year 1990, or fiscal year beginning _____ , 1990, and ending _____ , 19 ___

| Use IRS label. Other-wise, please print or type. | Name of organization | **A** Employer identification number (see instruction S2) |
|---|---|---|
| | Number, street, and room (or P.O. box number) (see instruction S1.) | **B** State registration number (see instruction E) |
| | City or town, state, and ZIP code | **C** If application for exemption is pending, check here ▶ ............ ☐ |

**D** Check type of organization—Exempt under section ▶ ☐ 501(c) ( ) (insert number), OR ▶ ☐ section 4947(a)(1) charitable trust (see instruction C7 and question 92.)

**E** Accounting method: ☐ Cash ☐ Accrual ☐ Other (specify) ▶

**F** Is this a group return (see instruction Q) filed for affiliates? . . . . . ☐ Yes ☐ No
If "Yes," enter the number of affiliates for which this return is filed _____
Is this a separate return filed by a group affiliate? . . . . . . . ☐ Yes ☐ No

**G** If either answer in F is "Yes," enter four-digit group exemption number (GEN) ▶

**H** Check box if address changed ▶ ☐

**I** Check here ☐ if your gross receipts are normally not more than $25,000 (see instruction B11). You do not have to file a completed return with IRS; but if you received a Form 990 Package in the mail, you should file a return without financial data (see instruction A5). **Some states require a completed return.**

Note: *Form 990EZ may be used by organizations with gross receipts less than $100,000 **and** total assets less than $250,000 at end of year.*

**Section 501(c)(3) organizations and 4947(a)(1) trusts must also complete and attach Schedule A (Form 990). (See instruction C1.)**

**Part I**    **Statement of Revenue, Expenses, and Changes in Net Assets or Fund Balances**

| | | | |
|---|---|---|---|
| **Revenue** | **1** Contributions, gifts, grants, and similar amounts received: | | |
| | **a** Direct public support . . . . . . . . | **1a** | |
| | **b** Indirect public support . . . . . . . | **1b** | |
| | **c** Government grants . . . . . . . . | **1c** | |
| | **d** **Total** (add lines 1a through 1c) (attach schedule—see instructions) . . . . . . | **1d** | |
| | **2** Program service revenue (from Part VII, line 93) . . . . . . . . . | **2** | |
| | **3** Membership dues and assessments (see instructions) . . . . . . . . . | **3** | |
| | **4** Interest on savings and temporary cash investments . . . . . . . . | **4** | |
| | **5** Dividends and interest from securities . . . . . . . . . | **5** | |
| | **6a** Gross rents . . . . . . . . . | **6a** | |
| | **b** Less: rental expenses . . . . . . . | **6b** | |
| | **c** Net rental income or (loss) (line 6a less line 6b) . . . . . . . | **6c** | |
| | **7** Other investment income (describe ▶ ) | **7** | |
| | **8a** Gross amount from sale of assets other than inventory . . . . . . **(A)** Securities / **(B)** Other | **8a** | |
| | **b** Less: cost or other basis and sales expenses | **8b** | |
| | **c** Gain or (loss) (attach schedule) . . . . | **8c** | |
| | **d** Net gain or (loss) (combine line 8c, column (A) and line 8c, column (B)) . . . . . . | **8d** | |
| | **9** Special fundraising events and activities (attach schedule—see instructions): | | |
| | **a** Gross revenue (not including $_____ of contributions reported on line 1a) . . . . . . | **9a** | |
| | **b** Less: direct expenses . . . . . . | **9b** | |
| | **c** Net income (line 9a less line 9b) . . . . . . . | **9c** | |
| | **10a** Gross sales less returns and allowances . . . . . . | **10a** | |
| | **b** Less: cost of goods sold . . . . . . | **10b** | |
| | **c** Gross profit or (loss) (line 10a less line 10b) (attach schedule) . . . . . . | **10c** | |
| | **11** Other revenue (from Part VII, line 103) . . . . . . . . | **11** | |
| | **12** **Total revenue** (add lines 1d, 2, 3, 4, 5, 6c, 7, 8d, 9c, 10c, and 11) . . . . . | **12** | |
| **Expenses** | **13** Program services (from line 44, column (B)) (see instructions) . . . . . . | **13** | |
| | **14** Management and general (from line 44, column (C)) (see instructions) . . . . . . | **14** | |
| | **15** Fundraising (from line 44, column (D)) (see instructions) . . . . . . | **15** | |
| | **16** Payments to affiliates (attach schedule—see instructions) . . . . . . . | **16** | |
| | **17** **Total expenses** (add lines 16 and 44, column (A)). . . . . . . . | **17** | |
| **Net Assets** | **18** Excess or (deficit) for the year (subtract line 17 from line 12) . . . . . . | **18** | |
| | **19** Net assets or fund balances at beginning of year (from line 74, column (A)) . . . . | **19** | |
| | **20** Other changes in net assets or fund balances (attach explanation) . . . . | **20** | |
| | **21** Net assets or fund balances at end of year (combine lines 18, 19, and 20) . . . . . | **21** | |

For Paperwork Reduction Act Notice, see page 1 of the separate instructions.

Form **990** (1990)

**Figure 19.2    Copy of an IRS Form 990.**

details or provide leads to follow. Has your target been divorced? Legal struggles over assets can be revealing. Probate court files of your target's deceased associates may tell you something you need to know.

*Campaign and Conflict-of-Interest Reports.*    Federal—and most state—campaign laws now require political candidates to disclose, during and after each campaign, lists of who gave what to whom. Those filings can yield stories on who is supporting the candidates. They also can be used later for comparing who gets what from which officeholder. Many states require officeholders to file statements of their business and stock holdings. These can be checked for possible conflicts of interest or used as background for profile stories.

*Loan Records.*    Commercial lenders usually file statements showing property that has been used as security for loans. Known as Uniform Commercial Code filings, these can be found in the offices of state secretaries of state and, sometimes, in local recorder's offices.

*Minutes and Transcripts.*    Most elected and appointed governing bodies, ranging from local planning and zoning commissions to the U.S. Congress, are required by law to keep minutes or transcripts of their meetings.

## Using and Securing Public Records

The states and the federal government have laws designed to assure access to public records. Many of those laws—including the federal *Freedom of Information Act*, which was passed to improve access to government records—have gaping loopholes and time-consuming review procedures. Still, they have been and can be useful tools when all else fails. Learn the details of the law in your state. You can get information on access laws and their interpretations by contacting the Freedom of Information Center at the University of Missouri, Box 838, Columbia, Mo. 65205.

## Non-Public Records

Non-public records are more difficult, but often not impossible, to obtain. To get them, you must know that they exist, where they are and how to gain access. Finding out about those things requires good human sources. You should know about a few of the most valuable non-public records.

*Investigative Files.*    The investigative files of law enforcement agencies can be rich in information. You are likely to see them only if you have a good source in a particular agency, or one affiliated with it. If you do obtain

## ANALYZING SYSTEMS

In the past several years, a new and even more ambitious type of investigative reporting has begun to appear. Reporters are no longer content to expose a single miscarriage of justice; they want to examine how a state's parole system really works. Reporters no longer settle for tracking down a single source of air or water pollution; they explore the impact of the petrochemical industry on an entire region. Reporters no longer stop with revealing a crooked public official or an example of racial injustice; they unravel the bureaucracy or explain how a "reform" has failed.

This new analytical reporting invades what formerly was the sole province of the social scientist. It relies on the social scientist's tools—polling, systematic study of records, computer analysis of masses of data (see Chapter 18). Indeed, the keys to this important development are a broader vision of the role of journalism and the capacity of the computer.

The analysis of social systems is work for the best and the most experienced journalists. A few examples will illustrate both the possibilities and the complexities.

When a murderer released after less than half his prison term killed again, Michigan officials began a prison-building program and toughened sentencing. The Detroit Free Press began a computer analysis of the records of all 5,762 prisoners released during the year. The study showed that prison officials, pressured to relieve overcrowding and incompetent to maintain accurate records, were freeing hundreds of prisoners too soon, sometimes in actual violation of law.

The legislature reacted with its own investigation, the corrections department reversed hundreds of errors and some early-released convicts went back to prison.

Reporters David Ashenfelter and Michael Wagner and computer consultant Larry Kostecke—a key member of the team—then moved on to examine other breakdowns in one of society's most important systems.

They offered this advice: "Reporters contemplating such projects should begin by learning how to run a mainframe computer and a such files, treat them cautiously. They will be full of unsubstantiated allegations, rumor and misinformation. Be wary of accepting as fact anything you have not confirmed yourself.

***Past Arrests and Convictions.***   Records of past arrests and convictions increasingly are being removed from public scrutiny. Usually these are easier than investigative files to obtain from a friendly police or prosecuting official. And usually they are more trustworthy than raw investigative files.

***Bank Records.***   Bank records would be helpful in many investigations, but they are among the most difficult to get. Bankers are trained to keep secrets. The government agencies that regulate banks are secretive as well. A friend in a bank is an investigative reporter's friend indeed.

***Income Tax Records.***   Except for those made public by office-

sophisticated data-base program, if possible, with the assistance of a computer consultant.''

The Free Press, of course, is one of the nation's best and biggest newspapers. Analysis of systems, however, is not the province of only the best and biggest. The Baton Rouge (La.) Morning Advocate has just 12 city desk reporters. The paper decided to commit one-third of that staff for three months to explore an issue of special importance to oil-rich Louisiana—the impact on the state's environment of the massive petrochemical industry.

The 200 people interviewed included cancer researchers, biologists, chemical experts, state officials, environmentalists and chemical industry spokespersons. The team's requests for documents under the federal Freedom of Information Act set a record for the Environmental Protection Administration.

The pattern that emerged was one of lax law enforcement, of tax breaks to consistent polluters, of appalling official ignorance of environmental hazards. A 40-page tabloid report led to the start of groundwater testing, the passage of a state right-to-know law and improvement of the state's own ability to collect and analyze information.

Similarly, the Providence (R.I.) Journal used computer analysis of 30,000 property transactions to reveal a pattern of fraud in the state agency that was intended to help low-income people buy homes. The series led to state and federal grand jury investigations, 15 indictments, and an overhaul of the agency.

The Louisville (Ky.) Courier-Journal ran through its own computer 36 tapes of data pried loose by open-records laws to expose hypocrisy and failure in a desegregated school system that was far from truly integrated. Here, no criminality was suggested; but the breakdown in one of society's most vital systems could be even more serious.

The files of the Investigative Reporters and Editors contain other such projects. Beyond the specific value of each, they illustrate the development of a new stage in the American tradition of investigative reporting.

holders, income tax records are guarded carefully by their custodians, and properly so. Leaks are rare.

*Credit Checks.*    Sometimes you can get otherwise unavailable information on a target's financial situation by arranging through your newspaper's business office for a credit check. Credit reports may reveal outstanding debts, a big bank account, major assets and business affiliations. Use that information with care. It is unofficial, and the companies that provide it intend it to be confidential.

## Problems with Written Sources

Even when you can obtain them, records and other written sources present problems. They are usually dull. Records give you names and numbers, not anecdotes or sparkling quotes. They are bare bones, not flesh and blood. They can be misleading and confusing. Many highly skilled lawyers and accountants spend careers interpreting the kinds of records you may find yourself attacking without their training. Misinterpreting a document is no less serious an error than misquoting a person. And it's easier to do.

Documents usually describe without explaining. You need to know the "why" of a land transaction or a loan. Records tell you only the "what."

Most investigative reporters use both human and documentary sources. People can explain what records cannot. Documents prove what good quotes cannot. You need people to lead you to documents and people to interpret what the documents mean. And you need records to substantiate what people tell you. The best investigative stories combine both types of sources.

### Documents on Computer

Later in the chapter you will see how the computer revolution is making possible an important broadening of investigative reporting. But even in more traditional investigations the computer has become an important part of the reporter's life. For example, many government and business records today are stored on magnetic computer tape instead of paper. The question of access to such tapes is the new frontier of Freedom of Information Act enforcement. Once you gain access, you will discover that having the information in a computer makes possible analysis and comparisons that would be impossibly time-consuming otherwise. Computer analysis, however, requires skills that must be learned. In some cases, the information itself must be transferred from the storage tapes of agencies to the disks of reporters' smaller computers.

Help is available from the national organization Investigative Reporters and Editors, headquartered at the University of Missouri-Columbia. Both Missouri and Indiana University have launched training programs in computer-assisted reporting to teach journalists how to use this new tool.

# The Obstacles

You have seen now why investigative reporting is important and how it can be done. The picture would not be complete, though, without a brief look at the reasons why not every newspaper does investigative reporting. As a reporter you will face certain obstacles. You and your editors will have to overcome them if you are to do real investigative reporting. Good newspapers do overcome such obstacles.

The first obstacle is money. Investigative reporting is the most expensive kind of reporting. It takes time, and time is money. Steve Woodward spent months on his Frank Morgan story. Newsday's investigative team spent nine months on a series about heroin traffic. Two Miami Herald reporters spent most of their time for more than two years on an investigation of corruption in a federal housing program. Usually, the reporters doing investigations are the paper's best and highest-paid. Frequently, fees for experts are involved. Lawyers charge for looking over a story and much, much more if a suit is filed. Space to publish the results costs money, too.

The second obstacle is staffing. Most newspapers, large or small, are understaffed. When a reporter is devoting time to an investigation, somebody else must be found to fill the gap. Many editors are unable or unwilling to adjust for prolonged absences by a key reporter. You may be able to get around that obstacle by doing your investigating in bits and pieces, keeping up with routine assignments all the while. That kind of part-time probing requires a high level of dedication on your part and your editor's. Such commitment is hard to sustain over long stretches of time.

The third obstacle is a lack of courage. This is the great inhibitor. Investigative reporting *means* disturbing the status quo. It means poking into dark corners, asking hard questions about controversial, sensitive affairs. Investigative reporting upsets people. If you are looking into the right things, the people who get upset are likely to be important.

Violence or the threat of violence directed toward reporters and newspapers is rare. The 1975 murder of investigative reporter Don Bolles in Phoenix was shocking partly because such things hardly ever happen. But pressure, usually applied to your editor or publisher, is common enough. It takes courage to stand up to such pressure.

The Nixon administration threatened the lucrative television licenses of the Washington Post Co. during the Watergate investigation. The federal government sued The New York Times, Boston Globe and St. Louis Post-Dispatch to prevent publication of the Pentagon Papers. FBI and CIA agents investigated newspapers and harassed reporters during the era of Vietnam and Watergate. Those were dramatic cases. The papers involved were big and rich, and they resisted.

Other pressures are directly economic. A newspaper's survival can be threatened. The financially weak Miami News ran a series of stories on grocery pricing, and grocery chains—whose ads are the lifeblood of any paper—pulled out their advertising. The Philadelphia Inquirer, then also unprofitable, published exposés of police corruption. The spouses of police officers picketed the paper, and sympathetic unions of mailers and delivery workers refused to distribute the paper. The cost was in the hundreds of thousands of dollars.

More common and less visible are the social pressures and social influence of editors' and publishers' peers. It is common for the top executive of a newspaper to associate socially with the political and business leaders who may be the targets of investigative reporting. It is also common for the reporters who work for those executives to be pulled off such stories.

If you find yourself on a paper lacking money or staff, you can still find ways to do investigative reporting, at least part-time, if you want to badly enough. But if you find yourself on a paper lacking courage, you have only two choices—give up or leave.

Fortunately, investigative reporting is so important and its rewards are so substantial that more reporters than ever are finding the support to do it. You can, too.

# Suggested Readings

Downie, Leonard, Jr. ''The New Muckrakers.'' New York: New Republic Book Co., 1976. Personality sketches and descriptions of how some of the best contemporary investigative reporters work.

''The IRE Journal.'' Publication of Investigative Reporters and Editors Inc. Walter Williams Hall, University of Missouri, Columbia, Mo. 65205. Every issue has articles on investigations, guides to sources and documents, and a roundup of legal developments. Edited transcripts of IRE conferences also are available at the same address.

Rose, Louis J. ''How to Investigate Your Friends and Enemies.'' St. Louis: Albion Press, 1981. Very good on the nuts and bolts of investigating.

Ullmann, John and Colbert, Jan eds. ''The Reporters' Handbook,'' Second Edition. New York: St. Martin's Press, 1990. Tells you how to get and how to use the most important records and documents.

Weinberg, Steve. ''Trade Secrets of Washington Journalists.'' Washington, D.C.: Acropolis Press, 1981. Excellent guide to Washington sources, written and human.

Williams, Paul. ''Investigative Reporting and Editing.'' Englewood Cliffs, N.J.: Prentice-Hall, 1978. This classic in the field is good on both how and why to investigate.

## Exercises

1. School board member Doris Hart reported at last week's meeting of the board that major flaws, including basement flooding and electrical short circuits, have shown up in the new elementary school. She noted that this is the third straight project designed by consulting architect Louis Doolittle in which serious problems have turned up. School Superintendent Margaret Smith defended Doolittle vigorously. Later, Hart told you privately that she suspects Doolittle may be paying Smith off to keep the consulting contract, which has earned the architect more than $100,000 per year for the past five years. Describe how you will investigate:

   a. The sniff.

   b. Human sources. Who might talk? Where should you start? Who will you save for last?

   c. What records might help? Where are they? What will you be looking for?

   d. What is the most you can hope to prove? What is the least that will yield a story?

2. Choose a public official in your city or town and compile the most complete profile you can using only public records.

# PART SIX

## Broadcast News

# 20

# Writing News for Radio and Television

Earthquake!

The time was 5:04 p.m., Tuesday, Oct. 17, 1989. The place was San Francisco. People were expecting to watch an all-California World Series game. Instead, they stayed glued to their television sets to watch a different drama. Had the big one finally happened? What would the aftershocks bring? It was an event made for broadcasting.

Not many people first learned about the 1989 California earthquake from the newspapers. The broadcast media did what they do best: They made it possible for anxious people the world over to keep abreast of what was happening and what witnesses on the scene could say about it. Moreover, broadcasters were able to repeat what they had broadcast earlier for those who missed it the first time.

Of course, the broadcast media are not always present to record the news while it is happening. Much of the time broadcast journalists must write and report news after it has occurred.

Writing for broadcast news is a relatively new profession. Few people heard the first radio newscasts in 1920, and few watched the first news items broadcast over experimental television in the 1920s. Today large numbers of people say that television is their major source of news. Just how many say so depends on who is taking the survey, the newspaper industry or the television industry. The same is true regarding whether newspapers or television is the most credible news source.

We do know, however, that the number of daily newspapers in this country continues to decline while the number of radio and television stations continues to grow. Daily newspapers have decreased from 2,042 in 1920 to 1,626 in 1990. From 1980 to 1990, dailies have decreased by 119. Sixteen dailies died between 1989 and 1990. According to the 1989 Broadcast and Cable Yearbook, there are 4,932 AM radio stations, 5,529 FM radio stations and 1,395 television stations operating in the United States. That's an increase from 1979 to 1989 of 878 AM radio stations, 1,335 FM stations and 387 television stations.

Many, if not most, of these radio and television stations provide at least some news that is written for them by journalists working for the wire services or employed by the stations.

Selecting and writing news for television and radio is different from selecting and writing news for newspapers. The differences arise primarily from the technologies involved in print and in the electronic media. This chapter explores these differences and discusses news reporting and writing for the broadcast media.

### In this chapter you will learn:

1. How the selection of broadcast news differs from that of print news.

2. How to write broadcast news.

3. How to prepare broadcast copy.

# Criteria for Selecting Broadcast News

In Chapter 1, you learned the traditional criteria of news value: impact, proximity, timeliness, prominence, novelty and conflict. You also learned the criteria of journalism of the 1990s: relevance, usefulness and interest. All of these criteria apply to the selection of print and broadcast news. However, there are four criteria of broadcast news selection that distinguish it from print news. Broadcast newswriters emphasize:

1. Timeliness above all other news values.

2. Information more than explanation.

3. News that has audio or visual impact.

4. People more than concepts.

Let's consider each of these points.

## TIMELINESS

The broadcast newswriter emphasizes one criterion of news value—timeliness—more than the others. *When* something happens often determines whether a news item will be used in a newscast. The breaking story receives top priority.

Broadcast news "goes to press" many times a day. If an event is significant enough, regular programming can be interrupted. The broadcast media are the "now" media. This sense of immediacy influences everything in broadcast news, from what is reported to how it is reported. Even when televison and radio air documentaries or in-depth segments, they try to infuse a sense of urgency, a strong feeling of the present, an emphasis on what's happening now.

## INFORMATION

Timeliness often determines *why* a news item is broadcast; time, or lack of it, determines *how* it is reported. Because air time is so precious, broadcast news emphasizes the what and the where more than the why or the how. In other words, broadcasters are generally more concerned with information than with explanation. Most stories must be told in 20 to 30 seconds; rarely does a story run longer than two minutes. A minute of news read aloud is only 15 lines of copy, or about 150 words. After commercial time is subtracted, a half-hour newscast has only 22 minutes of news, which amounts to about one-half of a front page of a newspaper. Although broadcast newswriters may never assume that their audience knows anything about a story, they may often have to assume that listeners or viewers will turn to newspapers or to news magazines for further background and details.

## AUDIO OR VISUAL IMPACT

Another difference between broadcast and print news results from the technologies involved. Some news is selected for radio because a reporter has recorded an on-the-scene audio report. Some news is selected for television because it is visually appealing. For this reason news of accidents or of fires that may get attention only in the records column of the newspaper may get important play on a television newscast. If a television crew returns with good pictures of an event, that event may be part of the next newscast, regardless of its significance. Of course, this is not always the case.

## PEOPLE

Finally, an important difference between broadcast and print news selection is that broadcasting more often attempts to tell the news through people. Broadcasting follows the ''classic writing formula'' as described by Rudolf Flesch in ''The Art of Readable Writing'': Find a problem, find a person who is dealing with the problem and tell us how he or she is doing. Broadcast journalists look for a representative person or family, someone who is affected by the story or who is a chief player. Thus, rather than using abstract concepts with no sound or visuals, broadcasting humanizes the story.

# Writing Broadcast News

Good writing is good writing, and most of what you learned in Chapter 4 about writing applies also to broadcast news. However, the differences between broadcast news and print news affect how stories are written. Broadcast writing emphasizes certain characteristics that newspaper writing does not, and story structure may also vary.

## CHARACTERISTICS OF BROADCAST NEWSWRITING

Because of the emphasis on timeliness in the broadcast media, newswriters must emphasize immediacy, aim for a conversational style, and try to write very tightly and clearly. When preparing news copy for radio or television, you should do the same.

## Immediacy

Broadcasting achieves a sense of *immediacy* in part by avoiding the past tense and emphasizing the present tense as much as possible. Note the use of present tense verbs (*italicized*) in this Associated Press story:

South African President F.W. de Klerk *is taking* action that could clear the way for negotiations between the white-minority government and black leaders. *He's lifting* the state of emergency everywhere in the country except Natal (nuh-TAHL) province, where factional fighting has killed hundreds of blacks in recent months.

Anti-apartheid leader Nelson Mandela *calls* de Klerk's decision "a victory for the people." But *he's urging* Western nations to continue their economic sanctions against South Africa.

Notice, too, that the verb "is taking" is in the present tense, an accepted practice in broadcast writing. Of course, to be accurate, the past tense is sometimes necessary, as it is in the clause "where factional fighting *has killed* hundreds of blacks in recent months." If you must use the past tense, though, you should try whenever possible to use the present perfect tense because it points up immediacy. The present perfect tense also has the advantage of sounding natural and conversational.

Sometimes the sense of immediacy is underscored by adding the time element. You might say, "just minutes ago," or on a morning newscast, "this morning." If there is no danger of inaccuracy or of deceit, though, reference to time can be omitted. For example, if something happened yesterday, it may be reported today like this:

The latest of four strikes by East Coast longshoremen is over.

There is no need in this case to point out here that the strike ended the day before. But if the past tense is used in a lead, the time element should be included:

Negotiators for the trucking industry and the Teamsters union bargained in Washington until almost midnight last night, came "very close" on money issues and agreed to go back at it this morning.

The best way to avoid the past tense is to avoid yesterday's story. You can do that by bringing yesterday's story up to date. By leading with a new development or a new fact, you may be able to use the present tense. Broadcast writers need to be especially aware of the techniques of follow-up stories described in Chapter 13.

Remember, radio and television are "live." Your copy must convey that important characteristic.

## Conversational Style

"Write the way you talk" is questionable advice for most kinds of writing; however, with some exceptions, it is imperative for broadcast writing. "Read your copy aloud" is good advice for most kinds of writing; for broadcast writing, that's what it's all about.

*Conversational style* is simple and informal. The key is to remember that you are talking to people. Tell them what just happened. Tell them what you just saw or heard. Imagine yourself going up to a friend and saying, "Guess what I just heard!"

Write so that your copy *sounds* good. Use simple, short sentences, written with transitive verbs in the active voice. People rarely use verbs in the passive voice when they talk; it usually sounds cumbersome and awkward. You don't go around saying, "Guess what I was just told by somebody."

Because casual speech contains contractions, they belong in your broadcast copy, too. Conversational style also permits the use of occasional sentence fragments and of truncated sentences. Sentences are sometimes strung together loosely with dashes and sometimes begin with the conjunction "and" or "but," as in the following example:

There's a lot more talk about the Stars and Stripes than usual on this Flag Day. This year the day is being marked in the midst of a political furor over flag burning—and a proposed constitutional amendment to outlaw it.

President Bush stopped at the Vietnam Veterans Memorial this morning for a flag-raising. Bush, who's been taking every opportunity to speak out in favor of the amendment, said nothing at the ceremony. But a White House aide said the flag raised at the memorial was a gift from Bush—the flag that flew over the White House last night.

Writing in conversational style does not mean that you may use slang or colloquialism or incorrect grammar. Nor does it mean that you can use vulgar or off-color expressions. Remember that your audience is composed of people of all ages and sensitivities. The broadcast media have been given credit for raising the level of properly spoken English. Make your contribution.

## Tight Phrasing

Although actual conversational English tends to be wordy, you must learn to write in a conversational style without being wordy. That means you must condense. Cut down on adjectives and adverbs. Eliminate the passive voice. Use strong active verbs. Make every word count. Use tight phrasing.

Keeping it short means selecting facts carefully because often you don't have time for the whole story. AP broadcast newswriter Ed Golden says that what AP's member broadcasters want most is good, tight writing that is easy to follow. Let's look at how a wire story written for newspapers can be condensed for broadcasting. Here's the AP newspaper story:

WASHINGTON—Police seeking to curb drunken driving do not violate motorists' privacy rights by stopping them at sobriety checkpoints, the Supreme Court ruled Thursday.

The 6-3 decision upheld Michigan's checkpoint program and, by extension, similar operations in most states.

"The balance of the state's interest in preventing drunken driving . . . and the degree of intrusion upon individual motorists who are briefly stopped weighs in favor of the state program," Chief Justice William H. Rehnquist wrote in the majority decision.

The three dissenters said the decision sacrificed individual liberty in favor of a police tactic that might not make any difference in the fight against drunken driving.

The story then briefly summarizes three other decisions of the court and returns to the decision regarding checkpoints for seven more paragraphs. The story notes how each of the justices voted on the issue and gives some background to help readers understand the effects of the decision. "Traditionally," the story says, "police identified suspected drunken drivers by observing traffic. Recently states began experimenting with other detection methods."

Now note how the same story appeared on AP broadcast wire:

The Supreme Court is giving police a boost in the effort to catch drunken drivers. The justices approved the use of sobriety checkpoints in Michigan, saying the tactic is not a violation of privacy rights. Many other states also allow police to set up roadblocks to check drivers for signs of intoxication. Chief Justice William Rehnquist says the intrusion on motorists is minor— especially in comparison to the threat posed by drunken driving.

The story then summarizes one other decision of the Supreme Court.

In the broadcast version, listeners or viewers are given the bare facts. They must turn to their newspapers for the details. Researchers have found that those who watch television news generally spend more time reading their newspaper. They may be reading, in part, to get the background.

Golden gives two other tips for turning newspaper copy into broadcast copy. First, if the newspaper story is complicated, break it down into separate stories. Second, read the newspaper version to the end before beginning to write the broadcast version. Often, he says, the best angle for the broadcast story is at the bottom of the newspaper story.

In broadcast news, tight writing is important even when there is more time. Broadcast writers waste no words, even in *documentaries*, which provide in-depth coverage of events. Here's how the famous CBS correspondent Edward R. Murrow introduced the well-known documentary on the state of migrant workers in this country:

> This is an American story that begins in Florida and ends in New Jersey and New York State with the harvest. It is a 1960 "Grapes of Wrath" that begins at the Mexican border in California and ends in Oregon and Washington. It is the story of men and women and children who work 136 days of the year and average 900 dollars a year. They travel in buses. They ride trucks. They follow the sun.

Murrow's writing style consists of simple, declarative sentences, written in the present tense, tightly, carefully, dramatically. It is casual and conversational; most of the words have one or two syllables. It is simple but not oversimplified. It is vivid and clear.

## Clarity

Unlike newspaper readers, broadcast news viewers and listeners can't go back over the copy. They see or hear it only once, and their attention waxes and wanes. So, you must try harder to be *clear* and *precise*. All of the emphasis on condensing and writing tightly is useless if the message is not understood. Better not to report at all than to fill air time with messages that have no meaning.

Clarity demands that you write simply, in short sentences filled with nickel-and-dime words. Don't look for synonyms. Don't be afraid to repeat words or phrases. Oral communication needs reinforcement. Avoid foreign words and phrases; do not use Latin words (*sine qua non*) or Latinisms (*somnambulist*) for "sleepwalker"). Avoid phrases like "the former" and "the latter." Repeat the proper names in the story rather than using pronouns. The listener can easily forget the name of the person to whom the pronoun refers.

When you are tempted to write a dependent clause in a sentence, make it an independent clause instead. Keep the subject close to the verb. Close the gap between the doer and the activity. Look at this news item:

> A man flagged down a Highway Patrol officer near Braden, Tennessee, today and told him a convict was hiding in his house. The prisoner, one of five who escaped from the Fort Pillow Prison on Saturday, surrendered peacefully.

The second sentence contains 12 words between the subject, "prisoner," and the verb, "surrendered." By the time the broadcaster reaches the verb, many listeners will have forgotten what the subject was. The story is easier to understand this way:

> A man flagged down a Highway Patrol officer near Braden, Tennessee, today and told him a convict was hiding in his house. The prisoner surrendered peacefully. He's one of five who escaped from the Fort Pillow Prison on Saturday.

The third sentence is still a complex sentence, but it is easily understood. The complex sentence is often just that—complex—only more so in oral communication.

Clarity also requires that you resist a clever turn of phrase. Although viewers and listeners probably are intelligent enough to understand it, they simply will not have the time. A good figure of speech takes time to savor. If listeners pause to savor it (presuming they grasped it in the first place), they will not hear what follows. Clever columnists often fail as radio commentators. Too often the listener asks, "What was that?"

Of course, there are exceptions. The twist of a truism may convey a point with clarity and impact. In documentaries or commentaries the writer has more license. Even a literary allusion may be illuminating, as it was when Eric Sevareid concluded his remarks about the nation's farewell to Martin Luther King Jr.:

> So the label on his life must not be a long day's journey into night. It must be a long night's journey into day.

Generally, though, literary speech is undesirable in broadcast news. Even more dangerous than figures of speech are numerical figures. Don't barrage the listener or viewer with a series of numbers. If you must use statistics, break them down so that they are understandable. It is better to say, for example, that one of every four Americans smokes than to say there are 54 million smokers in the United States. You may have to say how many billion dollars a federal program will cost, but you will help listeners understand if you say that it will cost the average wage earner $73 for each of the next five years.

Remember that you are writing for the benefit of your viewers and listeners. You serve them best by emphasizing immediacy and by writing conversationally, tightly and clearly.

## STORY STRUCTURE

Now that you know the characteristics of broadcast writing, let's examine the story structure. Writers must craft broadcast leads somewhat differently from print leads. They must also construct special introductions and conclusions to filmed or recorded segments and synchronize their words with taped segments.

### Writing the Broadcast Lead

Both newspaper and broadcast reporters must attract the attention of their audience. Much of what you learned in Chapter 17 applies to broadcast leads. However, people tend to do things when listening to radio or watching television, so when you write for broadcasting you strive to attract their attention in different ways.

One way to do this is by preparing your audience for what is to come. You cue the listeners to make sure they are tuned in. In effect, you are saying, "Now listen to this." You introduce the story with a general statement, something that will pique the interest of the audience, and then go to the specific. For example:

| | |
|---|---|
| *General Statement* | Things are far from settled for Springfield's teacher strike. |
| *Specifics* | School officials and union representatives reached no agreement yesterday. They will not meet again for at least a week. |

Sometimes the lead, or setup, will be a simple phrase:

| | |
|---|---|
| *Setup* | Injuries and heavy wind damage in Braddyville, Iowa. |
| *Specifics* | A tornado swept through the farming village of Braddyville, Iowa, this evening. And authorities report at least half the town was leveled. They say four persons required hospitalization. |

Sometimes the opening sentence will cover a number of news items:

There were several accidents in the Springfield vicinity today.

"Cuing in" is only one method of opening a broadcast story. Other leads go immediately into the what and the who, the where and the when. In broadcast news the what is most important, followed by who did the what. The time and the place may be included in the lead, but seldom is the why or the how. If time permits, the why and the how may come later in the story, but often they are omitted.

The first words of the leads are most important. Don't keep the listener guessing as to what the story is about. Don't begin with a dependent clause as in this example:

> Despite continued objections from Governor Carlin, a second state spending-limit bill is scheduled for final Senate action today.

The opening words are meaningless without what comes later. The listener may not know what you are talking about. A better way to introduce this story is:

> The senate will vote today on whether to limit state spending -- despite continued objections from Governor Carlin.

As you do in a lead for a newspaper story, be sure to "tee up," or identify, an unfamiliar name. By introducing a person, you prepare listeners for the name that they otherwise may miss. Do it this way:

> Veteran Kansas City, Kansas, businessman and civic leader Ivar Larson died yesterday in a nursing home at age 83.

Don't mislead. The opening words must set the proper tone and mood for the story. Attract attention; tease a little. Answer questions, but don't ask them. Question leads are for commercials. Lead the listener into your story.

### Writing Lead-ins and Wrap-ups

Broadcast journalists must learn how to write a different kind of lead, called the *lead-in*, that introduces a filmed or recorded excerpt from a news source or from another reporter. The functions of a lead-in are to set the scene by briefly telling the where, the when and sometimes the what, and to identify the source or reporter. The lead-in should contain something substantive. Here's an example:

The word from the NATO foreign ministers meeting in Scotland is that the Soviets are relaxing their stance on German reunification, Bob Smith reports.

Lead-ins should generate interest. Sometimes several sentences are used to provide background, as in the following:

We'll all be getting the official word this morning on how much less our dollars bought last month. The consumer price index for March is expected to show another sharp rise in retail prices. The rate of inflation was one percent in January and one-point-two percent in February. Here's more on our inflation woes from Bill McKinney.

Be careful not to include in the lead-in what is in the story. Just as a headline should not be stolen word for word from a lead of a newspaper story, the lead-in should not use the opening words of the correspondent. The writer must know the contents of the taped report in order to write a proper lead-in.

After the recorded report, you may want to wrap up the story before going on to the next item. This is especially important in radio copy because there are no visuals to identify the person just heard. If the story reported by Evelyn Turner was about a meeting to settle a strike, you might wrap up her report by adding information:

Turner reports negotiations will resume tomorrow.

A wrap-up such as this gives your story an ending and clearly separates it from the next story.

## Writing for Videotape

Writing for a videotaped report really begins with the selection of the subject and how it is to be videotaped. The writing continues through the editing and selection process. And always, it is done with the pictures clearly in mind.

Words and pictures must be complementary, never interfering with each other. Neither should the words and pictures ignore each other. Your first responsibility is to relate the words to the pictures. If you do not, viewers will not get the message because they will be spending their time wondering what the pictures are about.

You can, however, stick too closely to the pictures by pointing out the obvious in a blow-by-blow account. You need to avoid both extremes and use what Russ Bensley, formerly of CBS News, calls the ''hit-and-run'' technique.

This means that at the beginning of a scene or when a scene changes you must tell the viewer where you are or what is happening. Once you are into the scene, the script may be more general and less closely tied to the pictures. For example, if the report concerns the continuation of a steel strike and the opening scene shows picketers outside the plant, you can explain the film by saying:

> Union members are still picketing Inland Steel today as the steel strike enters its third week.

Viewers now know two things that are not obvious in the film: who is picketing and where. If the film switches to people sitting around a table negotiating, you must again set the scene for viewers:

> Meanwhile, company officials and union leaders are continuing their meetings -- apparently without success.

Once you have related the words to the pictures, you may go on to tell other details of the strike. You are expected to provide information not contained in the pictures themselves. In other words, you must not only comment on the film but complete it as well. Part of completing it is to give the report a wrap-up or a strong ending. Don't be cute and don't be obvious, but give the story an ending. Here's one possible ending for the steel strike story:

> Experts agree on one sure result of the strike -- steel prices will rise again.

Now that you have learned some principles of writing broadcast news, you must learn how to prepare the copy.

# Preparing Broadcast Copy

Preparing copy to be read by a newscaster is different from preparing it for a typesetter. Your goals are to make the copy easy for the newscaster to read and easy for the audience to understand. What follows will help you accomplish those two goals.

```
west broadway

12-30

1-11-92

flanagan



        Members of Citizens for the Preservation of West Broadway

plan to gear up their petition drive again this weekend.  The group

began circulating petitions last weekend.

        The petitions request the City Council to repeal all previous

ordinances and resolutions on the widening.  Many residents of the

West Broadway area complain that the proposed widening project will

damage its residential nature.

        Petition-drive coordinator Vera Hanson says the group is pleased

with the show of support from residents all over Springfield . . .

but it won't know exactly how many signatures it has until next week.
```

**Figure 20.1
Sample of Radio
Copy.**

**Key for Figure 20.1**
"west broadway" is the slug for the story.
"12-30" is the time of the newscast.
"1-11-92" is the date of the broadcast.
"flanagan" is the name of the reporter.

*Format.*    Most broadcast news editors want triple-spaced copy. Leave two to three inches on the top of the page and one to two inches on the bottom.

For radio copy, set your typewriter so that you have 70 characters to a line (see Figure 20.1). Each line will average about 10 words, and the newscaster will average 15 lines per minute. Most stations require you to start each story on a separate piece of paper. That way, the order of the stories can be rearranged, or stories can be added or dropped easily. If a story goes more than one page, write "MORE" in parentheses at the bottom of the page.

```
six              6-17            art                jorgenson


MOC: JORGENSON              A lesson in art and architecture paid

                           off for some Buchanan High School students

SOT    :27                 today.  Ribbons were the prizes for winning
NAT SND UNDER
VOICE OVER
                           entries in a sketch exhibit of scenery and
SUPER: BUCHANAN HIGH SCHOOL
       :00-:05             buildings in the capital city area.

                               The Springfield art club sponsored the

                           show and called in Springfield College art

                           professor Bill Ruess to judge the artwork.

                               Ruess says he was impressed by the

                           students' skills, especially those who tried

                           their hand at the different art media for

                           the first time.
```

**Figure 20.2
Sample of
Television Copy.**

**Key for Figure 20.2**
"six" is the time of the newscast.
"6-17" is the day of the broadcast.
"art" is the slug for the story.
"jorgenson" is the name of the reporter.

"MOC:" means the person is live on camera with audio from his or her microphone.
"SOT:27" means there is sound on the tape lasting 27 seconds.
"NAT SND UNDER" means the tape sound should be kept at a low level.
"VOICE OVER" means the voice is from the anchor person in the studio speaking over the tape
     that is being shown.
"SUPER: BUCHANAN HIGH SCHOOL" indicates the title that should be shown over the tape.
":00-:05" indicates that the title should be shown five seconds after the report of this news item
     begins.

Television copy is written on the right half of the page in a 40-character
line (see Figure 20.2). Each line will average about six words, and the newscaster will average about 25 lines per minute. The left side of the copy is used
for audio or video information. This information, which is not to be read by
the newscaster, is usually typed in all caps. The copy that is read generally
appears upper- and lowercase. In television copy the stories are numbered,

and each story is on a separate page. If a story goes more than one page, write ''MORE'' in parentheses at the bottom of the page.

Do not hyphenate words, and be sure to end a page with a complete sentence or, if possible, with a complete paragraph. If the next page should be missing in the middle of a broadcast, the newscaster can end, at least, with a complete sentence or paragraph.

At many stations copy is prepared for a *videoprompter*, a mechanical or electronic device that projects the copy next to the lens so the newscaster can read it while appearing to look straight into the lens. Copy for the video-prompter is often typed down a column in the middle of the page.

Date the first page of your script, and type your last name in the upper left-hand corner of every page. Stations vary regarding these directions. The local news director determines the slug for a story and its placement. Some directors insist that the slug contain the time of the broadcast. If a story continues to a second page, write under the slug ''first add'' or ''second add,'' or ''page 2,'' ''page 3,'' and so forth.

***Names and Titles.***    In broadcast style, unlike that followed by news-papers, well-known names, even on first reference, are not given in full. You may say Senator Kerrey of Nebraska or Governor Gregg of New Hampshire. Middle initials should not be used unless they are a natural part of someone's name (Joe E. Brown) or unless they are necessary to distinguish two people with the same first and last names.

Titles should always precede names so that listeners are better prepared to hear the name. When you use titles, the first name and middle initial may be omitted. for example, broadcasters would say Vice President Quayle and Secretary of State Baker. Newspapers write out names like Elmer J. ''Lucky'' Cantrell. In broadcast, use either the first name or the nickname, but not both.

***Pronunciation.***    The writer's job is to help the newscaster pronounce the names of people and places correctly. To do this, you should write out difficult names phonetically in parentheses. NBC, for example, has its own reference list, and many individual stations have handbooks of their own. You may have to look up difficult names in unabridged dictionaries. If you don't find the name there, use your telephone. Call the person's office, or the consulate or embassy. If the name is of a U.S. town, try calling an operator in that town. There is no rhyme or reason to the way some people pronounce their names or to the way some names of places are pronounced. Never assume. Never try to figure it out. Find out. Here's an example of how you should write out difficult names:

The ethnic violence in the Soviet republic of Kirghizia (kihr-GEE-zhuh) is spilling over into the neighboring republic of Uzbekistan (ozz-behk-ih-STAN).

Perhaps everyone knows how to pronounce Lima, Peru, but not every-one can pronounce Lima (LIGH-mah), Ohio. You must note the difference between NEW-erk, N.J., and new-ARK, Del., both spelled Newark. And who would guess that Pago Pago is pronounced PAHNG-oh PAHNG-oh?

*Abbreviations.*   Generally, you should *not* use abbreviations in broadcast copy. It is easier to read a word written out than to read its abbreviation. Do not abbreviate the names of states, countries, months, days of the week or military titles. There are exceptions, and when you use them, use hyphens instead of periods because the final period in the abbreviation may be misread as the end of a sentence.

You may abbreviate U-S when used as an adjective, and the U-S-S-R; Dr., Mr., Mrs. and Ms.; a.m. and p.m. If initials are well known—U-N, G-O-P, F-B-I—you may use them. Hyphens are not used for acronyms such as NATO and HUD that are pronounced as one word.

*Symbols and Numbers.*   Do *not* use symbols in broadcast copy because a newscaster can read a word more easily than he or she can remember a symbol. Such symbols as the dollar sign ($) and the percent sign (%) are never used. Don't even use the abbreviation for number (no.).

Numbers can be a problem for both the announcer and the listener. As in newspaper style, write out numbers one through nine. But write out eleven, too, because 11 might not be easily recognized as a number. Use figures for 10, and from 12 to 999. The eye can easily take in a three-digit number, but write out the words thousand, million and billion. Hence, 3,800,000 becomes three million, 800 thousand. Write out fractions (two-and-a-half million dollars) and decimal points (three-point-two percent).

Some stations have exceptions. Figures often are used when giving the time (3:20 a.m.), sports scores and statistics (The score was 5 to 2), market reports (The Dow Jones industrial index was up 2-point-8 points) and addresses (30-0-2 Grand Street). In common speech no one would give an address as three thousand two.

Ordinarily, you may round off big numbers. Thus 48-point-3 percent should be written "nearly half." But don't say "more than one hundred" if 104 people died in an earthquake.

Use st, nd, rd, and th after dates: August 1st, September 2nd, October 3rd and November 4th. Make the year easy to pronounce: June 9th, 19-73.

*Quotations and Attributions.*   Most broadcast newswriters rarely use quotation marks. Because it is difficult and awkward to indicate to listeners which words are being quoted, use indirect quotes or a paraphrase instead.

If it is important that listeners know the exact words of a quotation (as when the quoted words are startling, uncomplimentary or possibly libelous), the quote may be introduced by saying "in his own words," "with these words," "what she called," or "he put it this way." Most writers prefer to avoid the formal "quote" and "unquote," though "quote" is used more than "unquote." Note the following example:

In Smith's words, quote, ''There is no way to undo the harm done.''

If you must use a direct quotation, the attribution always should precede the quotation. Because listeners cannot see the quotation marks, they would have no way of knowing the words are a direct quote. If by chance the words were recognized as a quote, listeners would have no idea who is saying them. For the same reason, the attribution must always precede the indirect quote.

And if you must use a direct quotation, keep it short. If the quote is long and it is important to use it, you should use a tape of the person saying it. However, if you are compelled to use a quote of more than a sentence in your copy, break it up with phrases like, ''Smith went on to say'' or ''and still quoting the senator.''

Punctuation.    In broadcast copy, less punctuation is good punctuation. The one exception is the comma. Commas help the newscaster pause at appropriate places. Use commas, for example, after introductory phrases referring to time and place, as in the following:

In Paris, three Americans on holiday met their death today when their car overturned and caught fire.

Last August, beef prices had reached an all-time high.

Sometimes three periods are used in place of the comma. Periods also take the place of the parenthesis and of the semicolon. They indicate a pause and are more easily visible. The same is true of the dash—typed as two hyphens. Note the dash in the following example:

Government sources say a study due out today will show that the number of teen-agers who smoke is decreasing -- for the first time since 1968.

The only punctuation marks you need are the period, comma, question mark, dash, hyphen and, rarely, quotation marks. To make the words easier to read, use the hyphen in some words, even when the dictionary does not use it: anti-discrimination, co-equal, non-aggression.

Correcting Copy.    When preparing broadcast copy, do *not* use the copy-editing marks you learned for editing newspaper copy. If a word has an error in it, cross out the word and write the corrected word above it.

Note this sentence with newspaper copy editing:

The Stag Brewery at Beleville, (illinois), soon will be (ph)pased out of operation, and it's workers already are looking for new jobs.

Here's how you correct it for broadcasting:

The Stag Brewery at ~~Beleville, illinois~~ *Beleville, Illinois*, soon will be ~~hpased~~ *phased* out of operation, and ~~its~~ *its* 230 workers already are ~~lo oking~~ *looking* for new ~~jobs~~ *jobs*.

Again, your function is to make the copy easier to read. Avoid making the newscaster go up and down to find the right words, as in the following:

The ~~pirce~~ *price* of ~~glod~~ *gold* in ~~london~~ *London* at the afternoon fixing was 240 dollars.

Better to correct it this way:

The ~~pirce of glod in london~~ *price of gold in London* at the afternoon fixing was 240 dollars.

And, of course, always make your corrections neatly and clearly. Stations may vary in their writing style and in the preparation of copy. But if you learn what is presented here, you will be well-prepared. Differences will be small, and you will adapt to them easily.

# Suggested Readings

Bliss, Edward, Jr. and Patterson, John M. ''Writing News for Broadcast,'' Second Edition. New York: Columbia University Press, 1978. A classic writing text that excels in good writing.

Block, Melvin. ''Writing Broadcast News—Shorter, Sharper, Stronger.'' Chicago: Bonus Books, 1987. An excellent book by a former network newswriter.

Flesch, Rudolf. ''The Art of Readable Writing.'' New York: Macmillan, 1986. This book explains the famous Flesch formula for assessing readability.

Stephens, Mitchell. ''Broadcast News,'' Second Edition. New York: Holt, Rinehart and Winston, 1986. Covers all aspects of broadcast writing and the business of broadcast news.

White, Ted, Meppen, Adrian J. and Young, Steve. ''Broadcast News Writing, Reporting, and Production.'' New York: Macmillan, 1984. The best book on all aspects of broadcast newswriting.

# Exercises

1. Watch a local evening television newscast. Make a simple list of the news stories. Then try to find those stories in the next morning's local newspaper and compare the coverage.

2. Check to see if the following AP stories written for broadcast follow acceptable broadcast style. Are they technically correct? Do they emphasize immediacy? Change the copy where you think necessary.

   a. Residents throughout areas of the midwest are getting no break from floodwaters that have chased thousands of people from their homes. Rising water has forced as many as 35 thousand people out of their homes—and thousands more may yet have to evacuate. The floods have caused millions of dollars in damage in eight states in the nation's midsection. At least eight deaths are blamed on the floods.

   b. A Senate vote at this hour could decide the fate of a major crime bill. Lawmakers are deciding whether to limit debate on the measure that includes controversial restrictions on semi-automatic weapons. It also includes nearly 250 amendments—and Majority Leader George Mitchell warns the Senate might never get to take action on the bill unless members limit debate to 30 hours.

   c. There's not much left of Limon (LY-muhn), Colorado's central business district except heaps of rubble. A tornado tore through the town southeast of Denver overnight. Officials report about three-quarters of the buildings in the business district were destroyed and a dozen people were hurt.

   d. This just hasn't been Donald Trump's week. Reports and jokes about the real estate mogul's financial problems have been flying for days. Now a fire has damaged one wing of his 118-room mansion in Palm Beach, Fla. The fire chief says it heavily damaged a bedroom and bathroom this morning. There's no word on the cause.

3. Rewrite the following AP newspaper briefs in broadcast writing style. Assume the news is current and that you have time for one paragraph of four or five lines for each story.

   a. BEIJING—China freed 97 pro-democracy protesters, including two student leaders, after the anniversary of the June 4 army attack on last year's demonstrations passed without major unrest, officials said Wednesday.

      The releases bring to 881 the number freed in the past six months, out of thousands arrested.

But new arrests have been reported as recently as last week, and the releases did not signal a softening by the aging leadership.

The leaders still maintain that last spring's massive protests for democratic reform and an end to corruption were part of a coup attempt, and that Western-style democracy is inappropriate for China.

b. JOHANNESBURG, South Africa—President F.W. de Klerk is likely to lift the 4-year-old state of emergency on Thursday, according to a report by the independent South African Press Association.

The news agency said de Klerk was expected to announce his plans when he addresses Parliament in Cape Town on Thursday. If de Klerk ends the emergency, it would remove a major obstacle to black-white negotiations on a new constitution. De Klerk says he wants the document to allow the country's 28 million blacks to share power with the 5 million whites.

Presidential spokesman Kobie Pieterse said the report was pure speculation.

c. KOBLENZ, West Germany—A former U.S. soldier was convicted of treason and sentenced to life in prison Wednesday after a court found that he had passed on classified secrets to the East bloc for more than a decade.

The case of former Army Sgt. 1st Class Clyde Conrad, described by a judge as "ice-cold and unscrupulous," marked the first time a foreign resident living in West Germany had been tried for espionage.

The court found Conrad, 43, a native of Sebring, Ohio, guilty of providing classified material to the Hungarian and Czechoslovak secret services from 1975 through 1985, and estimated he received $1.2 million for his efforts.

4. Read the news in a current newspaper. Then write a five-minute newscast of the story. Pay special attention to lead-ins and wrap-ups. (Do not include sports material in your broadcast.)

# PART SEVEN

# Rights and Responsibilities

# 21

# Press Law

**"I**f you write that, I'll sue."

That threat can be intimidating to the young reporter who hears it for the first time. Those with a bit more experience will have encountered the situation many times. In either case, such a threat should not be taken lightly. It is at least possible that the person making it is both serious about the threat and accurate in insisting that your information is incorrect. If you are wrong, both you and your newspaper could suffer.

Reporters who know their stories are accurate are never intimidated by such threats. If what you write is true, and you can prove it, you have little to fear when threats of lawsuits are tossed about. The laws that pertain to libel, invasion of privacy and protection of sources are among the many you should know about. In an era when people increasingly turn to the courts to solve their problems, it makes sense to have an understanding of your rights as a journalist to gather and write the news. In recent years, the courts have chipped away at those rights in instances ranging from investigating prisons to covering divorce actions.

In one particularly threatening case that almost resulted in the closing of the Alton (Ill.) Telegraph, the libel judgment was for $9.2 million. The case ended in bankruptcy court, where the award was reduced to $2.1 million, still a major loss. Despite those setbacks, the press has ample opportunity to report the news as long as those reports are fair and accurate. It is important that you learn the essentials of libel and privacy and understand the basics of contempt of court.

## In this chapter you will learn:

1. What rights you have as a journalist and the source of those rights.

2. How to spot potentially libelous situations and what to do about them.

3. When you might be invading someone's privacy.

4. What kinds of problems you may face in protecting confidential sources.

5. What rights you have in obtaining access to courtrooms and court documents.

6. What you should know about copyrights and fair use.

# Your Rights

The Constitution signed in Philadelphia in 1787 did not contain explicit protections of freedom of speech and of the press. Those protections were added two years later in the First Amendment, which states:

> Congress shall make no law respecting an establishment of religion, or prohibiting the free exercise thereof; or abridging the freedom of speech, or of the press; or the right of the people peaceably to assemble, and to petition the Government for a redress of grievances.

Read that again: "Congress shall make no law . . . abridging the freedom of . . . the press." No other business in the United States enjoys that specific constitutional protection.

Why should there be such protection for the press? The Supreme Court gave an eloquent answer to that question in a 1957 obscenity decision. The press is protected, the court ruled, to assure the "unfettered interchange of ideas for bringing about the political and social changes desired by the people."

The free flow of ideas is necessary in a democracy because people who govern themselves need to know about their government and those who run it, as well as about the social and economic institutions that greatly affect their day-to-day lives. Most people get that information through newspapers, radio and television.

In 1966 Congress passed the *Freedom of Information Act* to assist anyone in finding out what is happening in our federal agencies. This act, which was amended in 1974 to improve access to government records, makes it easier for you to know about government business. All 50 states have similar *open-records laws*. Though of great assistance to the press, the laws also are used by individuals and businesses to gain information previously kept secret by the government. There are other laws assuring access to government transactions. The federal government and all the states have *open-meetings laws*—often called *sunshine laws*—requiring that the public's business be conducted in public.

The First Amendment, the Freedom of Information Act and sunshine laws demonstrate America's basic concern for citizen access to information needed for the "unfettered interchange of ideas." However, there are laws that reduce the scope of freedom of the press.

# Libel

Traditionally, most of the laws limiting the absolute principle of freedom of the press have dealt with *libel*. These laws result from the desire of legislatures and courts to help individuals protect their reputations. This was explained by U.S. Supreme Court Justice Potter Stewart in a libel case:

> The right of a man to the protection of his own reputation from unjustified invasion and wrongful hurt reflects no more than our basic concept of the essential dignity and worth of every human being—a concept at the root of any decent system of ordered liberty.

Protection for reputations dates back centuries. In 17th-century England individuals were imprisoned for making libelous statements. One objective was to prevent criticism of the government. Another was to maintain the peace by avoiding duels. Duels are rare today, and government is freely criticized, but the desire to protect an individual's reputation is just as strong.

Two cases concerning generals, government and reputations are of special interest to journalists and help in understanding libel. These extensively covered trials were held in the winter of 1984–1985 in the same federal courthouse in Manhattan.

In one, against CBS correspondent Mike Wallace and producer George Crile, Gen. William C. Westmoreland said a 1982 report by CBS accused him, as commander of the U.S. forces in Vietnam, of participating in a "conspiracy at the highest levels of American military intelligence" to underreport enemy troop strength in 1967. The purpose of the alleged underreporting, CBS said, was to create the impression that the United States was winning the war.

The other case was based on a 1983 Time magazine cover story, "Verdict on the Massacre," about Israel's 1982 judicial inquiry into the massacre of several hundred civilians in two Palestinian refugee camps in Lebanon. The Time article was about Israeli Gen. Ariel Sharon's conversations with the Gemayel family on the day after Bashir Gemayel's assassination. Time said

Sharon had "reportedly discussed with the Gemayels the need for the Phalangists to take revenge for the assassination of Bashir."

Libel is damage to a person's reputation caused by bringing him or her into hatred, contempt or ridicule in the eyes of a substantial and respectable group. Both generals sued. Their attorneys knew they would have to show that their clients had suffered hatred, contempt or ridicule because these statements were serious attacks on their clients' reputations and not just unpleasant comments.

Westmoreland was concerned that the CBS broadcast about a "conspiracy" to underreport enemy troop strength would cause people to believe he had deceived President Lyndon Johnson about the enemy. Sharon's concern was that the Time report suggested he had allowed, even encouraged, "revenge" killings of hundreds of civilians while he was in command in Lebanon.

The Westmoreland case ended before being submitted to the jury when both parties signed a joint statement announcing an out-of-court settlement on Feb. 19, 1985. The sudden and surprising end to the case has been attributed to the damaging testimony of two former subordinates, one a former classmate of Westmoreland at West Point.

In the joint statement CBS said it made no concessions and paid no money to Westmoreland. Both parties said they were satisfied "that their respective positions have been effectively placed before the public for its consideration and that continuing the legal process at this stage would serve no further purpose." Legal fees in the case amounted to an estimated $8 million to $10 million.

The Sharon case is more helpful in understanding the complexities of libel. The jury's decision was in three parts. The first part of the verdict was in answer to the question: Was the paragraph concerning Sharon defamatory? The jury said it was. This means the Time article had damaged Sharon's reputation and brought him into hatred, contempt or ridicule.

The second question for the jury was this: Was the paragraph concerning Sharon and revenge false? Again the jury answered affirmatively. If the answer had been "no," the case would have ended here. Truth is a complete defense for libel.

The third question for the jury: Was the paragraph published with "actual malice"—with knowledge that it was false or reckless disregard of whether it was false ("serious doubt" that it was true)? The jury answered "no." Thus the trial ended in favor of Time magazine, despite the jury ruling that the article was defamatory.

There are four categories courts use to help jurors like those in the Sharon case decide if someone's reputation has been damaged because he or she has been brought into hatred, contempt or ridicule. They are:

1. Accusing someone of a crime. (This may have been the basis in the Sharon case.)

2. Damaging a person in his or her public office, profession or occupation.
   (If the statements by CBS and Time against Westmoreland and Sharon
   did not accuse them of crimes, they did damage them in their profession
   as military men.)

3. Accusing a woman of being unchaste. Many states have statutes that
   make an accusation of unchastity a cause of action in a libel suit.

4. Accusing someone of having a loathsome disease. This category was fad-
   ing as an area of defamation. However, with the advent of AIDS, it may
   reappear.

This does not mean you never can say a person committed a crime, was
unethical in business, was adulterous or had a loathsome (contagious) disease. It does mean you must be certain that what you write is true.

## LIBEL SUIT DEFENSES

There are three traditional defenses against libel: truth, privilege, and fair
comment and criticism. Two other constitutional defenses—the actual malice
and negligence tests—also help libel defendants.

### Truth

*Truth* is the best defense against libel. However, knowing the truth is one
thing; proving it is another. In April 1986, the Supreme Court ruled that a
person who sues for libel must prove that the news account was false. This
now sets a uniform rule for all 50 states—the burden of proof in libel cases
concerning matters of public concern is on the plaintiff. This decision does
not, however, change the responsibility of the reporter to seek the truth in
every possible way.

You cannot be certain, for example, whether a person charged with
arson actually started the fire. Who told you that Joe Jones started the fire?
The first source to check is the police or fire report. If a police officer or fire
marshal says that Jones started a fire, you can report not that he did it but that
he has been accused of doing it. You should go no further than this unless you
have information you would be willing to present in court.

Be sure you report no more than what you know is true. You might, for
instance, learn that Helen Greer has not paid any of her bills for two years,
and the only way she can get merchandise is to pay cash when goods are
delivered. Who gave you this information? If the truth is that a former
employee of Ms. Greer told you, that is all the truth you have. The truth, then,
is not that Helen Greer has not paid any of her bills for two years and has a

bad credit rating. The only truth is that a former employee said it. Without supporting evidence for charges such as these, careful newspapers will not print the charges. If you do and your newspaper is sued for damaging Helen Greer's reputation, you would have to try to convince the court that the charge was true. But what if Ms. Greer presents canceled checks and calls suppliers who deny that she owes them any money? You would lose the libel suit. You must be able to prove that Helen Greer is a credit risk before you print it, not just that she was accused of bad business practices by a former employee.

When a newspaper in Oklahoma reported that a wrestling coach had been accused of requiring a sixth-grader, who wanted to rejoin the team, to submit to a whipping by his fellow students while crawling naked through the legs of team members, the coach sued. He claimed damage to his reputation.

In cases like this, the reporter has to be certain that not just that one or more participants told of the incident but also that the statements were true. In court some participants might testify to an occurrence and others might testify the incident never took place. A jury would have to decide on the credibility of the participants.

While you must always strive for absolute truth in all of your stories, the courts will settle for what is known as *substantial truth* in most cases. This means that you must be able to prove the essential elements of all you write.

## Privilege

In addition to truth, the courts traditionally have allowed another defense against libel: *privilege*. This defense applies when you are covering any of the three branches of government. The courts allow legislators, judges and government executives the *absolute privilege* to say anything—true or false—when acting in their official capacities. The rationale is that the public interest is served when an official is allowed to speak freely and fearlessly about making laws, carrying them out or punishing those who do not obey them. Similarly, a participant in a judicial proceeding, such as an attorney, court clerk or judge, is absolutely privileged to make false and even defamatory statements about another person during that proceeding.

In the executive branch it isn't always clear whose statements are privileged and when. The head of state and the major officers of executive departments of the federal and state governments are covered. However, minor officials might not enjoy the protection of absolute privilege.

As a reporter you do have a *conditional* or *qualified privilege* to report what public officials say. Your privilege is conditioned on your report's being full, fair and accurate coverage of the court session, the legislative session or the president's press conference, even if any one of those includes defamatory statements.

You can quote anything the president of the United States says without fear of losing a libel suit. But there are many other levels of executives in federal, state and local government. Mayors of small towns, for instance, often hold part-time positions. They are absolutely protected from libel suits, and you are conditionally privileged to report on what those officials say when they are acting in their official capacities. The problem arises when the mayor says something defamatory when not acting in an official capacity.

## Fair Comment and Criticism

In some writing you may be commenting or criticizing rather than reporting. The courts have protected writers who comment on and criticize the public offerings of anyone in the public eye. Included in this category are actors and actresses, sports figures, public officials and other newsworthy persons. Most often, such writing occurs in reviews of plays, books or movies, or in commentary on service in hotels and restaurants.

The courts call this *fair comment and criticism.* You are protected as long as you do not misstate any of the facts on which you base your comments or criticism, or as long as you do not wrongly imply that you possess undisclosed, damaging information that forms the basis of your opinion.

## The Actual Malice Test

It was a small but momentous step from fair comment and criticism to the case of New York Times vs. Sullivan. In 1964 the U.S. Supreme Court decided that First Amendment protection was broader than just the traditional defenses of truth and privilege and that the press needed even greater freedom in coverage of public officials.

The case started with an advertisement for funds in The New York Times of March 29, 1960, by the Committee to Defend Martin Luther King Jr. and the Struggle for Freedom in the South. The advertisement contained factual errors concerning the police, according to Montgomery, Ala., Commissioner L.B. Sullivan. He thought the errors damaged his reputation, and he won a half-million-dollar judgment against The New York Times in an Alabama trial court.

The Supreme Court said it was considering the case "against the background of a profound national commitment to the principle that debate on public issues should be uninhibited, robust and wide open." Thus Justice William Brennan wrote that the Constitution requires a federal rule prohibiting a public official from recovering damages from the press for a defamatory falsehood relating to his or her official conduct, *unless* the public official can prove the press had knowledge that what was printed was false or that the story was printed with reckless disregard of whether it was false or not.

The justices thereby gave you protection to write virtually anything about officeholders or candidates unless you know that what you are writing is false or you recklessly disregard the truth of what you write. They called this the *actual malice test.*

The actual malice test was applied later in a case involving a story on CBS's "60 Minutes" about a retired Army officer. Col. Anthony Herbert contended the broadcast falsely portrayed him as a liar. He tried to prove that producer Barry Lando recklessly disregarded whether it was a false broadcast or not. Herbert asked some questions that Lando claimed were protected by the First Amendment because they inquired into his state of mind and into the editorial processes during the production of the program.

The Supreme Court said in 1979 that the "thoughts and editorial processes of the alleged defamer would be open to examination." The court pointed out that protecting the editorial process "would constitute a substantial interference with the ability of a defamation plaintiff to establish . . . malice" as required by The New York Times case. The press greeted the ruling with displeasure, though some attorneys noted that the inquiry into the editorial process could help newspapers as much as hurt them. It could help by permitting journalists and their attorneys to demonstrate how careful they were in gathering and selecting the information printed.

Assume, for example, you are told that years ago your town's mayor had been involved in a bootlegging operation. Your source is a friend of the mayor who knew him 30 years ago in Idaho. You print the story. After it is published, you find it was not the mayor but his brother who was the bootlegger. The mayor sues. You are in trouble. You must try to convince the court that you should have been able to trust your source and that you did not act with actual malice. If the source had given you many valid stories in the past, you might be able to convince the court that you had good reason to believe what you were told. You also would have to show what else you did or failed to do before you printed the story. Did you call anyone in Idaho to check? Did you talk to the mayor? Did you try other ways to verify the information? All these questions could be asked as the court tries to decide whether you recklessly disregarded the truth.

Usually a reporter who has tried diligently to do all possible research for a story will be able to meet the actual malice test and win a libel action. The key is verification: checking the information with as many sources as possible.

The decision in the Sharon case discussed earlier in the chapter is an example of the burden of proving actual malice against the press. The jury decided that Time did not know at the time the article in question was printed that its statement about Gen. Sharon was false.

## STANDARDS APPLICABLE TO PUBLIC FIGURES

The actual malice protection was expanded in two cases in 1967 to include not only public officials but also *public figures*—persons in the public eye but not in public office.

The first case stemmed from a Saturday Evening Post article that accused Coach Wally Butts of conspiring to fix a 1962 football game between Georgia and Alabama. At the time of the article, Butts was the athletic director of the University of Georgia. The article, titled ''The Story of a College Football Fix,'' was prefaced by a note from the editors of the Post stating:

Not since the Chicago White Sox threw the 1919 World Series has there been a sports story as shocking as this one. . . . Before the University of Georgia played the University of Alabama . . . Wally Butts . . . gave (to Alabama's coach) . . . Georgia's plays, defensive patterns, all the significant secrets Georgia's football team possessed.

The Post reported that, because of an electronic error about a week before the game, George Burnett, an Atlanta insurance salesman, accidentally had overheard a telephone conversation between Butts and the head coach of Alabama, Paul Bryant.

Coach Butts sued Curtis Publishing Co., publishers of the Post, and won a verdict for $60,000 in general damages and $3 million in punitive damages. The Curtis Co. appealed the case to the Supreme Court and lost, though the amount of damages was reduced.

The second case was decided the same day. The Associated Press was sued by Gen. Edwin Walker for the distribution of a news dispatch giving an eyewitness account by an AP staffer on the campus of the University of Mississippi in the fall of 1962. The AP reported that Gen. Walker personally had led a student charge against federal marshals during a riot on the Mississippi campus as federal efforts were being made to enforce a court decree ordering the enrollment of a black student.

Walker was a retired general—a private citizen—at the time of the publication. He had won a $2 million libel suit in a trial court. The Supreme Court, however, ruled against him.

In both cases the stories were wrong. In both, the actual malice test was applied. What was the difference between the Butts and Walker cases? The justices said the football story was in no sense ''hot news.'' They noted that the person who said he had heard the conversation was on probation in connection with bad-check charges and that the notes he had made were not even viewed by Post personnel before publication. The court also said, as evidence of actual malice on the part of the Post, that no one looked at the game films to see if the information was accurate; that a regular staffer, instead of a football expert, was assigned to the story; and that no check was made with someone knowledgeable in the sport. In short, the Post had not done an adequate job of reporting.

The evidence in the Walker case was considerably different. The court said the news in the Walker case required immediate dissemination because of the riot on campus. The justices noted that the AP received the information from a correspondent who was present on the campus and gave every indication of being trustworthy and competent.

In an earlier case the Supreme Court had defined a public official as a government employee who has, or appears to the public to have, substantial responsibility for or control over the conduct of governmental affairs. In the Butts and Walker cases the court used two definitions of a public figure. The first, like Butts, is a person who has assumed a role of special prominence in the affairs of society—someone who has pervasive power and influence in a community. The second, like Walker, is a person who has thrust himself into the forefront of a particular public controversy in order to influence the resolution of the issues involved.

There are other examples of public figures. A college professor who has become involved with any public controversy ranging from grading practices to gay rights may have made himself or herself a public figure. A police officer who is the leader of the Police Association may be a public figure because of his or her power and influence.

In 1979 the Supreme Court decided three cases that help journalists determine who is and is not a public figure. The first case involved Mrs. Russell A. Firestone, who sued for libel after Time magazine reported that her husband's divorce petition had been granted on grounds of extreme cruelty and adultery. Firestone, who had married into the Firestone Tire and Rubber Co. family, claimed that those were not the grounds for the divorce. She also insisted that she was not a public figure with the burden of proving actual malice. The Supreme Court agreed. Even though she had held press conferences and hired a clipping service, the court ruled that she had not thrust herself into the forefront of a public controversy in an attempt to influence the resolution of the issues involved. The court admitted that marital difficulties of extremely wealthy individuals may be of some interest to some portion of the reading public but added that Firestone had not freely chosen to publicize private matters about her married life. The justices said she was compelled to go to court to "obtain legal release from the bonds of matrimony." They said she assumed no "special prominence in the resolution of public questions." The case was sent back to Florida for a finding of fault, and a new trial was ordered. Firestone remarried, and the case was settled out of court.

The second of the 1979 cases involved Sen. William Proxmire of Wisconsin, who had started what he called the Golden Fleece Award. Each month he announced a winner who, in his opinion, had wasted government money. One such winner was Ronald Hutchinson, a behavioral scientist who had received federal funding for research designed to determine why animals clench their teeth. Hutchinson had published articles about his research in professional publications. In deciding that Hutchinson was not a public figure, the court ruled that he "did not thrust himself or his views into public controversy to influence others." The court admitted there may have been legitimate concerns about the way public funds were being spent, but said this was not enough to make Hutchinson a public figure.

The third 1979 case concerned an individual found guilty of contempt of court in 1958 for his failure to appear before a grand jury investigating Soviet espionage in the United States. Ilya Wolston's name had been included in a list of people indicted for serving as Soviet agents in a 1974 book published by the Reader's Digest Association. Wolston had not been indicted, and he sued. The Supreme Court, in deciding that he was not a public figure, found that Wolston had played only a minor role in whatever public controversy there may have been concerning the investigation of Soviet espionage. The court added that a private individual is not automatically transformed into a public figure merely by becoming involved in or being associated with a matter that attracts public attention.

Lower courts have ruled that in other situations individuals have become public figures by the nature of their activities. These include an attorney in local practice for 32 years who had been involved in major disputes and social activities, a newspaper publisher who regularly had taken strong public stands on controversial issues, and a college dean who had attempted to influence the proposed abolition of his position.

Assume you are covering a proposal to fluoridate the water of your town. Among those you may write about are:

- The mayor (or town or county supervisor) who obviously is a public official.

- A doctor who has a private medical practice but is so concerned about the effects of fluoridation that he has made many public speeches. He has become a public figure because he has thrust himself to the forefront of the fluoridation controversy.

- A former state senator who now owns a radio station and is well-known in the community. She, too, is a public figure because of her prominence in the affairs of the city.

But how about the attorney who is handling the litigation for the individuals opposed to fluoridation? If he also is a spokesman for this group, he may be treated as a public figure. However, if he does no more than file the legal papers with the courts and leaves the press conferences and public appearances to others, he has not thrust himself to the forefront of the controversy. Do you have the same protection from a libel action when you write about him as you do with the persons you are certain are public figures or public officials?

In 1974 the Supreme Court said the answer usually is no. The justices said states may give more protection to private individuals if a newspaper or radio or television station damages their reputations than if the reputations of either public officials or public figures are damaged. The important phrase "may give more protection" is found in the landmark Gertz vs. Welch case.

## STANDARD APPLICABLE TO PRIVATE CITIZENS

Private citizens who sue for punitive, or punishment, damages must meet the same actual malice test as public officials and public figures do. Because of the *Gertz* case, states have been allowed to set their own standards for libel cases involving private citizens who sue only for actual damages. Roughly 20 states and the District of Columbia have adopted a *negligence test*, which requires you to use the same care in gathering facts and writing your story as any reasonable reporter would use under the same or similar circumstances. If you make every effort to be fair and answer all the questions a reasonable person may ask, you probably would pass the negligence test.

One state, New York, has adopted a *gross irresponsibility test*. Four states have established a more stringent standard that requires private citizens to prove *actual malice*. In the remaining states the matter is *unsettled* because of conflicting cases or cases that are still pending, or because there have been *no cases* to resolve the issue. Here is a state-by-state listing of the tests applicable to media defendants in the 50 states and the District of Columbia:

| | |
|---|---|
| Alabama | Unsettled |
| Alaska | Actual Malice |
| Arizona | Negligence |
| Arkansas | Negligence |
| California | Unsettled |
| Colorado | Actual Malice |
| Connecticut | Unsettled |
| Delaware | Negligence |
| District of Columbia | Negligence |
| Florida | Unsettled |
| Georgia | Unsettled |
| Hawaii | Negligence |
| Idaho | No Cases |
| Illinois | Negligence |
| Indiana | Actual Malice |
| Iowa | Unsettled |
| Kansas | Negligence |
| Kentucky | Negligence |
| Louisiana | Unsettled |
| Maine | No Cases |
| Maryland | Negligence |
| Massachusetts | Negligence |
| Michigan | Negligence |

| | |
|---|---|
| Minnesota | Negligence |
| Mississippi | No Cases |
| Missouri | Unsettled |
| Montana | Unsettled |
| Nebraska | No Cases |
| Nevada | No Cases |
| New Hampshire | Negligence |
| New Jersey | Unsettled |
| New Mexico | Negligence |
| New York | Gross Irresponsibility |
| North Carolina | Unsettled |
| North Dakota | No Cases |
| Ohio | Negligence |
| Oklahoma | Negligence |
| Oregon | Unsettled |
| Pennsylvania | Unsettled |
| Rhode Island | No Cases |
| South Carolina | Negligence |
| South Dakota | No Cases |
| Tennessee | Negligence |
| Texas | Actual Malice |
| Utah | Negligence |
| Vermont | Unsettled |
| Virginia | Unsettled |
| Washington | Negligence |
| West Virginia | Negligence |
| Wisconsin | Negligence |
| Wyoming | No Cases |

# Invasion of Privacy

Libel is damage to an individual's reputation. *Invasion of privacy* is a violation of a person's right to be left alone.

As a reporter you may be risking an invasion of privacy suit under any of the following circumstances:

1. You physically intrude into a private area to get a story or picture—an act closely related to trespass.

2. You publish a story or photograph about someone that is misleading and thus portray that person in a ''false light.''

3. You disclose something about an individual's private affairs that is true but also is offensive to individuals of ordinary sensibilities.

4. You use someone's name or picture in an advertisement or for similar purposes of trade. Called *appropriation*, this does not affect you when you are performing your reporting duties.

Your basic defense in an invasion of privacy suit is that you're a reporter covering a newsworthy situation. The courts usually protect the press against invasion of privacy suits when it is reporting matters of legitimate public interest. There are exceptions, however.

One exception arises when you invade someone's privacy by entering private property to get a story. You cannot trespass on private property to get a story or take a picture even if it is newsworthy. The courts will not protect you when you are a trespasser. Two Life magazine staffers lost an invasion of privacy suit because, posing as patients, they went into a man's home to get a story about a faith healer. They lost the case even though they were working with the district attorney and the state board of health. You may enter private property only when you are invited by the owner or renter.

The court also will not protect you if you invade someone's privacy out of carelessness. For example, a legal problem arises if a photograph or information from a true story about a careful pedestrian struck by a careless driver is used again in connection with a story, say, about careless pedestrians. The pedestrian who was hit could file a lawsuit charging libel, ''false light'' invasion of privacy or even both in some states.

Some states do not recognize ''false light'' invasion of privacy and insist that libel is the appropriate form of suit. But ''false light'' suits can cover situations where a picture or story is misleading but not defamatory. Even flattering material can place a person in an unwanted, false light.

The third category of invasion of privacy that the courts recognize—unwanted publicity—concerns stories about incidents that, because they are true, cannot be defamatory but can be offensive to a person of ordinary sensibilities. An example is a picture published by Sports Illustrated in which a football fan's pants zipper was open. The fan sued for invasion of privacy but lost. Also in the area of unwanted publicity, the Supreme Court held in 1975 and again in 1989 that truthfully reporting the name of a rape victim is permitted. In 1976 and in 1979 the justices upheld the right of the press to publish the names of juveniles involved with the law because the information was truthful and of public significance.

The courts say that in order for privacy to be invaded, there must be a morbid and sensational prying into private lives. Merely being the subject of an unflattering and embarrassing article is not enough.

# Protection of
# Sources and Notes

Another area you must know about is your ability—or inability—to protect your sources and notes. The problem may arise in various situations. A grand jury that is investigating a murder may ask you to reveal the source of a story you wrote about the murder. You may be asked to testify at a criminal or a civil trial. Or the police may obtain a warrant to search the news room, including your desk.

The conflict here is between a reporter's need to protect sources of information and the duty of every citizen to testify to help the courts determine justice. By the nature of your work as a reporter, you will be at the scene of events that are important and newsworthy. Anyone wanting the facts about an event can subpoena you to bring in all the details. Journalists usually resist. They work for their newspaper or radio or television station, not a law enforcement agency. Their ability to gather information would be compromised if the sources knew that their identities or their information would go to the police.

By 1990 some protection against testifying—*shield laws*—had been adopted by the legislatures in 28 states. The states are:

| | | |
|---|---|---|
| Alabama | Kentucky | New York |
| Alaska | Louisiana | North Dakota |
| Arizona | Maryland | Ohio |
| Arkansas | Michigan | Oklahoma |
| California | Minnesota | Oregon |
| Colorado | Montana | Pennsylvania |
| Delaware | Nebraska | Rhode Island |
| Georgia | Nevada | Tennessee |
| Illinois | New Jersey | |
| Indiana | New Mexico | |

Congress had not acted in this area in part because journalists themselves were divided about the desirability of such legislation.

However, Congress did pass the *Privacy Protection Act* of 1980. Under that act, federal, state or local enforcement officers generally may not use a search warrant to search news rooms. Instead, they must get a subpoena for documents, which tells the reporters to hand over the material. Officers may only use a warrant to search news rooms if they suspect a reporter of being involved in a crime or if immediate action is needed to prevent bodily harm, loss of life or destruction of the material.

The difference between a *search warrant* and a *subpoena* is great. If officers can search with a warrant, they knock on the door, enter the news room, and search on their own. With a subpoena for documents, reporters are asked to turn over the material to authorities at a predetermined time and place. A subpoena does not permit officers to search the news room. In addition, it gives reporters time to challenge in court the necessity of turning over the material.

Even in states with shield laws, judges in most criminal cases involving grand juries will not allow you to keep your sources secret. In civil litigation you may be permitted to keep sources confidential in most cases unless the court finds that the information sought is:

1. Unavailable from other sources.

2. Relevant to the underlying litigation.

3. Of such critical importance to the lawsuit that it goes to the heart of the plaintiff's claim.

If you are sued for libel, you will find it very difficult both to protect your sources and to win the lawsuit. The court might very well rule against you on whether a statement is true or false, if it came from a source you refuse to name.

There has been only one Supreme Court decision to guide journalists on protection of sources. In this case, Branzburg vs. Hayes, decided in 1972, the justices said the sole issue was the obligation of reporters to respond to grand jury subpoenas as other citizens do and to answer questions relevant to the investigation of a crime. According to the court, then, reporters cannot protect their sources before a grand jury.

William Farr, now a Los Angeles Times reporter, spent 46 days in virtual solitary confinement in a Los Angeles jail in 1971 for refusing to disclose to a judge his source for a newspaper article about the trial of Charles Manson, the mass murderer. Myron Farber spent 40 days in a New Jersey jail and his paper, The New York Times, was fined more than $250,000 in 1978 for failure to comply with subpoenas directing the paper to produce documents and materials during a murder trial.

Despite the publicity, the Farber case is of limted legal importance outside New Jersey. The precedent-setting case is U.S. vs. Nixon. The Nixon case requires a showing in court of the need for tapes, documents or other materials before people not directly involved in a court case can be ordered to comply with subpoenas.

That principle is relevancy, and it extends back to the Marie Torre case in

1958. Torre spent 10 days in jail in New York for refusing to disclose a confidential source the court said was relevant in a libel action by Judy Garland against CBS. Others have been jailed or threatened with jail by judges since John Peter Zenger, editor of the New York Weekly Journal, refused to reveal the name of the author of a letter in the Journal in 1735.

The only way to avoid such confrontation with the courts is not to promise a source you will keep his or her name confidential. Only for the most compelling reason should you get yourself into this judicial conflict between the First Amendment right of a free press and the Sixth Amendment right to a fair trial.

In 1991, the U.S. Supreme Court ruled in Cohen vs. Cowles Media Company that the First Amendment does not prevent a source from suing a news organization if a reporter has promised the source confidentiality but the newspaper publishes the source's name anyway.

# Access to Courts

Judicial acknowledgement of the right of access to courtrooms has had a sudden, cometlike history since 1979. The Supreme Court held in 1979 that "members of the public have no constitutional right" under the Sixth Amendment to attend criminal trials. In a reversal exactly one year later, the justices held that the public and the press have a First Amendment right to attend criminal trials.

The justices said the right was not absolute, but that trial judges could close criminal trials only when there was an "overriding interest" to justify such closure. The basic concern of judges when they close trials is to protect the accused person under the Sixth Amendment right to an "impartial jury"—often translated by attorneys into "a fair trial."

In addition, the First Amendment prevents the government from conducting business—even trials—in secret. In fact, in the Richmond Newspapers case in 1980, Chief Justice Warren Burger traced the unbroken and uncontradicted history of open judicial proceedings in England and the United States. He concluded that there is a "presumption of openness" in criminal trials and pointed out the important role of the news media as representatives of the public.

The next question for the justices was the role of the state legislatures in closing trials. Massachusetts had a statute mandating closure of the courtroom for specified sexual offenses involving a victim under 18. The Supreme Court said in 1982 that the mandatory closure statute violated the First

Amendment right of access to criminal trials even though safeguarding the physical and psychological well-being of a minor was a compelling concern.

The court said it was up to the trial judge to decide on a case-by-case basis whether closure is necessary to protect the welfare of a minor victim. The trial court should weigh the minor's age, psychological maturity and understanding, the nature of the crime, the desires of the victim, and the interests of parents and relatives.

So by 1982 the Supreme Court had decided that openness in criminal trials "enhances both the basic fairness of the criminal trial and the appearance of fairness so essential to public confidence in the system."

But when does a trial actually begin? At what point does the presumption that trial proceedings should be open first apply? Is there a right of access to jury-selection proceedings? The justices said in 1984 that the process of jury selection is a matter of importance "not simply to the adversaries but to the criminal justice system." In writing the opinion, Chief Justice Burger said openness has what can be described as a "community therapeutic value" after especially violent crimes. He said seeing that the law is being enforced and the criminal justice system is functioning can provide an outlet for the public's understandable reactions and emotions.

Public proceedings vindicate the concerns of victims and the community in knowing that offenders are being brought to account for their criminal conduct "by jurors fairly and openly selected." Proceedings of jury selection could be closed, the chief justice said, only when a trial judge finds that closure preserves an "overriding interest" and is narrowly tailored to serve that interest.

Finally, in 1986 the Supreme Court decided the issue of right of access to a preliminary hearing. A California court had held a 41-day closed preliminary hearing on the pretext of protecting the accused under the Sixth Amendment right to an impartial jury trial.

Chief Justice Burger in a 7–2 decision said the right of the accused to a "fair trial" and the public right of access "are not necessarily inconsistent." Plainly, the defendant has a right to a fair trial, the chief justice said, but he added, "As we have repeatedly recognized, one of the important means of assuring a fair trial is that the process be open to neutral observers."

In cases dealing with the claim of First Amendment right of access to criminal proceedings, the chief justice said, "Our decisions have emphasized two complementary considerations," experience and logic. Experience shows "whether the place and process has historically been open to the press and the public." As to logic, he said the court "has traditionally considered whether public access plays a significant positive role in the functioning of the particular process in question."

The chief justice acknowledged that some kinds of government operations "would be totally frustrated if conducted openly." A classic example is the grand jury system. However, "other proceedings plainly require public access," he said.

Finally, the chief justice said only an overriding interest found by a trial judge can overcome the presumption of openness of criminal proceedings. (See Chapter 12 for more on crime and the courts.)

# Copyright and Fair Use

The purpose of copyright law is to ensure compensation to authors for contributing to the common good by publishing their works. The Constitution provides for this in Article 1, Section 8, by giving Congress the power to secure ''for limited times to authors and inventors the exclusive right to their respective writing and discoveries.'' The same section indicates that this provision is intended ''to promote the progress of science and useful arts'' for the benefit of the public.

The most recent copyright statute went into effect Jan. 1, 1978. Key elements of this law include:

- That copyrightable works are protected from the moment they are fixed in tangible form, whether published or unpublished, but that the copyright owner has five years to register his or her work.

- That copyright protection begins with a work's ''creation and . . . endures for a term consisting of the life of the author and 50 years after the author's death.''

- That works for hire and anonymous and pseudonymous works are protected for 75 years from publication or 100 years from creation, whichever is shorter.

- That there is a ''fair use'' limitation on the exclusive rights of copyright owners. In other words, it may be permissible to use small excerpts from a copyrighted work without permission. According to the Supreme Court, factors that govern fair use are:

  1. The purpose and character of the use.
  2. The nature of the copyrighted work.
  3. The substantiality of the portion used in relationship to the copyrighted work as a whole.
  4. The effect on the potential market for or value of the copyrighted work.

Although a work is copyrighted from the moment it is fixed in tangible form, the copyright statute says certain steps are necessary to receive statutory protection. The author or publisher must:

- Publish or reproduce the work with the word "copyright" or the symbol ©, the name of the copyright owner and the year of publication.

- Deposit two copies of the work with the Library of Congress within three months of publication. Failure to do so will not affect the copyright but could lead to imposition of fines.

- Register the work at the Library of Congress by filling out the form supplied by the Copyright Office and sending the form, the specified number of copies (usually one copy with unpublished work and two copies with published work), and a $20 fee. The deposit and registration fee can be combined and usually are.

In 1989, however, some aspects of copyright law changed when the United States signed the 100-year-old *Berne Convention*, an international copyright treaty primarily intended to dissuade foreigners from pirating American film productions. The House of Representatives unanimously approved the treaty because of the losses to copyright holders in recent years. U.S. copyright holders lost an estimated $2.4 billion in 1986 alone, while in Japan pirated copies have been estimated to comprise up to 40 percent of the video market.

The Berne Convention went into effect on March 1, 1989. Other changes in copyright law under the Berne Convention include the following:

- *Placing a copyright notice on a work is no longer necessary to preserve a copyright after publication.* This is in line with the Berne Convention principle that the exercise of a copyright should not be subject to formalities. But the copyright notice is still useful in that it acts as a bar to an infringer's defense of innocent infringement.

- *Registration is no longer a prerequisite for access to the federal courts for an infringement action.* But registration is required for the copyright owner to recover statutory damages. (Without registration, the copyright owner can recover only the damages he or she can prove, court costs and "reasonable" attorney's fees.) The amount of statutory damages, generally between $500 and $20,000, is determined by the judge. However, if it is found that the infringer was not aware he or she was infringing a copyright, the judge may award as little as $200. Similarly, if it found that the infringement was willful, the judge can award up to $100,000. Copyright registration, then, remains highly advisable.

# Suggested Readings

Gilmor, Donald M., Barron, Jerome A., Simon, Todd F. and Terry, Herbert A., ''Mass Communication Law,'' Fifth Edition. New York: West Publishing Co., 1990.

Middleton, Kent R. and Chamberlin, Bill F., ''The Law of Public Communication.'' New York: Longman, 1988.

Nelson, Harold L., Teeter, Dwight L. Jr. and Le Duc, Don R., ''Law of Mass Communications,'' Sixth Edition. Foundation Press, 1989. Supplement: Mineola, New York: ''Notes to Update,'' 1990.

Pember, Don R., ''Mass Media Law,'' Fifth Edition. Dubuque, Iowa: Brown, 1990.

Watkins, John J., ''The Mass Media and the Law.'' Englewood Cliffs, N.J.: Prentice-Hall, 1990.

# Exercises

1. Which defense for libel discussed in this chapter would you have used in defending Time magazine in the lawsuit filed by Gen. Ariel Sharon? Why?

2. The New York Times v. Sullivan case was significant as a landmark decision in favor of the press. Discuss what the consequences for the press could have been if the decision had been different.

3. You are on an assignment with your photographer who enters a house without permission and photographs the sale of illegal drugs. Discuss the issues raised by the circumstances and explain why you would or would not publish the pictures.

# 22

## Ethics

- A doctor who prescribes medicine for a patient without a proper examination would be violating a code of ethics. He could lose the right to practice.

- A lawyer who deliberately misleads a client would be guilty of violating a code of ethics. She could lose the right to practice.

- A certified public accountant who knowingly signs a statement misrepresenting a company's financial position would be violating a code of ethics. He could lose the right to practice.

- A journalist who accepts a stolen document and poses as a police investigator to get private telephone records might be violating a code of ethics. She could win a Pulitzer Prize.

The doctor, the lawyer and the accountant all have mandatory codes of ethics, prescribed by their professions. Because it would be contrary to the idea of a free press, journalists have not established such a code. To be effective, a mandatory code requires an enforcement mechanism. That means some form of licensing, and licensing is a denial of freedom of the press. The power to license is the power to censor. So far, none of the proposals to license journalists has been approved. And none will be as long as most journalists act responsibly.

Although the industry doesn't have a common code, most newspapers have their own. According to researcher Harry Heath, by 1985 three out of four newspapers in this country had written codes of ethics. These codes help reporters pick their way through the maze of ethical and unethical practices. In this chapter, we establish some guideposts to help you through the maze. Although we pose many questions, we can provide answers only to some. The answers to the rest depend on the ethical code you have developed from teachings at home, in religion, in school and even in the streets.

You have a set of principles that guide your conduct. Some of the same principles that tell you when and if you should report someone in your class who cheats on an exam will help you to decide the ethical questions you will encounter as a journalist. Other principles you will learn in this chapter, in other classes and on the job.

Ethics is a system of principles that guides your conduct and helps you to distinguish between right and wrong or, in some cases, between two wrongs. Conduct is based either on motives or concern about the consequences of your acts, or both. Ethics also implies an obligation—to yourself or to someone else.

Simply stated, ethics is a standard of behavior. These days, it is especially important that journalists observe a high standard of behavior. The media, which have focused the public spotlight on unethical practices in so many of society's institutions, can afford to do no less for themselves. Some of the rocks the press has flung have ricocheted and cracked the glass.

The press holds up for scrutiny everyone from the captains of industry to the president of the United States, and many of them are found wanting. Now many of those who have felt the sting of the press—along with others who have not—are asking about our practices.

If it is wrong for the government to lie, why is it all right for the press to do it? If it is wrong for the Justice Department to obtain someone's long-distance telephone records clandestinely, why is it all right for the press to do it? If there is no other way to expose serious government wrongdoing than by having someone steal a document, should you do it?

The questions pile up at our door while we search for the answers. Some may never be found. Others will.

## In this chapter you will learn:

1. Three philosophical approaches that can provide answers to ethical questions.

2. Seven categories of ethical questions.

3. Some of the ways journalists have answered ethical questions without binding codes.

# Three Ethical Philosophies

Joseph Fletcher, author of the book "Situation Ethics," told a story about the time a friend arrived in St. Louis just before election day. The friend's cab driver started talking about the campaign:

> "I and my father and grandfather before me, and their fathers, have always been straight-ticket Republicans," the cabbie said.
> "Ah," said the friend, himself a Republican, "I take it that means you will vote for Senator So-and-so."
> "No," said the driver, "There are times when a man has to push his principles aside and do the right thing."

In his own way the cabbie was defining situation ethics, one of the three broad categories of ethical philosophies. The other two are absolutism and antinomianism. Let's look at each of these three categories.

## ABSOLUTIST ETHICS

*Absolutism* holds that there is a fixed set of principles or laws, from which there should be no deviation. Principles become rules that, in turn, are treated like laws. That is why some refer to this kind of ethical philosophy as *legalism*. If it is wrong to lie, it always is wrong to lie. If a murderer asks where his or her intended victim is, the absolutist could not lie to save a life. If the action is right, it does not matter whether a friend is killed. The consequences are irrelevant.

An absolutist or legalistic ethical philosophy could spawn a conscientious objector who not only would refuse to take up arms but who would also refuse even to go to war as a medic. If war is absolutely wrong, it is absolutely wrong to participate in war in any way.

The absolutist journalist is concerned only with whether an event is newsworthy. If it is interesting, timely, significant or important, it is to be reported, regardless of the consequences. That is the rationale some publications used for printing instructions for making bombs, for printing the names of undercover agents and for identifying rape victims. That some persons might make bombs, that the lives of the undercover agents might be endangered or that the rape victims may suffer public degradation is of no concern to the absolutist.

The philosophy is attractive to some journalists because it assumes the need for full disclosure. Nothing newsworthy ever is withheld from the public. In the end, these journalists believe, publishing without fear of the consequences or without favor for one group's interests over another is the highest ethical principle.

# ANTINOMIAN ETHICS

At the other end of the spectrum is *antinomianism*, which rejects all rules and, in effect, all ethics. The term literally means "against law." The antinomian has neither a predetermined standard of conduct nor moral rules. Actions in any situation are spontaneous and unpredictable.

Antinomian journalists are not concerned with motives, consequences or obligations. That does not mean that they would always lie, cheat or steal. Rather, antinomian journalists might pose as someone other than a journalist in an attempt to gather information on some occasions, and they would not be bothered by doing it. To them every situation is different. There are no principles that can guide decision making. Antinomians have faith in their ability to extemporize in any situation. No premeditation or preparation is required.

While the concept of absolutism is attractive to many journalists, few choose antinomianism. Most mainstream journalists reject the philosophy on the grounds that it is antithetical to their upbringing and inconsistent with a responsible press. The principle that the press has a responsibility to the reader implies a concern for the consequences that antinomians do not have.

# SITUATION ETHICS

Between the two extremes of antinomianism and absolutism lies another philosophy: *situation ethics* or *situationism*.

Unlike antinomianism, situationism does not hold that everything is relative. The situationist knows, understands and accepts the ethical maxims of the community and its heritage, and weighs them carefully before making a decision. However, unlike the absolutist, the situationist is prepared to compromise them or to set them aside completely if unselfish love for one's neighbor demands it.

For example, a situationist most likely believes that lying is unethical. But if a murderer asks where his or her intended victim is, a situationist would lie to save a life.

Hence, for the situationist, everything is relative to one absolute: unselfish love of one's neighbor. Christians base this ethic on the teaching of the New Testament: You shall love your neighbor as yourself. Others base it on various versions of the Golden Rule, found in Hebrew writing before the time of Christ. The book of Tobias states: What you hate, do not do to anyone. Hillel, a contemporary of Jesus, taught: What is hateful to yourself, do not do to your fellow men. Many religions profess love of neighbor as the highest good. The secular humanist, without an act of faith or promise of an afterlife, also professes human life, human values as the highest good.

In the broad sense then, for the person holding to situation ethics, people always come first. In every ethical dilemma, they always do what is best for people. Sometimes this takes the form of utilitarianism: They act in a way that is good for the largest number of people. Sometimes this means that they must act to benefit the most people in the long run. Unlike the absolutist, the situationist is always concerned with the human consequences.

Making an ethical decision is often not an easy matter for the situationist. Yet, most situationists hold that what is clearly unethical is not to decide; not to decide is to make a decision.

The nature of the news business demands dozens of decisions daily: to print or not to print. When The New York Times discovered that President Kennedy had approved an undercover invasion of Cuba in 1961, the editors had to decide whether the interests of the government or the need of the people to know was more important. The editors knew the consequences of printing the story: Knowledge of the pending invasion would have stopped it. They decided not to print the story. The invasion was a disaster for the United States. Later, President Kennedy and the Times' editors agreed the story should have been printed.

The Times case illustrates the problem situation ethicists have. If the rules are not absolute, there is opportunity for human error. On the other hand, when the rules are absolute, they also may be absolutely wrong.

Among the factors that the Times' editors used to make their on-the-spot decision was a concern for the nation's security as defined by the government. Fidel Castro had installed a Communist government in Cuba, and Kennedy argued that it was in the nation's interest to prevent the Soviet Union from gaining a strategic stronghold just 90 miles off the U.S. coast.

The absolutist would have printed the news without regard to the consequences. The Times' editors assessed the consequences and decided that the government's interest in national security was superior to the public's need to know. Ten years later when the Times obtained a copy of the classified ''Pentagon Papers,'' which traced the course of U.S. involvement in Vietnam, the Times had to weigh again what the government described as its national security interest against the people's need to know. This time, the editors decided to publish. The editors can be described as situation ethicists because in two similar situations they chose different actions.

In some situations the consequences are easily assessed and a decision is reached quickly. In other cases the consequences are troubling. What would you do, for instance, if you had a story about a married politician who kept a lover on the public payroll? Most journalists would print it. What would you do if the distraught politician told you he or she would commit suicide if the story were published? Reporters who use situation ethics would examine their motives for wanting to publish the story. They would balance the consequences—the public's need to know and the possible death of a person—before deciding whether to publish.

Most journalists today are situation ethicists. But unlike Fletcher and others whose philosophies of ethics have been developed against a theological background, a journalist's sense of ethics is more likely to come from a variety of influences. One of the most important is the profession itself. The journalistic ethic—the set of values governing conduct—asks its practitioners to be (1) honest, (2) independent of special interests, (3) dedicated to the best truth obtainable, (4) committed to open government and (5) protective of readers' interests. While the first four characteristics of the ethic are constant, journalists interpret the last one differently.

The Wall Street Journal perceives its readers' interests differently than The New York Times does; the same is true of The Miami Herald and The Los Angeles Times. When Joseph Pulitzer retired in 1907, he wrote a statement that still serves today as the platform for the St. Louis Post-Dispatch. The paper, Pulitzer wrote, "will always fight for progress and reform, never tolerate injustice or corruption, always fight demagogues of all parties, never belong to any party, always oppose privileged classes and public plunderers, never lack sympathy with the poor, always remain devoted to the public welfare, never be satisfied with merely printing news, always be drastically independent, never be afraid to attack wrong, whether by predatory plutocracy or predatory poverty."

Pulitzer may have expressed it more strongly than most journalists would, especially publishers, but that strong populist philosophy runs through much of journalism. Most journalists identify their readers as The Common People. Their answers to a question such as whether to print the information about the crooked politician would be weighed not just against the interests of the publisher, not just against the interests of the captains of industry, but also against the interests of all people. It would be weighed not just against the immediate impact, good or bad, but against the long-term impact as well. The prevailing ethic in journalism today is what John Stuart Mill called utilitarianism: the greatest good for the greatest number. For instance, a story about a person convicted of drunken driving would embarrass the driver and the family. But most journalists would argue that society needs to know about that driver and about how the courts are handling cases dealing with drunken drivers. The story may have a deleterious immediate impact on the family, but it will have a positive long-term impact on the community.

# Ethical Problems

Most ethical problems the reporter is likely to encounter fall into one of the following seven categories:

1. Plagiarism.

2. Payola.

3. Conflict of interest.

4. Withholding information.

5. Deceit.

6. Invasion of privacy.

7. Participation in the news.

Let's look at each of these problems in detail.

## PLAGIARISM

The American Society of Newspaper Editors once awarded a first-place prize to a writer for his story about a beauty queen on the race-car circuit. One of the people who read the winning article, Jerry Bledsoe of the Greensboro (N.C.) Daily News and Record, recognized his own work in it.

Bledsoe complained; Roy Peter Clark, who edited the book of winning entries, investigated and wrote a report. The ASNE board decided the offense was a misdemeanor, not a felony, and allowed the writer to keep the award. The winner wrote an apology and flew to Greensboro to apologize to Bledsoe.

In his account of the events, published in the March 1983 Washington Journalism Review, Clark wrote, "In reviewing the case, it became clear to me that there is little agreement among journalists as to how the rules against plagiarism should affect the behavior of reporters."

There may not be much agreement, but there is widespread plagiarism, according to the 225 editors who responded to a survey conducted by the ethics committee of the ASNE in 1986. One of every six editors said they had encountered plagiarism in the last three years at their newspapers.

There have been many publicized instances of plagiarism. In 1988 the St. Paul Pioneer Press drama critic resigned after it was discovered that there were many similarities between a review he wrote and one that had previously appeared in The New York Times. A Chicago Tribune correspondent quit after someone discovered similarities between a dispatch he wrote and one that had appeared earlier in the Jerusalem Post.

*Plagiarism* is the taking of another's words and representing them as your own. It is not only unethical, it is illegal. However, differentiating between plagiarism and research is often difficult. Events in a news story cannot be copyrighted, but the specific account of the event can. Journalists can rewrite the article without violating the law.

In the daily practice of journalism, reporters, consciously or unconsciously, deal with many situations that could involve plagiarism. Clark listed them:

1. *Taking material verbatim from the newspaper library.* Even when the material is from your own newspaper, it is still someone else's work. Put it in your own words or attribute it.

2. *Using material verbatim from the wire services.* It is fairly common for newspapers to take material from the Associated Press, add a few lines or paragraphs of local information, and publish the story as the work of the newspaper or under a staff member's byline. Even though it is common, it is not right.

3. *Using material from other publications.* Electronic data bases open a world of work to the reporter. It will become even more difficult to detect plagiarism with the multitude of sources available to the reporter through these data bases. Some plagiarism results from sloppy note taking; reporters who don't clearly indicate the source of their information in their notes risk using material—and even the exact words—as their own.

   Sometimes the reporter also uses the research of others. For instance, a researcher may find that tax breaks are not a high priority of corporations looking for new plant sites. Such a study may be published in a professional journal under the researcher's byline. Often, the findings will show up in news articles without any mention of the source.

4. *Using news releases verbatim.* This is a shadowy area because the companies and individuals who send the releases are delighted to see them published. Most newspapers, however, rewrite them. If they appear under a reporter's byline, the stories should be substantially the reporter's work. Except for quotes, the stories should not include verbatim repro-

ductions of portions of the release. If a release is used verbatim, the source should be credited.

5. *Using the work of fellow reporters.* Often more than one reporter will be assigned to a story, but the article will appear under one byline. Frequently, the work of the others is now credited in a note at the end of the story. Syndicated columnist Jack Anderson now credits his reporting aides.

6. *Using old stories over again.* Ann Landers admitted she had reused old letters and vowed not to do it again. Some reporters and columnists have used stories or columns they had done years earlier without attribution. The publication in which the original version appeared has a stake in that story, and your readers have a right to know that they are reading recycled material.

No one approves of plagiarism. Still, there is considerable argument about what constitutes it. As in many other shadowy ethical areas, however, most of the problems are avoided when reporters and editors think first. More plagiarism is committed unconsciously than knowingly.

## PAYOLA

- When sports reporters gather for the Kentucky Derby, they are treated to lavish parties with free drinks, expensive hors d'oeuvres and an orchestra. The scene is not much different the week preceding the Super Bowl and other major sporting events.

- Airlines inaugurating flights often invite media representatives to take the first flight free. Sometimes the destinations are attractive—such as Hawaii—and there is a stopover of at least a day.

- Television critics are invited to a whirlwind series of premiere showings, interviews and parties with celebrities. The networks offer to pay all expenses of the reporters.

- The mayor remembers a reporter on the city hall beat on each holiday and birthday with a gift. It may range from a bottle of liquor to an honorary key to the city.

The *payola,* or money and gifts such as those just described, is usually given in expectation of favorable coverage. Sports promoters attract reporters from around the country to their events. Reporters justify the trip by writing stories.

Airlines usually get stories in the travel or business sections announcing new flights. And if the reporter has taken the flight, there may be another story extolling the virtues of visiting Hawaii or Japan or Katmandu—all serviced, incidentally, by the host airlines.

Networks would prefer reviews to be favorable, but mainly they want publicity. Their preview week for the critics guarantees stories in papers around the nation.

Sponsors of the Los Angeles Summer Olympics gave accredited journalists an official Olympic duffel bag stuffed with such gifts as calculators, pocket radios, notebooks, Olympic medallions, sun visors and candies. Photographers were offered free film processing by Fuji and camera repairs and cameras on loan from Canon.

The mayor may not be looking for a specific favorable story but may instead be cultivating a relationship with the reporter. Eventually, however, the mayor may expect something in return.

Gifts, sometimes even outright cash payments, used to be common in the news business. At Christmas time some news rooms looked like department stores. Now many newspapers forbid reporters to accept gifts. If they are offered, they either are returned to the sender or donated to charity. Says Andrew Barnes, editor of the St. Petersburg (Fla.) Times, "We take nothing free from anybody."

Are reporters who don't pay their own way being bought? A good many persons inside and outside the press think that either they are being bought or that they may give readers the impression they are. The appearance of impropriety may be as damaging as actual impropriety.

## Standards within the Industry

In many cases the decisions about whether to accept gifts, tickets or trips is taken out of the reporter's hands. Nearly 75 percent of the newspapers and broadcast stations responding to a 1983 survey for the Society of Professional Journalists/Sigma Delta Chi (SPJ/SDX) said they had policies regarding acceptance of gifts. But the policies vary widely. Some papers prohibit reporters from accepting anything; others set specific limits. Many are more general, if not more ambiguous. The Scripps-Howard newspaper group says "When the gifts exceed the limits of propriety, they should be returned." SPJ/SDX says "Nothing of value should be accepted." Is a coffee cup "of value"? The Associated Press says staff members "are expected to return gifts and promotional materials of more than nominal value from public relations agencies, corporations and others hoping to encourage or influence AP coverage."

**Figure 22.1
Tough Choices.**
Journalists walk a
tightrope among
ethical dilemmas.
Can a journalist
accept a cup of
coffee? A free movie
ticket? Airfare to
Disney World?

Some newspapers have given their travel editors larger budgets instead of permitting them to accept free trips from airlines and travel agencies.

The issues involved are these:

1. Do reporters who accept free tickets or accommodations write more favorably about a subject than they would if the newspaper paid the expenses?

2. When promoters are paying the way, are stories written that otherwise would not be?

3. Does the public believe that a reporter is compromised by accepting free gifts or travel?

These issues are among the most easily addressed by the industry.

While it is by no means unanimous in its opinion, the industry is in general agreement that the press should avoid gifts and free travel. The issue that remains unresolved is whether there is a cutoff point. Is credibility impaired by a cup of coffee, a free meal or a free trip? Can journalists dashing about to cover a national political convention stop at a booth run by a special interest group, such as a railroad association, to grab a free snack? Thousands of journalists were invited to Disney World on its 15th anniversary. Disney World offered journalists three options: Disney World would pay for everything, including travel; journalists could pay $150 a day to cover a portion of the cost; journalists could pay their own way. Editor & Publisher magazine reported that the event cost its sponsors, which included area tourism bureaus, hotels and airlines, about $7.5 million. The number of journalists who accepted the free or subsidized offer is not known, although other reporters covering the event estimated it was a significant number.

The New York Times said in its editorial columns that those who had accepted the subsidy had "debased" the profession. Some of the Florida papers printed stories about junket journalism. A Disney World representative said the turnout would have been higher if it hadn't been for the stories that raised the ethics issue.

That sort of invitation to an event is easier to decline if you are one of several hundred journalists at Disney World than if you are the only reporter from the only newspaper or station in town covering the local fair and are being provided free tickets, food or gifts. Some news organizations will estimate the cost of meals or travel and reimburse the host organization.

## CONFLICT OF INTEREST

The third category of ethical questions is closely related to the second. With payola a reporter actually receives some material benefits. In the *conflict-of-interest* category the benefit often is intangible. This category differs from journalist as participant in that here the action is voluntary and outside the job. In the other category, which is discussed last, the journalist participates to get a story.

### Some Questions

Reporters have the opportunity to forward the causes of organizations to which they belong, and that intangible benefit raises many questions. Do reporters' allegiances interfere with their ability to be objective? Can a member of either the Democratic or Republican Party cover the political beat? Can religion editors objectively report on developments in their own churches? Can a reporter be a member of a city commission and report on city politics? Can a reporter objectively cover the school board if another reporter, an editor or a publisher is a member?

Some of the conflicts do involve material benefits. Can a financial reporter objectively report on a company in which he or she owns stock? Should a financial or business writer use inside knowledge to buy stocks, bonds or commodities? Can a sports reporter who is given four extra 50-yard-line tickets to sell or distribute to friends objectively report on a team? The Chicago Tribune requires members of its news staff to file annual statements disclosing outside income as well as civic and political activities. The San Jose Mercury News prohibits its business news reporters and editors from owning stock in local companies.

Not even annual financial disclosure would have helped The Wall Street Journal detect that a reporter for its sensitive "Heard on the Street" column was leaking information about upcoming stories and that he and others were profiting by trading stock based on the information that would be printed. Favorable mention in the column often sent the value of a stock up several dollars a share.

The Journal fired the reporter after he conceded to the Securities and Exchange Commission that he had leaked the information. The Journal then reported on the case to its readers. Soon after, a Business Week reporter was fired for acting on inside information.

The Honolulu Advertiser suspended a free-lance columnist when it learned he had accepted $500 to write an article favorable to the dairy industry.

Sometimes conflict of interest arises because the reporters are serving themselves or the paper instead of the readers. This occurs when a reporter elects to do a story or a series that may have little interest or importance for readers but that would be a good entry for a journalism contest. Many trade associations give substantial cash awards for stories about their special interests, ranging from food and furniture to cigars and cars.

A conflict can arise, too, because the journalist holds a second job. Most papers now have written policies on the subject, and few allow reporters to work for a competitor or to do work that conflicts with their primary jobs. The Boston Globe requires prior approval for any outside activity that may be a conflict of interest.

Finally, a conflict of interest may arise because of newspaper or management entanglements in the community. What is the newspaper's position with respect to the Chamber of Commerce if the publisher is the chamber's president? How does the paper treat the United Way when the editor is a member of the board of directors? If the newspaper corporation is involved in the creation of a special downtown taxing district, can the news room cover the issue objectively? Would the public perceive the coverage to be unbiased?

## Some Answers

To most of the questions raised about conflicts of interest, the answers, even to a situationist, are rather clear-cut. Sports reporters should accept no more than the press-box seat they need to cover the game. No stories should be written purely as journalism-contest entries. Some newspapers even forbid entry into trade-association contests, some of which exist only to encourage publication of stories about a certain topic such as fashions or wine.

Many newspapers, in fact, prohibit their reporters from engaging in activities that they might be assigned to cover. This means that reporters, like civil-service employees, forfeit some rights of citizenship: They may not participate in political campaigns or be stockholders in companies they may have to cover. They may not hold memberships, even in non-political governmental bodies such as city commissions. As of 1983, of the 115 Newspaper Guild contracts covering news room employees, 66 required permission from the employer to do outside work, 87 prohibited employees from working for a competitive enterprise, 81 prohibited employees from outside work or activity that would embarrass or exploit their position with the company, and 10 prohibited employees from being paid for working in public relations for any political group or candidate without the consent of the publisher.

The Guild contracts raise another complication. Publishers cannot simply impose codes on employees; the National Labor Relations Board has often ruled that many ethical concerns, such as the acceptance of freebies or what employees can do in their spare time, is subject to negotiation. A Knoxville, Tenn., reporter who won a seat on a suburban school board was given the choice of resigning from the board or being fired from her job. Her grievance was taken to binding arbitration. Among other things, she pointed out that her employer's statement prohibiting such elective office was not part of the Guild contract.

Some newspapers allow reporters to participate in activities if they are not involved with the coverage. This kind of severance is not clear enough, however. A reporter covering a commission on which a fellow employee is a member has at least the appearance of a conflict of interest. And any leaks coming from that commission are likely to be blamed on the newspaper member.

Many publishers argue vigorously that the newspaper and its management need to be good citizens of their community. The newspaper, like other businesses, should use some of its money and talent to improve the community.

That issue was debated emotionally and publicly in Florida when several newspapers contributed money to an organization campaigning against legalized gambling. The newspapers' involvement was debated nearly as much as the gambling proposal. Reporters bought advertising space to criticize their executives' decisions to become involved financially in the campaign. Other publishers also criticized the financial involvement even as their papers editorialized against the gambling proposal.

In an Iowa region beset by economic hardships, competing newspaper and broadcast managers contributed $73,500 to hire a consultant to advise the Quad Cities on how it could attract new jobs. When the plan was completed, the media managers tried to turn it over to a business group for follow-up action, but the group insisted that the media remain part of the implementation committee. Two of the managers served on the 23-member committee.

While some activities obviously must be proscribed, the newspaper can maintain its independence and be a good citizen. It has to be careful how it supports causes and activities.

A publisher cannot serve on a school board or with the Chamber of Commerce without causing problems for reporters and damaging the newspaper's credibility. But the paper can serve the taxpayers of the school district in many other ways: by providing in-depth, expert coverage; by encouraging good candidates to run for the board; and by supporting tax issues editorially when the newspaper feels they are deserving.

The newspaper also can serve the Chamber of Commerce in many ways without having the publisher on the board. The newspaper is a dues-paying member, as are most other businesses in the community. It can invite promotion experts, advertising experts or downtown development experts to present free seminars to the merchants. Or, it can donate time from its art and graphics departments to design pamphlets and booklets. The paper might do the same for the United Way.

In none of these activities is it necessary for the news department to become involved. And while the absolutist would frown, the involvement is no more serious than accepting a cup of coffee from a news source.

Deeper involvement does cause problems. Ray Spangler, retired publisher of the Redwood City (Calif.) Tribune, recalled the time he served on an "unidentified committee of five" to advise the school district on a bond issue. "At our first meeting, one of the five, a subscriber, turned to me and said, 'I'd rather see my publisher on the sidelines than here.'" Spangler added, "He was wiser than I."

## WITHHOLDING INFORMATION

The fourth category of ethical questions involves reporters and editors who must make decisions about *withholding information*. As a reporter you will make daily decisions about what will and will not be included in a story. Most of the decisions you make will be based on criteria of news value; if the news is timely, interesting and important, it should be reported. But there are times when other factors will influence your decision.

To what extent does the public have a need to know about an individual's private life? Does the public need to know details of the sexual entanglements of public officials? Is the inclusion of the addresses of elderly robbery victims who live alone an inducement for others to victimize them? Do you print the addresses of relatives in obituaries despite protests from police officials that publication is an invitation to criminals to enter the houses during the funeral services? When a private person commits suicide out of the public's view, should you report suicide as the cause of death? If the mayor is killed in a car accident and a dozen pornographic magazines are found in his car, would you report that? Would you withhold all or parts of a story if the subject of it threatened to commit suicide if you printed?

In Seattle, the Post-Intelligencer was about to reveal that a local judge had been accused of committing sexual acts with teen-age boys, some of whom had appeared before him in court. Informed that the story would run, the judge told a friend that he was going to commit suicide. The threat was never passed on to the newspaper. The day before the story was to run, the judge killed himself.

Critics said the paper should not have been working on the story. They pointed out that the judge had declined to run for re-election and had announced he was leaving the state. The editors replied that the State Commission on Judicial Conduct had quietly and secretly admonished the judge for out-of-court contact with some youths six years earlier. However, additional allegations had surfaced. The paper wanted to expose what it believed were inadequacies in the state judicial review system.

E&P magazine quoted J.D. Alexander, executive director of the Post-Intelligencer, as saying, "There was a system that allowed victims to report transgressions to what they believed were the proper authorities, never again to hear of their complaints."

Most cases are not quite so dramatic, however. Despite extensive efforts by some people in a political campaign, newspapers and stations covering a gubernatorial contest in Mississippi declined to disseminate evidence that one of the candidates was a homosexual. The evidence, affidavits from male prostitutes who claimed to have had relations with the candidate, was offered to several journalists. Finally, the candidate's opponents held a news conference to make the charges public themselves. The media covered the conference. Asked why he wanted to publicize the case, the spokesman for the other candidate said, "We simply seek the truth, which, I thought, was a common trait I shared with the media." The accused candidate won the election, and on the day he was inaugurated, the Jackson Clarion-Ledger reported that the prostitutes said they had been paid for their statements and recanted.

In El Paso, Texas, the media held a story of the kidnapping of two boys for two days because of threats, relayed by the FBI, that the kidnappers would kill the boys if the kidnapping were publicized. The boys were eventually freed unharmed.

A commonly accepted practice among both print and broadcast journalists is to withhold the names of sexual-assault victims because there is a perceived social stigma attached to being a rape victim. Two-thirds of the 375 editors who responded to a survey taken by Carol E. Oukrop of Kansas State University in 1983 said they would not print the name of a rape victim. Of those who thought it should be printed, nine out of 10 would wait until the trial to identify the victim.

When a woman accused the nephew of Sen. Edward Kennedy of rape in 1991, the case drew international attention. Soon, it became an exception in the handling of the accused rape victim's name.

First, a British tabloid printed her name. Then a U.S. tabloid, The Globe, printed her name and picture. Then NBC News broadcast her name and picture. Soon after, The New York Times and several other newspapers identified the woman.

Some critics charged that the media had identified the woman because the accused was a member of a powerful political family. They noted that the victim of a gang rape attack in New York's Central Park was never identified in the mainstream media despite intense coverage. Some critics suggested the difference was that the accused in the Kennedy case had connections and the accused in the Central Park case did not.

The case reopened the debate about whether withholding rape victims' names helps or hurts their cause. Those who argue that the names should be printed say that the female can unjustly accuse a male without suffering the consequences of public scrutiny; that the social stigma of being a rape victim will never fade until the media start handling it as they do other crime news; and that withholding those names make the media vulnerable to pressure to withhold names in other news.

Those who argue that the names should not be printed say that the act of naming the victim will not erase the stigma and that fewer women will report rapes if they know they will be identified in the media.

The courts have given some signs of turning voluntary actions into mandatory practices. In 1981 a Washington state Superior Court judge ordered reporters to abide by voluntary bench-bar-press guidelines as a condition of attending a criminal pretrial hearing. In 1980 the U.S. Court of Appeals for the Western District of Missouri cited a newspaper policy not to print names of rape victims as evidence the editors were aware of the consequences of printing the information. The court ruled that a woman who had been kidnapped briefly but not sexually assaulted could pursue a lawsuit against the newspaper for lawfully and accurately printing her name.

Cases such as these may slow or even reverse the growing number of media codes providing for the voluntary withholding of information.

Photography is another area of information that is being scrutinized more carefully these days. The most dramatic shots of tragedies, fires, rescues, crimes and accidents are no longer published routinely. That is because more and more, readers are saying that they find them offensive.

Because pictures are so powerful, they have impact beyond words. Some of the most offensive pictures ever taken are among the most widely praised and honored: the Saigon police chief shooting a Viet Cong soldier in the head at point-blank range; bodies stacked on each other in Guyana after the Rev. Jim Jones convinced his followers to poison themselves; a woman and child falling from a fire escape as helpless firefighters watch in Boston. Newspapers and television stations face the problem frequently on the local level. Do you show the face of a dead person? Do you show grieving relatives? Do you show death?

Editors have found that proximity is an important consideration. Readers are more apt to accept pictures that show the faces of dead people if the people are not local. A picture of a body under a blanket is much less offensive than one not covered, even if readers can't see the face. The larger such dramatic pictures are displayed, the more likely it is that some readers are going to believe the newspaper is sensationalizing the story.

Despite all this, few editors withhold pictures or film merely because some readers or viewers might object. The important thing is to know when and why they will object. Then if the decision is to print or broadcast, the editors can be prepared to answer the criticism with arguments considered before the decision was made rather than in hindsight.

Several surveys' results indicate that most editors are situationists. They are concerned about the consequences of their acts. While this concern helps them decide when and whether to withhold information, in the industry there still is a tradition of fierce independence and loyalty to the reader.

David Lipman, managing editor of the St. Louis Post-Dispatch, summed it up for situationists. ''If we sin, we should sin on the side of disclosures and not concealment.''

## DECEIT

The fifth category of ethical questions involves reporting techniques that might *deceive* readers, sources or those under investigation. Some of these practices are anathema to nearly everyone, others are more debatable, and still others may be illegal and yet be ethical. The question of deceit is perhaps the hardest one journalists must face.

### Generally Disapproved Practices

Some journalistic techniques can deceive readers into thinking a story is accurate and fair. One such practice involves picking up quotes from newspaper clippings and recycling them as if they were timely and presented in the right context. Another involves reporting charges against an individual without giving adequate opportunity for reply in the same article. A third is the subtle use of words to color a story, such as ''claims'' for ''says'' and ''demands'' for ''asks.'' And still another involves the subtle practice of ignoring news when it might be considered damaging to a newspaper's editorial or advertising interests.

No surveys are needed on these points. No ethical system can excuse these practices; no journalists brag of them. But a few do use them.

## Debatable Practices

The undesirability of some other techniques is not so clear-cut. Lying, surprisingly enough, is one. If it is wrong to lie, then the absolutists never would conceal their identity to gather information. If the only way to attend a meeting of the Ku Klux Klan were to go as someone interested in joining, the absolutists never would get in. The situationist, however, would balance the information to be gained against the deceit involved.

Jerry Thompson, a reporter for the Nashville Tennessean, spent 13 months posing as a member of the Klan. He and his editors believed it was the only way to be able to report fully on Klan activities and beliefs. After his identity was revealed in the newspapers, Thompson got 24-hour protection at his home because of threats.

Pat Harper of WNBC-TV dressed as a homeless person and spent five days and nights on the streets of New York. She carried a concealed microphone and was followed by a hidden camera crew. Harper and her station were accused by some critics of exploiting the homeless. The same year, a Baltimore Evening Sun reporter also spent days on the streets covering the homeless, but he didn't conceal his identity. ''I told them what I was doing, but I didn't ask a lot of questions,'' the reporter said.

The Ku Klux Klan and the homeless are important subjects. But instances of deception don't stop there. A reporter for the now-defunct Los Angeles Herald Examiner posed as a buyer in order to see the inside of the house Jim and Tammy Bakker were selling in Los Angeles. Jim Bakker was a television evangelist convicted of misusing money donated to the church. The reporter's editor told M.L. Stein, ''The press was barred. The Bakkers are news. They are in a public arena. Ordinary citizens could get into the house so why discriminate against the press?''

Although some media permit exceptions, usually only with the agreement of top editors, most, including The New York Times and Washington Post, have rules against concealing identity.

Frequently, reporters are requested to conceal not their own identities, but those of their sources. News columns and broadcasts are sprinkled with references such as ''highly placed sources,'' ''government officials,'' and ''sources close to the president.'' In stories involving the federal government, these descriptions are often code words understood by other journalists but usually not known to the reader.

Widespread use of anonymous sources may be necessary when covering volatile diplomatic issues and exposing mismanagement or crime in public offices. But it is not necessary in all of these instances, and the practice is subject to abuse. Politicians and private parties alike use anonymity to destroy other people's reputations, to test public opinion on new programs and to advance special interests. Reporters who allow themselves to be used by sources who have no legitimate reason for anonymity damage the credibility of their publications.

Even when the reporters decide that the requests are legitimate, they are obligated to doublecheck the accuracy of the information given. Verification is absolutely necessary.

Reporters use many techniques they would consider unethical in and of themselves but that, in a given situation, may be justifiable. Reporters have looked through garbage cans for information. They have asked clerks and secretaries for copies of private or classified documents. They have led sources to believe they knew more than they really did in order to force more information into the open.

Much of consumer reporting involves the reporter acting in the role of the consumer. A typical example is taking a car to repair shops to see if customers are being overcharged. Such a story would be impossible to get if reporters identified themselves.

## Lawbreaking Practices

Breaking into offices and receiving stolen documents are violations of the law. But laws do not make something ethical or unethical; they only make something legal or illegal. People who break the law must pay the penalty and suffer society's disapproval. People who say they have to break the law because obeying it would violate their principles risk being charged with setting themselves above the law.

Yet at times, journalists, among others, must consider breaking the law for ethical principles. Publication of the ''Pentagon Papers'' is an example. The editors of The New York Times knew that accepting the stolen papers could have been interpreted as a violation of the law. They had to balance that against the service they would provide to citizens by publishing the documents. Their ethical responsibility to the citizens apparently overrode what could have been a violation of the law. As it turned out, the courts never decided the legality of the Times' act.

The courts did get involved when a reporter for the Potomac News of Woodbridge, Va., was given a sergeant's badge for a day by the regional jail superintendent so the reporter could get into a state prison. He wanted to interview a prisoner there who said he had been raped by other prisoners. When the reporter told his superiors after he returned, they decided not to run the story because they could not condone his use of deception.

That would have been the end of it except that the regional jailer was suspended for his part in the incident. The paper then published a story explaining the reporter's role in it. Later, it published the interview with the prisoner under the headline, "LeVasseur the Murderer Now the Victim." State corrections officials charged the reporter with impersonating a law officer and falsifying an official document.

Nearly all journalists agree that the story was a significant one: It showed that the prison system was unwilling or unable to protect prisoners from each other. But was it worth the price?

Many journalists would say it was if there were no other way to get the information. Louis Hodges, director of Studies in Applied Ethics at Washington & Lee University, adds another consideration: "No one was put at risk by the deception in the way people might be at risk if the reporter posed, for example, as a doctor or fireman."

However, many journalists believe that no deception is acceptable. They are bothered by the contradictory position in which it places journalists: criticizing law officers for impersonating the media while they themselves are impersonating law officers. And finally, while the prisoner knew he was talking to a reporter, most of the time when reporters are undercover, the people they encounter do not know that their words may be printed or broadcast.

Laws complicate already complicated ethical questions for journalists. You cannot always assume that what is legal is the ethical thing to do; sometimes what is illegal is more ethical and, because it is illegal, even more difficult to do.

## The Rationale for Certain Kinds of Deceit

It would be a much simpler life for reporters if gathering information were a matter of asking questions and obtaining responses. But the information reporters are trying to secure often is more technical, more valuable and more protected than ever. The records that reporters need to investigate government officials are locked in safes or stored in computers. People who fear for their jobs are afraid to talk to reporters. Some documents are shredded to destroy evidence, while others are classified to avoid embarrassment rather than to protect national security. Newspapers have begun to look at white-collar crime, which even law enforcement agencies with subpoena power have difficulty investigating.

Many journalists believe that these extraordinary problems require extraordinary measures. That is why some journalists are willing to deceive people *in some situations*. That is why some journalists are willing to accept stolen documents *in some situations*. But just as most journalists believe that if they must err, they should err on the side of publication rather than suppression, most also believe that journalists must try every legal and unquestionable means of gathering information before considering more dubious techniques.

Absolutist reporters cannot operate successfully in today's society. The information they need often is not available by conventional means. Situationists are more successful because they balance the good to be gained against the transgression to be committed.

It is a fine line that situationists must draw. Journalists not deeply committed to a set of ethical principles will too easily and too often forget those principles in the heat of the hunt for information. As a journalist you must be prepared to defend the ethical against the unethical, sometimes against your own employer. And you must be prepared ultimately to give up your job to defend your principles.

## INVASION OF PRIVACY

Sometimes even a fullback chooses to run around, rather then over, a defender. The American public thinks that journalists too often simply run over people's private lives. For that reason and others, public confidence and respect for the press is relatively low. The perception that journalists peek in windows, crowd around private citizens who have been thrust into the public limelight and intrude into private spaces in pursuit of a story is based partly on fact and partly on fiction.

Journalists do change. Between 1976 and 1985, the percentage of editors who would publish the name and address of a clerk who had been a robbery victim fell from 48.3 to 9.1.

However, critics have much to criticize. When 241 servicemen died in a bombing in Lebanon, journalists rushed to interview the families of the victims. Some were with the families as they waited for word of their sons. One cameraman shot through a glass door as the parents were told that their son had died.

When the astronauts died in the Challenger explosion, journalists rushed to the hometowns for reactions and to cover the funerals. The editor of the Concord Monitor, one of the hometown papers, wrote, "For days after the shuttle tragedy the talk in bars and restaurants was of what vultures the media were, what heartless invaders of privacy."

When a Pan Am flight exploded over Scotland, the reverberations were felt most strongly in Syracuse, New York, where many of the victims attended school. As families waited anxiously in the airport for word, camera crews filmed and asked questions. The nation watched a mother fall to the floor screaming when she learned the fate of her child. Pan Am accidentally released a list of the students on the flight to a local television station before the parents were notified; the station broadcast the names.

All families have a right to their privacy. The activities of the media are invasive only when reporters and photographers stay around when the families do not want them there. The media and the public may have a *need* to know the impact of the deaths on the families, but they do not have a *right* to know. Courts give us a legal definition of *invasion of privacy*; journalists must supply their own ethical definition.

The definition of privacy was extended by journalists to include the last name of the family whose son, born with severe immunological deficiency, had become a worldwide news story. The boy lived in a sterile bubble for 12 years. Many journalists knew the boy's name; no one printed it or broadcast it even when the boy died. Although the local community knew who the boy was, he went to his grave known only as David, the "bubble-boy," to most of the world.

If the media continue to exhibit such responsibility, then public trust and confidence in the institution may grow. However, a decision to withhold information to protect someone's privacy is not made without cost. Every time it is done, the media get requests from others who want to be treated the same way. The extreme result of that type of policy is a nameless and faceless news report.

The two newspapers in Albuquerque, N.M., faced tough decisions about whether to show a face when covering the aftereffects of a fire that nearly killed a 5-year-old girl. Sage Volkman suffered burns on 45 percent of her body. She lost her fingers. The heat fused her toes and destroyed her eyelids, nose and left ear.

Two months later in a follow-up story, the Albuquerque Journal ran its least offensive color photo of her, taken at the burn center. The editors rejected several others because they were too "gruesome." The Albuquerque Tribune eventually printed a tabloid with a story and ten pictures of Sage as she came out of the burn center and re-entered society. Included in the package was a message from Sage's parents, who invited readers to share their thoughts with their children. Sage's mother also contributed parts of the diary she kept during the recovery period.

Clearly, the parents did not regard this coverage as an invasion of their privacy, even as some readers criticized the newspapers for providing it.

## PARTICIPATION IN THE NEWS

At their best, journalists are dispassionate observers. But it is hard to remain dispassionate when a man you are photographing is threatening to jump off the bridge and you might be able to grab him. It is hard to remain dispassionate when you are shooting TV videotape of someone rescuing a child from icy waters, and you could be helping. It is hard to remain dispassionate if you are on the front lines during a war and a soldier next to you is wounded. It is hard to remain dispassionate when you are observing police brutality.

Reporters have faced all of those situations, and they have reacted as most human beings would. They reached out to help. Should they?

**Figure 22.2
Participation in
the News.**
A reporter at the
scene of a suicide
attempt or other
crisis situation must
decide whether to
record the event or
to act.

In each instance, the journalist becomes a *participant in the news* rather than just a reporter of it. Yet, you must weigh the consequences of a man's committing suicide or a child's drowning against your obligation to remain a reporter and represent your readers. In a typical situation, a Sante Fe, N.M., photographer, first upon an accident scene, helped rescue a family from the cab of a semitrailer. After they were safe, he took pictures.

But there are some not-so-clear-cut instances where a journalist becomes a participant. A Dallas Times Herald reporter was arrested for aiding illegal aliens because he was found in the car with them as they drove across Texas. He said he was observing how a church group smuggled refugees from war-torn Central America into the country. The legal question is whether he had a right to be at the scene of a crime. Authorities didn't press the issue; they decided not to file charges. The ethical question is whether he ought to have participated, even if only by riding in the car with them once they were in Texas.

The television networks have found themselves at the eye of a storm because they are accused of being participants, rather than just reporters, of the electoral process. They have become participants, critics charge, by projecting election results before polls close. Critics are afraid that people will not vote if they believe the presidential race has already been decided. By staying away from the polls, non-voters affect other races. The networks argue that it is their constitutional right to report the news when they have it. It is now an ethical question; if enough politicians become aroused, it may become a legal one, too.

Members of a television crew from Anniston, Ala., became participants in a story when they filmed a man setting fire to himself. Oddly enough, the crew members became participants by not stopping him. The man had called the station several times to ask for coverage of his action, which he said was a protest over unemployment. The crew notified the police and then showed up at the park where the man said he would be. The police, however, did not find them. In the meantime, the cameraman filmed as the man doused himself with lighter fluid and tried to ignite himself. After 15 agonizing seconds, the first match went out. He poured more lighter fluid on and lit a second. This time, the fire quickly spread over his body. Not until the man was completely engulfed in flames did one of the journalists try to help him put it out.

The man survived. The journalists would not have become participants if they had not accepted the invitation to watch a self-immolation. The event might not have occurred if the TV crew had not shown up.

Journalists have often been participants in the news, sometimes trying to save lives, sometimes trying to get stories. When the action is taken to save a life, it is understandable. When the action is taken to get a story, it is questionable at best, despicable at worst. Yet, it is easy to criticize. Sometimes you become part of a story by covering it. Would you pick up a phone and call a hostage held captive in a house surrounded by the police if you could get an exclusive interview?

# The Media Response

Journalists' commitment to ethical practices is not a new one. For generations, journalism has been practiced by honorable people who have gone to jail, lost their jobs and suffered numerous other hardships in defense of their principles.

Journalism requires a commitment to truth, a sympathy for the public interest and a willingness to shun personal aggrandizement. But the journalist's ethical code is voluntary. As such, it has to be accepted on a personal, intellectual and moral basis. There are no licenses to be withdrawn, as in the case of the medical, legal and accounting professions. And that's as it should be, not only because a free press requires freedom from licensing, but also because ethical behavior cannot be legislated.

Even the existence of voluntary codes can be dangerous. As we indicated earlier, some judges have used them against journalists. In the one instance, a judge ordered all journalists who wanted to cover a trial to adhere to the voluntary press-bar guidelines in the state of Washington. His order was appealed but not overturned. In another case, a judge in a federal appeals court used a newspaper's policy to withhold the names of sexual assault victims against the newspaper when it printed the name of a female who had been kidnapped briefly. The judge ruled that the woman had a right to sue the newspaper for printing her name, even though it had been obtained lawfully.

The logical end of this type of judicial reasoning is that journalists are responsible for the consequences of everything they print. In Spain, a journalist was convicted of ''professional negligence'' because two people he named as government informers in a story were later killed. He was convicted despite the fact that the court never knew who the murderers were or why they killed the two men.

Although these are isolated examples, they are ominous warnings that, ironically, if a news medium has a voluntary code of ethics and does not adhere to it strictly, a court somewhere, sometime may use it against the medium. In those situations, a newspaper with a general statement of principles or even without a code may be better off legally.

The ethical codes for journalists are general statements of principles. The major ones—those of the Society of Professional Journalists/Sigma Delta Chi, the American Society of Newspaper Editors and the Associated Press Managing Editors—agree on the salient points: The press exists to serve reader interests and has a responsibility to do it fairly and accurately without fear or favor. Most of the ethical questions that we have addressed in this chapter are acknowledged in all three codes.

On payola and conflict of interest, the ASNE code says:

> The right of a newspaper to attract and hold readers is restricted by nothing but considerations of public welfare. . . . A journalist who uses his power for any selfish or otherwise unworthy purpose is faithless to a high trust.

On the same subject, the APME code states:

> The newspaper should report the news independent of its own interests. It should not give favored news treatment to advertisers or special interest groups. . . . Concern for community or business interests should not cause a newspaper to distort or misrepresent the facts. . . .
>
> The newspaper and its staff should make every effort to be free of obligations to news sources and special interests. . . . The newspaper should avoid even the appearance of obligation or conflict of interest.
>
> Newspapers should accept nothing of value from news sources or other outsiders. . . .

Active involvement in such things as politics, community affairs, demonstrations on social causes may compromise the ability to report and edit without prejudice. . . .

Outside employment that conflicts with news interests should be avoided.

Investments by staff members . . . that could conflict with the newspaper's ability to report the news or that would create the impression of conflict should be avoided.

Stories should not be written or edited primarily for the purpose of winning awards and prizes.

The guidelines are less specific when dealing with the question of deceit. The general principle stated by the SPJ/SDX is: "The public's right to know of events of public importance and interest is the overriding mission of the mass media." The SPJ/SDX code also states: "Journalists will seek news that serves the public interest, despite the obstacles. They will make constant efforts to assure that the public's business is conducted in public and that public records are open to public inspection." And, according to the APME code, the newspaper "should vigorously expose wrongdoing or misuse of power, public or private. It should oppose selfish interests regardless of their power, size or influence." Some journalists take these statements to be acknowledgments of the occasional need to balance two wrongs: the wrong being committed by someone in public office and the wrong that may be committed by a journalist trying to report on that official.

There also are general guidelines that acknowledge invasion of privacy. The ASNE code says this:

A newspaper should not invade private rights or feelings without sure warrant of public right as distinguished from public curiosity. . . .

A newspaper cannot escape conviction of insincerity if while professing high moral purpose it supplies incentives to base conduct, such as are to be found in details of crime and vice, publication of which is not demonstrably for the general good.

The SPJ code addresses itself to the same problem in these words:

Journalists at all times will show respect for the dignity, privacy, rights and well-being of people encountered in the course of gathering and presenting the news. . . .

The news media must guard against invading a person's right to privacy.

The media should not pander to morbid curiosity about details of vice and crime.

No codes, whether mandatory or voluntary, can anticipate all situations.

Even laws are constantly revised to accommodate omissions and changing social norms.

Taken as standards of behavior, the codes are adequate guidelines. Journalists must draw upon their own moral codes to provide specific answers to the complex questions faced in their daily work. The basic principle is stated in the SPJ code:

> Journalists must be free of obligation to any interest other than the people's right to know.

## Suggested Readings

Christians, Clifford, Rotzoll, Kim and Fackler, Mark. "Media Ethics." New York: Longman, 1984. Step-by-step analyses of 75 situations where ethical questions were raised in news, advertising and entertainment.

Fletcher, Joseph. "Situation Ethics; The New Morality." Philadelphia: Westminster Press, 1966. An overview of situation ethics from a Christian perspective.

Fry, Don. "The Shocking Pictures of Sage." "Washington Journalism Review," April 1988, pp. 35–41. A case study of how the Albuquerque newspapers handled the reporting and photography of a badly burned child.

Goodwin, H. Eugene. "Groping for Ethics in Journalism." Ames, Iowa: Iowa State University Press, 1984. Not only raises ethical questions but also suggests means to answer them. Has case histories and anecdotes.

Lambeth, Edmund B. "Committed Journalism." Bloomington, Ind.: Indiana University Press, 1986. Both a practical and a philosophical discussion of ethics.

McCulloch, Frank, ed. "Drawing the Line." St. Petersburg, Fla.: The Poynter Institute, 1984. Thirty-one newspaper editors describe the toughest ethical decisions they ever had to make.

Merrill, John. "The Imperative of Freedom: A Philosophy of Journalistic Autonomy." New York: Hastings House, 1974. A good look at press ethics from a philosopher's point of view.

Palmer, Nancy Doyle. "Going After the Truth—In Disguise." Washington Journalism Review, Nov. 1987, pp. 20–22. A roundup of instances when reporters concealed their identity.

# Exercises

1. You learn that the daughter of a local bank president has been kidnapped. The family has not been contacted by the kidnappers, and police officials ask you to keep the matter secret for fear the abductors might panic and injure the child. Describe how the absolutist, the antinomian and the situationist would react to the police request and what their reasons would be to justify their decision.

2. Is there an ethical difference between receiving a bottle of liquor and receiving a round-trip airline ticket from Chicago to San Francisco from a news source? Explain your answer, and identify the philosophical category (absolutist, situationist or antinomian) that your response fits.

3. You are a photographer for a newspaper. On your way back from a track meet, you see a man who looks as if he is thinking about jumping off a bridge. You have a camera with motor-drive action, which permits you to take pictures in rapid-fire sequence. Would you:

    **a.** Shoot pictures from a distance?

    **b.** Approach the man slowly, take pictures and try to talk him out of jumping?

    **c.** Step out of his sight and radio to the newspaper to send police?

    **d.** Take some other action?

    Justify your response.

4. A woman bank teller thwarts a robbery by alert thinking; the would-be robbers escape. The bank president, fearing the woman or her family might suffer reprisals, urges you to omit any identification in your story. Would you:

    **a.** Follow your usual style of carrying full name, age and address?

    **b.** Use only her name but no address?

    **c.** Omit her name and describe her only as a ''teller''?

    **d.** Handle the problem in some other way?

    Justify your response.

# APPENDIX

# Wire Service Style

A burro is an ass. A burrow is a hole in the ground. As a journalist you are expected to know the difference.

That piece of advice can be found in the United Press International Stylebook, a reference manual otherwise free of wit. If nothing else, the passage serves to dispel the myth that style rules encourage bland writing and conformity in newspapers.

Instead, style rules provide needed consistency throughout the paper so that the reader can focus on content, not differences of little substance. Some readers, for example, are irritated to find *employee* in one story and *employe* in the next. Both spellings can be found in dictionaries, but observing a style rule eliminates that annoying inconsistency. Style rules help reporters and editors avoid wasting time arguing about such details as the correct spelling of *OK* (or *okay*). Even more important, style rules provide guidance in the often troublesome areas of grammar, punctuation, capitalization, abbreviation and the like.

Despite that, editors are far from unanimous in their support of style. Louis D. Boccardi of The Associated Press wrote that journalists approach style questions with varying degrees of passion: "Some don't really think it's important. Some agree that basically there should be uniformity for reading ease if nothing else. Still others are prepared to duel over a wayward lowercase." Boccardi's comment appears in the foreword of The Associated Press Stylebook, a book designed as a reference manual as well as a stylebook. It is almost identical to The United Press International Stylebook. Indeed, the two news services collaborated in writing similar versions as a service to clients who subscribe to both.

Together, the AP and UPI stylebooks are the major source of American newspaper style. Many newspapers rely on them as their only source of style. Some issue supplements listing deviations from wire service style and establishing local style rules. Some, mostly large newspapers, have their own stylebooks.

Because newspapers depend so heavily on the AP and UPI stylebooks, this appendix focuses on the rules they establish. It is designed to point out the most common violations of style so that you, as a reporter, will learn to avoid them. It would be difficult, if not impossible, for you to commit to memory all the style rules in the AP Stylebook. But you can learn to avoid the most common mistakes while developing the habit of referring to your stylebook when in doubt.

In this appendix style rules are categorized under the headings of Capitalization; Abbreviations and Acronyms; Punctuation and Hyphenation; Numerals; and Grammar, Spelling and Word Usage. Following an introduction to each section, a listing of the most common style rules is provided. The appendix serves as an excellent reference for beginning reporters, but it should not be considered a substitute for the more comprehensive stylebooks. The authors thank the AP and UPI for granting permission to use excerpts from their stylebooks.

## CAPITALIZATION

In general, avoid unnecessary capitals. Use a capital letter only if you can justify it by one of the principles listed here.

Many words and phrases, including special cases, are listed separately in the complete stylebooks. Entries that are capitalized without further comment should be capitalized in all uses.

If there is no relevant listing in the stylebooks for a particular word or phrase, consult Webster's New World Dictionary. Use lowercase if the dictionary lists it as an acceptable form for the sense in which the word is being used.

As used in the stylebooks, *capitalize* means to use uppercase for the first letter of a word. If additional capital letters are needed, they are called for by an example or a phrase such as *use all caps*.

Some basic principles:

PROPER NOUNS: Capitalize nouns that constitute the unique identification for a specific person, place or thing: *John, Mary, America, Boston, England.*

Some words, such as the examples just given, are always proper nouns. Some common nouns receive proper noun status when they are used as the name of a particular entity: *General Electric, Gulf Oil.*

PROPER NAMES: Capitalize common nouns such as *party, river, street* and *west* only when they are an integral part of the full name for a person, place or thing: *Democratic Party, Mississippi River, Fleet Street, West Virginia.*

Lowercase these common nouns when they stand alone in subsequent references: *the party, the river, the street.*

Lowercase the common noun elements of names in all plural uses: *the Democratic and Republican parties, Main and State streets, lakes Erie and Ontario.*

POPULAR NAMES: Some places and events lack officially designated proper names but have popular names that are the effective equivalent: *the Combat Zone* (a section of downtown Boston), *the Main Line* (a group of Philadelphia suburbs), *the South Side* (of Chicago), *the Badlands* (of North Dakota), *the Street* (the financial community in the Wall Street area of New York).

The principle applies also to shortened versions of the proper names for one-of-a-kind events: *the Series* (for the World Series), *the Derby* (for the Kentucky Derby). This practice should not, however, be interpreted as a license to ignore the general practice of lowercasing the common noun elements of a name when they stand alone.

DERIVATIVES: Capitalize words that are derived from a proper noun and still depend on it for their meaning: *American, Christian, Christianity, English, French, Marxism, Shakespearean*.

Lowercase words that are derived from a proper noun but no longer depend on it for their meaning: *french fries, herculean, manhattan cocktail, malapropism, pasteurize, quixotic, venetian blind*.

## Common Problems

Newspapers conform to the basic rule of capitalization of the English language: Proper nouns—specific persons, places and things—are capitalized; common nouns are not. That rule is simple enough, but knowing when to capitalize words in other usages may not be as obvious.

When in doubt about whether to capitalize, refer to your stylebook. If that fails to solve the problem, refer to the primary supplemental reference established by the AP and UPI—Webster's New World Dictionary of the American Language, Third College Edition.

TRADEMARKS: Almost every editor has received a letter that reads something like this:

Dear Editor:

We were delighted to read your April 5 article about the popularity of Frisbees in your community.

Unfortunately, however, you failed to capitalize the word *Frisbee* throughout the article.

Because the word *Frisbee* is a trademark of our company, it should always be capitalized.

Such warnings of trademark infringements usually are nice enough. Businesses realize there are many trademarked words, and it is difficult for editors to keep up with them all. Only when violations repeatedly occur are threats of lawsuits tossed about.

Reporters and editors try to ensure that they don't turn words that are trademarks into generic terms. Companies register such words to protect their rights to them and have every reason to expect that newspapers will honor those rights.

Newspapers, however, are not eager to provide knowingly what amounts to free advertising for products in their news columns. Thus reporters and editors are encouraged to use generic words instead of trademarks. Here are some examples of substitution:

- Use *real estate agent* or *salesperson* rather than *Realtor*, a trademark of the National Association of Real Estate Boards.

- Use *soft drink* or *cola* rather than *Coke*, a trademark of the Coca-Cola Co.

- Use *gelatin*, not *Jell-O*.

- Use *bleach*, not *Clorox*.

- Use *refrigerator*, not *Frigidaire*.

The list of such words is lengthy, and some may be real sources of confusion. It is permissible to use *jeep*, for example, when referring to an Army vehicle, but the similarly named civilian vehicle is a *Jeep*. When in doubt, refer to the AP or UPI Stylebook for a list of many trademarked names.

PLURALS OF PROPER NOUNS: More confusion can result when referring to plurals of proper nouns. You would write about the *Tennessee Legislature* and the *Colorado Legislature* when each is used in the singular form. The plural, however, would be the *Tennessee and Colorado legislatures*. The same rule applies when referring to streets: *Ninth Street* and *Cherry Street*, but *Ninth and Cherry streets*.

RELIGIOUS TERMS: References to a deity often cause confusion. Style provides for the capitalization of proper names referring to a monotheistic deity, such as *God, Buddha, Allah, the Son, the Father*. However, pronouns used to refer to a deity—*he, him, thee, thou*—are lowercase.

TITLES: For the unwary reporter, titles are another source of trouble. Generally, formal titles used directly before a person's name are capitalized: *President George Bush, Secretary of State James Baker III, Queen Elizabeth II*. When used after a person's name, the title is lowercase: *George Bush, president of the United States; James Baker III, secretary of state; Elizabeth II, queen of England*.

Occupational titles—those more descriptive of a person's job than formal status—generally are not capitalized. Thus, you should lowercase references to *movie star Eddie Murphy, astronaut Neil Armstrong* or *outfielder José Canseco*.

DIRECT QUOTATION: Perhaps the most abused rule of capitalization deals with the first word of a direct quotation. That word should be capitalized following the source only when it:

1. Starts a complete sentence;

2. Is separated from the source by a comma; or

3. Appears in direct quotation marks.

Thus, it is permissible to write:

*Correct*                     Bush said, ''It was a tiring trip.''

                              Bush said ''it was a tiring trip.''

                              Bush said it was a tiring trip.

These constructions are incorrect:

| *Incorrect* | Bush said "It was a tiring trip." |
|---|---|
| | Bush said, "it was a tiring trip." |
| | Bush said, it was a tiring trip. |

## Alphabetized Listing

**academic departments**   Use lowercase except for words that are proper nouns or adjectives: *the department of history, the history department, the department of English, the English department.*

**administration**   Lowercase: *the administration, the president's administration, the governor's administration, the Bush administration.*

**air force**   Capitalize when referring to U.S. forces: *the U.S. Air Force, the Air Force, Air Force regulations.*
Use lowercase for the forces of other nations: *the Israeli air force.*

**animals**   Capitalize the name of a specific animal, and use Roman numerals to show sequence: *Bowser, Whirlaway II.*
For breed names, follow the spelling and capitalization in Webster's New World Dictionary. For breeds not listed in the dictionary, capitalize words derived from proper nouns; use lowercase elsewhere: *basset hound, Boston terrier.*

**army**   Capitalize when referring to U.S. forces: *the U.S. Army, the Army, Army regulations.*
Use lowercase for the forces of other nations: *the French army.*

**Bible**   Capitalize, without quotation marks, when referring to the Scriptures of the Old Testament or the New Testament. Capitalize also related terms such as *the Gospels, Gospel of St. Mark, the Scriptures, the Holy Scriptures.*
Lowercase *biblical* in all uses.
Lowercase *bible* as a non-religious term: *My dictionary is my bible.*

**brand names**   When they are used, capitalize them.
Brand names normally should be used only if they are essential to a story.
Sometimes, however, the use of a brand name may not be essential but is acceptable because it lends an air of reality to a story: *He fished a Camel from his shirt pocket* may be preferable to the less specific *cigarette.*

**building**   Capitalize the proper names of buildings, including the word *building* if it is an integral part of the proper name: *the Empire State Building.*

**bureau**   Capitalize when part of the formal name for an organization or agency: *the Bureau of Labor Statistics, the Newspaper Advertising Bureau.*
Lowercase when used alone or to designate a corporate subdivision: *the Washington bureau of The Associated Press.*

**cabinet**   Capitalize references to a specific body of advisers heading executive departments for a president, king, governor and the like: *The president-elect said he has not made his Cabinet selections.*

The capital letter distinguishes the word from the common noun meaning cupboard, which is lowercase.

**Cabinet titles**    Capitalize the full title when used before a name; lowercase in other uses: *Secretary of State James Baker III,* but *Richard B. Cheney, secretary of defense.*

**century**    Lowercase, spelling out numbers less than 10: *the first century, the 20th century.*

For proper names, follow the organization's practice: *20th Century Fox, Twentieth Century Fund, Twentieth Century Limited.*

**chairman, chairwoman**    Capitalize as a formal title before a name: *company Chairman Henry Ford, committee Chairwoman Anne Roberts.*

Do not capitalize as a casual, temporary position: *meeting chairman Robert Jones.*

Do not use *chairperson* unless it is an organization's formal title for an office.

**chief**    Capitalize as a formal title before a name: *He spoke to Police Chief Michael Codd. He spoke to Chief Michael Codd of the New York police.*

Lowercase when it is not a formal title: *union chief Walter Reuther.*

**church**    Capitalize as part of the formal name of a building, a congregation or a denomination; lowercase in other uses: *St. Mary's Church, the Roman Catholic Church, the Catholic and Episcopal churches, a Roman Catholic church, a church.*

Lowercase in phrases where *the church* is used in an institutional sense: *He believes in separation of church and state. The pope said the church opposes abortion.*

**city council**    Capitalize when part of a proper name: *the Boston City Council.*

Retain capitalization if the reference is to a specific council but the context does not require the city name:

BOSTON (AP)—The City Council . . .

Lowercase in other uses: *the council, the Boston and New York city councils, a city council.*

**committee**    Capitalize when part of a formal name: *the House Appropriations Committee.*

Do not capitalize *committee* in shortened versions of long committee names: the Special Senate Select Committee to Investigate Improper Labor-Management Practices, for example, became known as the *rackets committee.*

**congress**    Capitalize *U.S. Congress* and *Congress* when referring to the U.S. Senate and House of Representatives. Although *Congress* sometimes is used as a substitute for the House, it properly is reserved for reference to both the Senate and House.

Capitalize *Congress* also when referring to a foreign body that uses the term, or its equivalent in a foreign language, as part of its formal name: *the Argentine Congress, the Congress.*

Lowercase *congress* when it is used as a synonym for *convention* or in second reference to an organization that uses the word as part of its formal name: *the Congress of Racial Equality, the congress.*

**constitution**   Capitalize references to the *U.S. Constitution,* with or without the *U.S.* modifier: *The president said he supports the Constitution.*

When referring to constitutions of other nations or of states, capitalize only with the name of a nation or a state: *the French Constitution, the Massachusetts Constitution, the nation's constitution, the state constitution, the constitution.*

Lowercase in other uses: *the organization's constitution.*

Lowercase *constitutional* in all uses.

**courthouse**   Capitalize with the name of a jurisdiction: *the Cook County Courthouse, the U.S. Courthouse.* Lowercase in other uses: *the county courthouse, the courthouse, the federal courthouse.*

*Court House* (two words) is used in the proper names of some communities: *Appomattox Court House, Va.*

**court names**   Capitalize the full proper names of courts at all levels.

Retain capitalization if *U.S.* or a state name is dropped: *the U.S. Supreme Court, the Supreme Court; the Massachusetts Superior Court, the state Superior Court, the Superior Court, Superior Court.*

For courts identified by a numeral: *2nd District Court, 8th U.S. Circuit Court of Appeals.*

**directions and regions**   In general, lowercase *north, south, northeast, northern,* and so on when they indicate compass direction; capitalize these words when they designate regions.

**federal**   Use a capital letter for the architectural style and for corporate or governmental bodies that use the word as part of their formal names: *Federal Express, the Federal Trade Commission.*

Lowercase when used as an adjective to distinguish something from state, county, city, town or private entities: *federal assistance, federal court, the federal government, a federal judge.*

Also: *federal District Court* (but *U.S. District Court* is preferred) and *federal Judge John Sirica* (but *U.S. District Judge John Sirica* is preferred).

**federal court**   Always lowercase. The preferred form for first reference is to use the proper name of the court.

Do not create non-existent entities such as *Manhattan Federal Court.* Instead, use *a federal court in Manhattan.*

**food**   Most food names are lowercase: *apples, cheese, peanut butter.*

Capitalize brand names and trademarks: *Roquefort cheese, Tabasco sauce.*

Most proper nouns or adjectives are capitalized when they occur in a food name: *Boston brown bread, Russian dressing, Swiss cheese, Waldorf salad.*

Lowercase is used, however, when the food does not depend on the proper noun or adjective for its meaning: *french fries, graham crackers, manhattan cocktail.*

**former**   Always lowercase. But retain capitalization for a formal title used immediately before a name: *former President Reagan.*

**fraternal organizations and service clubs**   Capitalize the proper names: *American Legion, Lions Club, Independent Order of Odd Fellows, Rotary Club.*

Capitalize also words describing membership: *He is a Legionnaire, a Lion, an Odd Fellow, an Optimist and a Rotarian.*

**geographic names**   Capitalize common nouns when they form an integral part of a proper name, but lowercase them when they stand alone: *Pennsylvania Avenue, the avenue; the Philippine Islands, the islands, the Mississippi River, the river.*

Lowercase common nouns that are not part of a specific proper name: *the Pacific islands, the Swiss mountains, Chekiang province.*

**government**   Always lowercase: *the federal government, the state government, the U.S. government.*

**governmental bodies**   Follow these guidelines:

FULL NAME: Capitalize the full proper names of governmental agencies, departments, and offices; *the U.S. Department of State, the Georgia Department of Human Resources, the Boston City Council, the Chicago Fire Department.*

WITHOUT JURISDICTION: Retain capitalization in referring to a specific body if the dateline or context makes the name of the nation, state, county, city or town unnecessary: *the Department of State* (in a story from Washington), *the Department of Human Resources* or *the state Department of Human Resources* (in a story from Georgia), *the City Council* (in a story from Boston), *the Fire Department* or *the City Fire Department* (in a story from Chicago).

Lowercase further condensations of the name: *the department, the council.*

FLIP-FLOPPED NAMES: Retain capital letters for the name of a governmental body if its formal name is flopped to delete the word *of: the State Department, the Human Resources Department.*

GENERIC EQUIVALENTS: If a generic term has become the equivalent of a proper name in popular use, treat it as a proper name: Use *Walpole State Prison*, for example, even though the proper name is the *Massachusetts Correctional Institution-Walpole.*

PLURALS, NON-SPECIFIC REFERENCES: All words that are capitalized when part of a proper name should be lowercased when they are used in the plural or do not refer to a specific existing body. Some examples:

*All states except Nebraska have a state senate. The town does not have a fire department.*

*The bill requires city councils to provide matching funds. The president will address the lower houses of the New York and New Jersey legislatures.*

**heavenly bodies**    Capitalize the proper names of planets, stars, constellations and the like: *Mars, Earth, Arcturus, the Big Dipper, Aries.*

For comets, capitalize only the proper noun element of the name: *Halley's comet.*

Lowercase *sun* and *moon,* but if their Greek names are used, capitalize them: *Helios* and *Luna.*

**historical periods and events**    Capitalize the names of widely recognized epochs in anthropology, archaeology, geology and history: *the Bronze Age, the Dark Ages, the Middle Ages, the Pliocene Epoch.*

Capitalize also widely recognized popular names for periods and events: *the Atomic Age, the Boston Tea Party, the Civil War, the Exodus* (of the Israelites from Egypt), *the Great Depression, Prohibition.*

Lowercase *century: the 18th century.*

Capitalize only the proper nouns or adjectives in general descriptions of a period: *ancient Greece, classical Rome, the Victorian era, the fall of Rome.*

**holidays and holy days**    Capitalize them: *New Year's Eve, New Year's Day, Groundhog Day, Easter, Hanukkah* and so on.

**House of Representatives**    Capitalize when referring to a specific governmental body: *the U.S. House of Representatives, the Massachusetts House of Representatives.*

Capitalize shortened references that delete the words *of Representatives: the U.S. House, the Massachusetts House.*

Retain capitalization if *U.S.* or the name of a state is dropped but the reference is to a specific body:

BOSTON (AP)—The House has adjourned for the year.

Lowercase plural uses: *the Massachusetts and Rhode Island houses.*

Apply the same principles to similar legislative bodies, such as *the Virginia House of Delegates.*

**judge**    Capitalize before a name when it is the formal title for an individual who presides in a court of law. Do not continue to use the title in second reference.

Do not use *court* as a part of the title unless confusion would result without it:

- No *court* in the title: *U.S. District Judge John Sirica, District Judge John Sirica, federal Judge John Sirica, Judge John Sirica, U.S. Circuit Judge Homer Thornberry, appellate Judge John Blair.*

- *Court* needed in the title: *Juvenile Court Judge John Jones, Criminal Court Judge John Jones, Superior Court Judge Robert Harrison, state Supreme Court Judge William Cushing.*

When the formal title *chief judge* is relevant, put the court name after the judge's name: *Chief Judge John Sirica of the U.S. District Court in Washington, D.C.; Chief Judge Clement F. Haynsworth Jr. of the 4th U.S. Circuit Court of Appeals.*

Do not pile up long court names before the name of a judge. Make it *Judge John Smith of Allegheny County Common Pleas Court.* Not: *Allegheny County Common Pleas Court Judge John Smith.*

Lowercase *judge* as an occupational designation in phrases such as *beauty contest judge Bert Parks.*

**legislature**   Capitalize when preceded by the name of a state: *the Kansas Legislature.*

Retain capitalization when the state name is dropped but the reference is specifically to that state's legislature:

TOPEKA, Kan. (AP)—Both houses of the Legislature adjourned today.

Capitalize *legislature* in subsequent specific references and in such constructions as: *the 100th Legislature, the state Legislature.*

Lowercase *legislature* when used generically: *No legislature has approved the amendment.*

Use *legislature* in lowercase for all plural references. *The Arkansas and Colorado legislatures are considering the amendment.*

**magazine names**   Capitalize the name but do not place it in quotes. Lowercase *magazine* unless it is part of the publication's formal title: *Harper's Magazine, Newsweek magazine, Time magazine.*

Check the masthead if in doubt.

**monuments**   Capitalize the popular names of monuments and similar public attractions: *Lincoln Memorial, Statue of Liberty, Washington Monument, Leaning Tower of Pisa.*

**mountains**   Capitalize as part of a proper name: *Appalachian Mountains, Ozark Mountains, Rocky Mountains.*

Or simply: *the Appalachians, the Ozarks, the Rockies.*

**nationalities and races**   Capitalize the proper names of nationalities, peoples, races, tribes and the like: *Arab, Arabic, African, African-American, American, Caucasian, Cherokee, Chicano, Chinese* (both singular and plural), *Eskimo* (plural *Eskimos*), *French Canadian, Gypsy (Gypsies), Hispanic, Japanese* (singular and plural), *Jew, Jewish, Latin, Negro (Negroes), Nordic, Oriental, Sioux, Swede* and so on.

Lowercase *black* (noun or adjective), *white, red, mulatto* and the like.

Lowercase derogatory terms such as *honky* and *nigger.* Use them only in direct quotes when essential to the story.

**navy**   Capitalize when referring to U.S. forces: *the U.S. Navy, the Navy, Navy policy.*

Lowercase when referring to the naval forces of other nations: *the British navy.*

**newspaper names**   Capitalize *the* in a newspaper's name if that is the way the publication prefers to be known.

Lowercase *the* before the newspaper names if a story mentions several papers, some of which use *the* as part of the name and some of which do not.

**organizations and institutions**    Capitalize the full names of organizations and institutions: *the American Medical Association; First Presbyterian Church; General Motors Corp.; Harvard University; Harvard University Medical School; the Procrastinators Club; the Society of Professional Journalists.*

Retain capitalization if *Co., Corp.* or a similar word is deleted from the full proper name: *General Motors.*

FLIP-FOPPED NAMES: Retain capital letters when commonly accepted practice flops a name to delete the word *of*: *College of the Holy Cross, Holy Cross College; Harvard School of Dental Medicine, Harvard Dental School.*

Do not, however, flop formal names that are known to the public with the word *of*: *Massachusetts Institute of Technology,* for example, not *Massachusetts Technology Institute.*

**planets**    Capitalize the proper names of planets: *Jupiter, Mars, Mercury, Neptune, Pluto, Saturn, Uranus, Venus.*

Capitalize *earth* when used as the proper name of our planet: *The astronauts returned to Earth.*

Lowercase nouns and adjectives derived from the proper names of planets and other heavenly bodies: *martian, jovian, lunar, solar, venusian.*

**plants**    In general, lowercase the names of plants, but capitalize proper nouns or adjectives that occur in a name.

Some examples: *tree, fir, white fir, Douglas fir; Dutch elm, Scotch pine; clover, white clover, white Dutch clover.*

**police department**    In communities where this is the formal name, capitalize *police department* with or without the name of the community: *the Los Angeles Police Department, the Police Department.*

If a police agency has some other formal name such as *Division of Police,* use that name if it is the way the department is known to the public. If the story uses *police department* as a generic term for such an agency, put it in lowercase.

If a police agency with an unusual formal name is known to the public as a police department, treat *police department* as the name, capitalizing it with or without the name of the community. Use the formal name only if there is a special reason in the story.

If the proper name cannot be determined for some reason, such as the need to write about a police agency from a distance, treat *police department* as the proper name, capitalizing it with or without the name of the community.

Lowercase *police department* in plural uses: *the Los Angeles and San Francisco police departments.*

Lowercase *the department* whenever it stands alone.

**political parties and philosophies**    Capitalize both the name of the party and the word *party* if it is customarily used as part of the organization's proper name: *the Democratic Party, the Republican Party.*

Capitalize *Communist, Conservative, Democrat, Liberal, Republican, Socialist* and so on when they refer to the activities of a specific party or to individuals who are members of it. Lowercase these words when they refer to political philosophy.

Lowercase the name of a philosophy in noun and adjective forms unless it is derivative of a proper name: *communism, communist; fascism, fascist.* But: *Marxism, Marxist; Nazism, Nazi.*

**pontiff**   Not a formal title. Always lowercase.

**pope**   Capitalize when used as a formal title before a person's name; lowercase in all other uses: *Pope John Paul II spoke to the crowd. At the close of his address, the pope gave his blessing.*

**presidency**   Always lowercase.

**president**   Capitalize *president* only as a formal title before one or more names: *President Bush, Presidents Ford and Carter.*

Lowercase in all other uses: *The president said today. He is running for president. Lincoln was president during the Civil War.*

**religious references**   The basic guidelines:

DEITIES: Capitalize the proper names of monotheistic deities: *God, Allah, the Father, the Son, Jesus Christ, the Son of God, The Redeemer, the Holy Spirit.*

Lowercase pronouns referring to the deity: *he, him, his, thee, thou, who, whose, thy.*

Lowercase *gods* in referring to the deities of polytheistic religions.

Capitalize the proper names of pagan and mythological gods and goddesses: *Neptune, Thor, Venus.*

Lowercase such words as *god-awful, goddamn, godlike, godliness, godsend.*

LIFE OF CHRIST: Capitalize the names of major events in the life of Jesus Christ in references that do not use his name: *The doctrines of the Last Supper, the Crucifixion, the Resurrection and the Ascension are central to Christian belief.*

But use lowercase when the words are used with Christ's name: *The ascension of Jesus into heaven took place 40 days after his resurrection from the dead.*

Apply the principle also to events in the life of Christ's mother: *He cited the doctrine of the Immaculate Conception and the Assumption.* But: *She referred to the assumption of Mary into heaven.*

RITES: Capitalize proper names for rites that commemorate the Last Supper or signify a belief in Christ's presence: *the Lord's Supper, Holy Communion, Holy Eucharist.*

Lowercase the names of other sacraments.

Capitalize *Benediction* and *Mass.* But: *a high Mass, a low Mass, a requiem Mass.*

OTHER WORDS: Lowercase *heaven, hell, devil, angel, cherub, an apostle, a priest* and the like.

Capitalize *Hades* and *Satan.*

**seasons**   Lowercase *spring, summer, fall, winter* and derivatives such as *springtime* unless part of a formal name: *Dartmouth Winter Carnival, Winter Olympics, Summer Olympics.*

**senate**    Capitalize all specific references to governmental legislative bodies, regardless of whether the name of the nation or state is used: *the U.S. Senate, the Senate; the Virginia Senate, the state Senate, the Senate.*

Lowercase plural uses: *the Virginia and North Carolina senates.*

The same principles apply to foreign bodies.

Lowercase references to non-governmental bodies: *The student senate at Yale.*

**sentences**    Capitalize the first word of every sentence, including quoted statements and direct questions: *Patrick Henry said, ''I know not what course others may take, but as for me, give me liberty or give me death.''*

Capitalize the first word of a quoted statement if it constitutes a sentence, even if it was part of a larger sentence in the original: *Patrick Henry said, ''Give me liberty or give me death.''*

In direct questions, even without quotation marks: *The story answers the question, Where does true happiness really lie?*

**Social Security**    Capitalize all references to the U.S. system.

Lowercase generic uses such as: *Is there a social security program in Sweden?*

**state**    lowercase in all *state of* constructions: *the state of Maine, the states of Maine and Vermont, New York state.*

Do not capitalize *state* when used simply as an adjective to specify a level of jurisdiction: *state Rep. William Smith, the state Transportation Department, state funds.*

Apply the same principle to phrases such as *the city of Chicago, the town of Auburn* and so on.

**statehouse**    Capitalize all references to a specific statehouse, with or without the name of the state: *The Massachusetts Statehouse is in Boston. The governor will visit the Statehouse today.*

Lowercase plural uses: *the Massachusetts and Rhode Island statehouses.*

**subcommittee**    Lowercase when used with the name of a legislative body's full committee: *a Ways and Means subcommittee.*

Capitalize when a subcommittee has a proper name of its own: *the Senate Permanent Subcommittee on Investigations.*

**titles**    In general, confine capitalization to formal titles used directly before an individual's name. Lowercase and spell out titles when they are not used with an individual's name: *The president issued a statement. The pope gave his blessing.*

Lowercase and spell out titles in constructions that set them off from a name by commas: *The vice president, Nelson Rockefeller, declined to run again. John Paul II, the current pope, does not plan to retire.*

ABBREVIATED TITLES: The following formal titles are capitalized and abbreviated as shown when used before a name outside quotations: *Dr., Gov., Lt. Gov., Rep., Sen.* and certain military ranks. Spell out all except *Dr.* when they are used in quotations.

All other formal titles are spelled out in all uses.

ACADEMIC TITLES: Capitalize and spell out formal titles such as *professor, dean, president, chancellor* and *chairman* when they precede a name. Lowercase elsewhere.

Lowercase modifiers such as *history* in *history Professor Oscar Handlin* and *department* in *department Chairman Jerome Wiesner*.

FORMAL TITLES: Capitalize formal titles when they are used immediately before one or more names: *Pope John Paul II, President Washington, Vice Presidents John Jones and William Smith*.

LEGISLATIVE TITLES: Use *Rep., Reps.,* and *Sens.* as formal titles before one or more names in regular text. Spell out and capitalize these titles before one or more names in a direct quotation. Spell out and lowercase *representative* and *senator* in other uses.

Spell out other legislative titles in all uses. Capitalize formal titles such as *assemblyman, assemblywoman, city councilor* and *delegate* when they are used before a name. Lowercase in other uses.

Add *U.S.* or *state* before a title only if necessary to avoid confusion: *U.S. Sen. John Danforth spoke with state Sen. Joseph Carter*.

*First Reference Practice.* The use of a title such as *Rep.* or *Sen.* in first reference is normal in most stories. It is not mandatory, however, provided an individual's title is given later in the story.

Deletion of the title on first reference is frequently appropriate, for example, when an individual has become well-known: *Barry Goldwater endorsed President Bush today. The former Arizona senator said he believes the president deserves another term.*

*Second Reference.* Do not use a legislative title before a name on second reference unless it is part of a direct quotation.

*Congressman, Congresswoman, Rep.* and *U.S. Rep.* are the preferred first-reference forms when a formal title is used before the name of a U.S. House member. The word *congressman* or *congresswoman*, in lowercase, may be used in subsequent references that do not use an individual's name, just as *senator* is used in references to members of the Senate.

*Congressman* and *congresswoman* should appear as capitalized formal titles before a name only in direct quotation.

*Organizational Titles.* Capitalize titles for formal, organizational offices within a legislative body when they are used before a name: *Speaker Thomas Foley, Majority Leader Richard Gephardt, Minority Leader Robert Michel, Democratic Whip William Gray III, Chairman David Boren of the Senate Intelligence Committee, President Pro Tem Robert Byrd.*

MILITARY TITLES: Capitalize a military rank when used as a formal title before an individual's name.

Spell out and lowercase a title when it is substituted for a name: *Gen. John J. Pershing arrived today. An aide said the general would review the troops.*

ROYAL TITLES: Capitalize *king, queen* and so on when used directly before a name.

**trademark**   A *trademark* is a brand, symbol, word or the like that is used by a manufacturer or dealer and protected by law to prevent a competitor from using it: *AstroTurf*, for example, is a type of artificial grass.

In general, use a generic equivalent unless the trademark name is essential to the story.

When a trademark is used, capitalize it.

## ABBREVIATIONS AND ACRONYMS

The notation *abbrev.* is used in the AP and UPI stylebooks to identify the abbreviated form that may be used for a word in some contexts.

A few universally recognized abbreviations are required in some circumstances. Some others are acceptable depending on the context. But in general, avoid alphabet soup.

The same principle applies to acronyms—pronounceable words formed from the initial letters in a series of words: *ALCOA, NATO, radar, scuba.*

Guidance on how to use a particular abbreviation or acronym is provided in entries alphabetized according to the sequence of letters in the word or phrase.

Some general principles:

BEFORE A NAME: Abbreviate the following titles when used before a full name outside direct quotations: *Dr., Gov., Lt. Gov., Mr., Mrs., Ms., Rep., the Rev., Sen.* and certain military designations. Spell out all except *Dr., Mr., Mrs.* and *Ms.* when they are used before a name in direct quotations.

AFTER A NAME: Abbreviate *junior* or *senior* after an individual's name. Abbreviate *company, corporation, incorporated* and *limited* when used after the name of a corporate entity.

In some cases, an academic degree may be abbreviated after an individual's name.

WITH DATES OR NUMERALS: Use the abbreviations *A.D., B.C., a.m., p.m., No.,* and abbreviate certain months when used with the day of the month.

IN NUMBERED ADDRESSES: Abbreviate *avenue, boulevard* and *street* in numbered addresses: *He lives on Pennsylvania Avenue. He lives at 1600 Pennsylvania Ave.*

STATES AND NATIONS: The names of certain states, the *United States* and the *Union of Soviet Socialist Republics* (but not of other nations) are abbreviated with periods in some circumstances.

ACCEPTABLE BUT NOT REQUIRED: Some organizations and government agencies are widely recognized by their initials: *CIA, FBI, GOP.*

If the entry for such an organization notes that an abbreviation is acceptable in all references or on second reference, that does not mean that its use should be automatic. Let the context determine, for example, whether to use *Federal Bureau of Investigation* or *FBI.*

AVOID AWKWARD CONSTRUCTIONS: Do not follow an organization's full name with an abbreviation or acronym in parentheses or set off by dashes. If an abbreviation or acronym would not be clear on second reference without this arrangement, do not use it.

Names not commonly known by the public should not be reduced to acronyms solely to save a few words.

SPECIAL CASES: Many abbreviations are desirable in tabulations and certain types of technical writing. See individual entries in the Appendix.

CAPS, PERIODS: Use capital letters and periods according to the listings in the stylebooks. For words not in the books, use the first-listed abbreviation in Webster's New World Dictionary.

If an abbreviation not listed in the stylebooks or the dictionary achieves widespread acceptance, use capital letters. Omit periods unless the result would spell an unrelated word.

## Common Problems

Abbreviations save much space for newspapers in a year's time but editors use them only when readers will recognize them instantly. Newspapers are in the business of communicating to their readers. Saving space to the detriment of understanding is an intolerable offense.

There are many exceptions to the rules of abbreviation discussed in this section. They can be determined only by consulting a stylebook, and in each case the meaning of the abbreviation should be clear.

STATE NAMES: Although the U.S. Postal Service uses two-letter abbreviations for state names, they have been rejected for newspaper use because of the potential for confusion. *MS*, the post office abbreviation for *Mississippi*, could be mistaken for *Missouri* or the recently popularized courtesy title for a woman, *Ms*. Instead the AP and UPI use the more familiar state abbreviations that have won general acceptance through the years.

State names are abbreviated only when they follow city names.

The names of eight states never are abbreviated by the AP and UPI, though some newspapers make exceptions:

| | | |
|---|---|---|
| Alaska | Iowa | Texas |
| Hawaii | Maine | Utah |
| Idaho | Ohio | |

The most common mistakes are made when abbreviating *California* (*Calif.*, not *Cal.*), *Kansas* (*Kan.*, not *Kans.*), *Kentucky* (*Ky.*, not *Ken.*), *Nebraska* (*Neb.*, not *Nebr.*), *Pennsylvania* (*Pa.*, not *Penn.*) and *Wisconsin* (*Wis.*, not *Wisc.*).

The accepted state abbreviations are listed under the *state names* entry in the alphabetized listing that follows this section.

DATES: Confusion also can arise in abbreviating dates. Months are abbreviated only when followed by the day of the month in constructions such as *Sept. 13*. Five months are never abbreviated: *March, April, May, June* and *July*. These are easy to remember because they begin with March and are consecutive. Therefore, write *Nov. 6*, but *March 16*. Days of the week are never abbreviated in newspapers, except in tabular matter such as stock-market listings.

ADDRESSES: Street names also are a source of confusion. The words *street, avenue* and *boulevard* can be abbreviated, but only when preceded by a street name and number:

He lives at 311 Ninth St.

He rode down Ninth Street.

The same rule applies in abbreviating direction with an address. Write *311 S. Ninth St.* but *South Ninth Street*. Addresses with the directions northeast, southeast, southwest and northwest are abbreviated with periods:

He lives at 212 Westwinds Drive S.W. in Chicago.

OTHER ABBREVIATIONS: Generally, abbreviations of one- and two-word terms take periods, whereas abbreviations of terms consisting of three or more words do not. Thus, write *U.S.* and *U.N.*, but *FBI, CIA* and *mph*. An exception is made when an abbreviation without periods spells an unrelated word. Write *c.o.d.*, not *cod*, which is a kind of fish. Other exceptions are listed in the stylebooks, the most common of which is *TV* (no periods).

## Alphabetized Listing

**academic degrees** If mention of degrees is necessary to establish someone's credentials, the preferred form is to avoid an abbreviation and use instead a phrase such as: *John Jones, who has a doctorate in psychology.*

Use an apostrophe in *bachelor's degree, a master's,* and the like.

Use abbreviations such as *B.A., M.A., L.L.D.* and *Ph.D.* only when the need to identify many individuals by degree on first reference would make the preferred form cumbersome. Use these abbreviations only after a full name—never after just a last name.

When used after a full name, an academic abbreviation is set off by commas: *Daniel Moynihan, Ph.D., spoke.*

Do not precede a name with a courtesy title for an academic degree and follow it with the abbreviation for the degree in the same reference.

**addresses** Use the abbreviations *Ave., Blvd.* and *St.* only with a numbered address: *1600 Pennsylvania Ave.* Spell them out and capitalize when part of a formal street name without a number: *Pennsylvania Avenue.* Lowercase and spell out when used alone or with more than one street name: *Massachusetts and Pennsylvania avenues.*

All other street designations (*alley, drive, road, terrace,* and so on) are always spelled out. Capitalize them when part of a formal name without a number; lowercase when used alone or with two or more names.

Always use figures for an address number: *9 Morningside Circle*.

Spell out and capitalize *First* through *Ninth* when used as street names; use figures with two letters for *10th* and above: *7 Fifth Ave., 100 21st St.*

**AFL-CIO**    Acceptable in all references for the *American Federation of Labor and Congress of Industrial Organizations*.

**aircraft names**    Use a hyphen when changing from letters to figures; no hyphen when adding a letter after figures: *F-15, 747, 747B.*

**AM**    Acceptable in all references for the *amplitude modulation* system of radio transmission.

**a.m., p.m.**    Lowercase, with periods. Avoid the redundant *10 a.m. this morning.*

**Amtrak**    This acronym, drawn from the words *American travel by track,* may be used in all references to the *National Railroad Passenger Corp.* Do not use *AMTRAK.*

**armed services**    Do not use the abbreviations *USA, USAF* and *USN.*

**assistant**    Do not abbreviate. Capitalize only when part of a formal title before a name: *Assistant Secretary of State Thomas M. Tracy.* Wherever practical, however, an appositional construction should be used: *Thomas M. Tracy, assistant secretary of state.*

**association**    Do not abbreviate. Capitalize as part of a proper name: *American Medical Association.*

**attorney general, attorneys general**    Never abbreviate. Capitalize only when used as a title before a name: *Attorney General Richard Thornburg.*

**Bible**    Do not abbreviate individual books of the Bible.

Citations listing the number of chapter(s) and verse(s) use this form: *Matthew 3:16, Luke 21:1-13, 1 Peter 2:1.*

**brothers**    Abbreviate as *Bros.* in formal company names: *Warner Bros.*
For possessives: *Warner Bros.' profits.*

**Christmas**    Never abbreviate *Christmas* to *Xmas* or any other form.

**CIA**    Acceptable in all references for *Central Intelligence Agency.*

**c.o.d.**    Acceptable in all references for *cash on delivery* or *collect on delivery.* (The use of lowercase is an exception to the first listing in Webster's New World Dictionary.)

**company, companies**    Use *Co.* or *Cos.* when a business uses the word at the end of its proper name: *Ford Motor Co., American Broadcasting Cos.* But: *Aluminum Company of America.*

If *company* or *companies* appears alone in second reference, spell the word out.

The forms for possessives: *Ford Motor Co.'s profits, American Broadcasting Cos. profits.*

**Conrail**   This acronym is acceptable in all references to *Consolidated Rail Corp.* (The corporation originally used *ConRail,* but later changed to *Conrail.*)

**corporation**   Abbreviate as *Corp.* when a company or government agency uses the word at the end of its name: *Gulf Oil Corp., the Federal Deposit Insurance Corp.*

Spell out *corporation* when it occurs elsewhere in a name: *the Corporation for Public Broadcasting.*

Spell out and lowercase *corporation* whenever it stands alone.

The form for possessives: *Gulf Oil Corp.'s profits.*

**courtesy titles**   *Note:* Many newspapers consider the AP style (UPI style varies) on this subject to be sexist and have chosen to treat courtesy titles for women as those for men are treated—by first and last name on first reference and last name only on second reference. For the same reason, other newspapers use courtesy titles for both men and women on second reference. Despite those increasingly common deviations, the AP policy is presented here; it is still the predominant policy at U.S. newspapers.

In general, do not use the courtesy title *Miss, Mr., Mrs.* or *Ms.* with first and last names of the person: *Barbara Bush, Jimmy Carter.*

Do not use *Mr.* in any reference unless it is combined with *Mrs.*: *Mr. and Mrs. John Smith.*

On sports wires, do not use courtesy titles in any reference unless needed to distinguish among people of the same last name.

On news wires, use courtesy titles for women on second reference, following the woman's preference. If the woman says she does not want a courtesy title, refer to her on second reference by last name only. Here are some guidelines:

MARRIED WOMEN: The preferred form on first reference is to identify a woman by her own first name and her husband's last name: *Susan Smith.* Use *Mrs.* on the first reference only if a woman requests that her husband's first name be used or her own first cannot be determined: *Mrs. John Smith.*

On second reference, use *Mrs.* unless a woman initially identified by her own first name prefers *Ms.*: *Carla Hills, Mrs. Hills, Ms. Hills;* or no title: *Carla Hills, Hills.*

If a married woman is known by her maiden last name, precede it by *Miss* on second reference unless she prefers *Ms.*: *Diana Ross, Miss Ross, Ms. Ross;* or no title, *Diana Ross.*

UNMARRIED WOMEN: For women who have never been married, use *Miss, Ms.* or no title on second reference according to the woman's preferences.

For divorced women and widows, the normal practice is to use *Mrs.* or no title, if she prefers, on second reference. But, if a woman returns to the use of her maiden name, use *Miss, Ms.* or no title if she prefers it.

MARITAL STATUS: If a woman prefers *Ms.* or no title, do not include her marital status in a story unless it is clearly pertinent.

**detective**   Do not abbreviate.

**district attorney**   Do not abbreviate.

**doctor**   Use *Dr.* in first reference as a formal title before the name of an individual who holds a doctor of medicine degree. *Dr. Jonas Salk.*

The form *Dr.,* or *Drs.* in a plural construction, applies to all first-reference uses before a name, including direct quotations.

If appropriate in the context, *Dr.* also may be used on first reference before the names of individuals who hold other types of doctoral degrees. However, because the public frequently identifies *Dr.* only with physicians, care should be taken to assure that the individual's specialty is stated in first or second reference. The only exception would be a story in which the context left no doubt that the person was a dentist, psychologist, chemist, historian or the like.

In some instances it also is necessary to specify that an individual identified as *Dr.* is a physician. One frequent case is a story reporting on joint research by physicians, biologists and so on.

Do not use *Dr.* before the names of individuals who hold only honorary doctorates.

Do not continue the use of *Dr.* in subsequent references.

**ERA**   (1) Acceptable in all references to baseball's *earned run average.* (2) Acceptable on second reference for *Equal Rights Amendment.*

**FBI**   Acceptable in all references for *Federal Bureau of Investigation.*

**FM**   Acceptable in all references for the *frequency modulation* system of radio transmission.

**ICBM, ICBMs**   Acceptable on first reference for *intercontinental ballistic missile(s),* but the term should be defined in the body of a story.

Avoid the redundant *ICBM missiles.*

**incorporated**   Abbreviate and capitalize as *Inc.* when used as part of a corporate name. It usually is not needed, but when it is used, do not set off with commas: *J.C. Penney Co. Inc. announced . . .*

**IQ**   Acceptable in all references for *intelligence quotient.*

**junior, senior**   Abbreviate as *Jr.* and *Sr.* only with full names of persons or animals. Do not precede by a comma: *Joseph P. Kennedy Jr.*

The notation *II* or *2nd* may be used if it is the individual's preference. Note, however, that *II* and *2nd* are not necessarily the equivalent of *junior*—they often are used by a grandson or nephew.

If necessary to distinguish between father and son in second reference, use the *elder Smith* or the *younger Smith.*

**mount**   Spell out in all uses, including the names of communities and of mountains: *Mount Clemens, Mich.; Mount Everest.*

**mph**   Acceptable in all references for *miles per hour* or *miles an hour.*

**No.**   Use as the abbreviation for *number* in conjunction with a figure to indicate position or rank: *No. 1 man, No. 3 choice.*

Do not use in street addresses, with this exception: *No. 10 Downing St.,* the residence of Britain's prime minister.

Do not use in the names of schools: *Public School 19.*

**point** Do not abbreviate. Capitalize as part of a proper name: *Point Pleasant.*

**saint** Abbreviate as *St.* in the names of saints, cities and other places: *St. Jude; St. Paul, Minn.; St. John's, Newfoundland; St. Lawrence Seaway.*

**Saint John** The spelling for the city in New Brunswick. To distinguish it from *St. John's, Newfoundland.*

**Sault Ste. Marie, Mich.; Sault Ste. Marie, Ontario** The abbreviation is *Ste.* instead of *St.* because the full name is *Sault Sainte Marie.*

**state names** Follow these guidelines:

STANDING ALONE: Spell out the names of the 50 U.S. states when they stand alone in textual material. Any state name may be condensed, however, to fit typographical requirements for tabular materials.

EIGHT NOT ABBREVIATED: The names of eight states are never abbreviated in datelines or text: *Alaska, Hawaii, Idaho, Iowa, Maine, Ohio, Texas* and *Utah.*

ABBREVIATIONS REQUIRED: Use the following state abbreviations in these circumstances:

- In conjunction with the name of a city, town, village or military base in most datelines.

- In conjunction with the name of a city, county, town, village or military base in text (see examples in the punctuation that follows).

- In short-form listings of party affiliation: *D-Ala., R-Mont.*

| | | |
|---|---|---|
| Ala. | Md. | N.D. |
| Ariz. | Mass. | Okla. |
| Ark. | Mich. | Ore. |
| Calif. | Minn. | Pa. |
| Colo. | Miss. | R.I. |
| Conn. | Mo. | S.C. |
| Del. | Mont. | S.D. |
| Fla. | Neb. | Tenn. |
| Ga. | Nev. | Vt. |
| Ill. | N.H. | Va. |
| Ind. | N.J. | Wash. |
| Kan. | N.M. | W.Va. |
| Ky. | N.Y. | Wis. |
| La. | N.C. | Wyo. |

**TV**   Acceptable as an adjective or in such constructions as *cable TV*. Use *television* as a noun, except when *TV* is part of a quotation.

**UFO,UFOs**   Acceptable in all references for *unidentified flying object(s)*.

**U.N.**   Used as an adjective, but not as a noun, for *United Nations*.

**U.S.**   Used as an adjective, but not as a noun, for *United States*.

## PUNCTUATION AND HYPHENATION

Think of punctuation and hyphenation as a courtesy to your readers, designed to help them understand a story.

Inevitably, a mandate of this scope involves gray areas. For this reason, the punctuation entries in the AP and UPI stylebooks refer to guidelines rather than rules. Guidelines should not be treated casually, however.

### Common Problems

PERIODS: In school you may have been taught that there are times when the period is placed outside quotation marks at the end of a sentence, as in the following example:

Stephen Crane wrote ''The Red Badge of Courage''.

In newspapers, however, the period always goes inside the quotation marks:

Stephen Crane wrote ''The Red Badge of Courage.''

However, a period can be placed inside or outside a closing parenthesis, depending on the usage. If the parenthetical phrase is a complete sentence, the period goes inside the parenthesis. If it is not a complete sentence, it goes outside:

John bought all the dogs at the kennel (except the German shepherd).

John bought all the dogs at the kennel. (The total cost was $239.)

COMMAS: Like periods, commas always are placed inside quotation marks.

Newspapers often omit commas before conjunctions in series of items unless the omission confuses the meaning:

The school's colors are black, gold and white.

I had orange juice, toast, and ham and eggs for breakfast.

Newspaper style also calls for the elimination of commas between words that relate closely: *Martin Luther King Jr.*, not *Martin Luther King, Jr.*

Commas are used with appositives, adjacent nouns with the same relationship to the rest of the sentence, even before a conjunction:

> John Smith, a freshman, Ralph Jones, a sophomore, and Bill Keith, a senior, were elected.

> Milwaukee, Wis., and Melbourne, Fla., were selected as sites for the tournament.

When referring to dates, do not use commas when only the month and year are mentioned:

> President Bush was inaugurated in January 1989 on the steps of the Capitol.

When the month and year are accompanied by an exact date, however, commas are used to set off the year:

> President Bush was inaugurated on Jan. 20, 1989, on the steps of the Capitol.

Notice that the comma is needed after the year as well as before.

SEMICOLONS: Semicolons are used to indicate greater separation of thought and information than commas convey, but less than the separation a period implies:

> Survivors include a son, James Jones of Chicago; two sisters, Jane Thompson of Chicago and Jill Revel of Milwaukee; and several grandchildren.

Note that the semicolon is used before the final *and* in such a series.

The semicolon is rarely used in newspapers to link independent clauses when a coordinating conjunction is missing:

> His plane arrived at 10 p.m.; it was due at 9 a.m.

Despite the infrequent use of such a construction, it is permissible.

DASHES: To indicate an abrupt change, dashes are used:

> We will win the game—if I can play.

They also can be used to set off a series within a phrase:

> The flowers—white, yellow and red—adorned the flower box below the window.

Dashes should be used sparingly, though. When used to excess they make for difficult reading.

HYPHENS: The abused or forgotten punctuation mark in almost all writing in this country is the hyphen. Unfortunately, newspapers are among the worst offenders. Hyphens are plentiful on sports pages:

The Tigers won 14-7.

Too often, however, newspaper reporters and editors omit the necessary hyphen when two or more words function as a compound adjective:

He is an out-of-state student.

A 30-yard field goal led to the last-minute victory.

Omit the hyphen, however, in compound modifiers involving the adverb *very* or adverbs ending in *-ly*: *a very cold morning, an easily remembered rule.*

Increasingly, hyphens are disappearing when two words are joined to function as a noun: *makeup,* not *make-up; layout,* not *lay-out.*

Suspensive hyphenation also creates trouble for reporters, who frequently omit the hyphens. Write *a 10- to 30-year prison term,* not *a 10 to 30 year prison term* or *a 10 to 30-year prison term.* In this usage the writer refers to a 10-year prison term and a 30-year prison term. By omitting the first *year,* space is saved, yet the meaning is clear. Completion of the phrase is suspended until after the second numeral, which accounts for the term *suspensive hyphenation.*

APOSTROPHES: Apostrophes are used most often in possessives. They also are used to indicate omitted letters (*I've, rock 'n' roll, ne'er-do-well*) or omitted figures (*Spirit of '76, class of '62, the '20s*). They also are used for plurals of a single letter: *your p's and q's, the Oakland A's.*

The apostrophe is not used for plurals of numerals or multiple-letter combinations: *1920s, ABCs.*

In newspaper usage, the possessive of plural nouns and singular proper names ending with the letter s is formed with an apostrophe: *the girls' books, the horses' stables, Dickens' novels, Texas' schools.* The possessive of singular common nouns ending with s is formed with *'s,* unless the next word begins with s: *hostess's invitation, hostess' story.*

Generally, the possessive of singular nouns ending with s sounds such as *ce, x* and *z* should be followed by *'s: justice's verdict, Marx's theories, Butz's jokes.* There are exceptions in some cases when words not ending in s have an s sound and are followed by a word that begins with s. Thus, you should write *appearance' sake* or *conscience' sake,* but you must add the *'s* in the case of *appearance's cost* or *conscience's voice.* A common error is to use the apostrophe in the possessive *its. It's* is the contraction of *it is; its* is the possessive form of *it.*

QUESTION MARKS AND EXCLAMATION POINTS: Question marks often are placed improperly in relation to quotation marks. The meaning dictates how a question mark is used:

Who wrote ''Gone with the Wind''?

He asked, ''How long will it take?''

In the first example, the entire sentence, not just the quoted material, is the question posed, so the question mark .belongs outside the quotation marks. In the second example, only the quoted portion of the sentence is a question, so the question mark is placed inside the quotation marks.

The question mark supersedes the comma normally used when supplying attribution for a quotation:

''Who is there?'' she asked.

Similarly, an exclamation point replaces the comma in attributing a direct quotation:

''Halt!'' the guard shouted.

## Alphabetized Listing

**ampersand (&)**   Use the ampersand when it is part of a company's formal name: *Baltimore & Ohio Railroad, Newport News Shipbuilding & Dry Dock Co.*
The ampersand should not otherwise be used in place of *and*.

**all-**   Use a hyphen:

all-around (*not*                all-out
   all-round)
all-clear                        all-star

**anti-**   Hyphenate all except the following words, which have specific meanings of their own:

| | | |
|---|---|---|
| antibiotic | antiknock | antiphony |
| antibody | antimatter | antiseptic |
| anticlimax | antimony | antiserum |
| antidote | antiparticle* | antithesis |
| antifreeze | antipasto | antitoxin |
| antigen | antiperspirant | antitrust |
| antihistamine | antiphon | antitussive |

* And similar terms in physics such as *antiproton*.

This approach has been adopted in the interests of readability and easily remembered consistency.

**apostrophe (')**    Follow these guidelines:

POSSESSIVES: See the **possessives** entry.

OMITTED LETTERS: *I've, it's, don't, rock 'n' roll. 'Tis the season to be jolly. He is a ne'er-do-well.*

OMITTED FIGURES: *The class of '62. The Spirit of '76. The '20s.*

PLURALS OF A SINGLE LETTER: *Mind your p's and q's. He learned the three R's and brought home a report card with four A's and two B's. The Oakland A's won the pennant.*

DO NOT USE: For plurals of numerals or multiple-letter combinations.

**by**    In general, no hyphen. Some examples:

| | |
|---|---|
| byline | byproduct |
| bypass | bystreet |

*By-election* is an exception.

**co-**    Retain the hyphen when forming nouns, adjectives and verbs that indicate occupation or status:

| | | |
|---|---|---|
| co-author | co-owner | co-signer |
| co-chairman | co-partner | co-star |
| co-defendant | co-pilot | co-worker |
| co-host | co-respondent (in a divorce suit) | |

(Several are exceptions to Webster's New World in the interests of consistency.) Use no hyphen in other combinations:

| | | |
|---|---|---|
| coed | coexist | cooperative |
| coeducation | coexistence | coordinate |
| coequal | cooperate | coordination |

*Cooperate, coordinate* and related words are exceptions to the rule that a hyphen is used if a prefix ends in a vowel and the word that follows begins with the same vowel.

**colon**    The most frequent use of a colon is at the end of a sentence to introduce lists, tabulations, texts and the like.

Capitalize the first word after a colon only if it is a proper noun or the start of a complete sentence: *He promised this: The company will make good all the losses.* But: *There were three considerations: expense, time and feasibility.*

INTRODUCING QUOTATIONS: Use a comma to introduce a direct quotation of one sentence that remains within a paragraph. Use a colon to introduce longer quotations within a paragraph and to end all paragraphs that introduce a paragraph of quoted material.

PLACEMENT WITH QUOTATION MARKS: Colons go outside quotation marks unless they are part of the quotation itself.

**comma** The following guidelines treat some of the most frequent questions about the use of commas. Additional guidelines on specialized uses are provided in separate entries.

For more detailed guidance, consult ''The Comma'' and ''Misused and Unnecessary Commas'' in the Guide to Punctuation section at the back of ''Webster's New World Dictionary.''

IN A SERIES: Use commas to separate elements in a series, but do not put a comma before the conjunction in a simple series: *The flag is red, white and blue. He would nominate Tom, Dick or Harry.*

Put a comma before the concluding conjunction in a series, however, if an integral element of the series requires a conjunction: *I had orange juice, toast, and ham and eggs for breakfast.*

Use a comma also before the concluding conjunction in a complex series of phrases: *The main points to consider are whether the athletes are skillful enough to compete, whether they have the stamina to endure the training, and whether they have the proper mental attitude.*

WITH EQUAL ADJECTIVE: Use commas to separate a series of adjectives equal in rank. If the commas could be replaced by the word *and* without changing the sense, the adjectives are equal: *a thoughtful, precise manner; a dark, dangerous street.*

Use no comma when the last adjective before a noun outranks its predecessors because it is an integral element of a noun phrase, which is the equivalent of a single noun: *a cheap fur coat* (the noun phrase is *fur coat*); *the old oaken bucket; a new, blue spring bonnet.*

WITH INTRODUCTORY CLAUSES AND PHRASES: A comma normally is used to separate an introductory clause or phrase from a main clause: *When he had tired of the mad pace of New York, he moved to Dubuque.*

The comma may be omitted after short introductory phrases if no ambiguity would result: *During the night he heard many noises.*

But use the comma if its omission would slow comprehension: *On the street below, the curious gathered.*

WITH CONJUNCTIONS: When a conjunction such as *and, but* or *for* links two clauses that could stand alone as separate sentences, use a comma before the conjunction in most cases: *She was glad she had looked, for a man was approaching the house.*

As a rule of thumb, use a comma if the subject of each clause is expressly stated: *We are visiting Washington, and we also plan a side trip to Williamsburg. We visited Washington, and our senator greeted us personally.* But do not use a comma when the subject of the two clauses is the same and is not repeated in the second: *We are visiting Washington and plan to see the White House.*

The comma may be dropped if two clauses with expressly stated subjects are short. In general, however, favor use of a comma unless a particular literary effect is desired or it would distort the sense of a sentence.

INTRODUCING DIRECT QUOTES: Use a comma to introduce a complete, one-sentence quotation within a paragraph: *Wallace said, ''She spent six months in Argentina and came back speaking English with a Spanish accent.''* But use a colon to introduce quotations of more than one sentence.

Do not use a comma at the start of an indirect or partial quotation: *He said his victory put him ''firmly on the road to a first-ballot nomination.''*

BEFORE ATTRIBUTION: Use a comma instead of a period at the end of a quote that is followed by attribution: *''Rub my shoulders,'' Miss Cawley suggested.*

Do not use a comma, however, if the quoted statement ends with a question mark or exclamation point: *''Why should I?'' he asked.*

WITH HOMETOWNS AND AGES: Use a comma to set off an individual's hometown when it is placed in apposition to a name: *Mary Richards, Minneapolis, and Maude Findlay, Tuckahoe, N.Y., were there.* However, the use of the word *of* without a comma between the individual's name and the city name generally is preferable: *Mary Richards of Minneapolis and Maude Findlay of Tuckahoe, N.Y., were there.*

If an individual's age is used, set it off by commas: *Maude Findlay, 48, Tuckahoe, N.Y., was present.* The use of the word *of* eliminates the need for a comma after the hometown if a state name is not needed: *Mary Richards, 36, of Minneapolis and Maude Findlay, 48, of Tuckahoe, N.Y., attended the party.*

IN LARGE FIGURES: Use a comma for most figures higher than 999. The major exceptions are: street addresses (*1234 Main St.*), broadcast frequencies (*1460 kilohertz*), room numbers, serial numbers, telephone numbers, and years (*1976*).

PLACEMENT WITH QUOTES: Commas always go inside quotation marks.

**dash**    Follow these guidelines:

ABRUPT CHANGE: Use dashes to denote an abrupt change in thought in a sentence or an emphatic pause: *We will fly to Paris in June—if I get a raise. Smith offered a plan—it was unprecedented—to raise revenues.*

SERIES WITHIN A PHRASE: When a phrase that otherwise would be set off by commas contains a series of words that must be separated by commas, use dashes to set off the full phrase: *He listed the qualities—intelligence, charm, beauty, independence—that he liked in women.*

ATTRIBUTION: Use a dash before an author's or composer's name at the end of a quotation: *''Who steals my purse steals trash.''—Shakespeare.*

IN DATELINES:

NEW YORK (UPI)—The city is broke.

IN LISTS: Dashes should be used to introduce individual sections of a list. Capitalize the first word following the dash. Use periods, not semicolons, at the end of each section. Example:

*Jones gave the following reasons:*

*—He never ordered the package.*

*—If he did, it didn't come.*

*—If it did, he sent it back.*

WITH SPACES: Put a space on both sides of a dash in all uses except the start of a paragraph and sports agate summaries.

**ellipsis ( . . . )**   In general, treat an ellipsis as a three-letter word, constructed with three periods and two spaces, as shown here.

Use an ellipsis to indicate the deletion of one or more words in condensing quotes, texts and documents. Be especially careful to avoid deletions that would distort the meaning.

**ex-**   Use no hyphen for words that use *ex-* in the sense of *out of*:

excommunicate          expropriate

Hyphenate when using *ex-* in the sense of *former*:

ex-convict               ex-president

Do not capitalize *ex-* when attached to a formal title before a name: *ex-President Carter*. The prefix modifies the entire term: *ex-New York Gov. Nelson Rockefeller*; not *New York ex Gov*.

Usually *former* is better.

**exclamation point(!)**   Follow these guidelines:

EMPHATIC EXPRESSIONS: Use the mark to express a high degree of surprise, incredulity or other strong emotion.

AVOID OVERUSE: Use a comma after mild interjections. End mildly exclamatory sentences with a period.

PLACEMENT WITH QUOTES: Place the mark inside quotation marks when it is part of the quoted material: *"How wonderful!" he exclaimed. "Never!" she shouted.*

Place the mark outside quotation marks when it is not part of the quoted material: *I hated reading Spenser's "Faerie Queene"!*

**extra-**  Do not use a hyphen when *extra-* means *outside of* unless the prefix is followed by a word beginning with *a* or a capitalized word:

extralegal                    extraterrestrial
extramarital                  extraterritorial

But:

extra-alimentary              extra-Britannic

Follow *extra-* with a hyphen when it is part of a compound modifier describing a condition beyond the usual size, extent or degree:

extra-base hit                extra-large book
extra-dry drink               extra-mild taste

**fore-**  In general, no hyphen. Some examples:

forebrain                     foregoing
forefather                    foretooth

There are three nautical exceptions, based on long-standing practice:

fore-topgallant               fore-topsail
fore-topmast

**full-**  Hyphenate when used to form compound modifiers:

full-dress                    full-page
full-fledged                  full-scale
full-length

See Webster's New World Dictionary for the spelling of other combinations.

**great-**  Hyphenate *great-grandfather, great-great-grandmother* and so on.
Use *great grandfather* only if the intended meaning is that the grandfather was a great man.

**hyphen**  Hyphens are joiners. Use them to avoid ambiguity or to form a single idea from two or more words.
Some guidelines:

AVOID AMBIGUITY: Use a hyphen whenever ambiguity would result if it were omitted: *The president will speak to small-business men. (Businessmen* normally is one word. But *The president will speak to small businessmen* is unclear.)

COMPOUND MODIFIERS: When a compound modifier—two or more words that express a single concept—precedes a noun, use hyphens to link all the words in the compound except the adverb *very* and all adverbs that end in *ly: a first-quarter touchdown, a bluish-green dress, a full-time job, a well-known man, a better-qualified woman, a know-it-all attitude, a very good time, an easily remembered rule.*

Many combinations that are hyphenated before a noun are not hyphenated when they occur after a noun: *The team scored in the first quarter. The dress, a bluish green, was attractive on her. She works full time. His attitude suggested that he knew it all.*

But when a modifier that would be hyphenated before a noun occurs instead after a form of the verb *to be,* the hyphen usually must be retained to avoid confusion: *The man is well-known. The woman is quick-witted. The children are soft-spoken. The play is second-rate.*

The principle of using a hyphen to avoid confusion explains why no hyphen is required with *very* and *ly* words. Readers can expect them to modify the word that follows. But if a combination such as *little-known man* were not hyphenated, the reader could logically be expecting *little* to be followed by a noun, as in *little man.* Instead, the reader encountering *little known* would have to back up mentally and make the compound connection on his or her own.

TWO-THOUGHT COMPOUNDS: *serio-comic, socio-economic.*

COMPOUND PROPER NOUNS AND ADJECTIVES: Use a hyphen to designate dual heritage: *Italian-American, Mexican-American.*

No hyphen, however, for *French Canadian* or *Latin American.*

AVOID DUPLICATED VOWELS, TRIPLED CONSONANTS: Examples:

anti-intellectual          pre-empt
shell-like

WITH NUMERALS: Use a hyphen to separate figures in betting odds, ratios, scores, some fractions and some election returns. See examples in entries under these headings in the section on numerals.

When large numbers must be spelled out, use a hyphen to connect a word ending in *y* to another word: *twenty-one, fifty-five* and so on.

SUSPENSIVE HYPHENATION: The form: *He received a 10- to 20-year sentence in prison.*

**in-** No hyphen when *in-* means ''not'':

inaccurate
insufferable

Often solid in other cases:

| | |
|---|---|
| inbound | infighting |
| indoor | inpatient (n., adj.) |
| infield | |

A few combinations take a hyphen, however:

| | |
|---|---|
| in-depth | in-house |
| in-group | in-law |

Follow Webster's New World when in doubt.

**-in**    Precede with a hyphen:

| | |
|---|---|
| break-in | walk-in |
| cave-in | write-in |

**parentheses**    In general, be sparing with parentheses.

Parentheses are jarring to the reader. Because they do not appear on some news service printers, there is also the danger that material inside them may be misinterpreted.

The temptation to use parentheses is a clue that a sentence is becoming contorted. Try to write it another way. If a sentence must contain incidental material, then commas or two dashes are frequently more effective. Use these alternatives whenever possible.

There are occasions, however, when parentheses are the only effective means of inserting necessary background or reference information. The stylebooks offer guidelines.

**periods**    Follow these guidelines:

END OF DECLARATIVE SENTENCE: *The stylebook is finished.*

END OF A MILDLY IMPERATIVE SENTENCE: *Shut the door.*
Use an exclamation point if greater emphasis is desired: *Be careful!*

END OF SOME RHETORICAL QUESTIONS: A period is preferable if a statement is more a suggestion than a question: *Why don't we go.*

END OF AN INDIRECT QUESTION: He asked what the score was.

INITIALS: *John F. Kennedy, T.S. Eliot* (no space between *T.* and *S.*, to prevent them from being placed on two lines in typesetting).
Abbreviations using only the initials of a name do not take periods: *JFK, LBJ.*

ENUMERATIONS: After numbers or letters in enumerating elements of a summary: *1. Wash the car. 2. Clean the basement.* Or: *A. Punctuate properly. B. Write simply.*

**possessives**    Follow these guidelines:

PLURAL NOUNS NOT ENDING IN S: Add *'s: the alumni's contributions, women's rights.*

PLURAL NOUNS ENDING IN S: Add only an apostrophe: *the churches' needs, the girls' toys, the horses' food, the ships' wake, states' rights, the VIPs' entrance.*

NOUNS PLURAL IN FORM, SINGULAR IN MEANING: Add only an apostrophe: *mathematics' rules, measles' effects.* (But see INANIMATE OBJECTS below.)
Apply the same principle when a plural word occurs in the formal name of a singular entity: *General Motors' profits, the United States' wealth.*

NOUNS THE SAME IN SINGULAR AND PLURAL: Treat them the same as plurals, even if the meaning is singular: *one corps' location, the two deer's tracks, the lone moose's antlers.*

SINGULAR NOUNS NOT ENDING IN S: Add *'s: the church's needs, the girl's toys, the horse's food, the ship's route, the VIP's seat.*
Some style guides say that singular nouns ending in *s* sounds such as *ce, x,* and *z* may take either the apostrophe alone or *'s.* See SPECIAL EXPRESSIONS below, but otherwise, for consistency and ease in remembering a rule, always use *'s* if the word does not end in the letter *s: Butz's policies, the fox's den, the justice's verdict, Marx's theories, the prince's life, Xerox's profits.*

SINGULAR COMMON NOUNS ENDING IN S: Add *'s* unless the next word begins with *s: the hostess's invitation, the hostess' seat; the witness's answer, the witness' story.*

SINGULAR PROPER NAMES ENDING IN S: Use only an apostrophe: *Achilles' heel, Agnes' book, Ceres' rites, Descartes' theories, Dickens' novels, Euripides' dramas, Hercules' labors, Jesus' life, Jules' seat, Kansas' schools, Moses' law, Socrates' life, Tennessee Williams' plays, Xerxes' armies.*

SPECIAL EXPRESSIONS: The following exceptions to the general rule for words not ending in *s* apply to words that end in an *s* sound and are followed by a word that begins with *s: for appearance' sake, for conscience' sake, for goodness' sake.* Use *'s* otherwise: *the appearance's cost, my conscience's voice.*

PRONOUNS: Personal, interrogative and relative pronouns have separate forms for the possessive. None involves an apostrophe: *mine, ours, your, yours, his, hers, its, theirs, whose.*
Caution: If you are using an apostrophe with a pronoun, always doublecheck to be sure that the meaning calls for a contraction; *you're, it's, there's, who's.*
Follow the rules listed above in forming the possessive of other pronouns: *another's idea, others' plans, someone's guess.*

COMPOUND WORDS: Applying the rules above, add an apostrophe or *'s* to the word closest to the object possessed: *the major general's decision, the major generals' decisions, the attorney general's request, the attorneys general's request.*
Also: *anyone else's attitude, John Adams Jr.'s father, Benjamin Franklin of Pennsyl-*

*vania's motion.* Whenever practical, however, recast the phrase to avoid ambiguity: *the motion by Benjamin Franklin of Pennsylvania.*

JOINT POSSESSION, INDIVIDUAL POSSESSION: Use a possessive form after only the last word if ownership is joint: *Fred and Sylvia's apartment, Fred and Sylvia's stocks.*

Use a possessive form after both words if the objects are individually owned: *Fred's and Sylvia's books.*

DESCRIPTIVE PHRASES: Do not add an apostrophe to a word ending in *s* when it is used primarily in a descriptive sense: *citizens band radio, a Cincinnati Reds infielder, a teachers college, a Teamsters request, a writers guide.*

Memory Aid: The apostrophe usually is not used if *for* or *by* rather than *of* would be appropriate in the longer form: *a radio band for citizens, a college for teachers, a guide for writers, a request by the Teamsters.*

An *'s* is required, however, when a term involves a plural word that does not end in *s*: *a children's hospital, a people's republic, the Young Men's Christian Association.*

DESCRIPTIVE NAMES: Some governmental, corporate and institutional organizations with a descriptive word in their names use an apostrophe; some do not. Follow the user's practice: *Actors Equity, Diners Club, the Ladies' Home Journal, the National Governors' Conference, the Veterans Administration.* See the stylebook entries for these and similar names frequently in the news.

QUASI POSSESSIVES: Follow the rules above in composing the possessive form of words that occur in such phrases as *a day's pay, two weeks' vacation, three days' work, your money's worth.*

Frequently, however, a hyphenated form is clearer; *a two-week vacation, a three-day job.*

DOUBLE POSSESSIVE: Two conditions must apply for a double possessive—a phrase such as *a friend of John's*—to occur: (1) The word after *of* must refer to an animate object, and (2) the word before *of* must involve only a portion of the animate object's possessions.

Otherwise, do not use the possessive form on the word after *of*: *The friends of John Adams mourned his death.* (All the friends were involved.). *He is a friend of the college.* (Not *college's*, because college is inanimate.)

Memory Aid: This construction occurs more often, and quite naturally, with the possessive forms of personal pronouns. *He is a friend of mine.*

INANIMATE OBJECTS: There is no blanket rule against creating a possessive form for an inanimate object, particularly if the object is treated in a personified sense. See some of the earlier examples, and note these: *death's call, the wind's murmur.*

In general, however, avoid excessive personalization of inanimate objects, and give preference to an *of* construction when it fits the makeup of the sentence. For example, the earlier references to *mathematics' rules* and *measles' effects* would better be phrased: *the rules of mathematics, the effects of measles.*

**post-**  Follow Webster's New World. Hyphenate if not listed there. Some words without a hyphen:

| postdate | postgraduate | postscript |
|---|---|---|
| postdoctoral | postnuptial | postwar |
| postelection | postoperative | |

Some words that use a hyphen:

post-bellum          post-mortem

**prefixes**   See separate listings for commonly used prefixes.

Three rules are constant, although they yield some exceptions to first-listed spellings in Webster's New World Dictionary:

- Except for *cooperate* and *coordinate*, use a hyphen if the prefix ends in a vowel and the word that follows begins with the same vowel.

- Use a hyphen if the word that follows is capitalized.

- Use a hyphen to join doubled prefixes: *sub-subparagraph*.

**pro-**   Use a hyphen when coining words that denote support for something. Some examples:

| pro-business | pro-life |
|---|---|
| pro-labor | pro-war |

No hyphen when *pro* is used in other senses:

produce
pronoun
profile

**question mark**   Follow these guidelines:

END OF A DIRECT QUESTION: *Who started the riot?*
*Did he ask who started the riot?* (The sentence as a whole is a direct question despite the indirect question at the end.)
*You started the riot?* (A question in the form of a declarative statement.)

INTERPOLATED QUESTION: *You told me—Did I hear you correctly?—that you started the riot.*

MULTIPLE QUESTIONS: Use a single question mark at the end of the full sentence:
*Did you hear him say, ''What right have you to ask about the riot?''*
*Did he plan the riot, employ assistants and give the signal to begin?*
Or, to cause full stops and throw emphasis on each element, break into separate sentences: *Did he plan the riot? Employ assistants? Give the signal to begin?*

CAUTION: Do not use question marks to indicate the end of indirect questions:

*He asked who started the riot. To ask why the riot started is unnecessary. I want to know what the cause of the riot was. How foolish it is to ask what caused the riot.*

QUESTION-AND-ANSWER FORMAT: Do not use quotation marks. Paragraph each speaker's words:

*Q. Where did you keep it?*
*A. In a little tin box.*

PLACEMENT WITH QUOTATION MARKS: Inside or outside, depending on the meaning:

*Who wrote ''Gone With the Wind''?*
*He asked, ''How long will it take?''*

MISCELLANEOUS: The question mark supersedes the comma that normally is used when supplying attribution for a quotation: *''Who is there?'' she asked.*

**quotation marks**    The basic guidelines for open-quote marks ('') and close-quote marks (''):

FOR DIRECT QUOTATIONS: To surround the exact words of a speaker or writer when reported in a story:

*''I have no intention of staying,'' he replied.*
*''I do not object,'' he said, ''to the tenor of the report.''*
*Franklin said, ''A penny saved is a penny earned.''*
*A speculator said the practice is ''too conservative for inflationary times.''*

RUNNING QUOTATIONS: If a full paragraph of quoted material is followed by a paragraph that continues the quotation, do not put close-quote marks at the end of the first paragraph. Do, however, put open-quote marks at the start of the second paragraph. Continue in this fashion for any succeeding paragraphs, using close-quote marks only at the end of the quoted material.

If a paragraph does not start with quotation marks but ends with a quotation that is continued in the next paragraph, do not use close-quote marks at the end of the introductory paragraph if the quoted material constitutes a full sentence. Use close-quote marks, however, if the quoted material does not constitute a full sentence.

DIALOGUE OR CONVERSATION: Each person's words, no matter how brief, are placed in a separate paragraph with quotation marks at the beginning and the end of each person's speech:

*''Will you go?''*
*''Yes.''*
*''When?''*
*''Thursday.''*

NOT IN Q-AND-A: Quotation marks are not required in formats that identify questions and answers by *Q.* and *A.*

NOT IN TEXTS: Quotation marks are not required in full texts, condensed texts or textual excerpts.

IRONY: Put quotation marks around a word or words used in an ironical sense: *The "debate" turned into a free-for-all.*

UNFAMILIAR TERMS: A word or words being introduced to readers may be placed in quotation marks on first reference:
*Broadcast frequencies are measured in "kilohertz."*
Do not put subsequent references to *kilohertz* in quotation marks.

AVOID UNNECESSARY FRAGMENTS: Do not use quotation marks to report a few ordinary words that a speaker or writer has used:
Wrong: *The senator said he would "go home to Michigan" if he lost the election.*
Right: *The senator said he would go home to Michigan if he lost the election.*

PARTIAL QUOTES: When a partial quote is used, do not put quotation marks around words that the speaker could not have used.
Suppose the individual said, *"I am horrified at your slovenly manners."*
Wrong: *She said she "was horrified at their slovenly manners."*
Right: *She said she was horrified at their "slovenly manners."*
Better when practical: Use the full quote.

QUOTES WITHIN QUOTES: Alternate between double quotation marks ("or") and single marks ('or'):
She said, *"I quote from his letter, 'I agree with Kipling that "the female of the species is more deadly than the male," but the phenomenon is not an unchangeable law of nature,' a remark he did not explain."*
Use three marks together if two quoted elements end at the same time: *She said, "He told me, 'I love you.'"*

PLACEMENT WITH OTHER PUNCTUATION: Follow these long-established printers' rules:

- The period and the comma always go within the quotation marks.

- The dash, the semicolon, the question mark and the exclamation point go within the quotation marks when they apply to the quoted matter only. They go outside when they apply to the whole sentence.

**re-** The rules in **prefixes** apply. The following examples of exceptions to first-listed spellings in Webster's New World are based on the general rule that a hyphen is used if a prefix ends in a vowel and the word that follows begins with the same vowel:

| | |
|---|---|
| re-elect | re-enlist |
| re-election | re-enter |
| re-emerge | re-entry |
| re-employ | re-equip |
| re-enact | re-establish |
| re-engage | re-examine |

For many other words, the sense is the governing factor:

recover (regain)          resign (quit)          reform (improve)
re-cover (cover again)    re-sign (sign again)   re-form (form again)

Otherwise, follow Webster's New World. Use a hyphen for words not listed there unless the hyphen would distort the sense.

**semicolon**   In general, use the semicolon to indicate a greater separation of thought and information than a comma can convey but less than the separation that a period implies. The stylebooks offer guidelines.

**suffixes**   See separate listings for commonly used suffixes.
Follow Webster's New World Dictionary for words not in this book.
If a word combination is not listed in Webster's New World, use two words for the verb form; hyphenate any noun or adjective forms.

**suspensive hyphenation**   The form: *The 5- and 6-year-olds attend morning classes.*

# NUMERALS

A *numeral* is a figure, letter, word or group of words expressing a number.
*Roman numerals* use the letters *I, V, X, L, C, D* and *M*. Use Roman numerals for wars and to show personal sequence for animals and people: *World War II, Native Dancer II, King George VI, Pope John XXIII.*
*Arabic numerals* use the figures *1, 2, 3, 4, 5, 6, 7, 8, 9* and *0*. Use Arabic forms unless Roman numerals are specifically required.
The figures *1, 2, 10, 101*, etc. and the corresponding words—*one, two, ten, one hundred one*, etc.— are called **cardinal numbers**. The term **ordinal number** applies to *1st, 2nd, 10th, 101st, first, second, tenth, one hundred first*, etc.
Follow these guidelines in using numerals:

LARGE NUMBERS: When large numbers must be spelled out, use a hyphen to connect a word ending in *y* to another word; do not use commas between other separate words that are part of one number: *twenty; thirty; twenty-one; thirty-one; one hundred forty-three; one thousand one hundred fifty-five; one million two hundred seventy-six thousand five hundred eighty-seven.*

SENTENCE START: Spell out a numeral at the beginning of a sentence. If necessary, recast the sentence. There is one exception—a numeral that identifies a calendar year.
Wrong: *993 freshmen entered the college last year.*
Right: *Last year 993 freshmen entered the college.*
Right: *1976 was a very good year.*

CASUAL USES: Spell out casual expressions:
*A thousand times no! Thanks a million. He walked a quarter of a mile.*

PROPER NAMES: Use words or numerals according to an organization's practice: *Colgate-Palmolive, Twentieth Century Fund, Big Ten.*

FIGURES OR WORDS? For ordinals:

- Spell out *first* through *ninth* when they indicate sequence in time or location—*first base, the First Amendment, he was first in line.* Starting with *10th,* use figures.

- Use *1st, 2nd, 3rd, 4th,* etc. when the sequence has been assigned in forming names. The principal examples are geographic, military and political designations such as *1st Ward, 7th Fleet* and *1st Sgt.*

OTHER USES: For uses not covered by these listings: Spell out whole numbers below 10, use figures for 10 and above. Typical examples: *The woman has three sons and two daughters. He has a fleet of 10 station wagons and two buses.*

IN A SERIES: Apply the appropriate guidelines: *They had 10 dogs, six cats and 97 hamsters. They had four four-room houses, 10 three-room houses and 12 10-room houses.*

## Common Problems

Whether a numeral is written out or shown in figures usually depends on usage. Because of that, reporters frequently are confused about which form is correct.

THE GENERAL RULE: Figures are used in address numbers, ages, dates, highway designations, monetary units, percentages, speeds, sports, temperatures and times. They also are used to identify aircraft and weapons by model number and following the abbreviation *No.,* as in *No. 1 man.*

EXCEPTIONS: Casual references to temperatures, other than actual thermometer readings, are written out:

The temperature at 9 p.m. was 8 degrees, a drop of four degrees since noon.

Casual numbers are written out when the numbers one through nine are used infrequently in a story:

The baker made eight pies last night.

The school will accept only three more students.

## Alphabetized Listing

**act numbers** Use Arabic figures and capitalize *act: Act 1; Act 2, Scene 2.* But: *the first act, the second act.*

**addresses** Always use figures for an address number: *9 Morningside Circle.* Spell out and capitalize *First* through *Ninth* when used as street names; use figures with two letters for *10th* and above: *7 Fifth Ave., 100 21st St.*

**ages** Always use figures. When the context does not require *years* or *years old,* the figure is presumed to be years.

**aircraft names** Use a hyphen when changing from letters to figures; no hyphen when adding a letter after figures.

Some examples for aircraft often in the news: *B-1, BAC-111, C-5A, DC-10, FH-227, F-4, Phantom II, F-86 Sabre, L-1011, MiG-21, Tu-144, 727-100C, 747, 747B, VC-10.*

**amendments to the Constitution** Use *First Amendment, 10th Amendment,* and so on.

Colloquial references to the Fifth Amendment's protection against self-incrimination are best avoided, but where appropriate: *He took the Fifth seven times.*

**Arabic numerals** The numerical figures *1, 2, 3, 4, 5, 6, 7, 8, 9, 10.*

In general, use Arabic forms unless denoting the sequence of wars or establishing a personal sequence for people and animals.

**betting odds** Use figures and a hyphen: *The odds were 5-4. He won despite 3-2 odds against him.*

The word *to* seldom is necessary, but when it appears it should be hyphenated in all constructions: *3-to-2 odds, odds of 3-to-2, the odds were 3-to-2.*

**Celsius** Use this term rather than *centigrade* for the temperature scale that is part of the metric system.

When giving a Celsius temperature, use these forms: *40 degrees Celsius* or *40° C* (note the space and no period after the capital C) if degrees and Celsius are clear from the context.

**cents** Spell out the word *cents* and lowercase, using numerals for amounts less than a dollar: *5 cents, 12 cents.* Use the $ sign and decimal system for larger amounts: *$1.01, $2.50.*

Numerals alone, with or without a decimal point as appropriate, may be used in tabular matter.

**congressional districts** Use figures and capitalize *district* when joined with a figure: *the 1st Congressional District, the 1st District.*

Lowercase *district* whenever it stands alone.

**court decisions** Use figures and a hyphen: *The Supreme Court ruled 5-4, a 5-4 decision.* The word *to* is not needed, but use hyphens if it appears in quoted matter: *''the court ruled 5-to-4, the 5-to-4 decision.''*

**court names** For courts identified by a numeral: *2nd District Court, 8th U.S. Circuit Court of Appeals.*

**dates** Always use Arabic figures, without *st, nd, rd* or *th.*

**decades** Use Arabic figures to indicate decades of history. Use an apostrophe to indicate numerals that are left out; show plural by adding the letter *s: the 1890s, the '90s, the Gay '90s, the 1920s, the mid-1930s.*

**decimal units**    Use a period and numerals to indicate decimal amounts. Decimalization should not exceed two places in textual material unless there are special circumstances.

**dimensions**    Use figures and spell out *inches, feet, yards,* and the like to indicate depth, height, length and width. Hyphenate adjectival forms before nouns.

Use an apostrophe to indicate feet and quote marks to indicate inches (*5'6"*) only in very technical contexts.

**distances**    Use figures for *10* and above, spell out *one* through *nine: He walked four miles.*

**district**    Use a figure and capitalize *district* when forming a proper name: *the 2nd District.*

**dollars**    Use figures and the $ sign in all except casual references or amounts without a figure: *The book cost $4. Dad, please give me a dollar. Dollars are flowing overseas.*

For specified amounts, the word takes a singular verb: *He said $500,000 is what they want.*

For amounts of more than $1 million, use the $ and numerals up to two decimal places. Do not link the numerals and the word by a hyphen: *He is worth $4.35 million. He is worth exactly $4,351,242. He proposed a $300 billion budget.*

The form for amounts less than $1 million: *$4, $25, $500, $1,000, $650,000.*

**election returns**    Use figures, with commas every three digits starting at the right and counting left. Use the word *to* (not a hyphen) in separating different totals listed together: *George Bush defeated Michael Dukakis 48,881,221 to 41,805,422* (this is the actual final figure).

Use the word *votes* if there is any possibility that the figures could be confused with a ratio: *Bush defeated Dukakis 16 votes to 3 votes in Dixville Notch.*

Do not attempt to create adjectival forms such as *the 48,881,221-41,805,422 vote.*

**fractions**    Spell out amounts less than *1* in stories, using hyphens between the words: *two-thirds, four-fifths, seven-sixteenths.*

Use figures for precise amounts larger than *1,* converting to decimals whenever practical.

Fractions are preferred, however, in stories about stocks.

When using fractional characters, remember that most newspaper type fonts can set only ⅛, ¼, ⅜, ½, ⅝, ¾, and ⅞ as one unit; use *1½, 2⅝,* etc. with no space between the figure and the fraction. Other fractions require a hyphen and individual figures, with a space between the whole number and the fraction: *1 3-16, 2 1-3, 5 9-10.*

**highway designations**    Use these forms, as appropriate in the context, for highways identified by number: *U.S. Highway 1, U.S. Route 1, U.S. 1, Route 1, Illinois 34, Illinois Route 34, state Route 34, Route 34, Interstate Highway 495, Interstate 495.* On second reference only for *Interstate: I-495.*

**mile**    Use figures for amounts under 10 in dimensions, formulas and speeds:

*The farm measures 5 miles by 4 miles. The car slowed to 7 miles per hour. The new model gets 4 miles more per gallon.*

Spell out below 10 in distances: *He drove four miles.*

**millions, billions**   Use figures with *million* or *billion* in all except casual uses: *I'd like to make a billion dollars.* But: *The nation has 1 million citizens. I need $7 billion.*

Do not go beyond two decimals: *7.51 million persons, $2.56 billion, 7,542,500 persons, $2,565,750,000.* Decimals are preferred where practical: *1.5 million.* Not: *1½ million.*

Do not mix *millions* and *billions* in the same figure: *2.6 billion.* Not: *2 billion 600 million.*

Do not drop the word *million* and *billion* in the first figure of a range: *He is worth from $2 million to $4 million.* Not: *$2 to $4 million,* unless you really mean $2.

Note that a hyphen is not used to join the figures and the word *million* or *billion,* even in this type of phrase: *The president submitted a $300 billion budget.*

**minus sign**   Use a hyphen, not a dash, but use the word *minus* if there is any danger of confusion.

Use a word, not a minus sign, to indicate temperatures below zero: *minus 10 or 5 below zero.*

**No.**   Use as the abbreviation for *number* in conjunction with a figure to indicate position or rank: *No. 1 man, No. 3 choice.*

Do not use in street addresses, with this exception: *No. 10 Downing St.,* the residence of Britain's prime minister.

Do not use in the names of schools: *Public School 19.*

**page numbers**   Use figures and capitalize *page* when used with a figure. When a letter is appended to the figure, capitalize it but do not use a hyphen; *Page 1, Page 10, Page 20A.*

One exception: *It's a Page One story.*

**percentages**   Use figures: *1 percent, 2.5 percent* (use decimals, not fractions), *10 percent.*

For amounts less than 1 percent, precede the decimal with a zero: *The cost of living rose 0.6 percent.*

Repeat *percent* with each individual figure: *He said 10 percent to 30 percent of the electorate may not vote.*

**political divisions**   Use Arabic figures and capitalize the accompanying word when used with the figure: *1st Ward, 10th Ward, 3rd Precinct, 22nd Precinct, the ward, the precinct.*

**proportions**   Always use figures: *2 parts powder to 6 parts water.*

**ratios**   Use figures and a hyphen: *the ratio was 2-to-1, a ratio of 2-to-1, a 2-1 ratio.* As illustrated, the word *to* should be omitted when the numbers precede the word *ratio.*

Always use the word *ratio* or phrase such as *a 2-1 majority* to avoid confusion with actual figures.

**Roman numerals** They use letters (*I, X*, etc.) to express numbers.

Use Roman numerals for wars and to establish personal sequence for people and animals: *World War I, Native Dancer II, King George V, Pope John XXIII, John Jones I, John Jones II, John Jones III.* See the **junior, senior** entry in the section on abbreviations and acronyms.

Use Arabic numerals in all other cases.

**scores** Use figures exclusively, placing a hyphen between the totals of the winning and losing teams: *The Reds defeated the Red Sox 4-3, the Giants scored a 12-6 football victory over the Cardinals, the golfer had a 5 on the first hole but finished with a 2-under-par score.*

Use a comma in this format: *Boston 6, Baltimore 5.*

**sizes** Use figures: *a size 9 dress, size 40 long, 10½B shoes, a 34 ½ sleeve.*

**speeds** Use figures. *The car slowed to 7 miles per hour, winds of 5 to 10 miles per hour, winds of 7 to 9 knots, 10-knot winds.*

Avoid extensively hyphenated constructions such as *5-mile-per-hour winds.*

**telephone numbers** Use figures. The forms: *(212) 262-4000, 262-4000, (212) MU2-0400.* If extension numbers are given: *Ext. 2, Ext. 364, Ext. 4071.*

The parentheses around the area code are based on a format that telephone companies have agreed upon for domestic and international communications.

**temperatures** Use figures for all except *zero.* Use a word, not a minus sign, to indicate temperatures below zero.

**times** Use figures except for *noon* and *midnight.* Use a colon to separate hours from minutes: *11 a.m., 1 p.m., 3:30 p.m.*

Avoid such redundancies as *10 a.m. this morning, 10 p.m. tonight* or *10 p.m. Monday night.* Use *10 a.m. today, 10 p.m. today* or *10 p.m. Monday,* etc.

The construction *4 o'clock* is acceptable, but time listings with *a.m.* or *p.m.* are preferred.

**weights** Use figures: *The baby weighed 9 pounds, 7 ounces. She had a 9-pound, 7-ounce boy.*

**years** Use figures, without commas: *1975.* Use an *s* without an apostrophe to indicate spans of decades or centuries: *the 1890s, the 1800s.*

Years are the lone exception to the general rule in that a figure is not used to start a sentence: *1976 was a very good year.*

# GRAMMAR, SPELLING AND WORD USAGE

This section lists common problems of grammatical usage, word selection and spelling.

**a, an** Use the article *a* before consonant sounds: *a historic event, a one-year term* (sounds as if it begins with the letter *w*), *a united stand* (sounds like *you*).

Use the article *an* before vowel sounds: *an energy crisis, an honorable man* (the *h* is silent), *an NBA* record (sounds as if it begins with the letter *e*), *an 1890s celebration.*

**accept, except**   *Accept* means to receive. *Except* means to exclude.

**adverse, averse**   *Adverse* means unfavorable: *He predicted adverse weather. Averse* means reluctant, opposed: *She is averse to change.*

**affect, effect**   *Affect*, as a verb, means to influence: *The game will affect the standings.*
*Affect*, as a noun, is best avoided. It occasionally is used in psychology to describe an emotion, but there is no need for it in everyday language.
*Effect*, as a verb, means to cause: *He will effect many changes in the company.*
*Effect*, as a noun, means result: *The effect was overwhelming. He miscalculated the effect of his actions. It was a law of little effect.*

**aid, aide**   *Aid* is assistance. An *aide* is a person who serves as an assistant.

**ain't**   A dialectical or substandard contraction. Use it only in quoted matter or special contexts.

**allude, refer**   To *allude* to something is to speak of it without specifically mentioning it.
To *refer* is to mention it directly.

**allusion, illusion**   *Allusion* means an indirect reference: *The allusion was to his opponent's record.*
*Illusion* means an unreal or false impression: *The scenic director created the illusion of choppy seas.*

**among, between**   The maxim that *between* introduces two items and *among* introduces more than two covers most questions about how to use these words: *The funds were divided among Mondale, Hart and Jackson.*
However, *between* is the correct word when expressing the relationships of three or more items considered one pair at a time: *Negotiations on a debate format are under way between the network and the Dukakis and Jackson committees.*
As with all prepositions, any pronouns that follow these words must be in the objective case: *among us, between him and her, between you and me.*

**anticipate, expect**   *Anticipate* means to expect and prepare for something; *expect* does not include the notion of preparation:
*They expect a record crowd. They have anticipated it by adding more seats to the auditorium.*

**anybody, any body, anyone, any one**   One word for an indefinite reference: *Anyone can do that.*
Two words when the emphasis is on singling out one element of a group: *Any one of them may speak up.*

**apposition** A decision on whether to put commas around a word, phrase or clause used in apposition depends on whether it is essential to the meaning of the sentence (no commas) or not essential (use commas).

**because, since** Use *because* to denote a specific cause-effect relationship: *He went because he was told.*

*Since* is acceptable in a casual sense when the first event in a sequence led logically to the second but was not its direct cause: *He went to the game, since he had been given the tickets.*

**blond, blonde** Use *blond* as a noun for males and as the adjective for all applications: *She has blond hair.*

Use *blonde* as a noun for females.

**boy** Applicable until 18th birthday is reached. Use *man* or *young man* afterward.

**brunet, brunette.** Use *brunet* as a noun for males and as the adjective for both sexes.

Use *brunette* as a noun for females.

**burglary, larceny, robbery, theft** Legal definitions of *burglary* vary, but in general a *burglary* involves entering a building (not necessarily by breaking in) and remaining unlawfully with the intention of committing a crime.

*Larceny* is the legal term for the wrongful taking of property. Its non-legal equivalents are *stealing* and *theft*.

*Robbery* in the legal sense involves the use of violence or threat in committing larceny. In a wider sense it means to plunder or rifle and may thus be used even if a person was not present: *His house was robbed while he was away.*

*Theft* describes a larceny that did not involve threat, violence or plundering.

USAGE NOTE: You *rob* a person, bank, house, etc., but you *steal* the money or the jewels.

**collective nouns** Nouns that denote a unit take singular verbs and pronouns: *class, committee, crowd, family, group, herd, jury, orchestra, team.*

Some usage examples: *The committee is meeting to set its agenda. The jury reached its verdict. A herd of cattle was sold.*

PLURAL IN FORM: Some words that are plural in form become collective nouns and take singular verbs when the group or quantity is regarded as a unit.

Right: *A thousand bushels is a good yield.* (A unit.)
Right: *A thousand bushels were created.* (Individual items.)
Right: *The data is sound.* (A unit.)
Right: *The data have been carefully collected.* (Individual items.)

**compose, comprise, constitute** *Compose* means to create or put together. It commonly is used in both the active and passive voices: *He composed a song. The United States is composed of 50 states. The zoo is composed of many animals.*

*Comprise* means to contain, to include all or embrace. It is best used only in the active voice, followed by a direct object: *The United States comprises 50 states. The jury comprises five men and seven women. The zoo comprises many animals.*

*Constitute*, in the sense of form or make up, may be the best word if neither *compose* nor *comprise* seems to fit: *Fifty states constitute the United States. Five men and seven women constitute the jury. A collection of animals can constitute a zoo.*

Use *include* when what follows is only part of the total: *The price includes breakfast. The zoo includes lions and tigers.*

**contractions**     Contractions reflect informal speech and writing. Webster's New World Dictionary includes many entries for contractions: *aren't* for *are not*, for example.

Avoid excessive use of contractions. Contractions listed in the dictionary are acceptable, however, in informal contexts or circumstances where they reflect the way a phrase commonly appears in speech or writing.

**contrasted to, contrasted with**     Use *contrasted to* when the intent is to assert, without the need for elaboration, that two items have opposite characteristics. *He contrasted the appearance of the house today to its ramshackle look last year.*

Use *contrasted with* when juxtaposing two or more items to illustrate similarities and/or differences: *He contrasted the Republican platform with the Democratic platform.*

**dangling modifiers**     Avoid modifiers that do not refer clearly and logically to some word in the sentence.

Dangling: *Taking our seats, the game started.* (*Taking* does not refer to the subject, *game*, nor to any other word in the sentence.)

Correct: *Taking our seats, we watched the opening of the game.* (*Taking* refers to *we*, the subject of the sentence.)

**either**     Use it to mean *one or the other*, not *both*.
Right: *She said to use either door.*
Wrong: *There were lions on either side of the door.*
Right: *There were lions on each side of the door. There were lions on both sides of the door.*

**either . . . or, neither . . . nor**     The nouns that follow these words do not constitute a compound subject; they are alternate subjects and require a verb that agrees with the nearer subject:
*Neither they nor he is going. Neither he nor they are going.*

**essential clauses, non-essential clauses**     These terms are used instead of *restrictive clause* and *non-restrictive clause* to convey the distinction between the two in a more easily remembered manner.

Both types of clauses provide additional information about a word or phrase in the sentence.

The difference between them is that the essential clause cannot be eliminated without changing the meaning of the sentence—it so "restricts" the meaning of the word or phrase that its absence would lead to a substantially different interpretation of what the author meant.

The non-essential clause, however, can be eliminated without altering the basic meaning of the sentence—it does not "restrict" the meaning so significantly that its absence would radically alter the author's thought.

PUNCTUATION: An essential clause must not be set off from the rest of a sentence by commas. A non-essential clause must be set off by commas.

The presence or absence of commas provides the reader with critical information about the writer's intended meaning. Note the following examples:

- *Reporters who do not read the stylebook should not criticize their editors.* (The writer is saying that only one class of reporters, those who do not read the stylebook, should not criticize their editors. If the *who . . . stylebook* phrase were deleted, the meaning of the sentence would be changed substantially.)

- *Reporters, who do not read the stylebook, should not criticize their editors.* (The writer is saying that all reporters should not criticize their editors. If the *who . . . stylebook* phrase were deleted, this meaning would not be changed.)

USE OF WHO, THAT, WHICH: When an essential or non-essential clause refers to a human being or an animal with a name, it should be introduced by *who* or *whom*. (See the **who, whom** entry.) Do not use commas if the clause is essential to the meaning; use them if it is not.

*That* is the preferred pronoun to introduce essential clauses that refer to an inanimate object or an animal without a name. *Which* is the only acceptable pronoun to introduce a non-essential clause that refers to an inanimate object or an animal without a name.

The pronoun *which* occasionally may be substituted for *that* in the introduction of an essential clause that refers to an inanimate object or an animal without a name. In general, this use of *which* should appear only when *that* is used as a conjunction to introduce another clause in the same sentence: *He said Monday that the part of the army which suffered severe casualties needs reinforcement.*

**essential phrases, non-essential phrases**  These terms are used in this book instead of *restrictive phrase* and *non-restrictive phrase* to convey the distinction between the two in a more easily remembered manner.

The underlying concept is the one that also applies to clauses:

An *essential phrase* is a word or group of words critical to the reader's understanding of what the author had in mind.

A *non-essential phrase* provides more information about something. Although the information may be helpful to the reader's comprehension, the reader would not be misled if the information were not there.

PUNCTUATION: Do not set an essential phrase off from the rest of a sentence by commas:

- *We saw the award-winning movie ''One Flew Over the Cuckoo's Nest.''* (No comma, because many movies have won awards, and without the name of the movie the reader would not know which movie was meant.)

- *They ate dinner with their daughter Julie.* (Because they have more than one daughter, the inclusion of Julie's name is critical if the reader is to know which daughter is meant.)

Set off non-essential phrases by commas:

- *We saw the 1976 winner in the Academy Award competition for best movie, "One Flew Over the Cuckoo's Nest."* (Only one movie won the award. The name is informative, but even without the name no other movie could be meant.)

- *They ate dinner with their daughter Julie and her husband, David.* (Julie has only one husband. If the phrase read *and her husband David*, it would suggest that she had more than one husband.)

- *The company chairman, Henry Ford II, spoke.* (In the context, only one person could be meant.)

- *Indian corn, or maize, was harvested.* (*Maize* provides the reader with the name of the corn, but its absence would not change the meaning of the sentence.)

DESCRIPTIVE WORDS: Do not confuse punctuation rules for non-essential clauses with the correct punctuation when a non-essential word is used as a descriptive adjective. The distinguishing clue often is the lack of an article or pronoun:

Right: *Julie and husband David went shopping. Julie and her husband, David, went shopping.*

Right: *Company Chairman Henry Ford II made the announcement. The company chairman, Henry Ford II, made the announcement.*

**every one, everyone**   Two words when it means each individual item: *Every one of the clues was worthless.*

One word when used as a pronoun meaning all persons: *Everyone wants to be happy.* (Note that *everyone* takes singular verbs and pronouns.)

**farther, further**   *Farther* refers to physical distance: *He walked farther into the woods.*

*Further* refers to an extension of time or degree: *She will look further into the mystery.*

**fewer, less**   In general, use *fewer* for individual items, *less* for bulk or quantity.

**flaunt, flout**   To *flaunt* is to make an ostentatious or defiant display: *She flaunted her beauty.*

To *flout* is to show contempt for: *He flouts the law.*

**flier, flyer**   *Flier* is the preferred term for an avaitor or a handbill.

*Flyer* is the proper name of some trains and buses: *the Western Flyer.*

**girl**   Applicable until 18th birthday is reached. Use *woman* or *young woman* afterward.

**good, well**   *Good* is an adjective that means something is as it should be or is better than average.

When used as an adjective, *well* means suitable, proper, healthy. When used as an adverb, *well* means in a satisfactory manner or skillfully.

*Good* should not be used as an adverb. It does not lose its status as an adjective in a sentence such as *I feel good*. Such a statement is the idiomatic equivalent of *I am in good health*. An alternative, *I feel well*, could be interpreted as meaning that your sense of touch was good.

**hopefully**    It means in a hopeful manner. Do not use it to mean it is hoped, let us hope or we hope.
　　Right: *It is hoped that we will complete our work in June.*
　　Right: *We hope that we will complete our work in June.*
　　Wrong as a way to express the thought in the previous two sentences: *Hopefully, we will complete our work in June.*

**imply, infer**    Writers or speakers *imply* in the words they use. A listener or reader *infers* something from the words.

**in, into**    *In* indicates location: *He was in the room.*
　　*Into* indicates motion: *She walked into the room.*

**lay, lie**    The action word is **lay**. It takes a direct object. *Laid* is the form for its past tense and its past participle. Its present participle is *laying*.
　　**Lie** indicates a state of reclining along a horizontal plane. It does not take a direct object. Its past tense is *lay*. Its past participle is *lain*. Its present participle is *lying*.
　　When **lie** means to make an untrue statement, the verb forms are *lie, lied, lying.*

**like, as**    Use *like* as a preposition to compare nouns and pronouns. It requires an object: *Jim blocks like a pro.*
　　The conjunction *as* is the correct word to introduce clauses. *Jim blocks the linebacker as he should.*

**majority, plurality**    *Majority* means more than half of an amount. *Plurality* means more than the next highest number.

**marshal, marshaled, marshaling, Marshall**    *Marshal* is the spelling for both the verb and the noun: *Marilyn will marshal her forces. Erwin Rommel was a field marshal.*
　　*Marshall* is used in proper names: *George C. Marshall, John Marshall, the Marshall Islands.*

**obscenities, profanities, vulgarities**    Do not use them in stories unless they are part of direct quotations and there is a compelling reason for them.
　　Confine the offending language, in quotation marks, to a separate paragraph that can be deleted easily.
　　In reporting profanity that normally would use the words *damn* or *god*, lowercase *god* and use the following forms: *damn, damn it, goddamn it.* Do not, however, change the offending words to euphemisms. Do not, for example, change *damn it* to *darn it.*
　　If a full quote that contains profanity, obscenity or vulgarity cannot be dropped but there is no compelling reason for the offensive language, replace letters of an offensive word with a hyphen. The word *damn*, for example, would become *d--- or ---.*

**off of**    The *of* is unnecessary: *He fell off the bed.* Not: *He fell off of the bed.*

**on**   Do not use *on* before a date or day of the week when its absence would not lead to confusion: *The meeting will be held Monday. He will be inaugurated Jan. 20.*

Use *on* to avoid an awkward juxtaposition of a date and a proper name: *John met Mary on Monday. He told Bush on Thursday that the bill was doomed.*

Use *on* also to avoid any suggestion that a date is the object of a transitive verb: *The House killed on Tuesday a bid to raise taxes. The Senate postponed on Wednesday its consideration of a bill to reduce import duties.*

**over**   It is not interchangeable with *more than*.
*Over* refers to spatial relationships: *The plane flew over the city.*
*More than* is used with figures: *More than 40,000 fans were in the stadium.*

**people, persons**   Use *person* when speaking of an individual: *One person waited for the bus.*

The word *people* is preferred to *persons* in all plural uses. For example: *Thousands of people attended the fair. Some rich people pay few taxes. What will people say? There were 17 people in the room.*

*Persons* should be used only when it is in a direct quote or part of a title as in Bureau of Missing Persons.

*People* also is a collective noun that takes a plural verb when used to refer to a single race or nation: *The American people are united.* In this sense, the plural is *peoples*: *The peoples of Africa speak many languages.*

**principal, principle**   *Principal* is a noun and adjective meaning someone or something first in rank, authority, importance or degree: *She is the school principal. He was the principal player in the trade. Money is the principal problem.*

*Principle* is a noun that means a fundamental truth, law, doctrine or motivating force: *They fought for the principle of self-determination.*

**prior to**   *Before* is less stilted for most uses. *Prior to* is appropriate, however, when a notion of requirement is involved: *The fee must be paid prior to the examination.*

**reign, rein**   The leather strap for a horse is a *rein*, hence figuratively: *seize the reins, give free rein to, put a check rein on.*
*Reign* is the period a ruler is on the throne: *The king began his reign.*

**should, would**   Use *should* to express an obligation: *We should help the needy.*

Use *would* to express a customary action: *In the summer we would spend hours by the seashore.*

Use *would* also in constructing a conditional past tense, but be careful:

Wrong: *If Soderholm would not have had an injured foot, Thompson would not have been in the lineup.*

Right: *If Soderholm had not had an injured foot, Thompson would not have been in the lineup.*

**spelling**   The basic rule when in doubt is to consult the stylebooks followed by, if necessary, a dictionary.

Memory Aid: Noah Webster developed the following rule of thumb for the frequently vexing question of whether to double a final consonant in forming the present participle and past tense of a verb:

- If the stress in pronunciation is on the first syllable, do not double the consonant: *cancel, canceling, canceled.*

- If the stress in pronunciation is on the second syllable, double the consonant: *control, controlling, controlled; refer, referring, referred.*

- If the word is only one syllable, double a consonant unless confusion would result: *jut, jutted, jutting.* An exception, to avoid confusion with *buss,* is *bus, bused, busing.*

Here is a list of commonly misspelled words:

| | | |
|---|---|---|
| adviser | council | likable |
| accommodate | counsel | machine gun |
| Asian flu | drought | percent |
| ax | drunken | percentage |
| baby-sit | employee | reconnaissance |
| baby sitter | embarrass | restaurant |
| baby-sitting | eyewitness | restauratuer |
| cannot | firefighter | rock 'n' roll |
| cave in (v.) | fulfill | skillful |
| cave-in (n., adj.) | goodbye | subpoena |
| chauffeur | hanged | teen-age (adj.) |
| cigarette | harass | teen-ager |
| clue | hitchhiker | under way |
| commitment | homemade | vacuum |
| consensus | imposter | weird |
| consul | judgment | whiskey |
| copter | kidnapping | X-ray (n., v., adj.) |

**subjunctive mood**  Use the subjunctive mood of a verb for contrary-to-fact conditions, and expressions of doubts, wishes or regrets:
*If I were a rich man, I wouldn't have to work hard.*
*I doubt that more money would be the answer.*
*I wish it were possible to take back my words.*
Sentences that express a contingency or hypothesis may use either the subjunctive or the indicative mood depending on the context. In general, use the subjunctive if there is little likelihood that a contingency might come true:
*If I were to marry a millionaire, I wouldn't have to worry about money.*
*If the bill should overcome the opposition against it, it would provide extensive tax relief.*
But:
*If I marry a millionaire, I won't have to worry about money.*
*If the bill passes as expected, it will provide an immediate tax cut.*

**that (conjunction)**  Use the conjunction *that* to introduce a dependent clause if the sentence sounds or looks awkward without it. There are no hard-and-fast rules, but in general:

- *That* usually may be omitted when a dependent clause immediately follows a form of the verb *to say: The president said he had signed the bill.*

- *That* should be used when a time element intervenes between the verb and the dependent clause: *The president said Monday that he had signed the bill.*

- *That* usually is necessary after some verbs. They include: *advocate, assert, contend, declare, estimate, make clear, point out, propose* and *state.*

- *That* is required before subordinate clauses beginning with conjunctions such as *after, although, because, before, in addition to, until* and *while: Haldeman said that after he learned of Nixon's intention to resign, he sought pardons for all connected with Watergate.*

When in doubt, include *that*. Omission can hurt. Inclusion never does.

**that, which, who, whom (pronouns)**   Use *who* and *whom* in referring to persons and to animals with a name: *John Jones is the man who helped me.* See the **who, whom** entry.

Use *that* and *which* in referring to inanimate objects and to animals without a name.

See the **essential clauses, non-essential clauses** entry for guidelines on using *that* and *which* to introduce phrases and clauses.

**under way**   Two words in virtually all uses: *The project is under way. The naval maneuvers are under way.*

One word only when used as an adjective before a noun in a nautical sense: *an underway flotilla.*

**verbs**   In general, avoid awkward constructions that split infinitive forms of a verb (*to leave, to help,* etc.) or compound forms (*had left, are found out,* etc.).

Awkward: *She was ordered to immediately leave on an assignment.*
Preferred: *She was ordered to leave immediately on an assignment.*
Awkward: *There stood the wagon that we had early last autumn left by the barn.*
Preferred: *There stood the wagon that we had left by the barn early last autumn.*

Occasionally, however, a split is not awkward and is necessary to convey the meaning:
*He wanted to really help his mother.*
*Those who lie are often found out.*
*How has your health been?*
*The budget was tentatively approved.*

**who, whom**   Use *who* and *whom* for references to human beings and to animals with a name. Use *that* and *which* for inanimate objects and animals without a name.

*Who* is the word when someone is the subject of a sentence, clause or phrase: *The woman who rented the room left the window open. Who is there?*

*Whom* is the word when someone is the object of a verb or preposition: *The woman to whom the room was rented left the window open. Whom do you wish to see?*

See the **essential clauses, non-essential clauses** entry for guidelines on how to punctuate clauses introduced by *who, whom, that* and *which.*

**who's, whose**   *Who's* is a contraction for *who is,* not a possessive: *Who's there? Whose* is the possessive: *I do not know whose coat it is.*

**widow, widower**   In obituaries: A man *is survived by his wife,* or *leaves his wife.* A woman *is survived by her husband,* or *leaves her husband.*

Guard against the redundant *widow of the late.* Use *wife of the late* or *widow of.*

# Glossary

**absolute privilege**   The right of legislators, judges and government executives to speak without threat of libel when acting in their official capacities.

**absolutism**   The ethical philosophy that there is a fixed set of principles or laws from which there is no deviation. To the absolutist journalist, the end never justifies the means.

**actual malice**   Reckless disregard of the truth. It is a condition in libel cases.

**ad**   An advertisement.

**add**   A typewritten page of copy following the first page. "First add" would be the second page of typewritten copy.

**advance**   A report dealing with the subjects and issues to be dealt with in an upcoming meeting or event.

**advertising department**   The department of the newspaper responsible for advertisements. Most advertising departments have classified and display ad sections.

**anecdotal lead**   A newspaper story beginning that uses humor or an interesting incident.

**angle**   The focus of, or approach to, a story. The latest development in a continuing controversy, the key play in a football game, the tragedy of a particular death in a mass disaster may serve as an angle.

**antinomianism**   The ethical philosophy that recognizes no rules. An antinomian journalist judges every ethical situation on its own merits. Unlike the situation ethicist, the antinomian does not use love of neighbor as an absolute.

**AP**   The Associated Press, a worldwide news-gathering cooperative owned by its subscribers.

**APME**   Associated Press Managing Editors, an organization of managing editors and editors whose papers are members of The Associated Press.

**arraignment**   A court proceeding at which a defendant is informed of the charge. At the proceeding, the defendant is asked to enter a plea, and bail may be set.

**background**   Information that may be attributed to a source by title, but not by name; for example, "a White House aide said."

**backgrounder**   Story that explains and updates the news.

**beat**    A reporter's assigned area of responsibility. A beat may be an institution, such as the courthouse; a geographical area, such as a small town; or a subject, such as science. The term also refers to an exclusive story.

**books**    Assembled sheets of paper, usually newsprint, and carbon paper on which reporters prepare stories. Books are not used with modern OCR and VDT processes.

**brightener**    A story, usually short, that is humorous or pleasing to the reader. It is also called a *bright*.

**bureau**    A news-gathering office maintained by a newspaper at other than its central location. Papers may have bureaus in the next county, in the state capital, in Washington, D.C., or in foreign countries.

**business department**    The newspaper department that handles billing, accounting and related functions.

**byline**    A line identifying the author of a story.

**chain**    Two or more newspapers owned by a single person or corporation. Also known as *group*. The American chain owning the most newspapers is Gannett.

**change of venue**    An order transferring a court proceeding to another jurisdiction for prosecution. This often occurs when a party in a case claims that local media coverage has prejudiced prospective jurors.

**circulation department**    The department responsible for distribution of the newspaper.

**city editor**    The individual (also known as the *metropolitan*, or *metro*, *editor*) in charge of the city desk, which coordinates local news-gathering operations. At some papers the desk also handles regional and state news done by its own reporters.

**civil law**    Statutes under which an individual or a group can take action against another individual or group.

**clips**    Stories clipped from your own or competing newspapers.

**closed-ended question**    A direct question designed to draw a specific response; for example, "Will you be a candidate?"

**conditional privilege**    The right to report on the three branches of government if the report is full, fair and accurate, and the reporter does not seriously doubt the truth of the material.

**control**    The process of structuring an experiment so that the only forces affecting the outcome are the variables you are observing.

**controller**    The computer that drives a video display terminal (VDT) or optical character recognition (OCR) system.

**copy**    What reporters write. A story is a piece of copy.

**copy desk**    The desk at which final editing of stories is done, headlines are written and pages are designed.

**copy editor**    A person who checks, polishes and corrects stories written by reporters. Usually copy editors write headlines for those stories, and sometimes they decide how to arrange stories and pictures on a page.

**cover**    To keep abreast of significant developments on a beat or to report on a specific event. The reporter covering the police beat may be assigned to cover a murder.

**criminal law**   Statutes under which a grand jury or an officer of the court can take action against an individual.

**cub**   A beginning reporter.

**cursor**   A rectangle of light on a video display terminal (VDT) that indicates the writer's or editor's position within the text of a story. Changes in text are made with the keyboard and appear on the screen where the cursor is located.

**data base**   A computerized information bank, usually accessed by newspapers on a subscription basis.

**deadline**   Time by which a reporter, editor or desk must have completed scheduled work.

**deep background**   Information that may be used but that cannot be attributed to either a person or a position.

**delayed-identification lead**   Opening paragraph of a story in which the "who" is identified by occupation, city, office or any means other than by name.

**dependent variable**   See *variable*.

**desk**   A term used by reporters to refer to the city editor's or copy editor's position, as in, "The desk wants this story by noon."

**developing story**   One in which newsworthy events occur over several days or weeks.

**dig**   To question or investigate thoroughly, as in, "Let's do some digging into those campaign reports."

**directory**   The index of stories within a video display terminal (VDT) system.

**documentary**   In-depth coverage of an issue or event, especially in broadcasting.

**editor**   The top-ranking individual in the news department of a newspaper, also known as the *editor in chief*. The term may refer as well to those at any level who edit copy.

**editorial department**   The news department of a newspaper, responsible for all content of the newspaper except advertising. At some papers this term refers to the department responsible for the editorial page only.

**editorialize**   To inject the reporter's or the newspaper's opinion into a news story or headline. Most newspapers restrict opinion to analysis stories, columns and editorials.

**editorial page editor**   The individual in charge of the editorial page and, at larger newspapers, the op-ed (opposite editorial) page.

**fair comment and criticism**   Opinion delivered on the performance of anyone in the public eye. Such opinion is legally protected if reporters do not misstate any of the facts on which they base their comments or criticism, and it is not malicious.

**felonies**   Serious crimes punishable by death or imprisonment.

**field experiment**   A research technique in which the reporter deliberately takes some action to observe the effects. For example, a perfectly tuned automobile could be taken to several repair shops to find out if the mechanics would invent problems that required fixing.

**follow**   A story supplying further information about an item that has already been published; *folo* is an alternate spelling.

**Freedom of Information Act** A law passed in 1966 to make it easier to obtain information from federal agencies. The law was amended in 1974 to improve access to government records.

**futures file** A collection, filed according to date, of newspaper clippings, letters, notes and other information to remind editors of stories to assign.

**general manager** The individual responsible for the business operations of a newspaper. Some newspaper chains award this title to the top-ranking local executive.

**graf** A shortened form of *paragraph*, as in "Give me two grafs on that fire."

**handout** See *news release*.

**hard lead** A lead that reports a new development or newly discovered fact. See also *soft lead*.

**hard news** Coverage of the actions of government or business; or the reporting of an event, such as a crime, an accident or a speech. The time element often is important. See also *soft news*.

**human-interest story** A piece valued more for its emotional impact or oddity than for its importance.

**hypothesis** In investigative reporting the statement a reporter expects to be able to prove, as in, "The mayor took a bribe from that massage parlor." In an experiment the statement of what a researcher hopes to find.

**immediate-identification lead** The opening paragraph of a story in which the "who" is reported by name.

**independent variable** See *variable*.

**indictment** A document issued by a grand jury that certifies there is sufficient evidence against a person accused of a crime to warrant holding that person for trial.

**invasion of privacy** Violation of a person's right to be left alone.

**inverted pyramid** The organization of a news story in which information is arranged in descending order of importance.

**investigative reporting** The pursuit of information that has been concealed, such as evidence of wrongdoing.

**IRE** Investigative Reporters and Editors, a group created to exchange information and investigative reporting techniques. IRE has its headquarters at the University of Missouri School of Journalism.

**lay out (v.)** The process of preparing page drawings to indicate to the composing room where stories and pictures are to be placed in the newspaper.

**layout (n.)** The completed page drawing, or page dummy.

**lead** (1) The first paragraph or first several paragraphs of a newspaper story (sometimes spelled *lede*); (2) the story given the best display on Page One; (3) a tip.

**lead-in** An introduction to a filmed or recorded excerpt from a news source or from another reporter.

**lead story** The major story displayed at the top of Page One.

**libel** Damage to a person's reputation caused by a false written statement that brings the person into hatred, contempt or ridicule, or injures his or her business or occupational pursuit.

**linecaster**   A device used in hot-metal composition to set type. The cold-type equivalent is a photo digital or laser typesetter.

**managing editor**   The individual with primary responsibility for day-to-day operation of the news department.

**misdemeanors**   Minor criminal offenses, including most traffic violations, which usually result in a fine or brief confinement in a local jail.

**more**   Designation used at the end of a page of copy to indicate there are one or more additional pages.

**morgue**   The newspaper library, where published stories, photographs and resource material are stored for reference.

**multiple-element lead**   The opening paragraph of a story that reports two or more newsworthy elements.

**negligence test**   The legal standard that requires reporters to use the same care in gathering facts and writing a story as any reasonable individual would under similar circumstances.

**news conference**   An interview session, also called a *press conference*, in which someone submits to questions from reporters.

**news editor**   The supervisor of the copy desk. At some newspapers this title is used for the person in charge of local news-gathering operations.

**news release**   An item, also called a *handout*, that is sent out by a group or individual seeking publicity.

**news room**   The place, sometimes called the *city room*, where reporters and editors work.

**news value**   How important or interesting a story is.

**not for attribution**   Information that may not be ascribed to its source.

**OCR**   Optical character recognition. The process in which reporters write their stories on electric typewriters and a device called an optical character reader translates the typed material into electrical impulses for processing.

**off the record**   Usually means, "Don't quote me." Some sources and reporters, however, use it to mean, "Don't print this." Phrases with similar, and equally ambiguous, meanings are "not for attribution" and "for background only."

**op-ed page**   The page opposite the editorial page, frequently reserved for columns, letters to the editor and personality profiles.

**open-ended question**   One that permits the respondent some latitude in the answer; for example, "How did you get involved in politics?"

**open meetings law**   State and federal laws, often called *sunshine laws*, guaranteeing access to meetings of public officials.

**open records laws**   State and federal laws guaranteeing access to many—but not all—kinds of government records.

**participant observation**   A research technique in which the reporter joins in the activity he or she wants to write about.

**payola**   Money or gifts given in the expectation of favors from journalists.

**photo editor**   The individual who advises editors on the use of photographs in the newspaper. The photo editor also may supervise the photography department.

**piece**   See *story*.

**plagiarism**   The use of any part of another's writing and passing it off as your own.

**play**   A shortened form of *display*. A good story may be played at the top of Page One; a weak one may be played inside.

**poll**   The measurement of opinion by questioning members of some small group chosen at random so as to be representative of the entire group. A poll is also referred to as a *survey* or *public opinion poll*. See also *randomization*.

**population**   In scientific language the whole group being studied. Depending on the study the population may be, for example, voters in St. Louis, physicians in California or all residents of the United States.

**preliminary hearing**   A court hearing held to determine whether there is probable cause that a defendant committed a crime and whether the defendant should be bound over for grand jury action or trial in a higher court.

**press**   The machine that prints the newspaper. Also a synonym for journalism, as in the phrase "freedom of the press." Sometimes used to denote print journalism, as distinguished from broadcast journalism.

**press agent**   A person hired to gain publicity for a client. The tactics used, often called *press agentry*, might include the staging of interviews or stunts designed to attract the attention of reporters.

**press box**   The section of a stadium or arena set aside for reporters.

**press conference**   See *news conference*.

**production department**   The department of the newspaper that transforms the work of the news and advertising departments into the finished product. The composing room and press room are key sections of this department.

**profile**   A story intended to reveal the personality or character of an institution or person.

**public figure**   A person who has assumed a role of prominence in the affairs of society and who has persuasive power and influence in a community or who has thrust himself or herself to the forefront of a public controversy. Courts have given journalists more latitude in reporting on public figures.

**publisher**   The top-ranking executive of a newspaper. This title often is assumed by the owner, although chains sometimes designate as publisher the top local executive.

**Pulitzer Prize**   The most prestigious of journalism awards. It was established by Joseph Pulitzer and is administered by Columbia University.

**queue**   A holding area within a video display terminal (VDT) system. It is the electronic equivalent of an in-basket.

**quote**   As a noun, the term refers to a source's exact words, as in, "I have a great quote here." As a verb, it means to report those words inside quotation marks.

**randomization**   The mathematical process used to assure that every member of a population being studied has an equal chance of being chosen for questioning or observation. See also *poll*.

**records column**   The part of the newspaper featured regularly that contains such information as routine police and fire news, births, obituaries, marriages and divorces.

**reporter**   A person whose job it is to gather and write the news for a publication or a broadcast outlet.

**rewrite**   To write a story again in an effort to improve it. It also means to take information over the telephone from a reporter in the field and mold it into a story.

**roundup**   A story including a number of related events. After a storm, for example, a reporter might do a roundup of accidents, power outages and other consequences of the storm.

**sample**   A portion of a group, or population, chosen for study as representative of the entire group.

**sampling error**   The allowance that must be made in any survey for the possibility that the sample questioned may not be exactly like all other members of the population.

**scanner**   The popular term for an optical character reader. See also *OCR*.

**scenic lead**   A lead that concentrates on a description of an environment.

**second-cycle story**   A second version of a story already published, also called a *second-day story*. It usually has new information or a new angle.

**series**   Two or more stories on the same or related subjects, published on a predetermined schedule.

**shield laws**   Legislation giving journalists the right to protect the identity of sources.

**sidebar**   A secondary story intended to be run with a major story on the same topic. A story about a disaster, for example, may have a sidebar that tells what happened to a single victim.

**situation ethics**   The philosophy that recognizes that a set of rules can be broken when circumstances dictate the community will be served better by it. For example, a journalist who believes it normally unethical to deceive a news source may be willing to conceal his or her identity to infiltrate a group operating illegally.

**slug**   A word that identifies a story as it is processed through the newspaper plant. It is usually placed in the upper left-hand corner of each take of the story. See also *take*.

**sniff**   The preliminary phase of an investigation.

**soft lead**   A lead that uses a quote, anecdote or other literary device to attract the reader. See also *hard lead*.

**soft news**   Stories about trends, personalities or lifestyles. The time element usually is not important. See also *hard news*.

**sources**   People or records from which a reporter gets information. The term often is used to describe persons, as opposed to documents.

**spot news**   A timely report of an event that is unfolding at the moment.

**story**   The term most journalists use for a newspaper article. Another synonym is *piece*, as in, "I saw your piece on the mayor." A very long story may be called a *takeout* or a *blockbuster*.

**stylebook**   A book of standard usage within newspaper text. It includes rules on grammar, punctuation, capitalization and abbreviation. The AP and UPI publish similar stylebooks that are used by most papers. (Portions of the AP and UPI stylebooks are reprinted in on appendix to this book.)

**substantial truth**   The correctness of the essential elements of a story.

**summary lead** The first paragraph of a news story in which the writer presents a synopsis of two or more actions rather than focusing on any one of them.

**sunshine laws** See *open meetings laws*.

**take** A page of typewritten copy for newspaper use.

**30** A designation used to mark the end of a newspaper story. The symbol # is an alternate designation.

**tie-back** The sentence or sentences relating a story to events covered in a previous story. Used in follow-up or continuing stories or in parts of a series of stories. Also, the technique of referring to the opening in the ending of the story.

**tip** A fragment of information that may lead to a story; also called a *lead*.

**transition** A word, phrase, sentence or paragraph that moves the reader from one thought to the next and shows the relationship between them.

**TTS** Teletypesetter, a system used to produce coded paper tape that is read by an automated typesetter to produce type.

**universal desk** A copy desk that edits material for all editorial departments of a newspaper.

**update** A type of follow that reports on a development related to an earlier story.

**UPI** United Press International, a worldwide news-gathering organization that is privately owned.

**variable** In an experiment, one of the elements being observed. The independent variable is what is thought to be a cause; the dependent variable is the effect of that cause.

**VDT** Video display terminal or visual display terminal, a computer-assisted device with televisionlike display and attached keyboard for writing stories and headlines and editing copy.

**videoprompter** A mechanical or electronic device that projects broadcast copy next to the television camera lens so that a newscaster can read it while appearing to look straight into the lens.

## Acknowledgments (cont. from p. iv)

*Page 160.* ''Mandela's Visit Prompts Rerun of Old Ethnic Battles.'' From the July 1, 1990 edition of *The Miami Herald*. Reprinted by permission of The Miami Herald.

*Page 230.* ''Hundreds Dead in Huge Quake.'' From October 1989. Copyright © *San Francisco Chronicle*. Reprinted by permission.

*Figure 15.2, page 352.* Cover from Sept. 23, 1991 issue of *Consumer Reports Magazine*. Copyright © 1991, *Consumer Reports Magazine*. Reprinted by permission.

*Figure 16.1, page 371.* Photo by Duan Burkson/AP. Courtesy of *Sports Illustrated*.

*Page 395.* By Walt Harrington, ''The Making of a Muckraker,'' *The Washington Post Magazine*, June 10, 1990, The Washington Post Company. The article is part of a full-length book by Harrington tentatively entitled, *American Profile* to be published by the University of Missouri Press in 1992.

## Photo Credits

*Part One opener, page 1:* Charles Gatewood/Stock, Boston
*Figure 2.1, page 18:* Hiroshi Nishikawa/MIT Media Laboratory
*Figure 2.2, page 27: New York Times*, photo by Bill Aller
*Figure 2.14, page 45:* © Cliff Schiappa
*Figure 2.15, page 45:* © Cliff Schiappa
*Part Two opener, page 47:* Gale Zucker/Stock, Boston
*Figure 4.2, page 77:* Courtesy of the Mark Twain Memorial, Hartford, Connecticut
*Figure 4.3, page 77:* Harold Krieger, Courtesy of William Morrow & Company, Inc.
*Figure 5.1, page 108:* AP/Wide World Photos
*Figure 5.2, page 109:* Mike Kagan/Monkmeyer
*Figure 5.3, page 111:* AP/Wide World Photos
*Figure 7.1, page 152:* Paul Conklin/Monkmeyer
*Part Three opener, page 163:* Bob Daemmrich/Stock, Boston
*Figure 8.1, page 176:* Roberta Hershenson/Photo Researchers
*Figure 10.1, page 210:* Reuters/Bettmann Newsphotos
*Figure 11.1, page 221:* Virginia Schau, AP/Wide World Photos
*Figure 11.2, page 221:* Stanley Forman, *Boston Herald American*
*Figure 11.3, page 221:* George Mattson, *Daily News*
*Figure 12.3, page 266:* UPI/Bettmann Newsphotos
*Part Four opener, page 291:* Stephen Marton/Silver Image
*Figure 14.1, page 294: Miami Herald* photo
*Figure 14.2, page 301:* R. Maiman/Sygma
*Figure 14.3, page 303: Miami Herald* photo
*Figure 14.4, page 317:* AP/Wide World Photos
*Figure 15.1, page 349:* AP/Wide World Photos
*Figure 16.2, page 372: Washington Post* photo
*Part Five opener, page 375:* Margaret Miller/Photo Researchers
*Figure 17.1, page 379:* © Burk Uzzle
*Figure 17.3, page 390:* Pulitzer Prize Committee, Columbia University
*Figure 19.1, page 422:* Courtesy of the Pelletier Library, Allegheny College, Meadville, PA, 16335
*Part Six opener, page 443:* Dirck Halstead/Capital Cities/ABC, Inc.
*Part Seven opener, page 467:* John Coletti/Stock, Boston
*Figure 22.1, page 500:* Courtesy of *The Orlando Sentinel*/Merrit Weatherly
*Figure 22.2, page 513: The Oregonian*/Tom Trieck

# Index